AF521663

# The Washington Post

THE FIRST 100 YEARS

# The Washington Post

## THE FIRST 100 YEARS

Chalmers M. Roberts

Illustrated with Photographs,
Drawings, and Cartoons

Houghton Mifflin Company
Boston 1977

*Library of Congress Cataloging in Publication Data*

Roberts, Chalmers McGeagh, date
The Washington post.

Bibliography: p.
Includes index.
1. Washington post. I. Title.
PN4899.W31W35 071'.53 77-21907
ISBN 0-395-25854-5

Printed in the United States of America

v 10 9 8 7 6 5 4 3 2 1

# Acknowledgments

Four years ago Katharine Graham and I agreed that this centennial history of THE WASHINGTON POST should be written. She asked me to do it and made her extensive files freely available. Other POST executives, past and present, also were most cooperative.

There were four other prime sources. First, I have been through nearly 1500 rolls of microfilm of each day's paper since its founding in 1877. Obviously, I did not read every word or every advertisement, but the microfilm record was basic to the flavor of the times and to what the paper offered its reader. Second, I had the unpublished manuscript of Edward T. Folliard, for decades a leading POST reporter, who first undertook to write the paper's centennial history. Third, in 1927 THE POST published a mammoth 50th anniversary edition, essentially the work of reporter George Rothwell Brown. This was indispensable in writing of the years before Eugene Meyer, Mrs. Graham's father, bought the paper in 1933. Fourth, I myself worked for THE POST in 1933–1934 and 1949–1971 and I have continued since retirement to contribute to its editorial pages. All these years of association may have biased my view of the paper, although I hope not.

Nearly 100 POST employees past and present and others knowledgeable about the paper contributed memoranda, granted interviews, or answered queries. May they forgive me for not listing their names; some, in fact, prefer the anonymity. Special thanks go to these non-POST people who helped: Joseph W. Barr of Washington; Brady Black of the Cincinnati *Enquirer;* Mrs. Rothwell Hutton Brown of White Stone, Virginia; Edward J. Gallagher of the Laconia, New Hampshire, *Evening Citizen* whose biography of Stilson Hutchins filled a large gap and who granted permission to quote from it; the late Constance McLaughlin Green of Washington; Milton Kaplan, formerly of the Library of Congress; Alice Roosevelt Longworth of Washington; Nicholas W. Newbold of Chevy Chase, Maryland; Edward F. Prichard, Jr., of Frankfort, Kentucky; Mrs. Edward H. Rice of Atlantic City, New Jersey; Robert A. Truax of the Columbia Historical Society, Washington; Vernon E. West, Jr., of Bethesda, Maryland; and Marguerite Bone Wilcox of Santa Barbara, California. Felix Morley kindly granted permission to quote from his unpublished autobiography and Richard B. Norment IV from his unpublished thesis on THE POST and the League of Nations. Of all the books I found useful one deserves special mention: Evalyn Walsh McLean's *Father Struck It Rich.* Little, Brown and Company has granted permission to quote extensively from it. Other books and some magazine articles bearing in one way or another on THE POST are listed in the bibliography.

Additional thanks go to Mark Hannan, chief of THE POST library, and to his staff, most especially to Sunday Orme, formerly on that staff; to Elizabeth Hylton, Maureen Rogers, Pat O'Shea, Donna Crouch, Pamela Whitehead, Miriam Grant, Carol Krucoff, Virginia Rodriguez, and my daughter Patricia Roberts, all at THE POST; to Matthew Lewis, chief of POST photography; and to the Library of Congress' manuscript and prints and photographs divisions. Ferdinand Kuhn proved to be an invaluable critic and a meticulous editor. Joseph L. Gardner patiently but firmly worked his way through the several drafts of the manuscript and without his wise counsel and editing skill the book would never have reached fruition.

The one person who made this work possible by providing unstinting encouragement, constructive criticism, and proficient copy reading was my wife, Lois. How she stood it so long is a mystery.

Finally, for the inevitable errors doubtless herein I claim full responsibility.

CHALMERS M. ROBERTS

*Washington*
*July 4, 1977*

# Contents

# Illustrations

# Prologue

THE WASHINGTON POST and Watergate are the inseparable twins of modern American journalism. The newspaper's newsroom has been seen by more people than any other, thanks to a motion picture version of how two of its reporters pursued the Watergate story. The controlling owner ranks among the most powerful publishers in the nation's history.

But it did not all begin with Watergate. It began on December 6, 1877, in the wake of Reconstruction when Stilson Hutchins, a young man out of the West, first published in the small and provincial capital what he called "a Democratic daily." His was the first of four ownerships. He sold the paper to a partnership, Frank Hatton, a Republican, and Beriah Wilkins, a Democrat. John R. McLean, a Cincinnati publisher-politician, purchased control from Wilkins' heirs and passed it on to his son, Edward B. (Ned) McLean. Eugene Meyer, a millionaire Republican financier, acquired the paper at a 1933 bankruptcy sale and for two decades pumped his fortune into it before red ink turned to black. Control passed to his son-in-law, Philip L. Graham, and then to his daughter, Katharine Meyer Graham. His grandson, Donald Edward Graham, now is preparing to be her successor.

Two of the publishers came to sad endings: Ned McLean ran the paper into bankruptcy and lost it, then died in a mental hospital. Philip Graham, after brilliant years, fell into manic depression and killed himself. Oddly, these two, 40 years apart, were the closest of any POST publishers to presidents, McLean to Warren G. Harding and Graham to John F. Kennedy.

John Philip Sousa wrote the stirring "Washington Post March" for Hatton and Wilkins. One POST cartoonist created Theodore Roosevelt's Teddy Bear and coined the slogan "Remember the Maine." Another cartoonist coined the term "McCarthyism" and became Richard

Nixon's implacable foe. One publisher was caught in a lie trying to cover up for a Teapot Dome conspirator; his wife wore the Hope diamond. Under one owner THE POST helped destroy Woodrow Wilson's dream of American participation in the League of Nations. Under another, the paper was a leader in the fight against Franklin Roosevelt's plan to "pack" the Supreme Court. This is the newspaper that helped incite a race riot following World War I and that led the movement toward full rights for black citizens after World War II.

In its first 100 years 20 presidents, living a few blocks away, have been POST readers. Most were concerned about what it said of them. Many curried its favor and some received it; a few disdained the paper. One sought to damage, if not to destroy, it.

Because Washington is a political city — Henry James called it "the city of conversation" — THE POST throughout its life has paid more attention to government and to those who compose it than to anything else. It has observed them all — presidents to bureaucrats — with fascination, praise, scorn, and at times with verbal loathing. It has recorded their high aspirations and disclosed their foibles and unconscionable acts. Its pages have been flushed with five wars, the recurrent search for lasting peace, and the often roller-coaster economy.

For much of its early life THE POST's editorials were more powerful than its reporting was exact. The paper has spoken timorously, stridently, thunderously. In recent decades THE WASHINGTON POST has been the powerful voice of liberal American democracy.

At its founding the paper was bright and saucy, but it grew gray and dull, even outrageous and groveling. At times it was despised within the trade; today the door is jammed with job seekers. In the earlier and in the later decades THE POST well served the public interest, sometimes at great risk as in the McCarthy and Watergate eras. In short, its journalism has ranged from the obsequious and the sensational to the solidly exemplary.

For decades under different owners THE POST struggled against that proper and long profitable old lady of Washington journalism, the *Evening* and *Sunday Star.* Its current profitability dates from the achievement of morning-paper monopoly in 1954 with the purchase of Colonel Robert R. McCormick's reactionary *Times-Herald.* THE POST then raced past the *Star* and soon began to find a new target to challenge for the role of the nation's number one newspaper, the New York *Times.* This competition has become intense, today's most notable rivalry among all American newspapers.

THE WASHINGTON POST began as a private business and continued so until it went public in 1971, but control remains firmly in family hands.

Today it is the flagship of a larger communications empire that includes *Newsweek* magazine; a seven-day paper in Trenton, New Jersey; one radio and four television stations; a half interest in a major news service that distributes POST stories at home and abroad; a part interest in the *International Herald Tribune* published in Paris; and ownership of, or interests in, various supportive enterprises.

A daily newspaper is a transitory thing, a "first rough draft of history" as Philip Graham remarked. This particular newspaper is unique in having been published in the national capital almost every morning of every year for the past century. What the future holds for THE WASHINGTON POST is conjectural; what the past has been is recorded here.

# The Washington Post

THE FIRST 100 YEARS

# 1

# A Democratic Daily
# Mr. Hutchins Comes to Town
# 1877-1889

A robust figure with splendid shoulders, a fine Roman nose, a jaw of resolution, eyes of grayish blue, and a deep bass voice, Stilson Hutchins was a man of commanding presence. He was 38 when he arrived in Washington one summer day in 1877 to put into execution a plan he long had cherished — the founding of a daily Democratic newspaper in the national capital: THE WASHINGTON POST.

In two ways it was an auspicious moment. As Eugene Field, the poet who worked awhile for THE POST, later wrote: "The newspapers of that city were dreary mockeries of the profession. They gave the Associated Press dispatches, dull reports of the Congressional proceedings and platitudinous editorials that seldom interested and less frequently instructed the reader." The capital had five dailies published Mondays through Saturdays and four papers appearing only on Sundays. "For the news," Field went on, "and for intelligent comments upon the current topics of the time, the Washington public looked to the New York papers" that came down on the late night train.

The year of Hutchins' arrival, 1877, also marked the end of Reconstruction, that forcible alteration of race relations in the South under "radical" Republicans who considered the former Confederate States to be conquered territory. Not until March 2, only two days before the inauguration, was the bitterly contested presidential election between Samuel J. Tilden, the Democratic governor of New York, and Rutherford B. Hayes, the Republican governor of Ohio, finally settled. A partisan vote of 7 to 6 in the specially created Electoral Commission gave the victory to Hayes. Behind the decision lay what some have called a bargain — others a deal — between Southern Democrats and Northern Republicans that ended Reconstruction and set the nation on its new course. Once in office, Hayes withdrew the last federal troops from the South and white supremacy became the rule. One hundred years later Hayes' action was assailed as having "ushered in almost a century of apartheid in America."

The conjunction of the man, Stilson Hutchins, and the moment, 1877, was propitious. The capital was hungry for a first-rate newspaper of its own and Hutchins had the wherewithal to create it. Although he had limited financial resources (there are no exact records), his background and training in journalism was immense and impressive, his motivation intense and politically partisan.

"Hutch," as he was called, was born in Whitefield, New Hampshire, on November 14, 1838. His education went only as far as a Harvard College preparatory school. He wrote letters to the Boston *Herald* at 17; cofounded a country weekly, the *North Iowan,* in Osage, Iowa, at 19; and quickly demonstrated a taste for politics with a decided Democratic bent by serving as chairman of the party's state committee before his twenty-first birthday. Next, he was editor of the Des Moines *Telegraph* and, in 1860, became owner of the *Iowa State Journal.* In 1862 he and a partner took over the Dubuque *Herald,* known as a Copperhead paper for its southern sympathies and branded a "secessionist sheet" by its enemies. How he avoided service in the Civil War is not recorded but of his sympathies there is no doubt — he named his youngest son for Robert E. Lee.

A year after Appomattox, this vigorous, restless man moved to St. Louis. There he cofounded the *Times,* became its managing editor, and then bought the *Dispatch,* where his office became "a headquarters for Democratic henchmen." But the *Dispatch* did badly and in two years Hutchins had lost his stake. He returned to the *Times* until he was forced out by new owners in May 1877.

In Missouri Hutchins plunged into state politics, serving two terms in the legislature. He was a delegate to the 1876 Democratic convention that nominated Tilden. Joseph Pulitzer, who later published the St. Louis *Post-Dispatch* and the New York *World,* was a fellow legislator. Hutchins at the *Times* gave the foreign-born Pulitzer his first job writing for an English-language paper; Pulitzer remained a lifelong friend, occasionally contributing to THE WASHINGTON POST. Somehow, in St. Louis Hutchins also found the time to study law and be admitted to the bar, although he never practiced.

One Missouri newspaper described Hutchins' energy as "of that sleepless kind which neither grows weary nor despondent . . . Cool in every emergency . . . fertile in resources and daring in plan and attack, he would be formidable in any fight . . . He hates sham . . . He is as true as steel to his friends, unrelenting to his enemies." Another paper termed him "confessedly, recognizedly, the leader" of the Missouri legislature, concluding prophetically: ". . . when he reaches an arena where there are foemen worthy of his steel, he will make himself well known. He has . . . ability enough to carry him on the high tide wherever he goes." And thus he went to Washington to found a newspaper.

In 1877 the United States had a population of about 46 million, approximately 6 million of them blacks, in 38 states. The nation was in transition, painfully, slowly, but surely, from a country torn by war and the slavery issue to a power obsessed with industry, commerce, and growth. At the crossroads between victorious North and humbled South was the national capital on the banks of the Potomac.

Washington was not a city of commerce or industry but one of government and politics. The residents' own sympathies, like Hutchins', were more southern than northern. The city had only 130,000 inhabitants, a third of them black, of whom some 30,000 had flocked to the capital from the rural South after the war. Another 20,000 lived in the still separate community of Georgetown and on the farms of Washington County, all within the District of Columbia.

Pennsylvania Avenue, that grand thoroughfare from Capitol to White House, had recently been paved on the north side with concrete, but the south side remained a morass of decaying wood blocks. Many other streets alternated between dust and mud. Cows and goats grazed near the Capitol. It was a half-finished city, newly embellished by nearly 60,000 trees planted a few years earlier by Alexander R. (Boss) Shepherd, who also had graded and surfaced streets, installed 3000 gas lamps (turned off when the moon was due to shine, whether or not it was visible), and ripped up offending railroad tracks before he was driven from office. He piled up an $18 million debt despite a debt ceiling of $6 million. That extravagance also resulted in Congress decreeing that municipal affairs should be run by a three-person board of district commissioners. Local suffrage was ended, not to be revived by Congress until 1974.

The symbol of the city's incompleteness was the stump of the marble shaft dedicated to George Washington, only yards from the Potomac shore behind the White House. Begun in 1848, it had reached a mere 184 of its eventual 555 feet when the funds ran out six years later. Still, the national capital had promise. In 1877 Henry Adams wrote to an English friend: "One of these days this will be a very great city if nothing happens to it. Even now it is a beautiful one and its situation is superb."

Washington may have been small but it was lusty. Close by both

White House and Monument, only a few steps from the hotels and emporiums of Pennsylvania Avenue, were the city's Civil War–spawned bordellos. To appease the outcries against rampant vice, General Joseph Hooker had "colonized" the nearly 4000 women. They were easily recognizable by their rouge and by skirts so short they sometimes disclosed shoe tops. The area they inhabited was dubbed Hooker's Division and thus the general's name entered history, not for his wartime exploits but as a synonym for prostitute. (The "Division" lasted until February 7, 1914, when Congress, legally at least, abolished the red-light district.)

The city had eight substantial hotels, ready-made clothing stores (business suits from $1), and bars and restaurants featuring bourbon and oysters. Members of Congress and other part-time inhabitants of the capital could board at the Continental Hotel on the Avenue for $1.50 a day, American plan, with rooms only from 50 cents a day. Houses rented from $12 to $50 a month; a new ten-room home in the northwest section could be purchased for $40 a month at 8 percent interest. The President's salary was $50,000 a year, the Vice President's $10,000. A member of Congress received $5000, a Cabinet officer $8000. A good government clerkship paid $1200, though most of the 7500 federal employees earned little more than $800 per annum.

To Hutchins the outcome of the Hayes-Tilden contest was a fraud. His paper, consequently, was a child of the fierce passions of the times. Hutchins made no secret of his political views as he plunged with vigor into a city long known as the graveyard of journalism, so many were the partisan sheets that had come and gone.

That first edition of THE WASHINGTON POST had four pages, each with seven columns, printed on rag paper. The page size was quite large, two inches wider and one inch longer than THE POST of 1977, although the type was considerably smaller. Appearing six mornings a week, the paper cost three cents or $8 a year. Volume 1, Number 1, appeared on Thursday, December 6, 1877, published at 914 Pennsylvania Avenue Northwest, the former office of the defunct daily *Chronicle,* where the Department of Justice building now stands.

In a page 2 editorial, Stilson Hutchins stated his case:

> Human beings sometimes come into the world without being able to assign practical reasons for their coming. When a newspaper is born there is always a reasonable excuse. In the case of *The Post* it needed only be said that Washington city is too large and too important to be denied the benign influence of a Democratic daily journal . . .

> *The Post* will aim to be a thorough-going newspaper, always abreast the times. It will be Democratic in politics and modern in style. The Democratic party controls twenty-five of the most important States of the Union today, and is in a position to prevent bad legislation. *The Post* will do what it can to uphold the Democratic majority in the House and the majestic Democratic minority in the Senate. It will bring about the political millennium which is due in 1880 . . .
>
> We will do what we can to promote intelligence in this neighborhood, and will certainly increase the conditions most favorable to the success and prosperity of our institutions by preaching sound Democracy.

In short, Hutchins set up shop in the capital because he knew, as did so many before and after, that a Washington newspaper could command the daily attention of men of power in all branches of the national government. His was not a search for mass circulation and wealth. He was content to keep his monthly accounts in the black with a modest circulation in a small city because, both in the news columns and especially on his editorial page to which he devoted his greatest attention, his voice would be heard at what he considered the most influential breakfast tables in America. In this he succeeded extraordinarily well. Copies of the first day's paper were placed on every congressman's desk; 50 years later a man who then had been a House page recalled "the hearty expressions of approval."

In Hutchins' opening statement he referred to "Mr. Hayes"; while Hayes was in the White House, Hutchins refused, beyond a rare occasion and that probably a slip, to refer to him in print as "President." Rather, Hayes was called "the acting President," "the bogus President," "his fraudulency," or "his immaculacy, the de facto President." To drive home the point he also referred to "President Tilden." An early editorial said that "we do not recognize the Hayes Administration further than is absolutely necessary to insure peace and tranquility." A news story about a Hayes speech carried the headline: TWADDLE OF THE FRAUD. It was to be expected that Hutchins' "Democratic daily journal" soon would be embroiled in verbal exchanges with the city's Republican organ, the *National Republican,* and its publisher, A. M. Clapp. Hutchins mocked it as the "Gnashional Republican" and Clapp, in retort, called Hutchins "the Missouri renegade."

Partisan journalism was still very common in the post-Reconstruction era, although newspapers as strictly party organs were fast dying out. If THE POST, owing allegiance to a party in principle though not in ownership, had been only a partisan Democratic paper, it probably would have joined the journalistic graveyard. But Hutchins provided something more: news, more news than any other Washington paper offered.

Hutchins gathered a small but competent staff. His first managing editor, 32 the night the first edition went to press, was Colonel John A. Cockerill who had held that position at the Cincinnati *Enquirer* and who went on to journalistic fame in the same job at Pulitzer's New York *World.* Though he stayed only a year and a half at THE POST, Cockerill suggested the paper's name, hired its first woman reporter (Calista Halsey, in 1878), and was the first of many paragraphers who provided editorial page pungency. The last to leave THE POST each night, Cockerill was a dynamo who mixed sarcasm with ribaldry. Augustus C. Buell of New York State became the chief editorial writer, aided by Montague L. Marks (who became the New York correspondent in 1878) and Captain Charles H. Allen who stayed on for 25 years. Frederick Aiken, a Washington lawyer who had been a junior counsel for Mary Surratt at the trial of the Lincoln assassination conspirators, was the first city editor. The star reporter was Stanley Huntley. In 1883 Hutchins hired Mrs. Lucy H. Hooper as his first foreign correspondent — in reality a stringer rather than a staff member — who mailed a column of social, art, and theater news from Paris.

For THE POST's first 16 years the newspaper type was hand set by printers from the longhand copy of reporters and editors. To make a duplicate the reporter wrote with a stylus, an agate-pointed pencil, on thin yellow tissue paper known as a "flimsy." To gather the news, reporters walked, rode high-wheeled bicycles, or took a horse-drawn streetcar or a particular hack parked for such duties outside the office. The same hack hauled the mail editions of the paper to the trains. Henry Litchfield West, one of the early reporters, was paid $7 a week to cover Georgetown news in the mornings as well as activities at Treasury, Agriculture, Post Office, and Interior in the afternoons. After turning in his early copy, West took the horsecar back to his Georgetown home for dinner, returning to THE POST for night assignments, such as covering meetings, and taking his turn at reporting police news. When the paper had gone to press around 3 A.M., West had to walk the more than three miles home because the horsecars had ceased running for the night. The practice of using the reporter's by-line at the head of a story still was decades off; it was a rare mark of distinction even to have one's name or initials appear at the foot of an article.

Hutchins himself quickly explored the city. Three months after THE POST's founding he wrote his half sister that he had been "looking about and I can truthfully say so far excellent. I have seen all there is except the last remains of the individual called George W. which I eschewed, not liking to witness so much inanimate greatness. I have spent most of my time at the capital where I have sat in great joy listening to the cooings of the august senators and playful representatives. I am quite intimate with several of the former and a large number of the latter. Such is fame."

Visitors flowed into THE POST offices where, Field related, they were greeted by "the fashionably-attired colored boy who stood at the door" to intercept them and ask: "Beg pardon, sah, but de gemmen is all busy. Take your card in, sah?" Whether Hutchins was in or out depended "on the condition of the copy-hook and the object of the visitor's visit."

Hutchins bragged in his first day's paper that THE POST began with "an assured circulation of nearly 10,000 copies distributed through the entire Union." In this period editors avidly scanned each other's publications for news and thus THE POST quickly became something of a national newspaper. Eight months later, on August 8, 1878, Hutchins established the *Weekly Post* to circulate his news and his views around the nation. In time the weekly edition, culled from the product of the daily, reached as far south as Texas, west to Nebraska, and north to New Hampshire. It lasted until 1916.

THE POST was an instant success. Eugene Field, who later fathered the newspaper column as a device for comment, had followed Hutchins from St. Louis to Washington to work for the new daily. In 1881, having departed the paper, Field wrote that THE POST was launched under most favorable auspices.

> It was the marvel of Washington journalism. The newspaper world of the continent, who had no idea that any good could come out of Nazareth, gaped in astonishment when this bright, saucy, vigorous bantling pranced blithely into the ring. The paper took immensely. It had spurs and it used them to advantage. Poor old man Clapp, sitting up in the fourth floor of the Republican building, groaned and shivered, and penned many a jeremiad against "the Missouri renegade." But, somehow or other, the public fancied the renegade, and the subscriptions would insist upon floating in . . .

The first issue had a "special dispatch" from New York headlined WHAT THE GOTHAMITES ARE DOING; a cable from London on the ongoing war between Russia and Turkey; the latest report about a dying pope; and, above all, political news: what happened the day before in Congress and what was happening in California where the state legislature was about to elect a United States senator. On the second day there was listed among new presidential nominations: "Theodore Roosevelt of New York to be collector of Customs, District of New York." He was the future President's father and these were the first of millions of words about various Roosevelts over the coming century.

Standard fare in the paper was the triad of congressional, New York, and foreign news, each rating a column on page 1. Headlines were more intriguing than informative: UNDER THE DOME, FLASHED BY CABLE, GOSSIP FROM GOTHAM. On Mondays came PIOUS PABLUM or what the local preachers had said on Sunday. During the long congressional recesses there were columns of Executive News, Capital Gossip, Government Grist, or Departmental Droppings. POST reporters, despite the continuing row with the President, had as much access as any to the executive mansion and elsewhere. "What 'The Post' Reporters Found Out at the Departments Yesterday" included: "The White House — Mr. Hayes enjoyed the loquacity yesterday of Post-master General Key, the long sentences of Mr. Evarts, the Mephistophelian suggestions of Mr. Schurz, and the wisdom of Representatives Benning and Mills."

Among the Departments was brash but concise: "Nothing very well calculated to curdle the blood of the Nation occurred in any of the brain workshops of the Government yesterday. The meeting of the Cabinet yesterday was not important." When such reporting brought subscribers' complaints, which THE POST published, that the paper's "tone is not sufficiently solemn," Hutchins replied that he had no intention of reverting to the dullness that had sent so many papers to the grave.

"Diplomacy is duplicity," THE POST declared. The paper took a dim view of the "needless expenditures" for, and the "absolute inutility" of, American diplomats abroad. It called for abolition of all positions except those of consuls dealing with trade matters. Nonetheless, Hutchins printed a great deal of foreign news, taking advantage of the new Atlantic cable to record the story of European power politics, wars, and the growth of British and French colonialism.

There was plenty of local news, too. Under District Notes it was recorded that "the foot pavement on thirteenth street southwest, near Maryland avenue, fell in yesterday morning, making a dangerous trap for pedestrians." Turkeys were selling "at two-thirds of the cost of good cuts of beef. This is very unusual." The day before Christmas of 1878 sirloin was 25 cents a pound, chickens $3.50 to $5 a dozen, and dinner out ranged from 25 cents to $1.50. THE POST noted that Washington had 1165 saloons and 15 breweries but it added that 71 recruits were enlisted

Christmas Day at a temperance meeting. Items from Georgetown and Alexandria, the two towns predating the establishment of the capital city and which had been incorporated into the original ten-mile-square District of Columbia, were listed as Suburban News. (Because the city grew so slowly the Virginia portion of the District, including Alexandria, was retroceded to that state in 1846.) Boundary Street, now Florida Avenue, was the northern edge of the city. Only an occasional news item emanated from the open spaces beyond and across the Anacostia River, which together comprised Washington County, until legalized betting moved there after being outlawed in the city.

News of sports at first was limited to an occasional paragraph on sculling, regattas (with competition for THE POST cup), horse racing, billiards, prize fights, and baseball. The Nationals, a baseball team organized in 1859, were still playing an assortment of minor teams such as Springfield, Albany, Holyoke, New Bedford, Worcester, Utica, and a team called Hop Bitters after a patent medicine advertised in THE POST as a cure for "sinking spells, fits, dizziness, palpitation and low spirits." Not until the winter of 1885 could the paper headline IN THE LEAGUE AT LAST to signal admission to the old National Baseball League.

When John L. Sullivan knocked out Patrick Ryan in 1881 it was front-page news, but an editorial called the fight the "most disgraceful spectacle seen in this country for many years." From time to time THE POST ran a chess column. Racing news, both in and out of the capital, often was featured. Walking contests were a craze in the early POST years, especially among women. MAY MARSHALL'S GREAT WALK at the Gymnasium on E Street lasted for 2796 quarter miles and she was acclaimed as "the champion lady pedestrian of the world" with a "splendid physique." Bicycle clubs grew, especially once solid rubber tires were invented for the big wheelers. By 1888 THE POST was exclaiming that "incredible as it may seem, there are at least 150 lady bicyclists in Washington at present." That same year the first tandem bike, the "bicycle built for two," appeared in the capital.

Eleven days after the paper's founding, AMUSEMENT THIS EVENING included Joseph Jefferson at the National Theater in *Rip Van Winkle.* A fashion note said that "eighteen button kid gloves are the latest. They come up to the shoulder and meet the short sleeve." Soon THE POST was running frequent social notes signed "Miss Grundy." She was Austine Sneed who had written the same combination of society and fashion for the *Evening Star.*

THE POST managed to cram a lot of news into its few pages by the use of one-paragraph or even single-sentence items: "Victor Hugo has a new idea. He says that in the twentieth century war, capital punishment, monarchy, dogmas and frontiers, will all disappear." "Field Marshal Baron Von Manteuffel has arrived at Strasburg to assume the governorship of Alsace-Lorraine." Or: "Severe frosts have occurred in the French wine districts," "The Italian Senate by a vote of 65 to 11 have decided to abolish the grist tax," and "The harvest prospects in Upper Silesia and East Prussia are very gloomy."

Hutchins and his first wife, Teresa, quickly established what he called "fortnightly symposiums" at their home. "His parlors were thrown open," Field recounted, "and a dozen or fifteen friends were invited to enjoy an evening of anecdote, song and wine," concluding with a cold supper. Occasionally "a chorus of colored singers, imported for the occasion from a neighboring church or academy, would vary the programme with their strangely characteristic melodies. The evenings were always charmingly spent, and the symposiums became immensely popular among statesmanly circles. Senator Lamar . . . used to say he would give a hundred dollars any time rather than miss one of the Hutchins symposiums." Lucius Q. C. Lamar, a Confederate officer and Mississippi Democrat, had helped Hutchins found his paper. On other, more intimate, evenings friends such as Senator Allen G. Thurman, an Ohio Democrat, dropped in to "smoke his pipe and drink sour mash." As a member of the Electoral Commission, Thurman had voted for Tilden to become President. Soon the publisher was in demand as an after-dinner speaker. In that role, Field wrote, "he is exceedingly felicitous, and as the presiding man at a banquet there are few who can compare with him . . . He is full of fun, of humor, of wit, of pleasant sarcasm."

Hutchins shrewdly contended that the paper was a roaring success with constantly rising circulation. A week after the paper began THE POST ran a letter to the editor complaining that newsboys were asking five cents. "It is worth five but the newsboy who charges that for it is a swindler," the paper replied. "He makes a fair profit at three cents, and purchasers should insist on having the paper at that price." Four weeks after the founding of THE POST it claimed it had "received yesterday over nine hundred new subscriptions." In February 1878, however, when Hutchins printed his circulation for the previous week it varied between 6100 and 6750; still, Hutchins claimed THE POST had the largest circulation for a morning paper in the capital. And he went after potential advertisers: "If, therefore, merchants desire to reach the people they should advertise in *The Post;* if, however, they desire to make their advertisements an excuse for extending aid to a favorite journal, nobody has a right to complain."

Four months after its founding THE POST bought the *Union,* a Republican paper, and for two weeks the masthead read: THE WASHINGTON POST AND UNION. On buying the paper Hutchins moved THE POST from 914 Pennsylvania Avenue into the *Union* building at 339–341 on the Avenue, long known as Jackson Hall and now the site of the United States Court House. Hutchins reprinted the comment of the Philadelphia *Times* on the purchase of the *Union:* "[THE POST,] which has sometimes been very naughty, has always been enterprising and is the first real newspaper Washington has ever had." By mid-1879 Hutchins contended that his paper "is more generally quoted than any other paper in the country and aims to be as reliable in its statements as it is terse and vigorous in its way of putting them." THE POST, he added, "is no longer an experiment, but a profitable business enterprise."

A center of controversy from its birth, THE POST quickly encountered the problem of any provocative journal with strong editorial opinions, a problem that continued, with some lapses, through its first century. Six weeks after the founding, Hutchins put it this way: "We hope to be able, some time or other, to disabuse the public mind in this community that a newspaper attack upon a public man is not necessarily the explosion of private malignity or the echo of personal grievance." On its first anniversary, with a circulation now of 11,875, the paper proudly stated:

> No man has been able to say that he owned it except its owner, and no clique, faction or set of men have been able to say they controlled it. It has endeavored to do justice to all parties, subserve honestly the interests of the Democracy, build up the city of Washington, protect the rights of the humblest citizens, and crowd the largest amount of news into the smallest possible space. Thousands of Republicans read it daily with a gratitude they do not hesitate to express, and twice ten thousand Democrats swear by it from one end of the country to the other.

Three months later, certain now that his venture was a solid success, Hutchins installed a new Hoe press, "capable of striking off both sides of the paper at one impression." By now the paper was carrying 12 columns of advertising, nearly two of its four pages of 6 columns each.

Halftone photographs in newspapers were yet to come, but Hutchins introduced drawings made from photographs quite early, initially in advertisements and then in the news columns. Appropriately, the first to make page 1 was a drawing of a design for completion of the Washington Monument. In August 1880 work was resumed on the shaft after a quarter century of delay. In its very first issue THE POST had declared that "New York City may pine for Egyptian obelisks and Cleopatra's old darning needles, but the heart of the Washingtonian is gladdened when his eye rests upon that chaste, but unfinished shaft dedicated to George Washington which springs like a toad-stool from the bosom of the Kidwell Marsh." For decades white marble chips of Monument stones, lying by the stump, were sold in the city's curio shops. In mid-1879, when plans for resuming construction were being made, one scheme, known as the Story proposal, would have sheathed the shaft in Victorian ugliness. To its credit THE POST, while printing its drawing of the Story monstrosity, cried out editorially that "you hope as you gaze on the Great Unfinished that some special interposition of Providence will prevent the infliction on us of the Story design."

In the five years it took to complete the great Monument, Henry E. Eland was THE POST reporter who lived with the construction job. His reward was to "jump over the monument" once the capstone was placed on the squally afternoon of December 6, 1884, the seventh birthday of THE POST. Eland and two fellow POST reporters had their photo taken on the work platform at the top and Eland later confessed to vandalism: he had scratched his initials with a pin on the 100-ounce aluminum cap. The formal dedication ceremony was held on the snow-covered Monument grounds on February 21, 1885 (Washington's Birthday fell on a Sunday), before 10,000 people.

The national capital felt a glow of pride at the completion of what was then the world's tallest man-made structure. The first tourists began to ascend in the Monument's steam-driven elevator on October 9, 1888. The brave walked up the 898 steps, inspecting the 188 memorial stones — gifts from the states, church and temperance groups, and foreign countries — set into the interior walls.

THE POST had campaigned for completion of the Monument and for reclaiming the Potomac flats and marshes, beginning in the early 1880s. An 1881 flood, during which "the Potomac river flowed into the city" covering much of Pennsylvania Avenue, spurred a drive to fill in the flats and create the present river front. THE POST pressured Congress for financial help for the project:

> The people of this District are utterly at the mercy of Congress. The Constitution places this community in the hands of Congress . . . Is it not time for those who have this responsibility to take hold of their obvious and imperative duties? Must we be bathed in sewage, flooded with Potomac overflows, and killed by malaria through lack of interest on the

> part of our lawmakers in the welfare of the Capital and its people?

"There is no reason," another editorial stated, "why Washington should not be made the peer of Paris or any other city on the globe."

Hutchins' vision of the future Washington was strengthened by the honeymoon he spent in Europe with his second wife. Teresa Hutchins had won a divorce in 1882 on grounds of adultery after 24 years of marriage. The next year he married Sarita Brady to whom he had been introduced by Frances Hodgson Burnett, then writing *Little Lord Fauntleroy* in her Washington home at 1219 I Street. For Sarita, Hutchins built a handsome mansion at 1603 Massachusetts Avenue. She died in childbirth 13 months later. Hutchins married a third time in 1890, after he had sold THE POST.

Though the paper began to sprinkle its pages with woodcuts, it had no regular artists or cartoonists. Powerful political cartoons by Thomas Nast and others then were appearing in the weeklies. On May 1, 1879, THE POST printed what can be called its first political cartoon — a ballot box atop a bayonet — as a jibe at Hayes for his veto of a Democratic bill to protect elections in the South. There were a few others, but in the final years of Hutchins' ownership, during the editorship of his son, Walter S. Hutchins, THE POST grew more sedate in its makeup and less provocative in its headlines. An 1888 editorial foolishly said that "the day of the caricature and cartoon as a political power is about over, though it may still pay as an amusement to the populace."

In mid-1888 Hutchins bought out both the morning *National Republican* and the afternoon *Critic.* In announcing the purchase Hutchins disclosed that THE POST had made a profit ranging from $25,000 to $40,000 for every year since its founding. Small though such figures now sound, it was an amazing feat. He had begun the paper with a staff of perhaps 40 men and boys who, he reported in mid-1878, "make from five to 40 dollars a week." Thus his weekly payroll ranged around $1000. Printers earned $3 a day while streetcar drivers made from $1.35 for an 11-hour day to $2 for 16 hours of work. THE POST's circulation figures, sometimes published, often not, ranged from 6100 to 14,000. Some especially newsy editions ran to 17,000. An edition with drawings of President Garfield's assassin and other figures in the case sent circulation soaring for the day. A high of 52,000 was reached for the inaugural edition of 1885 when Grover Cleveland became the first Democratic President in 24 years. THE POST's chief rival, the *Evening Star,* founded in 1852, had a substantially larger circulation, averaging 18,137 in 1880 and 32,295 in 1890.

Frank Carpenter, the widely reprinted Washington correspondent of the Cleveland *Leader,* wrote soon after Grover Cleveland came to the White House that THE POST, "enterprising and spicy," was the President's "official organ." Carp, as he was known, went on: "*The Washington Post* will now make more money than ever. The advertisers here will patronize it because it is the court paper. The thousands of clerks who want to keep on good terms with the administration will subscribe to it, reading it ostentatiously in their offices to hide their actual Republican sympathies." But before that day arrived THE POST had had to live through, and prosper during, the four Republican years of Garfield and Arthur who followed Hayes.

THE POST's advertising ranged from what are now called classified ads, then mostly placed by job seekers, boarding houses, or small merchants, to patent medicines and, later, department stores. Not uncommon were ads such as this one on August 13, 1879, under "Wanted-Situations": "Wanted — I will give $300 for a position in any of the departments. Address, LOYALTY, this office." For most of Hutchins' ownership a three-line ad for three days cost 25 cents. Two local enterprises that advertised in THE POST's first issue, the National Theater and the jewelry store then known as M. W. Galt, Bro. and Co., are still in business a century later. The first of thousands of Woodward & Lothrop advertisements appeared on February 25, 1880, when the firm began business in the capital as the Boston Store. Another survivor at the end of the paper's first century is the Harvey & Holden restaurant, later simply Harvey's, which came to fame for its oysters and other seafoods. Willard's Hotel, which long preceded THE POST, succumbed before the first POST century ended. Of national companies both the Pennsylvania and Baltimore & Ohio railroads were advertisers in the first issue.

The volume of advertising, of course, affects the number of newspaper pages each day. Hutchins' POST began with four, a quarter of the space in advertising. After the first decade THE POST went to 8 and then 12 pages. Hutchins experimented typographically, ranging from a six-column-page format to seven and even nine columns. For a week in 1887, page 1 was composed exclusively of classified ads in the British fashion of that period.

On May 2, 1880, Hutchins launched a Sunday edition, called for nearly ten months THE SUNDAY POST. The result was Washington's first newspaper published seven days a week; the *Evening Star* did not begin its Sunday edition until 1905, a quarter century later. Sunday papers in the capital, up to this time, were one-day-a-week sheets composed largely of gossip and fiction; THE POST soon ran them out of business. Hutchins filled his paper not only with news but also with features, book reviews, sports, and fiction. The first Sunday POST, eight pages for five cents, sold 8400 copies. The Sunday paper varied at first from 4 to 8 pages but within a few years was either 12 or 16 pages, with nearly half the space in advertising. Among the early fiction writers were Bret Harte and Robert Louis Stevenson. A frequent contributor was Joaquin Miller, "the poet of the Sierras," who lived in a log cabin on Meridian Hill at the north end of the city.

In hopes of adding circulation, Hutchins at one point resorted to a gimmick — a word-hunt game. Mary R. Wilcox, granddaughter of Mrs. Andrew Jackson Donaldson, mistress of the White House in Jackson's day, won $30 for finding 2431 words in the letters of the name Frances Folsom Cleveland. Hutchins never tried that again. On election nights the paper regularly drew a crowd, on occasion by adding a band as an attraction, with the election results thrown on a screen in front of THE POST building by calcium light from a stereopticon.

In national affairs the news ranged from the trivial (a delegation of 20 from Alexandria called on Hayes to press the claim of Colonel Mott Ball for the consulship at Belfast, Ireland, to which the President was "favorably disposed") to the serious (the 1878 yellow fever epidemic in the South, which claimed 20,000 lives). THE POST reported that, under Hayes, Republican collectors assessed government employees 2 percent of their salaries as "voluntary" contributions. Though Hutchins' halfheartedly supported civil service reform under Republican administrations, he was quick to print a list of patronage jobs opening up when Garfield succeeded Hayes: private secretary to the President, $3250 a year; Assistant Secretary of State, $3500; Solicitor General, $7500; district court judge, $3500.

Newspapers of the period wallowed in scandal, both personal and political or, best of all, a combination of the two. THE POST's first extra (in reality, a second edition of the regular paper) on August 11, 1879, was juicy. Senator Roscoe Conkling, the powerful and vain New York Republican known for his "turkey gobbler strut," had been paying too much attention to the wife of ex-Senator and ex-Governor William Sprague of Rhode Island. Sprague had driven the senator, "whom he charges with having despoiled his home," from his Narragansett Pier house at shotgun point. The wife was Kate Chase Sprague, daughter of the Chief Justice of the United States and the belle of the capital when President Lincoln had attended her wedding. Mrs. Sprague protested that "Mr. Conkling never paid me any attention that a wife could not honorably receive from her husband's friend, and it is false to say otherwise." She called "outrageous slander" the stories "of my remaining out at late hours and meeting Mr. Conkling at the Capitol." Nonetheless, aspects of the Sprague-Conkling story recurred in THE POST for years.

There were other varieties of scandal, too. A story headed A NAKED MODEL CLASS recounted that 20 young artists who had studied in Europe were paying $3 a sitting for nude models, though the artists had rejected models "from the demi-monde" and those who did pose sometimes wore masks. After the story appeared the group had to abandon its room at the Washington YMCA and seek other quarters.

For the political capital of the nation THE POST provided reams of copy about state politics. There were constant battles over the election of senators by state legislatures and the paper came out for direct election. There was the quadrennial jousting for presidential nominations and election. Hutchins did not send out his own reporters; rather, he drew on other newspapers (as they did on THE POST) and on "special correspondents" or stringers who worked for other papers. The job of the New York correspondent, in addition to furnishing a column or more of news and gossip, was to scan first editions of the morning papers as they came off the presses and to telegraph the best items to THE POST, which held open until around 4 A.M. THE POST had begun with the services of the Associated Press but early in 1879 Hutchins shut down the wire in a row over his assessment. It had been $75 a week but when the AP raised it to $300 he said that to pay such a sum "absolutely excludes me from the newspaper field." Not until 1881 did he patch up the quarrel and resume the AP reports.

Newspapers of the period quoted at length from each other, favorably and unfavorably, and fired editorial salvos back and forth. The New York *Times* was a particular Hutchins target. In 1878 THE POST called the *Times* "a radical Republican sheet of the deepest dye and of the most obdurate Bourbonism. It is a bitter, savage and proscriptive organ of the bitter, savage remnant of the ultra sectional party of Eternal Hate in the Northeastern states. It is, in fact, but little short of a fanatic."

On March 4, 1881, as Hayes gave way to Garfield, THE POST printed one of the most bitter editorials ever to appear in it or any other newspaper. Titled "Exit the Fraud," it said: "There should be no spot of ground on the continent to give him harborage or shelter save the few feet of earth needed for a nameless grave. Exit Hayes, the fraud. Eternal hatred to his memory."

Garfield's Vice President was Chester Alan Arthur whom THE POST termed "a ward politician by education and natural taste." In 1879 President Hayes had fired him from the post of customs collector at New York "in order that the office may be honestly administered." But Arthur had powerful friends, especially Senator Conkling who was Hayes' bitter enemy in intraparty battles, and he had been given second place on the GOP ticket. Although THE POST had strongly supported the Democratic candidacies of General Winfield Scott Hancock and William E. English, predicting victory for the two men, when Garfield and Arthur won, Hutchins accepted the outcome as honest. He declared that "*The Post* really enjoys the privilege of being able, conscientiously, to refer to the incumbent of the Executive Office, as the President."

When Garfield was a House member, however, THE POST had excoriated him for having been a beneficiary in the Crédit Mobilier scandal of the Grant administration. After his election the paper said, "If it is proper to expect so much from a dishonest man, we desire to indulge in the hope that the new President will give the country a wise and honest Administration."

On his 199th day in the White House James A. Garfield was mortally wounded by assassin Charles Guiteau at the old Baltimore & Potomac depot at Sixth and B streets Northwest, where the National Gallery of Art now stands. It was 9:30 in the morning of July 2, 1881. The *Evening Star* had a man at the station to cover the President's departure for Massachusetts where he was to have attended the Williams College commencement; THE POST's nearest reporter was seven blocks from the station. It was an early lesson in the journalistic necessity of dogging a chief executive's every move. The *Star*'s extra shouted: ASSASSINATION! THE PRESIDENT SHOT. THE POST next morning: HE STILL LIVES! Both were single-column headlines.

Thereafter THE POST followed in detail every painful day until the President's death on September 19 at Elberon, New Jersey, where he had been moved in hope that the more salubrious climate would help recovery. There were medical bulletins and accounts of Professor Alexander Graham Bell's "induction balance" device vainly used to locate the bullet. (A POST story in 1954 reported that nobody had told Bell the President lay on a bed with then new metal coils that foiled his device.) Headlines ran from the hopeful POSSIBILITY THAT HE MAY SURVIVE to the dire VERY NEAR TO DEATH. Hutchins himself interviewed Guiteau.

The morning of the shooting Guiteau's former landlady, unaware of what had just occurred, walked up to THE POST's want-ad counter intending to put this advertisement in the paper: "WANTED — Charles Guiteau of Illinois who gives the President and Secretary Blaine as references, to call at 924 14th St. and pay his board bill." She was Mrs. William S. Grant "who keeps a first class boarding house" which Guiteau had abandoned on June 30, the day THE POST announced that Garfield was "expected to start on his New England tour on Saturday."

The new President, Arthur, soon was being described in THE POST as "handsome and knightly" and "dressed with immaculate nicety," wearing "on the left lapel of his broadcloth coat a large and beautiful buttoniere." A widower, he was a night worker, breakfasting at 11 A.M. and dining at eight, with callers often arriving at his request between midnight and 3 or 4 A.M. Arthur was a socializer: he attended receptions and weddings, including that of Colorado Senator H. A. W. (Silver Dollar) Tabor to his beautiful Baby Doe at Willard's Hotel; he made the White House once again a center of hospitality. His cellar was celebrated and his state dinners included Chablis, claret, sherry, Rhine wine, champagne, Burgundy, brandy, and other liqueurs.

On New Year's Day of 1882, THE POST reported: "From 11 o'clock until three a continuous stream of humanity poured into the mansion, and not even the humblest of citizens was denied the pleasure of taking the Chief Magistrate by the hand." Arthur received in the Blue Room, decorated with Spanish moss draped on mirrors and chandeliers.

Like Lincoln and Hayes, Arthur used a summer house at the Soldiers' Home three miles north of the Capitol. But as a New Yorker with an abiding interest in Empire State politics, Arthur frequently traveled there either by train or by the executive steamer, *The Despatch*. THE POST commended him because he "pays his own bills while he is away from home, and his trip upon the Despatch is no exception to the rules."

Through the four years of Hayes' administration Hutchins had yearned for a Democratic successor. He worried that General Grant would try for a third Republican term in 1880. THE POST reported the general's 1877–1879 tour of the world and at one point suggested, only half humorously, that he accept an alleged proffer of the throne of Bulgaria. When Grant partisans, led by Conkling, began to build up a third-term movement THE POST declared editorially that "there is no use mincing words . . . It will take from $20,000,000 to $50,000,000 to elect Grant to the Presidency." Grant's friends put up a fight at the Chicago Republican convention but Garfield was nominated on the thirty-sixth ballot. It was not until Grover Cleveland finally broke the long Republican hold on the presidency that Hutchins was truly jubilant. Even before the outcome of the close election was certain THE POST celebrated Cleveland's victory over James G. Blaine with a Democratic rooster cartoon.

The Cleveland campaign was marked by two political bombshells. First, the Buffalo *Evening Telegraph* disclosed that Cleveland had fathered an illegitimate child. The resulting Republican attack must have deeply distressed Hutchins. It was a week before THE POST referred to the story and then only obliquely in a condemnation of Republican "smut mills . . . still grinding." THE POST did print the second bombshell on page 1: the Reverend Samuel D. Burchard's devastating reference to the Democratic party as one "whose antecedents are rum, Romanism, and rebellion." The day before the election the paper reported from New York that "Mr. Blaine not only did not rebuke this charge, but in responding told Mr. Burchard and his zealous associates that he realized the full weight of that which had been said to him." That gaffe lost Blaine the Irish-American vote in New York and cost him the state — and the election.

When Cleveland entered the White House THE POST editorially backed him on such issues as a tariff for revenue rather than for protectionism. This was a subject of hot debate now that America's "infant industries" were becoming giants, and the farmers filling up the vast American continent were more than ever conscious of the prices they had to pay for industrial goods. In the Cleveland era THE POST also began to print verbal sketches of western ranch life but, lacking foresight, neglected to print the name of their young author, Theodore Roosevelt.

In February 1888 the Democratic National Committee met in Washington to choose among contending cities for the site of that year's presidential convention. The young publisher of the San Francisco *Examiner,* William Randolph Hearst, wanted the convention for his city. To aid the cause he published, as pages 5 and 6 of THE POST of February 22, a special edition of the *Examiner,* with its own masthead and written by its own staff. But the convention choice was St. Louis.

After Cleveland's election with Hutchins' strong support, THE POST declared that "President Cleveland will, we hope, run his administration, and we shall continue to run *The Post.*" The declaration turned out to be true; nonetheless, the paper's relations with the White House were far closer than they had been during the Republican administrations. Of the five correspondents known to have access to major news at the White House one was THE POST's Richard Weightman. On November 4, 1885, after THE POST had been defending Cleveland on civil service reform, the President agreed to Hutchins' request for an interview. Weightman was sent to the White House. Cleveland sat down at his desk, pulled a block of cheap yellow paper in front of him, and with a pencil wrote out his own interview. THE POST thus was able to publish the President's own defense of his handling of civil service reform.

Little seemed to escape THE POST's reporters, not even "a lamp is to be erected on the corner of 21st and N streets" or "ice harvesting in the East branch" of the Potomac in January. When the House District Committee, in 1878, complained to the local government that "the deposit of street sweepings and offal on the low grounds south of the Capitol" resulted in "a very unpleasant odor which is wafted through the rooms and corridors of the Capitol," THE POST reported the health officer's contention that the real problem was "the ponds of stagnant water" in the bed of the abandoned canal across the Mall and that money from Congress was needed to fill in the canal. THE POST reported, too, that in 1879 nearly 15,000 of the 25,000 houses in Washington and Georgetown "take" Potomac water. Citizens could tell the river's condition by the color of their drinking water since raw water ran to homes until 1906. The intake at Great Falls was uncovered and eels swarmed into the water mains, necessitating an "eel trap" at each house connection. Cleaner water came from wells.

Crime was regularly chronicled. A local minister contended in 1879 that "the morals of the city are 50 percent better when Congress is away." The police force never seemed adequate. Pay cuts in late 1878 reduced a private's salary from $90 to $70 a month. By 1880 THE POST was complaining that the city had had 200 police patrolmen since 1860 with only 125 actually on street duty, though the new census showed 177,624 living in the District of Columbia.

Local transportation was a constant issue. Horse-drawn vehicles were supplemented in 1880 by "herdics" — one-horse, eight-passenger, five-cent-a-ride cabs with yellow plush cushions developed by Peter Herdic, who already had made a fortune with his new omnibus in Philadelphia. The regular horse-drawn streetcars ran on rails (30 miles of track in 1880), but the tracks projected above ground level, and carriages and wagons often lost a wheel crossing the rails. In 1890 came the first cable cars; in 1895 electric streetcars that drew their power from an underground third rail, a system that lasted until 1962. Luckily for the beauty of the capital, it was decreed in 1893 that electric power lines for streetcars in the central city must be underground; the same rule applied to telephone lines after 1880. Such rules, as well as franchises for the various transportation companies, were set by Congress, not the local government.

THE POST was an opponent of any move to restore local suffrage. Hutchins' paper claimed to see in suffrage proposals during the Hayes administration a scheme to increase the Republican vote since most blacks had become Republicans in gratitude for emancipation and Reconstruction. The national capital, THE POST said, is "to all intents and purposes, a government reservation, as much as a navy yard or a fort" and the commission system "has inaugurated an era of magnificent prosperity." An 1878 editorial declared that "we have a very poor opinion of negro suffrage." Another editorial the next year favored the idea of a nonvoting delegate to Congress despite fears that "the hordes of negroes who swarm here will be used to elect a delegate who will misrepresent our people." But THE POST did campaign repeatedly for the 50–50 principle established in 1878, under which half the cost of running the local government was paid out of federal funds, the other half collected from local citizens. The extent of the federal "contribution" remained an issue through the formal abolition of the 50–50 rule in 1920 to the end of THE POST's first century.

On August 31, 1886, Washington was hit by a rare earthquake, a shock that made "buildings rock and totter" and "their occupants rush wildly to the streets." Richmond and New York also felt that temblor but it was Charleston, South Carolina, that four days later suffered the greatest shock, one that devastated the city. THE POST called for and helped raise a relief fund, as it did during many other disasters around the country.

Frequent winter snows immobilized the city, sometimes cutting it off from the rest of the nation for days. On the last day of 1880 THE POST reported:

> The cold was so intense that the snow gave out a sharp, metallic ring under the feet of the pedestrian, while the carriage wheels were followed by the musical crunching of the crisp snow. People whose business called them out early in the morning hurried along closely muffled up. The windows of the crowded street-cars were thickly encrusted with frost, and the flanks of the toiling horses were covered with a frozen fleece of white. The large plate glasses in the store windows became opaque, and the entire city presented a genuine winter appearance.

The temperature the next day was seven degrees below zero, and it reached ten degrees below later when sleigh enthusiasts organized a grand masquerade party on Pennsylvania Avenue. The Potomac was frozen from shore to shore.

For the lucky, Christmas was both gay and good. In December 1881 the Palais Royal, a fashionable department store, advertised that for 25 cents the buyer could select as a gift "a leather pocket-book, or a doll, or a fine all linen handkerchief, or an ink-stand, or a pair of ear-rings, or a card receiver, or a pocket comb in Russian leather case."

The White House offered the height of elegance. Five days before Christmas 1881, after seven weeks of work by Louis C. Tiffany & Co., the redecorated mansion was opened to inspection. THE POST's reporter was captivated.

> A new era — the era of stained glass, tiled fireplaces and high mantelpieces — has dawned upon the White House. Aestheticism reigns within the walls supreme. Peacock blue and silver, crimson brown and dead gold, delicate primrose and pale fawn — these are now the prevailing tints of the interior furnishings. No longer is the White House simply the home of a Republican President. Lo, it is the temple of high art!

Amusements aplenty there were. The D'Oyly Carte traveling company presented *The Pirates of Penzance* at the National Theater. In 1881 the "Divine Sarah" Bernhardt triumphed in *Frou Frou* and *Camille* at the National. The "Genuine Colored Minstrels" were at Ford's Opera House; and *Ten Nights in a Barroom* was a big box-office success. Henry George, a man with "sharp, steely, restless blue eyes," came to lecture on *Progress and Poverty*; Mark Twain raised a gale of laughter. In the summer it was P. T. Barnum's circus and the races at Pimlico. Many a POST column was devoted to the noted agnostic Robert G. Ingersoll, whom the paper called "the pagan prince" but whose lectures, in part derived from Tom Paine, it ran at length.

Oscar Wilde came to Washington in January 1882 during his grand tour of America, prompted by the fact that Richard D'Oyly Carte, the London producer, was about to present Gilbert and Sullivan's *Patience*, which satirized Wilde and his fellow aesthetes. THE POST described him as "elaborately attired in a black frock coat, knee britches, black silk stockings, Oxford ties, elaborately embroidered white vest and ruffled shirt, on which sparkled a solitaire diamond of great magnitude, quality unknown." On January 22, THE POST ran a two-column cartoon likening Wilde to the wild man of Borneo with this editorial caption:

> We present in close juxtaposition the pictures of Mr. Wilde of England and a citizen of Borneo, who, so far as we have any record of him, is also Wild, and judging from the resemblance in feature, pose and occupation, undoubtedly akin. If Mr. Darwin is right in his theory, has not the climax of evolution been reached and are we not tending down the hill toward the aboriginal starting point again?

The height of the capital's social season came between New Year's Day and Easter Sunday. On New Year's of 1881 the entire diplomatic corps turned up "in full court dress" to call at Secretary of State William

M. Evarts' "elegant house" on Lafayette Square. THE POST listed in advance New Year's Day receptions at more than 200 homes and hotel parlors. It must have cost some a pretty penny what with Mumm's Extra Dry advertised at $22 a case.

Social life in the capital, then as now, was not just a matter of visiting lecturers, belles and beaux, splashy embassy dinners, or fashionable soirees by the old families known as cliff dwellers. Social life bears a direct relationship to power and power means money as well as influence — and sometimes influence sold for money. In the early years of THE POST, as ever after, the capital, and the Capitol itself, swarmed with lobbyists seeking favors.

Of all Washington's lobbyists in THE POST's early years Sam Ward was doubtless the most famous, though not so famous a person as his sister, Julia Ward Howe, who had written "The Battle Hymn of the Republic" at Willard's Hotel in 1862. Ward boasted that he knew the dinner-table tastes of every man in Washington worth cultivating; stewed terrapin, Maryland style, was his own favorite dish. Many of his dinners were given at Welcker's on 15th Street just above New York Avenue, at the old Metropolitan Hotel in Georgetown, or at Chamberlin's at 15th and I streets.

On occasion Congress tried to discover just what Ward did in the way of lobbying. Once he admitted to an investigating committee that he worked "sometimes for a railroad man wanting information, sometimes for a patentee wanting a patent renewed, or a broker wanting to know what the Treasury was going to do" or sometimes for "a banker anxious about the financial movements in Congress, or a merchant about the tariff." The dinners he gave, he explained, demonstrated that "diplomacy is assisted by good dinners. Dinners give a chance to ask a gentleman a civil question and to get a civil answer." Uncounted thousands of lobbyists would use the same technique but none with more gastronomic elegance.

Ward avoided the Capitol but others did not. In 1879 the *Evening Star* reported that the correspondents covering Congress set new regulations on who could use the press galleries in House and Senate in order to prevent their being "overrun by dead beats and lobbyists." By 1884 the rules were further strengthened by excluding from gallery membership those who also held jobs on the side in government departments.

The "high rollers" gathered at John Chamberlin's establishment. Chamberlin had come to Washington in the 1870s to open a high-class gambling place at 1627 I Street, later combining food and drink with the cards. At Chamberlin's, it was said, enough senators would appear of an evening to constitute a quorum. One also could find actors, financiers, and such celebrities as William A. (Buffalo Bill) Cody. There were other gambling halls, with or without free food, for the less well heeled, including many a government clerk. Just outside the city limits members of Congress and others took in the cockfights with bets on the side or chuck-a-luck and over-and-under monte.

Rutherford B. Hayes, the embodiment of Victorian respectability, had enjoyed an occasional glass of wine before he came to the presidency. But once in the White House he deferred to his temperance-minded wife who promptly became known as "Lemonade Lucy." THE POST reported that "the absence of wines from the tables of the Cabinet officers, and from those of high social distinction was noticeable." Ben: Perley Poore, a famous Washington correspondent, reported that oranges on the White House dinner table concealed frozen punch, a large ingredient of which was rum. "Thenceforth (without the knowledge of Mrs. Hayes, of course) Roman punch was served about the middle of the state dinners . . . This phase of the dinner was named by those who enjoyed it 'the Life-Saving Station.' "

But was it really true? Hayes wrote in his diary on January 10, 1887, having read Poore's account in his just-published *Reminiscences,* that "the joke of the Roman punch oranges was not on us, but on the drinking people. My orders were to flavor them *rather strongly* with the same flavor that is found in Jamaica rum. This took! There was not a drop of spirits in them!"

Hutchins' POST preferred to believe that liquor really was secretly available at the White House. On February 28, 1879, it reprinted a savage account of official drunkenness from the Baltimore *Gazette* — including the charge that "Hayes was sitting in his private office trying to write a veto of the Chinese bill with a corkscrew."

If the Hayeses formally banned liquor from the White House, Mrs. Hayes did provide a new entertainment for children. When Congress forbade Easter egg–rolling on the Capitol grounds because the custom was ruining the grass, Mrs. Hayes opened the White House grounds and the practice continues to this day.

Pre-Lenten pleasures included a round of "dinners, suppers, balls, hops and receptions" at Willard's Hotel. Cabinet members' receptions fell on Wednesdays and senators' wives received on Thursdays. Irish-Americans and German-Americans held their rival St. Patrick's Day Parade and *Schuetzen Verein,* the latter often in honor of "King" Christian Ruppert, the brewer.

Of all Washington social news White House weddings have proved to be the most enthralling. Grover Cleveland, a bachelor of 49, was the only President to be married in the Executive Mansion. His bride, 21-year-old Frances Folsom, was the daughter of the President's former law partner. On April 18, 1886, THE POST printed its first marital rumor about Cleveland in the form of a New York *Sun* story that linked the President to Miss Folsom. The next day on page 1 under WILL HE GET MARRIED? there were more rumors. Then came the report that the President had bought a summer home in the hills northwest of the city. On May 25 a POST editorial said that Cleveland surely would marry and that would "not only restore the fulcrum of the local social world, but will tend to increase the sprightliness and gaiety of the Capital next winter."

Three days later the White House announced the wedding would be held June 2. The June 3 headline said simply MARRIED! with a full account of the eleventh White House wedding. The Clevelands went by train to Deer Park in western Maryland for their honeymoon, a clutch of reporters camping nearby. THE POST's man reported that the President sat on the front porch of their cottage in slippers while the new Mrs. Cleveland wore a "white morning wrapper." Cleveland was an avid fisherman and he soon took his bride along but, THE POST recounted, she had no luck the first day. In six days the couple was back at the White House and on June 19 came the first public reception with 4593 visitors shaking the hands of both the President and the new First Lady.

Lafayette Square was the scene of much social activity. A year and a half before the Cleveland wedding Emily Beale, daughter of General and Mrs. Edward F. Beale, was married in the drawing room of the family's residence on the Square, Decatur House, to John R. McLean. At that time McLean was the editor and publisher of the Cincinnati *Enquirer;* in 1905 he would buy THE WASHINGTON POST. In 1889 the McLeans instituted an annual children's party for those of the social world, a custom continued into the 1920s. At the corner of 16th and H streets, the acerbic Henry Adams and diplomat-historian John Hay shared adjoining houses that Henry Hobson Richardson had designed for them in 1885. Adams' breakfasts became an institution in the 1880s and an invitation a prize. Just off the Square lived the historian George Bancroft, who originated the American Beauty rose in the garden of his H Street home.

William W. Corcoran, Washington's leading philanthropist and art benefactor, whose Civil War sympathies for the South were no bar to his popularity in the capital, also lived on the Square, in Daniel Webster's old house. Of all the familiar figures to be seen on the capital's streets Corcoran undoubtedly was the most magnificent. He carried a gold-headed cane, wore gloves even in the hottest weather, and always had a red rose in his buttonhole. He delighted in giving oyster-roast suppers, supplying each guest with a pail for shucking. The flow of visitors to such houses as Corcoran's was unending — kings, princes, commoners of note from around the country and abroad. Diplomats and their ladies, at least those who did not leave the capital during the hot and humid summers, chartered a Chesapeake & Ohio canal boat for a gay ride up to the Great Falls of the Potomac. In 1878 scientists, artists, and writers organized the Cosmos Club; generals and bankers formed the Metropolitan Club.

For the less fortunate, however, Washington, especially in cold weather, was often grim. At noon and in the evening Mr. Hugh of the Morton House at 922–924 F Street served poor whites (provided they "be free from any sign of intoxication") a meal of soup, meat, two kinds of vegetables, bread one piece of pie or a plate of pudding, and coffee or tea, all for ten cents. There were others who ate on Ninth Street at "Abner's Five Cent Lunch," while the very poor, as many as 1600 a day, ate a "penny lunch" at Mrs. Roberts' place. For this latter establishment Congress provided some of the funds, though it was an annual battle to win approval of the money for such charity.

At the bottom of the capital heap were the blacks. A central problem of THE POST's early years, the post-Reconstruction era, was the future of the Negro in America. Hutchins backed the return to white supremacy in the old Confederacy. This was reflected in his acceptance of segregation in the District of Columbia, his opposition to local home rule including a Negro vote, and his printed quarrels with those newspapers that condemned the end of Reconstruction.

On September 23, 1879, when THE POST was 21 months old, the newspaper published a long editorial that outlined Hutchins' views and indicated the paper's handling of news about the race problem. Entitled "The Negro North and South," it said in part:

> It cannot be denied that in Southern society there is discrimination between the whites and blacks . . . There is no pretense of social equality in that section. The negro has a social world of his own. He is not admitted and does not expect admission to the social circles of the whites.
>
> The amended Constitution guarantees the negro equality before the law. He can sue and be sued in the courts, and can sit on juries. But there is no Constitutional or statutory provision requiring a white man to invite the negro to his home,

> or to make a companion of him. As a rule, the negroes of the South are rude and ignorant. Their personal habits and manners are disagreeable. Their animal nature has been well developed, but their intellectual powers are of a low order. They are not fit to mingle in refined society, and feel no regret at being excluded.

Nonetheless, the editorial continued, southern whites acted "generously and manfully" toward the blacks, principally by supporting education for Negro children. "When the ballot was given to the negro, it became not simply a question of justice or generosity, but a matter of the highest expediency to educate him, to put as much enlightenment as possible behind his ballot." In contrast had been the action of northern carpetbaggers, "banding the negroes together like herds of cattle or droves of mules, [using] them as a political force to despoil the whites, and do irreparable wrong to themselves." The blacks' ignorance had made this possible. "Had they been intelligent they would have seen that, in their poverty, owning no land and having no homes in their own right, their interests were identical with those of their late masters."

Education of the southern Negro had paid substantial dividends, THE POST contended:

> The rising generation of blacks in the South is vastly superior in mental force to the men and women who were set free by the war. The work of education will go on, the negro will continue to improve, he will become a more intelligent voter and a better citizen, but he will not be on terms of social equality with the whites until human nature is made over again and some of its traits are eliminated.

"How is it in the North? Is there any social equality between the races in any Northern state?" asked the editorial writer. The answer was a resounding no.

> The North offers the negro no inducement that he does not possess in the South . . . Wherever he may reside, he need not hope for admission to the social circles of the whites, nor should he desire it. Let the colored people stop striving for impossible recognition, be content with their own society, and make it as exclusive and high-toned as they please. They will thus show a degree of self-respect that will commend them to all classes.

In a September 1878 editorial THE POST had said that "there can be no doubt that Washington would be wealthier, healthier and happier for an immediate exodus of 15,000 or 20,000 of her negro population and the summary destruction of the huts and shanties in which they huddle to breed vermin and squalor." The next year THE POST, referring to "the wretched conditions of many thousand colored in this city," declared that "more than half of the blacks in this District have but a precarious, wretched existence. There is no hope of relief except in sending this surplus labor where it may find employment."

In 1878 THE POST reported there were 12,374 colored children, ages 6 to 17, in public schools compared to 26,426 whites; but the story did not disclose the inferior education available to the blacks or the fewer years they remained in school. The 1880 census listed 59.3 percent of the colored population, compared to 5.4 percent of the whites, as unable to write. The schools were segregated in a dual system. In 1869 Congress had voted to merge the two school boards but Negro leaders persuaded President Andrew Johnson to veto the bill lest their own schools suffer. By 1878 Negro leaders had abandoned the idea of integrated schools. In Washington, the board of health reported, the Negro suffered from a high mortality rate with diphtheria, scarlet fever, and malaria the principal diseases. According to THE POST, there had been a great increase in the death rate of Negroes "since they were thrown upon their own resources."

By 1883 a POST reporter's survey, run under the headline A COLORED MAN'S RIGHT, showed that the Reconstruction civil rights laws on "entertainment at hotels, saloons and eating houses" were "almost completely ignored except in the case of very light colored or distinguished members of the negro race. Yet this city has the reputation among colored people of being one of the most liberal in the country in this respect." At Harvey & Holden's on the south side of the Avenue at 11th Street, Harvey told the reporter that "he must either exclude colored people from his table or lose his white trade and close his place."

Frederick Douglass, born a slave, played a leading role in both abolition and enfranchisement for the freedmen. He believed that the solution of the race question lay in the amalgamation of the black and white races. Douglass, whose second wife was white, became a man of property and his Washington home is now a national shrine. Because, to the white majority, he was not a militant but a moderate and an educated man, he was rewarded with a number of public posts including that of minister to Haiti.

Douglass was favorably quoted in THE POST for urging the southern blacks not to accept schemes to leave the South, schemes the paper hinted were a radical Republican attempt to fatten the GOP vote in northern states. By 1887, however, the Negro's plight in the South was evident for those willing to see. Douglass was quoted as saying that conditions there were then worse than at any time since emancipation. To this THE POST loftily replied that there had "never been a time when the Southern negroes were doing so well." But there were no POST reporters touring the South to find out the facts.

During Hutchins' years, THE POST reported many stories of violent racial crimes, usually blacks against whites. On occasion, lynchings were reported including one or two of whites by whites. There was no editorial condemnation of the lynching in nearby Rockville, Maryland, of a Negro accused of attacking white women. But a June 25, 1881, editorial declared, with reference to race, that "lynching is becoming fearfully common all over the country . . . The mob spirit is a terrible thing to invoke. The man who incites a mob today may need the protection of the law tomorrow." The paper printed matter-of-factly the story of enforcement of Virginia's antimiscegenation law under which a Negro and his white wife were sentenced to two years in jail.

After Garfield's election, while the newspapers were speculating on his coming Cabinet selections, THE POST gleefully picked up the suggestion of the Washington *Advocate,* "a colored organ," that Blanche K. Bruce of Mississippi, then the one remaining Negro senator, should be appointed. A POST editorial commented that blacks had held the balance of power in the election and had thrown it to Garfield. Earlier THE POST had reported that "the chocolate-colored senator from Mississippi" had married in Cleveland a "pretty quadroon white" and the paper speculated, incorrectly, that when he brought her to Washington "the opening of the next social season will set 'society' to wrestling with one of those great questions that sometimes threaten demolition of the entire social structure."

The senator was a POST favorite. Born a slave in Prince Edward County, Virginia, he attended Oberlin College, served one term in the Senate, and became the District's recorder of deeds (as had Douglass before him, establishing a precedent for decades that a Negro should fill that post). Then, by Garfield's appointment, he served as Register of the Treasury.

In 1878 Bruce told "an inquisitive chap of *The Post*" that "my earnest advice to the colored people is to remain in the South . . . All the bitterness and prejudice seems to have worn away and both races are struggling together for the common good. You never hear any more of the antagonisms between the races that used to exist, and it is evident there is a better time coming for the entire South."

If both Hutchins and Bruce were blind to what really was happening to the former slaves in the South, others pressed to enforce the Reconstruction era Civil Rights Act and to make use of the post–Civil War 14th Amendment to the Constitution. THE POST left no doubt that it opposed both efforts. When the Supreme Court in 1880 declared that West Virginia had violated the 14th Amendment's equal protection of the laws by trying a Negro under a law requiring all-white juries, THE POST condemned the ruling as "sophistry, misnamed judicial logic, by which the Federal usurpation of State power is sanctioned."

On October 15, 1883, the Supreme Court, with only the first Mr. Justice John Marshall Harlan dissenting, struck down the Civil Rights Act. Headlined THE POST: AN IMPORTANT DECISION SETTLING THE STATUS OF THE COLORED RACE. THE LONG-VEXED QUESTION FINALLY AND WISELY DETERMINED. The court's ruling nullified prosecutions on behalf of Negroes who were refused equal accommodations and privileges in inns and hotels, railroad cars and theaters. The ruling legally affected all the states but did not include the District of Columbia and other territories. Nevertheless, for all practical purposes the effect of the ruling and of the general nonenforcement of local antidiscrimination laws was to fasten segregation on Washington for nearly three-quarters of a century. THE POST declared editorially that "we have no idea that it [the Supreme Court decision] will be injurious or that it will beget oppression. A race that has the ballot in this country can get along without laws regulating hotel accommodations and theaters."

But the decision created alarm among Negro leaders and some 2000 people, both blacks and whites, packed Lincoln Hall to protest. Bruce and Douglass were there along with Ingersoll, the agnostic, who called the ruling the most infamous since the Dred Scott decision. Yet both Douglass and Ingersoll advised that the law must be obeyed. Ingersoll praised the Harlan dissent; THE POST did not print it.

Segregation in the South, and in effect that included Washington, was coming into full force, though there were exceptions. In 1887, at an enormous reunion of Civil War veterans from both North and South, companies from Mississippi and Tennessee refused to march in the parade down the Avenue because colored companies of Union veterans also were to march. But President Cleveland shook the hands of blacks as well as whites at a White House reception.

Six months before the Supreme Court civil rights decision, on the twenty-first anniversary of the congressional act ending slavery in the national capital, THE POST had recounted the facts of emancipation in Washington. There had been some 3000 slaves in the city for whom their owners had been paid compensation of $914,942. The largest slave owner had been George Washington Young who owned 69 persons, for which he had received $17,771.85. An oddity was that three blacks had collected for either spouses or children. The largest sum paid for a slave was $788, the smallest $10.95 for an infant. No compensation was paid for 101 slaves judged too old or feeble to be of value.

America in the Hutchins years had two other minority race problems: the native Indians and the imported Chinese.

THE POST was full of stories on the army's forays "against the hostile Indians." A front-page story on June 4, 1878, began: "Dispatches received at Army headquarters from different points in the West indicate that the apprehended troubles with the Indians on the return of warm weather were not groundless. Great uneasiness prevails among the different tribes, and the old disposition to resent the presence of whites in their territory is becoming manifest." By July the headline on a story from Oregon and Washington Territory read: SLAYING THE SAVAGES. ANOTHER HEAVY BATTLE EXPECTED — THE SETTLERS ARMED. Next year: WAR TO THE KNIFE. A BLOODY BATTLE WITH THE UTE INDIANS. And: THE RED-HANDED UTES. A BELIEF THAT THEY HAVE BUTCHERED ALL THE WHITES. RED SCALP-LIFTERS. NARRATIVE OF BARBARITIES BY AN ONLY SURVIVOR. These last accounts came from Wyoming Territory.

To those in Washington, far from the Indian wars, delay in resolving Indian problems meant delay in developing the United States. A POST editorial on October 8, 1879, titled "Our Red Wards," expressed Hutchins' view of the problem and what should be done.

> Most of our troubles with the Indians have grown out of the original blunder of regarding the various tribes as so many nations, and entering into solemn treaties with them, as if they were foreign and independent powers. To the early colonial settlers this policy was a necessity. They were weak, and the Aborigines were strong. They were intruders on the possessions of the natives, and were glad to escape strife by entering into compacts of amity on the best terms they could get.

Indian tribes, "with habits, customs and modes of life directly antagonistic to our civilization," were in the track of Western migration, "closing all the avenues to the best portions of the continent." The treaties were broken. "Any other result was impossible. It would have been as easy to dam up the Mississippi by an act of Congress, and prevent its waters from reaching the Gulf, as to hold back 'the tide of Empire' by treaties with the simple red men." Even worse, new compacts were made only to be broken in the same way. "So we have gone on, placing ourselves always in the wrong by pledging impossible things, giving the Indians fresh ground of complaint by the abrogation of ridiculous and preposterous treaties."

THE POST proposed:

> The nomadic Indian must disappear. The race must become self-supporting, and must be compelled to obey the laws. To all tribes or fragments of tribes who will try to support themselves by tilling the soil, we should render all reasonable encouragement. But to the savage who will not submit to the inevitable, we should show the mailed hand of martial power and force them to accept the only conditions on which they can hope to live — industry and obedience to the law. We can't go on forever keeping up the delusion that these people are independent nations, fit subjects for solemn treaties . . . The War department should take charge of the Indians, and teach them the stern lesson that he who will not work shall not eat.

By 1885 most Indians had been forced into reservations. The holdouts were no match for the United States Army, which had the railroads as the line of supply and reinforcement. The Indian wars came to an end, for all practical purposes, in 1886 with the surrender of the Apache leader Geronimo and the 1890 army massacre of the Sioux at Wounded Knee, South Dakota.

THE POST was also unsympathetic to the Chinese minority. Imported by the thousands to build the western railroads, the Chinese continued to emigrate to the United States and some began to move to eastern cities, including Washington, to create Chinatowns. MOON-EYED WORKMEN, said one headline in 1879, CHEAP MONGOLIAN LABOR AND THE BANEFUL RESULT. The story declared that "a Chinaman can live on twenty cents a day" and "they even bring their clothes and food to the country." THE POST's policy was to support immigration from Europe, especially skilled workmen and farmers to fill up the vast empty spaces in midcontinent; but this open-arms policy did not apply to the Chinese. THE POST reported "indignation" in California when President Arthur vetoed a Chinese Exclusion Act. Anti-Chinese riots continued until passage of another act in 1882. Once when the Senate in executive session was considering a treaty with China, THE POST and other papers obtained the text and printed its contents. Of the resulting row over the leak, a POST editorial said what the paper would say in one way or another many times in subsequent years: "The Senate is able to survive ridicule but that is not a good reason for making itself ridiculous."

Women were not a minority in numbers in the United States but they clearly were second-class citizens. Barely a month after THE POST's founding an editorial presented what now seems a curious viewpoint. Instead of complaining about her subordinate position, THE POST advised, a woman "should be grateful for the kindly curbs that have been placed upon her for her own good here and hereafter. All the gentle traits that render her lovable have been developed by the system that the suffragists condemn, and all that would make her hateful are repressed by the same system." The absence of opportunity amounted to an immunity from the cares of government. "Let her be content with her lot."

Suffragettes, called in a POST headline THOSE FRANTIC FEMALES, were constantly besieging the capital. Belva A. Lockwood, Susan B. Anthony, and Dr. Mary E. Walker were frequently in the news. Dr. Walker was a dress reformer who preferred pantaloons. A March 1, 1878, story reported that she had applied for appointment as a District policewoman because, she told a POST reporter, a small boy had followed her on the city streets calling out "give me a chew of tobacco," "take off your pants," and "pull down your vest." Dr. Walker complained that a policeman refused to arrest the harasser.

Mrs. Lockwood, with a law degree from Washington's National University, began practicing in 1873. By the 1880s she was a familiar sight in Washington, having stormed the Supreme Court and forced the justices to admit her as the first woman to practice before them. An 1882 account called her "a finished scholar" and related, with an accompanying drawing, how she "asserts her independence in battling the world unaided and alone riding a tricycle in sunshine or in storm . . . flying up the Avenue on her three-footed nag, her cargo a bag of briefs for the Supreme Court or . . . for the Pension Office." In 1884 and again in 1888 Mrs. Lockwood ran for President as the candidate of the Equal Rights party. She received a few thousand votes.

The suffragettes provided what to THE POST was disquieting news of women. More to the paper's taste were such New York dispatches as one that began: "The absorbing topic among all classes of the community is the confession of Mrs. Tilton of her intimacy with the Rev. Henry Ward Beecher." Or this under the headline SUMMER RESORT SALAD: "At Rehoboth City [a Delaware resort patronized by Washingtonians] the young ladies are holding indignation meetings over the scarcity of young men. The few gentlemen who are still there are enjoying their vacation hugely." And, from Saratoga, New York, where Washingtonians favored the Grand Union Hotel, "young ladies at Saratoga who receive boxes of candy and confectionery from their gentlemen friends and admirers display them at the table d'hôte."

During Hutchins' years at THE POST the United States, safely isolated by the great oceans from the tribulations of the rest of the world, concentrated its energies on expansion and growth of its domestic economy. The leaders of big business who came to be known as the "robber barons" were the beneficiaries of government largess in the form of vast land grants and government help through protective tariffs. The inevitable reaction came first from the workingman, with some aid in time from his natural economic ally, the farmer, and eventually from the federal government.

The effect of these developments in Washington, a city having no sizable industry of its own, was reflected in the political struggles and controversies in Congress, at the White House, and in the Supreme Court. THE POST carried news stories about both capital and labor, early indicating the importance of the former by printing New York stock market tables. Three weeks after its founding the paper had listed quotations for 19 stocks and 10 bonds on the New York exchange as well as cotton and produce figures. By 1880 the tables were more extensive and the paper was carrying half a column of advertisements for mining company stocks.

However, Hutchins obviously was aware of the growth of big business and the corruption that the scramble for wealth engendered both in Washington and in the state capitals. From its beginning, THE POST had cast a jaundiced eye on unbridled business. An editorial of January 17, 1878, six weeks after the paper's founding, warned Hutchins' Democratic party that its members in Congress "must permit no legislation in favor of classes, corporations or monopolies as against the masses of the people and their interests." Existing legislation that "perniciously associated" the government with class and corporate interests "should be terminated in the speediest and most practicable way possible." The editorial cited abuses in the sale of Northern Pacific securities, as well as fraudulent activities involving the Union Pacific and Central Pacific railroads.

At that time, the railroads were by far the most important industry in the country, as the iron horse gradually tied the nation together, North to South, East to West. John D. Rockefeller and Andrew Carnegie were beginning to amass their vast fortunes in oil and steel, but until about 1890 the railroads were the dominant corporate structures.

When Jay Gould, in the course of a strike against one of his railroads, appeared at the Capitol a POST reporter described him thus: "Jay Gould — quiet and cool when he scored a point in his favor, evasive when closely pressed, a little hot-tempered when describing alleged wrongs, good-humored when it suited his purpose and keenly astute always — was for five hours yesterday a witness before the House committee now investigating the great strike." Gould and William H. Vanderbilt were becoming so unpopular that, when Republican presidential candidate Blaine dined with them and others before the 1884 election, the publicity helped his rival, Cleveland.

On October 2, 1882, Vanderbilt, angry at those who sought to curtail his power, was asked by a reporter whether or not he ran his Pennsylvania Railroad "for the public interest." To this the magnate blurted out: "The public be damned!" THE POST ignored that sensational quote but six days later reacted to the incident with an editorial under the heading "Vanderbilt and Anti-Monopoly." Noting that Vanderbilt had so cut expenses to increase profits that fatal accidents had occurred on his lines, the editorial perceptively commented that "the possessing of immense wealth often exerts a brutalizing influence on the possessor." Vanderbilt had complained of the "anti-monopoly movement" which he declared was "inspired by a set of fools and blackmailers"; he had commented contemptuously that "when I want to buy up any politician, I always find the anti-monopolists the most purchaseable. They don't come too high." In reply, the editorial said that the movement to curb the corporations was the most important issue to arise in the United States since the Civil War. Corporations owned legislatures and executives, the paper charged, and through these they dictated the appointment of judges. The indictment continued: "The power of enormous masses of capital in the hands of a few ambitious scheming men, whose interest is promoted by robbing labor of its just rewards to any extent short of the actual crushing out of labor, is the great danger that menaces our future."

While THE POST clearly defined the savagery of the corporations and called for their control, it put little faith in the one counterforce then beginning to rise in the nation — the labor unions. A principal reason for the paper's distaste apparently was the violence associated with early labor organizing efforts; a secondary reason evidently was Hutchins' own problems at THE POST with the printers' union.

A legitimate reason for labor organization was the growing demand for an eight-hour day, a movement that helped swell the ranks of the

Knights of Labor. Headed by Grand Master Workman Terence V. Powderly, the Knights were a precursor of the American Federation of Labor, organized in 1886 and long led by Samuel Gompers. Powderly's eight-hour-day agitation was duly noted in THE POST but, after an 1878 "workingman's parade" espousing that principle, an editorial declared:

> In our judgment the whole theory of trades' unionism is faulty, and the practice of the unions calculated to weaken rather than to advance the cause of labor. If half the diligence now spent by isolated organizations of workingmen in trying to coerce their employers to pay wages which the rules of business will not permit to be paid, should be exerted in shaping the political destinies of the country aright at the ballot-box, there would be no trouble about wages, no lack of work, no plethora of workmen, and hence no necessity for trades' unions.

THE POST condemned Pennsylvania "coal barons" who paid only a pitiful 90 cents a day to their miners, commenting that such employers were good producers of anarchists. But strikers led by the terroristic Molly Maguires in the Keystone State were regularly dubbed "communists" in the paper. THE POST declared its opposition to "socialism, communism and rowdyism, idlerism and loaferism," but insisted it was the honest workingman's friend. On occasion the paper adopted a plague-on-both-your-houses attitude, condemning "the arrogance of capital and the obstinacy of labor."

Hutchins had a running fight with the Columbia Typographical Union, for a year replacing union men with nonunion compositors in 1883–1884. The paper reported that the union wanted the same pay scale as that at the Government Printing Office, where the 1000 employees received what THE POST termed "salaries and wages which no legitimate business house in the country could pay." Hutchins told his readers that he paid the same rates as such papers as the New York *Tribune* and the Cincinnati *Commercial,* and that THE POST's "proprietors have done nothing to degrade labor, and they do not propose to abandon the luxury of managing their own business."

The paper continued to succeed — and along with it the capital prospered. From about the time that THE POST was founded and throughout the rest of the Hutchins ownership, Washington enjoyed a building boom. Land values rose, mansions were erected on Dupont and Scott circles and along Connecticut Avenue. The city began to move westward, though Seventh Street remained the principal shopping artery and Pennsylvania Avenue the center of the city's life. The first apartment house went up in 1879, the four-story Fernando Wood Flats, named for an ex–New York mayor and congressman, at 1418 I Street with rents considered high at $50 to $55 a month, unfurnished. Secretary of State Blaine and Senators Cameron and Windom were among those who built stately homes. Out-of-towners of substance began to come to Washington, too. In 1891 the Chicago merchant prince Levi Z. Leiter erected a mansion on Dupont Circle, now given way to the Dupont Circle Hotel. The Blaine home, still standing on Massachusetts Avenue at 20th Street, was sold in 1899 to George Westinghouse, the airbrake magnate from Pittsburgh.

In the mid-1880s the city began to explode into the countryside north of Boundary Street, the present Florida Avenue, and even farther to the northwest when an act of Congress opened the way for the extension of Massachusetts Avenue to the Tenleytown Road (Wisconsin Avenue), where the National Cathedral now stands. President Cleveland purchased part of the tract known as Pretty Prospect and a house called Forrest Hill (later known as Red Top and Oak View) located off Tenleytown and Woodley roads; the area now is called Cleveland Park.

Finally, in 1889–1890, came the creation of Rock Creek Park, a project strongly endorsed by THE POST after the idea had been initiated by such leading citizens as banker Charles C. Glover. Under an act of Congress 1400 acres, at a cost of $1,200,000, were purchased for the capital's major park. In 1890 funds were appropriated for the adjoining National Zoological Park. As a civic booster, THE POST eagerly covered all these developments and helped convince the public that the election of a Democratic President, Cleveland, would not halt the boom.

Hutchins was an avid follower of new inventions, especially those of Thomas A. Edison. His admiration for Edison led to this humorous 1878 editorial paragraph: "Mr. Edison, the inventor of the phonograph, telephone, aerophone, metric system and Keely meter, is now working on a boot-jack, which will kill two cats at one throw." A week later the 31-year-old inventor visited the Smithsonian Institution to demonstrate his phonograph. He gave a POST reporter a prophetic preview, declaring that "this tongueless, toothless instrument, without larynx or pharynx, dumb, voiceless matter, nevertheless mimics your tones, speaks with your voice, utters your words, and centuries after you have crumbled into dust will repeat again and again, to a generation that could never know you, every idle thought, every fond fancy, every vain word that you choose to whisper against this thin iron diaphragm."

When Edison opened his Menlo Park, New Jersey, laboratory to public view, Hutchins himself went to see it. He wrote a personal account published January 2, 1880, with a drawing of the new carbon filament bulb for which the inventor had applied for a patent two months earlier.

> As to the character of the light, there can be no question that the advantage [over gas lamps] is altogether with Edison. The electric lamp is a steady glow. There is no combustion or appearance of it. It is the flash of a thousand diamond facets perpetuated. It is in no sense dazzling to the eye, however. You can stare at it and feel no weariness of the vision. It is the highest form of illumination known. There is no flicker, subsidence or increase. It cannot be turned down or up. There is nothing between it and darkness. It consumes no air and, of course, does not vitiate any. It has no odor or color. It is simply light.

When electricity came to Washington THE POST built an addition to its building to house the United States Electric Light Company. The paper's first lights glowed on July 13, 1882. (The first telephone had been installed in 1878, number 28 of the original 140 in the city.) Three years after THE POST was illuminated electricity caused the paper a major disaster.

In August 1880 the paper had outgrown its second home, at 339–341 Pennsylvania Avenue, and Hutchins moved to a new three-and-a-half-floor Post Building that he erected at 10th and D streets, at the edge of Pennsylvania Avenue — now the site of the Federal Bureau of Investigation. To make the move THE POST missed the Sunday edition of August 8. The new building was trimmed in blue limestone and, with foresight, contained a shaft for an elevator if and when two more stories might be added. Part of the building was rented to its morning rival, the *National Republican,* and some rooms to the afternoon *Critic.* Hutchins later told his readers that the building had been built and paid for out of earnings, that it had cost $75,000, and that various tenants paid $8000 in annual rents.

On the morning of July 16, 1885, the addition caught fire. Next morning's paper headlined: THE POST BURNED OUT. OFFICES OF THREE DAILY NEWSPAPERS ALMOST ENTIRELY DESTROYED. The story began: "For the first time in its history *The Post* has met with a disaster." But THE POST did not miss an issue, thanks to the generous offer of the *Evening Star,* located a block away, to use its presses with the paper being composed in a job shop. The most enduring disaster was the loss of the *Weekly Post*'s list of 50,000 subscribers; they were urged to send in their names and addresses at once. After a month THE POST was "at home again" in its rebuilt building, now with five floors. The paper acknowledged "our heartfelt thanks" to the *Star* "for its unfailing courtesy and uniform kindness" in giving "friendly aid."

Hutchins' admiration extended to another inventor, and in time led to his selling THE POST in 1889. In January 1883 Ottmar Mergenthaler, a German-born inventor, unveiled a long-dreamed-of typesetting machine in his Baltimore workshop with Hutchins among the dozen interested spectators. The printer, instead of composing a line of type by picking up individual letters to make each word, sat at a keyboard. He arranged type matrices in a line, automatically adjusting to the correct length. A solid lead slug (hot type) then was cast and the matrices returned for future use. The speed of composition was vastly increased by this most important advance in printing. It endured at THE POST until the 1970s when the cold type process began the phasing out of the Mergenthaler machine.

Hutchins became the principal promoter of the National Typographic Company, receiving a $200,000 finder's fee from the syndicate formed in 1885 to market the machine. President Arthur attended a Washington demonstration arranged by Hutchins. The machine was named the "linotype" — according to some accounts by Hutchins, according to others by fellow syndicate member Whitelaw Reid of the New York *Tribune.* In 1888 the first 102 linotypes were ordered by the *Tribune,* the Louisville *Courier-Journal,* the Chicago *News,* the Chicago *Inter-Ocean,* and THE POST, which ordered 16 of the total. But because of opposition from the printers' union, as well as lingering misgivings as to its workability, the linotype did not come into regular use at THE POST until 1893, after Hutchins had sold the paper. Even then old-style hand compositors stood ready to go to work should the machines fail, although other papers had demonstrated the machine's effectiveness and quieted printers' fears that it would throw them out of work. In 1889 Hutchins went to Europe to negotiate patents and he later received a $250,000 commission for selling the English rights. When he died in Washington on April 12, 1912, his fortune, most of it in real estate, was variously estimated at from $4 million to $5 million. His income in 1911 from linotype stock alone had been $38,000.

If the linotype project proved to be a distraction to Hutchins in his final years of POST ownership, his personal political ambitions seem to have been ever present. Eugene Field wrote that at THE POST's founding he was "determined to take no active personal part in politics" but Hutchins quickly established legal residence in his birth state of New Hampshire. In 1880 he was mentioned for Congress and served as chairman of the State Democratic Convention. However, he never achieved what he apparently really wanted: either the governorship or election to the United States Senate; election in 1885 to one term in the state legislature was as far as he got. He remained active, nonetheless, in New Hampshire affairs and was a part owner of the Manchester *Union* while he owned THE POST.

To the national capital Hutchins presented two statues. In 1889 he gave the statue of printer Benjamin Franklin, in the costume of a diplomat at the Court of Versailles; it still stands on Pennsylvania Avenue at 10th Street. When erected it was almost outside the front door of THE POST. In 1900 he gave the Scott Circle statue of Daniel Webster. A great friend of horses, he was credited with setting up more drinking troughs for them in the capital than anyone else.

Hutchins became so deeply engrossed in the development, financing, and sale of the linotype that he arranged, in October 1888, to sell THE POST. The agreement was made public on October 16 by which The Post Company had been reorganized with control in the hands of a new syndicate of owners. The deal included syndicate purchase of the evening *Critic,* which henceforth would be published as the *Evening Post.* But the deal fell through within three months and ownership reverted to Hutchins who continued to publish the morning, evening, and Sunday papers. The *Evening Post* lasted only until January 5, 1889.

After the purchase of the *National Republican* in 1888 THE POST had begun to lower its Democratic profile. To one side of the paper's name on page 1 was printed in an "ear": "The Washington Post is an independent morning newspaper — the only one published in Washington. It has no rivals and is read by everybody." The proof of the shift away from the Democratic bias came when the two parties nominated their presidential candidates for the November election. For the first time since Hutchins had founded THE POST the paper published front-page drawings of both the Republican and Democratic candidates instead of only the Democrat. Circulation then was reported as exceeding 14,000 daily.

However, the old habits died hard. THE POST wanted a second term for Cleveland but in 1888 Benjamin Harrison won an electoral majority although he trailed Cleveland in popular votes. The news of Harrison's election boosted THE POST's circulation to a record 54,000 for the day and the presses did not stop running until 9:40 A.M.

On January 6, 1889, a firm sale of THE WASHINGTON POST was announced in the Sunday paper. Hutchins told his readers that he was giving up the paper for "other business interests." His last editorial ended: "Wishing every friend of *The Post* a happy New Year and its new managers unbounded prosperity, I bid them all adieu." Next day the new managers ran an editorial on "Mr. Hutchins' Retirement."

> . . . he first gave to morning journalism at the National Capital its modern and progressive stamp. It was his untiring enterprise and comprehensive sagacity that made an accomplished fact of what had come to be considered well nigh an impossibility — the establishment of a daily paper here upon new lines of management befitting the advanced and metropolitan progress of the city . . .
>
> The paper became a paying investment from the start; its growth in circulation, influence and patronage was continuous, if not under the circumstances phenomenal, and Mr. Hutchins now leaves it one of the most valuable newspaper properties in the country, and an enduring monument to his ability. His successors will feel amply rewarded if they succeed in maintaining at the same high standard a work so courageously begun and admirably done.

THE POST, indeed, was "an enduring monument" to Hutchins. Eugene Field called Hutchins "the inspiration, the life, the soul of a great newspaper." Inspiration, life, soul — yes. But great? Hardly. His POST was not in a class with contemporary metropolitan dailies in New York or other big cities. On many issues it had reflected narrow vision, southern bias, and, especially in the early years, political partisanship. Limited resources often had meant spotty news coverage. Still, it was an increasingly bright, attention-getting, and well-produced newspaper. In a small national capital, often ignored by most of an expanding nation, THE POST was exceptional.

Stilson Hutchins alone made that possible. He had the indispensable nose for news, an ability to spot talent and hire it, a willingness to plow back at least a portion of his profits, and a determination that THE WASHINGTON POST should achieve power and importance, as it did. Above all, he gave it the initial momentum that would carry it forward through good times and bad under his successors to that distant day when it would be a truly great paper in a national capital of an importance that few foresaw.

# 2

# Slow Change
# Mr. Hatton and Mr. Wilkins
# 1889-1905

The new owners of THE WASHINGTON POST were Frank Hatton and Beriah Wilkins. It was, in many ways, an odd alliance. Each was 42, Hatton the elder by only ten weeks; each was a native of rural Ohio. But their personalities and their paths to shared control of THE POST differed markedly.

Frank Hatton was born April 28, 1846. Both his profession and political party were early set. He had carried newspapers at 9; he had begun to learn the printer's trade at 10; and at 16 he was foreman and local editor of his father's paper, the Cadiz *Republican.* At 17, in the midst of the Civil War, Hatton joined the 19th Ohio as a private, mustering out three years later as a lieutenant. By his twenty-first birthday the young man had moved to Iowa to help publish his father's Mt. Pleasant *Journal.* Before he was 25, on his father's death, he became proprietor of the *Journal* and, four years later, of the Burlington *Hawkeye.* In 1881 Hatton was named first assistant Postmaster General by President Arthur and came to Washington. Three years later, at 38, he was named Postmaster General, the youngest Cabinet member up to that time except for Alexander Hamilton. A "stalwart" Republican, he held the post for the final five months of the Arthur administration.

After Cleveland was inaugurated Hatton spent two years at the *National Republican,* then helped found the New York *Press* and reorganize and edit the Chicago *Mail.*

Beriah Wilkins, born July 10, 1846, had come off the farm at 17 to begin his career as a young merchandiser. He joined the 136th Ohio in 1864 but saw no combat and was mustered out in four months. He then organized and became principal managing officer of the Farmers' and Merchants' Bank at Uhrichsville, Ohio. At 35 he was elected to the state senate for a two-year term, followed by membership on the Democratic state central committee in 1882. That November Wilkins was elected to the first of three terms in the House of Representatives.

An ardent Democrat, Wilkins was chairman of the Banking and Currency Committee at the time he joined Hatton in purchasing THE POST. John C. Spooner, a Republican senator from Wisconsin, and Levi Z. Leiter, then living in Washington, played "helpful parts in closing the deal."

On a 50–50 basis, Hatton and Wilkins agreed to pay Hutchins $210,000 for THE POST. They then sold back to him one of the paper's presses for $35,000, making the net cost $175,000 paid over a two-year period. They incorporated as The Washington Post Company with 600 shares of stock and a capitalization of $300,000.

Hutchins later was quoted as saying he had "made a fool of himself" in selling the paper. Judging from its continued success, that probably was true. In 1892–1894 the paper showed a profit averaging more than $100,000 a year. The new owners boasted in print of THE POST's success but modestly never put their names on the paper's editorial page masthead as Hutchins had done. Hatton was to die of a stroke only five years after the purchase. After he died his widow charged Wilkins with illegally taking majority control of the paper, but a settlement was reached and Wilkins carried on in sole control for another decade.

The Hatton-Wilkins division of labor was a natural one. "The combination is unique," wrote one amused observer. "M. Hatton writes all the pieces, takes in the champagne suppers and twists the tail of the civil service commission, while Herr Wilkins puts up the mail, runs the business office, and drinks beer and eats pretzels and wienerwurst at the Scheutzenfest." A crisp and pungent writer, Hatton was a man of "plain, incisive speech" often mistaken "for bluntness," as his obituary noted after his death on April 30, 1894. "He despised all shams, and against them he launched the shafts of his wit and sarcasms." A hard worker, Hatton reputedly twice brought out POST extras with the sole aid of the janitor.

Wilkins was a dapper man who liked to wear a rose in his buttonhole and who in later years waxed his mustache. It was he who in 1889 called together "a few of the representative business men" to organize the Washington Board of Trade. His "ideas were always conservative," read his obituary. "He never was tempted to adopt a radical change of any sort in the character of the paper . . . Fair-play was the motto he impressed upon his co-workers and associates." He remained a faithful Democrat but, once a newspaper proprietor, he withdrew from party affairs. Hatton and Wilkins agreed that strict nonpartisanship was good business.

The Hatton-Wilkins era, 1889–1905, was tumultuous and THE POST reflected — sometimes well, sometimes imperfectly, sometimes badly — the enormous changes both foreign and domestic. During this time the capital grew and prospered. An 1897 editorial put it this way: "Washington has felt the pressure of hard times less thus far than any other city in the United States, for this city is less dependent than any other on those branches of business that were crippled by the panic of '93." In short, the city had a steady, usually rising, government payroll as its base.

On January 7, 1889, under the caption "We Greet You," the new owners announced their plans in the lead editorial:

> The new management have no double-leaded promises to make. No effort or expense will be spared to make *The Post* a thoroughly first-class newspaper, giving the news and all the news, without personal or partisan bias . . .
>
> Editorially, *The Post* will have very decided opinions on all public and other questions, and it will endeavor to express them in such a manner as to leave no possible doubts as to its position.
>
> In addition to being a complete newspaper, *The Post* will be devoted to the interests of this great city of Washington. Less of its time will be devoted to discussing the interests of this and foreign countries than will be given in earnest effort to every project that has for its object the improvement and advancement of Washington city.
>
> *The Post* intends to stand for Washington, Washington interests, and Washingtonians, first, last, and all the time.

This was typical journalistic horn tooting; and the owners failed to live up to their promise. National and international news, rather than local affairs, dominated the paper's columns. Probably this was inevitable, given the fast though often erratic flow of national and international news compared to the molasses-slow progress of local affairs — affairs directed by a less than attentive Congress controlling the necessary money.

Throughout this ownership one public figure strode more than any other across the pages of THE POST. He was Theodore Roosevelt. Early in 1889 TR was appointed by President Harrison as one of the three members of the United States Civil Service Commission, a post he held for six years. Not until Congress created the commission in 1883 had there been any meaningful effort to protect the bulk of civil government employees from the ravages of quadrennial presidential politics. Roosevelt was an ardent believer in "good government" and that included civil service; Hatton, while in the Post Office Department, had served President Arthur as a patronage dispenser. A clash was inevitable.

In July 1889 Roosevelt publicly called Hatton a "spoilsman" and, in a private letter that month, called THE POST a "vile" newspaper. The POST responded, often with petty gibes. When the paper discovered that TR had written a letter on Civil Service Commission stationery to get a friend a job on the New York police force, an editorial was headed "Oh, Naughty, Naughty Teddy." When THE POST got hold of a handwritten Roosevelt letter it reproduced the hard-to-read scrawl and asked: "Could he pass an examination for a position as copyist?" Roosevelt's manner and speech were mocked, THE POST calling him "this distinguished, though somewhat sissified statesman."

There was, however, both substantive disagreement and grudging admiration: "*The Post* is not fighting Mr. Roosevelt . . . What this paper is after is the sham reform of which Mr. Roosevelt is the accidental representative." Then came an exposé; civil service examination papers, said THE POST, had been sold or furnished in advance. A two-column page 1 headline, a rarity at the time, proclaimed: SECRETS ON SALE. Questions were "purloined by a clerk," POST reporters had discovered, during the Cleveland administration. The sale had been made for $15 by the brother-in-law of Charles Lyman, one of Roosevelt's fellow civil service commissioners.

The next day Roosevelt retorted: "I decline to get into a controversy in the press on the subject because I have not the least idea of being used as a means to advertise an unimportant local newspaper, whose editor I have already publicly branded for his utter disregard of truth." To that THE POST replied: "This is Sunday morning and *The Post* must go to church. It will see Theodore later." A week earlier it had said that "there is much about him to admire. He is undoubtedly the strongest intellectual force on the commission." TR was not appeased; he retorted that THE POST was "an obscure spoilsman organ."

In February 1890 THE POST bore in on Lyman, charging he was covering up for his brother-in-law. The paper demanded that both Roosevelt and Lyman be fired if they would not resign. In June TR declared that "Mr. Hatton will never be able to do all the mischief to which his malignity prompts him, for he lacks the requisite physical courage." Hatton's editorial called TR "a sham, a fraud and a liar." "Teddy," it said, "is only dangerous to himself. His friends should muzzle and hand-cuff him." In May in a private letter, TR wrote that "Frank

Hatton flinched like the cur that he is" by failing to appear at a public hearing on the exam scandal.

In July THE POST published its own civil service reform platform: a single presidential term; Cabinet officers to be ineligible for the presidency for the term succeeding the administration in which they served; six-year terms for department employees, one-third to be ousted every two years; departmental patronage to be apportioned to members of Congress as with appointments to West Point; appointments, after recommendation by a member of Congress, to be subject to an examination; and removals from office to be made only "for cause." Roosevelt stayed on as a civil service commissioner and THE POST's reforms got nowhere.

By 1893 TR was being mentioned as a possible candidate for governor of New York. Said THE POST: "The people of New York might go further and fare worse. Mr. Roosevelt is a man of brains, of courage, of high purpose and clean record." But two years later when he became New York City police commissioner and insisted on closing saloons on Sundays in accordance with the law, THE POST revived its antipathy: "It seems to us that New York will be wise to rid itself of Roosevelt."

While police commissioner, Roosevelt wrote a magazine article on the Monroe Doctrine. His call for "robust patriotism," said THE POST, "is good, strong, wholesome talk" that "braces one like a fresh mountain breeze." A mutual interest in Manifest Destiny, to which TR long had been addicted but to which THE POST came more gradually, brought them closer together. When it was rumored that TR might become Assistant Secretary of the Navy, THE POST thought "it would be an interesting experiment." But when TR got the job in 1897, the news story on his nomination slipped into editorializing: "Whether rightly or wrongly, Mr. Roosevelt has established a reputation as a trouble-maker. He had been represented to the [McKinley] administration as a man who, whatever his position, would not permit things to run smoothly about him, who was fond of rows, utterly lacking in diplomacy, and who, unless he changed his disposition, would involve the department in no end of snarls."

But all doubts vanished after Roosevelt's speech at the Naval War College in Newport, Rhode Island, in which he said: "Peace is a goddess only when she comes with sword girt on thigh" and "We ask for a great navy, partly because we think that the possession of such a navy is the surest guarantee of peace, and partly because we feel that no national life is worth having if the nation is not willing when the need shall arise to pour out its blood, its treasure, and tears like water rather than to submit to the loss of honor and renown." To these sentiments THE POST exclaimed: "Well done, nobly spoken! Theodore Roosevelt, you have found your proper place at last — all hail!"

The United States was moving into a new age and THE POST was swept up in the popular feeling that America, indeed, had a Manifest Destiny. The phrase was an old one, going back to at least 1845. In the McKinley administration it came to mean territorial expansionism or, as its enemies put it, imperialism, with something of a moral righteousness about both the process and the goal. As Hatton and Wilkins took over, 7 of the 48 contiguous states were still territories. Nonetheless there was talk of annexing Canada and perhaps of chipping away another piece of Mexico. THE POST opposed senatorial thrusts at Mexico, chiefly on the grounds that that country was too revolution-prone to be of benefit as additional American territory. Canada seemed more attractive.

In the fall of 1891 THE POST declared that "the acquisition to us of the great Canadian territory would be valuable beyond comparison. It would give this country another century's boom. It would open up for settlement a vast new Northwest . . . It would give us the continent from subtropical regions to the North Pole, with untold resources in magnificent abundance, and it would make us practically unassailable among all the nations of the world." Some months later, when opponents of annexation pointed out that such an act would require American assumption of Canada's debt, THE POST backed off and soon the issue disappeared from the paper's columns.

Hawaii was something else again. On January 21, 1891, THE POST carried the news of the accession to the island throne of Queen Liliuokalani, described as "not friendly to the United States." On September 19 THE POST reported that England proposed to establish a protectorate over the islands. A September 24 editorial put forth the American claim in terms of "the commerce of the Pacific coast" and "the expanding influence and requirements of the American Navy." THE POST wanted "a virtual American protectorate . . . at an early date."

In January 1893, before Cleveland's second inauguration, came the revolt in Hawaii. The queen was deposed and the United States was asked to annex the islands — a step THE POST heartily endorsed. When William McKinley succeeded to the presidency a treaty was signed and THE POST greeted the event with an "Aloha, Hawaii!" editorial: "Freedom, civilization, progress will set up another stronghold on their line of march." Congress, however, did not immediately ratify the treaty. The Spanish-American War would bring the American flag to Puerto Rico, Guam, and the Philippines; THE POST argued that Hawaii was needed as a "stepping stone" to the new Pacific possessions. Finally, Hawaiian annexation was achieved by a joint resolution of House and Senate, requiring only a simple majority vote in each house. THE POST's comment rang true: "Had it not been for the war with Spain it is doubtful if annexation would have been accomplished this session."

It often has been said that the Spanish-American War was the product of yellow journalism, most specifically that of Hearst's New York *Journal* and Pulitzer's New York *World.* "You furnish the pictures, I'll furnish the war," Hearst was said to have instructed his artist Frederic Remington, though the quotation is of doubtful validity. There is no doubt, however, that the *Journal* and the *World* fought to outdo each other in sensational reports of Spanish cruelty in Cuba and that the often highly imaginative and downright false reports they carried aroused anti-Spanish fever in other editorial offices around the nation. THE POST, though it came to be a strong advocate of the war, disdained the sensational and long sought a solution short of war. In the spring of 1895, when Spanish rule in Cuba and the islanders' opposition to that rule were becoming news, THE POST supplemented its press association sources with the cables of James Gordon Bennett's New York *Herald.*

On March 31, 1895, THE POST took a hard look at the Cuban problem:

> . . . it is possible that the revolution now in progress may be of a character different from that of its predecessors. It may represent some intelligent and worthy purpose and have the support of honest and reputable men . . . If that be really the case . . . then it is safe to say that public sentiment throughout the Union is with the revolutionists and, for once at least, rightly with them. We want no monarchies on this hemisphere, especially monarchies whose home and inspiration are in Europe. To be sure we cannot as a nation involve ourselves in the conflict. We are bound by every consideration of duty, honor, and propriety to keep aloof.

THE POST's qualms about what was going on in Cuba were heightened by subsequent reports that "American capitalists," even "three U.S. Senators," were fomenting the troubles for reasons of economic gain. Nonetheless, on January 11, 1896, THE POST went wholeheartedly over to the rebel side, urging official recognition for the "patriots who seek personal liberty and free institutions for themselves and their descendants" in "a noble drama of a united people battling for their liberty."

By the fall of 1897, the New York *Journal* and the *World* were locked in a newspaper war of blood and sensation about Cuba. THE POST commented that "we are sadly afraid that those papers which reek with bloody war in every column are lashing themselves into needless fury." To see for itself, THE POST sent to Cuba its former White House reporter, now one of its editorial writers, Richard C. Weightman. This first venture in foreign correspondence by a staff member was disastrous. Weightman was a Confederate veteran credited with "luminous, breezy" editorials but with little ability, judging from his "letters" back to the paper, to discern what was happening. In his second letter he declared that "if those 20,000 Spanish officers and soldiers in Havana have not engaged in a conspiracy to delude me by a concerted and systematic comedy of false and impudent pretence, they are the most kindly and courteous and gentle human beings I have ever seen in military uniforms." Weightman concluded that the rebels were exhausted, that the Cuban affair was being worked out, that the Spanish held no Americans. The trains, he reported, ran regularly and besides the Cubans were less oppressed by taxes than were their Spanish rulers. Back home in Washington after his two-week trip, Weightman concluded that the "insurrection is a miserable farce."

Two events were soon to produce war. The Spanish ambassador in Washington, Enrique Dupuy de Lôme, incautiously wrote to a friend in Cuba that McKinley was "weak and a bidder for the admiration of the crowd," a "common politician." When the letter appeared on page 1 of both the New York *Journal* and THE POST of February 9, 1897, the ambassador promptly resigned. THE POST, hoping this would not be the incident to cause war, declared that, while he had to go, "no peril confronts our peace. No affront has been put upon us as a people. The incident is closed." It was closed only because a far more serious incident occurred six days later: the sinking of the American battleship *Maine* on a friendly visit to Havana.

THE POST issued two extras on February 16, the second including the dispatch from the *Maine*'s commander to Secretary of the Navy John D. Long, and cabled eyewitness accounts of the disaster in which 260 of the 350 men aboard died.

It was impossible to know — it still is — what had caused the disaster. But the lines quickly were drawn in the press between the jingoes and the cautious; THE POST was on the cautious side. The next day Hearst's *Journal* bannered its unproven conclusion that "an enemy's secret infernal machine" had done the deed. THE POST's story said that the administration was "strongly of the opinion that the disaster was accidental" and an editorial appealed for calm. Yet, in the next five weeks, until war was declared by Congress on April 25, THE POST's headlines grew bigger and the type used for the chief stories larger.

While the editorial line was to stand behind the President, THE POST reflected a growing appetite for having a go at the Spanish. Page 1 on April 3 carried the cartoon caption that provided the slogan: "Stout hearts, my laddies! If the row comes, remember the Maine, and show the world how American sailors can fight." Clifford K. Berryman drew Uncle Sam on the deck of a warship pointing to the sinking *Maine.* On April 20, Congress adopted a joint resolution of war. THE POST was elated.

> The die is cast. The country will go to war . . . The last lingering shred of peace has been blown away upon the gust, and we stand as one man behind the country's flag, and we give to it our love and our devotion — if need be, our fortunes and our lives. No other course is open to patriots.

Theodore Roosevelt was a young man in a hurry. On April 1 THE POST ran his picture on page 1 with: ROOSEVELT READY TO FIGHT. WILL ACCEPT AN ARMY COMMISSION IN EVENT OF WAR. An editorial later that month declared: "Mr. Roosevelt is a man in every fiber of his being"; the old enmity was now forgotten in the new patriotism. On May 7, THE POST presciently noted that "it seems quite probable that this war may make one or more Presidents." The war also meant higher circulation; that Sunday THE POST had a regular press run of 48,168 copies plus 25,000 more in extras.

News was erratic; some of it came from Spain, some from other European capitals, before it was confirmed in Washington. THE POST printed anything and everything it could lay a hand on. Admiral George Dewey's cable, via the American consul in Hong Kong, of his victory over the Spanish fleet in the battle of Manila Bay arrived at the Navy Department at 4 A.M. on May 7 and was in an 8:30 A.M. extra.

On June 3, 1898, THE POST gave its definitive approval to imperialism.

> The policy of isolation is dead . . . The taste of empire is in the mouth of the people, even as the taste of blood in the jungle. It means an imperial policy; the republic, renascent, taking her place with the armed nations.

The "taste of empire" indeed was in the mouths of many people. By the time these words were used — and THE POST's comment was often reprinted as symptomatic of the period — the "splendid little war," as TR called it, seemed to the public to be going swimmingly. On June 12 the marines landed at a bay on the south coast of Cuba called Guantanamo, a spot where the American flag still flies. TR's charge up San Juan Hill with the Rough Riders came on July 1. And then the navy: SPANISH FLEET ANNIHILATED. DEWEY DAY AT SANTIAGO proclaimed THE POST in a 6 A.M. extra. A week later, in the edition reporting Senate approval of Hawaiian annexation, came the inevitable political fallout: ROOSEVELT FOR GOVERNOR. THE FIGHTING COLONEL IS TO BE NAMED BY NEW YORK REPUBLICANS.

Within less than four months Spain was defeated in the Caribbean, and Cuba and Puerto Rico were under American control. American and Spanish peace commissioners met in Paris amid contradictory press reports on just what McKinley was seeking, especially what status would be given the Philippines. THE POST editorialized: "The Philippines are our affair. We shall take them now and do what we please with them afterwards." But a month after the peace treaty was signed on December 10 and the islands turned over to the United States, THE POST noted that "it must be evident to the dullest intelligence that trouble, and very serious trouble, for us is brewing in the Philippines." Some sought to justify the Philippine campaign against the insurgents by adopting the "white man's burden" viewpoint. THE POST, at least, was frank about such tactics. A January 14, 1900, editorial, "Let Us Be Honest," said:

> All of this gabble about civilizing and uplifting the benighted barbarians of Cuba and Luzon is mere sound and fury, signifying nothing. Foolishly or wisely, we want those newly acquired possessions, not for any missionary or altruistic purposes, but for the trade, the commerce, the power, and the money there are in them.

There were powerful pressures to expand Manifest Destiny to the Orient, with China the objective. When the Germans moved to take control of the Shantung Peninsula and when the Boxers began to rise against all foreigners, THE POST called for limiting American action to the protection of its own citizens. "Let us at least hold aloof from the banded vultures of Europe," said a May 31, 1900, editorial, "and keep our honor bright." The next month the Boxers were described as "devoted patriots" and not the "rabble," as "yellow journals depict" them. "Why should we take part in a crusade against China?"

The Boer War produced strains with England because American sympathy seemed to lie with "Oom Paul" Kruger. The war also introduced, on November 28, 1899, a new name to POST readers. An editorial quoted from a dispatch of "young Winston Churchill" who said that the conflict was likely to be "bloody and protracted."

Much space in THE POST was devoted to Russia. "Bloody Sunday" of January 22, 1905, produced the headline DAY OF FURY AND DEATH. The story included this: "Gorky, the Russian novelist, expressed the opinion that today's work will break the faith of the people in the Emperor. He said this evening: 'To-day inaugurates revolution in Russia. The Emperor's prestige will be irrevocably shattered by the shedding of innocent blood.' " Editorially, the paper felt that "a peaceful, gradual reform is possible. Obstinate refusal to enter upon that course must, sooner or later, and probably not far in the future, produce a revolution."

Four days before Christmas 1890 a western correspondent wrote a caustic story of the battle of Wounded Knee:

> To say that it was a most daring defeat — 120 Indians attacking 500 cavalry — expresses the situation but faintly. It could only have been insanity which prompted such a deed. It is doubted that if before night either a buck or squaw out of all Big Foot's band will be left to tell the tale of this day's tragedy. The members of the 7th Cavalry have once more shown themselves to be heroes in deeds of daring.

Three years later historian Frederick Jackson Turner declared that "the frontier has gone and with its going has closed the first period of American history." He was correct. Back East the nation was well launched into the new industrial age with its growing tensions between rich and poor, city and country. Immigrants now were arriving by the hundreds of thousands yearly.

Washington as a city had none of the problems of industry, nor the grime of factories. The capital, THE POST boasted, was "the prettiest city in the world, with the possible exception of Paris." The city's fortunes seemed to turn on the outcome of elections. Its largest single group of workers, the federal employees, felt a vital interest in the vagaries of politics despite the growing job protection of civil service. Few presidential campaigns have reached the peak of frenzy and importance of the 1896 McKinley-Bryan contest.

William McKinley, who became famous as the father of the protectionist tariff, was gerrymandered out of his House seat in 1890 by the Ohio Democrats in a move that turned out to bring fortune. Marcus A. (Mark) Hanna, a prominent Cleveland industrialist with a bent for politics, successfully backed McKinley for governor, and in 1896 the Ohioan was the leading Republican contender for the presidency. As Hanna presented him, McKinley was a "sound money" man as well as a high tariff backer, both essential in GOP eyes for the future of party and country.

All of this was well chronicled in THE POST. Reports that Hanna was "soliciting large sums of money from manufacturers" for his candidate led to an editorial entitled "Campaign of Boodle" in the spring before the convention. Three days later Hanna declared "absolutely and unqualifiedly false" stories that he had "levied contributions on the industrial interests of the East." This campaign set the popular belief that the Republicans were the party of big business.

Only four years earlier THE POST had sent its first reporter to the two major party conventions. Now, in 1896, the paper's political reporter, Henry Litchfield West, was allowed to sign his stories at the end. He detailed the internal party fight over gold and silver, interviewed Hanna, and correctly predicted the winning ticket of McKinley and Garrett A. Hobart. The GOP platform favored territorial expansion, sound money, and the high protective tariff; it condemned lynchings.

If the Republicans that year moved along the familiar track of American politics, the Democrats were another story. The party divided on gold versus silver, the majority for unlimited or "free" coinage of silver. This issue was the symbol of rural rebellion against urban bankers, debtors against creditors. Then, at the moment of wide national discontent, there came to the Democratic convention a young man from Nebraska, William Jennings Bryan, largely unknown to the nation but included by POST cartoonist George Y. Coffin as one of five potential candidates.

Arriving at Chicago, Harry West wrote that Missouri Representative Richard P. (Silver Dick) Bland was in the lead; West saw Horace Boies of Iowa his chief rival and John R. McLean of Ohio "a factor." Only in the ninth paragraph of his story printed on July 6 did West mention Bryan as a dark horse in case of a deadlock. The platform called for "free and unlimited coinage of both gold and silver at the present legal ratio of 16 to 1," enactment of a federal income tax, states' rights, and only "sympathy" for the Cuban rebellion against Spain.

Then, without warning, came the most electrifying speech ever made at a national political convention. The headline in THE POST on Friday, July 10, 1896: BRYAN IN THE FIELD. THE NEBRASKAN'S ORATORY TAKES THE CONVENTION BY STORM. West's long telegraph account included:

> [Bryan's] dramatic and theatrical entrance to the hall yesterday was but a part of a well laid plan to stampede the convention for him, and this program was carried out today to its fullest development . . . He was inspired with the possibilities which the occasion meant for his future, he knew his subject, he had the popular side of the controversy, he felt himself among friends. Combined with this, he had the rhythm of language, grace of oratory, and picturesqueness of presence.
>
> Certain it is that his speech was the only one of the convention to thrill, electrify, stir, and sway the throng. He struck fire with every word. Earnest as Savonarola, eloquent as Ingersoll, burning with fiery conviction, able enough to emphasize the points which would stick like burrs, artfully modulating his musical voice until it played like the wind upon aeolian strings, he stimulated and swelled the enthusiasm until the great audience was absolutely under his persuasive, yet powerful, domination.
>
> Of his speech . . . it is enough to say that demagogic and full of sophistry as it was, it suited the sentiment and temper of his audience, and nearly every sentence was wildly cheered . . . The peroration, evidently memorized with studied care, flowed from his lips with syrupy ease. "You shall not," he exclaimed in conclusion, stretching out his arms as if in benediction and voice trembling with passionate thrill, "place a crown of thorns upon the brow of Liberty or sacrifice mankind upon your cross of gold."

West did not quite catch the exact wording of the peroration but he had its tone and spirit. And he felt the response it produced and he understood why.

> The scene which followed beggars description. Words may tell what actually happened, but words cannot impart the strange and curious magnetism which filled the atmosphere. Bedlam broke loose, delerium reigned supreme. In the spoken word of the orator thousands of men have heard the unexpressed sentiments and hopes of their own inmost souls. The great mass of humanity threw forth the fiery lava of its enthusiasm like Vesuvius in eruption. The yells were so deafening that only at irregular intervals could the music of the noisy band be heard, the stamping of the feet was as the roll of thunder among the echoing Alps, and the hurricane of

sound almost caused the steel girders of the roof to tremble with its perceptible volume.

The Boy Orator of the Platte, as Bryan became known, next day became the first presidential candidate from west of the Mississippi. He was 36, only a year past the constitutional minimum for the presidency. The shock of what had occurred was reflected in THE POST's lead editorial:

> The nomination of Hon. William Jennings Bryan, of Nebraska, by the Democratic Convention yesterday, constitutes the most astounding spectacle in the history of American politics . . . What amazes us is that he should have been able, by the mere act of mounting a rostrum and delivering a twenty minute speech, to dislocate the process of the convention machinery, to obscure every veteran aspirant then in view, to change men's hearts, to divert the course of their passions and their preferences, and to transform a serious and deliberative body into an instrument upon which he played as Pan upon his pipe, as the blind prince of music upon his immortal harpsicord.

Arthur Sewell of Maine was nominated as Bryan's running mate. A millionaire industrialist, he was nonetheless a free-silver advocate and a believer in an income tax. Many expected him to foot the campaign bills. West wrote that "for four hours or more the Vice Presidency was hawked around as a cheap and undesirable thing."

THE POST later boasted, and rightly so, of "its absolute fairness" toward Bryan during the campaign "when nearly all the remaining metropolitan journals were treating him with bitter prejudice." THE POST endorsed neither candidate but it clearly leaned to McKinley. It accused Bryan of "commonplace twaddle" but said he was speaking "with amazing force and shrewdness." Ardent Democrat Wilkins, now the sole POST owner, was among the many in his party who could not stomach Bryanism; but Stilson Hutchins, the POST's founder, actively campaigned for Bryan. When McKinley won, THE POST said, "We are glad [Bryan] is defeated, but we recognize and here pay tribute to the purity, the candor, and the utter self-abnegation of his course." A 9 A.M. extra had the McKinley electoral vote, 271, exactly. That day 137,000 papers were sold and at least 15,000 had gathered election night to follow the returns at THE POST building.

A new batch of Republican senators soon took their seats, men who reflected the power of big business — Boies Penrose of Pennsylvania,

Thomas C. Platt of New York (who had been there before), and, soon, the elegant and eloquent Chauncey Depew of New York, the voice of the New York Central Railroad. When John Sherman resigned to become Secretary of State, Hanna got his Senate seat. For a while the Senate refused to seat Matthew Quay of Pennsylvania. At one time four Senate seats were vacant because of feuding state legislatures; yet Wilkins' POST continued to reject direct senatorial election.

The most spectacular Democratic senator, frequently in the columns of THE POST, was "Pitchfork Ben" Tillman, a one-eyed anti-black South Carolinian who spoke for the dirt farmer and who served from 1895 to his death in 1918. He had been in Congress only a few months when a POST news story described one of his speeches as "a torrent of invective, a Niagara of abuse, such as never before was listened to upon the floor of the Senate." An editorial declared that "the most charitable explanation of Senator Tillman's disgraceful outbreak . . . is that he is a fool and could not help himself."

On November 21, 1899, Vice President Hobart died, opening the way for a new political era. Roosevelt had been elected governor of New York the year before and had been in office only since January. Senator Platt, who controlled that state's Republican party and who disliked TR, had run Roosevelt for governor as a Spanish-American War hero in order to elect the GOP ticket. After Hobart's death it became widely known that Platt wanted to get rid of his uncooperative governor by running him for Vice President in 1900.

TR wavered on whether he would accept that nomination. But he was outspokenly indiscreet about the man he would be running with. THE POST on April 5, 1900, said it could not believe Roosevelt would say what he was reported to have said: "McKinley has about as much backbone as a toy chocolate man that you see on the confectioner's stand. He is a dreadful disappointment." But he had said it, or something very much like it.

By the time the Republican convention opened at Philadelphia in June, the pressure on TR to accept was immense. Reporter West led his story for June 18 with: "The lasso is around Roosevelt's neck. Platt and Quay have hold of the cord and are slowly dragging him toward the Vice Presidential nomination." TR, said West, is no longer "irrevocably declining." Three days later, the day before the balloting, West wrote: "Theodore Roosevelt of New York will be nominated for Vice President by the Republican national convention."

How was the reporter so sure? During the Spanish-American War West had been one of four newspapermen who met regularly at the Capitol with Senator Henry Cabot Lodge, Roosevelt's closest friend.

From this evolved a strong West-Roosevelt relationship, and so West had access to TR at the convention. When West asked if he would accept the second place, TR replied that "only one man ever declined the Vice Presidency." It was not an accurate statement but it convinced West that TR would accept. The reporter then ran into George Corteylou, McKinley's man, who told him that the President would not object to the nomination. The next day both McKinley and Roosevelt were nominated unanimously. Bryan was given a second nomination by the Democrats, with former Vice President Adlai Stevenson as his running mate.

THE POST had a hard time swallowing the GOP ticket. At the time of the nomination the paper noted that while it had "never been an admirer" of TR, he was acceptable. But less than two weeks later TR had rekindled the old suspicions and THE POST trumpeted: "It is simply ridiculous now. There is no excuse for his absurd and impudent pretensions. It is no longer possible to overlook his ignorant conceit." Two months later THE POST complained of TR's "crazy antics." Nonetheless, of all the candidates TR was by far the most interesting and, in THE POST, he made the most news.

THE POST considered prosperity the issue and it found that "prosperity is real, incontestible, practical. It is not an abstract question; it is a definite, enjoyable experience." It was, at least, for enough of the voters to elect the McKinley-Roosevelt ticket. Bryan's defeat was worse than that of four years earlier. Election night some 20,000 came to watch the returns on THE POST's screens. And that year four states — Colorado, Wyoming, Utah, and Idaho — allowed women to vote.

Roosevelt had hardly been installed as Vice President when THE POST referred to him as "a foaming, snorting demagogue." When he announced a trip to Colorado the paper snickered that "the poor man evidently is chafing under the terrible obscurity." McKinley, by comparison, was described as a President whom the people "love and trust . . . without measure or misgiving."

Everything changed at 4 P.M. on September 5, 1901, at Buffalo, New York, where the President had gone to visit the Pan-American Exposition. As McKinley was receiving a long line of citizens a young man named Leon Czolgosz, with a .32 caliber revolver wrapped in a handkerchief around his right hand, shot the President in the stomach. Eight days later, after murmuring "nearer, my God, to thee," McKinley was dead and Theodore Roosevelt was President of the United States.

Luckily for THE POST, Scott C. Bone, the paper's managing editor, was in Buffalo the day of the shooting and able to file a long account of the assassination. At 8:45 P.M. an extra was out and hawked around the city. Thousands came to THE POST as the latest reports on McKinley's condition were flashed on a hastily erected screen and shouted through a megaphone. "When the bulletin came at six o'clock that the wound might not necessarily be fatal," the paper recounted next day, "the great throng in front of The Post Building burst into prolonged cheers." But on September 14 THE POST's first eight-column banner proclaimed PRESIDENT IS DEAD in a 2:25 A.M. extra.

THE POST's uncertainty and unhappiness about the new President were well reflected in an editorial on September 15. As Mark Sullivan, a quarter century later, wrote in his monumental *Our Times*, THE POST editorial was "a wholly candid expression of the real feeling of conservatives."

> We need not tell our readers that up to this time we have discovered in Mr. Roosevelt very little cause for serious rejoicing. He has at all times been far too theatrical for our taste. He pranced too much in war. He vociferated too much in politics . . . That he has ever suggested to us the perfect model of a President we cannot truly say . . .
>
> But the day of Rough Rider Roosevelt is past . . . The curtain rises on a drama, and Mr. Roosevelt comes down the stage in a role gigantic enough to sober the most frivolous of men . . . History tells us of many men who made the worst and often the most dangerous of subordinates, yet ruled with strength and wisdom. We know that Mr. Roosevelt is a brave and upright gentleman. We feel sure that he is a patriot, jealous of his country's honor. Of his personal integrity we have no misgivings whatsoever. Of his loyal and pure purpose there cannot be a doubt. Why, then, shall he not rise to the full measure of his opportunity? May he not be one of those who, unfitted by temperament for service, develop splendid forces of command and leadership under the stimulus of vast responsibility?

On New Year's Day 1902, the official mourning for McKinley at an end, the Roosevelts received 9000 White House callers. Two days later they gave a ball to introduce 17-year-old daughter Alice, described in THE POST as "tall and slender" with "a profusion of very pretty blonde hair, worn in the prevailing pompadour style." She was dressed in a "clinging gown of white chiffon, built on taffeta, with elaborate garniture of tiny white rosebuds on shirt and bodice." It was the first of hundreds of stories about "Princess Alice" stretching far past the White

House years into her rule as a *grande dame* of Washington until after her ninetieth birthday in 1974.

Roosevelt began to travel about the country with West or other POST reporters in his entourage. He spent the summer at his Oyster Bay home on Long Island but unlike prior presidential vacations there seemed to be news almost every day. TR was "great copy" for the reporters for whom, incidentally, he established the first White House press room. William Allen White wrote that "he talked state secrets in a loud voice to statesmen in the presidential workroom, so that reporters could hear."

Roosevelt easily won the 1904 election against Judge Alton B. Parker. Two years earlier TR had named reporter West to be one of the three commissioners who ran Washington. West's successor as chief political reporter for the 1904 campaign was Edward G. Walker.

In 1905, in an editorial about presidential prospects for 1908, THE POST remarked that "sooner or later the 'unwritten law' that is said to stand against a third term will be set aside, not by 'the man on horseback' but by the American people." But that would involve a different Roosevelt of another party. Before that occurred, another name came to dominate American politics and life. On October 26, 1902, THE POST recorded that, in the presence of ex-President Cleveland, Princeton University had installed a new president, Professor Woodrow Wilson.

Two weeks after Hatton and Wilkins took over THE WASHINGTON POST in 1889 an English visitor to the capital was quoted as saying that "Washington is wholly given over to politics. When Congress is not sitting it is dead; when Congress is sitting it is delirious." But Washington was not all that dead without Congress and there was more to city life than politics. The bulk of Washingtonians remained in the capital year-round and for them THE POST offered a steady diet of crime, scandals, disasters, revolutions, and wars. Most readers either worked for the government or for those who did. And these readers also cared about sports and society and amusements.

A letter to the editor in 1889 revealed something of the life of government workers. The writer objected to reports that women employees were constantly "playing the sick game — coming with pale faces and hollow eyes and pleading illness, after they have spent the night in dancing, theater-going, or a thousand ways unnecessary to mention." What about the male clerks, the writer asked, "who come with red faces, bleared eyes and puffy bags beneath them from a night spent at the grogshop or other low places?"

THE POST, after the general fashion of Washington newspapers over the years, took the side of the government workers. "Don't be too hard on the department clerks," it said in May 1889.

> The weather is warm and oppressive. Most of the department buildings are gloomy, jail-like, and poorly ventilated . . . A clerk that does his or her work honestly, and most of them do, does not have the easy time that the outside world are made to believe that they do by reckless scribblers . . . If there are worthless and indolent clerks in the departments, turn them out, but do not punish the faithful and industrious employes because of the worthless few.

Some government buildings were worse than merely gloomy. One such was the former Ford's Theater on 10th Street where Lincoln had been assassinated, which had been turned into the War Department's pension office with 500 employees. On June 9, 1893, parts of three floors collapsed; 22 were killed and more than 80 injured. THE POST published a 3 A.M. extra with a "complete list of killed and wounded" and promptly opened a relief fund. In five days THE POST fund totaled $16,598.37 and eventually grew to nearly $30,000. A general committee collected $5122.65, the *Evening Star* took in $3553, and the *Evening News* $465.

THE POST approved of female typists in the government going to lunch with their bosses because, "as a rule," they "are very wise and well-behaved young ladies — at least in Washington." But in 1895 "a well dressed and fashionable young woman" was sent to the workhouse for 15 days for being "detected in the act of smoking a cigarette on Pennsylvania Avenue." THE POST was outraged: "The spectacle [of women smoking cigarettes] is a matter of every day occurrence. [It would be better to catch] pocketbook snatchers, razor and revolver carriers, burglars, thugs, and hoodlums . . . Is the whole force of our police to be directed against innocent organ-grinders, whose monkeys happen to attract a crowd, and foolish young women who think it is a fine thing to smoke a cigarette in public?"

Perhaps some government girls were intrigued by such "personal" ads as these: "A western gentleman of personal wealth, expecting to visit Washington soon, desires correspondence with agreeable young lady." "Wanted — the acquaintance of a bright young lady; object enjoyment; address Diplomat, this office." Some doubtless answered this one: "Ladies — mail two-cent stamp for sealed instructions how to enlarge your bust five inches by using Emma bust developer."

There were titillating stories headlined: HE LED A DOUBLE LIFE. AND

A TRAGEDY FOLLOWED EXPOSURE; SHOCKING MURDER OF A YOUNG GIRL IN PHILADELPHIA AND SUBSEQUENT SUICIDE OF HER SLAYER TO AVOID ARREST; ENTICED THEM TO HER ROOM. WASHINGTON MAN VICTIMIZED BY A HANDSOME NEW YORK BLONDE; and, THE FIRST WIFE ON HAND. SHE STOPPED A MARRIAGE CEREMONY IN SHORT ORDER.

The Easter egg–roll on the White House lawn attracted crowds of 10,000. "Such customs as were yesterday observed in Washington," THE POST remarked one year, "are the oil we put on the old world's wheels to keep them from rusting." Tourists came in constant flow, a million and a half annually as early as 1889, and 5000 a day in winter when Congress was in session.

On the Avenue one could enjoy a lantern parade of 1000 cyclists on high wheelers. But there were dangers: TWO BULLETS. A SENSATIONAL SHOOTING AFFRAY IN A WELL-KNOWN SALOON ON PENNSYLVANIA AVENUE. Or: THE CHINAMAN'S VICE. OPIUM SMOKING IS LARGELY ON THE INCREASE IN WASHINGTON. THERE IS NO LAW TO REACH IT. IN NEARLY EVERY LAUNDRY IS A "JOINT." Not until 1905 would the word "marihuana" appear in THE POST. Then, it was reported, Professor Frederick Starr of the University of Chicago had discovered in Venezuela the marihuana plant "which, when dried, resembles tobacco leaves. It is smoked in cigarette form or in a pipe. Its effects are immediate and exciting."

In 1890, to mark its tenth anniversary, Woodward & Lothrop took its first full-page ad in THE POST. Among the "anniversary bargains" were double bed muslin sheets for 75 cents, calico wrappers for $1, and, for $3, an "elegant imported white Coutil corset, with spoon busk, two side steels, two gores over the hips, bones fanned with silk and finished at top with fine Hamburg embroidery." If one indulged too much over the holidays there was "Dr. Pierce's Favorite Prescription." It advertised: "The trying ordeals which fashionable society imposes on its devotees are enough to severely test the physical strength and endurance of the most robust. Irregular and late hours, over-rich and indigestible food, late suppers, the fatigue of the ball-rooms, the bad air of the illy-ventilated, over-crowded theaters, are each, in themselves, sufficient to upset the system and ruin the health of the delicate and sensitive."

Others did not need remedies for such "ordeals." They ate at the Elks lunchroom where "ham and eggs, bread and butter," could be had for ten cents. Washington favored eating and entertaining at home. Private families needed cooks and Dick's Agency advertised in 1889 for "French, German, American and colored women cooks at once; wages from $15 to $40 per month."

The city was growing up. In 1889 it was proposed to substitute electric lighting for gas lamps in the area north of K Street. But two years later THE POST complained that the capital had only 170 electric street lamps compared to 1526 in Buffalo. Telephones were now so numerous that a bank advertisement offered its customers a card on which to list numbers. It advised them to ask for "the number please, not the name." THE POST now was available by 7 A.M. in the "suburbs" of Columbia Heights, Meridian Hill, and Mt. Pleasant, to the north of old Boundary Street.

By the fall of 1891 five theaters were live for the season, and that year Chautauqua came to the suburb of Glen Echo, accessible by streetcar. Lectures in the Hall of Philosophy included a series on the "causes for the existence of the present economic problems." THE POST reported that ladies were going to the theater without hats, jackets, or escorts. "Is this another evidence of the growing independence of the sex?"

In the summer some Washingtonians went to the seashore. At Ocean City, Maryland, "the coming seaside resort for Maryland, Delaware and Washingtonians," as a real estate ad had it, there was a "grand sale of lots." For $2 one could buy a round-trip rail ticket to go and inspect. Mosquito netting, a necessity for staying in the capital, could be purchased for $1.10 to $5 in white, pink, or blue and buff. A dollar would buy five bicycle riding lessons. Lots along the "palisades of the Potomac," on the way to Glen Echo, could be had for $300 and up, $25 cash required. The extension of electric streetcar lines opened new "suburban" areas in Bethesda and Rockville across the District line in Maryland, and in Fort Myer Heights over the Potomac in Virginia. Prices ranged from $200 to $750 and some business lots were advertised as "fronting immediately on the railroad."

In the winter the well-off could escape to the South. The Great Southern Fast Mail left Washington at 11:01 A.M., due in Jacksonville, Florida, at 9:30 the next morning. A "grand tour of Northern Europe" was advertised in mid-1890 for $280 "to cover all expenses" for 45 days.

THE POST had a typically Victorian attitude about some of the books of the day. An 1895 editorial noted:

> Just now there seems to be an unnatural and morbid craving for infidel and erotic literature. Men and women find time from their books of devotion to take sips from the deadly and prurient novels of the day, in which all the sores of modern civilization are painted with sickening realism. Their mental appetites are not unlike their stomachs, and after partaking of a ripe peach in the form of a pure and beautiful romance,

they like to wind up with a bit of limburger cheese from the factory of Zola or Bourget.

Lest THE POST seem too prudish, however, it should be noted that it approved of "bloomers and knickerbockers" as "the correct and sensible thing" for bicycle riding. "Sensibilities that can bear up under the apparition of the average seaside bathing costumes," said an editorial in 1895, "will hardly writhe in the presence of a pair of trim knee britches and knickerbockers." When a Chicago alderman proposed to ban such women's sports attire, THE POST retorted: "Does he think to veto the recrudescence of the female leg?"

The paper reported the Oscar Wilde case, in which the author was "charged with inciting young men to commit a foul crime, and also with having committed the crime itself." It would be many decades before the word "homosexual" would appear in THE POST or any other family newspaper. But THE POST did object when there were requests that Wilde's books be withdrawn from public libraries: "This is nonsense unworthy of intelligent and civilized human beings."

The paper reveled in recounting tales of both the royal and the rich. An 1895 feature story began:

> Never before has there been such a galaxy of rich weddings on the society tapis, and the fall and early winter promise to unite a larger number of millionaire families than any similar period in the social history of the country. To enumerate the dollars concerned by these alliances is a huge and somewhat delicate task. This table gives an approximate idea of the subject, however:

| | |
|---|---|
| Miss Gertrude Vanderbilt — Moses Taylor | $30,000,000 |
| Miss Pauline Whitney — A. H. Paget | 18,000,000 |
| Miss Edith Rockefeller — Harold McCormick | 28,000,000 |
| Miss Consuelo Vanderbilt — Duke of Marlborough | 25,000,000 |
| Miss Felicite Oglesby — G. M. Pullman, Jr. | 15,000,000 |
| Miss Ethel V. Phelps-Stokes — J. S. Hoyt | 9,000,000 |

If such matters seemed more the province of New York and Europe than of the capital city, Washington could boast a scandal or two. In 1904 the following breathless sentence began a page 1 story:

> Countess Esterhazy, one of the most prominent women in the society of the capital city and of a recognized position throughout this country and Europe, and who was the beautiful Sallie Carroll, of the Carrolls of Maryland, was made the

> defendant in a damage suit for $100,000 filed yesterday by Mrs. Laura M. DeLang, who charges in her bill that the Countess Esterhazy had alienated the affections of her husband, Mr. Martin DeLang, well-known as a friend of the defendant.

The New York versus Washington feud, as old as the existence of the national capital, burst forth in 1900. The New York *Times* remarked that "New York is surely as efficient as Washington is amiable and inefficient," and "When a New Yorker first comes to Washington he is struck with the uniform politeness of the population, from Cabinet officers to bootblacks. After he has been here a few days he longs for the rudeness of New York." At this rebuke THE POST snorted: "No doubt. The pig returns to his wallow."

The centennial of Washington as the national capital in 1900 found the city with a population of 278,718 with another 100,113 in adjacent Virginia and Maryland. Negroes were still just under a third of the city's total population, but the percentage was declining because of the large influx of whites. The 1900 census showed that almost 49 percent of Washington's whites were natives; 29 percent from south of the Mason-Dixon line, mostly from Maryland and Virginia; and 22 percent natives of the North and West. Of the city's blacks, 41.9 percent were Washington-born and another 50.8 percent from Maryland and Virginia. The figures on adults unable to write in 1900 were 1.86 percent for whites and a shocking 30.47 percent for blacks.

THE POST's economic views were very conservative. The paper opposed the idea of a federal income tax. In 1894, when the House Ways and Means Committee voted for a 2 percent tax on incomes over $4000. THE POST called the move "folly," declaring that "the list of those who vote against it will make the role of honor for this memorable year." Nonetheless, Congress enacted the income tax. When the Supreme Court ruled, 5 to 4, against the tax, THE POST shouted "Hallelujah!" The Court's majority, it said, had "stood between their country and the ignorant rabble led by demagogues. They have checked the ugly and abhorrent tide of class prejudice and reckless passion." The paper did print what it termed Justice Harlan's "bitter words" of dissent in which he called for a constitutional amendment to permit graduated taxes on incomes. That was to take another 18 years.

The political struggle over the economic issues of silver and the tariff filled column after column. In 1893 THE POST wrote of a "commercial depression which is daily closing once prosperous factories, throwing out of employment hundreds of thousands of laboring men, bringing distress to countless American homes, and destroying incalculable millions of values." The answer, to the paper, was repeal of the silver coinage law, a lowering of tariffs, and the generosity of the rich. Andrew Carnegie ordered his mills to run at capacity and he distributed $1000 a day "throughout the period of distress for the relief of the deserving poor in Pittsburgh, or $5,000 a day for the next two months if the people of Pittsburgh will be an equal contributor."

Two years later, when wages were raised 10 percent at the Carnegie Steel Company, THE POST editorialized that "it is evident that employers, capitalists, and corporations are not as wicked as some would have them appear . . . May it not, in fact, be possible that employers really desire the prosperity and happiness of their employes?"

Such conservative comments have to be read against the continuing news of labor agitation, disputes, and strikes. On principle THE POST now felt that labor unions "in the main" had "proved of great benefit to their members." Such organizations "can be made to serve good and lawful ends. It is only their mismanagement that brings them into discredit and destroys the relations of confidence which employers and employes should sustain to each other."

THE POST opposed unrestricted immigration into the United States. In 1891 it found that too many unskilled immigrants coming to America — "mainly Russians, Italians and Huns" — presented a "danger of unchecked immigration of the present quality and character" though "immigrants will always be welcome if they be healthy, honest, intelligent and industrious." Another editorial found that the "most desirable" come from Britain, Ireland, Scandinavia, and Germany. But finally, an editorial cried out: "Close the Gates."

The Chicago Haymarket Riot of 1886 brought the anarchists into prominence and THE POST was violently against this breed of social activist. The 1892 steelworkers' strike at the Carnegie works in Homestead, Pennsylvania, found THE POST with little sympathy for the men because of the violence, the "ghastly result" of the strike. When the company demanded protection for its Pinkertons who had tried to break the strike, THE POST said it did "not see how the authorities can refuse to respond to these demands unless they propose to connive at anarchy." An attempt on the life of Henry Clay Frick, general manager of the Homestead works, was denounced in an editorial concluding:

> Labor has its rights and suffers its wrongs; but law is not to be defied. Every man, whether master or servant, must be protected in his own. Life and property must be held sacred

from violation. Injustice has not yet reached a stage in this country that we must wade through blood for justice.

But America did, indeed, have to "wade through blood for justice." Samuel Gompers, the head of the American Federation of Labor, had initially been accepted by THE POST as a peaceful backer of such things as the eight-hour day and women's suffrage. But when he called Frick "a terrible despot" and his Pinkertons "cut-throats and murderers," the paper branded Gompers an "anarchist." Other labor battles, many of them bloody, brought POST support for putting down "at all costs" such "insurrection."

The depression of 1893 produced a march on Washington by hundreds of unemployed who became known as Coxey's Army after their leader, "General" Jacob S. Coxey of Massillon, Ohio. The "army" left Ohio on March 25, 1894, by horse, wagon, canal boat, and foot. By April it reached Frederick, Maryland, and THE POST had a reporter on hand. The marchers, said the paper, faced "nothing but failure." THE POST added that "we speak in sympathy and sorrow rather than in animosity"; the District had its depression problems and could barely take care of its own. On May 1, THE POST recounted, only 600 of a promised 10,000 "marched up Capitol Hill and marched down again" and even that number included some of the local unemployed. There was "the semblance of a riot," a reporter wrote. Coxey was arrested and later found guilty by a jury of "unlawfully trampling on the grass."

More serious that year were the strikes, especially the Pullman strike. When George M. Pullman, inventor of the sleeping and dining cars, cut wages, he failed to lower his company town rents. Workers signed up with the American Railway Union whose head was Eugene V. Debs, a believer in industrial unionism but not yet a Socialist. The union declared a boycott of railroads using Pullman cars. Soon THE POST headlined: MOB RULE SUPREME. When Debs defied a court order not to interfere with railway transportation of the mails, President Cleveland sent in federal troops with violence the outcome.

THE POST was on Pullman's side; the union, it said, had set up machinery for the "intimidation of capital, the terrorization of the country, and even defiance of the authority of the government." There was no effort to report or discuss the underlying causes of the strike.

Debs was arrested and later jailed for contempt; the union's lawyer was a young man named Clarence Darrow. Only after the strike was broken and THE POST had reported that Pullman was about to turn "his striking tenants into the streets" did the paper shed an editorial tear for the 5000 men, women, and children thus made homeless. As for Debs, when talk of his running for President began, THE POST said: "He is nothing but a light-weight agitator, a cheap demagogue — the inferior in ability, in moral character, and in substantial worth to nine-tenths of the men who earn their living by honest toil."

In May 1902, when anthracite miners in Pennsylvania struck for higher pay, THE POST again was on the side of capital; John Mitchell and his United Mine Workers Union, it said, were keeping men who wanted to go back to work from doing so. President Roosevelt forced arbitration, which brought the miners a 10 percent raise and a nine-hour day but also a ruling that there should be no discrimination against non-union men. When TR sought to prosecute the Northern Securities Company, a pooling arrangement of the railroad barons, for a violation of the Sherman Antitrust Act, THE POST's position at last began to change. The government's victory in the Court of Appeals was called "a great legal triumph." In 1904 the Supreme Court upheld the government, terming the railroad merger unlawful.

The limit of THE POST's shift was reflected in an editorial printed before that decision:

> Curb the power of the trusts, by all means. Limit them to a legitimate and useful exercise of their activities. There is much to do along these lines, and intelligent and courageous action is urgently desired. But to abolish them is impossible. That is the dream of a visionary, the hope of a brooding anarchist, the prattle of a silly demagogue.

While the government at last was beginning to curb the excesses of the "free enterprise" system, the men of great wealth were not exactly suffering. On February 15, 1905, THE POST reprinted from a financial journal a list of the twenty wealthiest Americans. Heading the list were Rockefeller, Carnegie, and Vanderbilt, and others included E. H. Harriman, James J. Hill, J. O. Armour, and Jacob H. Schiff. Their total wealth was put at $2,120,000,000 and their total yearly income was listed at $112,000,000 with Rockefeller alone worth $500,000,000 with a yearly income of $25,000,000. A 1905 POST editorial about Rockefeller commented that, while he was a pious man, "he sows demoralization throughout the land — in the mansion of the plutocrat and in the hovel of the beggar. And that is why Mr. Rockefeller's billions will not buy content."

That same month THE POST carried accounts of the New York State investigation into the chicaneries of insurance and banking leaders, including testimony by a vice president of the New York Life Insurance

Company that the company had contributed $150,000 to Republican presidential campaigns. The inquiry introduced to the nation a new name, that of the 43-year-old committee counsel, Charles Evans Hughes.

If THE POST's conscience was only slowly stirred by the issue of the trusts, it came to flame over the extraordinary case of Captain Alfred Dreyfus. At first THE POST brushed aside calls for judicial review of the notorious French court-martial case. But by January 1898 it was a multicolumn page 1 story. "No government can live," an editorial stated, "no people can respect themselves, under the suspicion of compounding an infamy so vile as the persecution of Dreyfus now appears to be."

THE POST was quick to see in the case the virus of anti-Semitism, signs of which were appearing in the United States, and denounced it in a January 1899 editorial:

> If there be in New York any ruffians who have brought anti-Semitism to this country from France, Russia, Germany, or Austria, and propose to maltreat the Jews here as they did in Continental Europe, they have made a mistake that should be corrected by stern methods without delay. There is no public sentiment in the United States that will tolerate Jew baiting.

The civil rights of black Americans were quite another matter. In many ways the conditions of American blacks deteriorated in the Hatton-Wilkins era, 1889–1905. The big decision of the white majority in the post-Reconstruction period had been made during the Hutchins era; now they would be refined to assure subjection of the Negro minority, both in the South and in the capital city.

There were essentially three major developments in this period: southern white-controlled state governments legislated to make the voting rolls lily-white; lynching and other forms of violence were employed to intimidate the Negro when he came into physical contact with whites, especially white women; and, finally, the federal government began to enforce segregation in Washington to eliminate pockets of racial commingling at places of work.

When, in 1890, Mississippi prepared to introduce "ballot reform" — establishing property and literacy qualifications — the paper approved, calling it "a way whereby, without fraud or violence, the minority may be enabled to govern the majority."

Lynching, and other forms of violence, began to increase and THE

POST was filled with accounts of such acts, not all of them in the South and not all of them against blacks. On January 8, 1896, THE POST reprinted from the Chicago *Tribune* these figures on lynchings: 1890 — 127; 1891 — 192; 1892 — 235; 1893 — 200; 1894 — 190; 1895 — 171. The story said that of the 171 lynchings in 1895 all but 27 had occurred in the South and that 32 of the 144 victims in the South had been whites.

THE POST obviously was troubled. After publishing the report of an 1892 lynching in nearby Warrenton, Virginia, an editorial declared that "mob law, under any circumstances, albeit the first law of nature, as sometimes claimed, is a dangerous thing to encourage. There is too much of it already throughout the country, and it spreads like a contagion so long as public sentiment tacitly approves it." Yet, most of the reports coming to, and printed in, THE POST, as well as editorial comments, assumed the blacks involved were guilty.

THE POST's basic prescription was to grant Negroes full legal rights but to accent social distinction. "The best plan," said an editorial in the first week of Hatton-Wilkins ownership, "is to see to it that the status of the negro, who is a citizen by virtue of the Constitution, is one of immutable equality before the law." A March 1895 editorial said:

> . . . the colored people should either drop the race issue themselves or stop complaining of the whites who take them at their word . . . They get together in numbers and listen to harangues by flashy, half-educated demagogues — professional negroes who thrive on the race issue — and adopt resolutions to the effect that the white people are persecuting them, trying to keep them down, jealous of their talent, their virtues and their worth. They segregate themselves, band together, accepting the hypothesis they themselves have offered us.

Washington remained closer to being a southern than a northern city in most of its mores, and that included race. Southern members of Congress, from the end of Reconstruction to the middle of the twentieth century, sought to enforce the southern pattern in the capital. In 1890 Congressman Thomas W. Grimes of Georgia, THE POST reported, refused to eat in the dining room of the Riggs House, one of the better hotels, when he found that blacks were present. There was a row at a local typing club when it was proposed that black girls should be admitted to learn that skill. In 1895 six black students about to graduate from Howard University were arrested on charges of excessive noise. THE

POST editorialized that "it is no secret that the police and the colored people of Washington do not love each other."

An incident in the summer of 1895 helps explain why. Miss Elizabeth M. Flagler, a general's daughter, shot and killed a 13-year-old black, Ernest Green, in front of the Flagler "country" home at Columbia Road and California Street. THE POST's news story, the most prominent on page 1, said that young Green, whose father was a messenger for the Secretary of the Treasury, was among half a dozen boys playing ball in the street. He had reached for a pear on a Flagler tree or else had picked up one that had fallen to the ground. Miss Flagler saw this, picked up a pistol, and fired the fatal shot from a second floor window. "Miss Flagler," the story recounted, "was greatly excited when she perceived the damage she had unwittingly done." She surrendered to police and at an inquest the same evening she was acquitted of wrong-doing. THE POST, some days later, objected to the "unprecedented" speed of this verdict. So great was the feeling, presumably among whites as well as blacks, that two months later Miss Flagler was charged with manslaughter. She pleaded guilty, was fined $500, and served a token two and a quarter hours in jail.

Two individual black leaders of whom THE POST did approve were Frederick Douglass and Booker T. Washington. When Douglass died in 1895, THE POST called him "one of the great men of the century." The paper endorsed Booker T. Washington just as enthusiastically, by 1901 calling him "a great negro" because "he is guided by wisdom, not vanity."

On October 16, 1901, five weeks after he became President, Roosevelt invited Washington to dine at the White House. Other blacks had been there before — Cleveland had received Douglass and his white wife at a reception — but this was different. TR, who approved of Washington's advice to his fellow blacks that they not seek social equality, intended to name at least a few Negroes suggested by Washington to federal jobs. There was no public announcement of the invitation and except for chance it would have passed unnoticed.

THE POST's White House reporter, in checking TR's daily activities, found Washington's name. But THE POST editors who handled the story either failed to see its significance or deliberately chose not to. The result was this one-sentence item on page 3 of next day's 12-page paper: "Booker T. Washington, of Tuskegee, Alabama, dined with the President last evening."

Washington correspondents of southern papers spotted the item and sent it flashing home. Two days later the playback hit page 1 of THE POST: SOUTH IS RESENTFUL. CENSURES PRESIDENT FOR DINING BOOKER

WASHINGTON, said the top headlines in column 1. THE POST noted, "No portion of the population is discussing the affair with more relish than the colored people of Washington. In passing about the department buildings it is a common occurrence to hear the colored messengers proudly rehearse the fact that one of their own race has dined with the President of the United States at the White House." Roosevelt was "surprised and dismayed" by the violence of the South's reaction to the incident, as one historian wrote, and he never again had a Negro to a White House meal.

THE POST on occasion praised some of the capital's blacks: "the negro scholar in silk hat and frock coat," lawyers, colored women college graduates, teachers, businessmen, and those with musical talents. But a 1905 editorial demonstrated a lamentable and basic prejudice in saying: "We still have in the National Capital a colored population which is by no means desirable. It is thriftless, prone to theft, lacking in moral sense, and contributes largely to the throngs which crowd the prisoners' pen in the Police Court."

In Washington legal equality existed on paper but restaurants, barbershops, and hotels barred all but an occasional well-known black. Jim Crow was the rule on railroads operating into the city from North as well as South. It was no wonder, then, that when on May 18, 1896, the Supreme Court majority upheld the "separate but equal" segregation device for trains THE POST printed only a three-paragraph item headed SEPARATE CAR LAW UPHELD. This was the case known as *Plessy* v. *Ferguson* that became famous when a later Court, in 1954, reversed the doctrine in the public school cases. The stinging one-man minority criticism of the majority view, uttered by the first Justice Harlan, went unreported. Harlan prophetically said that the majority ruling "will, in time, prove to be quite as pernicious as the decision made by this tribunal in the Dred Scott case," the pre–Civil War decision that had upheld the institution of slavery.

Blacks in the capital city were more and more segregated, even those with jobs in the federal government. In 1904 what was called a "Jim Crow corner" first made its appearance at the Bureau of Engraving and Printing where black employees were separated from their white coworkers. The process accelerated in the later years of the Roosevelt administration, and then under Taft and Wilson.

Fascination with things mechanical has been an American attribute throughout THE POST's first century. Few laymen followed such developments with more interest than did the editors of THE POST. In the Hutchins era interest had centered on Edison's lamp and Mergenthaler's linotype. In the Wilkins period came two inventions to further revolutionize the way of life — the automobile and the airplane.

The coming of the auto was long and well publicized. On July 26, 1895, an editorial titled "Horseless Carriages" noted that the American consul in the French port city Le Havre had just reported on an auto competition in which "one important result" had been that "electricity suffered a defeat and petroleum scored a victory." It was noted that "the vehicles run by gasoline at small cost and little trouble, vehicles of simple design and cheap construction, went 'over the hill and far away' at an average speed of fifteen miles an hour." To this the editorial added that "great improvement of country highways is a condition precedent to the general introduction of these vehicles into the United States. At present most of our roads are an insult to the horse and not very complimentary to the mule." Nonetheless, "in the suburbs of many of our cities there are roads as good as those of France, and on these horseless carriages may soon be expected to make their appearance in large numbers, to the still further depression of the horse-raising industry." Three years later THE POST concluded that "we shall probably witness, before many months, the introduction of such vehicles in all of our cities as delivery wagons" though they would be costly.

The historic day turned out to be Friday, April 2, 1897, but the story appeared next day not on page 1 but on page 11. MOTOR CARRIAGE HERE. THE HORSELESS VEHICLE CAUSED A STREET SENSATION. TRIAL TRIP ON THE ASPHALT. The account reported that "pedestrians, drivers and horses gazed after it in amazement as it sped noiselessly along at a speed of ten miles an hour," causing "more excitement than a circus." As a practical note, the story added that the "universal use" of such vehicles would bring a saving "in street cleaning alone in a city like Washington" of "almost $400,000."

Six weeks later the first auto advertisement appeared in THE POST, a two-column notice for the "Columbia motor carriage" which, it was stated, anyone could learn to drive in ten minutes. The first Washington auto show took place during the city's 1900 centennial. "One of the most popular of the exhibits," THE POST noted, was the Pennsylvania Horseless Carriage Manufacturing Company's vehicle, "the only motor carriage in the country which uses kerosene oil as fuel. A distance of sixty miles can be covered with this machine on two gallons of oil."

By mid-1901 there were enough automobiles to produce problems. "To be quite frank," a July 24 editorial said, "the private auto is far and away the most dangerous thing on wheels within the limits of the District"; and "scores of these machines" now were "flying along in all directions, manifestly far beyond the legal speed." THE POST called for cars to carry both lights and tag numbers. It also was suggested that perhaps cars should run on their own "paths" and not on "public streets." In February 1902 a boy killed by an auto in New York was front-page news. The paper began to ask "Are Automobiles Safe?" and gave a wary "yes and no" answer, depending on their speed.

Automobiles at first were only for the rich who generally employed chauffeurs. When the city proposed giving each car a number, the chauffeurs set up a howl. THE POST was for registration and control. "Our local automobilists," an editorial said on April 24, 1903, "talk freely of and pleasantly of machines with fifty to eighty horsepower, and of speed anywhere from thirty to sixty miles per hour." A Berryman cartoon depicted policemen handing out tickets to lady car drivers. And on June 1, a driver was fined $20 for going 17 miles per hour.

By 1904 the auto show produced advertisements for Oldsmobiles, Franklins, and Pierce-Arrows at prices ranging from $650 to $2500. That summer one could sightsee in Washington by electric car for 50 cents or a dollar in "perfect safety, no noise, no smell." But THE POST complained of "the recklessness with which the Washington chauffeurs dash around corners and plunge headlong through crowded thoroughfares, with machines that fill the air with noise and the most disagreeable odors."

The inevitable — Washington's first auto fatality — occurred on September 7, 1905, when an 11-year-old girl was struck by a car. Three women fainted when they saw the child, playing in the street, hurled through the air. The driver and his passenger were hustled off to the lockup on a manslaughter charge. There is no record of the eventual penalty.

Automobiles needed paved roads instead of the dirt and mud of the horse and buggy age. When in 1894 there was talk of improving highways, THE POST's conservative view was expressed in an editorial opposing "the paternalistic scheme of national aid in making or repairing roads. That is the business of the people of the localities where the roads are needed." Ten years later, after it was evident that the automobile had come to stay, THE POST held firmly to its position.

> *The Post* opposes road building by the national government because the proposition conflicts with our conception of the idea upon which this republic was established. It contributes, as we see the matter, to the general drift toward centralization, the effacement of state sovereignty, and the substitution of imperial for republican institutions. In this drift we see, or think we see, a national menace of alarming character.

The automobile, however, would contribute, perhaps more than any other development except world wars, to that very centralization of power in the national government.

The airplane, like the automobile, was well anticipated; but there were startling differences. Surrounding the Wright brothers' triumph was an incredible tale of journalism, and following it came another hardly believable story. Both involved THE POST.

An October 12, 1890, editorial, commenting on current balloon experiments, declared that "we are of the opinion that we are on the eve of great discoveries in this respect, and that any one of these days the world may be startled by an invention which will furnish the means of flying safely through the air." Seven months later a POST reporter interviewed Hiram J. Maxim, the inventor of the gun that bore his name, during a Washington visit. Maxim then planned a plane to be propelled by a "petroleum"-fired engine. To THE POST reporter he was prophetic: "If I can rise from the coast of France, sail through the air across the Channel, and drop half a ton of nitro-glycerine upon an English city, I can revolutionize the world." A September 5, 1895, editorial was perceptive in quoting some scientists as thinking that "the time is not far distant when the railways and steamboats will be left to handle heavy freights, while passengers and express packages will go to and from all parts of the world by aerial routes."

In 1896 THE POST noted dispatches from Berlin that a company was being formed "for the purpose of constructing air ships on plans submitted by Count von Zeppelin of Wurtenburg." Commenting on the Berlin dispatches, THE POST said that "the prediction that aerial navigation will be an accomplished fact at the end of the century does not appear extravagant. The prudent man does not apply 'impossible' to any proposition unless he knows it to be opposed to a law of nature."

Among those working on the problem was Samuel P. Langley, secretary of the Smithsonian Institution, a widely respected scientist with a passion to make flying possible. In 1896 he had flown a powered model plane along the banks of the Potomac, an event unnoted by THE POST but which impressed the War Department. Langley was given a $50,000 subsidy to build a flying machine capable of carrying a man. He was encouraged in his work by another Washingtonian, Alexander Graham Bell.

By July 1903 Langley had at last built his plane. THE POST of July 4, on page 2, headlined: AIRSHIP READY TO FLY. The story said that Langley would try it at Widewater, Virginia, about 30 miles southeast of Washington where the Potomac broadens, with his plane to be launched from a "large houseboat." Newspapermen camping nearby included THE POST's 23-year-old George Rothwell Brown.

Not until October 7 was the attempt made, with Charles V. Manley aboard but Langley himself absent. Reporters waited in boats offshore. The plane, named the *Buzzard,* was catapulted forward and, as Brown described it, "there was a roaring, grinding noise — and the Langley airship tumbled over the edge of the house-boat and disappeared in the river sixty feet below." Next day's POST headlined: BUZZARD A WRECK. LANGLEY'S HOPES DASHED. After a second failure on December 10, THE POST advised ending the government subsidy.

In the face of failure by the most respected American inventor known to be working on aeronautics, it was no wonder there was skepticism at THE POST, and at other newspaper offices around the nation, when on December 17, only a week after the second Langley failure, there arrived a telegraph message from the South. Editors were asked if they wished to buy a story about a successful plane flight by two unknown Ohio brothers named Wright.

The query came from Harry P. Moore, the marine reporter for the Norfolk *Virginian-Pilot.* Moore's later account of how he picked up the story is a journalistic classic. Early one September morning in 1903 he walked into a Norfolk restaurant and found a garrulous North Carolinian buying a barrel of oysters. The man was saying, as Moore sat down, "There are two looney Yankees down at Kitty Hawk trying to learn how to fly, and they want to eat some Lynnhaven oysters before they die." The man told Moore the names of the secretive fliers and described their kitelike contraption. Moore, who had friends in the Coast Guard at Kitty Hawk, was able to get close enough to see the site and the machine. On the morning of December 17, 1903, a coastguardsman gave Moore the critical message: the first flight had been made at 10:45 A.M.

The *Virginian-Pilot* put a double-line eight-column banner over Moore's account. But he received only five orders for his story — from the New York *American,* the Cincinnati *Enquirer,* the Chicago *Inter-Ocean,* the Philadelphia *Record,* and THE WASHINGTON POST. For the five stories he sent, Moore received a total of $170.

THE POST's editors, however, were wary. They did not print Moore's eloquent account that night but waited a day before transforming the news into the less dramatic and more cautious account published on December 19. Under a striking one-column headline, SOARED LIKE A BIRD, displayed on page 1 but with only moderate prominence, the rewritten story began:

> Norfolk, Va., Dec. 18 — It is reported here that a successful trial of a flying machine was made yesterday near Kitty Hawk, N.C., by Wilbur and Orville Wright, of Dayton, Ohio. It is stated that the machine flew for three miles in the face of a wind blowing at the registered velocity of twenty-one miles an hour, and then gracefully descended to earth at the spot selected by the man in the navigator's car as a suitable landing place. The machine has no balloon attachment, but gets its force from propellers worked by a small engine.

Even thus hedged THE POST's account was sensational news on page 1. But what followed was perhaps even more amazing.

The normal inclination of editors faced with a big event is to follow up, to send their own reporters to find out more. But no editor anywhere did so after the first Wright flight nor after further flights in 1904 and 1905. Not until 1908, when another local reporter queried editors about the continuing Wright flights at Kitty Hawk, did the press wake up and send its own reporters to find the facts. Not THE POST, however, although it did print an account of this round of flights. Still it remained doubtful of what it did print, editorially worrying lest "some fine genius of a correspondent," with "the aerial imagination of a Poe and the mendacity of a Munchausen, has set free his interesting tales upon an unresisting public."

A newspaper's influence depends on a combination of what it prints and who reads it. Lord Northcliffe, the British publisher, once said, "Of all the American newspapers I would prefer to own *The Washington Post,* because it reaches the breakfast tables of the members of Congress." He might have added the tables of the Presidents, administration officials, judges, and justices. But a Washington paper must have a wider local readership and THE POST in the Hatton-Wilkins era had that. It boasted that it was

> read at home, on the streetcars, and in the offices. It is ubiquitous. It comes around early Monday morning and snuggles up against the washtub. On Tuesday it holds the place of honor at the head of the ironingboard. Wednesday the housewife pauses at her mending to read its cheery contents. The labors of Thursday's cleaning are lightened by its presence. Friday's paper is no deadhead in the household, and Saturday morning brings the last bright number of the working week.

In 1901 THE POST proudly reprinted a comment from the *Trade Unionist:* "To thoroughly read the *Sunday Post* is as much as a man can comfortably do on that day in addition to the proper performance of his religious duties."

THE POST was an increasingly successful paper. A comparison between the editions of Christmas seasons ten years apart gives a measure: On December 22, 1889, THE POST printed 140 columns of which 78 were advertisements; on a comparable Sunday in 1899, 288 columns of which 177 1/2 were ads in what was proclaimed to be "the largest regular edition ever printed by a Washington newspaper." In 1901 the daily paper varied from 12 to 14 pages with the Sunday edition running 30 to 36. The big Sunday paper before Christmas carried 244 columns of ads in its 44 pages, "122 columns more advertising than ever carried in a single issue by any of *The Post*'s contemporaries."

In the Hatton-Wilkins era circulation figures were printed only for big special editions and for notable extras. The Audit Bureau of Circulation, which requires disclosure, was not established until 1914. However, in 1890 THE POST claimed that it sold around 16,300 daily and 19,900 Sundays. By 1905, when the paper again changed hands, these figures had slowly but steadily increased to 33,967 daily and about 45,000 on Sundays. The price remained three cents daily and five cents on Sunday.

The lucrative Sunday edition may have been one reason THE POST's chief competitor, the *Evening Star,* a two-cent daily, inaugurated the *Sunday Star* on March 26, 1905, at a time when its daily circulation was about that of THE POST. The April 16 Sunday POST carried 195 columns of advertising compared to 109 for the *Sunday Star* and only 66 1/2 for the other Sunday paper, the Washington *Times.*

THE POST's relationship to the *Star,* at least as reflected in its own columns, was a friendly one. In 1890 there was some editorial carping at the *Star* over its differing stand on the issue of getting the railroads off the Mall. In 1895 the New York *Sun,* as a POST editorial put it, "referred in most injurious terms" to Frank B. Noyes of the *Star,* then a director of the Associated Press, during a row between the AP and the United Press. THE POST declared that "we take pleasure in saying of a fellow townsman, albeit a competitor in business, that no one who knows him as well as we do will be in the very least disturbed by the *Sun*'s extraordinary attack." Editors of both papers shared various civic posts and both belonged to the prestigious Gridiron Club.

THE POST used many devices to promote itself. It sold readers books and encyclopedias; for a few years beginning in 1896 it published a 500-page almanac for 25 cents a copy, full of useful information plus a boastful account of the paper; it gave $100 in gold coins as prizes for the best guess of the city's 1900 census count, receiving some 300,000 replies from every state as well as from the District of which three entrants exactly guessed the preliminary figure of 229,796; it treated its newsboys to the annual circus; and it provided free trips to the Chicago World's Fair in 1893 to five public school teachers voted most popular by their students.

The greatest promotion ever for the paper unexpectedly resulted from its "amateur authors' association," begun in 1889 to encourage young writers and to make them constant readers. Frank Hatton and John Philip Sousa, fellow Gridiron members, met one day that same year on a Washington street. Hatton told Sousa about the plan to award prizes to the young authors at a gathering on the Smithsonian grounds and he asked the bandmaster to enliven the ceremony with a concert. A few days later Hatton again ran into Sousa and this time Wilkins was along. "One of them," Sousa recalled, "said it would be a great thing if I would write a special march for the occasion, to which I agreed, and the first performance of The Washington Post March was at this event on the Smithsonian grounds."

On Saturday afternoon, June 15, 1889, some 20,000 young authors congregated at the Smithsonian for the award of THE POST's gold medals.

> Promptly at 4 o'clock, John Philip Sousa took his place in front of his men and raised his baton and the instruments of the famous Marine Band poured forth the strains of the overture. Full as the space was all about people were still coming from every direction and the long lines of them looked like rays converging to the grand stand as a center. Hundreds arrived while the band was playing.
>
> Mr. Wilkins stepped to the front of the platform and said, "the meeting will come to order," but he was mistaken. There were too many boys in it for order to be evolved in any way, but when the Rev. Dr. Corey of the Metropolitan M. E. Church came forward, bowed his head and began "Our Heavenly Father," the noise was hushed. The clergyman's prayer was short and at its conclusion Mr. Wilkins said, "The Marine Band will now play a march composed by Professor Sousa, and dedicated to *The Washington Post.*" The announcement was greeted by applause and the march was generously applauded and before that died away the High School Cadets came marching up from the east, and their

appearance was greeted with a mighty cheer from the children.

The reporter covering the event described Sousa's new march as light and melodious; evidently no one present realized that the bandmaster had created an international hit. Sousa sold the sheet music rights for a mere $35, but he received performance royalties the rest of his life. Later the march king reminisced: "I have smiled incredulously many times at its popularity. It seems there is no getting away from it." The first edition of the sheet music carried a reproduction of the paper's front page and a dedication to owners Hatton and Wilkins.

The popularity of the march was both immediate and immense. It was played by the Austrian band at the Chicago World's Fair and, as a result, popularized at Viennese music gardens. Before long costermongers were whistling it on London streets; the tuneful cadences soon were heard all over the British Empire. It was played on Admiral Dewey's flagship during the battle of Manila Bay. The music has endured; in 1974 the Royal Band of Jordan unintentionally jarred visiting President Richard Nixon with a spirited rendition of the march honoring the newspaper that had first uncovered the Watergate scandal. The newspaper's auditorium is dedicated to Sousa, inaugurated in June 1962 by the Marine Band playing his march.

The Sunday POST began to carry fiction by writers such as Émile Zola, Bret Harte, and Arthur Conan Doyle. George Ade described his travels in Europe and Finley Peter Dunne's Mr. Dooley became a fixture. In 1895 Alfred Henry Lewis began to write a fabulously successful series of "Wolfville" stories in the picturesque language of the Old West.

Some of the fiction and a number of cartoons and illustrations came to THE POST from other papers or from news syndicates. THE POST had two editorial cartoonists, George Y. Coffin and Clifford K. Berryman. Both Coffin and Berryman depicted individuals in an almost photographic manner but with a pungency of point that added influence to THE POST.

After the fashion of the time Coffin, who graduated from a government clerkship to cartooning, sketched for magazines and various newspapers at the same time, gradually becoming a full-time POST employee. He kept drawing until ten days before his death at 46 in 1896. His obituary rightly said that his drawings were "never coarse, never brutal, never malignant." Berryman, at 26, became Coffin's understudy in 1895. In 1902, when TR during a Mississippi bear hunt refused to shoot a cub, Berryman created the Teddy Bear on THE POST's page 1. The bear became the cartoonist's symbol. Berryman stayed with THE POST until 1907 when he moved to the *Star*, becoming a fixture there for four decades.

Photography was invented before THE POST was founded but its transfer to newspapers by means of halftones did not come for half a century. In the case of THE POST the first halftone, a man's picture, appeared on January 10, 1891, and by the turn of the century both line drawings and halftones had become commonplace. In 1901, Theodore Roosevelt was the first President to appear in halftone; in 1905 came the first "action" photograph, a view of a group of strikers moving along a Chicago street.

The editorial paragrapher, a man capable of making a point, humorous or stinging, in a sentence or two was a journalistic staple before and after the turn of the century. Some POST samples:

> "Anthony Comstock has opened warfare on the figure of Hermes in the American Institute Hall, New York. It is understood that Anthony is getting so sensitive that he takes his bath with a pajama suit on." (February 21, 1889)
>
> "Vermont has appropriated $5000 for a World's Fair exhibit. It will probably consist of a few jugs of sugar sap." (March 31, 1891)
>
> "Every time President Harper hears of a Standard Oil spurt he makes a visit to Mr. Rockefeller, and the Chicago University is able to participate in the prosperity." (December 20, 1900)

The man who penned such lines from 1889 until his death in 1903 at age 44 was Harry (Pop) Merrick, the recognized "prince of paragraphers." James Hamilton Lewis, first a representative from Washington and later a senator from Illinois, sported reddish-pink whiskers which offered a constant Merrick target. One day Lewis dropped by THE POST to tell Merrick that "I would rather be mentioned in *The Post*'s paragraphs, even though ridiculed, than to be ignored all together." Merrick was succeeded by Harry Hunter and the quips became a column titled Post-scripts.

Until radio provided the almost instantaneous news that newspapers could never match, every major journal rushed extra editions into the streets after any seemingly important event. THE POST gloried in its extras, some still coming off the presses in the morning as the first Washingtonians were heading for work. A later description of the July 4, 1898, extra:

> All over the city the *Post*'s newsboys ran. Their ringing voices aroused the slumbering people from their beds. "Extra paper! Great naval victory! Spanish fleet is sunk! Extra *Post!*" Lights appeared in every window, until the whole town was illuminated, and soon the streets were swarming with cheering multitudes, gone mad with delight.

A feature of the Hatton-Wilkins era was the special edition. These multipage papers were turned out with great care and infinite detail on the occasion of such Washington gatherings as the Grand Army of the Republic, the Knights of Pythias, Presbyterian church leaders, and the Knights Templar. The GAR was a power in the land and it was a great civic catch to have the annual encampment in one's city. In 1891, when the GAR was meeting in Detroit, THE POST campaigned hard for the next year's encampment, even printing an extra edition that ran to 300,000 copies on the *Free Press* and *Tribune* presses of that city. This did the trick and when the veterans came to Washington the next September, THE POST ran off an 88-page special section one day and other special editions during the week-long gatherings of the 70,000 veterans. Papers were mailed home all over the nation; the major special edition sold 283,105 copies. An editorial recognized the general direction of the editions by Managing Editor West and News Editor Bone.

Undoubtedly Scott C. Bone was the most important POST employee in the Hatton-Wilkins era. In 1888 he came to the paper from his native Indiana to be telegraph editor under Hutchins, soon was news editor under Hatton, and in 1891 managing editor. Like his mentor, Hatton, the handsome Bone was a Republican and a conservative. After Hatton's death, Wilkins gave Bone control of both the news and editorial side of the paper, a role he continued until THE POST's sale in 1905. By then he was being paid $15,000 a year, $2000 more than the pay of the Chief Justice of the United States. Fellow journalists called him a "commanding personality," "a painstaking editor," and a "man of superlative talent." When he left, the head of the Associated Press wrote that "you have built your monument by long and efficient service, and hereafter every one going to Washington will speak of *The Post* as the paper which Scott Bone once edited." In 1906 he founded and edited the rival morning Washington *Herald.* In 1916 he was a delegate to the GOP convention and in 1920 the party's publicity director. In 1921 President Harding rewarded him with the appointive governorship of Alaska.

In the Hatton-Wilkins era THE POST varied its layout with either seven- or eight-column pages. Often in one week there would be four days of one makeup and three of the other, with no explanation to the reader. The addition of new presses was necessary several times. The paper finally outgrew its building at 10th and D streets and on October 23, 1893, it moved to the fourth of its six homes.

The new building was at 1339–41 E Street Northwest, facing Pennsylvania Avenue at an angle a few doors from 14th Street. At the time of the move "newspaper row," the offices of most out-of-town correspondents, was still around the corner on 14th Street. To the east on E Street was "rum row," a collection of saloons dating back to the Civil War. THE POST's new building initially housed correspondents of several papers. The structure, as THE POST described it, was "a combination of Gothic and Romanesque architecture." With two additional wings and some rented space next door it was the paper's home for 57 years. The building featured red cherry paneling, wrought iron, marble floors, and both gas and electric lights. About the time of the move the first two Remington typewriters were purchased for reporters after West, using the "hunt and peck" system, beat Hatton, using a pen, in a speed contest. In his 44 years at THE POST, West was reporter, city editor, managing editor, music and drama critic, political correspondent, and, finally, golf editor.

By 1903 Beriah Wilkins, the surviving partner of the 1889 purchase, was an ill man. To counter rumors that this meant THE POST was for sale, an editorial, the only one Wilkins ever signed, declared that "it is not on the market at any price, however large." Two months later, while in New York City, Wilkins suffered a partially paralyzing stroke. He died at 58 on June 7, 1905, at his home at 1711 Massachusetts Avenue Northwest, "the pathetic sequel to a long struggle for health." He left his POST stock to his widow and two sons, John F. and Robert G., both Princeton graduates. John was THE POST business manager and secretary, Robert the treasurer.

A June 12 editorial called the paper a monument to Wilkins' "foresight, his genius, and high ambition." A group of Washington correspondents, in a resolution, said that Wilkins "with his brains and capital, linked with the inspiring genius of Frank Hatton, built up" THE POST. The distinction was correct. Hatton was the partner who had emphasized the Hutchins tradition of aggressive news coverage and after his death THE POST lost considerable of its fire. Wilkins centered his attention on profit and the safe journalism that assured it. Although Managing Editor Bone was "highly competent," as H. L. Mencken described him, the quality of reporting and writing gradually declined. When Wilkins died the paper declared that it would continue "with conservatism and progress its watchwords."

John Wilkins carried forward a project of his father's, the first addition to the E Street building. But the widow and sons soon were negotiating the sale of THE POST and several papers reported the purchaser to be John R. McLean. On October 7 McLean bought 270 of the 600 shares of stock for $469,800, or $1740 a share. Some years later he obtained an additional 50, at the same price, to give him majority control. Wilkins' family lore is that McLean gained control by trickery: he persuaded John Wilkins that each should sell a small number of shares to a trusted employee who would not vote the stock. But McLean then announced he had bought that stock, that young Wilkins could continue as vice president at $25,000 a year but that he, McLean, was now in control. At any rate, McLean died owning 320 of the 600 shares which had cost him $556,800. John Wilkins held his remaining 270 shares until after McLean's death in 1916, then sold them to the McLean estate for $469,800, the same per share price McLean had paid in 1905 when Wilkins foolishly had signed an open-ended buy-sell agreement.

On October 13, 1905, as McLean moved into THE POST as his own managing editor, an editorial announced that Scott Bone had "resigned," his retirement "the cause of regret deep and sincere." In reality, Bone was fired. A new age had dawned at THE POST.

# 3

# Turn to Sensationalism Mr. McLean of Cincinnati 1905-1916

John Roll McLean, his daughter-in-law wrote of him, "loved power and nothing was too much trouble when he saw a chance to extend his reach and his control of other men." He was, as she remembered 20 years after his death, "the oddest hybrid of gentle friend and fierce monster that I have ever known. In Washington he exercised a power almost like that of a political boss."

However one may discount a relative's judgment, it is beyond doubt that McLean exercised power with his money and his newspapers. For years he bankrolled the Democratic party in Ohio and through his Cincinnati *Enquirer* influenced his party and his state. A delegate to the 1896 convention that nominated William Jennings Bryan, he was Ohio's favorite son in the presidential balloting; and he led the roll call for Vice President on the fourth ballot before withdrawing amidst a party fight. At least twice McLean hoped for election to the Senate but the Ohio legislature chose others. As the Democratic candidate for governor in 1899, he came close to winning in a Republican year. But unlike other politicians who never quite made it to elective office McLean did not then fade away; he had a secure base of power for the rest of his life, his newspapers, the *Enquirer* and THE WASHINGTON POST.

His father, Washington McLean, was "a sterling product of rugged Scotch ancestry" who began life as a boilermaker, rose to the manufacture of steamboats, and in 1857 joined with a friend to buy control of the *Enquirer*. He made it Ohio's leading Democratic daily. Washington McLean's only son, John R., was born on September 17, 1848. A handsome young man with blue eyes, something of a dresser and rather wild, he left Harvard after a year. According to one account he was expelled for fighting with a boy who had preempted his seat at chapel; according to another, he simply withdrew after being injured playing baseball. He did play baseball awhile for the famous Cincinnati Red Stockings. He was fluent in French and learned German when his father sent him to Heidelberg for a year. His daughter-in-law, Evalyn Walsh McLean, who had a love-hate relationship with him, concluded that he had been "infected with the harsh, ruthless philosophy of Kant and Nietzsche" by the time he returned from Germany. He began work on the *Enquirer* as an office boy, rose to police reporter, and before long was the managing editor.

In 1880 Washington McLean turned over his interest in the paper to his son and retired to the national capital. Within three years the son bought out his father's partner. In later years he liked to tell how he made even his father pay to subscribe. The Cincinnati paper circulated in what became known as the *Enquirer*'s Confederacy — Ohio, Indiana, Kentucky, and West Virginia — widening McLean's influence.

The *Enquirer* was a big moneymaker but John R. McLean hankered for more than that. In 1884 he too moved to Washington, though he kept his legal and political base in Cincinnati. His private railroad car, a mark of the wealthy, he named the *Ohio.* To reformers who saw state and local politics as a cesspool, McLean, as one of them described him, was part of "an oligarchy of business bosses" of both parties who strangled the state. The New York *Herald* called him "an apostle of practical politics. He never manifested sympathy with so-called sentimental statesmanship." Not until 1901, with the election of a reform mayor in Cleveland, was McLean's power in Ohio broken.

From Washington, John R. McLean supervised the *Enquirer* while joining the capital's business world. From 1892 to 1911 he was president of the Washington Gas Light Company. He cofounded the Washington and Old Dominion Railway in 1911 and was a director and large stockholder in both the American Security and Trust Company and the Riggs National Bank. The first appearance of his name in THE WASHINGTON POST, on July 12, 1891, indicated his social status: "Mr. and Mrs. John R. McLean have leased Briarfield cottage at Bar Harbor."

On May 9, 1895, a POST editorial noted that McLean, "one of Washington's most generous and public-spirited citizens," had just acquired the New York *Morning Journal.* "That he will be successful in his undertaking there is not the least room for doubt." The judgment could not have been more wrong. McLean paid a million dollars for the *Journal,* a paper with a reputation as "the chambermaid's delight." He raised the price to two cents, turned it into a serious Democratic paper, and began to lose money rapidly. After only a year, in desperation, he offered a half interest to William Randolph Hearst for $360,000. Hearst laughed and then bought it all for $180,000, thereby gaining entry to the nation's biggest city where he fathered yellow journalism. McLean retreated to Washington.

In his mid-thirties when he had moved to the capital, McLean paid $112,500 for a historic house at 1500 I Street Northwest. John Russell Pope transformed what had been a comparatively small, old-fashioned home by adding a big wing "nobly fashioned" for regal entertaining. There on February 24, 1897, McLean gave a dinner for nearly 100 in honor of defeated presidential candidate Bryan.

THE POST of Beriah Wilkins, a fellow Ohioan, was highly favorable to McLean. When he ran for governor the paper called him "a shrewd and potent quality in any campaign," and when he lost, congratulated him on "a gallant fight." It is apparent that Wilkins and McLean were well acquainted. It is doubtful, however, that Wilkins knew that in 1896 McLean had made a loan to Frank Hatton's widow secured by an option to purchase her stock in THE POST. McLean was never able to exercise that option; he nonetheless gained control from Wilkins' heirs in 1905. Thus began the 28-year McLean era at THE POST, nearly 11 years under John R. and another 17 under his only son, Edward Beale (Ned) McLean.

Upon gaining control of the Cincinnati *Enquirer,* McLean transformed it from a conventional newspaper into a more popular one designed for all classes: political news, sports, theater, society — all with a splash. He brought the same approach to THE WASHINGTON POST. In 1905 Washington had three dailies and a fourth would be established a year later. The *Evening Star* had added its Sunday edition six months earlier. The Washington *Times,* founded in 1894 by unemployed printers, was owned for four years by Stilson Hutchins who in 1901 sold it to Frank A. Munsey. Munsey turned it into a seven-day-a-week afternoon paper. In 1906 the morning Washington *Herald* appeared. McLean was stepping into a battle royal for circulation and advertising — a battle the *Star* was winning at the time of his death in 1916.

McLean took a couple of years to settle on his management team and recreate THE POST in his own image. In March 1905, Ira E. Bennett, a largely self-educated Washington correspondent for West Coast papers, came to THE POST, first as a reporter and then as an editorial writer. Three years later McLean called Bennett into the small office Frank Hatton had used and asked: "Do you like this room?" Bennett replied that it was snug and had a nice fireplace. "Take it then, and use it," was McLean's way of making him editorial page chief, a position he held for a quarter century, with one brief interruption. William P. Spurgeon and then Edward S. Rochester, as managing editors, were placed in control of the news departments. In 1906 McLean plucked Arthur D. Marks from the *Times* to be his business manager, a position he held, like Bennett, into 1933.

McLean considered himself editor-in-chief of both THE POST and the *Enquirer,* but most of his journalistic time was spent in Washington. There was virtually no combination of the news gathering resources of the two papers. In the capital he used as his office a home at 1508 H Street, a locale that became famous in 1921 when some of Warren Harding's Ohio gang moved in. There McLean received callers from 10 to 12:30 daily on non-newspaper business; evenings he spent at THE POST building on E Street, at least in the early years.

John R. McLean, a 1911 magazine article reported, was "full of humor and sarcasm," a "character" both "the lovable and the unthinkable in one, the cruel and the merciful, the sage and the savage." As he grew older, he wore a stubby mustache and became heavy for his medium height. His large eyes appeared to bulge and hostile cartoonists seized upon this to picture him with "eyes that hang out." To daughter-in-law Evalyn, writing in 1935, McLean was both "potent" and "crafty" with "an acid stomach" and "an acid heart." He was "always a businessman" who knew "the force of money, what true wealth was and how to store it" as well as "a newspaper proprietor who had a trick of getting his own way with men or women." His "most effective trick in life was to uncover something compromising about a highly placed individual — and then not print what he learned. He kept such secrets as loaded guns." In 1974 Alice Roosevelt Longworth recalled him as "a dreadful man," "not a splendid brigand," just a brigand with "a big belly and a big chest."

William Randolph Hearst was McLean's friend, and McLean was clearly influenced by Hearst's brand of journalism, not the least because Hearst was so successful financially. This influence was evident in flashy new feature sections, the addition of a four-page color comic section, and a sports section printed on pink paper, all in the Sunday POST. Columns of "Situation Wanted," "Rooms for Rent," and some other classified advertisements were printed free. Big news began to appear under increasingly larger headlines on page 1 of his eight-column paper. The editorial page was brightened typographically by switching to six columns.

Unlike Hearst, McLean never put his own name, or that of any of his editors, on his editorial page masthead. Nor did he trumpet in his ever-expanding society columns his own or his family's social life. (The only exception was Admiral George Dewey, the hero of Manila Bay, whose wife Mildred was McLean's sister. Dewey's birthdays and public appearances received more space than such events deserved by any standard of news judgment.) On July 22, 1908, when his son Ned married Evalyn Walsh, the only daughter of Thomas F. Walsh, who had struck it rich in the Colorado mines, THE POST carried no photographs, only a six-paragraph story on page 7. McLean allowed no more family pride in print than that "she is an unusually handsome girl, vivacious, accomplished and extremely popular." When the McLeans made Friendship, their 75-acre estate "out in the country" on Wisconsin Avenue, available for charity functions there would be lengthy stories about the event but no mention of the owners. He was not, however, above accepting special privileges. For years Friendship was protected by three regular members of the Washington police department, men paid by the city.

McLean once wrote a friend that "self-praise, you know they say, is half scandal, and I have found it a pretty good rule that so long as you are doing well — silence is a great thing." It was a rule befitting a backroom political operator and a powerful newspaper publisher.

Essentially McLean was THE POST's proprietor, in the business office sense, while also setting the general course for Bennett's editorials and for news handling by Spurgeon and Rochester. From a distance he supervised the *Enquirer* via mail and telegraph. McLean's philosophy centered on business prosperity for the nation, the cities of Washington and Cincinnati, the merchants who advertised in his papers, and for himself. Two letters he wrote to William F. Wiley, who handled the editorial side of the *Enquirer,* applied as well to his attitude toward THE POST. On January 22, 1913, he described the "proper course" for the Cincinnati paper:

> The *Enquirer* should be progressive, in that wise progressivism which never endangers but always produces sound development or growth. It should not be used to further personal ambitions costly to the public or subversive to our institutions, nor be allowed to advocate wild and untried theories dangerous to the industrial, or commercial, or financial prosperity . . . Remember, the paramount duty is to publish all the news without malice.

And on July 20, 1914, McLean wrote:

> I would try my best to print always the good about the city — both in the news and editorial departments — for the people don't want to hear or read unpleasant news, no matter how true.

These views, as applied to THE POST, meant that the paper would lose what a later editor, Felix Morley, called "the stimulating and distinctive personality which was Stilson Hutchins' great contribution and which had continued, in more matured and dignified form, under Beriah Wilkins and Scott Bone." Perhaps the change, wrote Morley in THE POST in 1937, was "traceable to the fact that John R. McLean, while personally directing the paper, was at the same time almost equally interested in his Cincinnati organ and other business projects. Perhaps it was due to his weakness for politics, always dangerous indulgence in the case of the newspaper owner whose ambition is to conduct a first class paper." Slowly, but surely, as Morley aptly put it, "in rather intangible ways, *The Post* began to deteriorate spiritually under the McLean ownership."

News is the prime requisite of a newspaper but McLean's POST became more and more erratic. Reporters and their by-lines came and went until by-lines all but disappeared except for sports, society, and features. Political coverage, a strong point in both the Hutchins and Hatton-Wilkins eras, became spotty, with reporters allowed to cover few major out-of-town events. Wire service copy and stories bought from various New York papers began to fill more and more columns, even on Washington events of the highest interest. There was no investigative reporting; local news coverage became casual and routine. There were no book reviews and, until the beginning of World War I, only occasional letters to the editor.

One important event in the early McLean years was the loss, in 1907, to the *Evening Star* of political cartoonist Clifford K. Berryman. After 11 years at THE POST, Berryman found the new owner personally objectionable, colleagues later said. He worked to the last possible moment, a cartoon appearing January 31 in the morning POST, and his first for the *Star* that same afternoon. Berryman added immensely to the *Star*'s prestige and growing strength in the competitive capital journalism of the pre–World War I years. The last few Berryman cartoons were run inside THE POST instead of on the usual page 1. New cartoonists — K. L. Russell, Robert Ishbell, "Wex," and "June" — were tried in the more prominent position, but all were inferior. Within a month THE POST abandoned cartoons, except for an occasional reprint, and not until 1923 did the paper again have a cartoonist of its own.

In the years 1905–1909 the five-cent Sunday edition was a big paper, running during the pre-Christmas shopping season from 60 to 80 pages chock full of advertisements. At times circulation hit 40,000 on Sundays, largest in the city, while the daily average of about 30,000 was slowly declining. The *Star, Herald,* and *Times* all were or became penny dailies, however, compared to THE POST's three cents. The *Times* soon topped all the others in daily circulation by a slim margin.

The papers battled for advertising as well as for circulation. On April 22, 1908, THE POST boasted in a page 1 box that its business in the past 15 months had been "greater than for any 15 months of its history." The previous Sunday THE POST had carried 154 columns of advertising, crediting the unnamed second paper with 128. That was the end of boasting about advertising or circulation supremacy, save for reports of extras such as that on the 1912 *Titanic* disaster when 100,000 papers were sold; by then THE POST was third of the four papers in daily circulation.

On February 28, 1911, without any announcement in the paper, McLean dropped the price of the daily POST to two cents. This had an immediate effect, raising the circulation from the 20,000 to the 30,000 range, about the level of the *Herald,* its morning competitor. The Sunday paper was selling 40,000 or more copies, less than the *Star* but more than the *Times.*

Within four months of taking control, McLean initiated contests to hold and win circulation with prizes ranging from pianos, a building lot, a Ford car, and movie projectors to free trips to the Jamestown Exposition, to Europe, and, finally, in 1914, free trips for 15 area clergymen to the Holy Land. Some contests were decided on the number of subscriptions turned in, others simply were puzzles. Contests always demean a paper and THE POST was no exception, devoting big gobs of space to self-serving stories as the contests grew larger while the circulation battle grew more fierce.

In 1906 THE POST added a Sunday "art supplement," then switched it to once a month. In 1911 came a twice-a-month Sunday magazine composed largely of fiction. The Sunday comics came and went, depending on which ones THE POST could buy from the New York syndicates. In 1915 Bringing Up Father began to appear as a daily strip. That same year THE POST ran on Sundays the popular sketches of Charles Dana Gibson and James Montgomery Flagg. Once in a while fiction was serialized in the daily paper.

Crime and scandal always have been a newspaper staple and they were never absent from THE POST. But McLean's paper ran far more than ever before. A sample of 1910–1911 headlines: KILLS EXTRA WIFE, HEIRESS AN ELOPER, LAYS BARE HER PAST, GHOULS GET GEMS, KILLS WIFE IN RAGE, SLAYS HIS SISTER, KILLS TWO AND SELF. There were features on Enrico Caruso's love affairs and on whether American heiresses who married foreigners should be taxed on their dowries.

Only occasionally did a picture by a staff photographer appear; most came from photo organizations, chiefly Harris & Ewing. Many halftones were badly printed. Carelessness reached the ridiculous in 1911 when the Mona Lisa was stolen from the Louvre: THE POST reproduced the wrong Leonardo and had to apologize next day.

McLean himself was withdrawing more and more from management of all but the financial side of the paper. Two incidents, however, demonstrate his use of the news and editorial columns to help his friends. One friend was Harry M. Daugherty, the Ohio lawyer-lobbyist who would become the disgraced Attorney General of the Harding era. In 1911, after Taft had entered the White House, Daugherty appealed to McLean to help spring Charles W. Morse from the Atlanta penitentiary. Morse, described in THE POST as a "former New York banker and ice king, convicted of misappropriating the funds of institutions with which he was connected," was interviewed by POST reporter Thomas P. Logan who wrote that the prisoner said he was dying and should be released. An editorial called for mercy and a lengthy Daugherty plea for Morse's release was printed on page 1. A month later Taft commuted Morse's sentence on grounds that he was incurably ill. However, Morse lived another 15 years and gossip had it that he had fooled the Taft-appointed medical board by eating a bar of soap before his examination. What McLean or Daugherty knew of Morse's true state of health is unrecorded.

In mid-1913 McLean wrote Bennett from his summer retreat asking him to "write a short editorial — a stick — speaking kindly of Thomas F. Ryan," the millionaire Democrat and financier. Bennett responded with a piece captioned "Mr. Ryan's Great Service," commenting on Ryan's explanation in a magazine article, which McLean presumably had read, of his role in a life insurance scandal. "Time did justify Mr. Ryan," wrote Bennett, "and it is now acknowledged that his foresight, courage, and public spirit were of invaluable service to the people."

THE POST, for all its growing faults, enjoyed the fun, fights, and excitement of a daily newspaper. On December 29, 1909, McLean threw a staff luncheon at the New Willard for 80 of his news and editorial employees and the paper ran a four-column photo of the group. Ned McLean, now the paper's 23-year-old business manager, was there, too. The story caught the mood: "The usual nightly friction between the telegraph editor and the city room and the inevitable appeal to the managing editor over the allotment of space; the disagreements between the reporters and the telephone switchboard operators; the quiet atmosphere of the society room and the noisy accompaniments of the sporting department, and other branches of a newspaper office were burlesqued [at the staff luncheon] in amusing fashion."

A job on THE POST remained a prize. One young reporter, John J.

Daly, recalled that the then city editor, Edward Rochester, a small, immaculate man who wore high collars and was known as "the Duke," seldom had to worry about replacements. "Always there was somebody knocking at his door in quest of a job." The Duke used this line to head off those who braced him for a raise: "You know what? I'm thinking of firing you. There are several good reporters looking for your job."

By 1912 the paper had a fair share of incompetents and there were plenty of reasons for firing reporters. After one man described in print the court testimony of a witness who had not even been there, Rochester posted this notice:

> Two men were dismissed last week for inaccuracy and carelessness. Two others this week are to follow for the same offense. And others — the entire staff — if necessary, will meet the same fate unless more respect is observed for facts and absolute accuracy.
>
> The reputation of a newspaper depends upon its ability to present the news in an impartial and accurate manner. Its reputation is as sacred and as vital as that of an individual. If a man is irresponsible, careless, dishonest and utterly devoid of a conception of truth, he is shunned and regarded as worthless. If a newspaper is irresponsible, careless and lax in its treatment of facts, it is shunned and regarded as worthless.

At the time, THE POST had a city staff of 13 men, paid from $10 to $27.50 a week. To Ned McLean, Rochester lamented that "it is an unfortunate fact that the great majority of reporters cannot be relied upon." Reporters, in turn, complained about the editor's parsimony. The practice was to report weekly how many streetcar tickets, at six for a quarter, had been used but Rochester often repaid less than the reporter's cost. He once shouted at Daly: "What in the hell do you do with these things, paper your room with them?"

When McLean took over THE POST in late 1905 Theodore Roosevelt was starting his fifth year in the White House, daughter Alice was the belle of the capital albeit its leading social maverick and prankster, "Uncle Joe" Cannon was the autocrat of the House of Representatives, and Standard Oil Company was fast becoming the bête noire of the trustbusters. The United States was now a world power, or TR acted as though it were, and the national capital was booming.

The Messrs. Shubert in partnership with David Belasco opened the Belasco Theater on Lafayette Square, across Pennsylvania Avenue from the White House, with *The Girl of the Golden West* featuring Blanche Bates. In January 1906 the "Divine Sarah" Bernhardt played the Belasco in *La Sorcière* to "a very large audience, which greeted her with enthusiasm and every mark of sincere cordiality." Comedian Lew Fields was at the National and George M. Cohan was booked the next week at the Columbia. Harry Houdini, to advertise his show at Chase's, went down to the city jail, was manacled, locked in a cell, and escaped in 15 minutes. (Chase's, on Pennsylvania Avenue between 14th and 15th streets, had begun in 1884 as Albaugh's Grand Opera House and later became Poli's Theater, the largest in Washington.)

The city was ON A WAVE OF PROSPERITY UNPRECEDENTED IN HISTORY OF CAPITAL, headlined THE POST; "apartment houses spring up in a night and are filled with tenants in a day." But there was growing concern over what were called "superannuated" government employees, those among the 35,000 who were past 65 or even 70 and who did not retire because there was no pension system. A congressional study proposed lowering pay at age 65 for clerks to $1400 a year, at 68 to $1200, at 70 to $840, with a proviso for compulsory retirement at 70 to begin in 1913. A POST editorial called this "unjust and absurd" and the paper then began a year-long campaign for a government pension system. Such a system, on a contributory basis, did not begin, however, until 1920.

In 1909, 200 women employees of the Bureau of Engraving and Printing organized a union and asked for a pay increase from $1.50 a day to $2 plus 30 days' leave with pay a year. A hundred black women in the same bureau met separately to form their own union. THE POST rushed to the defense:

> Government employes in Washington are not merely penmen, stenographers, or accountants. Many of them with small salaries and inconspicuous names do work which, if widely known, would be distinguished. Nor is the government clerk in Washington a sort of fatted nabob, living on wine and honey, and enjoying a fabulous salary at his ease, as some of the critics like to think of him. He probably does more work for less pay than any man of his intelligence, sobriety, and energy.

Washington's policemen were unhappy, too. In 1906 they asked for a raise on the grounds that their monthly cost of living, $60.25 in 1900, now had risen to $79.21, divided this way: house rent $22.50, groceries and provisions for a family of four $35, fuel $7.50, gas $3, laundry $4.50, uniform $5.71, and pension fund $1. The city budget that year was just over $9 million. As usual, only a few in Congress paid attention to District affairs. In 1906, when the House voted for compulsory education between the ages of 8 and 14, so few members were on hand that Speaker Cannon ordered "arrested" and brought to the bar of the House ten members who had been playing hooky at the ball park.

By the time McLean gained control of THE POST Theodore Roosevelt had shaken the city politically. But this concerned only the top officials in the executive branch and in Congress, diplomats, journalists, and a few others. The city itself was still essentially a southern town with a rather rigorous social code for those who counted. It was a pleasant, though often hot and humid, place for the middle class to live. At the bottom of the civil heap was the 30 percent of the population that was black.

Spring is always Washington's most glorious season, never more so than reflected in this May 14, 1906, POST story:

> Yesterday was a gala day for walks in the country and wild flower hunting. Not only were the woods and fields filled with pedestrians, but the drives out of the city and in the parks were teeming with natty looking rigs, while every auto in the city was in commission. The river, too, was alive with all manner of craft, many of the occupants fishing . . . In the evening the incoming cars were veritable floral displays, even the motormen wearing nosegays.

A month later the summer heat had come to stay, Congress was ready to close down until December and the President equally anxious to escape to his Oyster Bay home on Long Island. Some of those who remained behind took the streetcar that Fourth of July, the day the line opened, across the Potomac and out to the Virginia side of Great Falls, a 30-minute ride into the countryside. One of the trolley stops, now grown into a fashionable suburb, was named McLean, since he was coowner of the line.

Those who compute such facts figured that in 1891 the city center of Washington was at Pennsylvania Avenue and 7th Street; by 1906 it had moved west to New York Avenue between 13th and 15th streets, close to the Treasury building and the White House. The center continued to move relentlessly north and west, especially after 1908 when the "million dollar bridge," later named for President Taft, spanned Rock Creek Valley to open up the far northwest. It also opened up lucrative real estate advertising for McLean's POST as the subdivisions began to multiply toward the District line. Washington was a growing city but the rate of population increase was slowing: 34.9 percent between 1870 and 1879, 29.7 between 1880 and 1889, 21 between 1890 and 1899, and would be 18.8 between 1900 and 1909. By 1910, the District population reached 331,069 with nearly 150,000 more in the adjacent Maryland and Virginia countryside.

THE POST was a civic booster, accenting the positive. Rare was a story such as that of February 21, 1908, which reported Samuel Gompers as saying that Washington's beauty was "hypocritical" because of "the outward show and the inward uncleanliness of slums, courts, and alleys." Far more attention was accorded signs of growth, even in periods of national recession. An editorial a week before the Gompers remarks was headed "No Hard Times Here": "Washington makes no talk of 'recovering' from anything. The gay National Capital has never been sick. Business, pleasure, the social whirl, the glitter and magnificence of state functions have all gone on through the panic days and the days following them without a jot of abatement."

THE POST in McLean's years was attuned to the city's southern atmosphere. A 1906 editorial declared that "the race question is a problem the South will solve if left alone. If the North shall persist in intermeddling, the solution will be long deferred." As to the city of Washington, where citizens both black and white had no vote whatsoever, THE POST the same year remarked that "the total subjugation of our people to rule by other people is un-American and, indeed, uncivilized." That may have been principle but what to do about it was something else again. THE POST suggested that Negro voting in the city could be curbed by use of the 15th Amendment, as in the South. "The Republican Party," said an editorial, "has an opportunity . . . to prescribe tests which will exclude from the ballot box all elements that are dangerous." The "bugaboo of 'negro supremacy' would thereby be abolished in our political vocabulary."

The bulk of news of blacks in THE POST concerned involvement in crime. After a spate of reported black attacks on white women, a southern senator attached a rider to a District appropriation bill introducing a stiff vagrancy law with the alternatives of a $500 bond for good behavior or a year in jail. THE POST approved. A southern attempt to legislate Jim Crow streetcars failed in 1908, but the city's swimming pools, in reality large ponds close to the Washington Monument, were segregated. Negro Sunday School children of the city were not allowed to join the 1909 parade of an international Sunday School convention and Negro delegates were denied convention seats. A month later a court ordered a child, judged to be one-eighth to one-sixteenth black, ousted from one of the city's white public schools and sent to a black school in the segregated system.

Perhaps the clearest indication of racial attitudes and tensions was provided by Washington's reaction to the July 4, 1910, prize fight in Reno, Nevada, where the white hope, James J. Jeffries, lost to Jack Johnson, a Negro. Some 15,000 gathered in front of THE POST building to hear a round-by-round account, shouted through a megaphone as the description came over a special wire. The aftermath was described next day on page 1:

> Following the announcement in Washington of the results of the Reno battle, and lasting until early this morning, incipient riots between white men and negroes, small crowds and mobs, occurred in all parts of the city . . . two hospitals were filled to the crowding point with black and white persons . . . Negroes were chased, captured, and beaten in many instances without apparent provocation. In a few cases negroes were attacked and maltreated because they had dared to hurrah for Johnson.

It should not be forgotten, in viewing racial attitudes in this era, that the 1910 census showed only two cities north of the Potomac, Washington and New York, with more than 90,000 Negro inhabitants. New York, however, had nearly 15 times as large a total population. Until the World War I era 90 percent of the nation's blacks remained in the South.

As a rule, photographs of Negroes were not to be found in THE POST. One exception was that of William L. Houston, "colored lawyer," whose picture did appear — though in smaller size — along with three whites when the four were named to the Board of Education by the judges of the District Supreme Court in mid-1912.

The Roosevelt and Taft administrations, being Republican, at least paid lip service to their historic role as the blacks' champion. But when the Virginia-born Wilson became President and Congress came under Democratic control, things began to change for the worse.

One of the new Democrats, Representative Joseph B. Thompson of Oklahoma, offered a bill to segregate the government departments. THE POST story on this move reported that "in many of these offices white women and negro men have been closely associated, and the prevailing opinion is that this proximity does not promote the welfare of either class of employes." Most critical was the attitude of the first Mrs. Wilson and of politically ambitious Secretary of the Treasury William G. McAdoo who was soon to marry one of the Wilson daughters.

THE POST of September 30, 1913, in a page 2 story, reported that "an interesting occurrence followed a recent visit of Mrs. Wilson, wife of the President, to the bureau of engraving and printing. There she saw white and negro women working side by side. Mrs. Wilson came from Georgia and seemed very surprised. Shortly afterward Assistant Secretary of the Treasury John Skelton Williams issued an order segregating the races in the bureau." By fall, Negro employees at Treasury not only were segregated by rooms but also forbidden to use the lunch tables and toilets they had long shared with whites. The southern Democratic tone of Wilson's first administration thus fastened racial inferiority on Washington's black population more firmly than ever.

All Presidents have what they consider problems, or worse, with the press, but few worked at them the way Theodore Roosevelt did. His flair for the dramatic and his gift for words, coupled with an activist view of a strong presidency, had quickly made TR the center of Washington's journalistic life. TR was the first modern chief executive who saw the importance to himself and his administration of the flow of news, and thus of the need, as he saw it, to control that flow.

TR had favorites, and played favorites, among the newsmen covering the White House. Colleagues who were excluded from the group's meetings with the President called them "fair haired boys." One who did attend was POST reporter George Rothwell Brown, who later wrote of interviewing Roosevelt while TR was being shaved in the anteroom of his office by a Negro barber.

> I can see him now, in my memory, his muscular bulk stretched out in a regulation barber chair, his face covered with lather, while the dusky tonsorial artist scraped away at the presidential chin, the newspaper men standing around in a little circle, firing a veritable broadside of questions at him.
>
> The colonel would sputter his answers through the suds, and now and then, when he might have been in the midst of an important disclosure, the barber most exasperatingly would calmly take him by the presidential nose, and pull the presidential head around and the reply would be smothered in a gurgle.

Those who Roosevelt felt wrote untruths were assigned to his Ananias Club or, on occasion, banned from the White House by presidential ukase. TR so attempted to control the news flow that there was something of an uprising in early 1906. A POST editorial on January 7 declared:

> At the White House new rules multiply. The executive department there is always in secret session . . . The most ordinary transactions, which were always in times past treated as news, are now important state secrets. Cabinet officers are not permitted to speak of common affairs. There is a substantial censorship of the press.

If THE POST balked at the news gag, which eventually was loosened but never totally removed, it was on TR's side in his stricture against the "muckrakers." Roosevelt appreciated those writers who plowed new ground about social and economic problems but had a distaste for those he felt went too far, the "lunatic fringe" he later called them. He had just read one such article before going to the Gridiron Club dinner on March 17, 1906. There, lifting a phrase from *Pilgrim's Progress,* he attacked those who rake "the filth of the floor." The speech, under club rules, went unreported but word of it soon was all about. A month later TR decided to seize the opportunity afforded by laying the cornerstone for what is now the Cannon House Office Building. There, THE POST reported, he "delivered his much heralded speech, 'the man with the muck rake.' " The paper boxed the most pertinent phrases, including: "The man who never does anything else, who never thinks or speaks or writes, save of his feats with the muckrake, speedily becomes not a help to society, but one of the most potent forces of evil."

THE POST did not neglect, as did many others, what else TR said that day. Most notable was his proposal for income and inheritance taxes designed to tap "fortunes swollen beyond all healthy limits." But the paper totally disagreed on this "astonishing suggestion" that would affect not only "swollen" fortunes but more modest fortunes of men such as John R. McLean.

TR was an avid newspaper and magazine reader. Having been governor of the Empire State, he paid special attention to the New York City papers. What attention he paid to THE WASHINGTON POST is not of record. If he read THE POST of November 27, 1905, five weeks after McLean took over, he found an editorial praising "the recognized rugged honesty of Theodore Roosevelt, whose unsullied record as man and as President insures the people a square deal." On February 1, 1906, another editorial said of TR that "the masses applaud him. They love him for his impulsive nature. They trust him for his honesty. They believe in him for his 'Americanism,' as any political thing that is signally audacious is come to be called." On March 18 an editorial critical of anti–third term talk declared that "the question which appeals to us is, 'Why shouldn't the American people elect him if they want to, not only in 1908, but in 1912, 1916, and so long as he endures the strain and they want him?" Whether such extravagant language altered TR's low opinion of THE POST of Frank Hatton's years is questionable, however.

When Congress assembled in December 1905, Roosevelt made a deal with Speaker Cannon by which he agreed not to press for tariff reforms in exchange for support of his proposal for federal regulation of railroad rates. The rate bill led to an odd alliance between the President and Democratic Senator "Pitchfork Ben" Tillman. THE POST remarked that "the pitchfork and the big stick are buried together, and two strange bedfellows again illustrates the mysterious ways of Providence and politics." To push the measure through, Roosevelt began to release portions of a report by his Commissioner of Corporations on the oil industry and Standard Oil's habit of forcing rebates from what the railroads charged to transport petroleum. On February 5, 1906, THE POST headlined: PRESIDENT FLAYS THE OIL TRUST. HOME COMPETITION CRUSHED BY UNLAWFUL METHODS. ALLEGES GROSS FAVORITISM. COMPANY SAID TO HAVE BENEFITED ENORMOUSLY BY SECRET RATES. When a compromise amendment providing for limited court review of the new rates was worked out, THE POST credited TR with "wisdom and patriotism in the concessions he has made."

Almost concurrently came Roosevelt's efforts to have enacted a pure food law and a meat inspection measure. Both passed, in time, the latter because of a startling book, *The Jungle* by Upton Sinclair, published in February 1906. THE POST reported that the President was "shocked" by what the paper characterized as "the hideous revelations" in the book, but offered no summary of its contents. The packers hastily sought to clean up their plants. On June 8 eight firms, led by Armour and Swift, published a full-page advertisement in THE POST asking the public to "make a personal inspection of our plants . . . in view of the highly colored, sensational, and untruthful reports." This was the first of thousands of such "public service" advertisements in the paper, designed in one way or another to influence public opinion, the administration, and Congress, in succeeding decades.

THE POST based its editorial stance on the states' rights argument: ". . . the responsibility for most of the wrongs with which corporations are charged" lay with the states. If they had dominated, instead of being "dominated by" the corporations, "the public would not have been preyed upon by railroad corporations, by the coal combine, the Standard Oil trust, the meat packers, or any other combination of restraint of trade." When TR made public a report confirming Sinclair's disclosures, a POST editorial said it was "sufficiently full of filth and horror to arouse the envy of the most enterprising muckraker . . . It deals with many matters with which the government of the United States has nothing whatever to do, and it is difficult to understand why the attention of Congress has been called to abuses for which the authorities of Chicago and the state of Illinois are responsible."

By fall THE POST was reporting that the government soon would take on Standard Oil itself, the fiefdom of John D. Rockefeller, Sr., the nation's richest man. When the suit to break up the company was filed on November 15, 1906, THE POST commented: "The public will welcome a contest that will be decisive, whatever the result may be. It is tired of prosecution of the Standard Oil and other trusts by the magazines, with nothing but confusion as the outcome . . . The public has a right to know something of the facts concerning the relations of this great trust to the laws of the land." The final order to dissolve Standard Oil did not come from the Supreme Court until 1911 in the Taft administration.

In October, when a big New York bank suffered a massive run by depositors, Rockefeller, J. P. Morgan, E. H. Harriman, Henry Clay Frick, and other magnates banded together to support the stock market and end the panic, aided by government financial support. An editorial shrewdly commented on TR's tactics and suggested what, in fact, would be the outcome of the Panic of 1907:

> Mr. Roosevelt has, it is true, conducted his trust and railway prosecutions with an almost constant blare of trumpets, and in the few instances when he has stopped to take breath his Attorney General has piped up his shrill little fife. But there has been a certain amount of method in the President's madness, aside from his natural taste for the spectacular, for he has appreciated that unless he made his prosecutions sufficiently interesting to attract public attention and enlist public support he would fail of his purpose.
>
> When the present financial flurry shall have passed . . . and Wall Street shall have recovered from its scare, business conditions generally will have benefited from the violent purgative which is now gripping them, and it is a safe prediction that safer and more conservative methods will prevail and American railway and industrial securities will regain the full value to which they are entitled.

Meanwhile THE POST continued to cast a jaundiced eye at the technique of TR's news management:

> It is pretty safe to guess there will be nothing doing at the White House until something big can be announced. The politicians there understand the art of administering to the public. Like medicine to the sick, forty grains at a gulp will give the patient a thrill that he would never experience if he took one grain a day for forty days. The White House political news is to be given out in thrilling doses, and if there are no thrillers there will be no news.

If TR was effective, as he was, in bringing some measure of federal control to the nation's trusts, he did go off on one surprising tangent where he suffered an ignominious defeat. This was his 1906 campaign for simplified spelling. A POST story from Oyster Bay where TR was summering contained ridicule as well as fact: "At the luncheon hour the clerks and under-secretaries might have been observed hurrying to the local book store to unload their supply of dictionaries before the market went down. When the afternoon papers arrived with the complete list of the reformed 300, the clerks lined up on boxes in front of the grocery stores under the executive building and held a spelling bee." THE POST printed the 300 words, which included bark for barque, ax, check for cheque, carest for caressed, envelop, jail for gaol, mist for missed, past for passed, rapt for rapped, surprize, subpena, theater, valor, vapor, tho, thoro, thru, thruout, and whisky.

The London press called TR a linguistic "anarchist" and one paper there wrote of "Yanky Panky." A POST feature story was headed: SUM FU WURDZ, FONETIC, AZ TO TH NU SPELIN and came up with "President Rusefelt." In the end the House rebuked Roosevelt and TR capitulated. He always contended that the one simplified word that had defeated him was "thru."

McLean's POST eventually, albeit reluctantly, fell in step behind Roosevelt on the trusts issue but it offered little sympathy to organized labor. After a unanimous 1908 Supreme Court ruled in the Danbury hatters case, holding the union to be in restraint of trade and thus in violation of the Sherman Act because it had conducted a boycott of the company's products moving in interstate commerce, THE POST editorialized:

> The privilege conferred on labor is just as vicious as a privilege enjoyed by capital. Let the two stand before the law upon a plane of exact equality . . . It is the abuse of the right

> to organize by labor and the misuse of the right to combine by capital whence comes all mischief. When labor drives from employment nonunion men, it is just as vicious, just as criminal, as capital when it drives out of the market an independent competitor.

The John R. McLean era was dominated by two events: the Roosevelt-Taft split in the Republican party that led to Wilson's election and domestic reforms; and the outbreak of World War I with the resulting struggle to bring America into the war and thus into a new international role. The paper, though it often was leery of TR's own brand of reform and obviously preferred the quieter Taft pace, took no sides in the intraparty row. But it had very definite opinions about the possibility of involvement in Europe's war and in the civil war in Mexico, both major concerns of the first Wilson administration.

In 1908 Roosevelt skillfully managed a transfer of power to his Secretary of War, William Howard Taft. An amiable man who disliked fights and longed for a seat on the Supreme Court, Taft was clearly the Republicans' second choice. At the June convention in Chicago the delegates could scarcely be restrained when TR's friend Senator Lodge referred to the President as the "most abused and most popular" man in the country. ROOSEVELT TORRENT RAGES 49 MINUTES headlined THE POST. The paper sent no correspondent to the convention but it did send a man over to the War Department where Taft and his wife received news of his nomination. Of Mrs. Taft, whose political ambitions for her husband outweighed his own desire for the Court, he wrote: "Her eyes were aglow with excitement and her voice suppressed with emotion as she grasped his hand and expressed the joy that possessed her over the achievement of her husband in this great political struggle."

THE POST sent no one to Denver to cover Bryan's third presidential nomination. It did, however, hold open the paper close to daylight to make the story since the nomination came at 3:14 A.M. Denver time. While the paper gave reasonable coverage to Bryan its sympathies obviously were for Taft. When a reader asked why THE POST "had it in for Mr. Bryan," an editorial replied with criticism of his proposals for government ownership of the railroads, his approval of the referendum and recall movement, his advocacy of insuring bank deposits, and his backing of a national child labor law "that wipes out state lines."

Taft's victory, said THE POST, meant the public had approved TR's policies and had selected Taft "to carry them forward." McLean and his wife were among those invited to a postelection White House luncheon given "to bring together the leading factors in the recent Republican success." White House aide Archibald Butt wrote of McLean that, "while a Democrat, he did much for the success of Taft."

Roosevelt rounded out his term in strenuosity. In January 1909, accompanied by Butt and two others, TR rode 98 miles to Warrenton, Virginia, and back to demonstrate that an order requiring officers to ride 90 miles in three days was not excessive. They left the White House at 2:40 A.M. and returned at 8:30 P.M.; TR's "hair, mustache, clothing, and boots [were] netted with snow, ice, sleet, and mud," THE POST reported.

The day before his inauguration Taft played golf at the Chevy Chase Club, then dropped in for a call at the home of Thomas F. Walsh, Evalyn McLean's father. Taft spent the night at the White House, waking up to a snowstorm. THE POST's weather ear had predicted "fair and somewhat cooler today." Snow and slush forced the ceremony indoors in the Senate chamber though the temperate low was only 35 degrees. THE POST and other Washington papers were able to publish despite the Taft snowstorm, but the wires to the rest of the nation were knocked out until 11 that evening. Trains and cars bringing inaugural guests from Baltimore failed to get through.

The four Taft years were turbulent. Although Taft was not so standpat as his enemies painted him, it was during his White House years that the Republican party split into liberal and conservative factions, both in and out of Congress. Taft called a special session of Congress to enact the first tariff revision in 20 years. He had a premonition of the political retribution the upward revisions in the ultimate bill would bring in the next congressional election; the Democrats would capture the House in 1910. On the other hand, Taft did please Republican insurgents by proposing a constitutional amendment to permit an income tax. A POST story from New York reported that the National Association of Manufacturers endorsed an income tax for all citizens. As an illustration of what it had in mind, however, the NAM suggested a rate of one-eighth of 1 percent on all incomes, saying that "this would require 75 cents from the man who receives $600 a year and $1250 from the man who receives a million a year. Every man would, therefore, enjoy a patriotic sense of citizenship and become and be a part of the government and one of its defenders." The income tax amendment passed Congress in 1909 and came into force in 1913. THE POST, which had cheered rejection by some states, called the tax "radical"; the Democrats' proposal of a 2 percent rate on income in excess of $4000 was termed "huge."

By June 1910 ex-President Roosevelt had returned from his African and European travels to a triumphant welcome. His return marked the beginning of a long TR-Taft skirmish that became a feud. Two months later THE POST published its first account of the impending break — an AP story. Yet an editorial the same day derided the idea of "a death struggle" for the 1912 nomination. When TR proffered his "new nationalism" platform, very much on the insurgents' side, an editorial saw not a new Roosevelt but the same TR, "radical as a propagandist, conservative as to working out of principle."

The November election, among the Democratic gains, had made Wilson governor of New Jersey and THE POST viewed him as "a conspicuous figure in the calculations for 1912." Champ Clark became Speaker of the House; in the Senate a dozen Republican insurgents forced the 39 regulars to give them proportional representation on committees. During 1911 both houses approved the constitutional amendment to provide for direct election of senators.

Taft-Roosevelt relations were massively strained when the President ordered an antitrust suit against United States Steel for absorbing Tennessee Coal and Iron, a merger that TR as President had approved. Taft didn't help matters by calling the insurgents "political emotionalists or neurotics." On February 22, 1912, a dispatch from Cleveland reported that TR had declared that "my hat is in the ring." It omitted what Roosevelt had added: "The fight is on and I am stripped to the buff." THE POST recognized that the two men, "in destroying each other, are destroying the chances of the party."

On the Senate floor, THE POST reported, Mississippi Senator John Sharp Williams parodied the Apostle's Creed:

> I believe in Theodore Roosevelt, maker of noise and strife, and in ambition, his only creed. He was born to the love of power and suffered under William H. Taft, was crucified, dead, and buried . . . I believe in . . . the big stick, the Ananias club, the forgiveness of political activities, the resurrection of political ambitions, and the third term everlasting.

The 1912 GOP convention was more dramatic than any since the Democrats had first nominated Bryan in 1896. POST reporter James W. Faulkner wrote on the evening of June 17: "Passions have been unloosed, anger has been unbridled, and prejudice permitted a free rein. Every artifice to arouse the baser nature in men has been and is being used. As this dispatch is being written, Roosevelt, with uplifted arms and clenched fists, is speaking to a crowded auditorium, jammed with cheering, shrieking people, to whom he is telling over again the story of the attempt to cheat the people and deprive him of what he says is honestly his, a third [sic] nomination for the Presidency."

TR had won most of the primaries but Taft had more delegates from convention states. Taft won the contested seats and the nomination. By the time victory came on a roll call from which the Roosevelt backers abstained, the Democrats were headed for their convention in Baltimore.

Alice Roosevelt Longworth had gone to the GOP gathering to root for her father although her husband, Nicholas, was loyal to Taft. Both went to Baltimore and stayed with the John R. McLeans, who had taken a house. This time Bryan played his last important role in a Democratic convention. On June 27 Faulkner reported his first move.

> Like a lightning bolt from a cloudless sky, like the outpouring from a latent volcano, like the rising of a tidal wave upon a peaceful beach, was the bomb which William Jennings Bryan tonight exploded in the Democratic national convention, when, at the opening of the evening session, unheralded, he presented a resolution to purge the assemblage of its Ryans and its Belmonts, the representatives of "predatory wealth and self-seeking interests."

Thomas F. Ryan of Virginia and August Belmont of New York were convention delegates.

Two days later THE POST's double eight-column banner proclaimed: TWENTY-SIXTH BALLOT SHOWS WILSON STORMING THE RAMPARTS OF SPEAKER CHAMP CLARK. The delegates, wrote Faulkner, "sweltered in the awful heat while the monotonous march of the unvarying roll calls went on." Bryan then switched from Clark, who had a majority on nine ballots but not the necessary two-thirds, to Wilson, who went on to win the nomination on the forty-sixth ballot.

THE POST at first predicted that "it will be a clean cut fight" between Taft and Wilson, declaring that "the political situation . . . absolutely forbids the growth of a third party." But, when it became clear that TR would run on the Progressive ticket, the paper said: "It is evident that the approaching campaign will not be an Alphonse and Gaston affair. Women and children should be removed from the scene before the carnage begins." Roosevelt, with Governor Hiram Johnson of California as his running mate, was nominated by the Progressives in August but McLean sent no reporter to cover the third-party convention.

THE POST printed a New York *Herald* poll the Sunday before the election giving Wilson the election with only 41 percent of the popular vote; he received 41.9 percent but won nearly 82 percent of the electoral vote. Election night THE POST mounted a searchlight on the roof of the E Street building so those in suburban Maryland and Virginia could see the results: a white beam for Wilson, blue for Roosevelt, or red/yellow for Taft.

The inauguration of 1913 and the coming of the new Congress represented a major political change which THE POST pointed up well in its inaugural edition. The lead story on Wilson's swearing in, without a by-line, included this:

> There they stood — Taft, standard bearer of a vanquished party after sixteen years of power; Bryan, persistent plodder of progressive Democracy, thrice defeated, accepting a commission [as Secretary of State] from a new chieftain, and Wilson, the man of the hour, victorious, mustering, as he expressed it, "not the forces of party, but the forces of humanity."

Inauguration day temperatures ranged from 44 to a pleasant 58. Wilson and Vice President Thomas R. Marshall watched a parade of nearly five hours that included 1000 Princeton students who gave "the Princeton Locomotive" as they passed and 500 West Point cadets, including 22-year-old Dwight D. Eisenhower. At night there were fireworks behind the White House. From the Capitol to Washington Circle, west of the White House, Pennsylvania Avenue "from end to end was transformed into a fairyland of light by hundreds of incandescent lamps spanning the street in graceful arches." THE POST recorded but one discordant note: "[Several women in one grandstand group] were smoking cigarettes and drinking cocktails, to the evident disgust of the people in the stands."

On inauguration day Theodore Roosevelt was in New York. A two-paragraph item on page 12 of THE POST under the heading T.R. STUDIES FUTURISTS reported that the colonel "took the time to view the collection of paintings of the futurists on exhibition here. The colonel wandered leisurely about the improvised gallery and seemed to take delight in trying to solve the hidden meanings of the cubist paintings he found there." It was the famous Armory Show with Marcel Duchamp's *Nude Descending a Staircase* as its centerpiece. This was the only mention the paper made of that historic artistic event.

One of the thousands in the capital inauguration day in search of a job with the new administration was 31-year-old Franklin D. Roosevelt. He ran into Josephus Daniels, the new Secretary of the Navy, from whom he obtained a conditional promise. Five days later, THE POST, on page 6 almost at the end of a story, reported that "Franklin D. Roosevelt, State senator from Dutchess County, N.Y., probably will be appointed Assistant Secretary of the Navy, succeeding Beekman Winthrop, who has resigned. This post was filled prior to the Spanish-American war by Theodore Roosevelt." Two days later came this item: " 'Wonder if he'll raise the hob that the other Roosevelt did when he was Assistant Secretary of the Navy?' This is the question asked by naval officers." A feature story headed IS A FIGHTER LIKE T.R. described him as "a young man, with the finely chisled face of a Roman patrician" and handsome enough "to make hearts flutter." The first editorial about FDR, on August 6, 1913, approved of his proffer of a cup to the best navy swimmer, after discovering how many men could not swim at all. The young Roosevelts occasionally turned up in THE POST's social lists; they attended, for example, a Wilson dinner for Speaker Clark in 1914.

Theodore Roosevelt as President had led the strenuous life, charging about on foot or horseback. Taft walked, golfed, and went driving to escape the White House. On occasion he and Colonel Butt drove out to McLean's Friendship and walked the four and a half miles back. Wilson motored, golfed, went to baseball games and especially the theater. His first summer in the White House Wilson set the pace "for white clothes" and "aroused somewhat of a flutter . . . when he arrived at the State Department in white linen" and white shoes as well. Soon everybody who was or pretended to be anyone was in white.

One September evening in 1913, THE POST reported, Wilson went downtown, "brushed shoulders of busy buyers in the shopping section, enjoyed the demonstration of a safety razor in a drug store window, laughed heartily at a parody on 'September Morn,' broke the District of Columbia traffic regulations, and nearly got run over by a streetcar." The President stopped at THE POST building "long enough to glance at the bulletin board and note the results of the baseball games." He had one Secret Service man and his physician along. On June 15, 1913, the President and Mrs. Wilson were on hand at a National Press Club spelling bee between 14 members of Congress and 14 newsmen. POST editor Bennett was the last newsman to drop out, misspelling "gneiss."

John R. McLean's POST was more critical of Wilson than it had been of Roosevelt and Taft. McLean had been a Democratic politician but his business interests required more conservative policies, he evidently thought, than those of Wilson's "New Freedom."

Two letters McLean wrote in early 1913 throw light on his lack of rapport with the new President. On March 28 he wrote to an Ohioan of Wilson: "I have never known him" and "Some of the members of the administration are unfriendly." On April 29 he refused a request for a letter of introduction to either Wilson or Vice President Marshall, saying: "As you may know, I have taken no part in politics for a long time . . . I know very few" in the administration "and very slightly the men who are active in it." A third letter, however, of August 13 referred to Ira Bennett as "a very close friend of Mr. Bryan's." Thus while reporters and the editor had a working relationship with the Wilson administration they got no help from their boss who seemed to be more and more withdrawn from the daily flow of news.

Wilson began his presidency with a sensation, an announcement that he personally would read his message to a joint session of Congress, the first time this had been done in the 112 years since John Adams' day. THE POST reported that "all official Washington was agape" at the idea. Opponents likened it to "a speech from the throne" in Britain.

The first Wilson administration thus began in a burst of energy with the accent on domestic reforms, especially a reduction in the tariff and creation of the Federal Reserve System. THE POST was largely negative on both issues. One editorial said that putting wool and sugar on the free list would "reduce the cost of living only by reducing wages and destroying prosperity." Another, predicting that the monetary reform measure "would create a colossal political machine in Washington," questioned "whether it is desirable that such enormous, untried, and dangerous power should be lodged in a few hands." After 18 months of turmoil over these issues, both of which Wilson won, THE POST declared that "the work necessarily disturbed the business affairs of the country to a very great degree . . . The great majority of the business men of the country ask, Mr. President, for a period of time for business to recuperate in."

Wilson was a careful newspaper reader, and on October 8, 1913, he read a POST story that raised his ire. Under a single-column head, HE IS A REBEL, the story, without a by-line, began: "President Wilson yesterday announced that the pending currency bill should henceforth be considered an administration measure," a correct statement. Further down, however, the account said: " 'The Democrat who will not support me is not a Democrat,' is the way the President put it yesterday [to Congressional leaders]. 'He is a rebel.' "

Wilson immediately wrote THE POST: "I am quoted in your issue of this morning saying that anyone who does not support me is no Democrat but a rebel. Of course, I never said any such thing. It is contrary both to my thought and to my character, and I must ask that you give a very prominent place in your issue of tomorrow to this denial." THE POST boxed Wilson's letter at the top of page 1. The lead editorial was apologetic:

> The aim of *The Post* is fairness and accuracy. Politics and issues may suggest honest disagreement, but *The Post* would feel derelict in its duty to the public if it at any time wilfully exaggerated or misrepresented any public man's views on any question. In the making of a great daily newspaper, however, it is sometimes impossible to investigate as thoroughly as desirable all the information that comes into the office . . . *The Post* employs accurate and painstaking news gatherers and writers, but in obtaining the complete history of a day's events there are times when their informants make statements that are inaccurate.

Of all Wilson's proposals THE POST most vigorously differed on the repeal of toll-free passage through the Panama Canal for American coastal shipping. The paper built up the fight in both its news and editorial columns, and when the measure passed the House, 247 to 162, the story was headlined HOUSE SURRENDERS SOVEREIGNTY OF PANAMA CANAL. A stream of editorials opposed the bill. One said that Secretary Bryan's "defense of the tolls exemption repeal measure is palpably weak, obviously illogical, plainly evasive, manifestly labored, the very opposite of convincing." THE POST was bitter to the end but the Senate also accepted the change.

A major domestic issue that was not resolved until Wilson's final year in the White House was women's suffrage. In 1911 when Sarah Bernhardt was making her seventh and "positively my last engagement" in Washington, she was interviewed by THE POST at her suite in the Arlington Hotel on Vermont Avenue, where the Veterans' Administration building now stands. "Women should not engage in politics," she said. "They possibly might be allowed to vote, but as for holding office — never! We all know that woman at times is irresponsible; her mental being is changed. If she holds an important position, the result can easily be imagined."

Year after year the suffrage leaders appeared on Capitol Hill to lobby for a constitutional amendment. After Wilson's election they planned a big parade for the day before his inauguration. THE POST welcomed the idea and indeed Wilson's arrival in Washington was overshadowed by the parade. Reported THE POST:

> Five thousand women, marching in the woman's suffrage pageant yesterday, practically fought their way foot by foot up Pennsylvania Avenue, through a surging mass of humanity that completely defied the Washington police, swamped the marchers, and broke their procession into little companies. The women, trudging stoutly along under great difficulties, were able to complete their march only when troops of cavalry from Fort Myer were rushed into Washington to take charge of Pennsylvania Avenue . . . As a spectacle the pageant was entrancing. Beautiful women, posing in classic robes, passed in a bewildering array, presenting an irresistible appeal to the artistic, and completely captivating the hundred thousand spectators who struggled for a view along the entire route.

There were jeers as well as cheers. One woman of the "pettycoat brigade . . . struck a man a stinging blow across the face with her riding crop in reply to a scurrilous remark as she was passing." The women gathered later at Continental Hall to complain bitterly about the police. On the House floor Representative Richard P. Hobson of Alabama rebuked Police Chief Richard Sylvester, to which Republican Minority Leader James R. Mann of Illinois retorted, "They ought to have been at home." The disruptions of the parade "filled to overflowing" the Emergency Hospital, to which a hundred women had to be taken.

When Britain's militant suffragette Emmeline Pankhurst sought to come to the United States, it took President Wilson's intervention to permit her to enter. THE POST commented: "If Mrs. Pankhurst wants to discuss the issue of suffrage calmly and decently with American women, by all means let her talk. But if she begins to preach anarchy and destruction of property, she should be picked up by the first policeman who hears her and sent back to England on the first ship."

A 1914 Senate vote on the suffrage amendment won a bare majority, 35 to 34, but not the required two-thirds. The vote came after the Senate defeated, 48 to 19, an amendment that would, in addition, have repealed the 15th Amendment granting Negroes the right to vote. Another failing amendment, by 44 to 21, would have limited suffrage to white women only. A 1915 House vote failed to rally even a majority for the amendment.

If blacks remained second-class citizens and their situation deteriorated during the Wilson administration, and if women had yet to win their battle for the vote, let alone much later efforts to achieve full equality through another constitutional amendment, American Jews often were viewed with suspicion by Protestants and Catholics. Two very different cases reported in THE POST illuminated this.

The first, in 1914, was that of Leo M. Frank, convicted and sentenced to death for the murder of a girl employed in his Atlanta factory. THE POST's first comment on the verdict was that "there should be a new investigation into this strange case." The editorial made no mention of the fact that Frank was a Jew but a caption on his photograph said "Prejudice May Be His Doom." When the Georgia governor commuted Frank's sentence to life imprisonment, troops had to be sent in to guard his home. Frank was taken from jail by a band of armed men who hanged him in the nearby home town of his supposed victim. THE POST, in an editorial titled "The Shame of Georgia," asked: "Who would live in a state where the very peace officers are murderers?" though it offered no evidence of police involvement in the lynching.

The other case was that of Louis D. Brandeis, appointed to the Supreme Court by Wilson on January 28, 1916. THE POST reported the initial Senate surprise but the account did not mention that Brandeis was a Jew. Opposition during the more than four months before the Senate voted confirmation, 47 to 22, centered on his "radical" past. The only POST reference to Brandeis as a Jew — he was the first ever to sit on the Supreme Court — came in a page 1 reprint of a New York *World* dispatch from Washington. Listed as the number one point of opposition was "the fundamental, though tabooed, reason that Mr. Brandeis is a Jew." THE POST remained editorially silent on Brandeis throughout the controversy and even after his confirmation.

"The currents in the social world flow along in the same channel from week to week," observed the writer of THE POST's "social and personal" column as 1906 began. "Dynasties may totter and kingdoms be rent in twain, but as long as the social fabric remains, dinners and dances, teas and receptions will take place." The "younger dancing set" held its cotillions, with chaperones, at Rauscher's at Connecticut Avenue and L Street. Cabinet and congressional wives held "days at home" when callers left their cards but were not invited in. The White House, however, was the sun of society around which all else orbited. The Roosevelts were "fond of entertaining," said THE POST, and "both possess the happy knack of drawing congenial people around them." With the White House the center, "the homes, clubs, and hotels of Washington radiate a glow of gaiety."

Summer was something else again. By June a story recounted that "many houses still open are ready for the drawn blinds and boarded doors which give Washington in summertime the appearance of a city asleep." This was coupled with a page and a half of summer resort advertisements, plus railroad and steamship timetables.

Before the blinds were drawn came the spring charity fetes, most notable at McLean's Friendship. "Society was on parade," said THE POST, of the 1907 fete. There was an animal show, a tintype photographer, the "streets of Paris," a cavalry drill, and a fireman's display, as the participants drank lemonade and bought souvenirs. The fete was given by the George Washington University hospital's board of managers, and a Negro social settlement house was among the sponsoring organizations. The story led the paper.

Society and the social life provided prime copy. In 1908 the romance of the hour was that between Katherine Elkins, the Gibson Girl daughter of wealthy Senator Stephen B. Elkins of West Virginia, and handsome Prince Luigi Amedeo of Savoy-Aosta, Duke of the Abruzzi, who stood in line for the throne of Italy. "I remember that one night," Evalyn recounted in her book, *Father Struck It Rich,* "when I was going to a small dinner party Katherine was giving for the Duke just before he was to return to Italy early in 1908, Mrs. John R. McLean called me on the telephone. 'Evalyn,' she said, 'everyone thinks Katherine is going to announce her engagement at this dinner party. Don't forget we own the *Washington Post* and the Cincinnati *Enquirer.* Such a scoop, my husband tells me, would be worth an extra. I want you to slip out as soon as you learn and telephone me.' "

There was no extra. Just before the party THE POST had run photos of the Duke and Katherine, saying that "Washington may expect within a few days the announcement" of their engagement. But after the "small dinner party" THE POST lamely ran a reprint of a story from the New York *Herald* saying the wedding was off. This account added that the Duke wanted $2 million at 5 percent put up in Italy to guarantee him a $100,000 annual income.

Mrs. John R. McLean died suddenly of pneumonia at the Bar Harbor house on September 9, 1912. The New York *Times* reported that "Washington loses her foremost hostess of resident society"; the New York *Herald* said she "had become a national social figure"; the Washington *Times* remarked that "her charities were widespread." McLean ran his wife's obituary on page 1.

The White House wedding on February 17, 1906, of Alice Roosevelt, 22, the President's only child by his first wife, to Representative Nicholas Longworth, 36, Republican of Cincinnati and later Speaker of the House, was the first at the executive mansion of a President's daughter since that of Nellie Grant. The day the engagement was announced Longworth walked over to the Senate floor where he received congratulations. THE POST reported that the Senate "was all a-chatter like a girl's seminary" and that "blushes deep and rapid chased each other over his face and up the broad expanse of his Patrician brow back to where there is a mere rim of black hair left upon his head."

THE POST devoted all of page 1 to the wedding, later reporting that it had sold out "a very large edition" and more copies were being printed for souvenir keepers. The Longworths drove to Friendship "to stay there a couple of days before we went to Cuba," as Alice wrote in her autobiography. The honeymooners tried to outrace a carload of photographers to Friendship but did not succeed. However, THE POST did not disclose the honeymoon locale.

In 1910 the wife of the Austrian ambassador, then dean of the diplomatic corps, was indiscreet enough to be quoted in New York as saying that "Washington life is dull and stupid and society provincial." THE POST put the story on page 1, reported that the comments had "caused a distinct stir" in the capital, and gently editorialized: "As far as perfection can be reached down here, Washington comes pretty close to the head of the list. All in all, it is a very nice place, indeed." There was another stir when Mrs. John B. Henderson, a senator's widow converted to temperance, produced an antiliquor spectacular with "gallons of rare old vintage prized for age and quality" dumped into the gutter outside Boundary Castle on 16th Street.

McLean, for all the entertaining in which he and his family indulged, worried lest his newspaper exceed good taste. In 1913 he wrote from a vacation retreat to Managing Editor Rochester about splashy illustrated accounts of new women's fashions: "I think they seem attractive, but Mr. Rochester I rely on your good judgement not to let them go too far. *The Post* has always been conservative. Being there you are the best judge of public opinion and must regulate yourself accordingly."

Apparently Rochester had few qualms. The previous week THE POST had run photos of four shapely legs with "snakes" and "bugs" on "female hose," then the latest from Paris. A sketch of a gauze dress which outlined the female form was accompanied by a description of "the shimmering maze" of the latest "diaphanous creations" under the headline HAS THE EVE-LIKE CRAZE IN MODERN FASHIONS GONE TOO FAR? And two months after McLean's letter there appeared an account, with photograph, of an Arizona woman who had scandalized Tucson by wearing a Paris creation described as "an X-ray gown through which the limbs may be displayed."

On July 2, 1913, the White House announced that Jessie Wilson would marry Francis B. Sayre. She would be the thirteenth White House bride, reported THE POST, adding rather haughtily that Sayre, however, was "not known to Washington society." The paper nonetheless gushed over the wedding gifts, the gowns, and other prenuptial rites, and largely devoted page 1 to the wedding. Less than a year later Jessie Wilson's younger sister, Eleanor, 24, married Secretary of the Treasury McAdoo, a widower. THE POST reported that "though over 50, he is said by his friends to be as young as a man of 30."

THE POST's fascination with great wealth was ceaseless. In 1906 editor Bennett journeyed to Andrew Carnegie's Hot Springs, Virginia, retreat to interview the multimillionaire philanthropist. He described Carnegie as "the center of attraction to baggy-eyed pork packers, obese dowagers and young fellows who strut about in riding breeches. There is nothing about this small, unobtrusive, white-haired gentleman to cause the crowd to stare at him open-mouthed, but it stares, and nudges, and whispers, just the same."

In Washington the annual horse show was important page 1 news. When the winters were cold enough there was ice skating and sometimes a carnival. In January 1912 THE POST reported that "Potomac park was a fairyland of twinkling lights, where happy laughter mingled with the strains of sprightly music, the clink of skates on gleaming ice, the tinkle of sleigh bells, and the shrill warnings of automobile sirens." Some 15,000 turned out to skate at the Tidal Basin near the Washington Monument.

THE POST modestly reported, as the third item in the February 3, 1912, society column: "The Russian ambassador and Mrs. Bakhmeteff were guests at a dinner in their honor last night by Mr. and Mrs. Edward Beale McLean. A musicale followed the dinner, with Mme. Gluck and Mr. Ricardo Martine, of New York, as the artists." This Thursday evening affair was the social event of the season and, together with a second dinner on Sunday, the culmination of a long family relationship. Mrs. Bakhmeteff, born Marie Beale, was the sister of Mrs. John R. McLean, who was then in the last year of her life. Bakhmeteff was a professional diplomat for the czar.

After John R.'s only son Ned married Evalyn Walsh in 1908, they honeymooned in Europe, managing to run through in short order the $200,000 they had received as wedding gifts from their fathers. Prior to a planned visit to the Bakhmeteffs in St. Petersburg, Ned conceived the idea of getting the diplomat appointed ambassador to the United States. Most indiscreetly, Ned wrote that he was anxious to help arrange the appointment when he reached St. Petersburg. In alarm, Bakhmeteff wired back to do no such thing. He also must have cabled the elder McLean for Ned was ordered by his father to "stay out of Russia." McLean, however, did some lobbying on his own. According to Archie

Butt, McLean asked President Taft to request that Bakhmeteff be sent to Washington. But Mrs. McLean's brother, Truxtun Beale, told Taft to pay no attention to the suggestion, saying, as Butt put it, that "it would be no time before the McLeans would be at the White House again, asking to have them sent back to Russia." At any rate, Bakhmeteff got the coveted post. The two dinner parties, costing $40,000 according to Evalyn, were to welcome him to Washington. The decorations were orchids and 4000 yellow lilies, costing $2 each, brought from London.

Archie Butt wrote in a letter that

> as wonderful as the dinners were and the singing and the color scheme, nothing created half as much interest as the Hope diamond. It's a hideous thing too. It looks like a piece of light blue coal. It was set in a bandeau and worn just above [Evalyn's] forehead. Around her neck as a pendant she wore the "Carafe Stopper," as most people call it. It also has some history and is a far more beautiful jewel than the Hope diamond, to my way of thinking.

Butt was referring here to the pear-shaped Star of the East, a diamond of almost 95 carats that the McLeans had bought on their honeymoon trip.

The next year Butt wrote of another dinner at another house where "much to the disappointment of everyone there" Evalyn did not wear the Hope diamond. "Even the President," recorded Butt, "expressed the desire to see it." Evalyn's account to Butt inflated the price to $250,000. (Cartier's bill of $180,000 had been bargained down to $154,000.) Butt added:

> It would be interesting to follow its history from now on. If any unhappiness should ensue in the McLean family, it could hardly be charged to the Hope diamond, though of course it would be. Evalyn told me last night she could stand any disaster except being murdered, as some of its former possessors have been, or having the child struck by lightning.

Disaster, indeed, did strike the McLean family. Their first son, Vinson Walsh McLean, who came to be known as the "one hundred million dollar baby," died at age nine after being struck by an auto outside the gates of Friendship.

Evalyn first saw the Hope diamond, named for a London banker who once owned it, in Paris in 1910. The previous year THE POST had run two items on the stone. A feature story said it carried "the most relentless hoodoo known" but an editorial commented that "superstitions of this kind are a survival of the weaknesses of the sun worshipers." Evalyn was a jewel worshiper. She was intrigued by the stories Cartier's told of the 45 1/2-carat Indian stone supposedly stolen from a statue of a Hindu god, owned by Louis XIV and worn by Marie Antoinette among others. The great diamond became the symbol of Evalyn's wealth and social position and she kept it, through many vicissitudes, until her death. Today it is on display at the Smithsonian Institution's National Museum of Natural History.

In Washington the makings of scandal were never absent. One reason, aside from the human condition itself, was the custom of Washington wives of means to pack themselves and their children off to seashore or mountains during the hot and humid summer months. The result was "The Summer Widower," the title of a POST editorial on September 4, 1912.

> For three months he has been as foot-loose as the cat that was turned into the alley to shift for itself when the family departed for the mountains . . . He took in the moving-picture shows, and the "palm" gardens, and was a gay Lothario and a dead game sport.

Beginning in 1915, one such "gay Lothario" was President Wilson's handsome Assistant Secretary of the Navy, Franklin D. Roosevelt. Alice Roosevelt Longworth, in 1974, recounted that FDR, then 33, brought the "slim and attractive" 24-year-old Lucy Mercer, then Eleanor Roosevelt's social secretary, to dine at her house on a couple of summer days. Alice recalled that she teased FDR after having seen him driving Lucy about in a car, saying, "Franklin, that was a lovely girl," to which he smilingly replied, "Isn't she." But this FDR romance was not to surface until long after his 12 years in the White House. It was Lucy Mercer Rutherfurd who was with him as he sat having his portrait painted in Warm Springs, Georgia, the day he died.

Wilson's first wife, Ellen, died after a long illness in the White House on August 6, 1914. The President, the story said, was "completely unnerved by the shock." Fourteen months later Wilson's engagement to the widowed Mrs. Norman Galt, the former Edith Bolling, was announced by the White House. They were married at the Galt home, 1308 20th Street Northwest, on December 18, 1915. He was ten days short of 59, she was 43.

The romance had been rumored for some months in the capital before their October engagement but THE POST avoided any mention.

When the engagement was announced the paper reprinted a photograph it had run the previous spring of Mrs. Galt with Wilson when the President had thrown out the first baseball of the season. Once the news became public THE POST gushed. MRS. GALT'S DIMPLED BEAUTY LENDS CHARM TO STERLING MERITS headlined one story.

Before the wedding, Evalyn Walsh McLean wrote in her book, her husband "brought home from the office of *The Washington Post* a hint that a certain Mrs. Peck was offering to sell to newspapers her correspondence with the President. It covered a period of years, extending into his past at the time he was president of Princeton University. 'Editorial dynamite is what it is,' Ned told me." None of the Peck letters ever appeared in print although rumors of their existence and of her supposed "mysterious friendship with the President," as Evalyn put it, produced "just about the most exciting topic we had ever had." Evalyn said she later read the letters and that they cast Wilson in a more human, and less cold, light than was the public view. Wilson's relationship with Mrs. Peck, by all accounts, was entirely innocent and known to his first wife.

On November 2, 1905, Mrs. Howard Gould arrived in Washington in her chauffeur-driven French automobile. She told a POST reporter that "from the moment we left New York it was all bumps where it was not sandy." Nonetheless interstate auto travel had begun. THE POST campaigned for good roads and sponsored auto "marathons" in Washington — 50,000 watched a 1909 run of 15 miles.

By 1908 the city had some 2400 autos including 200 electrics. Most of them were driven by chauffeurs and owned by the rich, including the McLeans, father and son. By now THE POST was running an occasional "automobile section" and campaigning for better rules of the road. A four-cylinder, 20 horsepower Ford was advertised in December 1909 for $950 and there were agencies for 30 other cars as well. That same year both THE POST and the White House got their first motor vehicles, the former a truck to haul the papers, the latter White and Pierce-Arrow cars for President Taft.

Many of the first cars were right-hand drive. Not until shortly before World War I did the left-hand drive become standard. Although Washington traffic regulations called for driving to the right, a June 3, 1908, POST editorial complained about drivers who persisted in keeping to the left. Auto tags in the District cost $2 and were good indefinitely. By 1909 the gasoline engine was so common that new regulations included a downtown ban on any vehicle that "emits from the exhaust or muffler of said motor vehicle any prolonged, dense, or offensive quantities of smoke, gasses, or disagreeable odors." The pace of change was evident: in 1908 there were 400 horse-drawn vehicles for hire, in 1909 only 160 due to the increase in auto taxis. License plate reciprocity had not yet begun. District residents had to buy both Maryland and Virginia tags in order to venture across the city line. Not until mid-1913 were Washingtonians assured they could enter Virginia for two periods of one week each per year "without fear of molestation."

Speed, however, caused the most problems. Through Glen Echo, a town just outside the District line in Maryland, ran Conduit Road (now MacArthur Boulevard), then one of the few passable scenic routes in the area. Town officials set the limit at six miles per hour in the spring of 1907 and before long Conduit Road was a notorious speed trap. Marshal Charles P. Collins lay in wait for passing motorists, ready to jump on his bicycle, complete with speedometer to clock them. Many prominent Washingtonians were fined as much as $50 with payment on the spot. It took a ruling by the Attorney General that the road was under federal, not state or local, jurisdiction to raise the speed limit to a reasonable 12 miles per hour.

THE POST was an early advocate of the automobile and McLean quickly turned the new mode of transportation into a bonanza. The paper soon was stuffed with auto ads and tie-in features on driving tips, maintenance advice, and speed trap warnings. By 1914 a Ford could be bought for only $500. A 1912 editorial declared that automobilists "have become an important political, as well as commercial, factor in this country."

In the air it was the balloon that first created a sensation in the national capital. On June 15, 1906, THE POST reported that Lincoln Beachey, "the boy aeronaut," sitting perilously in a triangular frame slung under a balloon powered by a gasoline engine, "sailed around the monument twice, visited the White House, and went down Pennsylvania Avenue above *The Post* building, alighting on the south side of the Capitol amid the cheers of several thousand spectators." Clerks, proprietors, and customers poured out of stores, and both houses of Congress virtually halted business to gape. THE POST concluded that "not in many days has Washington had such an upheaval as the air ship caused." Before long there was an army balloon squad, part of the Signal Corps. After the Wright flights of 1908, however, the airplane became the center of attention both in Europe and the United States. In mid-1908 the War Department announced a contest with a $25,000 prize for a plane that it could accept; the chief entry, and eventual winner, was the Wright brothers' aircraft.

In 1908 and 1909 watching summer flights at Fort Myer, Virginia, proved to be a major attraction. The rich and powerful came by automobile, the less affluent by streetcar. On September 17, 1908, the propeller broke in flight and the plane plunged to the ground, injuring Orville Wright and killing Army Lieutenant Thomas E. Selfridge, the first American military death in an airplane. THE POST, however, was no more daunted than was Orville. An editorial said that the government should fund the Wright experiments because "if he succeeds in his efforts, he will have placed a new and powerful weapon of offense and defense in the hands of the government."

Both Wright brothers were in Washington for the 1909 flights. The June 29 POST reported that more than 40 senators and 3000 others were at Fort Myer but the Wrights did not try to fly that day because of a stiff wind. "Every trolley car that reached Fort Myer was crowded to the bumpers and the roofs with visitors." They did fly next day, however, and again during July. On the 12th, German ambassador von Bernstorff commented: "It is very wonderful, but I cannot see how it stays up in the air. A balloon I can understand, but this I cannot understand. It is what you Americans would call quite beyond me." That afternoon Alice Roosevelt Longworth, a constant visitor, went over in her electric, "taking a picnic basket and half a dozen vacuum bottles filled with ice tea and 'Tom Collins.' Indeed I ran a most popular 'lunch wagon.' " THE POST recounted that Alice had been photographed 28 times in one day but it did not mention the Tom Collins.

On July 30 Orville Wright with Lieutenant Benjamin S. Foulois, later a famous American aviator, flew from Fort Myer to Alexandria and back, the flight that sealed the Wright contract with the army. "It was an inspiring spectacle," wrote THE POST reporter, "and the successful termination of the journey evoked from the large crowd which witnessed it a spontaneous outburst of enthusiasm."

THE POST offered a $10,000 prize for a Washington-to-Baltimore-and-return flight. Aeronaut Claude Grahame-White accepted the challenge, wrecked two planes in the process, and failed to win the money. But on October 14, 1910, he landed a plane on West Executive Avenue "at the very gates of the White House," as the reporter put it. The following July 14 another aviator, Harry Atwood, did even better; he landed a biplane on the back lawn of the White House, stopping within ten feet of the roadway behind the executive mansion, as President Taft watched. After receiving a medal, Atwood somehow took off successfully.

At College Park, in the nearby Maryland countryside, the army by 1911 had established a flying school. That year a young flier of 25, Lieutenant Henry H. Arnold, piloted a plane at 3000 feet from College Park to Fort Myer. As he flew over the capital, THE POST reported, "every street corner was packed with sky-gazing people." "Hap" Arnold would lead the U.S. Air Force in World War II against both Germany and Japan. The month after Arnold's flight, Admiral Togo, the visiting Japanese "conqueror of the Russian fleet" in the 1904 war, provided a classic example of a military man's short vision when he told newsmen that "I do not think an aeroplane will ever be built that can in itself be a positive menace or destroy a battleship."

Sports in Washington, as everywhere else in the nation, ranged from the genteel to the brutal. Horse racing, boating, boxing, football, all had their partisans. But in the McLean era baseball became preeminent in the capital because of one man: Walter Johnson, "The Big Train." THE POST sent reporters to cover the team out of town and the world series, even if the Washington Senators had yet to get into one, when it was not doing the same to cover national political conventions or foreign wars. This policy may not have done much to enhance the paper's reputation among the capital's movers and shakers but it did a lot for THE POST with the mass of sports fans.

In the summer of 1907, fresh from the Idaho State League, the rookie "phenom" Johnson, as POST sportswriter J. Ed Grillo dubbed him, came to the Senators. Manager Joe Cantillon, Grillo reported in the August 2, 1907, sports page, announced he would pitch the 19-year-old Johnson in the second game of a double-header, forced to do so, Grillo added, because his pitching staff was "shot to pieces." Johnson pitched eight innings, allowed six hits, and lost. But Grillo knew his pitchers better than POST political writers knew their men. He wrote:

> Walter Johnson, the Idaho phenom who made his debut in fast company yesterday, showed conclusively that he is perhaps the most promising young pitcher who has broken into a major league in recent years . . . He has terrific speed, and the hard-hitting Detroit batsmen which included Cobb and Crawford found him about as troublesome as any pitcher they have gone against on the present trip.

Johnson won only five while losing nine that first season. Next year he was late reporting and the first baseball news of note in 1908 was that the Senators' catcher, Charles (Gabby) Street, to settle a $500 wager between two sports fans, managed to catch a baseball tossed nearly 555 feet from the top of the Washington Monument. Said Street: "Though my mitt is three or four inches thick, the force of the ball benumbed my hand." Then, even as Orville Wright was flying his airplane at Fort Myer, Walter Johnson in New York pitched three shutouts in four days against the Highlanders. Grillo, reacting to those who scorned the feat because the Highlanders were even lower than the Senators in the league, claimed Johnson to be "a pitching marvel."

On April 14, 1910, Taft inaugurated the custom of the chief executive throwing out the first ball at the opening game of the season. Johnson won, 3–0, against Connie Mack's Philadelphia Athletics. THE POST account said Johnson would have had a no-hitter had not some of the 14,000 fans spilled over the field so that a simple fly ball fell for a hit when the outfielder stumbled into the crowd. During his career Johnson opened 14 seasons, winning eight games of which seven were shutouts. He had to win a lot of games that way, so weak was the rest of the team for so many years. The team changed managers and THE POST changed sportswriters but Johnson seemed to go on forever.

In 1911 Clark Griffith appeared on the scene as the Senators' manager; he remained in Washington for 44 years as manager and then owner of the team in its best years. In June 1912 the Griffmen, as they sometimes were called, won 17 straight games, the last one with Taft in the stands the day he was on the point of winning renomination over Roosevelt. During the out-of-town part of the winning streak great crowds gathered in front of THE POST building, even on rainy days, to watch the play-by-play on a simulated diamond. The Senators finished second that year. Johnson was ablaze, winning 16 games in a row for a new record. Again in 1913 the team was second with Johnson recording a string of 56 consecutive shutout innings. But a pennant eluded the team until 1924.

THE POST sponsored Potomac River regattas, horse shows, marathons, auto runs, and other sports as newspaper promotion. Football news, especially of the Ivy League, got a lot of attention. This was particularly true in 1909 after a long series of fatalities among players. That year both Georgetown University and the local high schools temporarily gave up the game because of deaths and injuries.

The end of the Edwardian Era, with the death of King Edward VII on May 6, 1910, began a sea change in foreign affairs for the United States as well as for many other nations. The United States by then had become an important power because of the Spanish-American War and what flowed from it. Roosevelt enhanced that power. Under Taft and then, above all, Wilson, the American role in the world would change forever.

POST stories and editorials reflected problems of the new involvement. In 1906, during the course of a Senate row over sending American representatives to the Algeciras Conference on the Moroccan problem, the State Department invoked national security, refusing to give the Senate relevant documents. A POST reporter was told by Secretary of State Elihu Root that the "only objection" was that "some of the correspondence of the State Department with its confidential agents [in Europe] might gain publicity and thereby cause embarrassment" to the nations involved. The same year an editorial commented with amazing foresight: "This thing of being a 'world power' is annoying; it is expensive; it may be dangerous."

When the anti-Japanese movement in California produced war talk in Tokyo, THE POST took a hard line: "If our fleet in the Pacific angers Japan, then the Pacific is the very place for [war]. This may be jingoism — it is also wisdom." The paper agreed wholeheartedly when Roosevelt in 1907 sent the Great White Fleet around the world. POST reporters saw the ships off and when they returned to Virginia the paper ran off an extra 15,000 copies of a "fleet edition," rushed to the men by chartered tug.

The American dichotomy over intervention or nonintervention was growing. Asia, now that the United States was ensconced in the Philippines as well as in Hawaii, was regarded as an area of direct concern. Europe, the Old World whose conflicts so many had fled to come here, and its quarrels, in the Balkans and in the African colonies, were to be avoided. The third area, Latin America, in the aftermath of the Spanish-American War was widely regarded as of direct concern to the United States. In respect to the Caribbean and Mexico, THE POST took a jingoist position despite the continuing efforts of Roosevelt, Taft, and especially Wilson to limit American interventions.

As it turned out, Mexico was the all-absorbing focus of American interests from the 1910–1911 revolution to the disclosure in 1917 of Germany's effort to so embroil the United States south of the border that it would not enter the European war. The episodes of these years have faded into history's footnotes. But THE POST of the time illuminates how critical the issues seemed and how relations with Mexico were to shape Wilson's views on Europe before, during, and after World War I.

Initially THE POST was skeptical of involvement but by 1911 it was asking, "Why not take Mexico?" In April 1914 when some Americans were killed after Wilson ordered troops ashore at Vera Cruz following a minor incident involving American sailors, the paper called for planting the flag "once more . . . upon the towers of Chapultepec" as in the Mexican War of a century before. But Wilson was less enthusiastic. A page 1 story on April 23 made this evident. "Yesterday the President was sad and disheartened. As he walked slowly to his office through the White House, his head was bowed and his face a study in deep feeling and gravity."

The troops occupying Vera Cruz were withdrawn in the fall. THE POST, however, scorned "compromise," contending that "the Mexican problem is one that can be settled only by the strong arm of the United States." The withdrawal order was termed "a blunder."

THE POST sent no reporter to cover the war though it did use some stories by Richard Harding Davis, advertised as its "special correspondent." A cameraman, Arthur J. Sutton, who later was THE POST's chief photographer for nine years, promptly got himself arrested in Mexico City. He was released, with British diplomatic help, and the paper printed a batch of his nonaction pictures. One of them showed young Captain Douglas MacArthur "inspecting outposts" at Vera Cruz. Wilson had badly bungled the Mexican affair, and he knew it. But suddenly on June 28, 1914, a far more menacing shadow appeared on the horizon.

June 28 was a Sunday. The Washington temperature ranged pleasantly from 66 to 88. The big 74-page, five-cent Sunday POST was chock-full of news, as well as four pages of color comics: the Katzenjammer Kids, Jiggs and Maggie, Happy Hooligan, and Polly. THE POST's Sunday magazine featured "The Prince of Graustark," a serial by George Barr McCutcheon. Saturday had been ladies' day at the city pools and THE POST reported that "the favorite costume among the fair swimmers seems to be a combination of the vest of a boy's swimming suit and the full bloomers of a girl's suit, although many of the more daring frequently appear in one-piece, tight-fitting suits. Stockings are not essential to the bathing costume, according to many of the bathers, and shapely limbs, innocent of any covering, may be seen in great numbers."

On Friday the Wilsons had had a few friends in to see movies on the south lawn of the White House. "Picnic dinners in Rock Creek park, introduced in the spring by Mrs. Peter Gerry, have become a popular wind-up of the day," a society item reported. Walter Johnson lost Saturday's game to the Athletics, 4–2. Maude Adams, the "idol of playgoers," was at Poli's in *Camille.* Four free Sunday band concerts were promised at Glen Echo.

On Monday morning readers picked up their 12-page, three-cent POST to see a two-column head at the left side of page 1:

HEIR TO AUSTRIAN THRONE,
ARCHDUKE FERDINAND, AND
WIFE SLAIN BY ASSASSIN.

The great conflict did not begin immediately. The Balkan wars had been on-and-off news for years and assassination a commonplace. THE POST's Monday editorial took a limited view.

> The extinction of Ferdinand as a factor in the Balkan situation may have far-reaching consequences, when it is borne in mind that the kingdom of Servia is rent with internal strife, and that Greece and Turkey are bent upon a renewal of hostilities. The map of the Balkans, radically altered within the last three years, seems to be subject to further alterations as a result of the weakening of Austria-Hungary's influence.

For three weeks Mexico remained the prime foreign news. Wilson was anxious for Congress to adjourn so he could get away from steamy Washington to his summer retreat at the Cornish, New Hampshire, home of the American novelist Winston Churchill. The White House office wing, built under Roosevelt, had been doubled under Taft with an oval office for the President. It was equipped with "a novel refrigeration system . . . installed in the walls." Thus "by a system of chemical influences, cold fresh air is generated in an apartment between the walls, and by a ventilating fan, wafted through the room." Wilson refused to use this early air conditioning system because the windows had to be closed and he was "a stickler for fresh air." Instead he tried using a tent on the White House lawn for an office but found that too hot. The President escaped to the golf course for walks or motor rides until he could get away. But that was very difficult in the summer of 1914.

On July 25 came the first danger signal to POST readers. Under a one-column headline, EUROPE FACING WAR, a story from Britain began: "The possibility of a general European war transcends all other interests in London." On August 1, the day a German ultimatum to Russia ran out and the Kaiser declared war, the New York exchanges were closed, and would remain closed until December 12. Wheat prices soared. The first alarm was over the thousands of American tourists likely to be stranded in Europe.

A July 27 editorial, probably by Bennett, fully faced up to the consequences:

> War between Austria and Servia would almost certain embroil all the great European powers and develop into the most colossal struggle in history . . .
>
> No one with a shred of comprehension of what war means will welcome the ominous news from Europe. Nothing imag-

> inable could compensate the world for the losses incurred in a general European war . . .
>
> Those who hold the United States to be immune from the consequences of a general war in Europe do not reckon upon the interdependence of nations under modern conditions. Every dollar made by European demands for war supplies would be offset by a hundred dollars of loss in depreciated securities, commercial demoralization, disappearance of gold, and disrupted markets. If Americans were the most cynical and heartless of people, they would still fervently desire peace in Europe, out of pure selfishness.

Triple eight-column banner headlines raced across page 1 of THE POST on the first five days of that fateful August 1914 culminating in:

ENGLAND HURLS DEFIANT DECLARATION OF WAR AT GERMANY;
KAISER RUSHES TROOPS INTO BELGIUM AS HOSTILE COUNTRY;
GERMAN AND FRENCH FLEETS GRAPPLE IN MEDITERRANEAN.

With no foreign correspondents of its own, THE POST relied largely on AP dispatches "for its news from the front." On August 7 it reported complaints from readers asking why it was not printing accounts of German victories. It explained that cable connections to Germany had been cut but it promised that it would "give the public the latest news first of any military operations which may take place, and the success of German forces on land and sea will be transmitted as promptly, accurately, and completely as possible whenever and wherever it is physically possible for this information to reach the outside world."

THE POST's editorial position was clear from the outset: keep out of war — but profit from it. Several factors doubtless contributed: McLean came from Cincinnati, a city of German-American concentrations, and he still owned the *Enquirer* there; moreover, McLean had a business turn of mind that made American prosperity important to him; then too, there were important German-American groups in Washington and in Congress. Basically, the paper was simply continuing its noninvolvement-in-Europe policy.

On August 8, at the end of the first week of war, THE POST took the unique step of running an editorial in German as well as English, in parallel columns. It protested the "German policy of rigidly prohibiting the transmission of news from Germany" and blamed Germany for thus "establishing a censorship which works to the prejudice of Germany itself." Nine days later THE POST announced that it would print daily accounts of the two sides from the New York *Staats-Zeitung* and the

New York *Courrier des États-Unis,* German and French papers. It did so for many months, both sets of articles being essentially propaganda to bolster the rival causes with Americans.

On August 19 THE POST reported President Wilson's public appeal to all Americans to be "impartial in thought as well as in action" and "neutral in fact as well as in name." An editorial expressed approval but presciently added:

> There will be plenty of attempts to embroil the United States. We do not doubt that schemes are afoot, concocted by brilliant, audacious, and desperate men, having for their purpose the advantage of their own countries in drawing the United States into conflict with their enemies.

The New York *World* was regarded in London by those conducting British propaganda as "the mouthpiece of the administration" whereas its chief rival, the New York *Times,* was rated as friendly to the allies. THE POST was the only leading newspaper in the East that Wellington House, the British propaganda center, considered unfriendly. Indeed THE POST was unfriendly in two respects: it fully backed Wilson's nonintervention stance and it fought the continuing British interference in American commerce with neutrals and with the Germans. The fatal flaw in THE POST's position, however, was its expressed desire to see the nation profit from the war, something that the British-French blockade of its enemies meant was possible only by sales, shipments, and credits to the allies.

In August 1914 THE POST stated flatly that "the plain duty of all Americans is to refrain from taking sides in this war; to steer clear of any get-rich-quick schemes for furnishing contraband of war to any country; to keep on his own side of the Atlantic, and attend strictly to his own business." However, a September 5 editorial said that "the best citizen just now is the one who girds up his loins and gets into the thick of the peaceful war that the United States must wage for business and commerce."

The fall of 1914 brought a flood of defeats for the allied cause in Western Europe, recounted to POST readers under almost daily eight-column headlines and in a myriad of dispatches. "The President feels," read a September 21 story obviously based on one of his nonattributable meetings with newsmen, "that the opportune moment for the United States government to exert its influence for peace in Europe has not yet arrived. This was stated yesterday on the highest authority." Editorially, THE POST commended Wilson:

> Americans are justly proud of the majestic figure of the United States, looming up above the world's battle clouds, serene in its own right, with good will in its heart toward every nation. They are grateful to the President for the great and simple dignity with which he has maintained the time-honored rule of Jefferson — "Peace, commerce, and honest friendship with all nations, entangling alliances with none."

But THE POST was soon calling for something more positive: preparedness. "The United States should be prepared for war," said an October 10 editorial. "The United States has no assurance whatever that it will escape war. It may be drawn into war at any time, however ardently it may desire peace."

The long controversy with Britain over seizure of American-owned ships and/or cargoes soon began. Although Wilson conceded that some American shippers had concealed contraband in cargoes manifested as noncontraband, THE POST contended that "Great Britain is wrong . . . She will have to recede from the position she has taken, and refrain from enforcing her new and offensive policy, or lose the friendship of the United States."

On February 4, 1915, Germany announced unrestricted submarine warfare against Britain, to the shock of many Americans. But to THE POST this declaration was "on all fours" with the earlier British creation of a war zone around its islands. "If the forces of either belligerent should wantonly destroy an American vessel it would be an act of war against the United States." Then, on Friday, May 7, a cable from the American embassy in London reached Washington at 3 P.M.: "The *Lusitania* was torpedoed off the Irish Coast and sunk in half an hour."

There had been warning of such a disaster. Five days earlier THE POST had carried on page 2, under the heading WARNED OFF LUSITANIA, a "special" from New York: "A wave of terror swept over the Cunard liner Lusitania just before sailing time today, when 50 anonymous telegrams, addressed to prominent persons who had taken passage on the ship, warned them that the vessel would be torpedoed and sunk before she reached Liverpool." In an adjoining column, under U.S. IGNORES WARNING, another story began: "The State Department had not decided to take any action, so far as could be learned last night, in regard to the German embassy advertisement in numerous newspapers warning American travelers of the risk they run in traversing the war zone in vessels belonging to Germany's enemies."

THE POST of Saturday, May 8, carried a double eight-column banner: STEAMER LUSITANIA TORPEDOED AND SUNK OFF IRISH COAST; OF 2,000

ON BOARD, ONLY 650 ARE KNOWN TO HAVE BEEN SAVED. The toll eventually came to 1198 dead, including 124 Americans, of the 1959 passengers and crew. An AP story reported that Wilson "had just finished lunch and was about to leave the White House for a drive when he heard the news." He made no immediate comment. Privately, however, the President soon was telling his secretary, Joseph P. Tumulty, that the sinking "hung over my head like a terrible nightmare."

Wilson agonized; so did THE POST. On May 9 an editorial said:

> In sinking this merchant vessel without warning the Germans have made a fearful mistake . . . Whatever the United States does must be based upon right and justice. Nothing is gained by mere bluster and angry denunciation. On the face of things, it appears that Germany has been guilty of a crime against the United States. Let us wait until this is proved or disproved.

But the storm was brewing. Ex-President Roosevelt called the sinking "piracy accompanied by murder" which "demanded instant action on our part." Wilson, however, in a Philadelphia speech, declared "there is such a thing as a man being too proud to fight." THE POST boxed those words below a banner proclaiming, PRESIDENT, FIRM FOR PEACE, WILL REBUKE BERLIN; GERMANY EXTENDS OFFICIAL REGRETS; LUSITANIA FOLLOWED ORDERS. THE POST took refuge in preparedness:

> The plain truth is that the United States is in no condition to declare war upon Germany. It could not make its demands effective by force of arms, because it has no navy and no army capable of waging war on the scale that would be required . . . Let a navy be built up that fitly represents the power and majesty of the nation . . . Let an army be raised that can defend this country.

What was not to become public until June 8 was the internal strain within the Wilson administration. Fearful that the American course was drifting toward involvement in the war and unable to convince Wilson to follow his own suggestions for proclaiming and enforcing neutrality, Secretary of State Bryan resigned. THE POST said the resignation was "not a surprise," praised the "firm" note to Berlin that Bryan had thought went too far, and referred to Bryan's "mischief making."

Five days before Bryan quit, a secret British résumé of the American press printed for the use of the Cabinet lumped THE POST in the general category of "pro-German newspapers" that pointed up "any shortcomings discoverable" in Britain's "previous conduct of the war" by their comments on the latest Cabinet reorganization. It was disclosed after the war that the German embassy had reported to Berlin that the only "neutral" newspapers were the New York *Evening Mail*, the Milwaukee *Free Press*, the Chicago *Tribune*, the ten Hearst papers, and THE WASHINGTON POST. If the British felt that THE POST was against its cause, the Germans had reason to complain, too. A May 31, 1915, editorial warned that Germany's "failure to measure the depth of American feeling over the Lusitania case will cause profound disappointment and uneasiness in the United States."

There was, to THE POST, a twin peril: German submarines and British blockade, both impeding American commerce and threatening to involve the nation in war. While these issues created daily serious concerns, the paper's editorial page paragrapher sought somehow to find a few smiles, if not laughs, in the conflict. He was not very successful, judging from these samples: "U-boats are rightly named, as they are usually found at the bottom of the list." "Rcports from the Western front indicate that Great Britain continues to be a strong sympathetic ally of Canada." "Trench statistics indicate that hand grenades are almost as deadly as the old fashioned Fourth of July cap pistol."

In 1915 a series of revelations of German intrigue in the United States further tipped the American public opinion balance toward the allied side. THE POST broke none of these stories; instead it printed, simultaneously, those of the New York *World* and, a day or two late, those of the Providence *Journal* and the New York *Sun*. Incriminating documents, contained in a briefcase thoughtlessly left behind in a New York elevated car by Germany's Heinrich Albert, were snatched up by an American agent following him. Secretary McAdoo gave them to the *World*, which exploited them serially. THE POST printed great gobs of these and other sensational stories, but refrained from all but the most limited criticism of Germany for such overt intrigue. Yet the paper kept hammering away at the British for reading the mail of neutrals, including Americans, and for "illegal attacks upon our freedom of the seas."

THE POST, and it was not alone, failed to realize the strain that German submarine warfare had imposed on Britain, so effective was London's censorship. One telltale sign, however, was the appeal for American financial aid. J. P. Morgan & Co., by the spring of 1915, was discussing commercial loans to both Britain and France. A $500 million loan agreement, half of what the British and French had wanted, for five years at 5 percent, was agreed on in the fall of 1915. THE POST approved such private loans on the grounds that they would add to American prosperity, since the funds would be used to buy American goods, though others saw it as leading to American involvement on the allied side. But in February 1916, when Rudyard Kipling wrote an article hinting that Britain might repudiate its war debts after the conflict, THE POST snapped that in view of Kipling's "indiscreet but obviously sincere utterance, it is incumbent upon Americans to beware of financial entanglements in Europe's troubles."

In November 1915 Wilson called for 400,000 citizen soldiers though he hopefully declared that "the country is not threatened from any quarter. She stands in friendly relations with all the world." The army secretary wanted to boost the regular forces to 141,843 but Bryan, now leading the pacifists, wanted to use the money on such internal improvements as public roads. THE POST already had called for a million men under arms. It also ran a scare story on the defenseless capital, complete with an artist's conception of bombs falling on the city, even one at THE POST's front door.

Although Wilson sought to avoid involvement, he did not go far enough to satisfy some Americans. One of them was Henry Ford. The automobile magnate — whose company on December 10, 1915, would roll out its one-millionth car, an event unrecorded in THE POST — was an idealist, and an innocent, in foreign affairs. He was appalled at reading that 20,000 soldiers had been killed in a single day without altering the military balance. On November 25 Ford announced in New York that he had chartered the Scandinavian liner *Oscar II* to sail for Europe on December 4 to "establish a neutral conference in the interests of peace . . . We are going to see if we can't get the men out of the trenches on Christmas day." THE POST's editorial page paragrapher quickly came up with: "Hank Ford wishes to deny the rumor that the peace ship on which he proposes to sail will be ball bearing." An editorial called the peace ship "Ford's Wild-Goose Chase."

Ford sailed, amidst much hoopla and with the public approval of such pacifists as Bryan and Thomas A. Edison. A Christmas Day editorial, as the expedition was slipping into futility and obscurity, called Ford "Don Quixote II" but ended on a note of charity: "Let the world laugh, but let its laugh be kindly. Henry Ford's heart is big and in the right place."

To the south, the Mexican problem kept recurring and THE POST kept pushing for stronger American action. A long article by "noted editor" Hearst, attacking Wilson's "weak" policy, appeared on page 1. Wilson was quoted as saying that "I haven't even men to guard the Mexican border." Martial law was declared in El Paso after fights between American soldiers and Mexicans; Texans appealed for help and Roosevelt called Wilson's nonaction "criminal apathy."

On March 10, 1916, THE POST blazed with a double eight-column banner: VILLA BAND KILLS 23 IN RAID ON U.S. TERRITORY; BURNS AND LOOTS COLUMBUS, N. MEX.; CAVALRY PURSUES THE BANDITS 15 MILES INTO MEXICO; 100 KILLED AND 200 WOUNDED. For the next 11 months as many as 6000 American troops, commanded by Brigadier General John J. Pershing, chased the elusive Pancho Villa forces in northern Mexico. THE POST applauded but kept its editorial eye on the larger problem, saying that the Pershing campaign demonstrated "the utter inadequacy of the present armed forces of the United States."

By April the German submarine warfare had grown so intense that Wilson told a joint session of Congress that unless this "relentless and indiscriminate warfare" was stopped, the United States would "sever diplomatic relations altogether." But THE POST did not want to see the sword flash. It hoped Wilson's "solemn and final admonition to Germany will have its effect, beyond question . . . Germany has shown that she seeks no war with the United States. Doubtless she will now take precautions that will avoid further cause of offense. This will mean a change of methods, not the abandonment of the use of submarines."

To what amounted to an American ultimatum, the Kaiser responded with a qualified pledge to curb the U-boats. "The German government goes as far as could be expected," said THE POST with evident relief. Now, it added, the United States would "be able to devote its attention to Great Britain's violations of law."

American entry into World War I was only 11 months away. But first the constitutional calendar called for a presidential election that could be a referendum on Wilson's conduct of American foreign policy. Charles Evans Hughes, the former governor of New York who had been appointed to the Supreme Court by Taft in 1910, won the Republican nomination on the third ballot at Chicago. THE POST had always treated Hughes with respect. An editorial on November 17, 1915, when he was being boosted for the nomination, said: "In common with a large proportion of his countrymen, *The Post* thinks Mr. Justice Hughes would make a fine President. If a majority of the people make up their minds he should serve them, we hope they will not hesitate a moment to conscript him."

As the Wilson-Hughes contest began to shape up, there were other worries at THE POST. John R. McLean was a dying man.

In the spring of 1916, Evalyn revealed in her book, "the old man developed jaundice and a case of hiccoughs that could not be ended, seemingly." Evalyn and Ned began to worry about more than McLean's health; they nurtured a suspicion that "a certain woman might take advantage of his feeble state and jump herself into the queen row by way of marriage."

After a wild scene during which McLean snatched up a million dollars' worth of bonds and threw them at a doctor, the physician certified that his behavior "convinced me that legal measures should promptly be taken to prevent him from endangering himself or his property." Unpleasant family encounters ensued, with servants, guards, doctors, lawyers all struggling for or against the dying publisher. There was a final-hours reconciliation with son and daughter-in-law before John Roll McLean died of cancer at Friendship at 2:50 in the afternoon of June 9, 1916, with eight physicians at his bedside. He was 67.

The 16-page WASHINGTON POST for Saturday, June 10, contained the news that Hughes was far in front after the second ballot at Chicago, that Villa in Mexico was attacking American troops, and that at Verdun there had been a new German bombardment.

At the top of the first of three columns of editorials, between two black bars, ran this single sentence: "*The Washington Post* announces with profound sorrow the death of its editor-in-chief, Mr. John R. McLean." There was not another line in the paper about the man who had controlled it for more than a decade.

In Cincinnati, the *Enquirer* announced McLean's death in its lead editorial, followed by a column-long sketch of his career. While it mentioned his ownership of the two newspapers, the editorial closed not on a journalistic but on a personal note:

> Deeply absorbed as he was constantly in the great problems of business and in public affairs, he found time for the bestowal of a gracious hospitality in which he took keenest pleasure . . . An unusually retentive memory enabled him to bring instantly to command the wealth of information he had acquired through the years of his busy life. His ability to quote spontaneously from history or the classics was no less surprising than it was pleasing . . .
>
> It were inappropriate here to recount his kindliness of spirit, his benevolences, his private charities, but the thousands who have personal knowledge of those things will ever cherish the memory of the strong, earnest, human man, who, in extending succor and help, let not his left hand know the deed of the right.

Whatever his personal virtues, John R. McLean turned THE WASHINGTON POST into a second-rate newspaper. His own impulses centered on the acquisition of wealth, not on creative journalism. He allowed the paper to slip into sensationalism, aping his friend Hearst. Especially in his later years he left management of news and opinion to subordinates whose visions were limited and whose talents were largely unequal to the new challenges of the time. But for THE POST the worst was yet to come.

# 4

# Headed for Disaster
# Ned McLean Inherits
# 1916–1933

Edward Beale McLean, Ned to one and all, was the third generation in the worst sense. Pampered and indulged as a child, early addicted to drink, his problems, as his wife wrote, were "the natural consequences of unearned wealth in undisciplined hands." Born January 31, 1886, Ned was "educated by private tutors, supplemented by travel and study abroad," as he put it in *Who's Who in the Nation's Capital.* "A spoiling mother from his babyhood," Evalyn Walsh McLean added, "saw no wrong in anything he did, a doting but a selfish father would not take the time to study, as he studied any problem of business or politics, the problem of his son."

Father John R. once wrote son Ned:

> All well here. Tell Pop the truth, how are you? Are you over your cold or not? Everything is going all right here at *The Post.* All you have to do in this world is to keep well. Pop will take all the responsibility. I am only holding *The Post* for you.

John R. came to think better of "only holding *The Post*" for Ned. Before he died, it was rumored that McLean had created a trusteeship for both THE POST and the Cincinnati *Enquirer.* Yet to Evalyn it was "a stunning discovery" when her father-in-law's will was read. John R. had made the American Security and Trust Company of Washington the sole trustee of his estate; Ned was to receive all the net income for life and Ned's three children were to (and did) receive $100,000 each at ages 25, 30, and 35.

The McLean estate was appraised at about $7,000,000, not the $100,000,000 of rumor. It included the *Enquirer* at $3,000,000; stocks

$2,701,597.82; bonds $886,607.50; household effects $173,555; jewelry $128,759.75 — and books $47. The stocks included John R.'s 320 of the 600 shares of The Washington Post Company, appraised at $556,800, or $1740 a share. If, as Evalyn felt, the *Enquirer* was undervalued, so was THE POST. The share price was the same figure at which McLean had purchased control a decade earlier, yet at his death the paper was booming, with nearly $350,000 in undisposed accumulated earnings and both tangible and intangible assets.

Ned and Evalyn set out to break his father's will. On July 3, 1916, Ned declared that his father had not been "of sound and disposing mind, nor capable of making or executing a valid deed or contract." To settle the suit, the bank, on August 30, 1917, agreed to make Ned cotrustee of his father's estate. The previous December the bank had agreed that Ned should be editor-in-chief of the two newspapers. THE POST masthead for the next 15 years listed him as Editor and Publisher. Under this live-and-let-live arrangement, Ned had effective control of the paper, when he chose to exercise it, while receiving in the years 1916–1930 a total of $8,093,465.81 from father's estate. He had no trouble spending that as well as a good part of Evalyn's income from her father's estate. They lived in the fabulous $835,000 Walsh mansion at 2020 Massachusetts Avenue, now the Indonesian embassy, which had 60 rooms, an elevator, and a staff of 23 to run the place.

Ned McLean was 30 when his father died. He stood six feet two at around 220 pounds. He had a mustache, a sulky look, and a receding chin. He was fond of race horses, dogs, and fast automobiles. He had little use for society, Evalyn's world, preferring to sit in a duck blind warmed by a flask of whisky. "If a child was sick," wrote Evalyn, "Ned could be as tender as a woman; but he could also be, when his mean qualities were brought up by drink, a complete beast."

Ned and Evalyn met at mother McLean's dancing class when each was 11; he was "a gawky creature so extraordinarily tall he seemed more like fourteen." Mother bribed his playmates to let him win at Parcheesi and baseball. Ned and Evalyn were engaged from age 12 at least a dozen times. She was his favorite companion, although on occasion he took Alice Roosevelt for a spin in his motorcar, chauffeur and dog in the back seat. At 21 Ned was drinking so much he carried an arm in a sling to steady his drinking hand. Evalyn broke off with him for many months; but finally he promised to stop if she would marry him, as she did in 1908.

Ned McLean had a measure of his father's shrewdness but not his brains. While John R. ran the newspapers, Ned did make an effort to learn the trade; he attended the 1908 Republican convention in Chicago, acting the role of cub reporter. "But," Evalyn recounted, "he would not have recognized a piece of news — not even if the man who bit the dog likewise bit Ned McLean." Then came marriage and the fantastic honeymoon abroad. Home again, Ned put in time at THE POST but more often he was wintering at Palm Beach or summering at Bar Harbor or at Evalyn's favorite resort, Newport. Between times there was his 2600-acre Belmont Farm at Leesburg, Virginia. He boasted that his racing colors, maroon with yellow polka dots, were "familiar all over the United States and Canada." It was not unusual for his father to say, as he wrote in mid-1913, that "I haven't seen Ned or his wife for a month."

When John R. died, Ned made a show of taking over management of the papers, especially THE POST, which was on his home grounds. The *Enquirer,* run by competent men of his father's choice, served chiefly as a cornucopia into his bank accounts. In her autobiography, written after she and Ned had separated and THE POST had been sold, Evalyn described her initial hopes:

> I think I still believed, in 1916, that given his father's authority, Ned could make the *Enquirer* and *The Washington Post* pedestals for real power of his own. I wanted him to have the admiration and acclaim that go to greatness. I wanted him to rule his father's fortune when the time should come, and above all else I wanted our sons to be fit to play and work with the leaders of the nation. They do not teach so plainly as they should, in any school I ever went to, that these things cannot be bought as swift horses, jewels, furs, and lawyers' services are bought.

The United States was then less than ten months from entry into World War I. Washington and the nation were bitterly divided on America's course. THE POST had been in the forefront of those crying "keep out," damning both sides in the European conflict. The paper was still influential and prosperous, its circulation rising. It had a momentum that would carry it forward through the war years into the era of Warren G. Harding's "normalcy."

Ned did try; often he stayed late at the office — when he was in town. For his first years he was supported by the journalistically capable, if uninspired, trio he inherited: Ira E. Bennett as editorial page boss, English-born William P. Spurgeon who again became managing editor, and Arthur D. Marks as business manager. Marks had a habit of standing in the E Street building lobby at 9 A.M. to check on latecomers. Bennett complained that he spent half his time in the same lobby waiting for the single dawdling elevator. But momentum lasts only so long. It is evident that Ned McLean's direction, to the degree that he gave the paper any at all, was sadly deficient as the competition increased, especially from the afternoon and *Sunday Star.*

Wilson's 1916 reelection campaign was dominated by the Democratic cry that "he kept us out of war." Politics at home and dispatches from the ever-enlarging war fronts dominated the columns of THE POST. What was billed as "local news tersely recorded" was largely confined to the back page: the opening of the new Potomac bridge named after Francis Scott Key whose home had been at the Georgetown end; a Haynes-six touring car lowering the New York–Washington auto record to 7 hours and 26 minutes; free lunch at saloons henceforth to be limited to pretzels, crackers, cheese, and olives — no more soup, fish, hot sandwiches, or salads. Six days after John McLean died, Wilson, attired in dark blue jacket, white trousers, white shoes, and straw hat and holding an American flag, led a Preparedness Day parade down the Avenue. THE POST childishly cropped from the photo the man walking at his side, *Star* Managing Editor Rudolph Kauffmann.

The Germans captured THE POST's headlines on July 10: GIANT GERMAN SUBMARINE ARRIVES IN CHESAPEAKE BAY CARRYING DYES AND MESSAGE FROM KAISER TO PRESIDENT. THE POST editorialized that the adventure "adds another brilliant chapter to the history of German seamanship during the war" and that "it is now incumbent upon Congress to stimulate the planning and construction of submarines that will equal the best." The British soon produced their own surprise: the tank. The word initially was used in quotation marks.

THE POST clung tenaciously to neutrality and sought to give its readers Germany's side of the war through New York *World* dispatches from behind German lines. Most of the allied news came from the Associated Press and the United Press. There were dispatches from the Balkans by William Bayard Hale, a Hearst correspondent later exposed as a paid German agent.

At home, candidate Hughes crossed the country, in time followed by the President, but no POST reporter traveled with either. Editorially, THE POST did not take sides though it called Hughes the champion of protectionism, which it termed the "real issue." The real issue, however, to most voters was who would keep America at peace. Wilson on October 1 said a Hughes victory meant "the certain prospect" that "we shall be drawn in one form or another into the embroilments of European war." Hughes answered that "we do not want war. I am amazed at the audacity of the assertion that a vote for me is a vote for war."

The newspaper polls, then hardly scientific but in this case accurate, saw a drift to Wilson in a close race. THE POST, declaring that both men had "conducted an honorable campaign," felt that "Mr. Wilson is stronger and Mr. Hughes weaker than his party." On election night the paper's main edition double eight-column banner read: HUGHES LEADS, APPARENT WINNER; DEMOCRATS STILL CLAIM ELECTION. Hughes' picture as "President-elect" ran that night; the next night it was Wilson's with the caption: "Makes astonishing gains in returns after his defeat had been conceded by many of his warmest supporters." The election fell on November 7; Hughes did not concede formally until November 23. Only 3773 California ballots had made Wilson the electoral vote winner.

By 1917 Wilson knew war was inevitable and he awaited only some "overt act" before asking for a declaration. It came in dramatic fashion four days before Wilson's second inauguration: the Zimmermann telegram, an incredible piece of German stupidity and British cleverness.

The British had intercepted and decoded a telegram from German Foreign Minister Arthur Zimmermann to the Kaiser's ambassador in Mexico. The telegram said that if the United States entered the war, "we make Mexico a proposal of alliance on the following basis: make war together, make peace together, generous financial support, and an understanding on our part that Mexico is to reconquer the lost territory in Texas, New Mexico, and Arizona." Mexico was to ask Japan, technically a British ally, for "immediate adherence" to the scheme, a step designed to help immobilize the United States. The telegram had been sent on January 16, tied to the proposed beginning of unrestricted submarine warfare. On February 24, the British sent the Zimmermann text to the President. On the twenty-eighth, under a pledge of secrecy as to its origin, Secretary of State Robert Lansing gave the telegram to E. M. Hood of the Associated Press. Next morning's POST screamed in eight columns: GERMAN PLOT TO CONQUER U.S. WITH AID OF JAPAN AND MEXICO REVEALED.

At the moment Wilson had been attempting to win congressional approval to arm American merchantmen; the House's reaction to the Zimmermann telegram was quick passage. But, as THE POST boxed it in boldface on page 1, Wilson declared the government was rendered "helpless and contemptible" by a Senate filibuster of a "little group of wilful men representing no opinion but their own." They were the last ditch isolationists who talked the bill to death as the session came to an end. Up to that day Senate rules had permitted unlimited debate. But on March 8, as a result of the filibuster amid the clamor over Zimmermann, the Senate changed its rules; cloture, the cutting off of debate by a two-thirds vote, would henceforth be permitted. In the end, Wilson ordered the arming of ships on his executive authority alone.

The Capitol dome was illuminated for the first time the night before March 4, inauguration day. The crowd was small, only 40,000, for the swearing in as a 36-mile wind sent temperatures below freezing. THE POST noted that Wilson was guarded more than any President since Lincoln's second inaugural, that soldiers lined the Avenue with loaded rifles, and that seven machine guns were emplaced on the inaugural stands. The White House gates had been closed to the public a month earlier, not to swing open again for four years.

Before the President asked for the inevitable declaration of war came a mad rush of events, at home and abroad. In Washington a streetcar strike erupted and strikebreakers were imported; nationally, a railroad strike was averted by Wilson's intervention. On March 16 came shattering news from the Eastern front: CZAR YIELDS THRONE AS REVOLT BY PEOPLE AND ARMY TRIUMPHS. A myopic editorial next day saw Russia "transformed" from "an autocracy into a government of, by and for the people."

On April 2 Wilson stood before a joint session of Congress to ask for war because the "world must be made safe for democracy." THE POST, so long and so bitterly an opponent of every step toward war, became a total convert. Even before Wilson's war address Bennett, who wrote all the major editorials during the war years, cried out: "The hour has come for the world to hear the eagle scream again." THE POST boasted that its extra anticipating Wilson's war speech beat the rival *Herald* to the street by half an hour and had been read that evening between acts from Keith's stage.

THE POST took out after "slackers," men of military age it found sitting in theaters instead of volunteering. It called for legislation "forcing able-bodied vagrants" to work on farms. An editorial charged that "Americans are skulking behind skirts and taking to the bush, with a cowardice that is worse than sudden panic." Half a dozen POST men in service were proudly listed.

With the western front a stalemate, the Allies awaited American manpower while the Germans hoped to shift troops from the crumbling Russian front to the west. Accounts in THE POST from Russia came from the wire services or from New York *Herald* correspondents, especially Herman Bernstein. The accounts reflected confusion as Aleksandr Kerensky became premier. Lenin in THE POST was "the pro-German agitator," an "agent of the German general staff." Leon Trotsky was "one of the agitator Lenine's lieutenants." When Lenin toppled Kerensky THE POST called it "a Hun victory" produced by "German intrigue backed by German gold . . . a victory whose injury to the cause of democracy throughout the world cannot yet be estimated." THE POST naively declared that "the Russian people are united in the determination to crush German autocracy" and that civil war represented "more pangs of the birth of freedom." From such dreams and the subsequent disillusionment sprang a bitterness, not confined to THE POST, that poisoned American-Russian relations in the postwar decades. While the last czarist ambassador to Washington was Ned McLean's uncle, there is no evidence this fact did more than add, at the most, a modicum to his paper's stridently anti-Bolshevik attitude.

Wartime Washington was a boom town. In the first month more than 3900 out-of-towners were added to the government payroll with thousands more to come. Herbert Hoover, famous for having fed the Belgians while America was neutral, became the "arbiter of the diet of more human beings than any Roman Caesar ever dreamed of feeding," when Wilson made him national food administrator. Prices soared; shortages appeared. Agitation for pay increases mounted; THE POST for several weeks ran daily solicited statements from members of Congress who "favor higher pay for government clerks." By spring Congress voted a flat $120-a-year raise for federal and District clerks earning from $480 a year to $2000; a $240 bonus was added in 1919. The government workday was eight hours six days a week. District schoolteachers, whose basic pay was $600 a year, wanted a $1000 minimum. They listed these annual expenditures: rent $128; heat $26; light $12; food and laundry supplies $180; clothing $112; savings and investment $12; recreation $48; transportation, etc. $10; incidentals $72.

Coal, the almost universal heating and cooking fuel, was so scarce in the winter of 1917–1918 that THE POST offered it free for needy families "who have not the means to buy it." It was delivered largely by volunteers, one bushel at a time, to those certified by settlement houses, the Salvation Army, Boy Scouts, and "colored social settlements." Clearly, THE POST reported, "most of the suffering" during the cold winter "is among the colored people." Mrs. Wilson lent a White House truck and socialites their cars to deliver THE POST's coal from a hidden cache.

In January 1918 the fuel shortage was so severe Wilson ordered 14 "workless days" east of the Mississippi to last through March. The New York *World* called the ruling a "disaster" and the New York *Times* asked that the President "reconsider." THE POST, however, said that "the patriotic course is to comply with the government's regulations as faithfully as possible." Department stores decided to close when told to keep temperatures at 40 degrees; it was too cold for their employees' health. Theaters and pool halls shut down until warmer weather.

The crush in Washington was immense. The city's population peaked at the end of 1918 at about 525,000, up some 130,000 in 12 months. In the first year of war the number of government clerks more than doubled from 30,000 to 75,000 with 30,000 more expected by year's end. The greatest need continued to be for stenographers, typists, bookkeepers, and other clerical workers. In the winter and spring of 1917–1918 everybody faced two wheatless days a week and one meatless day (two for pork). All were presidentially proclaimed as Hoover struggled to send more and more food across the seas to Allies and troops — if the ships could escape the ravaging U-boats.

Housing quickly became a major problem. Senator Charles S. Thomas of Colorado thundered against "the greed and unscrupulousness, the avarice and extortion which seems to be a common practice in this city." THE POST countered that it was all due to the law of supply and demand. Witnesses came before Congress to tell terrible tales of rent gouging. Finally, near the end of 1918, Congress ordered rent controls which lasted into the mid-1920s.

World War I spawned the ubiquitous "tempos" for both offices and housing, the last of which was not demolished until after three more wars and more than half a century. These temporary structures, mostly of wood, were chilly in winter and steamy in summer, but they did provide much needed office space for thousands of war workers. Beginning in 1917 the tempos cluttered the Mall that stretched from Capitol to Washington Monument; others were erected on each side of that greensward. What is now the plaza between Union Station and Capitol was filled with three-story dormitories to house government clerks.

Gasless Sundays arrived on August 27, 1918. A POST paragraph: "You got along without a motor car on Sundays when you courted her. Now try the buggy again." The President set the example: he rode to church "and took the air in the afternoon in an old-time horse-drawn victoria." Most but not all obeyed the voluntary edict. "On Fourteenth street in the evening a large crowd collected when a policeman stopped a driver, who said that he was carrying a sick friend. It developed that the sick friend was suffering from the effects of alcohol. Both the car and the ailing friend went to the police station. The crowd followed the officer up the street, cheering him whenever he stopped a car."

The demand for workers was ceaseless. Women began carrying the mail. Twenty-two retail stores and banks joined in another appeal to the "thousands of capable women in this beautiful city who are not engaged in any work other than their various home duties." Even those with plenty of money had problems. The POST's society column recorded:

> Washingtonians are literally on the hunt. Those who are not hunting houses, apartments, or "quarters" are hunting carpenters and painters, or cooks and maids, and even hunting all of them. It seems as if the cooks had turned elevator men, all the household maids were waiting on customers in shops, and the clerks in the shops had turned into yeomen in the navy, or enlisted in some branch of Uncle Sam's great force helping to win the war.

The government needed money, too, and that meant four wartime Liberty Loan drives plus a final postwar effort. In Washington the four raised over $119 million and the victory drive another $28 million. All totals were over the city's quotas despite the fact that many who subscribed had their figure credited back home. Mary Pickford sold bonds behind the White House; Charlie Chaplin at the Capitol.

On the home front half a million died during the Spanish influenza epidemic between August 1918 and July 1919, five times as many deaths as there were among soldiers and sailors. Washington lost 3500 with hundreds more credited, perhaps erroneously, to pneumonia during the most critical weeks, compared to 525 who died in the wars.

The flu hit the capital area in September and by early October schools and theaters were closed, government working hours were staggered, many people wore gauze masks, and fear stalked the city. THE POST tried to calm: "If you do get it, the chances are that within a few days you will be well and about again." But the daily headlines soon belied such optimism: FLU GROWS BY 1,300; FLU KILLS 24 MORE; 91 MORE DIE OF FLU; D.C.'S HIGH RECORD. The epidemic slowly receded as spring arrived, trailing off in midsummer.

From the beginning of his presidency, Wilson was a daily reader "with care" of THE POST, the New York *World,* and the New York *Times.* After his reelection, Ned McLean sent him a congratulatory note. Wilson replied on November 23: "Your message gives me the keenest gratification. It means a great deal to me to be approved of by those who speak so nearly in the name of the great public itself." But if the President thought such flattery would boost the POST's support for his administration, he was wrong. Indeed, on occasion THE POST's news columns sent Wilson fuming to his typewriter over what he perceived as irresponsibility.

On July 7, 1917, a new POST by-line appeared: Ryley Grannon. That month Grannon wrote critical pieces about Wilson's failure to set up a war council, described Wilson as "intensely angered" by his subordinates' "blunders," and said that half a million troops would soon go to France. A prime Grannon topic was Mexico; he wrote that the Mexican ambassador in Washington, Ignacio Bonillas, showed a "hatred for America." Bonillas complained to Secretary Lansing who turned to Joseph P. Tumulty, Wilson's secretary. Tumulty sent the protest to the President along with a note saying: "I do not believe that there is any such person as Mr. Grannon." He also drafted a letter which Wilson signed and sent by messenger to Ned at THE POST.

> I do not believe that you would permit *The Post* to be used for the embarrassment of the nation, especially now that it is engaged in war, but I am bound in frankness to say that the character of [the Grannon] articles has made me feel that *The Post,* consciously or unconsciously, is conducting a propaganda for the embarrassment of the nation in its relations with the Allies and in the conduct of its own war against the German government. I am loath to believe that these misrepresentations have been made by your direction.
>
> I have no desire to suggest any limitation on criticism of the Government, but in view of our friendly talk at the White House shortly after you assumed control of *The Post,* I do feel free to call your personal attention to this series of misrepresentations by the unknown writer who calls himself "Ryley Grannon."

McLean responded:

> I regret exceedingly that any matter has appeared in *The Post* which is a cause of embarrassment to you or which might injuriously affect the nation.
>
> It is contrary to my standing orders for injurious matter to be printed, and so far as possible I know there is no intention on the part of *The Post* staff to deviate from these instructions.
>
> Now that you have courteously called the subject to my attention I shall redouble my efforts to avoid publication of any objectionable matter.
>
> If mistakes should be made, I trust you will attribute them to the unavoidable differences of judgement in the handling of the news, and not to any desire to publish that which should not be published.

On July 16 Wilson replied:

> Thank you for your generous letter . . . It was characteristic of you. May I not say that it has given me the greatest sense of encouragement and support to feel conscious that I could resort to you with the greatest frankness at any time for such assistance and clarification of the public mind as might seem possible and necessary . . .

Apparently McLean paid little attention to the news columns, but he did try to improve relations with the White House. On January 17, 1918, he sent Tumulty a proof of a POST editorial, asking his opinion. "Remove the Incompetents!" advised the President to "use the axe" on those impeding his war efforts.

At the time THE POST had three recurring page 1 by-lines: George Rothwell Brown, Albert W. Fox, and Ryley Grannon. The Grannon stories were similar in style and subject matter to those of Brown. Several POST staffers of this period said nearly 40 years later that Grannon, as Tumulty guessed, was a fake by-line, used chiefly by Brown. It is probable that the name was invented by either Brown or McLean, or both, and that it was an adaptation of Riley Grannan, a famous and colorful Kentucky racehorse follower and gambler known to one or both of them.

Fox covered politics and Wilson's White House; later he became a Washington lawyer for Mrs. McLean and others. Fox was the cause of another presidential complaint. In THE POST of March 4, 1918, he wrote:

> With President Wilson believed to be ready to address Congress on the international situation in general, and the Russian situation in particular, there are plain intimations that this next utterance will definitely dissipate the false impressions which pacifists and peace-by-compromise advocates have given of the President's last message.

Wilson wrote McLean:

> You have kindly given me leave to make suggestions as to any way in which *The Post* can help in the conduct of the war, and I am, therefore, going to take the liberty of saying to you that I am almost daily distressed by the articles of Albert W. Fox appearing in *The Post* . . . It might become necessary, if Mr. Fox's articles of this sort were continued, for me to make a public statement that they were without authority and that the man was absolutely inventing what he chose to put into

> my mind and to represent as my purpose. I, of course, would be extremely loath to do this because of the injury it might do the paper . . .

Wilson's chilling threat brought a reply the same day from McLean: "I regret that anything should have appeared which is a cause of annoyance to you, and I assure you that I shall take pains to see there is no recurrence of such utterances."

The final Wilson-to-McLean letter came amid one of the President's most serious political blunders. The chief headline in the October 26, 1918, POST read: WILSON URGES VOTERS TO ELECT DEMOCRATS; REPUBLICANS HIT BACK. The President had taken the calculated gamble of breaking the largely bipartisan approach to the war by asking for election of a Democratic Congress in the midterm balloting. A POST paragraph quipped: "President Wilson proposes to make American safe for the Democratic party."

The day of Wilson's public appeal he wrote a "personal" note to McLean: "I sincerely hope that you approve of what I have done in making a frank appeal to the people of the country to support me, and I hope most sincerely that if you do approve, you will take occasion to say so." In its news columns, THE POST reported that "the capital was a veritable hornet's nest of politics." Editorially, the paper waffled: "When the election is over, no matter who wins, the President will have a united support." Ten days after the appeal the voters returned a Republican majority in both House and Senate.

Bennett, the energetic editorial page editor, also engaged in some diplomacy. One of the many Europeans who swarmed Washington in hopes of getting the presidential ear was Professor Thomas G. Masaryk, president of the Czech National Council in Paris. Attracted by Bennett's editorial assaults on Austria-Hungary, Masaryk became a friend. He accepted the editor's advice to "declare your independence as a matter of national right. Your time has come." Masaryk's declaration subsequently won Wilson's approval and helped lead to the creation of Czechoslovakia of which he was president from 1918 to 1935.

THE POST prospered from the war and in the first postwar year, 1919, had its best 12 months of Ned McLean's era: a profit of $183,088.71. Circulation rose, especially for the Sunday paper, which neared 75,000, much more than the Sunday *Times* and only a few thousand less than the Sunday *Star.* Still McLean held down on expenses; except for sports he severely limited out-of-town reporting and he sent no correspondent to cover the war. Reporter Brown did go in mid-1918 but he cabled only a single story from Paris before returning home to write a series. Photos he took abroad appeared in profusion. That fall Brown returned to France and Italy. In France he was shot in the hand observing the front lines and he nearly lost his life in an Alpine mountain slide. Again, he wrote when he got back, beginning with a stirring account of Yanks living in mud swamps at Brest awaiting ships to bring them home. But, shamefully, there was no POST reporter with Wilson at the Paris peace talks.

The old pro-German reputation of THE POST, dispelled during the war, resurfaced in the month after the armistice when Congress began to probe prewar German propaganda. A message of October 17, 1914, from Count von Bernstorff, the Kaiser's last envoy to Washington, to German propaganda agents operating in New York was fished out of the Justice Department's file of captured documents. It included this astonishing statement:

> *The Washington Post* was offered to me to buy for $2,000,000, with the understanding to buy it back again after the war for $1,500,000. A second offer was made to put the paper entirely at our disposal for two months for $100,000. The paper is of importance, as the only large newspaper of the Capital. How do you stand on the question of the money.

The day an Associated Press account of that letter and other testimony appeared, THE POST ran a front-page denial signed by Ned McLean.

> My father purchased *The Washington Post* for me. He managed it in my interest. If any proposition had been on foot to sell the paper or ruin it by handing it over to any special interest, I would have known it.
>
> Von Bernstorff . . . often lied to his government and he was often fooled by sharpers, as previous disclosures have proved. This lie regarding *The Washington Post* is on a par with the rest of the German propaganda.
>
> I am proud of *The Washington Post* and jealous of its reputation. It never has been and never will be controlled by any foreign government or by any special interest or any political party.

No evidence was produced about the alleged offer nor is there any reason to think John R. would ever have contemplated such a sale or lease.

The American role in shaping the peace to follow, if, indeed, there should be an American role, was a most contentious issue. In this THE POST was to play an erratic but important part. Crusading liberal editor Oswald Garrison Villard, a fierce critic of THE POST, wrote that "its news pages and headlines undoubtedly exerted some influence on the breakfast tables it reached, and it did play an important role during the fight against the Treaty of Versailles and our entering the League of Nations . . . it demonstrated, through the tremendous propaganda carried on in its news columns, that a cause ably served by a Washington daily could make an impression upon the political public."

As Wilson developed and slowly disclosed his idea of a league, THE POST went along. During the Wilson-Hughes campaign the paper commented that "a world league may not be always able to prevent war, but it will minimize the danger."

On January 22, 1917, in a speech to the Senate, Wilson declared that the war must end in a "peace without victory." If both sides would agree to that formula, the United States would take part in a "concert of powers that will make it virtually impossible that any such catastrophe should ever overwhelm us again." He added that "it is inconceivable that the United States should play no part in that great enterprise." The sense of shock this speech engendered, despite previous hints of Wilson's thinking, is evident from these words in THE POST's account next morning.

> Washington gasped with amazement when the President announced he would make his address, sat in tense silence while he demanded for this country the right to determine what shall constitute a lasting peace in Europe and last night floundered helplessly in its efforts to appreciate the magnitude of the step.

That day's editorial indicated the tug of Wilson's idealism against America's historic isolationism.

> It constitutes a shining ideal, seemingly unattainable while passions rule the world, but embodying nevertheless the hopes of nations both large and small . . . a large proportion of the American people would have to be won over before the United States would exchange its present place as an exclusive guardian of the New World for a place in a concert of nations exercising guardianship over both the Old World and the New.

One of the senatorial comments printed that day came from the freshman Republican from Ohio, Warren G. Harding: "A beautiful conception, clothed in President Wilson's best expression, but impossible." By this time the Hardings were good friends of the McLeans. Some scholars have attempted to link that relationship to THE POST's subsequent virulent attacks on the League and American participation in it. The record is devoid of any clear relationship, however, although it is evident that McLean and Bennett were listening to anti-League talk not only from Harding but more importantly from Henry Cabot Lodge and other senior Republicans. Considering the isolationist, or Americanist, attitude of John R. McLean so long expressed in Bennett's editorials, an anti-League stance would have come naturally to Ned McLean and to Bennett. THE POST at first was tempted by Wilsonian idealism but the apple was ultimately rejected. This was curiously demonstrated in 1921, after the League's defeat, by a book of Bennett's 1917–1920 editorials on the war and the League, published with Ned's preface. The early editorials, approving then wavering on the League, were not included in Bennett's own selections.

THE POST approved Wilson's Fourteen Points, including the call for "a general association of nations." Likewise it approved his going to Paris after the armistice though it suggested he should take some senators along. One editorial noted that "opposition has suddenly developed in this country to the proposal for a league of nations to guarantee the permanency of the peace . . . It is unexpected, because from the beginning of America's participation in the conflict by common consent it was understood that once the issues of the war were decided steps would be taken jointly by the powers to protect the world against a possible repetition of it." A November 19, 1918, editorial characterized the League as "a magnificent, a glorious dream! May it be realized." This was the high point of enthusiasm.

Ex-President Roosevelt was against the League, ex-President Taft for it — articles by both appeared in THE POST *in extenso.* As Wilson sailed for Paris, with no senators along, THE POST recognized that "for good or ill" he was leaving "without the united support of the American people." Soon the lines hardened. Wilson declared the League was inseparable from a peace treaty; Lodge warned no treaty could include the League. THE POST concluded that efforts to commit the nation "to the principle of a league of nations empowered to enforce peace [had] failed." The United States "must and will retain its complete sovereignty."

Wilson returned to Washington from his second trip to Europe on July 8, 1919, to the cheers of 100,000 who jammed Union Station plaza.

By now, however, what THE POST had said editorially a month before was a widely held attitude: "Americans who were ready to give their all to the cause of liberty are becoming more and more disgusted with the selfishness and greed of the old and new nations in Europe." The paper began to take a poll — blanks to be cut out appeared daily — which quickly showed an anti-League majority. It was hardly scientific; the first day, for example, questions were asked of officials and customers at Woodward & Lothrop, Hecht's, the Union Trust Co., and "patrons of soda water fountains."

To combat the anti-League attitude, Wilson announced his "swing around the circle." THE POST approved this "campaign of education" but sent no reporter with Wilson on the fateful trip. Instead it used "specials" from Robert T. Small of the Philadelphia *Public Ledger*, soon to become a POST staffer. From the West Coast, Small reported that the President had been "greeted in Washington, Oregon and California by greater crowds than ever turned out before to see a chief executive." The day Wilson became so ill in Pueblo, Colorado, that the remainder of the trip had to be canceled, Small wrote that he was "continuing to burn all his bridges behind him. He says the fight for the ratification of the treaty of Versailles had come at last to the straight-cut line. There can be no qualification whatever. We must go into the league of nations as equals or stay out."

Wilson was a desperately ill man but for some days that was concealed. The September 29 lead story began:

> President Wilson returned to Washington yesterday to all outward appearances on the road to recovery from the nervous exhaustion which interrupted his speaking trip for the peace treaty . . . The President walked unsupported and smiling through the railway station to a waiting automobile, and later in the day took a two-hour motor ride through Rock Creek Park.

On October 2, the White House admitted that "the President is a very sick man" requiring "absolute rest." That same day the Senate demonstrated, as THE POST put it, that "the opposition to an unqualified ratification is insurmountable." A roll call, the first on the treaty, showed more than a third of the senators opposed to outright approval.

Wilson now was almost totally cut off from the world. Albert Fox wrote that Secretary Lansing, "so far as international affairs are concerned," was "Acting President of the United States." Talk of resignation was in the air. But the country knew only what Mrs. Wilson, through Dr. Cary T. Grayson, would disclose. The visiting king and queen of the Belgians paid a brief visit; the queen found the President in an old gray sweater "with a rip in the right shoulder." The Prince of Wales also called, finding Wilson "propped up in the mahogany bed" in which the future King Edward VII had slept when he visited Washington in 1860.

That evening, November 13, the Senate voted, 46 to 33, to add the Lodge reservation to Article X, declaring that the United States had no obligation to "preserve the territorial integrity or political independence of any other country" or to use military force without expressed congressional approval. Finally, on November 19 came the crushing votes: the original treaty that Wilson wanted was defeated, 53 to 38, then the treaty with the Lodge amendments was beaten, 51 to 41. Despite the small group of all-out opponents known as "the irreconcilables," more than two-thirds of the Senate did favor membership with limited reservations. But Wilson would not yield. It was all over. After the voting, THE POST advised: "Take the people's verdict, Mr. President! Take the treaty with the reservations, and let the country go forward!"

In December "Ryley Grannon" reappeared to write that the Senate was asking whether the President was "capable of exercising the powers of commander-in-chief of the army and navy." Republican Senator Albert B. Fall of New Mexico introduced a resolution calling for a visit to the President; he and Democratic Senator Gilbert Hitchcock of Nebraska were picked by Lodge to make a call. Much to their surprise the White House agreed. A three-column headline on December 6: PRESIDENT WILSON, MIND ALERT, JOKES WITH HITCHCOCK AND FALL. Editorially, THE POST said the visit showed that Wilson "is able to direct the executive government, notwithstanding his severe illness." But Wilson was called "the greatest irreconcilable of all." An editorial page paragraph best summed up the paper's, and the nation's, attitude: "Billions for defense, but not a bauble for the integrity of foreign territory."

News of Washington blacks in THE POST was close to totally absent in the war years. The end of the war, however, saw a major race riot in Washington in which THE POST played a highly provocative and shamefully irresponsible role.

On July 1, 1919, buried on page 5, a headline said: TWO WOMEN ATTACKED — POLICE HOLD FOUR NEGROES AS SUSPECTS IN OUTRAGE. On the tenth, this time on page 8, it was reported that more than 100 Negroes had been "arrested or examined" by police. Meanwhile, the National Association for the Advancement of Colored People wrote all four newspapers in the capital, warning that "they were sowing the seeds of a race riot by their inflammatory headlines and sensational news articles." On July 11 the story moved to page 1 of THE POST. By now there had been attacks (the word "rape" never appeared) on five women, the murder of a storekeeper, and "numerous minor offences." All had occurred in "the northern suburbs of Washington," the outer white fringe of the city, or in adjacent Montgomery and Prince Georges counties in Maryland.

July 19 was a Saturday, the beginning of a sultry weekend with temperatures in the 80s. White men still in uniform but with little to do roamed the downtown streets. The military police had been withdrawn the previous month. Under a one-column headline — ATTACKS ON WOMEN LEAD TO RACE RIOTS — this was the beginning of the lead story in Sunday morning's paper:

> Aggravation of District citizens and soldiery stationed in Washington at the recent attacks on women by negroes led to race riots last night when more than 400 men of mixed civilian and military dress, armed with revolvers and clubs, marched into the southwest section of the city on an avowed mission of terrorism.

Further down, the story said that the police, warned of an "impending racial clash," had called out 75 soldiers and marines to help. It also was reported that the white groups had formed after it had been rumored that the woman most recently "attacked" was the wife of a soldier.

The lead story in Monday's POST also carried a one-column head, SCORES ARE INJURED IN MORE RACE RIOTS. That there were no deaths in these fights along Pennsylvania Avenue, the story said, was "attributable solely to the fact that few weapons were employed, most of the encounters being with fists." The account, however, did not stop with telling what had occurred. It went on to say that "last evening's development was more significant in its augury than in its enactment. The uniformed men . . . were outspoken in their threats against the negro population of the capital [and] were loud in proclaiming their intentions for the near future."

Then came, in the seventh and eighth paragraphs, the inflammatory statements that would bring strong condemnation of THE POST.

> It was learned that a mobilization of every available serviceman stationed in or near Washington or on leave here has been ordered for tomorrow evening near the Knights of

> Columbus hut, on Pennsylvania avenue between seventh and eighth street.
>
> The hour of assembly is nine o'clock and the purpose is a "clean-up" that will cause the events of the last two evenings to pale into insignificance.

The prophecy was self-fulfilling. Tuesday's paper carried three eight-column banners:

> POLICE OFFICER, TWO NEGROES AND ONE WHITE KILLED; OTHERS ARE FATALLY HURT, AS RACES BATTLE IN THE STREETS OF WASHINGTON, DEFYING CAVALRY, INFANTRY AND MARINES

The subhead read: "Nation's Capital Held at Mercy of the Mob; Stern Action Tonight." The story began:

> Blazing race hatred turned the streets of Washington into battlefields last night. Surging mobs of blacks and whites proved themselves stronger than the law in the nation's capital.

Hospitals were "thronged throughout the long night of turmoil with wounded whites and negroes," the story continued. Negroes were reported barricading themselves in their houses, "crouched behind their guns, firing an occasional shot to ease the panic of hatred and terror which stirred in them." THE POST story went on to say that pastors of Negro churches and "other colored citizens" had met to petition President Wilson to withdraw leave from the military men. These leaders complained that "notwithstanding" police "knowledge of the mob's threat of a second attack . . . they took no precaution that a competent police department would have employed."

Two thousand federal troops and a driving rain ended the rioting after four nights. Nine men had been killed during the fighting and more than 30 died later of injuries; thousands were arrested, most of them soon released. THE POST started a benefit fund for slain policemen with a $500 contribution of its own. The paper ran a single editorial comment, on Wednesday morning:

> The disgraceful and dangerous disorders that have prevailed in Washington the last three days and nights are directly attributable to the inadequacy of the police system as a whole. The first disturbance might have occurred in spite of any precautions, but an efficient police superintendent with an adequate police force would have made further outbreaks impossible. From night to night race feeling has been permit-

> ted to intensify until now the entire city is terrorized after nightfall, not because the white and black peoples are intent upon making trouble, but because hoodlums of both colors have roamed about making life unsafe for any person, however unoffending. It is an intolerable situation.

There was, however, no note of contrition for the inflammatory paragraphs of the Monday story. There were no by-lines on any of the riot stories.

THE POST, unlike many American papers at this time, did not run separate columns of "colored news." It had no Negro reporter until 1925; then Assistant City Editor John J. W. Riseling was told to hire a black. The man chosen was Edward H. Lawson, a public school teacher and Rutgers graduate. For five years he covered civic meetings ("civic" was the code word for black whereas "citizens" meant white associations in the city) and Howard University and wrote feature stories. After he left the staff he became a "special correspondent" handling educational, athletic, and neighborhood assignments for another decade. Racial identification of blacks remained in the McLean era standard Washington newspaper practice.

Two great constitutional issues that long had roiled the nation came to a climax in the early years of Ned McLean's proprietorship — women's suffrage and prohibition. Suffrage was harder to put over but it was a long-run success; prohibition seemed to come almost by default and it was a disastrous failure.

In July 1917 suffrage pickets were arrested and sent to the city's Occoquan workhouse. Nearly all of them, said THE POST, were ladies "of wealth and distinction." Wilson was furious at District Commissioner Louis Brownlow for having made martyrs of them and he tried to limit publicity. He consulted *Star* editor Theodore W. Noyes and Arthur Brisbane of the *Times,* but not McLean. Wilson concluded that "nothing that they do should be featured with headlines or put on the front page but that a bare, colorless chronicle of what they do should be all that was printed. That constitutes part of the news but it need not be made interesting reading." At THE POST, however, arrests were front-page stories, and at length.

THE POST editorialized: "By all means pass the suffrage amendment and get on with the war." Not until June 4, 1919, did the Senate on the fifth try pass the amendment, the House having twice approved it. Ratification by the states was completed in August 1920; by that time 15 states had permitted women to vote, now all could do so.

In Washington, however, neither men nor women could vote. The

1919 race riot ended postwar hopes that Congress might grant the city home rule. But the District of Columbia became the guinea pig for prohibition, under the prodding of Senator Morris Sheppard and a powerful Anti-Saloon League, because the Constitution gave Congress exclusive power to enact legislation for the city.

In January 1916 Congress abolished the city's saloons and prohibited local manufacture of liquor. The wets' last hope, a city referendum, failed in the Senate on a tie vote. The House went along and WASHINGTON DRY NOV. 1 was the March 1 headline. The wets drank to the last moment of midnight, October 31. One of the city's favorite drinking spots, Shoomaker's, the birthplace of the "gin Rickey," was two buildings east of THE POST. The paper described the finale.

> Shoomaker's closed about 10 o'clock. At that time there wasn't anything to drink in the place except water. Some patrons had prolonged the festivities by opening privately-owned packages to aid in singing that they'd "take the Kaiser Billy and the Crown Prince Willie and put 'em where they both belo-o-o-ong" — or words to that general effect.

At the Ebbitt Hotel, where the National Press Building now stands, "as the hands of the clock pointed to 12, four bearers entered the dining room bearing aloft a casket in which reposed the 'remains of John Barleycorn.' Heads were bowed. A minute later the crowd was lustily singing, 'Where do we go from here?' "

Someone discovered, however, that liquor still could be imported into the District where, as elsewhere, citizens legally could drink what supplies they had on their own premises. Congress had forbidden interstate liquor shipments as of that November 1 but the courts held this did not apply to the District since there had been no such reference in the law. This loophole was closed, however, and the city went "bone dry" on February 25, 1919. Hundreds of last-minute shipments arrived, chiefly from Baltimore. National prohibition, under the 18th Amendment, followed in 1920.

Evasion was widespread in Washington as elsewhere. Ned McLean had a well-stocked cellar, indeed several. Alice Longworth wrote that "outside of the official houses Prohibition in Washington was ignored from the start." THE POST called prohibition's enforcement act a "stupid, fanatical" statute, pointing out that while it now was legal to offer a drink to a guest in one's home, the act made it illegal if the guest carried it away. District merchants, the paper noted, reported rising sales of cornmeal, the ingredient of "sour mash," and of raisins for "raisin hootch," said to have "a surprising kick." Other stories recounted rumrunning from Havana and the Bahamas. From the numerous stills in nearby Maryland poured corn whisky, the drink of the poor retailing at $8 a gallon.

In November 1922 John F. Major, McLean's handyman of many pursuits, listed in THE POST the Washington "curb quotations" for "choice liquors": $10 to $12 a quart for rye, bourbon, imported cognac, rum and London bottled gin. Imported extra dry champagne was $150 a case, California champagne $100. More ominously, Major reported that "it is a nightly occurrence on the main roads leading to the city for gun battles to be staged between bootleggers and 'knock-off men' who lie in wait for the bootlegger coming over the roads from Philadelphia and Baltimore."

Many times the paper published pictures by Chief Photographer Hugh Miller of confiscated liquor being poured into the Potomac behind the Lincoln Memorial. There were accounts of "B.Y.O.B." parties — bring your own bottle. When the Shriners arrived in the capital for a 1923 convention, it was reported that 3000 cases of Scotch and other liquors also arrived. But THE POST refused to recognize its own reporting, editorializing in 1923 that prohibition "becomes more effective every day."

World War I produced what might be expected by way of spy stories in a nation with a large German-American population. Within hours of the American declaration of war "60 alleged ringleaders in German plots, conspiracies and machinations" were rounded up across the country. THE POST called for exclusion of enemy aliens from the capital; on November 19, 1917, some 1000 resident German males over 14 living in the city were ordered out by a Wilson proclamation. The next year Congress banned the teaching of German in Washington schools. A bronze statue of Frederick the Great, presented to the United States by the Kaiser in 1904, was banished from the War College grounds, not to return until 1927; THE POST reported it had been "interned with the other enemy aliens." The Katzenjammer Kids became the Shenanigan Kids for the duration of the war. In September 1918 Attorney General–designate A. Mitchell Palmer charged the brewers — he mentioned such Germanic names as Hamm, Pabst, Miller, and Ruppert — had "bought" a Washington newspaper, the *Times.* Arthur Brisbane, who had bought the *Times* for $500,000 from Frank Munsey in June 1917, conceded that he had borrowed purchase money from a brewers' association. Next day the brewers took a full page in THE POST to declare that more than 95 percent of their number were American born.

If German-American disloyalty and German espionage were a wartime worry, what became known as the postwar "red scare" was a major concern of ballooning proportions. No newspaper in the nation yielded to THE POST in its pursuit of what it saw as the communist menace — traced less to Kremlin agents than to Americans who, in the phrase of Lincoln Steffens, thought that in the Soviet Union they had seen "the future and it works."

The red scare came to Washington with a bang on February 2, 1919. Under an URGE RED AMERICA headline, THE POST story next morning began:

> Bolshevism was lauded and advocated in preference to American democracy, before a big audience that packed Poli's theater yesterday afternoon, in an address on "the truth about Russia," by Albert Rhys Williams, a war correspondent who recently returned from Siberia. For three hours Williams and Miss Louise Bryant, who spent several months in Russia, interspersed descriptions of conditions in Russia, with praise of the soviet system and the bolshevik leaders, and frequently disparaged the American form of government.

The article was read on the Senate floor, and a congressional investigation was inevitable. THE POST roared that "within the very shadow of the Washington monument, bolshevism has shown its reptile head and desecrated a beautiful and peaceful Sabbath with venomous aspersions upon American liberty . . . One bolsheviki mass meeting for Washington is enough." And, "All anarchistic speech and action is treasonable."

Before a senatorial committee came Louise Bryant, by then identified as the wife of John Reed, who later wrote *Ten Days that Shook the World.* Miss Bryant, described by a POST reporter as an "extremely beautiful woman, with dark, bobbed hair, luminous eyes and vivid coloring," admitted that her husband, Williams, and another man "were engaged in propaganda from Petrograd to bring about a revolution in Germany." Reed, who had "paced nervously up and down the room during the examination of his wife," told the senators that he was a "revolutionary socialist" and that the bolsheviks were "doing great work."

The pastor of Washington's Church of the Epiphany declared that a proposal to recognize the Soviet regime was "a policy of weakness and dishonor." The pastor of the First Congregational Church characterized bolshevism as "anti-home, anti-marriage, anti-morality, anti-property, anti-civilization and anti-Christ." THE POST editorialized that the "whine about free speech and liberty is buncome . . . Lenine has set a covetous eye upon America and is attempting to direct the tide of bolshevism in this direction." On June 3, THE POST headlined:

"RED" BLOWN TO BITS AS HE DYNAMITES PALMER'S HOUSE;
BOMBS IN SEVEN OTHER CITIES SPREAD NATION-WIDE TERROR

"The engine of death exploded on the doorstep of Mr. Palmer's house, 2132 R Street northwest," THE POST reported, and "wrecked the front of the building and blew into fragments the terrorist bearing it. First hint of his being an anarchist came with the finding of revolutionary literature near the shreds of a suit case containing the bomb." No one else was hurt. Directly opposite the Palmer house lived the Franklin Roosevelts. Mrs. Roosevelt later wrote that "the police haven't yet allowed the gore to be wiped up on our steps and James glories in every new bone found!"

THE POST hammered away at the "red assassins" Palmer was after and declared that "there is treason of the tongue as well as of the head." The capital city, THE POST felt, was surpassed by none in "its Americanism" because of the nature of its population: "Some cities we could mention are more conspicuous for numbers than for quality . . . As for Washington it does not suffer from the indigestibility of foreign masses."

During six months of hysteria, until the spring of 1920, about 4000 aliens were rounded up, some deported, others jailed, in what became known as "the Palmer raids." THE POST had been a willing part of the hysteria and any idea of the United States recognizing bolshevik Russia now became unthinkable.

War and postwar excitement meant prosperity for THE POST. Some Sundays the paper even had to turn away advertising. The total of want ads declined but by now they were paid for, not free as in John R. McLean's time. The June 1, 1919, paper was the first Sunday edition to go over 100 pages. The June 1919 advertising of over one million lines was 126 percent above the prewar June of 1914. Ned McLean listed six national reporters and boasted of "the only six page comic section published by an American newspaper."

A new age was coming in America, to be known as "normalcy." McLean signaled its meaning for THE POST in a letter, after the onset of the Harding era, to a syndicate from which he bought feature stories: ". . . as affairs in Europe approach nearer to normal — assuming, of course, that the old world trend is toward normal and not toward a cataclysm — you should give more attention to stories carrying the personal element, social, sporting, insofar as they involve well-known persons, business, etc."

The day he wrote that letter, communists were in control of parts of Germany, Lenin was on the eve of his New Economic Policy, Harding had approved American bank loans to China, a former president of Cuba was in Washington seeking American aid, and Americans were under the illusion that allied war debts to be repaid through German reparations assured a continued prosperity.

Ned McLean will forever be associated with Warren G. Harding and his "Ohio gang," an association that began so auspiciously but ended so disastrously for both the publisher and THE POST.

Ned and Evalyn met the new senator and his wife Florence, "the Duchess," at one of Alice Longworth's poker parties. Evalyn found Harding "a stunning man. He chewed tobacco, biting from a plug that he would lend, or borrow, and he did not care if the whole world knew that he wore suspenders." The Hardings lived at 2314 Wyoming Avenue and there Evalyn tended "the Duchess" when she was ill, an act of compassion that bound them together. Ned and the senator became golf as well as poker companions.

As the 1920 election approached, THE POST began to boost Harding. His speeches were prominently though not excessively reported. At the Chicago convention, POST reporters John C. O'Laughlin and Robert Small listed him as only one of a quartet of dark horses. When Harding emerged as the nominee, Small wrote that "the Old Guard has reasserted its mastery over the Republican Party." Bennett's editorial called Harding "an American of the finest type" and his running mate, Governor Calvin Coolidge of Massachusetts, "well suited for the dignified and potentially fateful post" of Vice President.

A month later the Democrats, at San Francisco, picked their ticket: Governor James M. Cox of Ohio and 38-year-old Franklin D. Roosevelt of New York. THE POST termed Cox "an attractive, alert, courageous American." FDR, it found, was "genial and companionable" and "well equipped" for the vice presidency.

Both Harding and Cox owned Ohio newspapers and both hoped for endorsement by McLean's *Enquirer* and THE POST. Cox and FDR came to Washington to see President Wilson and back his League of Nations. Cox also went to see the McLeans. Evalyn recounted:

> "We've got to make up our minds," said Ned. "We're for Harding, you and me, but the readers of the *Enquirer* and *The Post* may be less ready for a shift than we should like to have them." . . .

> Just what to do came to me clearly in the night! Harding was going to win hands down, and everybody loves a winner. I put it plainly up to Ned, and he to me; we convinced each other . . . There was no open break with the party, but Ned made it clear that he wanted nothing printed that would interfere even a little with the success of the Harding campaign.

The McLeans spent some time with the Hardings during the senator's front-porch campaign in Marion, Ohio; Ned's private railroad car, the *Enquirer,* was attached to the campaign train. Even so, THE POST, at Harding's own suggestion, never formally endorsed the GOP candidate. Editorial page paragraphs, however, were a tip-off: "As a campaigner Gov. Cox is demonstrating that he can stir up almost as much apathy as Cal Coolidge." "Gov. Cox was nominated on the forty-fourth ballot, and the former delegates are wondering now why they were in such a rush." A new reporter joined THE POST to cover Cox for a time: William D. Hassett, who became White House secretary to FDR and Harry Truman. He stayed with THE POST 11 years.

Only at the very end of the campaign did THE POST go all out for Harding in its news columns. An old tale that Harding had Negro blood had circulated by word of mouth; now it broke into print on election eve. Ned was "in a rage over the slander that had been so quietly and skillfully launched in the closing days of the campaign," Harry M. Daugherty wrote in his 1932 memoirs. In Cincinnati just before election day, Ned showed Daugherty "the proof sheet of a leading article denouncing the Democratic party for this outrage" and "swinging his paper," the *Enquirer,* "squarely into the Republican column." Daugherty told Ned: "You mustn't print that" for "many reasons. Among them, it would have broken your father's heart. Your father was one of the finest men I've ever known. But he was a dyed-in-the-wool Democrat. He built up a great piece of property in the *Enquirer* as a Democratic paper. That editorial would destroy in a day the work of his life." Daugherty prevailed.

But back in Washington THE POST acted differently. Ned's hand in this, however, remains obscure. The man who for years had propagated the Negro blood story was William A. Chancellor, a professor at Wooster College in Ohio who once had been superintendent of schools in the District. It was the Chancellor connection to Washington's schools that gave THE POST a tie for the story by City Editor James V. FitzGerald on page 1 the Monday morning before the election:

> The most dastardly conspiracy in the history of American politics was exposed yesterday. In an effort to steal the election the Democrats have been sending out hundreds of thousands of circulars asserting that Senator Harding has negro blood in his veins. Many of these unsigned circulars have found their way into Washington. There has been an organized movement to give them wide distribution and to carry on further the defamatory, insidious attack by word of mouth.

The McLeans had a hand in one other part of the Harding campaign. The senator's sister, Mrs. Heber Votaw, a Washington policewoman who had been a missionary in Burma, agreed to speak to a group of colored citizens. The McLeans alerted the Hardings and, on Harding instructions, got her to come to Friendship where, Evalyn recounted, "we persuaded her to remain with us for dinner" and "we kept her with us until we learned, through one of *The Post* reporters, that the meeting had been held and the audience dispersed. After that, Mrs. Votaw was put aboard a train and shipped to Marion to stay for the remainder of the campaign."

All these last-minute campaign jitters were unnecessary. Fox's November 3 lead began: "Harding has swept the country. The great and solemn referendum on the league of nations covenant has resulted in the smothering of internationalism by an avalanche of 'American first' votes."

Some 25,000 had gathered in a drizzling rain in front of THE POST to hear the returns; the paper proclaimed Harding and Coolidge the winners at 8:15 P.M. POST boys shouting extras were mobbed. "Tens of thousands of Washingtonians deserted their homes" to congregate "on the streets of the downtown section, seeking election news . . . Practically every theater in the city staged an extra midnight show, and gave election returns between the acts. The hotels were filled with election news seekers."

THE POST exulted. Reporter Brown wrote that Harding "brings high character and strong mental equipment to solve the nation's problems." Editorial page paragraphs said: "America may now proceed to attend to its own tangled business." "The funeral of the dear departed league will take place on March 4." And, succinctly: "Wilson — that's all."

The press and the politicians had known of the McLean friendship with the Hardings but Ned had let little of it show in THE POST. Now the relationship intensified and some aspects began to appear in print.

When Harding returned to the capital, still a senator, he and the Duchess stayed with Ned and Evalyn at the I Street house. Mrs. Wilson sent a note there to the Duchess, asking her to call; Mrs. Harding replied on Evalyn's stationery, asking if she could bring Evalyn; Mrs. Wilson answered that, as THE POST had opposed her husband, Evalyn would not be welcome. Mrs. Harding went alone to look over her new residence.

The day Harding first appeared again on the Senate floor, as THE POST modestly described it, "Mrs. Harding, with Mrs. E. B. McLean, was in the senators' private gallery." That night the Hardings dined at the home of a senator and Ned was one of the eight guests listed by THE POST. Next morning Harding breakfasted with four, including Ned. Then Ned was at luncheon with Harding, and when the Hardings left for a Texas holiday, the McLeans were in the party. Later Evalyn journeyed to New York with Mrs. Harding and shared the applause at the theater.

Harding named Ned the inaugural chairman. When the dazzling celebration planned by Ned produced cries of extravagance, the President-elect wired him that "there is such a widespread desire for economy that I believe most heartily in a practical keeping of faith in the very beginning" and therefore a "wholesome example of economy and thrift" should be set. Undaunted, the McLeans threw their own inaugural ball. Evalyn described it this way:

> . . . we felt like celebrating; our home town was going to be a gayer place because two friends of ours had skyrocketed to power. What I proceeded to arrange was an enormous dinner at the I street house. I invited the new Cabinet members, the Justices of the Supreme Court, the diplomatic corps, the Senators and, as guest of honor, the new Vice-President, Calvin Coolidge. That was our first meeting with the Coolidges, who became our good friends.

When she took Coolidge's arm to go into dinner "I was astonished to discover that he was shaking." He wouldn't eat, complaining of a stomach ache which Evalyn fixed with bicarbonate of soda. The dinner went unreported in THE POST.

Power changed hands in Washington on March 4, 1921. Harding after "his usual breakfast of Ohio ham and eggs and buckwheat cakes" rode with a frail and still incapacitated Wilson to the Capitol where, THE POST headlined: 100,000 WITNESS SOLEMN INDUCTION OF WARREN G. HARDING; PROCLAIMS RETURN TO PRO-AMERICAN FOREIGN POLICIES.

The March 6 Sunday edition set the new scene. "The big iron gates" at 1600 Pennsylvania Avenue "had swung open" and "the atmosphere had changed entirely." Vice President Coolidge walked home from the Senate to the Willard after his first day on the job, a "warm and spring-like" afternoon. Poli's advertised *The Passing Show* with Mae West and Chaplin's *The Kid* was at Crandall's. The Boston Symphony with Pierre Monteux conducting would be next at the National. A Hungarian restaurant on 9th Street offered "regular dinner 60¢, with chicken 90¢." S. Klein advertised a Victrola for $100. The Young Men's Shop had spring suits for $27.75. A new Ford touring car could be rented for a dollar an hour, "all new 1921 cars with self-starters." Shannon & Luchs offered first mortgages at 7 percent and an 11-room, 3-bath, 4-fireplace, 2-car garage house at 10 East Lenox Street in fashionable Chevy Chase was for sale at $30,000.

As the Harding era began, THE POST was in favor at the White House as it had not been since the Cleveland administration and the paper prospered. In 1921–1923 the paper netted $376,612 and increased its surplus by the end of 1923 to $636,612, the highest figure reached in Ned's years. In these same three years Ned received from his father's estate $2,904,650. There thus was plenty of money to build the paper but Ned McLean's sporadic attention to his publisher-editor role, his long absences from Washington, and his increasing habit of drink mitigated what lasting advantage the relationship might have produced.

By the 1920s the comics were an important newspaper ingredient, especially on Sundays. THE POST had obtained its Sunday strips from Hearst's King Features but in 1921 they were withdrawn to go to the rival *Times* run by Hearst himself beginning in 1922. Ned complained, but to no avail, that this was "an absolute contradiction to a most clear understanding and assurance that I had with Mr. Hearst." New comics came first from the New York *Tribune* and then in late 1922 from the Chicago *Tribune* syndicate. The Gumps was the main attraction.

In 1921 came new competition in the form of the Washington *Daily News,* a breezy afternoon tabloid in what became the Scripps-Howard chain. It lasted 51 years. Of the five dailies, the *Star* was dominant for the rest of the decade. Conservative, often stodgy, but full of Associated Press dispatches, the *Star* was the city's big money maker; "gossip puts the annual profit at considerably more than $1,000,000 — some say $2,000,000," wrote Oswald Garrison Villard in 1923.

Of THE POST Villard wrote that Washington correspondents "despise, dislike, and distrust it; to them it is not only a poison sheet — it is also a contemptible one and they question its moral integrity." The two Hearst papers, the morning *Herald* and the afternoon *Times,* in Villard's view, were "typical Hearst newspapers, peas out of the same pod, typographically ugly and messy, with all the usual Hearst standardized features." To Villard, a Wilson liberal, Washington lacked a "thunderer." Indeed, it did.

To garner new subscribers THE POST ran a mélange of contests: free autos; a house worth $15,000 at 5312 Reno Road Northwest; a search for a "pretty bobbed hair girl" and another for "the prettiest feet" (tied to shoe advertising); a runners' marathon (with President Coolidge watching the finish at the zero milestone behind the White House); life insurance ($3.60 for $500 worth if the buyer subscribed daily and Sunday for a year at $8.40); cooking and bridge lessons; a free trip to Hollywood to meet Mary Pickford.

McLean added cartoons to the editorial page but at first they came from the syndicates: Louis Raemaekers during the war; then Carey Orr, Jay N. (Ding) Darling, and John T. McCutcheon, all of the Chicago *Tribune;* and finally William A. Rogers of the New York *Herald.* Occasionally local artists were given a try but none survived. Rogers, a distinguished veteran of *Harper's Weekly* and *Harper's Monthly,* at 69 became a regular, joining THE POST in 1923. He drew local as well as national cartoons for three years. James North began to appear in the mid-1920s and continued regularly until the end of the decade.

Of all the by-lines in THE POST during Ned's years, the most popular was that of George Rothwell Brown. From January 23, 1923, through June 1, 1929, six days a week, he wrote a combination of political comment, doggerel, pun, and parody that occupied column 1 on page 1 under the heading Post-Scripts. The initial column stated its purpose:

> Good morning, busy people! Here's something to prop against the coffee pot and read, with one eye on your eggs, without turning the page. All the news in the world between half a grapefruit and a slicc of bacon.

A prodigious worker and chatty commentator, Brown was conservative, often reactionary, and in tune with the paper's isolationist and Tory economic views. But he was never dull. When his column was missing, the paper had to explain that he was on vacation. He often worked into the night, changing items to comment on late-breaking news. He had the skill of the old-time editorial page paragrapher, catching in a phrase the core of the news with an interpretative, witty, often sardonic twist. "The question in the Illinois primaries," said a 1926 item, "is not so much the amount contributed by the utility boys as it is how they expect to get it back." At times he was writing not only his column but also an editorial page satirical feature, political stories, and reminiscences of bygone Washington. For the paper's 156-page 50th anniversary issue in 1927, the largest edition yet, Brown lovingly compiled and largely wrote a detailed history of THE POST intertwined with national politics and the history of the capital, all illustrated with over 700 drawings and photographs. Part was printed in rotogravure, a Sunday addition McLean had begun a decade earlier. Two years after the golden jubilee, however, Ned let Brown go to Hearst, who had been after him for years; it was a sure sign that THE POST was skidding downhill.

Sunday features ran from Sarah Bernhardt's love letters, a serialization of H. G. Wells' *Outline of History,* and E. Phillips Oppenheim fiction to Eddie Rickenbacker on spectacular deaths on the auto racetrack. There were bland book reviews, crossword puzzles, a radio column by Milton D. Meyerson. It was the Sunday paper that made money.

The evening street edition, off the press at 9 P.M., was aimed at downtown theater and movie audiences. For a decade John J. Daly served as drama critic, also writing a Footlights and Shadows column on Sundays. Once when he was refused a raise he did get approval for an assistant to cover movies. Daly invented "Neil Sheridan," did the job himself, and collected an extra $35 a week. Daly wrote in 1924 that in Washington "for the most part Shakespeare is a bugaboo. There are those who would rather have their tonsils removed than go to a performance of Hamlet."

For the most part Ned McLean's POST was a shallow paper, devoid of any intellectual or artistic ferment, content to chronicle the obvious and that usually in a superficial way. In-depth reporting was a rarity. Only applied science was of interest, including a fascination for recurrent cancer-cure stories; the new morality was viewed with alarm, not understanding; art, music, painting, and literature were treated, if at all, as intruders. In the final McLean years there was little anticipatory sense of the gathering storms of fascism abroad and economic woe at home.

In the post–World War I decade, as pressures relaxed and temporary employees left, Washington reverted to its leisurely ways, though it kept on growing. As a municipality, Washington had come through the war years in rather good financial shape, so good, in fact, that in 1920 Congress ended the 50-50 division of federal and local financing that dated back to 1878. The city budget had grown from under $7 million in 1900 to more than $20 million in 1920. The new 60–40 formula, with local taxpayers putting up the major share, lasted until 1924; then Congress introduced the "annual payment" or "fixed sum" system. Ever since, each year has seen a battle to fix that sum equitably.

One of Wilson's last acts for the city was to appoint the first, and only, woman commissioner. She was Mabel T. Boardman, "the noted Red Cross leader" who thus held "the highest political position of any woman in the United States." Six months later, however, she was out as the new President picked two men to be the civilian commissioners. One of them was James F. Oyster, 70, a butter businessman, former Board of Education head, and director of the Richmond Federal Reserve Bank. Harding had given Ned and THE POST the kind of municipal patronage that so long had been, and later would again be, the prerogative of the *Star* management. Ned thought that he had made a deal with Oyster under which the publisher could pick both the chief of police and the chief of detectives in exchange for having Harding name Oyster commissioner. But, as John F. Major, Ned's general factotum, later described it, once in office Oyster did not go through with his end of the bargain. Ned retaliated by banning Oyster's name from THE POST; when he had to be identified, the paper referred to "the commissioner in charge of the police department." This childishness continued more than three years.

Municipal news was run of the mill for much of the 1920s except for Saturday night, January 28, 1922. A snowstorm had dumped 12 to 30 inches on Washington and the roof caved in on Crandall's packed Knickerbocker Theater at 18th Street and Columbia Road. Sunday's triple eight-column headline: HUNDREDS, DEAD OR INJURED, BURIED UNDER RUINS AS ROOF OF KNICKERBOCKER THEATER COLLAPSES; RESCUERS BATTLE STORM THAT PARALYZED CITY. The movie was George M. Cohan's *Get-Rich-Quick Wallingford* and 97 lost their lives in what THE POST correctly termed "the most terrible disaster in the capital's history."

Wars recede from Washington like the tides, leaving much jetsam behind them. Thousands leave but thousands more "never go home to Pocatello," as the saying has it. Thus the 1920 census showed a 32.2 percent population rise in a decade, making the capital, with 437,571, the fourteenth largest American city, more populous than seven of the states. Farm towns on the District periphery were becoming suburbs although Bethesda, just beyond the city line, was characterized as "the quaint Maryland village." The "speedway" along the Potomac onto Hains Point "became the Washington equivalent of the Champs-Élysées." It had a tea house, a golf course, and garden plots of 100 by 40 feet rentable for $5 including plowing. Part of the Tidal Basin was a bathing beach including one area for ladies only. On the Monument grounds were picnic tables and tennis courts. The beaches remained segregated.

Washington's Negro population in 1920 was 25.1 percent of the total, the lowest proportion since the Civil War. The capital had its "high yellow elite" but this went unrecognized in THE POST. Nor was there any mention of the anti-Negro, and sometimes anti-Jewish, covenants in real estate deeds. At the 1922 dedication of the Lincoln Memorial, blacks, including one of the speakers, were relegated to an all-Negro section of the stands (another item unrecorded in THE POST). There were occasional black protests; in 1925, 200 Negro singers refused to take part in a music festival when told they must sit only on the left side of the hall. Racial contact was as nominal as possible and the white view of blacks often came more from the popular radio program "Amos 'n Andy" than from firsthand experience. By 1928, however, there was a slight change when the city organized the Community Chest and a black was made committee chairman — for black contributors. Blacks and whites, without protests, sat down together at the initial Chest luncheon. The fact was ignored by THE POST but the paper felt obliged to put on page 1 a "correction" when it misidentified a divisional school superintendent in Fairfax County, Virginia, as "colored."

In the Harding era America turned inward and THE POST reflected this fact. Foreign news centered on postwar troubles in Germany, post-revolution problems in Russia, the rise of Mahatma Gandhi in India, the never ending squabbles over Ireland, the appearance of Benito Mussolini in Italy. Adolf Hitler first appeared in the paper in 1922 as "the Bavarian Mussolini." When Lenin had a stroke in 1923, a POST editorial caught something of the bolshevik leader:

> The good qualities which he possesses — industry, foresight, fidelity to friendship, courage — have all been employed by him in the furtherance of plans which strike at the heart of civilization as it has been developed in the great nations . . . He is a master of cunning sophistry and of insinuating propaganda . . . His iron will, animated by a keen and tireless brain, shaped the formless mass of the Russian revolution into a movement which has worked with destructive effect upon the foundations of society.

Two events coincided on Armistice Day, November 11, 1921. The nation buried its first unknown soldier at Arlington National Cemetery, and the Washington conference on naval arms limitation began. One symbolized the end of America's military participation in what it considered Europe's war; the other marked the limit of American cooperation in trying to prevent another conflict. Harding prayed for peace at Arlington where, Brown wrote, "wrapped in the brooding silence of eternity in the nation's Valhalla, where the white marble temple to its war gods on the wooded hills of Arlington stands guard above the Capital, the well-loved son of the republic sleeps at last shrouded in his immortality." Harding opened the arms conference but left it to Secretary of State Hughes to announce the American plan to scrap designated capital ships and establish a naval ratio of 5:5:3 for Americans, British, and Japanese battleships and aircraft carriers.

While President, Harding read THE POST, the Chicago *Tribune,* and "for the home town touch" the Columbus *Dispatch.* His easy relationship with the press was a vast change from the Wilson years but he showed at one session during the arms conference that he was not master of the facts. He answered a question erroneously and Hughes had to issue a correction. Harding then revived the rule that questions must be submitted in advance. THE POST reported the presidential gaffe but did not criticize Harding. The paper backed the 5:5:3 agreement and even swallowed the related four-power treaty binding the United States, Britain, France, and Japan to consult about any threat to peace in the Pacific. The Senate isolationists attached a reservation to the treaty declaring that "there is no commitment to armed forces, no alliance, no obligation to join in any defense." This THE POST termed "a wise and far-reaching safeguard that projects into the future the pure Americanism of the past."

The major concern of the Harding era was domestic; the major aim of the Ohio gang was plunder. It was the latter that led to the Teapot Dome scandal, the first of two that would rock the capital and the nation in the twentieth century and which deeply involved THE POST, although in sharply contrasting ways.

Harry M. Daugherty, the old McLean family friend and the new Attorney General, lived for nine months in Ned's little house at 1509 H Street, adjacent to both the old Shoreham Hotel and the palatial McLean home at 1500 I Street; Mrs. Daugherty, an invalid, remained in Ohio. The H Street house became both a social and a patronage center for the new administration. The building was well stocked (the liquor was stored in John R.'s old wall safe) and tended by a cook and a valet-butler provided by Ned.

There were two poker evenings a week in the White House library, with occasional games at the big I Street house and at Friendship. Mrs. Harding, "the Duchess" to her husband and "the boss" to Ned, was on hand to mix drinks for her "Wur-r-ren" as she pronounced it. Ex-President Taft, whom Harding appointed Chief Justice, was surprised that the Hardings were growing so close to the McLeans and their extravagant life. "Of course," Taft remarked, "it is easy to see why the McLeans coddled the Hardings, because it will give them an even greater social importance than their wealth and means of entertainment in Washington would give, but it is a very dangerous relation for a president to have, and I fear that it is an evidence of the lack of conventional social experience of the Hardings."

While President, Harding played golf at several of the capital's country clubs, often with such newsmen as Henry Litchfield West who returned to THE POST in 1922 as its golf writer. In 1921 Ned added an 18-hole course at Friendship, the sod imported from Switzerland. One day when Harding came to play, Ned had a new caddy for him, a youngster he had met at his Bar Harbor estate and to whom he had taken a shine. His name was Shirley Povich and he would work for THE POST for 51 years, from copyboy to sportswriter, editor, and columnist. In his memoirs Povich wrote:

> There I was, a small-town boy . . . on my first morning in Washington, D.C. I found myself standing at the first tee of a private golf course with a man I knew to be a millionaire, and his friend, a distinguished gentleman with white hair and dark eyebrows who looked as if he should be President of the United States. He was.

The closeness of the Harding-McLean relationship, both husbands and wives, was apparent one Christmas. The Duchess, worried by threatening letters the President had received, wanted to be out of the White House that evening. So Evalyn invited them to I Street where they stayed until 2 A.M., the men, including Daugherty and Senator Charles Curtis, playing poker or bridge and the women watching a private showing of Mary Pickford in *Little Lord Fauntleroy.*

POST readers, however, did not find such stories in their paper. What they did read there were sympathetic editorials and favorable news stories. What newsmen called a "puff job" about Harding appeared on October 16, 1921, under Albert Fox's by-line. What the reader did not know was that the idea for the story came from George Christian, Harding's private secretary, and that Ned had sent an advance proof to the President who sent back his "O.K." The following March Harry Price produced a feature headed: RECORD OF ACCOMPLISHMENT IN BRINGING WAR-RACKED NATION BACK TO PEACE-TIME BASIS MARKS

FIRST YEAR OF HARDING ADMINISTRATION, AS PROGRAM FULFILLS PLATFORM PLEDGES.

Four days later the McLeans' association with the Hardings did appear in print. The Hardings, said the AP account in THE POST, had departed for Florida with "a small party of friends" and, next day, the President was golfing at St. Augustine with "E. B. McLean, the Washington publisher," in his foursome. Price went along to cover Harding as he, the First Lady, the McLeans, Daugherty, and others cruised in a McLean-provided houseboat with frequent stops for golf.

On June 20, 1923, the Hardings left for Alaska, a trip that ended with the President's death in San Francisco. The Hardings had urged the McLeans to come along but they preferred to spend the summer in Bar Harbor. A POST editorial the day the Harding train pulled out of Union Station commented that "his health . . . is robust, thanks to timely exercise, and the long trip of 15,000 miles will be restful in the sense of being a decided change from official life in Washington."

Harding died on Thursday, August 2, in the Palace Hotel in San Francisco at 10:30 P.M. Washington time. The news reached the capital 25 minutes later by wire "and through the air by radio." A POST extra soon was on the streets. No POST reporter had been among the 14 who had made the trip with the President; the paper used the AP account of the President's death, a beat scored by Stephen Early who became FDR's press secretary. In the composing room, George Rothwell Brown changed the first two items in his page 1 Post-Scripts column and had a black border around his opening: "Ill news is wing'd with fate, and flies apace . . ."

The new President, Calvin Coolidge, took the oath of office from his father at his Plymouth, Vermont, farm. He arrived next day after "a record breaking" train run from New York of 4 hours and 33 minutes. Ned and Evalyn hurried back to Washington; she consoled Mrs. Harding, Ned joined the funeral train to Marion. That same night the Coolidges went to Friendship for dinner. Later, when Mrs. Harding left the White House she stayed awhile at Friendship.

A POST editorial called Harding "a statesman" who "will take rank with the greatest of Americans as time brings its perspective to bear upon his administration." The reverse turned out to be true; Harding would go down in history as the leader of one of the nation's three most corrupt administrations.

When Harding died, the smell of corruption was evident to some, at least, in Washington but the public at large was unaware. Harding himself, at the end, had realized that some of his friends had betrayed him. To Ned, his Harding connection was one of bonhomie and association with power, not money. The most he received were small favors, including a starred badge as a dollar-a-year special agent of the Department of Justice. With this went a copy of the department's code, an item that would play a part in Ned's undoing.

On April 7, 1922, Secretary of the Interior Albert B. Fall had secretly leased the government oil reserve in Wyoming known as Teapot Dome to Harry F. Sinclair's Mammoth Oil; on December 11 he likewise leased the Elk Hills reserve in California to Edward F. Doheny's Pan-American Oil. A week later, on page 5, came a POST story reporting Harding's approval of "the plan for developing the naval oil reserve through contracts with private companies." By then a Senate investigation was under way. Democratic Senator Thomas J. Walsh of Montana emerged as the chief prober, for 18 months quietly preparing for public hearings. They began October 25, 1923, nearly three months after Harding's death. Fall, the first witness, had been a frequent McLean guest and poker companion. He had resigned his Cabinet post nine months earlier.

In THE POST Fox depicted the inquiry as "the first political rumblings from the opponents of the Coolidge Administration" with a view to providing "advance ammunition for the next Presidential campaign." Fall defended the oil leases and denied that he had received anything in return. But Walsh, on a tip from Carl Magee in his Albuquerque *Morning Journal,* kept probing into Fall's apparent new wealth.

Fall took to drink and wandering around the United States. From Chicago he phoned McLean asking to see him. Finally, Ned and two of his men, John Major and William O. Duckstein, went to Atlantic City in Ned's private car just before Christmas of 1923. He found Fall "in a very nervous, bad physical condition," he later testified. Fall denied he had taken any bribe but asked Ned to say that he, Ned, had lent Fall $100,000; Ned agreed. Fall then wrote Walsh's committee about the loan and Ned confirmed it in a telegram from Palm Beach to which he had retreated. Since McLean was known both as a millionaire and a close friend of Fall's, this explanation seemed reasonable.

THE POST editorialized after Fall's appearance before Walsh that his "character and ability are such as to make his testimony absolutely dependable." Fall's statement, including the $100,000 explanation, was run in full. Brown wrote in Post-Scripts that "Mr. Fall and Mr. Sinclair submit their statements as American business men at the bar of the Inquisition and innuendoes scatter to cover like rats in the Senate basement." Sinclair admitted nothing more than selling Fall some cattle.

As 1924 began Walsh persevered and McLean got the jitters. "Ned's only part," as Evalyn correctly put it, "was that he lied to help a friend." Ned began to ponder the penalty for perjury. In December, before leaving for his cottage in Palm Beach, he had hired A. Mitchell Palmer, formerly Wilson's Attorney General, as an extra lawyer. On January 2, on page 1, THE POST headlined: PALMER EXPLAINS LOAN OF $100,000 TO ALBERT B. FALL. The story consisted of the text of Palmer's letter to Walsh saying that McLean was in Florida "for the winter, and is obliged to remain there owing to the condition of his own health and that of his wife." More substantively, Palmer quoted this message from Ned: "In 1921 I loaned Fall $100,000 on his personal note. I have never met Harry Sinclair nor have I ever met Doheny or any of the so-called oil crowd. I have never owned any Sinclair oil stock . . . I have never owned any stock in Mr. Doheny's company . . . There is no stock of these oil companies pledged with the note. It is absolutely unsecured." Doheny, in fact, had suggested to Fall that he say the $100,000 — which he, Doheny, had paid Fall — had come from McLean.

Before he left for Palm Beach, McLean had installed a leased private wire between an office in THE POST building and his cottage. The wire was kept open from 6 P.M. to 6 A.M. daily. To man the key at the paper, Ned's secretary, Duckstein, hired a White House telegrapher who wanted the extra work to supplement his $2500 annual salary. What made all this most fascinating to Walsh, who obtained copies of the messages, was that the telegrams were sent in code. Duckstein and McLean were using the Justice Department code that Ned had obtained as a special agent as well as the Bentley commercial code book that could be purchased in bookstores. Duckstein encoded and decoded telegrams, with the approval of William J. Burns, head of Justice's Bureau of Investigation, in a Justice office. Duckstein's wife was Burns' confidential secretary.

Walsh knew McLean was pulling strings among his friends in the Senate, for some of them had approached him to go easy on "poor Ned." Editor Bennett was busy at the Capitol seeing senators.

To Walsh it was obvious that Ned's explanation of the Fall loan was short of the truth. He decided to go to Palm Beach as a one-man subcommittee to take Ned's testimony after Ned insisted his health — he spoke of "severe sinus trouble" — made a return north impossible. Fall arrived at the Breakers Hotel — "a trembling wreck," Evalyn said — just before Walsh. The night Walsh was asleep in his Pullman headed south, Ned's private wire carried this message: "Jaguar baptismal stowage beadle 1235 huff pulsator commercial fitful. Lambert conation fecund hyberdize." It was to Ned, signed "W.O.D." by Duckstein. Decoded: "Walsh leaves Coast Line 12:35 tonight instead of Seaboard.

Lambert on same train." Wilton J. Lambert was Ned's regular attorney.

Walsh interrogated McLean in private; Fall refused to see him. Ned told Evalyn, "I won't go back on Al Fall"; but before the stern gaze of Tom Walsh he did. Back in the capital, Walsh released the hearing transcript and THE POST on January 12, 1924, had this three-column head over the AP account: M'LEAN TELLS STORY OF LOAN AND FALL SUBSTANTIATES IT. In sum, Ned admitted he had not loaned Fall the $100,000. As Mark Sullivan later wrote, "That answer was the first climactic sensation of the oil scandal."

Sensation now piled on sensation. Reappearing on the witness stand, Doheny admitted he had given Fall the $100,000. Burns, Mrs. Duckstein, a White House phone operator, Duckstein, Bennett, Major, the White House doorkeeper, Secret Service agent Edmund W. Starling, the White House telegrapher, former POST editors Edward S. Rochester and James V. FitzGerald, all took the witness stand. Of the lot, Bennett was the most evasive; his testimony was sprinkled with "I can't remember" and "I may have sent one of those telegrams." Yet he obviously knew the most about Ned's efforts to avoid being called before the senators and he admitted that Ned had told him to ask Republican Senator Curtis, the future Vice President, about his prospects before the committee. The embarrassed Curtis rushed to the witness chair to deny the hint of using influence for Ned; he did concede to having seen Bennett.

Recalled to the stand, Bennett now said that the real message he had conveyed from McLean to Curtis was "regarding the attitude of *The Washington Post* . . . I told the senator the question was arising as to how *The Post* should handle this investigation; whether it should be noncommittal, or should publish matters that had come in, or whether it should publish merely the official reports, or what it should do. And that Mr. McLean, having great confidence in his judgement, would like to have him give his opinion. He gave me his opinion, and that opinion has largely influenced me and Mr. McLean in the editorial policy of *The Post* and also, I think, through Mr. McLean, has influenced Mr. [John J.] Spurgeon [the managing editor] in handling the news." Curtis came back again to say all that he had told Bennett was that THE POST "should stress tax reduction."

While the public read with fascination the often confusing testimony, Republican politicians were growing more nervous. At the White House, the new President could feel the heat. In late January, "the White House made known" that Coolidge was prepared to protect the public interest; that afternoon he took several members of Congress for a Potomac cruise on the *Mayflower.* Next morning THE POST headline read: PRESIDENT ORDERS OIL LEASES INTO COURT; CANCELLATION BEFORE SENATE TOMORROW. Coolidge also announced he would name "special counsels of both parties" to probe Teapot Dome, the precedent for a "special prosecutor" in a later scandal. The two men were Owen J. Roberts, whom President Hoover later appointed to the Supreme Court, and Atlee Pomerene, a former Democratic senator from Ohio.

By now Washington was awash with rumors of all sorts of Teapot Dome–related scandals. In the Senate Lodge read a parody which THE POST delightedly printed:

*Absolute knowledge have I none,*
*But my aunt's washerwoman's sister's son*
*Heard a policeman on his beat*
*Say to a laborer on the street*
*That he had a letter just last week —*
*A letter which he did not seek —*
*From a Chinese merchant in Timbuctoo,*
*Who said that his brother in Cuba knew*

. . .

*That a wild man over in Borneo*
*Was told by a woman who claimed to know*
*Of a well-known swell society rake*
*Whose mother will undertake*
*To prove that her husband's sister's niece*
*Has stated plain in a printed piece*
*That he has a son who never comes home*
*And who knows all about the Teapot Dome.*

But Teapot Dome could not be washed away with laughter. The Senate voted to annul the oil leases and to ask Coolidge to fire Navy Secretary Edwin N. Denby. A probe of Daugherty's conduct was demanded. Coolidge said dismissal of Cabinet officers was "exclusively an executive function" but he promised "immediate, adequate, unshrinking prosecution, criminal and civil, to punish the guilty and to protect every national interest." Since some Democrats outside government also were involved in the scandal, Coolidge struck a bipartisan note: "I am a Republican, but I cannot on that account shield anyone because he is a Republican. I am a Republican, but I cannot on that account prosecute anyone because he is a Democrat."

THE POST cheered; Coolidge's stand was "in refreshing contrast" to Senate Democrats seeking "to obtain partisan advantage." Coolidge, however, was to have a narrow escape from involvement because of

McLean's foolishness. While Vice President, Coolidge had played golf at Friendship and when he became President Ned continued to have entrée at the White House. Employees there had sent some telegrams to McLean in Palm Beach and, as the Senate inquiry grew, that seemed to involve the new President. One of Ned's associates had cryptically written that the McLean leased wire would provide "easy and quick access to the White House."

On March 7 THE POST headlined: COOLIDGE TELEGRAMS PUT INTO OIL INQUIRY. The AP story began: "Two telegrams from President Coolidge, to Edward B. McLean, caught in the dragnet of the oil committee, stirred up another breathtaking commotion yesterday in official Washington." The first read: "Prescott is away. Advise Slemp, with whom I shall confer. Acknowledge. Calvin Coolidge." C. Bascom Slemp was Coolidge's secretary and he had been in Palm Beach when Ned was there. The White House at first explained that the telegram "related to the District Commissionership. Samuel J. Prescott is Republican city chairman and the President desired to confer with him regarding District matters." A second explanation was that the President had wired Ned, since he could not locate Prescott, "asking whom he should talk to about District affairs in Prescott's absence."

There was another embarrassing message. Bennett had sent McLean a telegram that, decoded, read: "Saw principal; delivered message. He says greatly appreciates and sends regards to you and Mrs. McLean. There will be no rocking of boat and no resignations. He expects reaction from unwarranted political attacks." Bennett contended that "principal" was Senator Curtis, but Curtis denied it. Ned later testified that at first he had thought Daugherty was the man. Walsh said his view was that Bennett's "no rocking of boat" was "a deduction which he drew from a conversation he had with the President." But no tie with Coolidge could be confirmed and the President escaped the scandal unscathed.

Finally, on Wednesday, March 12, 1924, Edward B. McLean himself took the stand for about two and a half very uncomfortable hours. The resulting double eight-column banner in next morning's 24-page WASHINGTON POST probably was the most humiliating ever printed in a publisher's own paper.

E. B. MCLEAN ANSWERS CLEARLY AND FRANKLY
ALL QUESTIONS OF SENATE OIL INVESTIGATORS

The AP story said nothing about clear and frank answers; it simply began by saying that McLean "told the oil committee yesterday that he had been drawn unwittingly into the oil scandal through a well-intentioned effort to aid his trusted friend, Albert B. Fall." THE POST printed in four full pages the complete text of the day's testimony by McLean and others.

Ned retraced the now familiar Fall story. He denied he had sought immunity from prosecution in exchange for his testimony. When asked what "service you have rendered as a special agent of the Department of Justice," he replied: "Not of any very brilliant character, senator"; the "only advantage" was that in "travelling with the President, if you would get outside of the police line in a strange city" a "Department of Justice badge" got you back inside.

As to his conversation with Fall in Palm Beach as Walsh arrived there to question them both, Ned testified he had told Fall: "Albert, this thing has gone as far as it can go. I have gone down the line for you. I have done everything, but it has come to the point where I have got to tell the truth."

POST Managing Editor Spurgeon, on the stand, provided an insight into Ned's thinking and probably the justification for the paper's running full AP stories and texts of the hearings. He said that just before Ned had gone to Florida the publisher had said to him: "It may come out in this Teapot Dome investigation that I made a personal loan to Mr. Fall. If it does, why you are to print anything that you think should be printed in the paper about it, and not to suppress anything because of my connection with it. I wish you would act as if you were working for somebody else and not for me." John Spurgeon, whom Villard called "a liberal at heart, a clear thinker, a humane man, saddened and rendered rather cynical by his experience of life," was fired by McLean a year later. He was succeeded by City Editor Henry R. Jones, known as "Hen-rye" for his reputed bottle-a-day consumption.

Bennett never mentioned McLean's role in any editorial; rather he sought at first to buoy Fall and then to protect the Republicans. The day after Ned testified, Brown's Post-Scripts included: "Mr. McLean before the oil committee dissipates a lot of coded mystery by a frank statement of plain facts."

But Washington, and the nation, was laughing at Ned McLean. Mark Sullivan wrote in *Our Times* that Washington initially had "thought of him as trying earnestly, according to his lights, to live up to the responsibilities attending the ownership of great newspapers." Sullivan concluded that Washington, which had considered him "a strange person with many queer traits," now "recognized that McLean was a 'boob,' a 'dub.' " Later historians of the era saw McLean variously as a "playboy" lacking character and intelligence, or "dapper" and "good natured if not quite bright." In retrospect, Alice Longworth thought him a "pathetic" man with "no chin" and "no character."

Ned McLean's involvement in Teapot Dome was the turning point in the paper's fortunes. The profitable newspaper he had inherited went into the red in 1924 for the first time in all the McLean years of ownership. In only two of the remaining eight years before THE POST was sold at bankruptcy did it turn a profit. More important, Ned McLean had destroyed the reputation the paper had achieved during the years of control by Hutchins, Hatton-Wilkins, and his father. Seldom has there been a more striking case of a publisher — even though Ned was hobbled to a degree by the terms of his father's will — tearing down a newspaper of good record and unlimited prospects.

McLean made one valiant effort to rescue THE POST from the shambles of Teapot Dome. He hired a big name as editor. On May 19, 1924, two months after his appearance on the witness stand, while Washington was still laughing at him, he signed this page 1, two-column box:

> I have much pleasure in announcing that I have arranged with George Harvey, former United States ambassador to Great Britain, to become Editorial Director of the *Washington Post* on June 1.
>
> Col. Harvey needs no introduction to the American reading public. Signal as were his achievements in the field of diplomacy it is as a journalist that he is best known to his countrymen. Successively staff member of the Springfield *Republican* and Chicago *Daily News,* managing editor of the New York *World;* president of Harper Brothers, and editor of *Harper's Weekly;* editor and publisher of the *North American Review,* briefly epitomizes his journalistic career. . . .

Harvey, then 60, a "colonel" thanks to the governors of New Jersey and South Carolina, had played a small role in Cleveland's second-term campaign. In 1906, when he was the archconservative editor of *Harper's Weekly,* Harvey had publicly proposed Wilson, then president of Princeton, for the presidency and from that had grown an intimate relationship — which later soured. It was from a "smoke filled room" of Harvey's Blackstone Hotel suite at the 1920 GOP convention that Harding's name emerged as the presidential candidate. Subsequently Harding appointed Harvey ambassador to Great Britain.

McLean hired Harvey "in the kind of mood that would send me forth to buy a jewel," recounted Evalyn, who wrote Harvey's one-year agreement on her Friendship notepaper. Ned sent Major to offer the job without proposing a salary. Harvey suggested $75,000 a year and Ned, as Major later put it, was "tickled to death. He said 'I thought you'd have to go to $100,000.' " Major concluded that Ned's idea was to remove "the heat" on his boss, "I mean, every publisher in the United States was on his neck." The salary was more than half THE POST's total profit in 1923 and helped account for the paper going into the red by $162,938 in 1924.

On departing Britain, Harvey wrote King George V that he had turned down a job offer from Coolidge because of "a wider opportunity" to make THE POST "a truly National journal capable of serving the great cause of Anglo-Saxon civilization and unity." Archie Butt felt that Harvey "would be an interesting talker if he were not such a dogmatist. He eliminates all conversation by the first remark or comment he makes. He closes all avenues for discussion by his announcement of his opinion."

The new editor — he controlled only the editorial page though his influence was felt in the news department — started with a bang. He revamped the editorial page makeup, especially on Sundays, with wider columns and larger type after the manner of the London *Observer.* He signed the chief Sunday editorials, many of which ran to inordinate length, and sprinkled them with Latin and French phrases and erudite historical allusions. Often he rambled; frequently he reviewed last week's events or forecast next week's happenings. But he did create interest, and his most important editorials were widely quoted and commented on around the country and in some cases abroad.

Harvey's first, and principal, effort was to elect Coolidge to a term in his own right. A Harvey biographer wrote that Coolidge "did not, it is true, depend upon Harvey for aid as much as Harding did, yet he took counsel with him much more frequently and had him often as a guest, sometimes for days together, at the White House." Major recounted going to the White House to pick up some of Harvey's editorials and he also claimed that Harvey wrote some of Coolidge's campaign speeches. That this tie went far beyond any norm of journalistic ethics never bothered McLean.

The Colonel early wrote of Coolidge that "I think that he will be elected" and "not for what he has said nor what he has done, but for what he is." When Coolidge was nominated in 1924, with Charles G. Dawes as his running mate, Harvey declared that "the party is electrified with fresh energy, courage and confidence." Harvey was out to make it so by saying so. When the Democrats, wracked by bitter differences over prohibition and the Ku Klux Klan, battled on for days in New York's Madison Square Garden, Harvey advocated John W. Davis, the eventual nominee, as a man of "tact, eloquence, popularity, character" who "would make a President of the first class." But when Senators Robert M. La Follette and Burton K. Wheeler joined in a Progressive party ticket, La Follette's backers were tagged as "radicals" and their platform was described as "addressed to the elements of discontent, unrest and radicalism." A Rogers cartoon labeled Wheeler "Bolshevik Bert" and Harvey named La Follette "Calamity Bob."

The culmination of Harvey's campaign for Coolidge came in a Sunday, September 7, editorial headed with what became a prime GOP slogan: "Coolidge or Chaos." Harvey plugged away at that theme up to election day when the Coolidge-Dawes ticket easily won an electoral sweep. Coolidge wrote him an "acknowledgement of the fine contribution which you have made to the success of the campaign. Your work was one of its real features, and your many acts of helpfulness will not be forgotten."

Sycophancy now was rampant at THE POST. Reporter Price, who covered part of the campaign, wrote Harvey that "among newspaper men your work for the President is looked upon as one of the great achievements of political history." Managing Editor Spurgeon added his "tribute to the rare skill with which you have steered this campaign." Evalyn was less impressed. She described how Harvey, visiting the McLeans at Bar Harbor, had "burst out" that he had found *the* campaign slogan in "Coolidge or Chaos." She thought "it sounded pretty flat" and hard to imagine that conservative Wall Street banker Davis "could be a synonym for 'Chaos.' "

Harvey seemed restless after the election and his editorials wandered. He created a ministorm with a December 25 satirical piece entitled "The Devil's Christmas," which began: "As we approach the season of Yuletide, when hearts are warmed by emotions of forebearance for saints and charity for sinners, it would seem fitting that somebody should say a good word for the devil." He proceeded to do so. The editorial was denounced from many pulpits, and a frightening number of POST readers canceled subscriptions. McLean felt it necessary, six weeks later, to apologize in print: "I regret that it was misinterpreted by some of our readers and that offense was taken where none was intended."

An even more offensive editorial just missed getting into print. Harvey composed, or copied, a bit of verse about a mouse climbing up the altar of a Catholic church and eating the sacred host. The new managing editor, Henry Jones, appalled when he saw the verse, appealed to

Major for help and Major tried in vain to reach McLean in Palm Beach. Finally, Major faked a telegram from McLean telling Jones to kill the anti-Catholic verse. How much this sort of thing had to do with the nonrenewal of Harvey's contract is unknown. Harvey's friendly biographer contended there had been "no thought" of renewal despite unspecified "willful and malicious misstatements." At any rate, Harvey, after having indelibly stamped the Republican label on THE POST, departed at the end of his year. Ned saw him off with a friendly signed editorial page item regretting that "other obligations now demand his time and energies." Harvey's name came off the masthead; the sidelined Bennett moved back in as chief editorial writer.

McLean probably felt the $75,000 paid Harvey had been worth it; at least he seemed never to care about THE POST's balance sheet if only because he had so much income from his father's estate. In the fall of 1924 the public got a glimpse of just how wealthy he was. Earlier that year Senator George W. Norris somehow had managed to get passed a measure to make public the income taxes paid by American citizens. On October 23, reporters combed through the figures for 1923 payments. THE POST ran the list of the best known Washingtonians and McLean led all the rest: he had paid $422,849.27. That year Ned had received $1,012,697.53 from his father's estate, the peak payment. THE POST itself paid $20,141.06; by comparison, the *Star* paid $151,273. (The man who a decade later would buy THE POST, Eugene Meyer, Jr., paid $152,466.) Despite howls, income tax totals were made public one more year. The 1924 figures again showed McLean the city's biggest taxpayer with $281,125.32 for a year in which he received $793,628.13 from his father's estate. But THE POST this time was not listed; it had gone into the red. In contrast, *Star* taxes were up slightly to $156,620.

McLean's relations with President Coolidge gradually cooled. In the fall of 1923 he was among those who had their picture taken with the President as "leaders directing the Harding Memorial Association." But in 1931, when President Hoover, with ex-President Coolidge on hand, finally dedicated the Marion memorial, Ned was absent.

Teapot Dome, probes and then trials, went on for years, sometimes reported on page 1 and later inside THE POST. Ned again testified about the $100,000 "loan" at the 1926 Fall-Doheny trial in Washington. The two were acquitted, as were Fall and Sinclair in another trial. As the result of a third trial, however, Fall went to jail; he served 9 months and 19 days in a New Mexico state penitentiary and was fined $100,000. It was the first conviction in American history of a Cabinet officer. In a legal paradox, Fall was found guilty of taking a bribe from Doheny but Doheny later was acquitted of giving the bribe. Sinclair went to jail twice for contempt, once of the Senate and then of the court, because he had hired detectives to shadow jurors. The oil leases were canceled. Fall's release from jail on May 9, 1932, a broken man of 70, was the finale of Teapot Dome, ten years and one month after he had granted the first oil lease.

To some, the Harding scandals were symptomatic of what they saw as the lax postwar morality of "the roaring twenties." THE POST was full of personal scandals, sensational murder cases, and evils of prohibition. The paper was never so sensational as the Hearst press although Sunday sections aped the Hearst display of big headlines and splashy photographs. Headlines give the tone: HUNT BLACKMAILERS IN DEATH OF MODEL; FOLLIES GIRL TO WED EARL, LONDON HEARS; FORBIDS PETTING PARTIES; GIRL IS FOUND DEAD, WEALTHY MAN HELD.

The Reverend James Edward Freeman, Episcopal bishop of Washington, saw "the problem of our times" as "the revolt of youth," the "breaking down of conventions" where "love interprets itself in terms of lust." George Washington University banned the student magazine for "some very objectionable material" such as a cover depicting "a flapper, bobbed of hair and bare of limbs," and such gag lines as "the girls don't wear fraternity pins anymore. There's nothing to pin them on." THE POST paragrapher quipped: "The woman who wears one of this year's bathing suits relies upon herself absolutely." Lieutenant Colonel U. S. Grant III, in charge of Washington's public parks, announced a crackdown on those who "neck," "pet," "spoon," or otherwise "outrage public decency" in dimly lit parked cars.

The movies, now "talkies," were a prime contributor to the new social standards. After the Fatty Arbuckle scandal, the movie magnates hired Will Hays, a politician, to clean up things in Hollywood; he declared that salacious sex was out but the line of distinction was blurred. The stage was less restrained. In the capital in 1931, United States Attorney Leo A. Rover closed down Mae West's show *The Constant Sinner,* because, as a POST review described it, Mae "took the part of Babe Gordon in the presentation of 16 scenes which include murder, dope selling, miscegenation, and lots of sex." Nelson B. Bell, for nearly four decades the paper's theater and movie critic, wrote in his opening-night review: "Richly caparisoned in a succession of costumes that utterly baffle a reviewer of this gender, Miss West presents a dazzling figure of blonde and uncorseted seductiveness throughout the three acts of her merry harlequinade of harlotry." In contrast, Washington's own Kate Smith appeared at the Earle "in a cycle of ballads and popular numbers."

The social event of 1926 was the wedding at the National Cathedral of Ailsa Mellon, daughter of the Secretary of the Treasury, to David Kirkpatrick Estes Bruce, son of Senator William Cabell Bruce of Maryland. Not since Princess Alice's wedding in 1906, said THE POST, had there been such society interest. Congress adjourned early so members could attend. Only THE POST had the full story next morning; the press was barred from the ceremony but reporter Bill Peake "bribed a member of the choir to give him his vestments, stood there in the group throughout the ceremony faking all the numbers sung by the choir and fooling even the choirmaster."

Social precedence — who outranks whom in official Washington — became front-page news in 1925 with a contretemps between Alice Longworth, wife of the Speaker of the House, and Dolly Curtis Gann, sister of the widowed Vice President. The Eugene Meyers invited both couples to dinner but the Longworths did not come; gossip had it that Longworth would not allow Alice to be outranked by Dolly at the dinner table. Faced with a terrifying Curtis-Longworth problem, the diplomatic corps, to whom social precedence is holy writ, called on the State Department for a ruling. Secretary Henry L. Stimson passed the buck back to the diplomats who generally solved the issue by not inviting the two leaders and their ladies to the same function.

To its credit, THE POST took most seriously the Ku Klux Klan revival early in the Harding years. In 1922 Brown wrote from Louisiana a sensational story of how the state was controlled by the revival of the post–Reconstruction era antiblack organization — now with both anti-Catholic and anti-foreign characteristics. When the governor damned the account as a "slander on Louisiana and its chief executive," the paper ran a story "from the Klan point of view." Nonetheless, THE POST editorialized that the Klan "professes to champion American ideals, yet it devotes itself to fostering racial and religious antagonisms . . . There is no place for fascism of this sort in America."

On September 17, 1923, THE POST ran as forceful an editorial as it had ever printed on any subject.

> . . . The extent to which the Ku Klux Klan has usurped the functions of the government in several parts of the United States is just cause for anxiety among citizens who strive to keep the ancient landmarks intact. The growth of this masked organization has been very rapid, and the boldness of its leaders in some States is amazing. Under the pretext of patriotic motives, this secret society has taken upon itself to

> regulate the morals of communities, and in some places has taken possession of juries and attorneys, if not of judges . . .
>
> They organize flogging and lynching mobs, and drag men from their beds or their cells and flog or hang them . . .
>
> This is not the first time that crime has been committed in the name of patriotism. It is an old trick . . .
>
> The Ku Klux Klan must obey the law or die . . . No matter how pretentious may be the ostensible aims of the Ku Klux Klan, in its workings it is an enemy of the United States, and so it must perish.

Such condemnations did not halt the Klan but they did encourage its enemies. On August 8, 1925, THE POST recounted that "phantom-like hosts of the Ku Klux Klan spread their white robes over the nation's most historic thoroughfare yesterday in one of the greatest demonstrations this city has ever known," a three-and-a-half-hour parade down Pennsylvania Avenue. There was a second parade in September 1926 but, after several Klan leaders were exposed in a number of scandals, the organization petered out.

Prohibition was more enduring. In the capital, police engaged in periodic "clean ups" which succeeded chiefly in driving up liquor prices, at least temporarily. The drunk arrest statistics soared from 3565 in 1920 to 13,904 in 1926, when 26,421 gallons of whisky were seized. One bootlegger tactic was to carry the liquor in a lead car while a second auto laid down a smoke screen to foil police. THE POST ran a series by "the man in the green hat" who declared that "for nearly 10 years I have been supplying liquor at the order of United States senators and representatives at their offices" and that he served "more Republicans than Democrats and more drys than wets." But he was careful not to name names.

In 1926 Representative Thomas L. Blanton called on Coolidge to prosecute THE POST for printing George Washington's recipe for making "small beer," declaring that the paper was "known far and wide" as the "administration mouthpiece." THE POST then published a citizens' poll that showed 8262 favoring wine and near-beer sales with 1016 against; this was part of a national press poll with the results nearly ten to one for at least that much legal liquor. Prohibition's days were numbered but did not formally end until 1933, first with the legalization of beer with 3.2 percent alcoholic content, 4 percent by volume, and then with repeal of the 18th Amendment by adoption of the 21st.

The Roaring Twenties were great years for sports. Through the pages of THE POST's sports section, and occasionally on page 1, paraded all the greats: Jack Dempsey and Gene Tunney, Bobby Jones and Bill Tilden, Knute Rockne, Earle Sande, Gertrude Ederle, Suzanne Lenglen and Helen Wills, Babe Ruth and Washington's own Walter Johnson. There were other local heroes, Georgetown's all-American guard, Harry (Babe) Connaughton, among them. Norman Baxter was the sports editor in the first half of the decade and when he became managing editor he was succeeded by Shirley Povich. At 21, Povich was the youngest of his breed, assisted by Bob Considine on tennis, Henry Litchfield West on golf, and Walter Haight on racing. Westbrook Pegler's syndicated sports stories were a regular feature for years.

Washington was a sports-hungry town and McLean at least recognized that. He sent Povich to cover the World Series when he was cutting down on all other out-of-town assignments. Chief photographer Hugh Miller, whose POST career spanned nearly 50 years, used trains and planes to rush photos back to E Street from out-of-town games, a fact printed as news in itself. The city's baseball team finally responded to the cry for a winner. In 1924, the Senators, or Nationals (Nats), under second baseman–manager Bucky Harris and in Johnson's eighteenth year with the team, finally won both the American League pennant and the World Series over the New York Giants. For six consecutive days THE POST carried double eight-column page 1 banners on the games, topped with a triple-liner:

JOHNSON IS HERO AS NATIONALS WIN
DECISIVE GAME OF WORLD SERIES, 4–3;
CITY IN CARNIVAL, CELEBRATES VICTORY

In 1924 Johnson lost on his first two tries but won the crucial seventh game. The next year, in the series against the Pittsburgh Pirates, it was the reverse; Johnson won his first two tries but lost the final game, and the series. The Nats won the pennant again in 1933 but not the series. Johnson retired in 1927, later coming back as the Senators' manager but without success.

Povich was even more enduring than Johnson. His column, first called Following Through, then retitled This Morning in what he himself called "a dead steal" from Brisbane's popular Today, allowed Povich to roam the world of sports. It was an age in which Povich loved to knock out, and fans loved to read, such sentences as "The staccato crack of Yankee bats today tolled the virtual demise of Cardinal hopes."

In sports THE POST was competing against big-name writers hired for special occasions by the Hearst papers, big names whose copy actually was turned out by ghostwriters. "So," Povich recalled, "we decided that our only recourse was to poke fun." On the eve of the 1927 series Povich composed and ran across the entire top of THE POST's sports section the following ad:

> Col. Charles Lindbergh, Vice President Charles G. Dawes, Aimee Semple McPherson, the King of England, and Charles Chaplin will NOT cover the world series for THE WASHINGTON POST. This baseball classic will be covered by our baseball writers.
>
> "REACH FOR A POST INSTEAD OF A GHOST."

Racing bookies were big in the twenties, too. The paper posted results of each race on a huge blackboard on the front of the E Street building; two bookies set up shop just to the west and three to the east of the paper. The result was such a swarm of gamblers that "the sidewalk resembled a huge alfresco betting parlor."

Calvin Coolidge, who took three-month summer vacations and slept as much as 11 hours a day, believed in a minimum of government. His 1925 advice, as THE POST reported, was that "it would be a good thing for the country if business and industrial interests would forget about Washington for a time." In June 1927, after welcoming Lindbergh to the capital following his transatlantic flight, Coolidge left for a vacation in the Black Hills of South Dakota. With him went a new POST reporter, Carlisle Bargeron. The big political question now was whether Coolidge would run again in 1928. On August 2, as Bargeron described it, Coolidge, smoking a cigar in an ivory holder, "his hands trembling," passed out to the newsmen small slips of paper on which was typed: "I do not choose to run for President in 1928" and nothing more. THE POST took this as a flat "no" but others did not. Eight months later a "sense of the Senate" resolution, approved 56 to 26, said that presidents should retire from office "after their second term." Efforts to make it read "after two elective terms," so as to exclude Coolidge, were defeated, 75 to 3. THE POST editorial, titled "The Ass Brays," ascribed the resolution to a "mongrel majority" of Democrats and insurgent Republicans.

Secretary of Commerce Hoover won the 1928 Republican nomination on the first ballot at Kansas City. Candidates rarely went to conventions; Hoover remained at his desk in Washington and the next day inspected the foundation work for the new Department of Commerce building. "In the bright sun," recorded THE POST, "busily engaged with maps and concrete foundations, no one recognized him as the Republican candidate." Late that same June, Alfred E. Smith finally attained the Democratic prize, having been placed in nomination for the second time by Franklin D. Roosevelt.

Radio had become an important element in politics. A POST editorial after the GOP convention noted that "the spread eagle" orator had a hard time adjusting to the demands of the microphone: "The thunder and passion with which generations of Fourth of July orators have addressed public gatherings became absurd and offensive as it went out over the air. The flowery periods, which with gesticulation and a bellowing voice, were once the requisites of a public speaker, were handicaps in effectiveness when heard over the air." After FDR offered "the happy warrior" candidacy of Smith, THE POST's radio editor, Robert D. Heinl, noted that Roosevelt's "voice seemed almost ideally suited to the radio." That fall, FDR was nominated for governor of New York; he was elected although Smith lost the state.

It was Hoover's year. From Tennessee, reporter Edward T. Folliard wrote one of the clear, crisp, concise leads for which he became known among fellow journalists: "From this verdant valley in the Blue Ridge the voice of Herbert Hoover called out to the Southland today to support him and his party in November." Editorially, THE POST called both candidates "men of such high character and distinction" that a choice was difficult; but Smith did not "possess the intimate knowledge and masterly grasp of national affairs that are possessed by Mr. Hoover." THE POST once again provided election returns at its building, though it noted that "the radio and prohibition have completely changed the character of the old-fashioned bulletin-board crowd — nowadays there are no intervals between announcements to be filled up by going down to Shoomaker's to get a drink." Shoomaker's, in fact, had given way to the Munsey building a dozen years earlier.

Hoover came to the presidency on March 4, 1929, declaring that "we have reached a higher degree of comfort and security than ever existed before in the history of the world . . . I have no fears for the future of our country. It is bright with hope." Coolidge, for a year, wrote a short column of homilies for which he received one dollar a word. THE POST was happy to be a column subscriber and prominently displayed the first on page 1, on July 1, 1930.

"Coolidge prosperity" and the attendant big bull stock market had been well established by 1928. A Brown Post-Script on March 28 that year reflected the happy mood:

*The boom in Wall street shows no*
*end —*
*trend.*
*upward*
*an*
*note*
*we*
*Instead*

The POST's economic survey for 1929 saw "good times" ahead and reporter Robert C. Albright predicted a "highly prosperous" year for the city. In February, the Federal Reserve Board spoke out against speculative credit. The stock market shuddered; up, down, up again it went as sales mounted and attention was more and more focused on Wall Street. On July 1, Secretary of the Treasury Andrew W. Mellon announced a fiscal year surplus of $185 million and reported that for the first time since the World War the national debt had been reduced below $17 billion, down $673 million in the past year alone. Next day THE POST announced that on July 8 its newsstand price would rise from 2 cents to 3 cents daily; seven-day home delivery remained at 70 cents a month. The 2-cent daily rate had endured for more than 17 years. In 1928 the paper had again gone into the red and by the end of the year its surplus was down to $231,909, hardly a third of what it had been five years earlier; 1929 would see a small profit, the last in the McLean era. Circulation in 1929 averaged 77,072 daily and 85,058 Sundays. The comparable *Star* figures were about 100,000 and 110,000.

In October came the crash. Headlines progressed from STOCK PRICES CAVE IN FRANTIC SELLING, through CRUSHING BLOW AGAIN DEALT STOCK MARKET, to HUGE SELLING WAVE CREATES NEAR-PANIC AS STOCKS COLLAPSE. THE POST correctly commented that "speculation has boosted the price of stocks to insane figures, without regard to earnings." But it saw no need to fear "a collapse of legitimate business and commerce. The country is economically healthy and the readjustment of stock prices . . . will not be injurious in the long run. The readjustment has come as a violent shock, but it should not be mistaken for the collapse of prosperity itself." The truth was otherwise.

March 1930 produced what the hopeful American Communist party called "Red Thursday." On March 6 THE POST headlined: TEAR GAS IS USED TO QUELL REDS IN WHITE HOUSE RIOT AS JOBLESS AND POLICE FIGHT IN MANY CITIES. By spring, the paper was saying that "the winter of discontent is over" and citing the vast public building program, above all the Federal Triangle then under way between Pennsylvania and Constitution avenues, at a total cost of $324,065,000. But the calamity was worldwide. Hoover proposed a war debt moratorium, a step THE POST called both "bold and perilous." The Europeans simply could not pay. Congress passed, and Hoover signed, the Hawley-Smoot Tariff Act to protect American jobs; THE POST saw it as "a guarantee of American prosperity." The tariff added to the international woe. Coolidge finally used the word "depression" in his column.

In Washington the economy began to crumble. In the fall of 1930 Harry Wardman was forced to turn over to a syndicate his $30 million worth of hotels and apartments; the next year the Shoreham, Hay-Adams, and Mayflower hotels went into receivership. The Kennedy-Warren advertised dinners for 75 cents. Government wages were frozen. Taxi drivers began a price war with rates as low as 15 cents for a ride in the downtown area.

Many banks across the nation were in trouble. On February 5, 1931, THE POST hopefully headlined the city's first overt financial scare: RUN ON BUILDING ASSOCIATION IS STEMMED; REWARD OFFERED TO TRACE FALSE RUMORS. Jittery depositors withdrew $800,000 from the Perpetual Building Association, apparently because of rumors started by a man denied a loan. The Riggs National Bank rushed half a million dollars over to Perpetual and Riggs president Robert V. Fleming jumped on a desk, opened the bank bag, and "drew forth bundles of hundred- and thousand-dollar notes, which brought applause." Newbold Noyes of the *Evening Star* "climbed into a window nitch at the bank and reassured the crowd, declaring that he had just deposited $25,000 on behalf of the afternoon paper he represented." More ominously, THE POST also reported that "on the balcony running above the barricaded vaults, a picked squad manned a machine gun, prepared for any eventuality."

THE POST stood with Hoover against a veterans' bonus, against a "dole" for drought-suffering farmers, and for the Red Cross as "the nation's great relief agency." "The willingness of states and cities to take charity from the United States government," said a January 18, 1931, editorial, "is a reproach to the old American spirit. Several communities have brought shame upon themselves by asking for federal relief before taxing their own resources."

A March 1931 editorial said "the worst is over" although the Census Bureau said there were 6,050,000 unemployed in the nation. Farmers were dumping milk and the Federal Farm Board called on southern planters to destroy a third of their cotton crop. In September, U.S. Steel, Bethlehem Steel, and General Motors all cut pay rates and wage scales. THE POST remarked that "eagerness to restore dividends by cutting workers' wages may work havoc to all concerned, including the recipients of dividends."

Government employees were no longer immune. Hoover rejected a scheme to compel them to divide their jobs with the unemployed, but he called on them to give part of their pay for relief of the jobless. The inevitable reports of "coercive charity" ensued. THE POST worried about "damage to the esprit de corps." The President and his office staff of 48 donated three days' pay to the local emergency fund. Still, some people had money; there was a long line at the National Theater to buy tickets, at $4 tops, for the Ziegfeld Follies.

The 1930 election produced a slim Democratic House majority, and thus made John N. Garner the Speaker, while Republicans retained only nominal control of the Senate. That new Congress, however, did not convene until 13 months later. By then the city was full of "hunger marchers," THE POST was publishing 23 pages in tabloid size of delinquent real estate tax notices, and Hoover did his 1931 Christmas shopping for his grandchildren in a 5-and-10-cent store.

The depth of the Great Depression, in Washington and elsewhere, was reached in 1932. There were more marches on the capital by the unemployed and the Reconstruction Finance Corporation was set up to bail out businesses. Congress ordered a one-month furlough, spread over the year, for most government employees. For those exempted, pay cuts ranged from 8.3 percent to 20 percent. Hoover took a voluntary 20 percent cut, the Cabinet 15 percent.

Amid these dire events the Lindbergh baby was kidnapped on March 1, 1932, and murdered. For weeks the story of possible ransom dominated THE POST. Evalyn McLean tried to rescue the child through Gaston B. Means, a convicted swindler to whom she paid $105,000 and for which he went to jail. But no POST reporter was sent to cover the kidnap drama.

That July the Bonus Expeditionary Force assembled in the capital, clamoring for immediate payment of a bonus not due World War I veterans until 1945. On July 28 violence erupted after Hoover, in some panic, ordered the army to clear the BEF shacks, some of them on the Mall at Pennsylvania Avenue and Third Street, just below the Capitol. The resulting photos of the dome shrouded by blaze and smoke were reproduced around the world. THE POST's lead on the "bonus riot," written by Daniel B. Maher, began:

> Tear gas bombs and torches, unleashed by federal troops in a sweeping offensive, routed the ragged bonus army yesterday from every major encampment in the Capital in a day of wild disorder that took the life of one veteran.

Army Chief of Staff Douglas MacArthur, personally in charge and assisted by his aide, Major Dwight D. Eisenhower, said he believed that if the President had not taken decisive action when he did "the government would have been threatened." The "mob," he added, "was animated by the essence of revolution." THE POST found Hoover "fully justified" and blamed "the fanatics in Congress" for inciting the uprising "by their crazy schemes to pay the bonus from an empty Treasury."

Two days after the BEF was dispersed Adolf Hitler's Nazis won 229 of the 604 Reichstag seats with 37 percent of the vote. The next month the Democratic nominee for President, Franklin D. Roosevelt, called for a "new deal" in government. Reporter Folliard covered the Hoover renomination convention but then was fired in a POST economy move; nobody covered the FDR convention for the paper. When Managing Editor Norman Baxter protested a 15 percent pay cut for the remaining staff, McLean retorted: "I'm cutting your pay 100 percent."

THE POST, like most everybody else, knew FDR would win and he swept the country, bringing in Democratic majorities in both houses of Congress. Between election and inauguration the banks were closed; in Miami FDR was shot at but it was the mayor of Chicago who was killed. On March 4, the new President declared that "the only thing we have to fear is fear itself."

An era had ended for the United States. But THE POST was journalistically comatose; it did little more than record events. There was no sense of understanding of the great change so implicit in the end of Republican rule or of the meaning of FDR's New Deal and its implementation in the hectic First Hundred Days.

Evalyn's verdict on Ned now was that his "wild behavior was at last revealed to be a progressive madness caused by dissipation." He was an alcoholic. Evalyn, too, had a drinking problem and at one point a morphine addiction, but she was far the stronger of the two. By 1925, each was suing the other for divorce. In 1928, she wrote, "We went apart for keeps." Ned was seldom in evidence at THE POST. Without Evalyn he was, as John Major put it, "like a ship without a rudder. He didn't give a damn where he went or what he did." He went to California and at a Santa Monica party thrown by Marion Davies, Hearst's movie actress mistress, Ned met her sister, Rose Douras Davies. Soon Ned leased a house in Beverly Hills — it belonged to actor Tom Mix — installed Rose, and lived it up for awhile.

The background of this escapade appeared on page 1 of THE POST on

November 8, 1930, when Evalyn charged Ned with nonsupport and sued for separate maintenance.

> Mrs. McLean asserted that up until June, 1929, Mr. McLean lived with her and the children at Friendship . . . At that time, she alleges, he left and took up separate residence at his home on H street northwest. Beginning July 1, 1929, and ending March 30, 1930, Mrs. McLean states, Mr. McLean paid her $7,500 a month. Since then he has paid her nothing except $7,500 on July 3, 1930, and $2,500 on September 8 . . .
>
> Mrs. McLean states that after her husband left Friendship and took up his residence at the H street address he went to Los Angeles, Calif., where he maintained an establishment for some months. During the winter of 1929–30 she avers he went to Palm Beach, Florida, and maintained an establishment there. In the summer, she says, he went to Atlantic City, N.J. All these establishments, the wife tells the court, were maintained for the benefit of her husband, his friends and associates.
>
> Mrs. McLean also points out to the court that her husband maintains an apartment at the Ritz Hotel, New York City; has two Rolls Royce, one Packard and one Dusenberg autos, and at one time owned a private railway car.
>
> In addition, Mrs. McLean states that it requires the expenditure of at least $4,000 a month to support the minor children in their usual station of life.

In 1931, with his income from John R.'s estate drastically down and THE POST deeper in the red, Ned decided to sell the paper. In 1929 there had been, in secret, a cash offer of $5 million from Eugene Meyer but Ned had blocked that sale. Now in 1931 the best offers were from David Lawrence and from Hearst, each for $3 million but only partly in cash. On June 16 the *Daily News* reported that Hearst planned to kill THE POST and thus give his *Herald* a morning monopoly. Lawrence, it was said, planned to publish the paper from his own plant then producing the United States *Daily*.

Evalyn declared she would "never permit sale of *The Post*," that she wanted to keep it for her two sons, John R. II, then 15, and Edward B., Jr., 13. A sale agreement was discussed in the District Supreme Court before Judge Jesse C. Adkins. On June 18, THE POST finally headlined: POST SALE ACTION DELAYED BY COURT. Frank J. Hogan, Evalyn's attorney, fought for a delay and talked of rounding up money for her to purchase the paper. Meanwhile the American Security and Trust Company urged approval of the Lawrence bid.

THE POST did not report what happened next. Ira Bennett, apparently on Ned's behalf, approached Hoover's Secretary of War, Patrick J. Hurley. Bennett — who told his colleague Merlo Pusey that "we must be especially careful to keep this paper respectable because the publisher himself is such a s.o.b." — was determined to prevent a sale to Hearst. The upshot was that Hurley gave Ned $100,000 to keep the paper going for what amounted to a hidden mortgage on his Leesburg estate. On June 27, THE POST headlined: POST WILL REMAIN IN M'LEAN FAMILY. The subhead read: "Publisher Decides to Retain Paper for Sons; Offers for Sale Rejected." Ned sat silently in court, along with Lawrence, Arthur Brisbane, Hearst's attorneys, and Mrs. Eleanor Patterson, editor of Hearst's *Herald.* Judge Adkins said Ned had a right to change his mind although the bank now favored sale to Hearst but did not insist.

Next day, THE POST chapel of the printers' union published an ad in the paper thanking Ned and noting that he had "stated that one of the prime considerations determining his course is his interest in the personal welfare of the 300 employes." The ad concluded with: "P.S. Washington without *The Washington Post* is incomplete and unthinkable."

A suit filed in 1931 by Evalyn to have her husband removed as the cotrustee of his father's estate said that Ned took off with the $100,000 for Europe "where he squandered much of the aforesaid sum in extravagant living with the said Rose Davies." In October, THE POST ran an AP story reporting Evalyn's suit for limited divorce, alleging "marital unfaithfulness and misconduct of the affairs of the McLean estate. No correspondent was named." In a separate suit, the account continued, Evalyn alleged that "he had appropriated trust funds to his personal use, and by refusing to pay personal bills and otherwise had offended business men and damaged the interests of *The Post.*" The story added that McLean had already filed suit for divorce in Mexico but was enjoined by the local court from prosecuting it.

Ned and Rose indeed blew the $100,000 in Europe and Ned ended up in the American Hospital in Paris. He had long been a sick man. The story got around the capital that he had "a urination syndrome," exercised once in the White House East Room fireplace during the Harding administration and again down the leg of the Belgian ambassador. The ambassador story indirectly got into THE POST on May 15, 1929, when Ned filed a million-dollar libel suit over a Philadelphia *Record* story that, the account said, "referred to a dinner at the Belgian embassy, to news and editorial matter published in *The Post* concerning the Belgian ambassador, and declared that McLean had been 'squelched' by President Hoover." McLean averred that he "did not attend a dinner at the Belgian embassy . . . did not at such a dinner 'dine too well' and did not annoy any guests at such dinner nor shock said guests and did not subject the Belgian ambassador to embarrassment by reason of his conduct and was not requested to leave such dinner." Ned won a partial retraction from the *Record.*

THE POST crisis reached the inevitable dénouement in May 1932 close to the very depth of the Great Depression. It all appeared in the paper, written by an unnamed reporter.

May 18: M'LEAN OUSTER SUIT TESTIMONY IS BEGUN. Corcoran Thom, president of the bank, the other trustee,

> said his relations with the publisher had been "difficult" during the past several months. He added that he had been unable to get hold of Mr. McLean to talk over business matters and that this had been detrimental to the trust. The bank president said he had protested strongly after learning that money due *The Washington Post* had been used to pay Mr. McLean's personal debts and that he told the publisher he would have to resign as co-trustee if that continued. Most of the day's testimony centered about *The Post.* Arthur D. Marks, its business manager, said they felt the paper had lost circulation and advertising through "unfavorable publicity" given Mr. McLean within the last two years.

May 20: Ned's attorney, Julius Peyser, told the court that lack of capital was the paper's problem "and that $500,000 would make it a success."

May 28: M'LEAN OUSTER SUIT AGREEMENT REACHED. The subhead: "Publisher Yields *Post* Control; Retains Voice in Remainder of Estate." The stipulation provided that Ned "resign forthwith and immediately from the offices he now holds as publisher of *The Washington Post* newspaper and as president and as a member of the board of directors of the Washington Post Company." Ned would be limited to his role as a cotrustee of the estate and he would "have no voice in the sale or lease of the corporation or the newspaper." For the first time in over 15 years, Ned McLean's name was off the paper's masthead in the June 14 POST.

Two years later McLean was committed to the Sheppard and Enoch Pratt Hospital in Towson, Maryland, after being declared of unsound mind because of excessive use of alcohol. He died there July 27, 1941, at age 55.

Before the paper's sale in 1933 THE POST was down to a thin 14, or even 12, pages daily as readers and advertisers awaited a change in ownership. In a last frantic effort, THE POST reduced its advertising rates and in a house ad reproduced replies praising the move. THE POST had been forced into receivership in March when it could not pay newsprint bills it owed the International Paper Company. Banker Thom testified on March 19 that the paper now had nearly $500,000 in debts, that it had lost $150,000 in the first six months after Ned's removal, and that economies aggregating $200,000 a year had been made. He also testified that the bank had put in $155,000 to keep it afloat and was preparing to put up $200,000 more but that that would be the end. The John R. McLean estate's assets now included Friendship, assessed at $773,073 with no encumbrance, the I Street house assessed at $2,228,355, but with encumbrances of $1,260,000, and these by now depressed stocks: 23,071 shares of American Security & Trust Co., 81 shares of Riggs National Bank, 135 shares of National Savings & Trust Co., 50 shares in the Munsey Trust Co., and 6 shares of Virginia Brick Company.

Thursday, June 1, was one of those pleasant summer days, the temperature ranging from 56 to 67, with men in straw boaters and white Panama hats. President Roosevelt was in Annapolis handing out diplomas to the new naval officers. On E Street at the Avenue "important personages of the worlds of finance and journalism mingled with the merely curious in the crowd that swarmed about the historic *Post* building" at midday. On hand were Alice Longworth, Mrs. Robert Low Bacon, another of the capital's social leaders, diplomat David K. E. Bruce, the *Star*'s Victor Kauffmann, the *Herald*'s Eleanor Patterson, the *U.S. News*' David Lawrence, numerous lawyers, and a score or more of newspapermen.

Evalyn McLean, wearing the Hope diamond on her breast, her pink-tinted hair set off by her black dress, watched from an upstairs window the proceedings on the well-worn steps below. POST employees crowded other windows to await news of their fate; staff photographer Arthur Ellis had camera ready for his allotted two shots. The two McLean boys were in the crowd; Ned was in a Montreal hospital.

The bidding was brief, beginning at $250,000 by Bascom Timmons, a Washington correspondent who declined to disclose whom he was representing. A $500,000 bid was made on behalf of Mary Harrison Rumsey, her brother W. Averell Harriman, and Vincent Astor with the idea of installing Raymond Moley, the FDR braintruster, as editor. Soon there were but three bidders: George E. Hamilton, Jr., "an attorney, representing an undisclosed principal"; Evalyn's attorney, Nelson T. Hartson; and Geoffrey Kenta for Hearst. In jumps of $25,000, the bidding reached $800,000. The *Herald* next day recorded the finale:

> A pleading note in his businesslike voice, the auctioneer [Thomas J. Owen] exhorted:
>
> "Eight hundred thousand dollars bid. Do I hear 825? I have $800,000. Will you offer 25?"
>
> From Hamilton, wedged in the center of the throng, near the auctioneer, came an offer of $825,000.
>
> Bidding ended at this point, but not until Hartson had again run back to see Mrs. McLean. Impatient at this further delay, Hamilton threatened to withdraw his bid unless the sale was promptly closed.
>
> Three short words marked the passing of *The Post* into new hands: "Going, going, sold."

After the sale Evalyn remarked to reporters: "I have done everything I could to save *The Post.* I love this old paper. I bid $600,000 to keep *The Post* for my boys but I could go no higher. Some day, perhaps, the paper will pass back to us. Who knows?"

THE POST of Friday, June 2, 1933, at the top of page 1 contained the famous photograph of the circus midget on Morgan's lap at the Senate hearing. In a single column, underneath the two-column picture, was this headline:

WASHINGTON POST
SOLD FOR $825,000

Below was an Associated Press account of the sale of "the *Washington Post,* for 56 years one of the outstanding daily newspapers of the Capital" to attorney Hamilton.

Rumors of the real buyer's identity floated about the capital but Hamilton would disclose nothing. On leaving THE POST after the sale, the attorney managed without detection to reach the Crescent Place mansion of Eugene Meyer. With Floyd Harrison, his long-time associate, Meyer had hidden in the closed-for-the-summer home, careful that no light inside could be seen outside. After Hamilton's report, pleasing because Meyer had authorized him to bid up to $2 million, the new owner left town on reservations in his secretary's name. On June 4, the *Star* carried a Meyer denial to the AP in New York that he was the purchaser. There was a ten-day delay for the necessary court approval.

At the end of that period attorney Charles Evans Hughes, Jr., tried to reopen the bidding for Evalyn, but the bankruptcy receiver objected and the court ruled the sale both legal and final. On Tuesday, June 13, 1933, THE POST carried at the top of page 1 a two-column box headed:

EUGENE MEYER ANNOUNCED
AS WASHINGTON POST BUYER

# 5

# Rescue and Revival Mr. Meyer Begins Anew 1933-1945

Eugene Meyer stood five feet nine, wore pince-nez glasses, and in later life had a tendency to rotundity. He looked like the financier he was. As a young man, he had developed a sharp tongue, a combative instinct, a stubborn streak, an air of cocksureness, and an explosive temper. His background seemed totally void of the attributes needed to make a successful newspaper publisher when — a vigorous 57 — he bought THE POST, a distinguished ruin. Yet he did have characteristics that helped mightily: self-confidence, persistence, a receptivity to new and even unconventional ideas. Moreover, he had the vision of a newspaper of integrity and the wealth to make that possible. He never put a limit on the money he was prepared to pour into THE POST, and before red ink permanently turned to black, it had cost him more than $20 million.

Born in Los Angeles on October 31, 1875, to Jewish parents — his father was a well-to-do Alsatian-French immigrant; his mother, half-German and half-English — Meyer spent a year at the University of California, moved to Yale, compressed three years' studies into two, and graduated at 19. Soon he had worked out a plan of life: 20 years for schooling; the next 20 to earn a "competence," marry, and start a family; another 20 to devote to public service; thus at 60 to retire and "grow old gracefully."

In 1901, at 26, Meyer bought a seat on the New York Stock Exchange, then established his own brokerage and investment banking house. His ability to run against the speculative mob at precisely the right moment led J. P. Morgan to warn a partner to "watch out for this fellow Meyer, because if you don't he'll end up having all the money on Wall Street." Dealings in railroads, copper, oil, and chemicals swelled his fortune; he was the chief organizer of the giant Allied Chemical and Dye Corporation, the dividends of which helped finance THE POST. He passed up an opportunity to become one of the two largest General Motors stockholders, but he made millions with the Fisher auto body brothers. By 1915 Meyer's fortune was in the $50 to $60 million range.

In 1910 at 34 Meyer married Agnes Ernst, a 23-year-old New York beauty, in a Lutheran ceremony; by now he had dropped his Jewish affiliation. She was strong-willed, tough-minded on civic issues, bursting with opinions, and always ready to express them verbally or in writing for THE POST and other publications. Their marriage was boisterous, sometimes rocky, and the five children she bore him were both delight and problem. Daughter Katharine thought her father "very shy and remote on one level, witty but very distant and unable to be intimate" even with her. Agnes was not close to her children. She became an expert on Chinese art; another indulgence was romantic attractions to the great, ranging from Auguste Rodin and Thomas Mann to Adlai Stevenson and Earl Warren.

In 1917, two years behind in his life plan, Meyer began his public service. But it was not easy; he was well known as a Republican and Woodrow Wilson's Democrats ruled Washington. So he began as a dollar-a-year adviser to the army in the purchase of shoes and cotton duck. In short order, however, he was working for Bernard Baruch's War Industries Board, then as a director of the War Finance Corporation. Meyer was preparing to leave Washington after World War I ended, when President Harding reappointed him to the War Finance Corporation, now engaged in helping economically distressed farmers. Next, he headed President Coolidge's Farm Loan Board, a post he quit in May 1929, only to be named 16 months later by President Hoover to the Federal Reserve Board. Soon he was both governor (chairman) of the Fed and an ex-officio board member of the Reconstruction Finance Corporation, his mornings spent at the first job, afternoons and late into the night at the second. Meyer's term at the Fed carried over into the New Deal's First Hundred Days, ending with his resignation on May 10, 1933. He had given 16 years to government service.

During most of these years, and subsequently, the Meyers lived in Washington at a sumptuous mansion at 1624 Crescent Place, just off 16th Street, escaping when possible to their 262-acre estate, called "the farm," at Mt. Kisco in Westchester County, New York. Both establishments saw a constant parade of important people, Americans and foreigners, along with the normal clutch of children. Family life was competitive and ferment was constant. In the Washington of the 1920s the

Meyers were among the many who attended the lavish parties of Ned and Evalyn McLean.

The final Hoover years were bitter and Meyer, as a Hoover appointee, received his share of blame. The rabble-rousing Father Charles E. Coughlin included him in his financial (and conveniently alliterative) Four Horsemen of the Apocalypse: Morgan, Mellon, Mills, and Meyer. In the first New Deal months, Huey Long called Meyer "an ordinary tinpot bucketshop operator up in Wall Street . . . not even a legitimate banker." Harvard professor Felix Frankfurter, on the other hand, had described Meyer as "the only brave and effective leader in [the Hoover] Administration in dealing with [the] depression." All these comments, at least, were a measure of Meyer's prominence in the capital.

Four years short of his sixtieth birthday, Meyer left government physically exhausted and mentally irritated. After two weeks at Mt. Kisco his health was restored but with it came restlessness. One morning he came downstairs, running his fingers along a slightly dusty banister, to announce to Agnes: "This house is not properly run." She replied: "You'd better go buy *The Washington Post.*" And so he did.

In the front-page box on June 13, 1933, announcing Meyer as the purchaser, the new owner stated simply:

> It will be my aim and purpose steadily to improve *The Post* and to make it an even better paper than it has been in the past. It will be conducted as an independent paper devoted to the best interests of the people of Washington and vicinity, and hopes to have their interest and support.

Then, to allay speculation that this Republican financier was likely to be beholden to his party, Meyer added:

> I think I should, in this connection, make it clear that, in purchasing *The Post,* I acted entirely on my own behalf, without suggestion or discussion with any person, group or organization.

The new Washington Post Company, with paid-in capital and surplus of $1,250,000, had Meyer as president, his wife as vice president, and Floyd R. Harrison, long Meyer's right-hand man, as secretary-treasurer. The anemic POST that day printed only 18 pages with a mere 19 columns of display advertisements plus less than 2 pages of classified ads. Circulation had shrunk to 51,728, and even that figure was suspect.

Thus began the family control of THE POST which, over the next 44 years, through Meyer, his son-in-law, and then his daughter, carried the paper to the end of its first century — with his grandson the prospective third generation in control.

What Meyer had bought was chiefly a name and an opportunity. THE POST'S physical plant was close to a shambles, but the E Street building, with an additional wing built in 1935 and rented space in a structure next door, continued to be home for another 17 years. Meyer spent $367,000 for the addition and for press and mechanical improvements. The staff, what was left of it, was mostly second rate. The Associated Press franchise, exclusive in the morning field, was perhaps the most valuable asset except for the historic name itself.

Meyer thought he knew how to hire competent help but he later conceded that "in my first two years I made every mistake in the book." He began by hiring Eugene MacLean, a San Franciscan, as THE POST's general manager, the first of many bad choices; he lasted two years. Harrison, the secretary-treasurer and then comptroller, later was moved to New York to handle family finances. The new managing editor, Ralph E. Renaud, formerly of the New York *World,* was a disaster. Felix F. Bruner, Jesse O. Irwin, Luther Huston, and John Riseling all were city editors in quick succession; Riseling, a holdover, served long and well, however, as night city editor. For a long time the local side of the news received scant attention from the publisher, whose interests were national and international.

Ira Bennett, who had been running the editorial page for more than 28 years except for the Harvey year, was worn out; in any event, he was too conservative and too isolationist for Meyer. He hung on, his page persistently vapid, until fall when Meyer found a splendid replacement. He was Felix Morley, a 39-year-old Rhodes scholar, who had been a correspondent in the Far East, had worked for the Philadelphia *Public Ledger* and the Baltimore *Sun,* and now was at the Brookings Institution. He took over on December 18. Merlo J. Pusey, who had joined the editorial staff in 1928, was the only long-time holdover; he remained, a "splendid workhorse," for another 38 years. Bett Hooper and Anna Youngman became the first female editorial writers. Eugene (Gene) Elderman, who at 22 had become THE POST's editorial cartoonist in 1932, also remained; his drawings soon reflected the views of the new owner and the new editorial page editor. But Elderman, a charming nonintellectual, in time drank himself into a state of nonproductivity.

To create a national news staff Meyer quickly hired Elliott Thurston of the New York *World,* whose writing on finance had attracted him. Thurston was a good choice, both as writer and manager. He soon brought Meyer two men who became staff mainstays: Franklyn Waltman from the Baltimore *Sun* and Raymond Clapper from United Press. The one holdover to join them in national reporting was Robert C. Albright who concentrated on Congress with great skill and whose Sunday column, Gallery Glimpses, a lighthearted collection without malice of the facts and foibles of Capitol Hill, remained a feature for three decades. At the end of Meyer's first month the paper again had a man at the White House, first Lawrence Sullivan and then Sidney Olson. When Meyer took over, the paper had no serious columnist. Within six weeks Carlisle Bargeron, who had gone to the rival morning *Herald*, returned to write an Along the Potomac column of political whimsy and biting conservative comment, a feature until 1935.

Meyer paid close attention to the editorial page and he followed the news. Nightly at 9:30 he would call in, or drop by, to find out what would be in the next day's paper. Initially, he paid less attention to business, advertising, and circulation details. Meyer wanted THE POST to be a financial success, of course, not to make money for its own sake, but because, as he once put it to a reporter, "I am not going to endow this newspaper." He knew that the product had to be improved before the paper could turn a profit.

A new, cleaner typeface — Excelsior — was soon introduced, but the presses were still in bad shape and the printed result often included smudgy photographs. On July 7, 1933, the period after the name of the paper was dropped from the page 1 masthead; otherwise the name, THE WASHINGTON POST, in Old English type, remained the same from the first issue in 1877 through the 100th year except when, for a while, it was combined with names of rival papers THE POST had bought out.

A deluge of news pressed on Meyer as he struggled with management and staff. Roosevelt's First Hundred Days came to an end just as he took over. The day he assumed the role of Publisher, Congress passed the National Industrial Recovery Act and FDR quickly named Brigadier General Hugh Johnson to run the new National Recovery Administration (NRA), initiating the second frantic era of New Deal recovery efforts. Meyer promptly put the NRA's Blue Eagle in the left-hand masthead "ear."

But before he could tackle the serious issues he found himself in a monumental fight over, of all things, the comics. McLean's POST had been running four famous daily and Sunday strips — Andy Gump, Dick Tracy, Gasoline Alley, and Winnie Winkle — under contract with the New York *News*–Chicago *Tribune* syndicate; Meyer assumed that the contract continued. But Mrs. Eleanor (Cissy) Patterson, a major *News-Tribune* stockholder then editing the Washington *Herald* for owner Hearst, tried to get the strips for her paper by contending that the sale of THE POST voided the contract.

Meyer had never read a cartoon strip; his first query was: "Are comics important?" Once told they were, indeed, vital to his new venture, he battled to save them. When Cissy advertised that the comics would shift to her paper, Meyer obtained a court injunction. As insurance he also took on some new ones, Dixie Dugan and Joe Palooka among them. The legal struggle finally reached the Supreme Court, which on April 8, 1935, refused to hear Cissy's case. On page 1 THE POST proclaimed SUPREME COURT GIVES POST EXCLUSIVE RIGHTS TO 4 FAMOUS COMICS and Elderman drew a larger than usual cartoon of a black-robed justice sternly ordering the comic-strip characters back to THE POST. There they remained until the contract expired 22 months later, whereupon Cissy finally got them. THE POST lamely explained their absence as due to a change in "the taste of readers."

At times before the final legal action, both the *Herald* and POST were running the contested strips. The color pages for the Sunday paper following the court ruling already had been printed and Cissy asked Meyer to let them be used. He agreed, provided she would print a front-page box saying this was done through his courtesy and that henceforth THE POST had sole rights. That, coupled with the Elderman cartoon, was too much. Her revenge came in the form of a florist's box, sent to the Meyer home. Agnes carried it to THE POST where Meyer and Morley were meeting. As Morley wrote in his diary:

> A small package, beautifully beribboned, rested on a bed of orchids and on it was Cissy's card reading: "So as not to disappoint you." Eugene smilingly tore the wrapping apart — and out fell a chunk of raw beef. For a few moments none saw what it meant. Then Felix faltered: "It must be a pound of flesh!" Mrs. Meyer took it icily . . . "Of course," she said, "a dirty Jewish Shylock." But Eugene . . . was too hurt to say anything. He looked half-stunned — the only time I have ever seen him really taken aback. And it really was a foul and swinish gesture.

Meyer never disclosed the affront but Cissy could not resist spreading word of her deed around Washington.

The next year Cissy pounced on THE POST when it bannered an erroneous AP bulletin: HAUPTMANN GUILTY BUT ESCAPES ELECTRIC CHAIR. The bulletin was quickly corrected, for the verdict on the kidnapper of the Lindbergh baby was death. No papers hit the street with the error, but a POST printer sold a copy to the *Herald* for $50 and Cissy gleefully ran a photograph of it on page 1 under the headline: FALSE VERDICT FOOLS READERS — WRONG AGAIN! Later on Cissy referred in print to "our venerable lady friend, *The Post*" and "our narsty-nice morning contemporary." Meyer was too much the gentleman to retaliate in kind. THE POST did, however, constantly trumpet the fact that it was "the only morning newspaper" with AP wirephotos, a new development that added a sense of immediacy to pictorial news from afar.

The twin pillars of the New Deal were recovery and reform. Eugene Meyer was deeply interested in both, especially as they affected financial matters, in which he had had so much experience. Inevitably, FDR's improvisations, his economic twists and turns, his seemingly cavalier handling of the American dollar, and the vast expenditures and rising national debt ran athwart Meyer's conservative fiscal and monetary views. The President and the publisher were very opposite personalities and clearly disliked each other.

Eugene and Agnes Meyer had met Franklin and Eleanor Roosevelt when all were in Washington during the Wilson administration. Meyer wondered why his wife had invited the Roosevelts to dinner "because I thought they were very dull people." During the first Roosevelt year Meyer privately criticized FDR's "fondness for expediency against principle." Agnes "suffered acutely . . . while young New Deal whippersnappers for whom I had no respect strutted around as if no American had ever before raised a hand to make our society more truly democratic."

In February and March 1934 THE POST ran a series of 31 articles called "The New Dealers," written by "Jay Franklin," a pseudonym for John Franklin Carter. It was a gossipy series, on the whole friendly to the New Deal's left wing and critical of the conservatives. The stories attracted much attention, including a blast from General Hugh S. Johnson, one of the targets. He took to the radio to declare that the series had been written by someone with "more than a trace of rodent blood" and "published by a dying newspaper, recently purchased by an Old Dealer — a cold-blooded reactionary — who was one of the principal guides along the road to the disaster of 1929. And the object of its purchase must have been to attack men for the purpose of destroying measures." In reply, THE POST ran a page 1 box saying circulation had risen 37 percent since Meyer had taken over and the advertising increase had been the third largest in the nation. *"The Post,"* it was added dryly, "has a high regard for the ability, energy and devotion of Gen. Johnson. It is a matter of regret that it can not also admire his self-control or temperance in public utterance."

The first New Deal year brought a measure of visible economic recovery and, above all, a new sense of national confidence. An editorial on March 4, 1934, revealed THE POST's ambivalence:

> The greatest disservice which can be done to the Administration . . . is to attribute to its policies all the measures of recovery now happily apparent. Such fulsome praise would not be merely totally unwarranted. It would also encourage a perpetuation, perhaps an intensification, of measures which are impeding rather than restoring prosperity . . . What the past year has unquestionably accomplished is a great revival in the morale and spirit of the American people. For this the magnetic personality and the sympathetic outlook of President Roosevelt have been in large part responsible. The credit which is his due is strengthened, not minimized, if it is not degraded into witless adulation.

Later that month when Dr. William A. Wirt, the head of the Gary, Indiana, public school system, suddenly broke into national headlines, THE POST seized upon the affair to drive home its point. Wirt had written that "a group of theoretically trained young men, sincere but inexperienced," were directing the country along "the road to communism." Headline-catching and emotion-arousing was Wirt's statement that one of these young men had called FDR "only the Kerensky of this revolution." THE POST quickly ran a Wirt interview proclaiming the revolution already under way.

Wirt's accusation was a springboard for the anti–New Dealers, and a House committee was created to probe the Wirt charges. Wirt named six persons who had attended a dinner with him at the home of a minor government employee "when an alleged plot to overthrow the social order of the country" had been discussed. THE POST conceded that Wirt's testimony was "a flop" but added that it did reveal "the extent to which the American public is fumbling in the dark — uncertain, anxious, befuddled and to an increasing extent irritated by a kaleidoscopic and disorderly program too vague for analysis, yet too provocative for uncritical acceptance."

In a speech on April 22, 1934, Meyer stated with candor his, and his paper's, views:

> If there is any feeling in Washington or elsewhere that *The Post* is an anti-Administration paper, that feeling is due to the fact that such criticism as we have made stood out with undue emphasis in a country where temporarily almost all criticism, however rational, has been quenched . . . [*The Post*]

> is unfriendly to the policy of extreme Federal regimentation of the present Administration. We are unequivocally opposed to inflational monetary manipulation. As a balanced budget is a prime necessity, we are opposed to unlimited and careless spending of public funds . . . *The Post* is particularly opposed to legislation put forward ostensibly for one purpose while deceitfully establishing powers for other purposes.

In this period Meyer wrote several signed page 1 editorials, usually on fiscal issues, while the editorial page hammered away at "waste," "extravagance," and what it perceived as duplicity. Because they thought Meyer wanted it, editors outdid each other to cover and prominently display stories on gold, money, discount rates, and other financial news. "The place went mad on money," one reporter recalled. At the same time the publisher loosened the purse strings enough to let some of his reporters travel the country. Sampling the public's reaction to the New Deal as the first midterm election approached, Clapper found "the average man generally favorable, and business leaders, bankers and other men of affairs inclined to be dubious or frankly hostile." On election day there were more "average men" at the polls and the New Deal tightened its grip on Congress. When the new Congress assembled, Clapper wrote that

> the dominating fact in Washington is the complete supremacy of President Roosevelt . . . It comes close to being a dictatorship, though one which does not in any sense rest upon force, or terrorism or suppression as in the case with European dictators . . . If what we have is a near-dictatorship it rests upon the common consent of the American people.

There were then no accepted government figures on unemployment; the American Federation of Labor published its own estimates and they were disquieting. Despite all that the New Deal had done, more than 10 million were jobless. Partly in response to pressure from the left by Huey Long, Father Coughlin, and Francis E. Townsend, FDR asked Congress for money to put 3.5 million to work at public jobs. He also proposed the first national social security pension system and jobless insurance in the nation's history. THE POST approved the concept of social security but relief was another matter, especially Roosevelt's request for vast sums to be doled out as he alone would decide. "Never before in peacetime," thundered an editorial, "has so flagrant a demand been made upon Congress to abdicate its Constitutional control over national expenditures . . . The whole affair is a travesty of responsible government." But the Congress promptly voted FDR $4.88 billion and he created the Works Progress Administration with Harry Hopkins in charge.

A former social worker with a passion for aiding the jobless and little regard for the financial cost, Hopkins was constantly lambasted. His management of WPA led THE POST on September 21, 1935, to fume against "the squandering of $4,880,000,000 in a fruitless fiasco intended to hoodwink the Nation into believing that constructive jobs have been or will be found for the unemployed."

Clapper got a laugh with his column of April 17, 1935, describing how the paper managed one aspect of the problem:

> After holding out against the New Deal for two years, thinking it might blow over, *The Washington Post* has surrendered — typographically. The publisher has had to buy skinny headline linotype matrices to take care of the billions of dollars that figure in the New Deal news.
>
> *The Post*'s Old Deal headline type, of broad Tory girth, was designed to deal only in millions thus:
>
> $4,880,000 [this filled a line of type]
>
> Since the works bill passed, billion-dollar type has been purchased. It looks like this:
>
> $4,880,000,000 [this equally filled a line]
>
> If Mr. Roosevelt throws one more digit at us, *The Post* will match the rubber money, dollar for dollar, with rubber type.

By now many of those who disagreed with FDR's policy had turned to malicious hatred. In August 1935 reporter Felix Bruner wrote from the Midwest that "false reports that the President is failing mentally and physically have spread like wildfire." After a Roosevelt speech later that month, THE POST commented: "If there had been any doubt in the Nation concerning the President's health, it must have been set at rest by his radio address . . . Vigorous and forceful, it reflected a marvelous vitality."

Roosevelt was an avid newspaper reader. He went through as many as eight each morning in bed and about the same number in the afternoon, including all five Washington papers. Before retiring he frequently would scan the early "bulldog" edition of THE POST, off the press each evening to catch the after-theater crowd. One such edition became famous. The President was suffering from a cold at the time but the single-column front-page headline on the news report contained a classic typographical error: FDR IN BED WITH COED. It was a lazy fall evening, probably in 1940, and cub reporter Barry Sullivan was manning the city desk when the phone rang. "This is Frank Roosevelt," said the familiar voice with a chuckle. "I'd like 100 copies of that first edition of *The Post.* I want to send it to all my friends." But the circulation department had discovered the error—some thought a printer had made it deliberately, others ascribed it to a sloppy copyreader's headline handwriting—and already had scurried about town to retrieve the edition and shred it. FDR never got his 100 copies.

Eugene Meyer was a fiscal conservative but he knew Roosevelt was right to curb the freebooters he himself had fought in his Wall Street years. What made Meyer and his POST so angry, and often so bitter, was not just the extent of reform; it was FDR's way of going about it, especially his frequently biting language about the business community. Regulation was necessary, but unrestrained power for the regulators was wrong; relief was vital, but waste intolerable. The use of relief, especially WPA, for political purposes was worse than a disgrace. Jim Farley was attacked for his "spoils" system; Hopkins' WPA was viewed as such a "fiasco" that THE POST suggested "reversion to a national system of community relief . . . supplemented by the social security program" as "the only hope of ending the debauchery."

The entrenched civil service was slow to respond to the New Deal dynamism and FDR's men circumvented it as much as possible. George D. Riley's widely read column devoted to the bureaucracy, The Federal Diary, once was topped with a black-bordered box: "Sacred to the Memory of Civil Service, 50 years. Born 1883—Died 1933 soon after celebration of its diamond [sic] jubilee."

When, in a precedent-breaking evening address carried by radio on January 3, 1936, the President belligerently told Congress that his program had "earned the hatred of entrenched greed," THE POST retorted that his speech dripped with "venom" and "indeed, the dictators of Europe, reading this speech by Mr. Roosevelt to its end, will be impressed by the sincerest form of flattery which the President pays them . . . For Mr. Roosevelt's whole technique is copied from that employed, in the early stages of their rise to power, by both Hitler and Mussolini." The Gallup poll, however, in mid-1936 produced a 55 percent "no" to the question: "Do you believe the acts and policies of the Roosevelt Administration may lead to dictatorship?"

George Gallup's American Institute of Public Opinion owed much to the lavish display THE POST gave it from the beginning. Gallup had asked Meyer what he would think of periodic polls; Meyer was enthusiastic. Many of Gallup's questions came from Meyer and reflected his and Morley's interests. The first of what was to be a fabulously successful POST feature over the next four decades appeared on Sunday, October 20, 1935. The initial question: "Do you think expenditures by the government for relief and recovery are too little, too great, about right?" brought responses of 9, 60, and 31 percent respectively.

The weekly polls were displayed in a new editorial and features section of the Sunday paper, soon known around THE POST as "brains." Here were concentrated articles on the momentous questions of the week, domestic and foreign, by staff writers and famous-name contributors. The section also included the editorial page, the columnists, and later, a review of the week's news much like that in the contemporary New York *Times.* "Brains," now called the Outlook section, was for only a small part of the readership, but that part included the powerful in Washington who made government policy.

Felix Morley had firm principles and a deft pen. He gave the editorial page élan and distinction and made it a topic of conversation, its pieces widely quoted. For editorials in 1935 Morley was awarded a Pulitzer Prize, the first ever for a POST writer. One editorial that impressed the judges, "A President Leaves His Party," followed the Supreme Court's unanimous nullification of NRA on May 27, 1935. The President told reporters that the Court had so limited the Constitution's commerce clause that that document had been turned back to "the horse and buggy days." Morley wrote that the President "definitely turned his back on the traditions and principles of his party and gave tremendous stimulus to the move for a complete political realignment in the United States."

With the NRA decision the Blue Eagle disappeared from page 1 of THE POST. The sharp-eared Clapper, who had picked up administration rumblings after earlier but less important decisions had gone against the New Deal, wrote on the day of the NRA judgment that "talk of blackjacking the court by enlarging its membership collapsed when all nine justices joined in the decision. That subterfuge of packing the court, a weak and uncertain one at best, becomes ridiculous to think of now." While the NRA went down 9 to 0 other New Deal and related state laws fell by narrower 5 to 4 and 6 to 3 decisions. Before the issue was joined, however, came the 1936 presidential election, a referendum on FDR himself.

On January 1, 1936, Ray Clapper left THE POST to write his column for the Scripps-Howard papers. In an all-too-rare act of journalism, THE POST announced his departure with regret and good wishes. Clapper's last column in the paper ended with praise of Meyer:

> He has never sought to influence the writer's interpretation, or to see the copy before it appeared in print the next morning. If he had seen this before it got into the paper, he might have broken his rule and killed it.

Clapper's departure left Franklyn Waltman as the paper's chief political writer and columnist as well as national news bureau chief. Waltman, who was to leave in another two years to be the Republican National Committee's publicity chief, was a first-rate reporter but his anti–New Deal bias frequently showed through.

The Meyers' dissatisfaction with FDR led them to look around for an alternative for 1936 and they found him in the person of Governor Alfred M. Landon of Kansas. Meyer stimulated first Clapper and then Waltman to write about this little-known figure. After a 1935 interview, Clapper wrote that Landon's "significance nationally is that he embodies in a warm, human, liberal outlook upon public affairs the hard-headed, practical business man who knows what it is to meet a pay-roll." Soon texts of Landon speeches began to appear in THE POST. In March 1936 the Meyers visited Topeka and Agnes wrote a full-page piece for "brains." She found Landon's "force not the boisterous, assertive kind" but "more nearly the easy stance of the skilled prize-fighter who does not waste an ounce of energy." In her 1953 autobiography Agnes claimed that she helped nominate Landon. However, by order of her husband, it was her last public campaign effort.

To the two 1936 conventions THE POST sent Waltman, Folliard (rehired in 1934), Albright, Bruner, and Olson, as well as Morley. The Meyers attended and Agnes wrote "the woman's angle." She found the GOP gathering a "man's world" with only 58 1/2 female votes out of 1003 while the Democrats allotted 219 votes to women with 300 alternates, all of them "starry-eyed with a new found happiness."

Albright was the platform specialist, as he would be in succeeding conventions through 1968; Waltman was the star in 1936. Morley was cooling on Landon but he pounded away at the New Deal: the Democratic platform represented "a new party." Elderman's cartoon buried the "Jeffersonian tradition — 1787–1936." Yet the fateful end of the Democratic rule requiring two-thirds for nomination passed without comment. When Roosevelt in his Franklin Field, Philadelphia, acceptance speech denounced the "economic royalists" and "their mercenaries," Waltman wrote that although it was "very moving and eloquent," it also was "the sort of speech which paves the way for fascism."

When Gallup's first postconvention poll gave FDR only 51.8 percent to Landon's 48.2 with an electoral majority for the Republican, an editorial said hopefully that the poll "clearly indicates the closest election since 1916." But FDR swamped Landon by a margin of more than 11 million votes, winning 531 electoral votes to Landon's 8. THE POST had endorsed no candidate; Meyer's rationale was that "the major part of our constituency does not vote" because most of the readers lived in the deprived District of Columbia. But the editorial slant was pro-Landon and anti-Roosevelt. The postelection editorial worried that "in trying to build hastily the President will construct nothing permanent but may on the contrary destroy past accomplishments of enormous value of which he often seems only faintly aware."

By chance, the sour note turned to sweet, at least for a moment. A visitor to Washington phoned THE POST the day after election to ask if there would be a public reception for FDR when he returned from Hyde Park. Nothing, in fact, had been planned. THE POST's public relations man, Charles F. Moore, Jr., seized on the idea, and the result was a last-minute, two-column page 1 call to action: LET'S GIVE THE PRESIDENT A REAL WELCOME! Next day, the paper recounted, "wearing an old suit and his irresistible smile, Franklin Delano Roosevelt yesterday rolled into the biggest, noisiest and most enthusiastic welcome the Capital ever gave any President." Some 200,000 turned out; FDR waved at Meyer standing in a POST window as his car passed down the Avenue.

For those at the top in the capital, 1937 got off to a gala start. Evalyn Walsh McLean gave her first New Year's party in many years with two orchestras and "trucks laden with champagne and other beverages" rumbling into Friendship. FDR had abolished the New Year's Day public reception but he was host at a White House dinner. Downtown, THE POST reported, "not since 1929, when Americans seemed a little demented, had there been such a hilarious New Year's celebration as Washington experienced last night." Waltman softened:

> As the year approached its end, most people had the feeling that it had, indeed, been a very good year — a year in which the country had its first real breathing spell after the rigors and horrors of the depression — had its first taste of the more abundant life.

The breathing spell did not last long. On Friday, February 5, Roosevelt startled the nation with his plan to "pack" the Supreme Court. Saturday's paper headlined: ROOSEVELT ASKS 6 NEW HIGH COURT JUDGES. THE POST plunged into the fight the next morning with a lead editorial, contending that the President's proposal "would paralyze the judicial arm as a separate and independent branch of government." Elderman drew a widely reprinted cartoon, blown up to an unusual five columns, of six smiling Roosevelts sitting behind the current "nine old men" on the Supreme Court bench.

Meyer and Morley were conservatives in the best sense of the term, not Neanderthals. When the Supreme Court struck down, 5 to 4, the New York law setting minimum wages for women workers, THE POST called it "an unfortunate decision," adding that "such an attitude will give unfortunate encouragement to those critics of the Court who are seeking to curb its powers." After the NRA, with its section 7(a) providing the right under each industrial code for employees to organize and bargain collectively, was declared unconstitutional, Congress passed the Wagner Act reinstating and strengthening those rights. THE POST called it "a bad law because it tries to secure for workers rights and privileges that they should obtain for themselves. Furthermore, it assumes that labor needs to be protected against the unfair practices of employers, but makes no provision for safeguarding employers against unfair union tactics."

Making use of that act, John L. Lewis' new Committee for the Industrial Organization began to organize auto and steel workers. THE POST left most of the reporting to the wire services; the national news staff simply was too small, lacked a labor reporter, and was not given the funds to range around the nation. Editorially, the paper called the auto sit-down strikes "patently illegal," but it also declared that "if our industrial leaders had listened more tolerantly in the past to the reasonable demands of organized labor for recognition, instead of trying to suppress spontaneous organizing movements by overt and insidious means, they would not now be menaced by these irresponsible guerrilla tactics." When General Motors signed up with the United Auto Workers, THE POST applauded; it did so again when United States Steel amazed the nation by accepting the CIO steel union.

Many anti–New Dealers attacked the Wagner Act in the courts. By the time FDR sprang his "court packing" plan it was questionable whether the law could win majority approval and the uncertainty increased pressure for the President's proposal. Meyer, not a lawyer and unaware of the unwritten rule that reporters do not ask Supreme Court justices about pending matters, suggested to Waltman that he go see Justice Owen J. Roberts. Waltman did nothing until Meyer said he would go himself. Waltman then saw Roberts who sent him to Chief Justice Hughes. The result was a series of POST articles, under Waltman's by-line and with a special "copyright" line to add authority. The series demonstrated, with figures supplied by but not attributed to Hughes, that the Court was not behind in its work, one of FDR's stated reasons for adding new justices.

The Court subsequently upheld the Wagner Act, 5 to 4, and it reversed itself on minimum-wage powers of the states. In each case Hughes and Roberts provided the critical swing votes. Of the wage case THE POST said the decision "should help terminate, once and for all, the idle charge that the court has arrogated to itself the use of super-legislative powers." On the Wagner Act decision the paper commented that while this and other decisions "give to the Federal Government a power over autocratic industrial policies which heretofore it has never securely achieved," they "destroy the last vestige of effective argument for the President's proposal to pack the court." Such was the tortuous pull and haul on the conservative Merlo Pusey, author of the bulk of the "court packing" editorials.

The Court battle was so intense and all-consuming that reporters covering other stories sought a related angle. Povich's lead on the opening game of the 1937 baseball season, at which FDR threw out the first ball: "By another one of those close decisions, 4 to 3, President Roosevelt saw another one of his pet projects, the Washington ball club, lose yesterday." As the crowd watched that day, an anti-Roosevelt lobbyist flew over Griffith Stadium, his plane trailing a chain of huge letters: "Play the game. Don't pack the court."

Gallup reported that the public favored by 64 percent to 34 a constitutional amendment requiring justices to retire at some age between 70 and 75. Six of the nine then were over 70, including all four of the ultraconservatives. On May 18 one of the four, Willis Van Devanter, age 78 with 26 years on the Court, announced his retirement. Waltman wrote that "the opinion is widespread that only an adverse decision by the court on the Social Security program can now save" the "court packing" program. A few days later that law also won approval, 7 to 2 and 5 to 4 on different sections. On July 23 the Senate formally killed FDR's plan. THE POST's victory editorial called for "restraint" and assumed that "Congress will now play a more important role in shaping the policies of the Nation."

Roosevelt supporters felt he had lost the battle but won the war; New Deal legislation now was winning Court approval and FDR appointments — there were five in the second term after none in the first — assured a liberal court for decades. THE POST felt a great constitutional principle had been saved. For the paper it had been the most powerful and effective campaign since the previous owner had helped defeat the League of Nations.

THE POST, however, was appalled when Roosevelt picked Senator Hugo L. Black of Alabama for the Van Devanter vacancy. An editorial said the nominee "combined lack of training on the one hand and extreme partisanship on the other." The day the nomination reached the Capitol, Waltman wrote that "there were some references in Senate corridors to the widespread reports which have persisted for 11 years that the liberal Alabaman was elected to the Senate as a candidate of the Ku Klux Klan." After Black's confirmation his Klan membership was established. THE POST thundered that "he cannot possibly take the oath." Elderman drew a klansman sitting behind the Supreme Court bench. On October 1 Black admitted his past membership but THE POST was unyielding: ". . . it is not entirely the fact that Hugo L. Black was a member of the Klan which makes him unfit to be on the court. More accurately, the traits which today make him unfit for the court made him years ago join the Klan for what he thought he could get out of it." Black said no more, took his seat, and went on to write one of the most distinguished records in Court history, generally praised in subsequent POST editorials.

Despite bitter POST-FDR differences over the Court plan and the Black appointment, the President, on the paper's 60th anniversary in December 1937, wrote a congratulatory letter to Meyer expressing the hope that "as *The Post* goes on from decade to decade it will ever uphold the noblest traditions of American journalism and thereby serve the highest interests of the community and the Nation."

The bitterness of the Court fight was deepened by the President's futile effort in 1938 to "purge" his party of several leading conservatives. THE POST saw the purge coming; a May 29 editorial reported "indications" that FDR was "out to purge his conglomerate party of all who have shown any spirit of independence." Three days later Maryland Representative David J. Lewis, a faithful FDR supporter, announced after a White House visit that he would run against Senator Millard E. Tydings, described in the story as "long a critic of Administration policies." On June 25 the paper's eight-column banner read: ROOSEVELT TELLS U.S. HE'LL AID "LIBERAL" CANDIDATES. The purge was on.

THE POST concentrated on the Tydings race and the Georgia primary where FDR sought to unseat Senator Walter F. George. Elderman cartoons showed FDR stabbing George in the back and FDR facing himself in a "legislative" mirror and saying "All in favor of the bill raise hands," which the President was doing. The purge was a disastrous political flop; only one FDR target, a New York House member, lost his seat. Moreover, in the midterm election the Republicans picked up 8 Senate and 81 House seats. A Republican–Southern Democrat coalition emerged and the New Deal, for all practical purposes, in domestic affairs, had come to an end after six exciting, and exhausting, years.

THE POST, read every morning by both FDR's supporters and his enemies, was naturally criticized by the former. Senator Sherman Minton, the Indiana Democrat whom President Truman would appoint to the Supreme Court, introduced a bill on April 29, 1938, making it a felony "to publish as a fact anything known to be false." He cited THE POST for "a fine exhibition of propaganda in the newspapers" because it had charged a government agency with abuse of the franking privilege. An editorial called this "fascist legislation"; it got nowhere.

Editorially, THE POST had fought Roosevelt time and again on both recovery and reform measures, often with strong words. But it never stooped to the personal attacks of the club-car crowd who so delighted in FDR's polio affliction and related it to everything they hated about the man. Curiously, Eleanor Roosevelt, the most energetic of first ladies, appeared in THE POST's pages more as an accompanying wife than as an activist, perhaps because THE POST regularly assigned no woman reporter to her as other papers did.

THE POST's posture on FDR's personal life reflected Eugene Meyer's own code of conduct. Federal Diary columnist Jerry Kluttz never forgot the time he told his publisher that he had heard of FDR's dalliance with Lucy Mercer Rutherfurd and of the extramarital activities of some of FDR's sons. Meyer heard him out,

> puffing away on his cigar, clearing his throat and spitting every 30 seconds or so. I could tell he was furious . . . He looked me in the eye and measured every word. It went along this line:
>
> "Mr. Kluttz, you must understand very clearly that *The Post* will never use any stories such as those you mentioned that would bring disrespect upon the President of the United States, and particularly in a time like this when we are looking to the President for leadership. I personally believe no representative of *The Post* should engage in such filthy and untrue stories . . . If we destroy the President, we destroy ourselves."

The turbulent New Deal years coincided with Meyer's initial efforts to build his newspaper. He personally solicited subscriptions from the driver of each taxi he rode in, and when Justice Douglas phoned to complain he was not receiving his paper regularly, Meyer investigated

POST distribution all over the suburban Silver Spring, Maryland, area where Douglas then lived. Circulation problems seemed continuous; in 16 years the paper ran through 13 circulation managers. By day and at night, sometimes in dinner jacket, the publisher roamed the E Street building — pressroom, circulation department, business office, printers' floor as well as the city room. Once when Meyer appeared in the city room a young reporter, Edward F. Ryan, who had never met him asked the apparent caller: "Can I help you?" The reply: "You are helping me." Once Meyer even shot craps with reporters. Ed McSweeney, a financial writer, dubbed him "Butch" and the nickname stuck to the end of his life. Meyer knew about it, though he didn't hear it to his face, and took it for what it was — a term of affection.

In a March 5, 1935, speech, the publisher drew up a set of principles for his paper:

> The first mission of a newspaper is to tell the truth as nearly as the truth can be ascertained.
>
> The newspaper shall tell *ALL* the truth so far as it can learn it, concerning the important affairs of America and the world.
>
> As a disseminator of news, the paper shall observe the decencies that are obligatory upon a private gentleman.
>
> What it prints shall be fit reading for the young as well as for the old.
>
> The newspaper's duty is to its readers and to the public at large, and not to the private interests of its owners.
>
> In the pursuit of truth, the newspaper shall be prepared to make sacrifices of its material fortunes, if such a course be necessary for the public good.
>
> The newspaper shall not be the ally of any special interest, but shall be fair and free and wholesome in its outlook on public affairs and public men.

In a separate guide for the editorial page Meyer many years later listed four principles: a belief in constitutional government; a belief that the civil liberties of all are best defended by protecting the civil liberties of each individual; a belief that an expanding free economy will best satisfy the material needs of the people; and a belief that in the nuclear age international cooperation is the only sane policy.

It was easier, however, to draft such general principles than for Meyer, a man of great wealth used to having his commands obeyed, to accept the peculiar nature of the newspaper business. Some found him gruff or brutally frank, others thought him patronizing, unfeeling toward subordinates. On one occasion Meyer held a staff meeting, at the suggestion of reporter Robert DeVore, during a Newspaper Guild negotiation. But the publisher's idea of frankness produced only snorts: he told the assembled staff that "we must all make sacrifices" and, as for himself, he had forgone his usual trip to Europe that year and "you should realize that I have made no addition to my collection of French Impressionists since I bought *The Post.*" As Morley noted, "It was an audience where more were interested in money than Monet."

On taking over the paper Meyer had canceled the 15 percent wage cut that the bankruptcy receiver had ordered. But in 1935 he raised a storm with an order that before making promotions or giving salary increases the managing editor must clear it with the new business executive, Donald M. Bernard. The managing editor, William Haggard, and 11 others, fearing business office control over journalistic freedom, threatened to walk out and in the end did so. By then the Newspaper Guild, just getting started nationally, had been organized at THE POST; there long had been contractual relations with the mechanical unions.

In late 1936, after discussion with the Guild, Meyer posted a statement of wages, hours, and working conditions: a $25 weekly minimum for reporters, rewrite men, and photographers, rising to $50 after three years' experience; a 40-hour week with compensatory time off for overtime; two weeks' vacation, a week's sick leave, and a minimum of two weeks' notice in case of dismissal. The first Guild contract was signed on June 11, 1938. Meyer, however, was adamant on the Guild's recurring requests for a closed shop because he opposed efforts "to impose involuntary obligations upon his employees."

At times it seemed amazing that the paper ever got printed. The old building shook and the lights flickered each evening as the presses, popularly believed to be held together by baling wire, began to roll. The second-floor city room, easier to reach by steep stairs than by the single rickety elevator cage, was jammed with desks and by ten o'clock was full of cigarette smoke. In the morning reporters wiped inky dust from typewriters. Acid from the engraving room dripped through the ceiling into the small "morgue," or library. Reporters and deskmen could still get away with drinking on the job; one editor who hid his in a popular mouthwash bottle was famous for his repeated gargling. An electrician and his girl, having a tryst on the roof, crashed through a skylight into the printers' proof room.

As much as anyone John Riseling, who served as both day and night city editor, held the news shop together and trained the cubs. A small, slight, and totally imperturbable veteran from the McLean era, Riseling knew the city block by block. When night's work was done, he often would ride the fire trucks or police cars. Riseling once was confronted by a squad of angry spit-and-polish marines, come to complain that a tongue-in-cheek story had cast aspersions on their corps' bravery. Riseling avoided what he clearly anticipated to be mayhem by phoning the officer of the day at the Quantico, Virginia, barracks to explain that a retraction would only spread the story. At the major's verbal phone order, the marines departed in peace. The early Meyer years often seemed madcap but bonhomie prevailed as conviction grew that THE POST would make it.

The publisher indulged in various devices to hold down the paper's expenses. Editor Morley was given a $15,000 no-interest loan to pay off a house mortgage and he was helped in creating a retirement fund. Not until just before World War II did he get a salary boost, to $15,000 a year. Nor was Morley the only one aided by the publisher in a personal capacity. On occasion Meyer paid out of his own pocket bills for some POST expenditure he wanted but which already had been vetoed by business office subordinates he had told to hold down costs.

More than two years of initial turmoil in the news operation came to an end in November 1935, when Alexander F. (Casey) Jones, city editor of the Milwaukee *Journal,* became the new managing editor. He held the post for 12 years to Meyer's great satisfaction. Casey was a gravel-voiced conservative of Welsh descent who constantly twisted his right eyebrow. He had the instincts of the "Front Page" school of journalism. *Fortune* magazine once described him as "cyclonic, convivial, incurably romantic about his profession." A subeditor felt that "his leadership tended to be exercised more by bursts of rage than by analysis of the news." Casey liked the flashy story and he soon began to brighten THE POST. He had an acute sense of "hard" news and knew how to display it, but he disdained the intellectual approach; he told reporters to avoid "interpretive writing" and instead to "write what the man said." When he took over, Sir Willmott Lewis, the London *Times* correspondent, shook his head and said: "Don't you know, old boy, that Pennsylvania Avenue is paved with the bones of former managing editors of *The Post?*"

Given the tight budget on which he operated, Casey Jones ran his shop with success. The big names — Thurston, Clapper, and finally Waltman — had departed or soon would; Jones fell back on Eddie Folliard, his kind of reporter, Bill Nessly, Bob Albright, and a handful of others on the national staff, and an ever-changing cast of local reporters, all of whom greatly respected his professionalism. On occasion, Jones himself wrote a story, usually on "hard" news such as the coming of transatlantic air service. Morale improved after Jones' arrival as THE POST began to pull itself up from the depths of its bankruptcy.

One contributor who filled many columns, often to the dismay of staffers fighting for the limited space, was Agnes Meyer. Just out of Barnard College she had broken into the hitherto all-male newsroom of the New York *Sun,* at $5-a-column space rate. Often at odds with her husband both personally and on policy, Agnes wrote spasmodically of her friend, novelist Thomas Mann, and his works, did interviews with John Dewey and Alexis Carrel, reviewed art books — she helped establish the Freer Gallery in Washington — and on occasion managed to get the full text of her own speeches into the pages of THE POST. Casey Jones often found himself caught between wifely pressure to publish and husbandly advice to resist. She promoted, and the paper for five years sponsored, an annual National Folk Festival. She also got the paper to run a series of photographs with text on "How a Baby Grows" by the pioneering Dr. Arnold Gesell.

THE POST's editorial page shone, the news was better edited (if all too much provided by the wire services), the paper twice won awards in the Ayer Cup contest for typographical excellence. It had 1700 employees on the first anniversary of Meyer's ownership when a former newspaper publisher, Senator Arthur H. Vandenberg of Michigan, wrote that it "has registered the most amazing improvement in the past twelve months ever to come to my attention."

Circulation rose from the dubious 50,000 at the Meyer takeover to the 100,000 range by 1938. By the end of that year THE POST's advertising surpassed that of the *Times, Herald,* and *News* but was still less than half the *Star*'s much higher cost linage. Advertising Director Bernard early on added a Friday food page to cajole grocery advertisers. Space was aggressively sold by Jack B. Sacks who rose to advertising manager during his 30-year career. The advertising department had to foot the food editor's salary (and a fashion editor's, too) because Jones refused to pay it from his budget. The ad staff had the laugh on Jones when a food page recipe for oysters won the paper's first national award. By 1934 the Sunday paper once again exceeded 100 pages.

In mid-1936 Meyer came close to buying the rival morning *Herald,* owned by Hearst and edited by Cissy Patterson, for something over $600,000. But Cissy talked Hearst out of the sale by lending him a million dollars and then leasing both his *Herald* and *Times* with an option to buy. She exercised the option in early 1939 and merged the two into the 24-hour *Times-Herald* with morning, evening, and Sunday editions. The competition had been fierce; it now grew fiercer. Nobody in Washington made money but the good, gray *Star.*

THE POST's reputation, however, was slowly improving within the journalistic profession. In 1937 Leo Rosten published *The Washington Correspondents,* a book based on research done the previous two years. A poll of 99 Washington correspondents found the New York *Times* considered far in the lead as the "most fair and reliable paper." The *Star* ranked fifth, THE POST only eighth. The "least fair and reliable" list was led by the Hearst papers in general, which included the *Herald* and *Times.* THE POST was seventh, the *Star* was not named. In short, nearly as many still rated THE POST as unfair and unreliable as they did the reverse.

THE POST's deficits were massive: $323,588 for the last half of 1933 after Meyer took over; $1,191,597 in 1934; $1,279,262 in 1935; $857,156 in 1936; and $838,937 in 1937. "One year," Meyer later remarked to a friend, paying THE POST losses "took more than my entire income." To another he said: "No one is rich enough to keep that up." But not only did Meyer keep on paying the losses, he plunged ahead to improve his paper.

On June 14, 1938, to mark the fifth anniversary of his ownership, Meyer announced with fanfare in the paper and on radio that THE POST, in agreement with the New York *Herald Tribune* Syndicate, would now carry the columns of Walter Lippmann, Dorothy Thompson, Mark Sullivan, book reviewer Lewis Gannett, theater critic Richard Watts, and others, 15 features in all including "cable correspondence from abroad" by the *Herald Tribune*'s first-rate staffers around the world. (THE POST had a few regular contributors from abroad but no overseas staffer for another 19 years.) THE POST was lucky; the *Star* had been offered the *Herald Tribune* package first but refused to buy it all. Meyer never hesitated.

Lippmann, whose name was misspelled in both the announcement headline and story by omitting the final "n," cabled Meyer from Europe that "you have made an honest, competent and liberal newspaper. Am happy in joining you." The addition of his column made THE POST required reading for the serious. In his subsequent three decades of association with THE POST, Lippmann was a quiet but constant prodder, at owners, editors, and reporters alike to strive for excellence.

By now THE POST was developing an "op-ed page," the page opposite the editorial page, for its columnists and features. The *Herald Tribune* writers appeared there along with Westbrook Pegler, who had switched from sports to general commentary, and Barnet Nover, a new editorial writer and foreign affairs commentator. Before long the commentary in the paper was superior to the news presentation, at least in what it told readers about the more complex issues of the prewar years, especially foreign affairs.

Barely a month after the acquisition of Lippmann, Meyer added another writer: Ernest K. Lindley of the *Herald Tribune* staff. Meyer told Lindley he wanted a New Deal columnist. Lindley was not eager to be tagged as such a spokesman and prided himself on his GOP connections; nonetheless, he agreed on the understanding that Meyer would stress his independence. Thus he was described in a page 1 box as "an admirer of the aims and policies" of President Roosevelt but one who also was "an objective reporter with unusual insight and broad experience." Lindley, who had come to Washington from Albany when FDR did, had invaluable pipelines into the New Deal, especially the White House, that no one on THE POST possessed. The result was that inside administration news often appeared in Lindley's columns, whereas in the past it had made page 1 under the by-lines of Thurston, Clapper, and Waltman. In 1939 Meyer added Hearst's International News Service and King Features when Cissy Patterson, in a moment of pique, threw them out of her paper. The publisher didn't even ask the price before agreeing.

Washington of the New Deal years was a boom town. Federal employment jumped from 63,000 at the time of FDR's first inauguration to 93,000 in 1935 and 166,000 by mid-1940. In addition the recision, in two steps in 1934 and 1935, of the last 10 percent of depression pay cuts generated more prosperity in the capital than in any other major city.

Georgetown swiftly changed from a largely rundown Negro section to a haven for young New Dealers who delighted in refurbishing the houses they found so quaint. The vast Federal Triangle complex of 12 government buildings, begun in 1928, was completed in 1938. Yet office space pressure was so great that the National Institutes of Health and the Naval Medical Center were built in Bethesda, Maryland, creating by 1941 a new satellite area in what had been a sleepy town.

These developments, when they were noted at all, were no more than routine news in THE POST. Most important in local coverage was the city's annual budget struggle with Congress. As always in the past, a handful of congressmen effectively ruled the city in money matters. Representative Thomas L. Blanton, the Texas Democrat so long a thorn, now chaired the District appropriations subcommittee; when he cut the federal payment below the 40 percent of the total budget legally required, THE POST shouted HEIL BLANTON! and said that "the local schools have been denied adequate funds, public health has been cruelly neglected, utility regulation is being slowly strangled and police protection is jeopardized." In 1936 when Blanton was forced into a run-off primary the paper cheered this welcome news for Washington "where the word 'Blantonism' has come to signify loudmouthed self-advertisement and arbitrary disregard of the first principles of self-government." When he lost the run-off and thus his House seat, he wrote THE POST a "You win. I lose" and no-hard-feelings letter, displayed on page 1.

Before he lost, however, Blanton had harassed the city's schoolteachers with what came to be known as "the red rider." This was a rider to a money bill, the idea of Blanton's superior, Appropriations Committee Chairman Clarence Cannon of Missouri, that forbade payment of salary to any instructor "teaching or advocating communism" in the schools.

When Superintendent Frank W. Ballou asked the city's legal officer what he should do, Corporation Counsel E. Barrett Prettyman ruled that, while "any shadow of favor or support of communism" was forbidden, "the mere recitation or study of factual data" was permissible. The Board of Education, 6 to 2, backed Prettyman's stand. THE POST applauded but letters to the editor were divided. Then Comptroller General J. Raymond McCarl, an instrument of Congress, swept aside the Prettyman ruling.

THE POST assailed McCarl's edict, declaring that "this insult to the patriotism of Washington's teachers can not be entirely wiped out until the Legislature repeals a clause showing such offensive lack of faith in the strength of American institutions." Mrs. Roosevelt, always interested in the city's schools, conjured up for reporters the vision of a teacher saying: "Here is an area two times the size of the United States. It is lived in by people called Russians," and letting it go at that until some student asked: "What kind of government do they live under?" Then, said Mrs. Roosevelt, it might be necessary for the teacher to say: "My dear, I cannot tell you."

Teachers signed an oath to get paid. THE POST hammered away at the "red rider" and at "witch burners" who scrutinized schoolbooks for signs of communism. In 1937 the House rejected outright repeal of the rider. Instead, it adopted and the Senate later accepted a "pink rider" substitute offered by Representative John W. McCormick of Massachusetts, who later became Speaker. This banned payment to teachers "advocating communism or treating any such doctrine with favor or support."

Teachers, at least, had jobs. While government employment rapidly increased, the city depended on New Deal relief and recovery agencies to help the less fortunate. Public Works Administrator and Interior Secretary Harold L. Ickes handed out the first checks to workmen repaving upper 16th Street in the fall of 1933. Soon 14,500 were on Civil Works Administration rolls, some of them to plant elms on the Mall and elsewhere. WPA workers helped improve the National Zoo. Federal funds were used to complete electrification of the Pennsylvania Railroad line to New York and to air-condition government buildings. In 1937 the WPA's Federal Writers' Project produced the monumental WPA guide to Washington, one of a series of American guides and one of a very few WPA efforts that won POST praise.

Much of the relief money went to the city's blacks. A 1934 editorial commented that "in good times and bad Washington is a haven for distressed colored people from the South" and noted that "75 percent of the families on relief here are Negro." It was about this time that the word Negro began to be capitalized in the paper; however, racial identifications in crime stories and in classified and real estate ads remained the rule for nearly two more decades. Likewise THE POST took for granted the continuation of the city's dual school system and the exclusion of blacks from most places of public accommodation.

On race, Meyer's POST thus far was benighted. The status of Washington Negroes was never the subject of investigative reporting; disgraceful facts appeared only when some report or prominent person mentioned them. The sports section ignored the great Satchel Paige though he often packed Griffith Stadium when he pitched in a Negro league. But the mass baptisms of blacks in a tank in the same stadium was news. The one POST avenue for helping Negroes was through slum clearance but the paper's efforts to get more money out of Congress were largely unsuccessful. Shockingly, THE POST took no editorial part in the national furor in 1939 when the famous Negro contralto Marian Anderson was barred from singing in the Daughters of the American Revolution's Constitution Hall. When she did sing on Easter Sunday before 75,000 at the Lincoln Memorial, Folliard reported that "the crowd roared its acclaim for the colored girl." She was 37; Folliard's choice of the word "girl" undoubtedly reflected the state of mind of most of the POST staff.

Washington had two adjacent and partially connected airports, near where the Pentagon now stands. The two fields, divided by Military Road, were called Washington and Hoover. Both were inadequate; a traffic light halted automobiles whenever a plane took off. THE POST, with Felix Cotten writing a flood of stories, campaigned loud and long for a new airport. The Army Engineers, in dredging a Potomac River channel, used the fill to build up what became known as Gravelly Point, site of the present Washington National Airport. From 1935 to 1938, as the work went on, Congress dallied over whether to locate a new airport on the filled land. In 1938 FDR recounted that he had dreamed of a terrible plane crash at Washington Airport and he was so moved by the experience that he acted to locate the new field at Gravelly

Point. Financed by WPA and PWA funds and providing nearly 5000 jobs, the airport, costing $15 million, opened for business on June 16, 1941.

In the New Deal years Washington was magnificently lively; the White House was the center around which all revolved and the working press shared in the White House fun. The Roosevelts, until the war, held an annual spring reception for the hundreds of newsmen and their families. FDR sat in an East Room chair shaking hands and chatting; Eleanor sometimes led a Conga line or the Virginia Reel; the gardens and the roof over the east wing were open to strollers. One POST White House reporter, George Bookman, and his date were still enjoying such a party at 2 A.M. when Mrs. Roosevelt said sweetly but pointedly, "Isn't it a little late for ice cream?"

The large Roosevelt clan provided never-ending news. A 1934 POST society-page item reported that "the swift-moving Roosevelts with their flair for informality have left hidebound society groggy." THE POST's women's pages, especially on Sundays, were expanded; the paper's new rule, publicized in a 1934 house advertisement, was that this part of the paper was "written by women for women." The pages were run by Malvina Lindsay who also wrote The Gentler Sex, a column of humor and satire without malice. There were other columns called The Merry Whirl and Top Hats and Tiaras. The author of the latter, paid $5 a column, was Betty Beale who later at the *Star* became one of the city's leading purveyors of social chitchat and hard news items gleaned on the party circuit. The social whirl in THE POST of this period was spotlessly white.

Without question the best read and most successful feature of the women's pages throughout the Meyer era was Mary Haworth's Mail. The column sprang from Meyer's long interest in psychology and psychiatry, and he saw it as an effort to use these tools to enhance the everyday lives of POST readers. Elizabeth Young, a $25-a-week reporter, began to write This Business of Living under the Haworth pseudonym. Meyer liked it and gave it the "Mail" title in 1936 after the column had begun to produce a torrent of letters which she answered in print. The column, written "with an astringent Irish wit," provided a free psychiatrist's couch for the capital though it directed many a reader to professionals as well as to clergymen. Mary Haworth's Mail soon was nationally syndicated.

Also expanded in the early Meyer years was the coverage of theater, art, books, and other aspects of the city's growing cultural life. Nelson B. Bell wrote of both stage and movies from 1927 until Richard L. Coe arrived in 1938 to help with films. Ray C. B. Brown, an accomplished pianist, brought to THE POST in 1933 by Meyer, covered music for 13 years, writing reviews and a Postlude column. Both the paper and the Meyers were strong supporters of the new National Symphony Orchestra. In 1935 the orchestra began a series of concerts at the river's edge behind the Lincoln Memorial, playing in a floating bandshell. To this locale, the original Watergate, soon came a crowd "dressed in flannels and ginghams and bathing suits. The bathing suits came in canoes." The first 1939 "sunset symphony" drew 20,000, among them FDR in a parked car at the top of the slope.

The premier cultural news of New Deal years was the 1936 gift by Andrew Mellon of the National Gallery of Art, both the building and his collection of paintings and sculpture. THE POST had been campaigning for an art gallery and it was enthusiastic about the Mellon gift. Mellon, incidentally, once tried to buy THE POST. In 1936 he offered to pay whatever Meyer had lost on the paper plus $1 million. Meyer replied: "Mr. Mellon, I didn't buy it to sell it." But he answered "certainly" when Mellon asked for "the first opportunity" if Meyer ever decided to sell. He never did.

Eugene Meyer was no more a sports fan than a comic strip reader; but once again he learned, and early on. A few days after he took over THE POST the Senators were in first place, headed toward their third — and last — American League pennant. The paper's scoreboard again was providing play-by-play accounts. As the race grew exciting Meyer was captivated; occasionally he helped run the copy from the Western Union telegrapher to the scoreboard operator. At one critical moment he handed word of the play to a copyboy with the admonition: "Wait until I can get to a window so I can see the fans' happy faces."

By now the great Walter Johnson was managing the Cleveland Indians. In July 28,000 crowded Griffith Stadium for a double-header. "They came to see Walter Johnson and they stayed to cheer the Nats" who won both games, Povich wrote. The Senators won the pennant, eight games ahead of the hated Yankees. They lost the first two World Series games in New York to the Giants but came home to triumph, 4 to 0, with Roosevelt throwing out the first ball. Meyer and his wife took a box with assorted guests including the British ambassador. The society page recorded, in a rare mention of the owner's wife, that Agnes "wore a smart costume of brown tweed with a three-quarter-length coat and a small brown hat." But the Giants took the final two games, both in extra innings. In 1934 Meyer asked Povich why the Senators were doing so badly; Povich explained they needed a good pitcher. "How much would it cost to buy one?" the publisher asked, suggesting he would put up

$50,000. Povich had to tell him this was not the way organized baseball worked.

THE POST's sports department had such syndicated columnists as Westbrook Pegler, Paul Gallico, Damon Runyon, and Bob Considine. For nearly four decades Walter Haight covered racing meets including 37 consecutive Kentucky Derbys. Boxing, especially with the rise of Joe Louis, got a big play and THE POST trumpeted an extra when Lewis knocked out Maxie Baer in their 1935 Yankee Stadium fight. That year the paper began an "early sports" edition, on the street at 8:45 P.M.

On September 16, 1937, "Big League football and 24,492 customers came to Griffith Stadium," as Povich put it. George Preston Marshall, a local laundry operator, had brought his team, the Redskins, from Boston. The Skins were a great success, inaugurating a new sport for the capital that in time would eclipse baseball and all other sports. The Skins' first hero was Slingin' Sammy Baugh; "glory fairly dripped from the lean, lank Texas kid." The Skins won the eastern division playoff the first year. Owner Marshall began to object to Povich's accounts and tried to get him fired. Managing Editor Jones told him, "You run your goddamn Redskins and I'll run *The Washington Post.*"

The journalistic world into which Eugene Meyer plunged in mid-1933 was concerned, above all, with the economic relief of Americans and recovery of their national fortunes. Yet almost from the beginning of the new regime at THE POST the paper inescapably faced, as Franklin Roosevelt already had begun to face, the world across the seas.

On October 11 THE POST ran a United Press story on page 7 about a book to be published next day in the United States with the English title *My Battle.* The one-column headline: ENVOY OF GOD TO CRUSH JEWS, HITLER'S CLAIM. It was a long time before many Americans took *Mein Kampf* seriously but they soon learned some of the things the one-time Austrian army corporal was up to. On October 15 the lead page 1 five-column headline read: HITLER BOLTS ARMS PARLEY, QUITS LEAGUE, RALLIES NATION; U.S. BACKS ALLIES IN CRISIS.

That part of the headline which said the United States "backs allies" was misleading; a few cautious words of encouragement, no more, were all the Roosevelt administration dared. The United States was still trapped in the isolationist vise. An editorial page paragraph put it succinctly: "The popular American chorus: 'Hands Off Across the Seas.' " The editorial page was still under holdover Bennett; Morley's arrival soon afterward improved the paper's perception of events in Europe and Asia, but editorial calls for American action were a long time in coming. Meyer himself set the paper's tone the next April, in a speech declaring that "in foreign relations we are neither for extreme nationalism nor extreme internationalism."

Morley long had considered the Versailles Treaty terms "intolerable stigmas" and thus he made no protest when Hitler scrapped that document. "The only ultimate alternative," he wrote in a March 18, 1935, editorial, "to acceptance of German equality is another war designed completely to destroy and dismember that nation. And that would involve collapse of the remainder of European civilization." Hitler's attacks on both Jews and the Catholic Church, however, were condemned as "Germany's back-to-barbarism movement." Stalin's purges were reported although their extent was far from evident to POST readers from the skimpy wire service stories. When Stalin in 1936 proclaimed his new constitution, THE POST let its hopes outrun its judgment. The headline: SOVIETS SET UP A DEMOCRACY GIVING PEOPLE WIDE LIBERTY.

There was one dramatic foreign story that riveted American attention: the constitutional crisis in 1936 created by the determination of the new British monarch, bachelor Edward VIII, to marry an American, Mrs. Wallis Warfield Simpson. THE POST printed a notable journalistic scoop on October 17:

> King Edward VIII of Great Britain plans to marry the glamorous American, Mrs. Ernest ("Wally") Simpson, *The Post* learned last night. He may not be able to make the erstwhile Baltimore belle his Queen, but he is determined to make her his wife, even if it costs him his throne.

Folliard wrote the story but the news came from Meyer who never thereafter ceased to boast about his coup as a reporter. At the time he had as his houseguest Lord Lothian, later the British ambassador in Washington, and the conversation produced enough information and hints to inspire the widely reprinted story. The British press was operating under a self-imposed gag on the romance though American papers printed every possible scrap of rumor or fact.

In the spring of 1937 Congress passed a new neutrality act, permitting the President to prohibit American ships from carrying goods to belligerents and thus abandoning the historic freedom-of-the-seas doctrine. Spain was in the midst of its civil war although foreign participation as yet was little known. An editorial condemned Franco's "rebel planes" which had "systematically and ruthlessly bombarded unfortified towns such as Guernica, the ancient Basque capital."

In this atmosphere the Meyers, in May 1937, went to Europe taking Morley with them. During their joint interviews of European leaders Morley was irked by Meyer's habit of expressing his own opinions rather than following the journalistic practice of trying to extract views and information. Since Meyer, as Morley later put it, "for all his keen thinking, was congenitally unable to write a single paragraph of comprehensible newspaper English," the editor had to "compose [stories for THE POST] to satisfy both." Furthermore, Meyer refused to visit Germany because of the Nazi persecution of the Jews. Morley, who did go there, was "disposed to think the police-state stories somewhat exaggerated."

Then, "in a frank discussion on the return trip the publisher accused his editor of undue resistance to the former's ideas. To this I replied tartly that if a Yes-man had been wanted I was a poor selection. The breeze blew over quickly and probably revealed, more than anything else, the anxieties which both men were bringing back." As Meyer's biographer Merlo Pusey, then an editorial writer, explained it years later, Meyer was "ready to move wherever logic and reason might dictate to save Western civilization from fascism." But "Morley's Quaker background would not allow him to pursue his passion for international cooperation to the point of supporting war."

Despite these differences, Morley enjoyed freedom to write his convictions on the editorial page. One editorial well expressed the American dichotomy: "No people is more fanatically isolationist than ours. We cling desperately to the belief that we can, with safety, ignore any and all developments abroad. But in our heart of hearts we know that this is an illusion."

Then, on October 6, 1937, reporter Waltman wrote from Chicago: "In perhaps the most momentous utterance of his career, President Roosevelt today suggested that peace-loving nations of the world take concerted action to quarantine international aggressors." Morley's response was an editorial displayed on page 1, declaring that "the effects of this speech . . . are certain to be momentous . . . The speech ends, for all time it may be hoped, the flabby, vicious, humiliating doctrine that America can see no difference between a ruthless aggressor and the innocent victim of his aggression."

But Morley's was a rare voice of approval. So negative was the outcry that FDR never made explicit what had been implicit. "It is a terrible thing," FDR would later say privately, "to look over your shoulder when you are trying to lead — and to find no one there." Aggression continued. "As long as this nation contents itself with the tactics of the ostrich," lamented a later editorial, "the cause of peace will be more rather than less uncertain."

The Japanese captured and sacked Nanking and their planes sank the American gunboat *Panay* in the Yangtze River. Next came Hitler's conquest of Austria and the Munich Pact dismembering Czechoslovakia. Such dramatic foreign news, from both the wire services and New York *Herald Tribune* correspondents, finally shoved aside domestic matters. At THE POST two young reporters wrote numerous long, and often perceptive, articles about the developing crises: Hedley Donovan, who succeeded Henry Luce as head of the *Time* empire, and John B. Oakes, who became the New York *Times* editorial page chief.

In his first column in THE POST Walter Lippmann wrote from Paris on July 5, 1938: "Barring incidents which cannot be foreseen . . . there would seem then to be no great probability of war in the near future . . . Neither Germany, nor her uneasy partner Italy, has the resources to conduct a great war." But Dorothy Thompson, in her POST debut in September, was more perceptive: "Today the world trembles on the brink of war."

Morley agonized. When Britain's Chamberlain and France's Daladier began the surrender to Hitler, the editor sought to strike an affirmative note. He drafted an editorial, showed it to Meyer, discussed it with Secretary Hull, and consulted British, French, Russian, and German diplomats. To many readers the editorial, titled "A Turning Point," was a shocker when it appeared on September 30 after the Munich Pact. "After three weeks for which history shows no parallel," wrote Morley, "constructive choice is being made. War is averted. Peace, at least temporarily, is confirmed." Morley argued that Czechoslovakia now could become "another Switzerland — secure, prosperous and respected." France and Britain were praised for making concessions. The indications that Germany alone had triumphed were "superficial." For the first time Hitler had been forced to yield, the editorial concluded. Morley later said he was influenced on Munich by East European diplomats who feared the Soviet Union more than Germany.

THE POST now began to back what Roosevelt saw as his only course, to rearm as rapidly as possible. This the public wanted although the isolationists in Congress were grudging at every step. THE POST's Barry Sullivan and John G. Norris filled pages with preparedness stories as event tumbled on event. Hitler took over the remains of Czechoslovakia; Mussolini occupied Albania; Franco completed his conquest of Spain; Britain signed a fateful mutual defense pact with Poland. Then, on April 10, 1939, THE POST carried, back on page 6, the President's seemingly offhand remark on leaving his Georgia vacation home: "I'll be back in the fall if we don't have a war."

Morley seized on the remark to editorialize:

> Most Americans realize today that the sweep of events has now brought Europe to the very edge of war. What is insufficiently realized is the tremendous implications of the impending catastrophe for every citizen of this country . . . By "we" he undoubtedly meant western civilization . . . In using the collective "we" the President told Hitler and Mussolini that the tremendous force of the United States must be a factor in their current thinking . . . To make this plain at this crucial time is to help in preventing war.

Next day FDR told reporters he heartily approved those words and ordered the editorial inserted in the press conference minutes. He added that the editorial had not been inspired by him and that he had almost fallen out of bed when he read it that morning.

When Hitler and Stalin on August 30 announced their nonaggression pact, a page 1 Morley editorial called it a "historic and world-shaking document." Indeed, it was. The next eight days saw a succession of triple banners march across the front page as the dénouement approached. For an extra on Friday, September 1, the paper mustered its largest type for a single eight-column line: NAZIS INVADE POLAND.

Idling by the sea at Rehoboth Beach, Delaware, POST columnist Harlan Miller wrote: "Now that little vermilion airplane sweeps low over the beach, too low, and all the young mothers say to each other, 'What if that were a bombing plane?' " Richard Coe reported that the 2500 who saw *The Merry Wives of Windsor* at the Sylvan Theater on the Monument grounds were "fully conscious of the evening's sickening implications." The day's picture page featured Mrs. Roosevelt's champagne christening at Newport News, Virginia, of the new $19 million passenger liner *America.* The American Federation of Government Employees offered a weekend rail trip to the New York World's Fair. A 6.2-cubic-foot refrigerator was on sale at Sears, Roebuck and Co. for $119.96; the Acme liquor store on the Avenue offered a quart of Kentucky bourbon for $1.49; Hahn's was selling fall Florsheim shoes for women at $9.75; Ourisman Chevrolet offered a used 1928 deluxe club sedan for $597; Giant food stores (three locations) advertised smoked hams at 15 cents a pound and the Sanitary groceries had coffee at two pounds for a quarter; Hall's restaurant near the waterfront featured whole broiled lobsters for a dollar. FDR, it was reported, hoped to get away to Hyde Park for his annual Labor Day picnic. And the list of "broadcasts from the war front today" included William L. Shirer, Berlin; Eric Sevareid, Paris; and Edward R. Murrow, London.

Two weeks later Lippmann observed that "the popular resentment against the radio which has been only too evident in the past ten days, has been caused by the broadcasters who threaten the listener in a hot, moist and fervent voice, conveying a mood of breathless alarm and mounting danger." The columnist suggested that radio news ought to be presented "perhaps only twice a day" to allow time for checking on what was reported.

But there was no time. Britain went to war over Poland on September 3. THE POST slowed the presses until after 5 A.M. to run off 47,000 extras. Assistant Managing Editor Lowell A. Leake, a new hand, had seen in a London dispatch arriving about midnight that Prime Minister Chamberlain would broadcast at 5 A.M. Washington time and he knew what to do.

Roosevelt told the nation that "I hope the United States will keep out of this war. I believe that it will." But "I cannot ask that every American remain neutral in thought," as Wilson had suggested at the onset of World War I. "Even a neutral cannot be asked to close his mind or his conscience."

THE POST asked: "Is there anyone, in Congress or out, who can search his heart and really say it is of no concern to us who wins? If so, he is truly neutral. But it may be doubted that he is truly an American."

On September 9 THE POST announced it was adding the New York *Times* War News Service and soon such by-lines as James Reston, C. L. Sulzberger, Turner Catledge, Hanson W. Baldwin, and Ferdinand Kuhn began appearing. The addition gave THE POST a vast choice of dispatches; it was up to the editors to weigh and choose from thousands of words now pouring in daily. Chiefly responsible was Cable Editor Shirley Hurst.

Newspaper expenses generally soar in wartime. Partly as a result of that, POST deficits continued. The loss in 1938 was $986,624; in 1939, $1,040,402; and it would be $776,519 in 1940 and $873,066 in 1941.

The war and its alliances were quickly reflected in Washington. Society Editor Hope Ridings Miller described FDR's diplomatic reception the week before Christmas as "brilliant but tension-shot . . . The entire political plight of Europe could be placed together by noting frigid nods, stiff bows, and the clever device more than one envoy employed of ignoring entirely diplomats from countries unfriendly to their own." On the last day of 1939 THE POST ran on page 1 its pledges for the new year: Managing Editor Jones saw 1940 as likely to be portentous, hence "America is going to need all the laughs it can get . . . A sense of humor will be priceless leaven in the inevitable drama." But there were not very many laughs. Bob DeVore did turn up Agriculture Department economist Frederick L. Thomsen whose story was headlined: SOLEMN SCIENTIST PROVES LENGTH OF SKIRTS IS BAROMETER OF BUSINESS: BOTH GOING UP. Jones put the story on page 1; he himself appeared on the picture page with Hollywood columnist Louella Parsons, in town with her *Stars of 1940,* including actor Ronald Reagan. Amusing *Zoo's Who* animal photographs ran on for weeks.

After the collapse of Poland, Hitler overran Denmark and Norway. Then came the period known as the "phony war," a term rarely used, however, in THE POST. Page 1 turned to a host of other topics: Thomas E. Dewey said he would be "glad to run" for President, Socialist Norman Thomas was nominated for a fourth try, and John L. Lewis said that if FDR ran for a third term he would suffer an "ignominious defeat." There also was page 1 space for local stories, including Lucia Giddens' series on baby brokers; Casey Jones had told her he wanted "red hot copy that will make people angry at this intolerable situation."

On March 4, 1940, columnist Lindley wrote, as THE POST headlined his story on page 1, that ROOSEVELT WON'T RUN, HULL HIS CANDIDATE. Lindley reported that the President had ruled out James A. Farley because he was a Catholic, but that FDR might "not desert the ship" if the Germans "overrun England and head in our direction." After an editorial called on the President to speak out, Roosevelt responded, denying he had told anyone that religion was a bar to a Farley candidacy and declaring Lindley's column was made of whole cloth. FDR, THE POST reported, said he considered Lindley's "one of the respected columns that he considered only about 20 percent wrong, as against other columns that are 80 percent wrong." Lindley stood his ground but the incident cooled their hitherto close relationship.

Meanwhile, there were indications of the coming Nazi storm. Undersecretary of State Sumner Welles, touring Europe, seemed to find no basis for peace. Louis Lochner of the Associated Press wrote from Berlin in March 1940 of "some signs pointing to a gigantic German offensive, on land and in the water and air, early this spring." The blow fell on May 10: NAZIS INVADE HOLLAND, BELGIUM, LUXEMBOURG; WIDESPREAD LAND AND AIR BATTLES RAGING; PLANES BOMB BRUSSELS; BRITISH OCCUPY ICELAND. The "phony war" was over.

Day after day, triple eight-column headlines reported the conquest of the Lowlands, the attack on France, and the rescue of the British army from the beaches of Dunkirk. The June 5, 1940, POST carried Churchill's stirring "we shall never surrender" speech, but that Eugene Meyer read those words that day is doubtful, and understandable. For on THE POST's society page it was reported that his third daughter,

Katharine, 22, the day before had married 24-year-old Philip Leslie Graham in the garden of the Meyers' Mt. Kisco, New York, estate. "The bride wore a wreath of orange blossoms in her dark hair and carried a spray of orchids." Graham had just finished a year as law clerk to Justice Stanley Reed and was to clerk the next year for Justice Frankfurter. "She is on the editorial staff of *The Washington Post.*" Only the immediate family was present. Meyer was approaching 65 and the thought crossed his mind that in Graham he might someday have a successor to run the newspaper he had owned for almost seven years.

After the fall of France, Morley wrote that Britain "knows . . . it has the full sympathy of the American people . . . The British must not be misled, however, into assuming from this that the United States is likely to enter the war. The resolve of the American people to avoid participation in this struggle is exceedingly strong."

The Meyer-Morley strain now was intense. Meyer saw American participation as necessary and inevitable; Morley resisted it. On August 6 the paper announced that Morley that day had surrendered control of the editorial page. He had, in fact, submitted his resignation the previous March 26 to become president that fall of Haverford College. The position of editorial page chief almost went to Elmer Davis, then a leading radio commentator, but it was Morley who suggested his successor: Herbert Elliston.

Yorkshire-born, the 44-year-old Elliston, although he never went to college, had a prodigious memory, sometimes "wrote with an imp on his shoulder," and had "the true genius of the editor." Often he could improve a colleague's editorial by cutting it in half. A liberal and an internationalist, he had spent years in Asia and the past ten on the *Christian Science Monitor.* He arrived at THE POST as associate editor on October 17, 1940, his editorial pen afire. Meyer now listed himself on the editorial page as Editor and Publisher.

Within a week, under the heading "It Is Later Than You Think," Elliston called for "speed, and more speed" in preparing for possible war because "every minute the heat of the European blaze is hotter — and closer!" And: "Our peril is so great, our time to prepare so limited." On top of the page 1 masthead ran the overline IT IS LATER THAN YOU THINK! both that day and for several succeeding days, keyed to stories that emphasized the point. THE POST was using page 1 to push its new editorial view.

The war, of course, was a major factor in FDR's third-term campaign and victory. THE POST sent Albright, Folliard, Donovan, Oakes, and Christine Sadler to the Republican convention in Philadelphia. On the eve of the balloting Folliard wrote that Wendell Willkie was "rushing ahead like a flame-throwing tank but old hands at the political game were busy laying mines under his path." It did not work; Willkie won on the sixth ballot. THE POST liked Willkie because he "candidly affirms that there is no miraculous solution, no painless panacea, no easy short-cut around the grievous and growing difficulties of democracies."

The same reporters went to Chicago for the Democratic gathering. When FDR announced that "all the delegates are free to vote for any candidate," Folliard put it succinctly in his lead story: "He didn't say no." The President's renomination was a cinch but there was a bitter struggle before the delegates would accept his choice of Secretary of Agriculture Henry A. Wallace for Vice President. Morley was still in charge and THE POST editorial on FDR was bitter: ". . . the Messianic complex . . . seems to be possessing Mr. Roosevelt even more firmly." Still, THE POST once more avoided any endorsement.

Elderman cartoons in the closing days of the campaign linked FDR's preparedness calls with "politics" and a November 2 editorial said:

> The sorry fact is that the American people cannot look back to any part of the last decade with any substantial degree of satisfaction. That fact now works to President Roosevelt's disadvantage just as certainly as it smoothed his way to the White House in 1932.

It was an outrageous statement; certainly the majority of voters did not agree. Roosevelt won a 531 to 82 electoral sweep and led Willkie by nearly 5 million votes although this was well below his first two victory margins. THE POST conceded only "a clear-cut and substantial margin." Some 4000 had stood in front of the E Street building to hear the returns even though they now came far faster by radio. Once again THE POST called for a big turnout to welcome FDR back from Hyde Park and some 200,000 lined the route to cheer. The Hecht Company ran a full-page ad with FDR's picture and a caption: "Local Boy Makes Good!"

THE POST staff by now was stretched thin and badly overworked. From the beginning of the war Folliard not only covered major news breaks but wrote a weekly roundup of the fighting, a chore Donovan took over during the election campaign. Albright was alone at the Capitol, while Jack Norris and Marshall Andrews covered military developments. George Bookman joined the paper in early 1940 and soon was covering the White House, but he rarely was sent on the President's out-of-town trips. Bill Nessly was both reporter and editor. No one concentrated on diplomatic developments. Dick Coe, the number two movie and theater man, was pressed into service to write about the Suez Canal. And Katharine Meyer pitched in to write local editorials, a feature on the chief phone operator at the defense mobilization office, and articles on the cherry blossom festival, Pan American Day, and the rivalry between the America First Committee and the Committee to Defend America by Aiding the Allies. The columnists, especially Lippmann and Lindley, provided the broader view and inside stories. Soon after the election a new pair appeared: Joseph Alsop and Robert Kintner joined to write Capital Parade five times a week until they left to join the war seven months later.

The 1940 census showed the District's population up a whopping 36 percent in a decade to 663,091, with blacks about 28 percent of the total. Suburban sprawl had begun. In addition to new federal workers the city was crowding with European refugees, including royalty and some British children sent out of harm's reach. Now 11th in the nation in population, the city was booming: in 1940 government jobs were up 16 percent; the monthly payrolls up 14 percent; new car sales up 13 percent; bank deposits up 18 percent.

THE POST's advertising was slowly growing but in 1940 it was still less than half the *Star*'s linage, below the *Times-Herald* although ahead of the *News*. Daily circulation averaged 126,708; the *Star*, 153,087. Meyer remarked that the *Star* was first in advertising, the *Times-Herald* first in circulation, and THE POST first in deficits.

FDR proposed to "lease" war material to Britain, a device, he said, to eliminate "the silly, foolish dollar sign" that had caused so much acrimony over World War I loans to the Allies. Thus was born the lend-lease program, American aid that would run to many billions. THE POST heartily approved: "Fortunately the President's method of easing the financial problems of the British in this war by providing for repayment in kind represents a learning from experience which is all too rare in contemporary history." Although Albright correctly wrote that the Lend-Lease Act was "reminiscent of blank check authority granted Mr. Roosevelt to deal with the depression emergency," this time there was no POST protest over unlimited executive power.

Meyer's vision, instinct, and sense of need to save Western Europe overrode all his old antagonisms toward Roosevelt; with Elliston's hearty approval and writing skill, the combination gave Washington, at a critical moment in history, a thunderer — THE POST editorial page. The paper declared flatly that "we are in a state of war, whether we call it war or defense or what-have-you. And it is none of our doing. In the circumstances the only alternative open to us is surrender or resistance." In powerful language a succession of editorials helped push lend-lease through Congress over bitter isolationist protest. Up to this point THE POST's news coverage of the war was hardly more than routine; its editorial page demanded, and received, attention.

To cover the burgeoning defense mobilization story THE POST picked Alfred Friendly who had come over from the *News* in the fall of 1939 to write The Federal Diary column. Casey Jones sent him to investigate strikes instigated by Communist-dominated unions, the first of many labor disputes he wrote about. Dillard Stokes joined the paper to cover the fascist and Communist fringe then under investigation by Representative Martin Dies. THE POST, in a February 13, 1941, editorial commended this work: "On the whole . . . Mr. Dies and his colleagues deserve the green light signal given them by the House. They have a real job to do."

On June 22, 1941, THE POST headlined: HITLER DECLARES WAR ON RUSSIA; NAZIS, FINNS AND RUMANIANS MARCH AGAINST SOVIETS IN "GREATEST CAMPAIGN" IN ALL HISTORY. Churchill argued that "Russia's danger is our danger, and the danger of the United States. Any man or state that fights against Hitler will have our aid." Folliard caught the Washington mood: "Two points of view on this question [of extending lend-lease aid to Russia] were quickly discerned in Congressional circles. One was that the United States ought to forget Russia's own record of betrayal and aggression and give her aid; the other was that the United States ought to remain aloof and regard the Nazi-Soviet war as a dog-eat-dog contest."

Once lend-lease became a fact FDR set up the National Defense Mediation Board to "end strikes that interfere with our armament program," as an editorial put it. He appointed Meyer as one of the industry representatives on the board after the publisher had gone to him to offer his services to the government. FDR was the fifth President whom Meyer served, but this time it was different — it cast a shadow on his paper's objectivity however much he avoided any effort to influence either Friendly's labor reporting or Elliston's editorial page. In short, it was a violation of a fundamental rule that publishers should not hold government positions.

On July 4, 1941, at the suggestion of Promotion Manager Raoul Blumberg, THE POST ran a four-page tabloid supplement with the words, music, and history of "The Star-Spangled Banner," so readers could join Lucy Monroe at the Monument grounds that evening in singing the national anthem prior to the fireworks. There were thousands of requests for reprints.

That July, *Time* magazine took a look at Meyer's POST, as he entered his ninth year of control, and pronounced it "the Capital's sole big-league newspaper . . . it has become a journal of national importance, a reading must on Capitol Hill, an institution of high character and independence, a force for good in its bailiwick." To this the paper replied on page 1 that "there can be no stretched hatbands around *The Post:* This newspaper has just started to grow."

One POST feature that became must reading for the increasing thousands of government workers was The Federal Diary column, begun under McLean in 1932 and continued by half a dozen writers until January 1, 1941, when it was taken over by Jerry Kluttz. The bureaucrats' friend, Kluttz was fabulously successful over the next 29 years, through peace and war, in pointing out job opportunities, disclosing raids against the civil service, uncovering scandals, and predicting changes in wages, pay, hours, and working conditions.

The larger story fell to the eager Friendly and he had a rough start. He had fallen in with the determined young government advocates of defense mobilization — Robert R. Nathan, Stacy May, Joseph L. Rauh, Jr., Edward F. Prichard, Jr., and Philip L. Graham, Meyer's son-in-law now working for the Office of Emergency Management and later the Lend-Lease Administration. Friendly, who needed no conversion himself, wrote a stinging indictment of the Office of Production Management's failure to produce enough steel, aluminum, and magnesium. Jones first sent the story to Meyer, and Meyer passed it to OPM head William S. Knudsen. It came back annotated "nonsense," "wrong," "not so" in the pen of a middle-level mobilizer, W. Averell Harriman. Jones told Friendly that he and Meyer chose to take the word of men who knew the facts; the story was spiked. Soon, however, when it became obvious that Friendly had been right, Jones apologized for missing a major scoop. From then on, he never touched Friendly's copy and Friendly became one of Meyer's reportorial confidants. Harriman, too, switched, becoming a driving force for war preparation.

Beginning August 21, 1941, Jones gave double-column, page 1 display to a series titled "Guns for Soldiers," designed to shock the defense mobilization establishment out of its continuing doldrums. Friendly was the spark for this series, aided by Norris, Folliard, Albright, and Marshall Andrews. It was a devastating critique of increasingly scarce raw materials needed for military supplies going instead to "an industrial cornucopia" of autos, washing machines, air-conditioning equipment, and refrigerators.

In the less than five months between the German invasion of Russia and Pearl Harbor the capital's pace intensified. Kluttz predicted that "an absolute minimum of 308,861 new employes will be hired by the

Federal Government in its defense agencies during the next 16 months," at least 35,000 of them in Washington. Mrs. Roosevelt announced that because the President was "so busy" there would be no formal functions in the fall or winter. Congress voted a rent freeze for the District, and 35,000 local volunteers signed up for civil defense. FDR approved more temporary wood buildings to house 1000 government girls. Five hundred girls turned out one evening to register as volunteer dance partners for the "warriors quartered in this area."

The biggest battle was for more office space; dozens of new tempos simply were not enough. The major result was the world's biggest office building, the Pentagon. On July 25, 1941, THE POST printed a drawing of the War Department's "dream building," about four times bigger than any existing federal structure and estimated to cost $35 million. FDR said the new building would be "emergency quarters," to become a storage and record building when no longer needed.

The last frantic "peacetime" months still left some time for amusement. Charles Chaplin's *Great Dictator* jammed them in at the Palace; Charlie himself had come to the third-term inaugural. Some 31,000 went out to Griffith Stadium to cheer Joe DiMaggio as he broke George Sisler's 19-year record by hitting in his 41st straight game. Then, on Sunday, December 7, as 27,102, including Navy Lieutenant John F. Kennedy, watched the Redskins' Sammy Baugh lead his team to a 20 to 14 victory over the Philadelphia Eagles, the AP machine at THE POST rang the maximum 12 bells to alert editors and then typed out: FLASH WHITE HOUSE SAYS JAPS ATTACK PEARL HARBOR.

In the pages of THE WASHINGTON POST the long route to Pearl Harbor, until the final days, was a very secondary story to events in Europe. Reporting from Asia largely concerned the Japanese efforts to conquer China, and American sympathies were clearly on China's side. FDR sought to hold off the Japanese at least until the tide could be turned in Europe; THE POST was equally Europe-minded. But when Russia and Japan signed their neutrality pact the paper saw its significance: "Japan has now been given the green light for any adventure she may decide to embark on in southeast Asia." In October the statements coming out of Tokyo grew more militant; one headline said: JAPAN'S NAVY TELLS NATION WAR MAY BE IMMINENT. The day before General Hideki Tojo took control, a POST editorial commented that "the possibility that Japan will now be on the warpath, either in the north or south, cannot be excluded." THE POST, however, was as blind as the American government to the possibility of a Japanese move east across the Pacific.

On November 15, the special Japanese envoy, Saburu Kurusu, arrived in San Francisco. Hedley Donovan, covering the story from Washington, sounded the first POST alarm by writing of "fateful negotiations which may settle the issue of peace or war in the Pacific." THE POST, however, did not keep Donovan on the story; he alternated with wire service reporters and Wilfred Fleisher of the New York *Herald Tribune* until the final four days. When Kurusu and Ambassador Kichisaburo Nomura met with the President and Hull on November 27, the headline read: U.S.-TOKYO SHOWDOWN NEAR AS SIAM BRACES FOR ATTACK. The editorial that day followed the administration line that Japan must give a "guaranteed renunciation of aggression" and not expect the United States to abandon China. The sequel dominated page 1 for the next nine days. A December 6 editorial concluded that "all the circumstances conspire to show that the Japanese are preparing for another snatch in their career of Asian conquest . . . There is no longer any need, let alone any warrant, for buying off an aggressor."

THE WASHINGTON POST of Sunday, December 7, 1941, cost ten cents and consisted of 96 pages in eight sections plus the new circulation-building supplement *Parade*, comics, and an eight-page tabloid section.

For some time THE POST had been running The President's Day, a chatty summary by the International News Service. Sunday's entry included: "Today the President has promised, somewhat vaguely, to take it easy; get in an afternoon snooze and a drive in the Virginia countryside. Personal friends are due for a small, informal supper this evening."

When AP's 12 bells rang out the first flash, the clock on THE POST city room wall showed 2:25 P.M. It was a dull, gray Washington Sunday, the temperature varying from 32 to 43 degrees. Casey Jones rushed to the office to get out an extra with a simple black line in the biggest type yet used: U.S. AT WAR. As Jones was putting the paper together, THE POST's church editor, Robert Tate Allen, fondly known as "the Bishop," rushed up to announce a scoop: a Georgetown minister had decided to leave for a pastorate elsewhere. Whatever the explosive Jones said, Allen never forgot that his "face turned a deep purple." Still, the *Times-Herald* beat THE POST to the street; Editor Frank Waldrop had been in his office reading his mail when the flash came.

Monday morning's paper gave only a hint of the carnage at Pearl Harbor. Locally, the news centered on the White House where cars drove by "at snail's pace, with heads thrust from their windows." At the Japanese embassy on Massachusetts Avenue other autos choked the street, policemen lined the sidewalk, and diplomatic documents were burned in the garden. Reporter John D. Morris was briefly held by FBI men after he demanded in vain to see the two key diplomats. His story that they had sent him word that they had not known of an impending attack, which was true, was spiked. Apparently, it was just too much to believe.

Herbert Elliston hurried to the office to whip off a thunderous editorial:

> With a blinding flash the true inwardness of the world crisis now stands revealed for the American people. This was never an "intra-European war." It was intended from the beginning as a world war. And America was marked out as the final object of attack . . . It would be fantastic folly to think of the Japanese engaging on their cosmic adventure alone. On that assumption — thank Heaven! — all our defense plans have been prepared.
>
> To whom is the credit due for this policy: To nobody but our President. This country, now that it is confronted by the stark facts, has reason to be grateful to the President for his prescience. He saw the war coming long before it came in 1939. He foresaw the time when Japan would carry out the obligations of the Axis compact. As a result this Nation is ready as never before to meet the mighty shock of the Japanese act.

FDR's strategy in fighting World War II was to give priority to defeating Hitler; with this THE POST heartily agreed. But before American GIs could grapple with the Wehrmacht came shocking retreat in the Pacific as the Japanese pressed south, and a confusing effort at home to organize men and machines, to produce soldiers, sailors, and airmen, and to give them the instruments of war. Washington was the nerve center; the city and the paper reflected the struggle to organize and then to turn from the defensive to the offensive on both major fronts and on many lesser ones.

At the White House the guard was trebled and "the blackout curtains were being tacked into frames. Fire buckets filled with sand were hung in convenient spots upstairs and down." THE POST reported that at the first air-raid test "an unappealing, disillusioned and funereal moan was produced by a 12-year-old reconditioned siren." Nonetheless, Hope Ridings Miller's Capital Whirl column four days after Pearl Harbor began: "Anybody who had an idea that a double-barreled declaration of war . . . would black-out the social calendar should have been out and about yesterday afternoon, when parties from 5 o'clock on had Washingtonians dashing all over town."

The initial war news was grim, and would become grimmer, as 1941 came to an end and the capital struggled to readjust. THE POST proclaimed "Remember Pearl Harbor!" in a box above the page 1 masthead, printing below a mass of often contradictory and false wire service reports from the Pacific.

Elliston called for disclosing the truth of the Hawaiian disaster: "Right now the country is fighting mad," he wrote on December 9. "It can take the bad news along with the good that must inevitably come." On December 13 an editorial on censorship said: "We can take it with the best, and this newspaper therefore hopes that the President will entrust the information job to men who are wise and technically proficient rather than to officers who are neither." The appointment of Byron Price of the Associated Press as chief censor won approval. Throughout the war THE POST fought with military censors but not with Price's office. It often quarreled, however, with Elmer Davis' Office of War Information although it supported Davis' efforts to pry facts from the military.

Victory in the end seemed inevitable but the anguish and turmoil in Washington at times were appalling. A POST editorial, written by Jones, on February 12, 1942, pinpointed the problem:

> *The Post* submits that if there is any one industry in this country which needs conversion to the wartime basis it is our Government . . . Department heads are running around town trying to grab this and that war activity to build up their own importance, and to perpetuate their own jobs . . . Half the parasites in Washington are coordinators and fancy titled people in screwball jobs, doing their best to think of something to start that will outstrip another department doing the same thing.

The editorial reference to "parasites" derived from Roosevelt's remark shortly before that such people should move out of town to make room for war workers. As to "people in screwball jobs," Jones the next month threw the paper into a ding-dong battle to belittle and destroy the Office of Government Reports, headed by Lowell Mellett, the former editor of the Washington *Daily News.*

A building to house this office, where those who wanted to help the government were to come and be told what agency to go to, was being erected in a park catty-corner across Pennsylvania Avenue from THE POST building, and the carpenters' hammers pounded in Jones' ears. He wrote a front-page editorial, "The Great Boondoggle," attacking the enterprise and dubbing the building "Mellett's Madhouse." For days he denounced "Mellett's overgrown information booth," contending Congress had never funded it. It was one of THE POST's sillier campaigns; the building was completed although the agency's usefulness had been badly damaged by Jones' blasts.

A later editorial best caught the mood of Washington in early 1942: "The problems of the day are so pressing that tempers are short, voices are angry, and men honestly engaged in the same high purpose are hurling accusations at each other." The snarling peaked early in April. Jesse Jones, the conservative Secretary of Commerce, had been under fire by THE POST and others for his management of the rubber shortage, and he had had to defend his program before a Senate committee headed by Harry S. Truman of Missouri. On April 9 THE POST claimed that "the chief reason for his failure is a boundless ambition for power that has led to his taking on more than he can successfully manage." Publisher Meyer had asked editorial writer Anna P. Youngman to include the reference to Jones' "boundless ambition."

By chance, Jones and Meyer were both guests of the Alfalfa Club at the Willard Hotel on the evening the editorial appeared. Years later Folliard recounted what happened:

> Mr. Jones, infuriated by the editorial, sought out Mr. Meyer in the Little Ballroom of the Willard. He seized him by the shoulders and shook him so hard that Mr. Meyer's glasses fell to the floor. Mr. Meyer was about to land a right on the chin of the taller and heavier Mr. Jones when friends stepped in and halted what was called the "elegant brawl."
>
> The fracas caused a sensation and was headlined in just about every newspaper in the United States, with one exception. *The Post* carried not a line about it. Mr. Meyer in killing the story, said it concerned something that happened in a private club. To make matters worse — from the standpoint of *Post* editors and reporters — he told the rival *Evening Star* how he had taken boxing lessons in San Francisco from "Gentleman Jim" Corbett, heavyweight champion of the world.

It was the *Times-Herald*'s George Dixon who dubbed it "an elegant brawl," describing Meyer as "swinging like a maddened walrus" and crediting Jones with "rattling the publisher about like an empty barrel." The *News* had Jones shaking Meyer "like a malted milk." *Time* magazine said Meyer "came up with a haymaker aimed straight at the Jones

The Washington Post.

NUMBER 1. WASHINGTON, THURSDAY MORNING, DECEMBER 6, 1877. THREE CENTS.

NEW YORK SPECIAL. | AT THE CAPITOL. | OVER THE WATER.

The first issue of THE WASHINGTON POST *(top)* came off the press December 6, 1877. Founder Stilson Hutchins *(right)*, an ardent Democrat, displayed the crowing rooster to celebrate an 1882 party victory. When his POST absorbed the rival *Union* he briefly used both names *(below)*.

The Washington Post and Union.

NUMBER 112. WASHINGTON, MONDAY MORNING, APRIL 15, 1878. THREE CENTS.

GOTHAM SUNDAY HASH | THE BOSS OF THE COUNT. | OUR CAPITOL GOSSIP. | THE SILVERY LINING.

Democrat Beriah Wilkins *(above left)* and Republican Frank Hatton *(above right)* bought out Hutchins in 1889. To them bandmaster John Philip Sousa dedicated the paper's most enduring advertisment, "The Washington Post March" *(below left)*. Cartoonist George Y. Coffin in 1893 created The Post Boy *(left)*, long the paper's emblem. Star reporter of this era was Henry Litchfield West *(below)*.

The POST building at 10th and D Streets *(above left)* was decorated for Garfield's 1881 inauguration. After an 1885 fire, it was rebuilt with two more stories *(above right)*. The E Street building with two additions housed the paper from 1893 (about the time of the snow scene, *below*) through arrival of the auto *(right)* to 1950. This building faced on Pennsylvania Avenue, a few doors from 14th Street.

Managing Editor Scott C. Bone *(above)* had both gas and electric lights, probably about 1891. Cartoonist Clifford K. Berryman created the Teddy Bear *(left)* when President Theodore Roosevelt refused to shoot a cub during a 1902 bear hunt. Berryman also provided the Spanish-American War slogan, "Remember the Maine," in the caption of a cartoon *(lower left)* after the battleship was sunk in Havana harbor. Coffin rapped William Jennings Bryan in an 1896 campaign cartoon *(lower right)*.

John R. McLean *(above)*, already publisher of the Cincinnati *Enquirer*, became THE POST's owner-publisher in 1905. Star reporter George Rothwell Brown *(above left)* and Editorial Page Editor Ira C. Bennett *(left center)* carried on long after McLean's death in 1916. In 1912 newsboys hawked an extra *(below left)* after the sinking of the *Titanic*. Woodrow Wilson's first inauguration and a suffragettes' parade were the big news of March 4, 1913 *(below right)*.

The Washington Post.

WOMAN'S BEAUTY, GRACE, AND ART BEWILDER THE CAPITAL

Miles of Fluttering Feminity Present Entrancing Suffrage Appeal.

PAGEANT, LIVING PICTURES, ORATORY

WOODROW WILSON ARRIVES TO BECOME NATION'S HEAD TODAY

Democracy to the Number of 250,000 Comes to Inaugurate President.

STATE EXECUTIVES AND SOLDIERY HERE

ROW IN THE HOUSE

CABINET LIST READY

The Washington Post.

JOHNSON IS HERO AS NATIONALS WIN DECISIVE GAME OF WORLD SERIES, 4-3; CITY IN CARNIVAL, CELEBRATES VICTORY

POST-SCRIPTS

WHIRLWIND OF JOY SWEEPS CAPITAL IN BIG DEMONSTRATION

PRESIDENT VOICES JOY AT RESULT OF SERIES

GRIFFMEN TRIUMPH IN 12-INNING BATTLE AS CITY GOES WILD

The Washington Post

LINDBERGH WILDLY HAILED AT PARIS FOR 3,800-MILE FLIGHT IN 33½ HOURS; AIRMAN TELLS OWN STORY OF TRIP

POST-SCRIPTS

SLEET AND MIST CHIEF HANDICAPS OVER THE OCEAN

ATE SANDWICH AND A HALF ON THE WAY; DRANK SOME WATER AND SLEPT LITTLE

LONE FLIER WHO BLAZED TRAIL ACROSS ATLANTIC

HERO IS MOBBED BY VAST THRONG ON FRENCH FIELD

GREATEST EVENT IN AVIATION HISTORY, EXPERTS ASSERT; ALL PRAISE HIS DARING

Edward B. (Ned) McLean *(above right)*, who succeeded his father, led THE POST into bankruptcy in 1933. His wife, Evalyn Walsh McLean *(above left)*, as the premier Washington hostess proudly wore the Hope diamond on a pearl necklace and the Star of the East on her bandeau. Sports and the Lone Eagle *(left)* were big news in the 1920s. Note Post-Scripts columns by Brown on page 1, column 1. Harding rode with McLean in the publisher's car *(below left)*. After the President's death McLean had to recant before a Senate committee *(below right)* for his role in the Teapot Dome scandal.

THE POST was sold at bankruptcy on the steps of the E Street building June 1, 1933 *(above).* The paper's Arthur Ellis photographed auctioneer Thomas J. Owen holding a notebook as attorney George E. Hamilton, Jr. *(next to Owen, wearing felt hat and with pocket handkerchief),* bought the paper for $825,000 on behalf of secret bidder Eugene Meyer. On hand *(top right in cloche)* was Eleanor (Cissy) Patterson, editor of Hearst's Washington *Herald.* That summer baseball fans watched THE POST's play-by-play board *(right).* In 1937 Meyer joined rival publishers at a Community Chest luncheon *(below). Left to right:* Frank B. Noyes of the *Star,* Meyer, Cissy Patterson and Lowell Mellett of the *News.*

Meyer's new editorial page chief Felix Morley *(top)* and Managing Editor Alexander F. (Casey) Jones were photographed with a young Morley assistant, Katharine Meyer, now POST publisher Katharine Graham. Two stellar reporters for decades were *(above left)* Edward T. Folliard *(left)* and Robert C. Albright.

Eugene Elderman's bitter 1937 cartoon *(above right)* titled "Reform of the Judiciary," appeared when newly appointed Supreme Court Justice Hugo Black was disclosed as once having been a Klan member. Four Meyer era stalwarts were *(below, left to right)* Federal Diary columnist Jerry Kluttz, District Line columnist Bill Gold, sports writer and editor Shirley Povich, and City Editor Ben Gilbert.

Meyer's son-in-law, Philip L. Graham *(above, third from left)*, came to THE POST in 1946 and here lunches in the new L Street building with *(left to right)* Managing Editor James Russell Wiggins, Meyer, and Editorial Page Editor Herbert Elliston. Meyer's wife, Agnes *(right)*, often wrote for THE POST.

After their 1948 upset victory Harry Truman and Alben Barkley *(below)* ride past THE POST, which displays its confession of a wrong prediction.

On March 17, 1954, Eugene Meyer, wearing a pressman's paper hat, started the presses for the combined WASHINGTON POST AND TIMES-HERALD *(above)*. Purchase of its rival, the climactic event of Meyer's career, gave THE POST a morning monopoly and assured its fortunes. Circulation instantly surpassed that of the afternoon and Sunday *Star*. Five years later THE POST took the lead in advertising. Three leading executives of the period were Alfred Friendly *(lower left)*, James Russell Wiggins *(lower center)*, and John W. Sweeterman *(lower right)*.

When Graham appeared on *Time*'s cover for April 16, 1956 *(above left)*, he and THE POST had reached a new high in public and professional esteem. His friendship with President Kennedy brought JFK to speak *(above right)* at a 1961 POST Book and Author luncheon. Frederick S. Beebe *(right)*, a New York lawyer hired by Graham, became the company's board chairman after the 1961 purchase of *Newsweek* magazine. The cartoons of Herbert Block, known as Herblock *(below center)*, have been a major POST feature since 1946. He created the monster bomb figure *(below left)* and he relentlessly battled Senator Joseph R. McCarthy as in this May 7, 1954, cartoon.

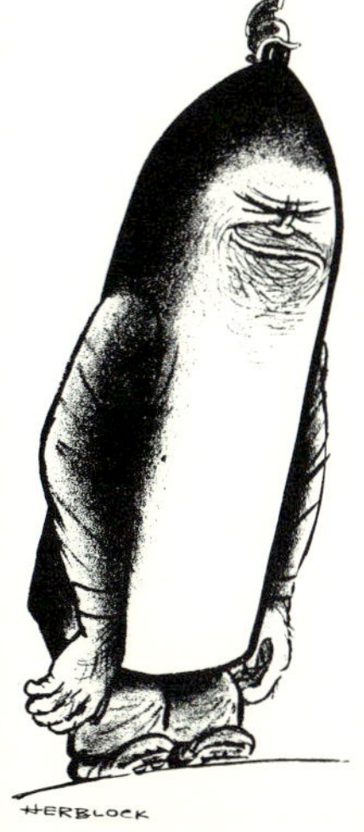

Katharine Graham's first major step was to hire Benjamin C. Bradlee as managing editor *(above)*. Together they read the 1971 Supreme Court decisions in the Pentagon Papers case which favored THE POST, the *New York Times*, and other papers *(right)*. Two of Bradlee's new stars were David S. Broder *(below left)*, Pulitzer Prize winning political reporter, and Sally Quinn *(below right)*, leading interviewer-writer for the Style section.

The Weather

The Washington Post

Index

94th Year ... No. 208 — THURSDAY, JULY 1, 1971 — Phone 223-6000

# Court Rules for Newspapers, 6-3

## Vote at 18 Ratified Into Law

### Move by Ohio Enacts 26th Amendment

The 26th amendment to the Constitution, giving those 18 to 21 years old the right to vote in all elections, became law last night as Ohio was the 38th state to ratify it.

## Decision Allows Printing of Stories On Vietnam Study

The Supreme Court settled a historic confrontation between government and press by ruling yesterday that The Washington Post and The New York Times are free to publish their stories about the secret Pentagon report on how America went to war in Vietnam.

## *War File Articles Resumed*

FBI Finds Nixon Aides Sabotaged Democrats

Key Nixon Aide Named As 'Sabotage' Contact

Lawyer for Nixon Said to Have Used GOP's Spy Fund

By Bob Woodward and Carl Bernstein

President Nixon's personal attorney, Herbert W. Kalmbach, was one of five persons authorized to approve payments from the Nixon campaign's secret intelligence gathering and espionage fund, according to sources in the Watergate bugging investigation.

The sources said that the FBI has determined that Kalmbach himself either authorized or actually made payments of thousands of dollars, mostly in cash, to Donald H. Segretti, a California lawyer.

Segretti, a former Treasury Department attorney, has been identified by the FBI

Testimony Ties Top Nixon Aide To Secret Fund

Bob Woodward *(left above)* and Carl Bernstein did the key work that led to a Pulitzer Prize for THE POST's public service in the Watergate scandal. Chief among their stories were four published in October 1972, shown here in library clipping form *(above center)*. Herblock was probably Richard Nixon's most persistent foe. His May 24, 1974, cartoon *(right)* linked the President with the tapes. The denouement was recorded August 9, 1974 *(below)*.

The Washington Post

FINAL

FRIDAY, AUGUST 9, 1974

# Nixon Resigns

When union pressmen struck THE POST October 1, 1975, some sabotaged the presses. The paper missed only one day's publication, however, and in the end broke the strike. *Above:* Mrs. Graham addresses non-striking newsroom employees on December 10. THE POST regained its strike losses and went on to new circulation highs in 1976. That year the paper ranked fifth among all newspapers in advertising and one reason was the fat classified sections. *Below:* Part of the classified ad team sports T-shirts boasting of their 1976 accomplishment.

When THE POST dedicated its new 15th Street building on October 16, 1972, the street was closed for the ceremony and this fish-eye photo *(above)*. The building joined with the smaller L Street structure *(below)* opened in 1950. Below right, Mrs. Graham takes a break during travel with the 1964 Goldwater press contingent.

News and editorial executives in THE POST's 100th year: *left to right above,* Executive Editor Benjamin C. Bradlee, Deputy Managing Editor Richard Harwood, Deputy Editorial Page Editor Meg Greenfield, Managing Editor Howard Simons, and Editorial Page Editor Philip L. Geyelin. Executive Vice President and General Manager Donald E. Graham *(left)* will succeed his mother as controlling owner. *Below,* the seven POST vice presidents in the board room with Graham and POST President Mark Meagher. *Left to right:* Robert M. McCormick, John M. Dower, Lawrence A. Wallace, Graham, Meagher, Jack F. Patterson, Virgil P. Schroeder, William A. Spartin and Christopher M. Little.

jaw. It missed." Everybody agreed that Meyer's glasses shattered as they hit the floor.

Meyer devised an important way to move from red to black in 1943 when his POST for the first time made a profit — exactly $13,732. As the large corporations converted to war production and thus had few or no products to sell to consumers, Meyer suggested they run "open presentation" advertisements, a way of telling both the government and the public of a firm's ideas, wartime problems, and accomplishments. These ads, now called "public service" or "institutional presentations," were and remain tax deductible. THE POST began to run such ads, often full pages, in 1942 and the volume grew during the rest of the war, with such linage far ahead that of the *Star.* One by-product of Meyer's idea was the creation of the Advertising Council which developed cooperative public service ads after the war.

The war, however, brought a newsprint shortage. All papers had to take a percentage cut and since THE POST's circulation was growing faster than its competitors' the paper had to cut newsprint usage sharply. Meyer chose to limit circulation rather than cut advertising while the *Star* decided to curtail only the advertisers. Meyer's choice was a major mistake; after the war the advertisers flocked back to the *Star* while THE POST struggled for several years to regain and then to increase circulation.

To save newsprint THE POST trimmed the size of its pages, ended headline "banks" or subheads, shrank the size of the comics, and omitted much local advertising from the bulldog and mail editions. The Sunday rotogravure section and many features were abandoned. The "news hole," space devoted to nonadvertising matter, dropped from 60 percent of the total columns in 1941 to 42.5 percent three years later. In 1944 in a page 1 box THE POST asked readers to turn in their old editions for salvage because "the paper on which this newspaper is printed today is literally worth its weight in gold in the war effort. The need for paper for the boxing, packaging and wrapping of war supplies cannot be overstated." On May 13, 1944, the newsstand price went from three to five cents daily; the Sunday paper remained at ten cents with no changes in home subscription rates.

As the war effort gathered momentum the services drained off THE POST's staff. The first employee to volunteer was John Keull, a linotype machinist. By April 1942, 60 men were in uniform, including John Oakes and Albon B. Hailey from the news side. In March and April the marines swept through Washington newspaper offices recruiting combat correspondents; from THE POST they included Alfred E. Lewis, Sam Stavisky, Jack Garrity, and Irving Schlossenberg. Others who left for the military included Donovan and Friendly. In July, Marshall Andrews, a World War I veteran, went to Northern Ireland to write about the American troops; when Jones called him home, he quit the paper to reenter the army. By 1943 the reporting staff was down to the redoubtable Folliard, who was spread far too thin over too many disparate stories, Bill Nessly, Ben Gilbert who succeeded Friendly in covering the civilian war effort, Scott Hart, James E. Chinn, Dillard Stokes, Edwin Gritz, George Connery, and a few others.

Some men in uniform, while assigned in the Washington area, moonlighted evenings on THE POST desks as did a few women who held government jobs. The inevitable result of the manpower drain was an influx, first, of female "copy boys" and then of women reporters; some from outside, others coming down a floor from the women's department to the city room. Some were confronted by one editor who, in the Hollywood casting couch tradition, demanded a sexual price for good assignments. Two who survived the war were Chris Sadler, a local reporter and feature writer who married Dick Coe, and Mary Spargo, who had a voice that rattled eardrums as she yelled "boy" for a copy girl. Marie Sauer, editor of the brains section, earned Jones' enmity by joining the Navy's Waves; when she returned, he banished her to head the women's department where she was topnotch. On July 19, 1942, Society Editor Miller declared that "for the duration — and probably longer — we are finished with society-as-such. We are interested only in contributing our bit toward preservation of the only kind of world in which any of us would care to live."

Richard Shea, a copy boy at the war's beginning, remembered the city room as "a fortress of glorious male isolationism. Jones had a secretary [Rae Lewis] who sat beside his office . . . but she left every afternoon at five o'clock. And that was the end of the female presence." Society and women's page employees were "quarantined" on the third floor. "The copy boys brought their copy down and there were always great roars of contempt and of satisfaction when — as frequently happened — their copy was late or contained mistakes." The war changed all that.

The first copy girl was Helene Champlain, sporting harlequin glasses and black fishnet stockings. Shea recalled that "she was, all at the same time, liked, sought after, admired, looked at and resented. Each staff member protested her arrival by scrupulously avoiding calling out 'girl!' when they wanted copy moved. It was always 'boy!' " Other early copy girls were Eileen Shanahan, Cherry Cook, and Jean Reiff, who became Mrs. Albon Hailey. Reiff was the first to graduate to reporter, including the night beat at police headquarters while Al Lewis was in the marines, and the only one to survive after the men returned.

With the staff so shorthanded and largely inexperienced, readers more and more had to depend on the columnists who went beyond reporting simply what had occurred. Pusey wrote explanatory Wartime Washington columns on both local and national issues. To make matters worse cartoonist Gene Elderman gradually drank himself out of a job; syndicated cartoons had to be used when he disappeared. For about a year LeBaron Coakley frequently filled in and then took over for some months. Finally, on January 1, 1943, THE POST dropped editorial cartoons from the daily paper and there was no staff man for another three years. This allowed the paper to cram more opinion columns onto the editorial page, but it left the paper with far less punch.

Publisher Meyer played a creative role in one aspect of the journalistic home front. At a luncheon in his third-floor office one day shortly before Pearl Harbor, Undersecretary of State Welles was expounding on the importance of giving American newspapermen background on foreign policy. But he added that that was difficult if not impossible in ordinary press conferences because of the presence of journalists from the Axis nations. Meyer volunteered to arrange private conferences at his home. These were backgrounders, with the rule of secrecy observed on some matters and use without attribution allowed on others. Both civilian and military leaders came to these sessions throughout the war years to talk with groups of Washington newsmen, not just those from THE POST.

On August 13, 1942, Drew Pearson's Washington Merry-Go-Round column appeared in THE POST for the first time. Pearson had been married to Cissy Patterson's daughter Felicia, who had written movie reviews for THE POST in Ned McLean's time, and despite the divorce the columnist's friendship with the *Times-Herald* publisher survived for a time. But after Pearl Harbor Cissy fell out with Pearson and his partner, Robert S. Allen; she cut the column or omitted it and castigated the authors in print as "the headache boys" after they began attacking such Cissy favorites as General MacArthur. In the spring of 1942, Allen encountered Meyer on the street and suggested moving the column to THE POST. Meyer offered to pay $100 a week; the *Times-Herald* had been paying only $35.

While Meyer never was an admirer of the "inside" journalism of the Merry-Go-Round variety he knew the column was widely read and would be a circulation booster, just as its loss to Cissy would hurt her paper's sales. By the time the column appeared in THE POST Allen was in the army and Pearson was writing it alone; the first words of that first column were typical: "It will probably be denied but . . ." THE POST began by displaying the column in a long box on the picture page but within a year it was shoved back amid local stories on the last page. Finally, on November 13, 1947, the column began running daily on the final comic page, and there it remained, as has its successor written by Jack Anderson after Pearson's death in 1969. The column was both a boon, for its scoops and its investigative reporting, and a bane, for its feuds and its often sloppy and tendentious reporting.

In 1944, during Roosevelt's third-term campaign, Pearson took out after John Foster Dulles, prospective Secretary of State should Dewey win, for his alleged ties to prewar Germans who had financed Hitler. Jones read the copy to Meyer who, considering the material both false and libelous, ordered it cut. In anger Pearson telegraphed Meyer, charging "continued sabotage of free and fair reporting" by Jones. Meyer fired back at Pearson that THE POST did not "lease its space and facilities to you for you to do as you like with them." In time Pearson apologized but the publisher ever after was leery of columnists.

As the war was moving to a climax in Europe there was increasing talk of a fourth term for Roosevelt. THE POST kept slamming away at the "delinquencies of his administration" and criticized FDR for "using his press conference time after time as a vehicle for the flaying of the free press." Before the July 1944 Democratic convention there was some talk and a few hints in print about the state of Roosevelt's health. Lindley, almost always a total FDR backer, responded with: "Mr. Roosevelt should be good for quite a few years more of active public life."

THE POST's staff at both conventions was led by Folliard and Albright. Among the Democrats the only issue, once FDR let it be known he would run, was whether Wallace would be dumped from the ticket. Marquis Childs, who had taken over the syndicated column of Raymond Clapper after his death in a Pacific plane crash and whose column would continue in THE POST for more than three decades, wrote that "the opposition to the shy, gangling Iowan within his own party is, of course, tremendous." Lippmann stated the central objection to Wallace: "The fundamental question before the Democratic Convention is whether, with the President running for a fourth term, they can nominate a Vice President, not unlikely to be President in this fourth term, who divides the people so deeply and so sharply." They could not, and they would not. Instead, with FDR's assent, they chose Harry Truman. THE POST editorialized that for Truman "we have a hearty respect. He is head and shoulders above his senator colleagues for wartime service."

As to FDR, however, the paper gagged at the Democratic view that there could be no other candidate: "The superior assumption of such a body of wisdom as to make Mr. Roosevelt indispensable for another four years has not enough back of it to warrant the claim." But to many the war seemed to warrant it. By the time Roosevelt won his fourth term, the Germans had been swept from France, the Russians were nearing Warsaw and Budapest, and the Japanese home islands were being fire-bombed by both air corps and navy carrier planes. POST headlines were now jammed with action verbs: *smash, drive, batter, seize, sweep, assault,* and *invade* for all fronts of the war.

Americans were never really deprived during World War II although there were hardships, and frills were cut out. Vests and cuffs quickly disappeared from men's suits; babies did without rubber pants; ruffles, pleats, and full sleeves were banned from women's nightgowns, slips, petticoats, and pajamas. When silk hose disappeared Mrs. Roosevelt complained that bare legs were ugly; wrote Anne Hagner in May 1942: "Washington women, at a wide divergence of opinion with the First Lady, would like to go barelegged this summer, if only the rules of strict ethics could be relaxed." They were.

The growing scarcity of food and clothing made rationing a way of life for every family; THE POST, by late 1942, was carrying numerous lost-ration-book ads. Gasoline was recurrently short as tankers were diverted or sunk, sometimes in view of local vacationers at the Atlantic coast beaches. THE POST backed a share-your-car plan; the transit company tried out streetcars with "stand-sit" seats only 18 inches apart; elongated autos to carry ten appeared.

A 1943 census report showed a 27.5 percent increase to 839,013 in the District with the metropolitan area total surpassing one million for the first time. Despite the removal from Washington of some nonwar agencies, a move fiercely resisted, housing remained a major problem to war's end. In early 1941 the District commissioners asked owners of the city's 104,000 private homes to rent "decent living accommodations" to at least one war worker. One government girl, ousted from her Dupont Circle apartment building, found herself back in her former bathroom as a typist. This was one of many wartime vignettes collected by Gerald Gross in his weekly This Capital of Ours column. Government hours went to 44 a week in January 1942 and to 48 on December 26 the same year, for the duration. Some jobs later were extended to a mandatory 54 hours until late 1944. Job reporting times were staggered to ease traffic; the nation went on daylight savings time, or "war time," on February 9, 1942.

How to make the government work better was a constant newspaper theme. THE POST produced some ideas itself by offering, at Jerry Kluttz's suggestion, a $100 war bond a month to the federal employee with the most constructive suggestion. One winner suggested, to save paper, "don't write a letter — use a refer slip." When Agnes Richards wrote Kluttz suggesting she and her friends would like to help buy an airplane, THE POST started a "government girl warplane fund" and in four weeks 155,000 women contributed $157,000 to buy a Mustang for the army and a Corsair for the navy. Shirley Povich suggested a war bond ball game and $1,953,775 worth of bonds were sold; Babe Ruth appeared, and Kate Smith and Bing Crosby sang.

Washington stores devoted much of their POST advertising to promoting bond sales, although Woodward & Lothrop also offered a "foxhole pillow" for $2 "to make his sleeping at the front a little easier." When the Japanese were reported to have executed some of the Tokyo air raiders, the same store used a full page, with a fist punched through a photograph of the story in THE POST, to spur bond sales. The paper's carrier boys sold war savings stamps. On August 17, 1942, Tommy Dorsey played and his "songster," the 4-F Sinatra, sang at a bond rally in what was described as Post Square. This recurrent effort to create a Washington counterpart of Times Square in New York never succeeded although reporters were put on the alert for any pretense that could call for use of the term to describe the wedge of park that partly separated the E Street building from Pennsylvania Avenue.

In August 1943 Meyer conceived the idea of bringing the army to the public "so that America could see what its money in war bonds was buying for its soldiers, and how some of that equipment looked in action." The result was a giant "Back the Attack" show to promote the third war loan drive at the foot of the Washington Monument. In all, 1,724,000 came to see such things as a walk-through bomber, tanks, flame throwers, infantry drills, a WAC band, and "a grave for Corporal Hitler." Meyer paid $6000 to clean up the Monument grounds afterward.

The paper's efforts to increase war fervor included serialization of such books as *Mission to Moscow, Victory Through Air Power,* and *Thirty Seconds over Tokyo.* Casey Jones wrote page 1 editorials calling on Roosevelt to "give air power its wings" by creating a separate air force. Before he joined the navy, Norris got big display for an article headed FLYING MEN HAVE LITTLE SAY IN NAVY'S COUNCILS. The paper began to campaign for a single Department of Defense.

Roosevelt had established a Fair Employment Practices Committee in the Office of Production Management six months before Pearl Harbor, after A. Philip Randolph and other Negro leaders had threatened a 100,000-person march on Washington in July 1941. The manpower shortage, coupled with occasional prodding by FDR, did open up defense jobs to blacks around the country. Yet the resistance in Washington, especially outside the government, remained strong.

Inferior housing and general crowding in the city on top of long-time discriminatory practices by private employers and labor unions came close to producing major racial confrontations, as had occurred at the end of World War I. The summer of 1943 was the time of trouble; in Detroit a bloody race riot forced the President to send in troops.

The issue in Washington was the adamant refusal of the Capital Transit Company to hire blacks although it had advertised for men to run its streetcars and buses. The Washington newspapers all avoided reporting the tension that gradually built up, lest they spark trouble. Finally, on Wednesday, May 12, THE POST did run an editorial saying that for the past fortnight the city had been filled "with ugly rumors of racial strife." The editorial went on to say that Police Superintendent Edward J. Kelly and Commissioner John Russell Young had defused the situation by marching with Negro protesters and that "the evening passed without the slightest disorder."

The transit company hired a few women, but its white male operators threatened to quit if blacks were taken on. A 1945 editorial noted that "the company made an effort in 1943 to train a Negro bus operator and encountered employe resistance" and the company lawyer, appearing at an FEPC hearing, said that the transit firm "cannot take upon itself the responsibility of employing Negro platform employes as long as the hazard of complete stoppage exists." To this THE POST replied: "To bar men from serving in these jobs because of their race or color is at once to hamper the war program and to subvert the principles for which the war is being waged." These were the words of Alan Barth, an editorial writer who came to the paper in 1943 and remained for 29 years as the vigorous exponent of civil rights and civil liberties. Meyer hired him, knowing him to be a strong liberal, with the admonition that he wanted editorial writers not to write what they were told, but to write with an assurance of freedom within their area of competence. It was Barth who turned around THE POST's editorial position on blacks, beginning the paper's enlightened commitment to civil rights that continued through the rest of its first century.

At war's end in the fall of 1945 THE POST commented on a report of the local Federation of Churches which said that "the only area of District life in which whites and Negroes stand on an absolutely equal footing is in the matter of the franchise — both are denied the right to vote." Noting that mortality among Negroes was about 150 percent higher than among whites, life expectancy 10 to 15 years less, and housing available for blacks was "too often shoddy and exorbitant in price," an editorial continued:

> Negroes face discrimination and segregation in stores, restaurants and places of recreation. Employment opportunities for Negro residents of Washington are limited — and likely to become more so with demobilization. All that can be discovered to offset the ugliness of this picture is some evidence that discrimination against Negroes has diminished during the war years . . . There have been substantial gains in Negro employment within the Federal Government and an abandonment of segregation in federally owned restaurants and recreation facilities.

Agnes Meyer wrote two long series of articles for the paper, the first on wartime Britain with emphasis on the role of women, the second on America at war. Her reports on the home front, in fact, provided POST readers with their best glimpse of reality in the rest of the nation. She wrote at length of the "accelerated race tensions that loomed like a threatening cloud over my whole journey through the country." In the South, she reported on March 28, 1944, "the uniform worn by a Negro affects the ignorant white population as a red flag does a bull . . . Southerners said to me quite frankly: 'You've got to teach a nigger in uniform that he's still a nigger.' "

When the army ordered Japanese-Americans and Japanese aliens ousted from the coastal areas of the West three months after Pearl Harbor, THE POST commented that the "move ought to be done in the full recognition that many of the persons involved are third-generation American citizens whose loyalty to this country is now subjected to the severest sort of tests." And when a legal test of the evacuation order reached the Supreme Court in late 1944, THE POST commented that "we do not think that Americans in times to come will be able to read of this without a sense of shame." When the high court ruled unanimously that the detention was wholly unlawful, at least for American citizens, Barth wrote: "Congress will be manifesting nothing more than simple Americanism if it acts promptly to afford them due compensation for their losses."

While THE POST formally backed neither FDR nor Dewey during the fourth-term election, Elliston and others were increasingly alarmed at the President's health and, at least, took satisfaction in Truman as his running mate. An October 18, 1944, editorial said: "If a fourth term is voted for the President, Mr. Truman may one day be President of the United States and many voters, we fancy, will be influenced by that possibility."

Four days after the inauguration Gallup reported that 30 percent of the voters already wanted FDR for a fifth term. But when the President, on his return from the Yalta Conference, sat in a chair in the well of the House and slurred some of his words as he reported to Congress, Albright wrote that he appeared

> gaunt but suntanned . . . for an hour he spoke in a low voice . . . in the chatty, conversational tone of a drawing room circle, with as many phrases adlibbed as appeared in his printed text. So often did he leave his text that he sometimes had trouble getting back to his original lines.

Roosevelt told his audience that "I was not ill for a second until I arrived back in Washington and there heard the rumors about my health." Forty-one days later he was dead.

Nearly all the next day's advertisements in THE POST were black-bordered tributes and announcements of store closings. The editorial said he had "put a stamp upon history which may well be unique in recorded time . . . The record puts Mr. Roosevelt in the company of the very greatest back to Pericles." As to the new President: "We should be less than candid at this grave moment . . . if we did not recognize the great disparity between Mr. Truman's experience and the responsibilities that have now been thrust upon him."

Franklin D. Roosevelt brought to office the unforgettable experiences of having run in 1920 as a pro–League of Nations candidate for the vice presidency and of seeing the United States turn its back on participation in the world political arena. The aspirations and defeats of Woodrow Wilson were much in his mind as he approached the problems of the post–World War II period. THE WASHINGTON POST likewise was much influenced by the same history. Central to FDR's plans and THE POST's hopes was the problem of the Soviet Union. Whatever history's final judgment may be on the origins of the Cold War, both the President and the paper sought to find a way to bring the Soviet Union into a new and lasting concert of nations.

In 1942 THE POST had said that a postwar peace-keeping organization would be "doomed to impotence and ultimately to destruction" if it did not have "the fullest cooperation" of the Soviet Union and the United States. The paper strongly backed every wartime effort in Congress to create what became the United Nations.

With Roosevelt's death both the finale of the war and the postwar problems landed on the largely unprepared Truman. Folliard was with the troops in Europe for the end in 1945 and he wrote that some of the captured Germans he saw "would be rated as worse than 4-F at home." Povich abandoned sports to see the war in the Pacific; he wrote of Joe Rosenthal, the 1929 McKinley Tech High School graduate who took the famous Iwo Jima flag-raising picture. But the penny-pinching Jones, who never realized that war correspondents traveled and lived practically free on the military, brought them both home. Folliard turned to covering the Truman White House and became a great admirer of the man he liked to describe as "the Missouri gamecock."

As Hitler died in his bunker and the European war came to an end, Meyer, Elliston, Albright, Gilbert, and later Nover were in San Francisco for the United Nations founding conference. From there in THE POST of May 10, 1945, with both foresight and accuracy, Elliston summarized Soviet policy and set the course for the paper's editorial response:

> There has never been any question that Moscow wants to see a world organization set up. But the Russians do not regard it as their first line of defense, nor do they bring to it the slightest faith. For their security they rely primarily upon their own resources. Their secondary line of defense is a periphery of dependent territories, coupled with an alliance system. The world organization comes third in Russian calculations . . .
>
> The assumption of our statesmen must be that Russia wants to live in peace with America . . . it is impossible to find any reason why Russia should want war with America. Russia, for at least 20 years, wants peace if only to recover from this war . . . Accordingly, the United States is in the position of a man with a 20-year credit at the bank. We may live on the capital, or we may invest it wisely. That is the problem of our statesmanship.

Returning to Washington after V-E Day, Elliston pondered the finale of the Pacific war. He would later say that "we on the paper missed the significance of the unconditional surrender formula" in Germany's case. As to Japan, he privately urged the new Secretary of State, James F. Byrnes, and Navy Secretary James Forrestal to amend that term. A May 9 editorial said "unconditional surrender was never an ideal formula." This brought "angry protest" from readers but Elliston replied that "to insist that a war be continued, after its purposes have been realized, is to make an end of the means, to make war for its own sake. That is militarism pure and simple." Then on May 30 an editorial said that if the Japanese monarchy "can be useful to us in ending the conflict and preserving order in Japan without militarism, we think there should be no hesitation in using it for these purposes."

The Elliston argument had both strong supporters and fierce opponents in the government. One who did agree was his friend Admiral Ellis M. Zacharias, a former navy attaché in Tokyo, who found that Elliston "was reaching conclusions startingly similar to my own." Zacharias, with top government approval, had been broadcasting to the Japanese, inviting them to ask for peace. With the first hint of a possible positive response, Zacharias decided to plant a letter to the editor as the vehicle for an answer. The letter, signed "A Constant Reader," appeared on July 21, 1945. Its pertinent sentences read:

> If the Japanese desire to clarify whether or not unconditional surrender goes beyond the conditions contained in the five documents [cited were various official statements] they have at their disposal the regular diplomatic channels . . . If, as Admiral [Kantaro] Suzuki [the Premier] revealed in the Diet, their chief concern is over Japan's future national structure (Kokutai), including the Emperor's status after surrender, the way to find out is to ask. Contrary to a widespread belief, such a question can be answered quickly and satisfactorily to all those who are concerned over the future peace of the Orient and the world.

This letter was picked up, somehow, by the Japanese ambassador in Switzerland and radioed to Tokyo. Zacharias then said much the same thing publicly and Folliard's account was given the lead spot on THE POST's page 1.

As the new formulation was discussed in Tokyo, American B-29s and navy planes rained fire bombs on the island empire. Undersecretary of War Robert Patterson said in a Washington speech that "the main body of the Japanese army is still strong and intact and free to move" and that there were two million men on the home islands "whipped into fanaticism for a last-ditch fight." It was this latter view, including military estimates that the scheduled invasion would mean a million American casualties, that led Truman to order use of the atomic bomb on Hiroshima as the Japanese procrastinated over surrender.

THE POST expressed no regrets over the mass slaughter at Hiroshima. Nor had it ever raised the issue of genocide at the equally destructive fire bombings of both German and Japanese cities, including the use of napalm in the final weeks; indeed, a 1944 editorial had endorsed the use of gas against the Japanese. After the second atomic bomb was dropped on Nagasaki, an editorial claimed that the bomb "may even make an invasion of the Japanese home islands a nonessential prelude to final victory. In any case, it is certain to make invasion infinitely less costly in lives of American soldiers."

Eight years later, however, Elliston in an interview said he regretted "our editorial support of the A-bombing of Japan. It didn't jibe with our expressed feeling that Japan was already beaten." Indeed, on September 2, 1945, after the Japanese had signed the surrender instrument, an editorial had said that "it is well to remember that the Japs were doing their best to get out of the war before they knew anything about our atomic bomb . . . The atomic bomb and the Russian declaration of war were merely additional straws on the back of a nation that was already broken." THE POST's, and Elliston's, comments on the bomb are vivid reminders that daily editorial writing often expresses the judgment, the mood, and the passion of the moment.

President Truman, standing in his oval office, announced the Japanese surrender at 7 P.M. on Tuesday, August 14. THE POST soon was on the street with a single black banner: HISTORY'S WORST WAR IS OVER! Many local stores devoted their advertising space to announcing they would close and adding their thanks. In front of THE POST building a crowd cheered as a soldier and his girl jumped from a taxi, stripped to applause, exchanged clothing, and drove off. Churches were jammed that evening and a crowd in front of the White House kept shouting "We want Harry" until the President came out on the portico to say, among other things, that "this is the day when fascism and police government ceases in the world."

From the moment of the Japanese surrender pressures mounted to demobilize the military services. War industries began laying off workers; Congress began to talk about how to legislate "full employment." THE POST was full of stories on who was leaving government and of the return of the 40-hour week for those remaining.

By fall the Truman administration had made clear its determination to keep the "secret" of the bomb. A November 16 editorial said that the United Nations would have no hope of success "unless the existing bombs as well as bomb manufacture are removed from the category of national armament." But in December when a POST poll, a new feature, asked local citizens: "Who do you think should have the secret of the atomic bomb?" the response was typical of the nation: 54 percent said the United States alone; 28 percent, the United Nations.

Most Americans wanted to get back to a more normal life. Prices were going up but Thanksgiving dinner at the Hot Shoppes still cost only $1.35. A survey showed some costs in the metropolitan area had risen 42 percent in five years. Sports fans had a good but not totally satisfactory year: the Senators finished a close second and the Redskins lost the National Football League title when the Cleveland Rams beat them, 15 to 14, in the final game. Air fares were becoming competitive: Washington to Los Angeles in "less than 16 hours" cost $111.35 compared to four days in a railroad Pullman for $120.55.

A million people turned out in October to hail returning Admiral Chester Nimitz, a celebration Meyer had suggested to the navy. But the June crowd that had welcomed General Eisenhower back from Europe had been more ecstatic; Folliard wrote of his "flashing, all-out smile." When Ike, as everybody called him, declared that "I am a soldier and I'm positive no one thinks of me as a politician," the POST applauded.

> We can only hope that this emphatic disclaimer of political aspirations will silence those wrong-headed, irresponsible hero worshipers among us who mistakenly regard the gift of high political office as a fitting reward for all kinds of service to the public.

At THE POST, the men began returning in numbers and the women, who had known they were only temporaries, either departed or moved to less star billing. Returning marine combat correspondent Sam Stavisky became the veterans' editor. The Alsop brothers began their new column at year's end.

Among the returnees was Alfred Friendly who had spent much of the war in Britain helping to decode German military messages. On December 23, 1945, he wrote the first of 26 annual Christmas poems. Appearance in these lighthearted lines became a mark of distinction among the capital's newsmakers. The first poem was displayed full page under the title "At This Season, Good Folks, an Abundance of Cheer! (All Sentiments Subject to Change Next Year)."

*God wot there is some little reason*
*For singing joyful songs this season*

. . .

*A host of toasts, a shoal of skoals*
*To Walter Lippmann, Chester Bowles*

. . .

*A fine and cheerful Christmas Day*
*To Edwin Johnson, Andy May*

. . .

*May wealthy clients fill the sox*
*Of Thurman Arnold, Oscar Cox*

. . .
*Atomic luck to Harry Truman,*
*McMahon, Condon, Jimmie Newman.*
*Joyful days and celebrative*
*To that High-Placed, Authoritative,*
*Reliable, Inform-ed Source*
*Whose Name Cannot Be Used, of course*
. . .
*To all these folks, a Tom-and-Jerry,*
*A fervent wish, "God rest ye merry!"*
*(But measles, mumps and chicken pox*
*To Bilbo, Rankin, Hoffman, Cox).*

The day after Christmas THE POST announced that beginning January 2 it would once again have its own cartoonist: 36-year-old Herbert L. Block, who signed his drawings Herblock, already a Pulitzer Prize–winner who was about to get out of the army. Meyer had been scouting for a cartoonist and when a mutual friend, Nelson Poynter, brought them together it was soon arranged.

Then, on December 28 at the bottom of page 1, ran this two-column headline over a short story:

PHILIP L. GRAHAM TO JOIN POST
JAN. 1 AS ASSOCIATE PUBLISHER

In 11 and a half years Eugene Meyer had succeeded in rescuing, reviving, and revitalizing THE WASHINGTON POST. As the newspaper entered its 69th year, a great deal remained to be done before it would become fully successful. But Meyer had given it the priceless ingredients of success: integrity, decency, and powerful idealism.

# 6

# New Energy
# Young Mr. Graham
# 1946–1954

Philip Leslie Graham was a lean six-foot-one bundle of nervous energy. Sensitive and shrewd, ingenious and innovative, direct and devious, benign and malicious, he seemed to be ever driven by some inner compulsion that in the end led him to take his own life. For more than 17 years at the helm of THE WASHINGTON POST — even after he entered what would be the fatal manic-depressive stage — Phil Graham was a vivid, lovable, dynamic publisher. A man with a salty vocabulary, he led, pushed, and prodded those who worked for him, vastly improving the newspaper during one of the most exhilarating periods in its history.

At Graham's death, POST Managing Editor Alfred Friendly wrote that he "could out-sleuth the paper's star reporters, out-think its sagest pundits, out-wit its most genial spoofers and out-write its fanciest — or most fancied — stylists." A dozen years later, Gordon Gray, who as a government official had known Graham well, described him as

> a *rara avis.* He was a complex person — seemingly a man of contradictions, but like a jig saw puzzle, he could and did put it all together. He was vibrant. He was brilliant. He was determined . . . He had serious drive and motivation, yet he had an impish humor. I could even describe him as an intellectual prankster . . . Phil had a wit like a flash of lightning; and he could be as forbidding as a thunder cloud . . . He was tolerant of almost anything except stupidity . . . He was, if you will, a practical dreamer. His was a restless mind, not content to leave undisturbed that which needed disturbing, and I think that he would say: "Remember me not for what I have

> done — but rather for the future that I may have helped to shape."

That Phil Graham helped to shape THE POST's future, and shaped it well, is beyond dispute. He became publisher and, later, controlling owner of THE POST by marrying Eugene Meyer's daughter and then demonstrating a capacity successfully to run and expand the enterprise. He was a less-than-affluent boy from the South, with politics, not printer's ink, in his veins. When he and Katharine Meyer were engaged he told her: "We're going to live in Florida and you're going to have only two dresses," and "I'm not going to take your father's money."

Graham, the son of Ernest R. and Florence Morris Graham, was born July 18, 1915, in Terry, South Dakota, a Black Hills mining town no longer on the map. His mother, a schoolteacher, died when he was in his teens. His father, who married again, was a Michigan native educated in agriculture and mining and an Army Corps of Engineers captain in World War I. The senior Graham moved to Dade County, Florida, in 1921 to manage a sugar cane project in the Everglades. Long a member of the state roads commission, he served in the state senate before losing a bid for the Democratic gubernatorial nomination in 1943. Until his death, the year after his son's suicide, he ran a dairy and cattle farm north of Miami.

Phil went to Miami High School, where he was voted "wittiest." At the University of Florida, where one of his roommates was the future Senator George Smathers, he majored in economics. After graduation he took a year off to drive milk trucks for his father. This southern background was ever in his mind; he used it as a ploy in blunting the wrath of southern congressmen over THE POST's liberal posture on racial and other issues. To one such he wrote in 1952: "What you must understand is that *The Post* is especially sensitive about people from the South, because all the people here have to put up with a publisher from the South."

His early years in Florida helped him understand the southern point of view but he was never a "southerner" himself. He graduated tenth in a class of 400 at Harvard Law School in 1939 where he was president of the *Law Review*. From Cambridge Graham went to Washington to clerk, first for Supreme Court Justice Stanley Reed and then for Justice Felix Frankfurter, to whom he always remained close. In 1941–1942 he was an attorney for the Lend-Lease Administration and then the Office for Emergency Management. In his brief government career, so eight of his colleagues testified when he became THE POST's associate publisher, Graham made "a major contribution to our war production and aid-to-our-Allies programs."

At Harvard Graham developed, politically, into something of a radical; as his close friend Edward F. Prichard, Jr., years later put it, the two of them were "sort of half-ass apologists" for the Soviet Union's position at the beginning of World War II. During his first year in Washington Graham was among a group of young bachelors who shared an Arlington, Virginia, house called Hockley. There he imbibed New Deal thinking, and there he met Katharine Meyer, already an ardent New Dealer, whom he married in 1940.

In 1942 Graham joined the Army Air Corps as a private. Commissioned the next year, he came to the Pentagon to work in G-2's "special branch" to help unravel Japanese military codes. Sent to the Southwest Pacific as an aide in that arcane branch of intelligence, he ended up a major, advising General George C. Kenney in the Philippine bombing campaigns. He was discharged in the fall of 1945.

Before Graham went off to the Pacific Meyer sat down for a talk with his son-in-law. I have to decide, Meyer said, about the future if nobody in the family is interested in the paper. His only son, Bill, by then was a physician. Of his four daughters only Katharine had shown any interest but he never thought of her in the role of publisher for the simple reason that she was a woman and his was a man's world. By now enchanted with Graham, Meyer asked: "Would you be interested?" Phil talked it over with Kay who told him: "You have to decide." He gave his father-in-law a "yes" before he left for the Pacific, a commitment that was to be fulfilled when he joined THE POST on January 1, 1946.

What Graham found was a paper that had shown a total profit of $249,451 in the wartime years of 1942–1945 after the initial nine and a half years of losses under Meyer. Circulation was growing but it was still well behind the *Star* and the round-the-clock *Times-Herald,* and advertising totaled barely a fourth of the linage in the city's four dailies. THE POST had gained an important measure of both public and journalistic standing but its physical plant was in bad shape, its staff too small, underpaid, and overworked. And this was a time of uncertainty about the economics of postwar Washington.

The 30-year-old Graham plunged into the job of learning the newspaper business. His quick mind and tenacious memory absorbed everything. A man of ideas and a craftsman with words, Graham's natural affinity was with writers and editors but he also "came out of the pressroom knowing as much as any pressman ever did," as business colleague Don Bernard put it. Graham needed perhaps a couple of years to absorb the business and plan its future. He had less than six months.

In June 1946 President Truman asked Meyer, then 70, to be the first president of the World Bank. Meyer went to his son-in-law to say that banking was "my first love and I'm interested" but "if you don't want me to, I won't go." Graham replied: "You must go." The bank post turned out to be such a bureaucratic jungle that Meyer found himself asking Graham for help rather than giving his son-in-law advice on handling the paper's problems. Meyer's tenure at the World Bank lasted only six months, but it was sufficient to launch that international organization and long enough to convince him that Graham was capable of running THE POST.

The formal announcement appeared on page 1 on June 18. While retaining his ownership interest in THE POST, Meyer stated, "I am withdrawing from the active direction of its affairs and shall have no control or responsibility over news or editorial matters." Graham became the publisher with Elliston the editor, Jones managing editor, Charles C. Boysen business manager, Bernard advertising director, and Wayne Coy assistant to the publisher, all their names appearing for the first time on the editorial page.

The shift of power was consolidated two years later after Meyer had returned to the paper as board chairman. On July 23, 1948, Meyer announced the transfer of voting stock to Philip and Katharine Graham. What he did not announce, however, was that Graham now would hold 3500 and his wife 1500 of the 5000 voting shares. When Meyer turned over the larger share to Graham he explained, "You never want a man working for his wife."

All these shares were placed in a trust to reinforce a Graham-suggested scheme that Meyer did announce, the creation of a committee of five to approve any further changes in control of THE POST. Amended articles of incorporation proclaimed the object of The Washington Post Company to be the publication of "an independent newspaper dedicated to the welfare of the community and the Nation, in keeping with the principles of a free press." Voting shares could only be transferred to persons considered by the new committee to hold that view of the newspaper's function and because, as Meyer put it, "control of *The Post* shall be treated as a public trust" and "shall never be transferred to the highest bidder without regard to other considerations." The committee was given "absolute discretion" to approve or disapprove any person to whom voting shares might be transferred. The group, however, would have "no authority over or responsibility for the policies or operations" of the paper.

The committee, which had the right to fill vacancies caused by death or resignation, continued in this role until it was dissolved when The Washington Post Company went public in 1971. The original members were Chester L. Barnard, president of the Rockefeller Foundation; James B. Conant, president of Harvard University; Colgate W. Darden, Jr., president of the University of Virginia; Bolitha J. Laws, chief judge of the United States District Court in the District of Columbia; and Mrs. Millicent C. McIntosh, dean of Barnard College. Successor committee members included Chief Justice Earl Warren and Davidson Sommers, a former general counsel of the World Bank and at the time an official of the Equitable Life Assurance Society. Committee approval was not required, however, for transfer of voting stock within the family; thus, on Graham's death, his widow became the majority voting stockholder, with other shares going to the four Graham children. In 1950 the Meyers turned over the bulk of their nonvoting, Class B, stock to the Eugene and Agnes E. Meyer Foundation, established in 1944, which supports Washington area charitable, cultural, and other civic activities.

Meyer's transfer of voting stock to the Grahams was a sale, not a gift. But Graham, by Meyer family standards, "didn't have a penny" when he married the boss' daughter. In their first years together Graham insisted that they live, rather frugally, on his salary; when he joined the army they used his wife's money from a trust fund set up by her father. To pay for POST stock Graham used a $75,000 gift from Meyer, what he saved from his salary, and a modest sum from the sale of Florida land his father had given him.

In his association with and control of THE POST Graham constantly faced a money problem. In the early years he wanted to make the paper profitable, not for the sake of making money — he once termed that "an essentially boring and dreary business" — but to demonstrate that he could manage finances like his father-in-law and that he did not have to depend on the Meyer fortune. In those years he did not seek money for himself but later, when illness overtook him, "the money thing built up in him" and he grew to have a compulsion both to make money and to wield power. Some came to feel that he had always had an inner insecurity because he was a poor boy who married into wealth. "To survive, a newspaper must be a commercial success," Meyer had said when he transferred the stock to his son-in-law and daughter; Graham could never forget.

The relationship between Meyer and Graham was extraordinarily close. Meyer, in the fashion of older and successful men, tended to retell stories of his career. His children fled from the repetition but Graham was a rapt listener who always wanted to hear more. Meyer's pre-POST story had been one of financial wizardry and Graham desperately wanted to find out how to be a wizard. Graham was a generous letter writer to his vacationing father-in-law, forwarding the latest company news and seeking advice. But Graham was in charge and Meyer's role was to advise and back his son-in-law.

The great turning point in THE POST's fortunes came in 1954 when it bought the *Times-Herald* and became the national capital's sole morning newspaper. But in the eight years before that, the paper barely broke even as Graham strove to earn, in the view of his peers, the right to his publisher's role, to meet THE POST's pressing need to grow and expand, and to cope with the changing city, suburbs, nation, and world of the post–World War II era.

Graham's first move to strengthen management was to find a new managing editor. With what little money was available, Casey Jones had built the core of a good staff; but Jones was a traditional old-school editor and times were changing. Quite conservative in outlook, Jones had a simplistic, black-hats-versus-white-hats view of affairs and he was uncomfortable with issue stories. It soon was evident that he was not Graham's kind of managing editor. So in the spring of 1947 Jones was booted upstairs to be assistant to the publisher until he left the paper three years later, and James Russell Wiggins became the new managing editor.

Russ Wiggins, then 43, had begun as a cub reporter in his native Minnesota. He then served for 25 years as editorial writer, managing editor, Washington correspondent, and editor of the Saint Paul *Dispatch–Pioneer Press.* Three months after Graham joined THE POST he offered Wiggins the job of Sunday editor but Wiggins chose to go to the New York *Times* as assistant to the publisher. In April 1947 Wiggins finally came to THE POST where he stayed 21 years until he left to become United States Ambassador to the United Nations.

Wiggins had never gone to college but he was a man of great erudition. A self-taught Jefferson scholar and an eloquent speaker, he was as ardent a believer in and advocate of a free press and "the people's right to know" as journalism has ever produced. In addition to his technical competence, Wiggins' enormous strength derived, above all, from his highly accentuated moral principles, his ethical standards, and his rigid integrity. In turn, however, these characteristics helped to account for what some perceived as a heavy-handedness and a remoteness from many of those who worked for him. His probity produced an often irritating ban on outside jobs that might constitute conflicts of interest and his fastidiousness was carried to a prohibition of food and drink at office desks.

He told the staff to avoid "the Jehovah complex," that "assumption of omnipotence." The function of a newspaper, as he saw it, was to "report what happens and what people do, say, think and feel about it." He fought with presidents, bureaucrats, and Congress to establish access to the news as a constitutional right of the press; therefore, he disdained anything that smacked of stealing government secrets for publication. In 1959 Graham wrote him: "It is clear to me that part of your individual talent — a major, admirable part — is to be a rock of integrity. *The Washington Post* would be nothing like as decent as it is today but for your steadfastness."

Not until more than two years after Wiggins' arrival did Graham find his counterpart for the business side. He was John W. Sweeterman, then 43 and working in Dayton, Ohio. On Advertising Director Bernard's recommendation, Graham initially tried to hire Sweeterman as retail advertising manager. He was so taken with Sweeterman that when he refused that offer, Graham proffered the business managership: Sweeterman became Bernard's boss, not his assistant. It took a $35,000 salary, $5000 more than Graham himself was getting, to hire Sweeterman and, when he accepted, Graham raised himself to $35,000.

Sweeterman, who in time became general manager and then publisher of the paper by Graham edict, found a dispirited business staff and his first task was to induce a belief that by more aggressive advertising solicitation THE POST someday could predominate in the morning field. But it was hard going because the *Star*'s philosophy was to keep its advertising rates low, a tactic profitable enough for that leading paper but which kept all the others financially strapped. Sweeterman was shrewd and he ran a tight shop which led some to view him as essentially a one-man operator. Tall, soft-spoken and handsome, he was penny-pinching, conservative and sometimes old-fashioned. He admitted years later that he had been shocked on first meeting Katharine Graham at home to find her in bare feet. During Graham's early years Sweeterman and Wiggins were more or less in continuous struggle over money for the news operation, with Graham the arbiter.

The winter before Sweeterman was hired, Graham plugged the other managerial weak spot: circulation boss. Harry Gladstein, a cheerful conservative who came from Hearst's Los Angeles *Examiner*, proved a great success though he, like Bernard and others on the business side, often moaned at the presumed detrimental effect on advertising and circulation of THE POST's liberal editorial policy and news slant. Gladstein stayed for more than 20 years, capping his career as business manager.

As a hedge against red-ink years and to make expansion possible, Graham, with Meyer's backing, bought into radio and television. In

1944 Meyer had bought WINX, a small local radio station. It made some money in the war years until Meyer discovered, and ended, broadcasting of the daily "number" for the benefit of local gamblers. After that WINX lost nearly half a million dollars before it was disposed of in 1949. That same year, Graham made a deal to buy a 55 percent interest in the Columbia Broadcasting System's local radio station, renamed WTOP. Together THE POST–CBS combination in 1950 purchased television station WOIC and changed the call letters to WTOP. In 1954 The Washington Post Company bought out CBS's 45 percent interest. The total cost came to $4,355,000. In 1953 The Washington Post Company purchased a Jacksonville, Florida, television station and in later years television stations in Miami and Hartford. After Graham's death the Miami station was renamed WPLG in his honor.

Revenues from radio and television were a major sustainer of the newspaper until its own consistent moneymaking era began with the *Times-Herald* purchase. More than one reporter remembered asking Graham for a raise and, as Sam Zagoria recalled it, hearing him reply, "Sam, did you get a check the last week from *The Post?* The funds for that came from WTOP. We lost money here." There was no raise. Wiggins was admonished, "There simply is no available money to award merit increases — except in the most extraordinary cases, and I hope none of these will arise." A number of good hands left for better-paying jobs; those who stuck it out through the lean years generally were well rewarded by salary boosts in the later profitable times.

Buying into television was like striking the mother lode for THE POST and for other publishers as well. The word "television" had first appeared in THE POST in 1927 but development was slow and World War II put it on the shelf. By 1948 there were still only 8600 sets in the city but televising the presidential conventions helped spiral sales. THE POST began listing TV programs that year and Sonia Stein, the paper's first TV reporter, wrote of the 1949 Truman inauguration that ten million had seen it in 14 cities, more than had viewed all previous inaugurations combined. In 1950 the Sunday paper began printing *TV Week*, a fold-in tabloid and the biggest single circulation booster since *Parade,* the Sunday supplement, had been added back in 1941.

Graham flooded THE POST with notes scribbled in his flowing handwriting. Early on they were cautiously worded but soon they were exuberant and forceful, sometimes ordering or demanding, but almost always with humor, even whimsy. When he discovered that a wire service story had "all the jollity blue-penciled out," he wrote Wiggins, "I hope we never stop struggling to make the important interesting

— even if some of the bill of fare may seem of less than cosmic importance." He asked: "Are we making front page too ponderous for general readership? . . . Should we have put just one or two national items inside and had a couple of general interest snappers outside for the Silver Spring housewife?" The rival *Times-Herald* ran a page 3 of scandal and other forms of titillation; Graham ordered THE POST's page 3 henceforth to be made up of "light news — local, human interest, popular feature stuff, etc."

Graham developed an antipathy for "jumps" from page 1, stories that told the reader to turn to another page for the rest of the account. Some days page 1 had as many as a dozen jumps and he ordered this cut to one or two or at a maximum four. But the nature of news made this a hard rule to follow and Graham complained that it was "violated frequently." The limited-jump rule became a Graham fetish, pursued relentlessly to the annoyance of both editors who made up the pages and reporters whose stories were chopped off to avoid a jump. As the paper grew a parallel mechanical problem was the placement of the editorial, sports, and financial pages. To readers' bewilderment one or the other would appear one day in the first news section, the next day somewhere back in other sections.

Graham criticized the wording of headlines, misspellings, even the content of the crossword puzzle. When Joseph M. Lalley, a gifted but eccentric editorial writer, used the word "avatar" Graham wrote to Elliston: "I really think that the use of rare and unusual words — and I mean to the common people, of which I have the honor of being one myself — gets them mad." A sportswriter, criticized for "carelessness," was admonished: "Moreover, as you probably know, the sports pages are in effect the English teachers of a great majority of the young boys in our area." Graham distributed to editors and reporters copies of Strunk and White's *Elements of Style* and to particular offenders he sent Fowler's *Dictionary of Modern English Usage.*

There was praise, too. One reporter was "certainly doing a brilliant job" covering a trial. Another's story was "the best written we have run in months." He told Folliard that his coverage of a political campaign had been "consistently a joy." Despite budget stringencies, Graham was always on the outlook for new talent. In 1949 he hired Chalmers M. Roberts, then on the *Star*, as a local and later foreign affairs reporter. Then 38, Roberts had been a POST cub in 1933–1934 and had been a wartime colleague of Graham's in military intelligence.

Wiggins received most of the internal prods: the book page was missing the "news" that some volumes made, and, "Do you think we are doing enough on food in the women's section, in view of our general importance in the food [advertising] field?" But to outsiders who complained, Graham knew how to turn away wrath.

> Now I will let you in on a terrifying secret. Occasionally things get into our paper with which I don't agree. And frankly, I haven't found how to keep bright and creative people around and happy if one exercises plenary control. Nor have I found how to be in two places at once so that I can always see all copy pre-publication.

He could sidestep. To an irate Harold Ickes he avoided a direct reply with: "Since you make it so difficult to get into a controversy with you . . ." But if the outsider had a point, Graham would send an editorial writer a note: "Were we wrong? If so, should we admit it?"

The publisher worried how to save precious news space, find new comics, place ads, use photographs, hold down payment of overtime. He sent a constant flow of news story tips to reporters and was responsible for a series that won Folliard the Pulitzer Prize for 1946, the first ever for a POST reporter. From his voluminous correspondence he had plucked a sentence in a letter from Georgia Governor Ellis Arnall: "Have you been reading about the Columbians, a brown-shirt organization fashioned on the Hitler pattern that is operating in my state?" Graham sent Folliard, at the moment enjoying a rest with Truman at Key West, Florida, to investigate. The reporter wrote four well-displayed page 1 articles about the "fanatic racists" who "dress and swagger in the manner of storm troopers."

The publisher's ever-growing circle of friends and acquaintances included leaders of the nation's businesses and advertising agencies. From them, without compunction but never crudely, he solicited advertising THE POST so much needed. No ad was too small; to one Washington businessman he wrote:

> As you know, I saved your waning reputation as a salesman by arranging for the new *Post* building to be heated with your fuel oil. Now my Advertising Department boys are giving me a loud raspberry because the first ad in what is apparently your fall campaign on fuel oil and oil burners has just appeared in the *Star*. What are you going to do to save my waning reputation?

He got the ad.

Graham was repelled by the First Amendment yammer that so often came from his fellow publishers. To the head of the national publishers' association he wrote: "I have always thought that we newspaper people should be careful not to cry 'Wolf' about our Constitutional protection. Otherwise, we are not going to have public support when real violations of Freedom of the Press arise."

Graham consumed books and sent copies to both reporters and friends outside THE POST. He put his wife Katharine to work in 1949 writing The Magazine Rack, a Sunday roundup of the best or most striking in the periodicals, a task she continued for several years. He serialized books ranging from John Hersey's *Hiroshima* and Joe Louis' *My Story* to Eleanor Roosevelt's *This I Remember* and General Eisenhower's *Crusade in Europe*, all circulation boosters. POST Book and Author Luncheons, which had begun the month before Graham's arrival, promoted literary and political authors — and THE POST. Theodore White and other big names wrote for the Sunday brains section; Arthur Schlesinger, Jr., did a weekly news roundup for some months.

The most irrepressible author was Agnes Meyer. When she sent in stories from New Mexico on the impoverished Chicanos, however, Casey Jones would have none of them: "Who the hell in Washington cares about a lot of Mexicans." But she persisted. In the early Graham years she alone wrote, with fervor and distinction, about the nation's larger postwar social problems. She lobbied President Truman to create a new department of health, education, and welfare but it was his successor who actually did so. Truman complained to a visitor: "There's hardly a day I don't get a letter from that woman or from Eleanor Roosevelt telling me how to run this job."

Reader surveys showed that THE POST's columnists — especially Jerry Kluttz, Mary Haworth, Drew Pearson, Shirley Povich, and Bill Gold — were the top attractions, "almost always read." In 1947 when William E. Gold, who had been news director at WINX, moved over to the paper, Casey Jones created a column for him and named it "The District Line." A sprightly compendium ranging from traffic problems to cat and dog giveaways, interspersed with birthday greetings, bits of philosophy, and humorous tidbits, The District Line continued year after year as a popular hometown corner in a paper of increasingly broader horizons. That first year a reader sent in a dollar in thanks for finding a home for a kitten and Bill passed it on to Children's Hospital. Thus began an annual campaign which, through 1977, enriched the hospital by nearly $1.25 million.

Reader surveys showed that the *Times-Herald* comics had more followers than those in the three other papers combined. In 1947 Graham restored the comics to prewar size. Soon THE POST was advertising 34, then 40, Sunday comics in color, "more comics than in any other newspaper in America." It was discovered, however, that a paper in Lancaster, Pennsylvania, of all places, actually outdid THE POST by two. There were other promotional efforts: for a number of years an annual National Celebrities Golf Tournament attracted big names, with the profits going to local programs to combat juvenile delinquency; a children's book fair begun in 1950 still continues annually.

In his search for new talent, Graham replaced retiring music critic Ray C. B. Brown with Paul Hume who had been music director at WINX. Hume was never one to pull critical punches and one review almost earned him a punch in the nose, or worse, from the President of the United States.

When Margaret Truman made her debut with the National Symphony Orchestra in November 1949, Hume wrote that "she is now beginning to acquire the first fundamentals of singing" but "Miss Truman is still too much of a vocal beginner to appear in public." Apparently father didn't see those words. A year later, however, he did read, back on the theater page in the second news section, what Hume had written the night before:

> Margaret Truman, soprano, sang in Constitution Hall last night [with] a pleasant voice of little size and fair quality. [While] she is extremely attractive on the stage . . . she is flat a good deal of the time — more last night than at any time we have heard her in past years . . . Miss Truman has not improved in the years we have heard her . . . She still cannot sing with anything approaching professional finish . . . It is an extremely unpleasant duty to record such unhappy facts about so honestly appealing a person.

The President, his wife, and the visiting British Prime Minister were in the presidential box that evening. When Truman read Hume's review next morning he penned a bitter letter, put his own three-cent stamp on the envelope, and dropped it in a mailbox while out on his morning walk.

> Mr. Hume: I've just read your lousy review of Margaret's concert. I've come to the conclusion that you are an "eight ulcer man on four ulcer pay."
>
> It seems to me that you are a frustrated old man who wishes he could have been successful. When you write such poppycock as was in the back section of the paper you work

for it shows conclusively that you're off the beam and at least four of your ulcers are at work.

Some day I hope to meet you. When that happens you'll need a new nose, a lot of beef steak for black eyes, and perhaps a supporter below!

Pegler, a gutter snipe is a gentleman along side you. I hope you'll accept that statement as a worse insult than a reflection on your ancestry.

H.S.T.

Hume was aghast; could it really have come from the President? He asked Folliard to look at the letter and Folliard was certain it was Truman's handwriting. An art display with the letter was about to go into the paper when Graham intervened; he notified the White House that he did not intend to publish it. He told Hume he had had similar letters from Truman that never would be printed. Hume, however, could not contain himself; he innocently let out the story in a chat next evening with fellow music critic Milton Berliner of the *News* and THE POST was badly scooped. The most Graham would permit was to allow a reprint of the *News* account, adding a gracious statement by Hume: "I can only say that a man carrying a terrible burden of the current world crisis ought to be indulged in an occasional outburst of temper." Margaret Truman commented: "I am absolutely positive my father wouldn't use such language as that . . . This is ghastly . . . Mr. Hume is a very fine critic. He has a right to write as he pleases."

Hume's review and other grievances against THE POST led Truman to dash off an acerbic handwritten note to Graham in December 1952: "Look at the attached editorial from Roy Howard's snotty little *News.* It should have appeared in Eugene Meyer's paper. How come it didn't?" The publisher's reply included: "We have never questioned, as did the editorial you enclosed from another newspaper, the patriotism of any of your Cabinet."

THE POST's attitude toward President Truman varied. The paper supported him for keeping wage and price controls after war's end and in his battles with John L. Lewis; it backed his major foreign policies. But it criticized many of his appointments, his seizure of the steel mills, and the corruption in his administration.

In July 1946 Gallup reported in THE POST that for the first time since Roosevelt's 1932 election a majority said they would vote Republican. That November the voters elected the GOP-controlled 80th Congress. After the voting Arkansas Democratic Senator J. William Fulbright suggested that Truman name a Republican Secretary of State, then resign, allowing the Republican to become President. Walter Lippmann agreed. THE POST, while calling the vote a "resounding repudiation" of the Truman administration, said that Truman should not resign but "the statesmanlike thing to do is for the President to name a new Cabinet of Republicans for all the portfolios except that of the State Department" and then announce that he would not run in 1948.

A particular villain to Truman, much of Congress, and THE POST was John L. Lewis, head of the United Mine Workers. Shortly after the election he risked jail by ordering a strike in defiance of a court order. The threat of new shortages and electricity brownouts led THE POST to declare that Lewis "is perhaps the leading example on the current American scene of the Actonian dictum that absolute corruption flows from possession of absolute power." Partly due to the ire against Lewis, Congress passed, over Truman's veto, the Taft-Hartley Act outlawing the closed shop and otherwise restricting organized labor. THE POST called the law "far from being perfect or even ideal" but rejected labor's contention that it was a "slave labor bill."

In June 1948 THE POST published a tabloid section, "Fifteen Exciting Years," to mark the period since Meyer's acquisition of the paper. But it did not seem a happy year for Truman. In April his "favorable" Gallup rating was down to a new low of only 36 percent. Two of Roosevelt's sons, Franklin and Elliot, were calling for Eisenhower, and a group of liberal Democrats, among them "Minneapolis Mayor Hubert Humphries" as his name was misspelled in THE POST, came close to endorsing Ike. Harold Stassen, the former "boy governor" of Minnesota, led Truman in a Gallup poll, 56 to 33.

A defiant Truman marched over to the Mayflower Hotel in May to tell the Young Democrats: "I want to say to you at this time that during the next four years there will be a Democrat in the White House and you are looking at him." And when "Mr. Republican," Ohio's Senator Robert A. Taft, referred disparagingly to Truman's "whistle stop" tour of the nation, the President grabbed the phrase, using it repeatedly along with his slam-bang attack on "the notorious do-nothing Republican 80th Congress." Truman drew big crowds, Folliard reported from the campaign train, but when the Republicans nominated New York's Governor Dewey and California's Governor Warren as their ticket, most of THE POST staff saw Truman as doomed.

With Eisenhower refusing to run, Wiggins wrote that "there are a lot of practical arguments for [the Democrats] surrendering to the inevitable" and nominating a "custodian" candidate such as 70-year-old Senator Alben Barkley. Wiggins was a better prognosticator at the convention, which picked a Truman-Barkley ticket. There he wrote of Humphrey, who led the fight for a strong civil rights plank in the platform, that he "left his indelible mark" and was "definitely 'on his way.'" The Dixiecrats walked out, later forming a "racial integrity" third party under the leadership of Governor Strom Thurmond of South Carolina. Albright described the Democratic convention as having "all the gaiety of a wake." THE POST spurned both the racially motivated Dixiecrats and the gathering that named Henry Wallace as the Progressive Party candidate. An editorial said, "The Communist minority had the [Progressive] convention in hand from beginning to end."

When Albright wrote from Dewey headquarters that the GOP candidate would give Truman "the silent treatment," an editorial remarked that "there are indications that Mr. Dewey can afford the luxury of this sort of campaign." THE POST came down hard on Truman's "ranting tactics" and said that Dewey "offers national unity, general good will and teamwork." The only note of uncertainty to creep into THE POST's political reportage came from the campaign-wise Bob Albright. He was number two to Folliard for political reporting so he went with Truman; Folliard followed the presumed new President. Albright wrote in a mid-October roundup: "Now and then a particularly large crowd or a noisy ovation starts a mighty surge of hope in the rear staff car [of the Truman train]. Some of it filters forward to the press car and hard-bitten reporters ask themselves, 'Could we be wrong?'"

Gallup predicted Dewey "will win the presidential election with a substantial majority of electoral votes." The final regular edition of THE POST on election night bannered disbelief:

> DEWEY GAINING ON EARLY TRUMAN LEAD;
> LATE RETURNS WILL DECIDE PRESIDENCY;
> DEMOCRATS WINNING HOUSE AND SENATE

The second of two extras bannered: HOUSE MAY NAME PRESIDENT. But the next day there was no doubt. Publisher Graham knew what to do. Seizing on a phrase in Folliard's election eve story — if Truman won, "the poll takers and the prognosticators would be forced into the greatest crow-eating debauche in the annals of American politics" — he rushed off a telegram to Truman in Independence, Missouri, and reproduced it on page 1:

> You are hereby invited to attend a "crow banquet" to which this newspaper proposes to invite newspaper editorial writers, political reporters and editors, including our own along with pollsters, radio commentators and columnists for the

> purpose of providing a repast appropriate to the appetite created by the late election.
>
> The main course will consist of breast of tough old crow en glace (You will eat turkey).
>
> The Democratic National Committee has agreed to furnish the toothpicks to be used by the guests who (it is feared) will require months to get the last of the crow out of their teeth.
>
> We hope you will consent to deliver the address of the evening. As the dean of American election forecasters (and the only accurate one) it is much desired that you share with your colleagues the secret of your analytical success.
>
> Dress for guest of honor, white tie; for others — sack cloth.

With delight, Truman read THE POST telegram to a crowd at Jefferson City, Missouri. Back in Washington, there was a victorious drive down Pennsylvania Avenue for Truman and Barkley. They rode past a huge sign stretched across the front of THE POST's E Street building: "Welcome Home from The Crow Eaters." From the White House, Truman sent a telegram, also displayed on page 1:

> I received on the train your very handsome invitation to me to attend a "crow banquet." I know that we could all have a good time together, but I feel I must decline. As I said en route to Washington, I have no desire to crow over anybody or to see anybody eating crow, figuratively or otherwise. We should all get together now and make a country in which everybody can eat turkey whenever he pleases. Incidentally, I want to say that despite what your commentators and polls said, your news coverage of my campaign was fair and comprehensive.

The year 1948 was "the greatest" in its history for THE POST, a house ad proclaimed, with both advertising and circulation at new highs. But the great hope of the Meyers and Grahams was not yet to come true. Cissy Patterson died on July 24, willing the *Times-Herald* to seven faithful employees. When they ran into financial troubles the next year, Graham secretly offered $4.5 million for the paper and Meyer was prepared to pay another $1,050,000 for part of Mrs. Patterson's share in the trust that controlled the Chicago *Tribune* and the New York *News.* The offer later was increased, but Colonel Robert R. McCormick, the crusty boss of the *Tribune,* alarmed that an outsider might buy into his organization, stepped in to purchase the *Times-Herald* on July 20, 1949. Graham went back to work saying, hopefully: "I think we'll make it another way." His wife wept. The bitter journalistic war between the two papers continued nearly five more years.

It was thus an act of faith as well as necessity when THE POST announced at the end of 1949 that a new building was being constructed at 1513–21 L Street Northwest, a "modern seven story newspaper plant" to replace its then 56-year-old E Street home. By now the company's nearly 800 employees spilled over into three other structures. The new building, THE POST's fifth, doubled press capacity and provided air conditioning for all. Meyer put up the necessary $6 million by selling some of his stock in other companies. The move was made in stages during November and December 1950. At the January 28, 1951, dedication, Secretary of Defense George C. Marshall declared that an independent paper like THE POST was "one of the most delicate instruments in America's arsenal of freedom."

In a 26-page new-building supplement on January 23, Graham wrote that "the paper has a personality bigger than anyone on it" and "is grounded in its local community, wedded to the traditions of our country, fixed with a love of liberty, capable of indignation over injustice and aware of the destiny and responsibility of America as a world leader." THE POST's positions did not always "gibe with prevailing opinion, conservative or liberal," he added. "Its independence invites attack. But if a newspaper professes to have a personality, and is known as disinterested, the mud in the long run fails to stick."

Despite THE POST's marginal financial position, Graham instituted two plans to reward employees; both were based on faith in the future and both turned out to be highly worthwhile for participants. In 1952 some 20 executives were granted stock options and later others participated. Shares bought that first year at $47.50 grew to $1173 by 1970. Graham arranged bank loans for some executives to buy stock; others helped the paper financially by investing their own funds. The company bought back all this nonvoting stock when an employee retired or left THE POST, and in due course 14 persons were worth more than $1 million each. In 1953 Graham began a profit-sharing plan, essentially a substitute pension system, for the many hundreds of employees with the company at least five years. Ten percent of profits before taxes went into the fund. In 1974 THE POST and some of its unions, at union requests, began shifting from profit-sharing to fully funded pension systems. At the end of 1974 the assets in the fund were worth $15.6 million. Since inception in 1953 through 1974 THE POST contributed $17.2 million and $24.2 million had been paid to employees who left the company or to their beneficiaries.

One of the last big stories at the E Street building was the November 1, 1949, attempted assassination of Truman, then living at Blair House while the White House was being reconstructed. It illustrated the element of chance in reporting. White House reporter Folliard had a day off and the paper had no one on duty at the Executive Mansion when at 2:19 P.M. a group of Puerto Rican independence activists attacked. Chal Roberts, en route to another assignment, happened at that moment to be walking through Lafayette Park, across from the White House and close to Blair House, when police car sirens began to scream. There were so many, all headed in one direction, that Roberts began to run. As a result, he was the first on the scene. The story by Roberts and Alfred E. Lewis detailed the "wild exchange of blazing guns which broke the early afternoon Indian Summer calm."

Truman was not hurt but his political fortunes continued to decline. Scandals, including the distribution of deep freezers, then something new and prized by a favor seeker, had rocked the administration. "Five percenters," those who collected for their influence in obtaining government contracts, were being investigated.

In 1949 Graham conceived the idea of a senatorial investigation of organized crime and the possible tie-in between gangsters and politicians around the country. Wiggins and Folliard talked to federal experts who named as the three top men of the American underworld Frank Costello, Joe Adonis, and Frank Erickson. Costello and Adonis had been rumrunners during Prohibition, then became big operators in the gambling world. Erickson was "king of the bookmakers." Folliard was sent to New York to interview them. It was a tricky business, for the underworld was not used to talking to newspapermen for quotation. Costello, however, blurted out, "I'm a gambler but I don't operate where I'm not wanted." The implication was clear: he would operate only where the local authorities gave him a green light, where "the fix" was on. Adonis said the same thing. Folliard had the gambler-politician tie.

Wiggins thought up the tagline "Tygoons" for a series of articles in November, syndicated across the nation. Graham found his senator to run the investigation in Estes Kefauver, the Tennessee Democrat who had licked the Crump machine in Memphis. A member of the District Committee, Kefauver had first taken an interest in crime in Washington and had discussed that problem with POST editors. But he was reluctant to take on a nationwide probe until Graham exploded at him, "Damn it, Estes, don't you want to be Vice President?"

The majority Democrats in the Senate were wary that criminal ties to big city machines would cause their party political embarrassment.

But the "Tygoons" series and other publicity forced their hand and Kefauver was permitted to run an investigation for nearly a year. Short of staff, the paper never put a full-time reporter on the crime story, however, and the result too often was hit-and-miss coverage.

Crime was not only a national problem. Barely ten weeks after Wiggins became managing editor, THE POST on June 29, 1947, kicked off an investigation of "pocketed" — hidden — city crime reports with a lead story by Robert Bruskin and John Singerhoff. The result was a nearly four-and-a-half-year running battle with Washington Police Chief Robert J. Barrett before he was forced into retirement and THE POST's facts shown to be true. It was no more than a normal local newspaper campaign against a crooked police hierarchy except for the fact that aroused local citizens lacked the usual means of retaliation — throwing out those responsible at the next election. Because the city had no vote the burden fell on the newspaper and THE POST got no help from its rivals.

In fighting back, Barrett discovered and publicized the fact that City Editor Ben Gilbert, who ran the investigation under Wiggins' direction, had once been, briefly, a member of the Young Communist League. Barrett's officers also harassed POST delivery trucks for such things as double-parking in the middle of the night. The chief turned on Alfred E. Lewis, the paper's police reporter since 1935, especially when Lewis and Richard Morris began describing "the charmed life" of local gambler Emmitt Warring who had operated "without serious police interference for 14 years." Lewis, who became the city's senior and best police reporter and continued indefatigably for the next three decades, was one of those newsmen who phoned in so many stories he lost the art of writing them himself.

The paper's inability to appeal to voters led Wiggins to call for and get a congressional investigation and Gilbert to turn over to a cooperative Senate committee THE POST's invaluable file of police corruption tips. At one point Graham even went to see President Truman to tell him the city had a bad police chief. To this Truman responded, "Mr. Graham, if I am any judge of character Major Barrett is a fine police officer." If so, said the publisher, there's nothing more to discuss but would you ask him to stop harassing our delivery trucks. The harassment ended the next night.

The outcome of the Barrett case was a cleaner police force, some encomiums for THE POST, and an intensification of the paper's efforts to win from Congress home rule for the city.

At home, before the capital and the nation had time to catch their collective breath after the wartime exertions, a new menace appeared:

spies and traitors among us. The investigations, political uproars, threats to and violations of civil liberties consumed hundreds of POST columns, created internal problems at the paper, and threats to it from without that could not be brushed off.

It began with a page 1 headline in the February 16, 1946, POST: CANADA NABS 22 IN SECRET LEAK. This was the result of the revelations of Igor Gouzenko, a Soviet code clerk who defected in Ottawa and brought with him numerous incriminating documents. THE POST got off on the wrong foot editorially. Its first reaction was to ridicule the Canadian revelations: "One cannot but wonder . . . what the Russians were really after. Were they hoping, by any chance, to steal the whole Columbia River [atomic] plant and to ship it, brick by brick, to the Ural Mountains?" Two weeks later, when Gouzenko's name had been disclosed in a Canadian Royal Commission report, an editorial complained that the document did not reveal what secrets the Soviets had obtained "but unless it was a great deal, the whole thing would seem to have been a great waste of energy and expense." The editorial went on to declare that "the practice of suspending civil rights on the pretext of national security," as had been done in the Canadian inquiry, "is quite as disturbing as the spy plot itself."

It was such editorial devotion to civil liberties that led THE POST onto some dangerous ground just as the Cold War between the United States and the Soviet Union was beginning. In large part this derived from THE POST's long-time antipathy toward the actions and methods of the House Un-American Activities Committee whose scattergun techniques and lurid accusations had been the paper's target in prewar and wartime years. This skeptical attitude was maintained toward the new spy scares that followed the Gouzenko revelations.

THE POST, however, assigned no one to dig out the facts of what was going on within the government. It simply printed what was made public: Truman's establishment of a loyalty board to check employees and FBI Director J. Edgar Hoover's warnings against a Communist "fifth column." THE POST viewed Truman's board as providing "a fair and systematic method to deal with a problem that has long called for vigorous and decisive action" with "no impairment of Constitutional rights of free speech."

Under the Truman order, investigations of new government employees now were in full swing. In June 1948 the State Department said it had fired ten as bad security risks and in July Federal Diary columnist Jerry Kluttz reported that at least 223 federal workers had been "either fired or forced out on disloyalty charges" in the nine months ending April 1. Soon there was a bitter row over the loyalty hearings and the rules of a loyalty review board. When that board announced that no accused employee could face and cross-examine his accuser, other than in exceptional cases, and that board members themselves could not question or identify accusers, THE POST erupted editorially. If the FBI is not willing to identify accusers to the board, the paper said, "its evidence deserves no credence whatever." Here was a position of principle to which the paper held until, in time, the rules were changed and accusers had to be unmasked.

The loyalty investigations shook bureaucratic morale. The prestigious Washington law firm of Arnold, Porter and Fortas represented a number of accused State employees and won for them the right of resignation without anything being placed in their records against them. The only relief from this grim business was an item in a women's page column. Truman had received a postcard saying:

> I read where the Government is giving out loyalty checks. I was employed by the Government during the war. I was loyal. Please send me my check.

THE POST did assign a reporter to cover the House Un-American Activities Committee. She was Mary Spargo, who previously had worked for the committee. On May 29, 1947, she reported that a freshman committeeman had announced that the group would call 30 film stars. He was Richard M. Nixon. Given THE POST's firmly established negative attitude toward the committee, it was inevitable that Nixon and the paper would collide. In his 1962 book, *Six Crises,* Nixon wrote that THE POST, "which was typical of a large segment of the national press and of public opinion, has always taken a dim view of the Committee." THE POST's opinion of Nixon was fixed when the committee cited what became known as the Hollywood Ten for contempt in refusing to answer queries about Communist associations; they were blacklisted by the film industry. Nixon first appeared in a Herblock cartoon on May 16, 1948, where he and two other representatives, attired as Puritans, were pictured building a fire under a chained Statue of Liberty and saying: "We've Got to Burn the Evil Spirits Out of Her."

THE POST began to come under considerable fire for its stand. On December 14, 1947, an editorial replied to a complaint about its attitude toward the committee:

> This newspaper's criticism of the committee has been directed consistently at its methods rather than at its aims . . . Because the committee under successive chairmanships has equated loyalty with conformity, has concerned itself

> with opinions rather than activities, has disregarded the most elementary rules of fair play in dealing with witnesses, its conduct has seemed to us to be more dangerously un-American than that of any of the groups or individuals it has investigated.

In early 1948 the paper ran a series of 12 editorials, titled "Turning on the Light," explaining in detail what it had capsulized in the earlier editorial. The final editorial said that a witness should have the right to put questions to another witness "who has reflected on his reputation," that attorneys should be present, hearings should be open, that contempt citations should be issued only by a majority vote of either House or Senate, and that hearings should be by regular committees and not by special committees such as HUAC. A day later, however, the House doubled the budget of that committee.

In March 1948 an article in an obscure monthly, *Plain Talk,* edited by the Russian-born anti-Communist Isaac Don Levine, attacked THE POST as "a Trojan Horse for totalitarianism." Targets were publisher Graham as "a constant apologist for the paper's editorial policy," cartoonist Herblock, and Alan Barth, "unmistakably the ideological guide of its editorial page," who was charged with "adherence to the party line." The attack quoted Representative George A. Dondero, a Michigan Republican, who had referred to THE POST as "the Washington edition of the *Daily Worker.*"

The article, Graham soon discovered, had been written by a former POST clerical employee who had been fired. Although it was inserted in the *Congressional Record,* the magazine article created no meaningful public ripple. But Graham was quite disturbed when he discovered that an advertising agency, not employed by THE POST, had circulated copies and that some POST advertisers were taking it seriously. These underground murmurs, or worse, against the paper continued until they surfaced in a 1951 attack, built on the *Plain Talk* article, in the Chicago *Tribune* alleging that THE POST had been "defending Reds and pinkos." But before that occurred, the paper was more deeply involved in a whole gamut of "loyalty" issues, most notably the Hiss case.

In August 1948 Spargo reported that the House Un-American Activities Committee had summoned Whittaker Chambers, associate editor of *Time* magazine, to testify. He issued a statement saying he had quit the Communist Party because he became convinced that "it was an evil and a threat to the entire Western civilization." Next day, after Chambers' public testimony, THE POST's five-column headline read:

FORMER HIGH U.S. OFFICIALS
NAMED AS ACTING FOR SOVIETS;
WITNESS IS EX-RED COURIER

The chief former official was Alger Hiss; the others included his brother Donald Hiss, Harry Dexter White, Nathan Witt, Lee Pressman, John Abt, and Victor Perle. Chambers was the self-confessed "ex-red courier." The Hiss brothers and White flatly denied Chambers' accusations under oath.

For THE POST the Hiss case was agonizing from the beginning and the paper's handling of it typed it for years to come in the view of readers on both sides. Graham knew Alger Hiss only slightly, Donald Hiss somewhat better. But many of the publisher's friends came to Alger Hiss' defense with both words and money; among them, to stand up for Hiss was a litmus test of decency. Chambers seemed a disreputable informer; his charges too fantastic to accept. One editorial said that "one wonders why the testimony of turncoats should be preferred to that of men whose reputations are otherwise unsullied and who have enjoyed the full confidence of many of the most eminent Americans in private and in public life." Another editorial said that either Chambers or Hiss had committed perjury and it should be left to a jury to decide. "As things stand," it added, "it is the committee which is subject to the most serious indictment of all."

After Hiss had conceded he had known Chambers but only under another name, the two men finally confronted one another, first in secret in a New York hotel room and then on August 25 in a packed House caucus room. At the latter confrontation, Hiss invited Chambers to make his accusations where they would not be privileged. Two days later Chambers appeared on Mutual radio's "Meet the Press" and in answer to a question by POST reporter Folliard said, "Alger Hiss was a Communist and may be now." For six days Hiss did not react. On the seventh, THE POST said editorially: "Mr. Hiss himself has created a situation in which he is obliged to put up or shut up . . . Each day of delay [in filing a suit for slander] does incalculable damage to his reputation." In his book, Nixon quoted those lines, written by Barth, adding: "Even *The Post* changed its tune." *Time* magazine later commented in an otherwise laudatory story about the paper that it had "doggedly sympathized with Alger Hiss during the early stages of his trials."

A month after the "Meet the Press" challenge, Hiss finally sued Chambers, asking $50,000 for defamation of character. The case disappeared from the front page as the Truman-Dewey campaign climaxed in the President's stunning victory on November 2. Chambers meanwhile was pondering his problem and he came up with "the pumpkin papers."

In his Federal Diary column of December 1, Kluttz dropped a hint picked up from a Justice Department attorney: "The Hiss-Chambers fight is slated to make news again very shortly . . . Some very startling information on who's a liar is reported to have been uncovered." Nixon later told Kluttz that the moment he read the item he issued a subpoena for all Chambers' documents. Kluttz always was jealously protective of his news items, often complaining that prime news was lifted from his column on an editor's orders to be turned over to other reporters to develop into front-page stories; this one was not. Three days later a New York *Herald Tribune* news service story by Bert Andrews recounted on THE POST's page 1 how Chambers had produced, from a hollowed-out pumpkin on his Westminster, Maryland, farm, microfilm of classified government papers he alleged Hiss had passed to him.

The initial editorial comment was grudging: "Mr. Nixon undoubtedly deserves credit for belatedly bringing forth what the Committee on Un-American Activities should have had months ago." Then, as the "pumpkin papers" story expanded, THE POST conceded that it was "pretty clear" that the committee "had got hold of something real this time — some genuine documentary evidence." On December 15 Alger Hiss was indicted by the New York grand jury for perjury; the statute of limitations precluded an espionage charge.

In the final days leading up to the indictment THE POST had rotated four reporters on the Hiss case, a sure prescription for poor journalism. When Hiss went to trial in New York federal court, Murrey Marder, a careful, precise, and conscientious reporter, was sent to cover the story. But before the trial began another spy case broke in Washington. Judith Coplon, a clerk in the foreign agents registration unit at the Justice Department, had fallen in love with a Russian agent, Valentine A. Gubitchev, and had attempted to provide him with FBI documents. Her trial in Washington was well covered by Bill Brinkley, a facile writer whose skill with words delighted Graham. Later the same year Brinkley discovered and wrote the story of a 14-year-old boy in suburban Mt. Rainier, Maryland, who was freed by a Catholic priest of possession by the devil. It was on the basis of Brinkley's story that William Blatty, at the time a Georgetown University student, wrote the best-selling book *The Exorcist.*

Barth's editorial on the Hiss verdict began:

> Alger Hiss had the misfortune of being tempted to betray his country in an era of widespread illusions about communism and of being tried for perjury in connection with his offense

> in a period of cold war when the pendulum of public sentiment had swung far in the other direction. That does not excuse him or minimize the enormity of the crime of which he has been convicted.

Enemies of THE POST seized upon the first sentence, quoting it out of context, to make the case that the paper was "soft on communism."

Asked about the Hiss verdict, Secretary of State Dean Acheson caused a furor by saying, "I should like to make it clear to you that whatever the outcome of any appeal which Mr. Hiss or his lawyers may make in the case, I do not intend to turn my back on Alger Hiss." THE POST criticized Acheson's defense of Hiss: "Mr. Acheson has played right into the hands of the yammerers in our midst who are trying to rend our society with the Alger Hiss conviction as the instrument — has, indeed, given them a handle . . . Judgment was obscured when Secretary Acheson decided to yield to a personal sentiment."

This analysis was correct; Acheson did give his critics on the right a new handle and for the rest of the Truman administration they used it effectively against him. But Acheson supporters on the liberal-left wrote in a letter to the editor that "we had reason to hope" that THE POST "would regard" Acheson's statement "as an act of personal courage and a declaration of principle rare in past history and virtually unprecedented in these times." The signers were Thurmond Arnold, Wendell Berge, Oscar S. Cox, A. Powell Davies, Paul A. Porter, Joseph L. Rauh, Jr., and Gerhard P. Van Arkel. In a private letter to Graham, Justice Frankfurter also took exception to the editorial.

Hiss was sentenced to five years in the penitentiary and served 44 months. To the public at large he seemed to have been guilty of espionage for the Soviet Union, although a dwindling group of loyal friends stuck with him in his constant disclaimers and his charges that the evidence had been framed against him by a punitive government. A quarter century after his conviction, when he came to Washington to give a talk and read some of the FBI documents finally released to him, a sympathetic POST article called him "a man whose case still nags at the American conscience."

On February 9, 1950, in a Lincoln's Birthday speech at Wheeling, West Virginia, Wisconsin's freshman Republican senator, Joseph R. McCarthy, Jr., charged that the State Department was filled with "bright young men born with silver spoons in their mouths" and presided over by Acheson, "a pompous diplomat in striped pants" with "a phony British accent." Brandishing a paper, he declared that "I hold in my hand a list of 205 names" of persons "known to the Secretary of State as being members of the Communist Party" who nonetheless were working "and shaping policy" in the State Department.

THE POST had no account at all the next day, but on February 12 an AP story from Reno, Nevada, placed on page 1, reported that McCarthy had telegraphed President Truman to demand that he ask State for the names of its employees who were "Communists." The story included State Department Press Officer Lincoln White's reply: "We know of no Communist members in the department and if we find any they will be summarily discharged." Next day, also from Reno, McCarthy was reported to have trimmed his number to 57 and to have named 4 of them.

The first POST editorial comment was to say, "In place of the 57-gun salute he promised the State Department, Senator McCarthy blew up four empty paper bags — all of which failed to produce even as much as a pop." Of the four named, it was added, one never worked at State, two had not been there since 1946, and one, John Stewart Service, was being belabored because he had seen that Chiang Kai-shek's regime "lacked competence and stability." The editorial title: "Sewer Politics."

THE POST's battle against Joe McCarthy — one of the most courageous and exemplary episodes in the newspaper's first 100 years — had begun; it continued, with increasingly bitter verbal assaults both ways and with a torrent of Barth editorials and Herblock cartoons against the senator, for more than four years. It was Herblock, in fact, who coined the term "McCarthyism," using it first in a March 29, 1950, cartoon as a label on a tar barrel.

Within three months after McCarthy's tirade his charges were being investigated by a Senate subcommittee headed by a conservative Maryland Democrat, Millard Tydings. McCarthy had named more names, chief among them Owen Lattimore, an Asian expert whom he charged with being the "top Soviet agent"; Lattimore had retorted that the senator was "a madman." Senator Robert A. Taft, urging McCarthy on, had defended him as a "fighting Marine who risked his life" for his country; McCarthy had attacked "the egg-sucking phony liberals who litter Washington," declaring that Acheson should be fired; the Secretary had called the campaign to picture his department as Communist-infected "a filthy business" and "vicious madness." All this was major news, with major display, in THE POST and everywhere else in the nation. Editors pondered whether such coverage was creating a monster but, for the most part, as at THE POST, they felt that reporting McCarthy's accusations, however reckless, was unavoidable.

One McCarthy target was Earl Browder, head of the American Communist Party. His appearance on the witness stand led to this POST editorial on April 28, 1950:

> In refusing to identify and stigmatize certain persons whose names were presented to him . . . Mr. Browder was patently in contempt of the committee's authority. But this contempt was pretty well earned by the drift and character of [the] questions . . . Mr. Browder was as responsive as anyone could have wished to those questions relating directly to the McCarthy charges . . . [Other senators] saved the subcommittee from engaging in a kind of persecution that might have resulted in its punishing Mr. Browder for adherence to fundamental American decencies. Not everyone in America tests a man's loyalty to his country by his willingness to betray his former friends. The apotheosis of the informer is not altogether accomplished in the United States.

The author of the editorial was Alan Barth, the libertarian whose editorials gave unwavering and resolute support to the constitutional rights of all, even to wrong-headed, unpopular, and sometimes odious characters and causes. He was the author of most of the editorials criticizing HUAC and its handling of the Hiss case and other spy probes and castigating all who impinged on or defiled civil rights and civil liberties. What he wrote won him, and THE POST, many plaudits and much esteem at a time when many American newspapers were pandering to the hysteria of the day; yet his single-mindedness on occasion left the paper open to vicious attack and put him on a collision course with his publisher. Barth was the conscience of THE POST in one important area; Graham had to consider the paper's fortunes as a whole. Barth was such a persistent backer of the less fortunate that Meyer once said to him, "Mr. Barth, didn't you ever stop to think that the underdog might be a cur?" Yet Barth was given such freedom to write, by Meyer, Graham, and Elliston, that he could say after his retirement: "I was never asked to grind anybody's axe or stuff anybody's shirt or pander to anybody's prejudices or pull any punches or consider the interests of any advertisers or politicians."

Among the staff, Herblock was Barth's closest friend; he and the cartoonist shared a deep antipathy for men like Nixon and McCarthy. Their mutual beliefs seemed to interact on each other's editorials and cartoons. Herblock, too, was a strong personality, paying minimal attention to the paper's editorial policy on particular issues. Like Barth, he was a civil libertarian and his powerful cartoons, widely syndicated, carried the same message. But other editorial writers, Pusey chief among them, worried more about Communist subversion and infiltration. Elliston not only tolerated these opposite views; he frequently ran editorials from both sides on the same issue, to the readers' confusion.

Graham first read the Browder editorial on the train from Washington to New York the day it appeared. He was furious, determined to fire Barth, until he talked it over with Justice Frankfurter who dissuaded him. Four days later, at the end of a pair of angry letters from readers, this "editor's note" was added:

> The purpose of the editorial which we regret did not seem to come through was to show what a sorry mess we have come to when a Communist can be put in the public position of upholding political freedom and opposing the doctrine of guilt by association . . . The real question is the value of the testimony of Communists, former Communists, and temporarily exiled Communists, where that testimony, of dubious credibility, may do permanent injury to persons of good character.

In a private memo months later Graham explained that the "editorial was, unfortunately, just plain wrong . . . In the rush of work it somehow slipped by Mr. Elliston."

THE POST had been damaged; the rival *Times-Herald* cackled that the paper was "Browder's organ" and other critics repeatedly cited the editorial. Some subscribers canceled the paper. Graham decided to take a positive tack; he wrote a massive editorial, "The Road Back to America," filling the entire three columns of editorial space on May 22, 1950. With it THE POST reprinted an earlier Herblock cartoon of a man labeled "Hysteria" climbing a ladder, bucket in hand, to put out the flame in the Statue of Liberty's torch.

The editorial was an all-out attack on "witch hunting" and "the mad-dog quality of McCarthyism." It called for creation of a commission on national security to seek out the facts and thus "elevate current debate" and "create an atmosphere" in which congressional committees "can again provide the country with the light it needs." Very importantly, Graham balanced THE POST's well-known devotion to civil liberties with an extensive account of the threat to America from Stalin's communism, the threat the paper's critics contended it had brushed aside or ignored. Graham drafted the editorial, lawyerlike, in a scribbled hand on a long, lined yellow pad. Now approaching his 35th birthday, the publisher poured into his message his knowledge of history, his legal training, and his political acumen, the result of voracious reading, and above all his spirit of a free man. He began:

> For weeks the Capital has been seized and convulsed by a terror. It is a terror akin to the evil atmosphere of the alien and sedition laws in John Adams' Administration . . . What has permitted this thing to come to pass?
>
> The rising distrust, the roaring bitterness, the ranging of Americans against Americans, the assault on freedom of inquiry, the intolerance of opposition — all this malaise . . . has its roots in a deep and troubled state of the Nation's mind. Fear and frustration are abroad — fear of the unseen struggle in which we are locked, and frustration because of our inability to get directly at it.
>
> Some among us, to be sure, have tried to distort this fear and this frustration for selfish political gain, and the fact serves to their eternal discredit. But that does not alter the feeling that real reasons for concern exist, that our country faces, and will continue to face, dangers greater than we have ever known. To defeat those dangers we must know them, and, knowing them, meet them with a constructive program rather than with hysterical fright.
>
> This is one newspaper's appeal to Americans to support action which will turn on the light of truth and restore the national harmony.

Graham cited three central aspects of the danger. First, "the unparalleled, cancerous evil of totalitarianism . . . The kinship of nazism, fascism, Japanese militarism and communism"; second, this evil's control over Russia, which put the United States "under the shadow of devastating or crippling attack"; and third, "the fanatical devotion of [Communist] fifth columnists in every country abroad, including our own."

Why not use any methods to fight the danger, Graham asked, if it was so real? Why not a purge or witch-hunt? "Ought we not to consider one scalp worth the incidental persecution of 10 innocents? Ought we not to change our concepts and put the burden of proof on the accused?" Such a course, he argued, "would be burning down the house of the American way of life to get at the rats in it." This would be doing the work of the fifth column and advancing the aim of its Kremlin masters rather than destroying it.

Witch-hunting would "drive out of Government the very brains which alone can give us victory in the cold war," Graham stated. "This kind of onslaught on character will leave us a government of spineless mediocrities." Hitler's subordinates were afraid to give him any information that did not suit his prejudices; Stalin's diplomats tell him only what he wants to hear. "Do we want to create a similar atmosphere of terror that deprives us of honest and fearless thinking?"

Graham expressed hope that the "mad-dog quality of McCarthyism has become so apparent that its power for sowing confusion and suspicion has probably spent its force." Despite the senator's "artful dodging," the American people knew that he had failed to support his basic charge that the State Department harbored large numbers of Communists.

> However, it would be reckless to ignore the circumstances that permitted this escapade and this aberration to paralyze American diplomacy and to thrust fears and doubts into the minds of our people. The urgent problem is to find a way back to a basic unity, to traditional American standards.

The commission the publisher proposed could "take a fresh look at our situation and give the American people a trustworthy, 'unpartisan' statement of the salient facts" — military, economic, legal — "affecting our security." Such a commission, named by the President and composed of eminent citizens, "would catalyze the decencies of America." The editorial concluded:

> Communism everywhere is on the march. The masters of the Kremlin have not taken a recess during the months we have ignored the real battles of the cold war for the sham battles of witch-hunting. Naked self-interest demands a halt to this diversion of our energies.
>
> Establishment of this "commission on national security" will start us on the road back to our America — a land of freemen marching forward with confidence in ourselves and in our mission.

Graham's editorial brought a flood of favorable responses, although largely from those already on his side, so tightly drawn were the pro- and anti-McCarthy lines. Less than two weeks later Maine's Republican Senator Margaret Chase Smith issued her "declaration of conscience," concurred in by six other Republicans, declaring that the Senate had been "debased" into a "forum of hate" and a "publicity platform for irresponsible sensationalism," and attacking "the Four Horsemen of Calumny — Fear, Ignorance, Bigotry and Smear." THE POST ran the

Smith text and Graham sent her a telegram of congratulations.

Truman at first spurned Graham's proposal for a citizens' commission, then in 1951 named a Committee on Internal Security and Individual Rights headed by retired Admiral Chester W. Nimitz, the World War II hero. But suspicious conservative Senator Pat McCarran, a Nevada Democrat whose thinking was close to McCarthy's, blocked legislative help and Truman had to dissolve the group before it could begin to function.

On January 4, 1946, three days after Graham's arrival at THE POST, Elliston outlined in a Sunday brains article the paper's view of the central issue in postwar American foreign policy:

> The planetary power of the United States is . . . a rapidly wasting asset as a result of the advent of the atomic bomb. Like money in time of inflation, it is bound to lose value. Scientists tell us that equalization of power will be the automatic consequence of the atomic equipment of other nations . . . [and] give us a five-year run of supremacy. Thus the problem confronting the Nation can be stated simply. It is the problem of evolving a five-year plan of foreign policy which will insure world peace.

Elliston offered these points: manufacture of the atomic bomb should be halted at once; a naval demonstration of the destructiveness of the bomb should be conducted; the British should be offered a loan for economic revival and colonial liquidation; a loan should be granted to the Soviet Union; there should be general freedom of information.

It was too late, as it turned out, for such ideas except for the British loan. The Cold War was about to begin. Those who place the responsibility on the Soviet Union cite Stalin's February 9, 1946, speech in which he declared that the last two world wars had resulted from the development of capitalist world economy. Those who blame the West cite Churchill's March 5 "iron curtain" speech at Fulton, Missouri, in the President's presence.

Eddie Folliard's lead from Fulton said simply: "Winston Churchill today cast a cold, apprehensive eye on Soviet Russia, on the 'indefinite expansion' of her power and the Communist 'peril to Christian civilization' and eloquently called for a British-American alliance." Folliard, normally a master at catching the key phrase, explained in a POST story 25 years later why he made no mention of the "iron curtain" paragraph. He had written his account from an advance text and missed the passage when Churchill interpolated the instantly famous words: "From Stettin in the Baltic to Trieste in the Adriatic, an iron curtain has descended across the Continent." The complete text, however, appeared in THE POST.

Truman seemed incapable of mastering the multitude of early postwar domestic problems; aging POST columnist Mark Sullivan reported that "to err is Truman" was the quip of the month in Washington. The Alsop brothers saw "very dark days ahead"; an editorial, "One World or Two," declared that "no grounds exist for one world unless Russia by compromise makes room for compromise."

THE POST as yet had no foreign correspondents. At home, however, Ferdinand Kuhn, Jr., a New York *Times* veteran, was hired by Meyer in August 1946 as the paper's first full-time diplomatic reporter. A careful, low-key journalist, Kuhn provided incisive news coverage and analysis that got to the heart of issues. There was too much occurring, however, for Kuhn alone to cover, and other staffers had to pitch in on a hit-and-run basis that showed in their stories. Graham did not have the funds to increase more than modestly the news staff; the paper in 1946 spent less than $1 million for its entire news, features, photographic and library costs, including salaries. To compensate for the lack of reporters stationed abroad Graham permitted many to take trips paid for by the military; he hired M. W. (Mike) Fodor, an old hand, and Frank Gervasi as European stringers whose fees were paid by syndicating their articles.

In the spring of 1947 two major challenges — military and economic — were perceived in Washington; in response, by the Truman Doctrine and the Marshall Plan, the United States set forth on a course of international conduct that would reach a peak in far-off Indochina a quarter century later. On March 5, a five-column headline read: U.S. FACES FOREIGN SHOWDOWN IN COMMUNIST DRIVE IN GREECE: BRITAIN SAYS SHE MUST END AID. After a background briefing by Secretary of State Marshall, Folliard wrote that "the United States is confronted with one of the gravest problems in its diplomatic history — whether to go to the rescue of Greece and give her the financial help that a desperate Britain says she is no longer able to afford." An editorial called for "a plan of action" for all Europe, not just Greece; but the Washington climate did not seem propitious. When the Senate, by 64 to 20, cut $4.5 billion from the Truman budget, Herblock pictured the globe with a sign: "For sale cheap — can be developed for democracy or communism," with a Republican saying, "It's not in the budget."

When the President went to Congress to announce what came to be called the Truman Doctrine, THE POST backed him totally but incorrectly forecast that "the aggression we will oppose is totalitarian, not specifically communism." If the United States were "to think only of communism and Russia as the foe," the editorial perceptively added, "we would be driven to line up with anti-Communists of the same stripe of totalitarianism as the Communists themselves."

In THE POST Lippmann asked whether the Doctrine was "policy or crusade," declaring: "A vague global policy, which sounds like the tocsin of an ideological struggle, has no limits. It cannot be controlled. Its effects cannot be predicted." An editorial reply to Lippmann welcomed "the President's resounding statement of what the United States stands for, as well as what it stands against. He has given us a compass with which to steer our foreign policy along a line that is neither naked power politics nor mere anticommunism."

When Secretary Marshall went to Moscow, Graham sent Kuhn along on what was THE POST's first postwar diplomatic assignment abroad; daily he reported the gap between Moscow and Washington. On his return, Kuhn wrote a notable series describing life in the Soviet Union, concluding that "Soviet propaganda will make normal relationships between our two countries difficult if not impossible."

As Congress was passing the Greek-Turkish Aid Bill (voting for it were three future presidents, Kennedy, Johnson, and Nixon), what came to be the Marshall Plan was born. THE POST of May 8, in a story written in Washington by Assistant Managing Editor Frank Dennis, gave prominence to Undersecretary Acheson's speech in Cleveland, Mississippi, in which he declared that the United States must reconstruct both Germany and Japan even without Soviet agreement. An editorial approved. For Marshall's historic speech at a Harvard commencement, THE POST used an AP account. Kuhn stayed home to write a sidebar: "Official Washington sees Secretary Marshall's speech . . . as the start of a new program as bold as lend-lease and as difficult as anything the United States has undertaken since the end of the war."

Marshall's proposal was an offer of help to East as well as West in Europe and on this THE POST backed him fully. "The way must be kept open for the Russians to join in, and we conjecture that, having failed to obstruct the others, the Russians would enter the new project rather than risk isolation." But THE POST was wrong. Stalin ordered the East Europeans, starved for help, to reject the proffered aid as he himself did. This, and events that soon followed, turned the Marshall Plan and the Truman Doctrine into anti-Communist projects in which the United States, despite THE POST's hopes, lined up with totalitarianisms of the right, as well as with the democracies, against the totalitarianisms of the left.

When a final Big Four effort at reconciliation collapsed, THE POST declared: "Now there are two worlds." The Greek civil war exploded with the Communists receiving aid via Yugoslavia; the Communists seized power in Czechoslovakia; Russian pressure increased on both Finland and Italy, where elections were impending; and the Soviets began the Berlin blockade.

During the summer of 1947, at Graham's suggestion, Meyer took Friendly to Europe with him and Friendly sent home dispatches, mostly by mail to save cable costs, depicting the mounting troubles and plugging the Marshall Plan. On November 23 THE POST, in cooperation with the Foreign Policy Association, ran a special 16-page tabloid section, titled "This Generation's Chance for Peace." All the top POST reporters pitched in in what was a major effort to aid the Marshall Plan and Truman Doctrine.

THE POST called the Communist coup in Czechoslovakia a "rape" and used the occasion to advance the idea of what would eventuate as the 1949 North Atlantic Treaty. Marshall Plan aid was not enough, an editorial of March 1, 1948, argued a month before congressional approval. It was "tragic but true" that the United Nations was an "inadequate safeguard" to "halt the spread of Soviet tyranny." Hence, the United States had "no rational alternative to a vigorous drive . . . for a defense alliance of the democracies within the framework and spirit of the United Nations." The idea of such an alliance, unprecedented for the United States in war or peace, had been percolating within the Truman administration and Elliston was privy to such consideration.

The Berlin blockade, part of Stalin's response to the Marshall Plan, only gradually became a crisis. Early stories and headlines treated Soviet interference with traffic mildly, although on April 5, 1948, an editorial declared: "To retreat under threats . . . would be gravely to undercut our influence in Europe and virtually to invite Moscow to go ahead with its conquests." When diplomatic efforts to resolve the blockade failed, a United Press story from Moscow led THE POST's page 1; the by-line: Walter Cronkite. Congress voted a peacetime draft to beef up the armed forces as the squeeze tightened on West Berlin.

A major alarmist in the Truman administration was Defense Secretary James Forrestal, who had been pressing the use of the atomic bomb against the Soviets if war came over Berlin. On September 14, at Forrestal's request, Graham invited to his R Street house 19 other leading American publishers and editors along with Wiggins. Forrestal wanted to check public opinion and he brought along Marshall and other top diplomatic and military figures. After the growing crisis over Berlin was described, someone mentioned the atomic bomb. Forrestal recorded in his diary that there was "unanimous agreement that in the event of war the American people would not only have no question as to the propriety of the use of the atomic bomb, but would in fact expect it to be used."

Whatever Graham's own opinion, THE POST never suggested the use of the bomb. Instead, in October, Kuhn wrote a series of articles exploring and explaining "the tug-of-war over Berlin," relating it to the long East-West struggle over the future of Germany. Norris rode the airlift into West Berlin to write about the siege. On page 1 Wiggins stated flatly that "World War III will not start in Berlin unless Soviet Russia starts it." He and Elliston had been in Undersecretary of State Robert Lovett's office when Lovett had made that clear to General Lucius Clay on the telephone to Berlin.

Before the blockade ended, Stalin broke with Yugoslavia's Marshal Tito and the Chinese Communists began their rout of Chiang's forces. As to China, THE POST strongly and repeatedly opposed sending troops to "bail out" Chiang, and it fought the growing China lobby intent on rushing him money and arms. As to the Chinese Communists, a January 5, 1949, editorial correctly said: "Mao Tse-tung is like Tito in this: he owes precious little to Moscow in a positive way for his success . . . Mao Tse-tung is his own architect of his Communist victories. And, if the present has any relation to the past, he is a nationalist." A few weeks before Chiang fled the mainland to Taiwan, THE POST called for de facto recognition of Mao's regime, arguing that such a step would not be "indorsement, even friendship" but only "convenience."

Elliston fell ill in the spring of 1949. Kuhn was taken off the diplomatic beat to write editorials soon after the 321-day Berlin blockade came to an end and just as the North Atlantic Treaty came to fruition. Kuhn wrote that the pact "tells Russia very quietly, without bombast, that an attack against any of the Western nations will in all probability mean war against all."

On September 24, 1949, Truman announced that the Soviet Union had exploded its first atomic device. Herblock, who had given the bomb a human face and a menacing presence, now drew him as Robinson Crusoe discovering another footprint in the sand. Editorially, THE POST said "the principal advantage to Russia is psychological" and called for a full atomic partnership with Britain and Canada.

That same fall Al Friendly, back from a leave of absence as a Marshall Plan aide in Paris, began picking up the strings of his old atomic energy beat. He discovered that former friends and sources had suddenly clammed up; it was evident something important was going on. He began to hear talk that scientists were working on a superbomb, the hydrogen, or H-bomb, and that there was a secret internal administration debate over whether to proceed to do so. An Atomic Energy Commission member in his cups one evening was a key source. Friendly mentioned what he had learned to AEC Chairman David Lilienthal who blanched and pleaded with him not to publish anything.

Then Friendly discovered that Senator Edwin C. Johnson, Colorado Democrat on the Joint Atomic Committee, had appeared November 1 on a local New York television station and blurted out half the story: what the senator himself called "top secret" information that the United States had "made considerable progress" in developing a "superbomb" with "1,000 times" the effect of the Nagasaki bomb. Curiously, newsmen in New York had failed to pick up the story. The Dumont Company which ran the telecast refused Friendly a transcript on the grounds that permission could not be had from all the participants but he finally got the text from a commercial monitoring firm. The page 1 story on November 18 created a national sensation.

Friendly discussed his findings about the internal debate with Graham, Wiggins, and Elliston; Wiggins and Elliston were for publication, Graham was against it as was Friendly himself. This was a mistake and Graham must instinctively have realized it for he turned to Friendly to say they would read the story anyway in the Alsops' column. On December 4 the Alsop brothers did indeed break the story of the debate.

The Alsop brothers were becoming a major POST feature. Although the paper was not responsible for what they wrote, their strident anti-Communism helped give THE POST a hard-line image in foreign affairs. This was especially true after Elliston's departure. The Alsops were the first alarm sounders as a new storm now developed in the French colony of Indochina. On January 13, 1950, they wrote that "the first test" of America's post-Chiang policy in Asia would "almost immediately" begin in Indochina and that the French had asked for American aid to "counterbalance Ho Chi Minh's advantage."

This was the moment when France was launching the Schuman Plan to pool the heavy industries of Western Europe, actually Jean Monnet's idea for a first step toward unification of the nations that so often had gone to war against each other. Helping France in Indochina seemed to serve two purposes: to further that American aim in Europe and to prevent a change in the world balance between the Communists and the West. The dream was partly realized in Europe, but in Indochina the long trek began into the morass.

No Americans were more passionate backers of a unified Europe than

Graham and Elliston. In this the publisher was greatly influenced by Monnet, whom he once called in a letter "my friend and teacher," and by David Bruce, who served as ambassador to France, Germany, Britain, China, and NATO. As the Cold War developed, Graham also was influenced by the Kremlinologists, Charles E. Bohlen and Llewellyn E. Thompson. Graham's circle of friends and acquaintances, in and out of government, now was immense and he constantly picked their brains at lunches in his office, which editors and reporters found highly valuable, or at dinners and receptions at his home.

By 1950 Graham's thinking about the Cold War was firmly fixed; he expressed it in the long May 22 editorial after the Browder row and three days later in an Akron, Ohio, speech. There he argued that a "successful cold war" was "the only morally acceptable and the only practically acceptable choice open to us. We must view a hot war as a possibility only if there is no alternative except capitulation." POST editorial writers and reporters involved in foreign affairs were, on their own, thinking along the same line; the publisher's words, public and private, simply reinforced the view they shared at the time with the vast majority of Americans. Then, suddenly, on Sunday, June 25, 1950, THE POST bannered a major new turn in the post–World War II world:

SOUTH KOREA INVADED BY REDS FROM NORTH;
WAR REPORTED DECLARED BY COMMUNISTS

From the founding of THE WASHINGTON POST in 1877 until well into the post–World War II years the national capital, by a combination of legal bonds and social customs, segregated the black minority from the white majority. And then the walls came tumbling down. Two presidents, Truman and Eisenhower, played a role in this as did citizens of conscience; but the prime mover was the Supreme Court. The result was the beginning of a new era in race relations in both Washington and the nation as a whole, one that continued with no clear end in sight as THE POST reached its second century. Nowhere in the United States was the change more striking and far-reaching than in the capital city. Here THE POST played a significant role.

The legislative branch, Congress, was impotent; southerners, through use of the filibuster in the Senate and seniority in the House, held the power to prevent passage of civil rights bills. Early in 1946 they blocked in the Senate an effort to create a Fair Employment Practices Committee at a time when THE POST declared that there was "urgent need for such legislation."

THE POST's editorial position was a matter of principle although the news pages still used racial identifications for Negroes and published a minimum of news about blacks. A 1946 reader survey showed that of the four capital dailies THE POST had the lowest percentage of Negro readership, its morning rival the *Times-Herald* the largest. In fact, THE POST deliberately centered its circulation-building efforts in the white community because the city's principal advertisers in large part ignored potential black customers.

Truman named a committee to investigate civil rights and THE POST called its 1947 report "a heartening as well as an appalling" document, "a signal service to the Nation." The report's section dealing with the District called the city "a graphic illustration of a failure of democracy," and asked for an end to Washington's segregated schools, a prohibition of segregation in places of public accommodation, and outlawing of racial covenants in real estate transactions. After the 1948 election, the Civil Aeronautics Board ended segregation at National Airport, a touchy move since the airport lay within Virginia, although it was, and still is, managed by the federal government. Eighteen Washington tennis courts controlled by the Interior Department were thrown open to everyone but 85 others run by the local Recreation Board remained segregated. After six swimming pools were desegregated in the summer of 1949 by Interior Department edict, there were two days of racial skirmishes. When a worried Interior Secretary Julius Krug came to THE POST to ask for minimal news coverage, Graham ordered the skirmishes downplayed as "disturbances."

The whites-only policy at the National Theater, in the early postwar years the city's chief live stage, brought together civic leaders, theater figures, and THE POST in a five-year battle that epitomized the racial struggle. Blacks appeared onstage at the National but none were permitted in the audience, save a then rare black diplomat who was willing to proffer credentials. When 33 playwrights, composers, and lyricists in the Dramatists' Guild announced "they would not permit their productions to play here unless race segregation is ended in the theaters," THE POST editorialized, "Our theater managers are called upon to do nothing more than honor tickets regardless of the racial origin of the purchasers or holders. They can do this without suffering the slightest loss of revenue and without causing a ripple in their audiences . . . They ought to be rivaling one another for the prestige of doing it first." But the National remained adamant, switching to movies in the fall of 1948, when the artists' ban took effect. Blacks also were refused permission to enter the three major downtown cinemas — the Capitol, Keith's, and Warner's. They could go only to segregated neighborhood houses.

THE POST's perspicacious and ebullient theater critic, Richard L. Coe, soon after his return from army service in 1946 succeeded the retiring Nelson Bell; he was shocked to find the city's theaters still segregated. Coe studded his columns with nudges and prods, and his desk in the paper's E Street building became a gathering place for those who wanted to break the racial barriers and return professional theater to the national capital. He campaigned tirelessly to find existing, though smaller, stages that might be used; for the success of Father Gilbert C. Hartke's Catholic University productions; for an eventual national theater; for the use of Ford's Theater where the stage had been dark since Lincoln's assassination; for the reopening of the old Belasco; and for the regional theater company which came into being in 1950 as Arena Stage. To nurture the Arena, Coe later confessed, "I found myself having to find the plusses for my reviews" in the early years.

In the end it was the Supreme Court that dealt the death blow to all legal segregation in Washington. On June 8, 1953, it unanimously upheld the validity of the so-called "lost laws" of 1872–1873, local legislation enacted in the spirit of Reconstruction which, among other things, made liable restaurant or hotel keepers who "refuse to sell or wait upon any respectable, well-behaved persons without regard to race, color, or previous condition of servitude." THE POST called the decision "a triumph for the proponents of civil rights legislation," among whom it counted itself. In anticipation, the National Theater and the movie houses took down the bars. The Court also ended restrictive covenants on real estate and segregation on buses crossing the Potomac to and from Virginia. Finally, on May 7, 1954, in *Brown* v. *Board of Education* came the historic unanimous decision ending segregated schools, not only in Washington but throughout the nation.

As the city moved toward an end to racial segregation, THE POST was making some adjustments in its own shop. In 1948 Wiggins promulgated a new set of rules to end the practice of writing stories such as "Sam Jones, 24, Negro, was arrested for larceny yesterday." For the first time in any Washington paper, racial identification henceforth would be used only (1) when that identification was a factor in the description of a wanted criminal, fugitive, or missing person; (2) in an achievement story when race was essential to evaluation of the achievement; (3) when usage sanctioned such description, such as "Irish tenor" or "Negro leader"; and (4) in reporting a racial dispute or happening that could not be explained without use of racial identification. (Racial designation in real estate advertising, however, was not ended until 1960.)

The logic of Wiggins' new rules, then still a rarity in American newspapers, was to use far more stories about Negroes throughout THE POST, including the society columns. When he approved use of the engagement announcement of the daughter of a Howard University professor, he took the angry phone calls himself. Graham was unhappy and told Wiggins to avoid raising such racial issues. Wiggins later banned all bridal pictures because they were taking up precious space for what he contemptuously termed "the breeders' gazette." When THE POST ran photographs of both black and white Korean War casualties, there were new cries of outrage from whites. Segregation in the capital was ending in legal but not in emotional terms.

In 1952 Graham and Wiggins agreed the paper must begin hiring black reporters. Ben Gilbert, the city editor, took on Simeon Booker without limiting him to Negro news. Booker had been a Nieman Fellow but resentment against him existed within as well as outside the newsroom. Two decades later he described in a POST interview some of his difficulties: "I had a hard time covering fires because the police wouldn't let me near the place if it was in a white neighborhood. And I could only use one washroom on the editorial floor of *The Post.*" He left after two years to reenter the black press because "it was a real tense situation and had me neurotic." In the view of civil rights activists Booker was only a token. In 1953, in reply to an Urban League inquiry, Graham could say only that THE POST had some Negro printers and a few blacks in clerical positions.

In all these problems involving blacks, both at THE POST and in the city, Ben Gilbert was a central figure. He was a bright, perceptive, and conscientious city editor, tireless in his determination to build a great newspaper. But he was humorless, abrasive, and without patience for error or incompetence. His city room enemies were numerous; some couldn't take his pressure and quit, at least one squared things by threatening loudly to punch him in the nose. He was 27 when Casey Jones made him city editor, a post he held for 21 years, longer than anyone else. During the early Graham years he worked miracles with a small budget and minimal staff. In retrospect, Gilbert felt that giving the capital's black population entry to the news columns was the most important advance during his early years. On the other hand, as he moved news coverage into this hitherto forbidden area, trying to educate the reporters as he went along, he became an advocate of many causes as well as an editor of news about them; in short, he became involved rather than standing above the battle. Thus he involved the paper, to the plaudits of activists, to the scorn of stand-patters.

Between 1940 and 1950 the city's population grew from 663,091 to 802,178 with the peak in mid-1945 estimated at 938,458, including

101,558 servicemen and women. Ever since, the city's population has been declining, first as the wartime establishment was dismantled and then as the flight to the suburbs began. Not until 1953 did the suburbs include more people than the District, but the trend to that crossing point and beyond was inexorable.

In the 1940s the Negro proportion of the city's population rose from 28.2 to 35 percent but it did not become a majority until 1957, although by 1950 more than half the pupils in public schools were blacks. Both a steady black migration into the city and a higher black than white birthrate accounted for the change, along with the white exodus. Washington was the first major American city to have a black majority. However, the metropolitan area as a whole, including the District, consistently remained about two-thirds white.

During these years THE POST led the agitation for home rule as the basic cure for the city's problems as well as a democratic right for its citizens. A 1946 plebiscite, at which a 250,000 turnout was anticipated, produced only 170,000 "voters" with 70 percent favoring home rule and 84 percent national representation in Senate and House, which the *Star* advocated. THE POST called the plebiscite "a disappointment" and rightly commented: "The liberation of Washington will not be hastened by Tuesday's puny and pathetic demonstration; it may be grievously retarded." The next year a southern-dominated Senate committee sidetracked a home rule bill and the House did the same thing in a floor vote. In 1949, however, the Senate for the first time voted to return self-government to the District; but in the House, although Graham was among those who testified in favor of home rule, the Southern Democratic–dominated District Committee, with conservative Republican help, tabled the measure.

Although the southerners would not publicly say so, race was the overwhelming reason why home rule was so long delayed in the House. But racc was only one of the factors creating the white flight to the suburbs; crowded city schools, increasing crime, a growing shortage of housing, rising taxes, and above all the desire of the multitude of new young families to have a home of their own with some open space also were important factors.

THE POST's first response to the changing metropolitan area was to add reporters specializing in suburban news (most notably Roger Farquhar in Maryland) and to begin regular Sunday columns of editorial comment on suburban Maryland and Virginia problems. By 1950 four suburban counties had populations of over 100,000 each. To serve these customers the city's major stores, first Hecht's, then Woodward & Lothrop and Kann's, opened large suburban department stores and the shopping center became a way of life. All these moves were duly noted in THE POST but essentially as business news. The department store dispersal, however, meant slowing sales within the central city and the economic toll finally produced a major reaction.

Not only were customers moving out of the city, the city itself was deteriorating. Some blamed continuing rent controls in a period of inflation. Others blamed the lack of self-rule. The District government — dependent on Congress to provide even such municipal ordinances as one debated in 1949 to permit spraying of weeds on private property to counter hay fever — seemed inadequate. A grandiose plan to mark the city's 150th anniversary in 1950 was a miserable flop.

Sam Zagoria wrote the first POST alarm story, based on a Board of Trade study that foresaw a no longer self-supporting Washington and that warned that this would lead to a "blighted area." In mid-1951 Graham, who had picked up the rising note of alarm among THE POST's major department store advertisers, businessmen, and bankers, called in Wiggins and Gilbert to consider the problem and what the paper might do about it. Here was an ideal opportunity to strike a blow for both Washington and THE POST. Roberts was charged with turning up the facts and writing them. The outcome of five months' work was a major series in the paper in January and February 1952, titled "Progress or Decay? Washington Must Choose." This series was given added impact by use of colored maps made possible by THE POST's new L Street presses.

The focus of redevelopment became the southwest portion of the city, a 113-block area south of the Mall in which 22,539 people lived of whom 78.6 percent were black. Roberts' series called for new apartments and homes "for all income brackets though predominantly within reach of middle and lower income families." THE POST argued that all new housing be offered on a nonsegregated basis, this at a time when the city still had segregated schools and most downtown theaters and restaurants still barred Negroes.

An editorial called for a new organization of civic leaders and businessmen to help "minimize the procrastination and the buck passing in public agencies, to mobilize community opinion and to interest private capital in rebuilding some of the areas to be cleared of existing slums." Graham then personally created the Federal City Council which continued to serve in succeeding decades as a useful civic prod. More progressive than the Board of Trade (long in conflict with THE POST over home rule which the Board looked on with alarm), the Council also was able, through the publisher's interventions, to obtain help from both the Eisenhower and Kennedy administrations in expediting federal aid programs.

Launched in 1952–1953, southwest redevelopment became a more than half-billion-dollar city-within-a-city project of new homes, offices, a hotel, and shops that required a quarter century to complete. THE POST brought New York builder William Zeckendorf and his brilliant but then little-known architect, I. M. Pei, to raise the sights for the project, which they did dramatically. Despite federal subsidies to write down land costs and provide construction money, the new homes were too expensive for almost all the previous residents. The area changed from more than three-quarters to less than one-quarter black and these were the more affluent blacks, including members of Congress. Some of the displaced blacks found better housing elsewhere but the majority added to the crowding and deterioration of other sections of Washington. Slum clearance was achieved but at a tremendous human cost.

In 1959 when Eleanor Roosevelt, a long-time advocate of better housing, toured the area she asked, "What has happened to the people who once lived here?" In partial reply, an editorial commented that "in all candor it must be conceded that the motivation has been more economic than social, and that a total assault upon poor housing here, as elsewhere, remains to be mounted." THE POST gained a new measure of civic respect, however, for its efforts; urban affairs reporting, with increasing emphasis on social problems, now became standard in the paper.

Despite redevelopment, the suburban trend continued. In 1951 for the first time a majority of THE POST's circulation was outside the city. In late 1952 the paper published the first map of the proposed belt highway around the city through Maryland and Virginia suburbs. Begun in 1958 and opened in sections beginning in 1961, the 65-mile Capital Beltway was finally completed in 1964. Its pull was immense. As Jack Eisen, who covered transportation for the paper for more than two decades, later put it in a magazine interview: "[The Beltway] sucked the guts out of the center city, especially in the warehousing industry. Previously the most accessible area was the city; now any point on the Beltway is most accessible." THE POST in the mid-1950s began an exurbia Land of Pleasant Living column, written for many years by Aubrey Graves.

By 1954 an Interior Department plan, backed by THE POST, to build a scenic highway between the Great Falls of the Potomac and Cumberland, Maryland, by filling in the old Chesapeake and Ohio Canal seemed likely to come to fruition. Justice William O. Douglas damned the project in a letter to the editor:

> The river and its islands are part of the charm. The cliffs, the streams, the draws, the benches and beaches, the swamps are another part. The birds and game, the blaze of color in the spring and fall, the cattails in the swamp, the blush of buds in later winter — these are also some of the story of the place.

All, he said, would be destroyed by a highway; so he invited POST editors to "come with me . . . Walk the 185 miles to Cumberland . . . Hear the roar of winds in thickets . . . Discover the glory there is even in a blade of grass." THE POST replied that "our idea . . . was not to make the littoral of the Potomac an artery of traffic . . . rather the [parkway] is designed to make the area accessible." Editors Robert Estabrook and Merlo Pusey agreed to make the much publicized walk; it took place in 1954, became an annual affair, and effectively killed the highway plan.

THE POST's attitude toward women was a long time in changing. Editorially, the paper continued to oppose the equal rights amendment. The women's pages had returned to social froth. After Evalyn Walsh McLean's death in 1947, the capital's new leading hostess was Perle Mesta; column after column was devoted to her parties and then, after Mrs. Mesta's appointment as ambassador to Luxembourg, to those of her would-be successor, Gwen Cafritz. For years Marie McNair daily reported such items as: "Saw Fleet Admiral William D. Leahy in summer whites and the Attorney General, Tom Clark, with Mrs. Clark looking like a Dresden figurine in a pale blue flowered frock." And: "Did you know: That Francesca Lodge, the wife of Connecticut's former Governor and former Representative in Congress, had added the Polynesian hula to her dance repertory. She took lessons from a Maui native while on summer holiday in Hawaii."

Washington social gatherings, however, always have been more than froth and an astute reporter could pick up news of real importance. The first to do so in the postwar era for THE POST was Mary (Molly) Van Rensselaer Thayer, a veteran hard news reporter, who wrote a sprightly column of nuggets picked up across the dinner table, at receptions, and elsewhere. To her editors' annoyance, however, she had a habit of flouncing off to far places without advance notice; but when she did she picked such good stories as the first train into Berlin after the blockade. In 1953 what had been called the "society" pages were renamed For and About Women and the tone became more serious. One of those responsible for the pages being carefully read was Dorothy McCardle.

She first began, in 1951, by contributing a column on parties and personalities and her reports became a standard feature after she joined the staff in 1960.

Still locked in the old conventions, THE POST ignored the January 1948 publication of the first Kinsey report, *Sexual Behavior in the Human Male.* However, it was news when the Reverend Billy Graham came to Washington early in 1952 to tell a crowd of 7900 in the National Guard Armory that immorality was "the scarlet sin" that could destroy the capital and the nation. An editorial the same year, noting that mass circulation magazines were running covers "of some actress or other current celebrity in extreme décolletage," thought this had "already gone beyond the limits of tolerance." In 1953, a chaperoned all-night party — dancing, a movie, swimming, and breakfast in the cafeteria — at Anacostia High School was termed "excessive and unwise."

It was all in vain; the new morality was sweeping in with a rush. THE POST did an about-face: the second Kinsey report in 1953, on female sex habits, was announced on page 1. Medical reporter Nate Haseltine prepared nearly a full-page summary on publication day in nondramatic language but including such hitherto forbidden terms as "climax," "homosexual stimulation," and even "sexual contact with animals." Herblock used the intense interest about the book to draw a man asking: "I've read about the Kinsey report. Am I big enough to know about the H-Bomb?" An editorial declared that it was "much to the good" that the report had "brought into frank general discussion matters that have long been distorted in the public mind by whisper, rumor and old wives' tales with resultant feelings of fear, guilt and neuroticism." Still, it was added, the work had "much of the trappings of pseudo-science" and "by seeming to fortify immorality with statistics, it contributes to the 'everybody's doing it' attitude as cheap justification."

The outbreak of the Korean War produced a momentary national unity in the face of outside danger. And, together with the Communists-in-government issue and corruption in the Truman administration, it brought Dwight D. Eisenhower to the presidency. Along the way Graham and THE POST climbed aboard the Republican bandwagon in a consequential move for the paper and its publisher.

THE POST's coverage of the war came from the wire services and such reporters as Homer Bigart and Marguerite Higgins of the New York *Herald Tribune* service. Graham had no money, he felt, to send his own reporter or photographer. One frustrated photographer, Gene Jones, left to join a television crew; military reporter Marshall Andrews took a leave of absence to make a study for the army in Korea. Herblock gave powerful support to the war and the United Nations, opening with a June 30, 1950, cartoon of a Communist holding an upside-down map of Korea and pointing to the invasion arrow to say: "You Can See How North Korea Was Invaded."

On February 12, 1951, the Chicago *Tribune* printed a story by William Fulton that began: "Sometimes called 'the *Washington Pravda'* after the Communist party newspaper in Moscow, the *Washington Post* is chalking up a telling record for defending Reds and pinkos, slavish devotion to the Truman Administration, and violent attacks on pro-American members of Congress." The long story went on to rake Graham, Agnes Meyer, Elliston, Gilbert, Friendly, and Barth, quoting the 1948 *Plain Talk* article along the way. Barth was a particular target, especially for writing "an editorial laudatory of Earl Browder." Graham took the attack seriously. Right-wing radio commentator Fulton Lewis, Jr., at the same time was calling THE POST "the Washington counterpart of the *Daily Worker,"* avoiding slander by quoting congressmen who had used that term of disparagement with immunity on the House floor. When these attacks had begun, Graham suggested that Meyer file a libel suit against the *Times-Herald* for its references to his paper as "the Washington edition of the Communist *Daily Worker."* But Meyer counseled against such a step. In the wake of the *Tribune* attack Graham wrote an internal memorandum, rebutting the charges in detail, for the benefit of skittish employees, especially conservative salesmen who were hearing about it from advertisers.

By now Graham was earnestly trying to counter the paper's, and his own, "radical" image. He had become an important figure in the Advertising Council and the Committee for Economic Development; he was a trustee of George Washington University and the University of Chicago. In the view of some who knew him well, Graham was "trying to get respectable."

In July 1951 he wrote a friend that "I think the most important thing ahead for us now is the election next fall. If we are going to blunder through four more years with leadership on either the Taft or Truman level, then I am nothing but a pessimist. As a result of this thinking, I am becoming a strong Ike man."

Graham began to take a direct part in politics. He went to see one potential Democratic nominee, Chief Justice Fred M. Vinson, after the Alsop brothers reported that Truman would not run and that Vinson was his first choice. Graham "personally felt this would be bad for the Court and I also thought it would be bad for Vinson of whom I was extremely fond." He urged Vinson to make a "Sherman statement" but Vinson said that would indicate he had been considering running. Graham next suggested that Albright be allowed to write, on the basis of "authoritative sources," that Vinson would not accept a nomination. Vinson replied that Graham himself would have to write it. Graham did a longhand draft, returned with it for Vinson's word-by-word approval and the deletion of some references to Truman. The story under the publisher's by-line, with a special copyright line, ran on page 1: "Chief Justice Fred M. Vinson will not permit himself to become the Democratic candidate for President even if drafted."

In mid-1951 Wiggins wrote that "if the GOP wants Ike it will have to draft him"; a view confided to Wiggins by Milton Eisenhower, Ike's favorite brother. Ike always referred to Wiggins as "Milton's friend," which, indeed, he had been for many years. What Wiggins wrote, the general later told importuners, was the clearest statement of his position. Gallup polls in THE POST showed Ike as the man to beat both Taft and the Democrats; and Meyer kept sending these reports to Eisenhower in Paris. Ike delayed a decision while Taft was running hard. Meyer and Wiggins went to Paris to see Ike and argue, as did many others, that he must come home and defeat Taft in the primaries in order to keep the Republican party on the internationalist track.

On March 24, while THE POST was serializing Kevin McCann's adulatory biography, *The Man from Abilene,* the publisher took the plunge. The editorial, drafted by Graham and agreed to by Elliston and Wiggins, was titled "We Stand for Eisenhower."

> The time for a change is overdue . . . The very air in the Nation's Capital is poisoned with scandal and corruption . . . Twenty years of enjoyment of office has left the Administration blind to error and obtuse about wrongdoing . . . Years of being hopelessly on the outside have bred a recklessness in [the Republican] opposition, an irresponsibility, a resort to devices which would otherwise be spurned . . . This newspaper feels that Eisenhower would be the dynamic force to rejuvenate our politics . . . Eisenhower has it in him to close the divisions which are outside the proper pale of political controversy . . .

This was the first time since Meyer bought the paper that THE POST had formally endorsed a presidential candidate. To explain the switch in policy the editorial argued that "this declaration of preference is an exercise of our independence, not an abandonment of it." But it left a good many in THE POST family unhappy; and after Truman took himself out and the Democrats nominated Adlai Stevenson the unhappiness vastly escalated.

Once Graham, with Meyer's full backing, put the paper behind Ike, the publisher plunged into the campaign, registering as a Republican and seconding the nomination of the Eisenhower candidates for delegates in Taft's own precinct in the city.

On July 3, a few days before the Republican convention was to meet in Chicago, Graham received a jolt from his mother-in-law, Agnes Meyer. In a Detroit speech carried in part next day in THE POST, she declared, "We must close the door tight against the present attempts of the Catholic hierarchy and reactionary Protestants to force our people to support sectarian schools whose rapid increase would destroy our secular schools and tear our Nation into irreconcilable factions." At the end of the story was this note credited to Mrs. Meyer: "The views expressed in my Detroit speech are my own and do not reflect the opinions of *The Washington Post* . . . I do not participate in the formation of editorial policies." When Graham read the speech story, he had drafted the note ostensibly by Mrs. Meyer and had Wiggins halt her train near Buffalo, New York, to show it to her. McCarthy had too many fervent supporters among fellow Catholics for the publisher to take on a church-school fight as well.

The GOP convention was well staffed by THE POST with Wiggins, Folliard, Albright, Edward F. Ryan, and Thomas Winship. On July 11 Eisenhower was nominated on the first ballot and Nixon became the vice-presidential candidate. The Nixon nomination troubled THE POST; the paper editorialized: "It is now up to him to repudiate both the Old Guard and the smear approach and to reflect the spirit of enlightened moderation that took over the convention." Two days later Graham wrote a friend that he had had "a pleasant afternoon yesterday at Burning Tree [golf club] with Senator Nixon, whom I had never known very well before." In fact, Graham came to have a certain admiration for Nixon.

Adlai Stevenson's welcoming speech to the Democratic convention, also in Chicago, with "laugh-provoking wit and humor," wrote Folliard, helped produce the closest thing yet to a genuine draft of a presidential candidate. Editorially, THE POST said of Stevenson: "The office chose the man" and that the top nominees of both parties were "men of stature, dignity and democratic instincts."

At the convention Graham had squeezed from the reluctant Stevenson a confession that it would be "an act of arrogance" to turn down the nomination. His selection put THE POST in an awkward position but Graham persisted in arguing, privately and through editorials, for Ike. The general would have "great advantage . . . in throwing out the corruptionists." When Eisenhower cut from a Wisconsin speech a favorable reference to General Marshall, one of McCarthy's targets, THE POST explained that "for purposes of getting elected Ike is being opportunistic." Another editorial denied that the newspaper had compromised with McCarthyism. If elected, Eisenhower would "leave McCarthy without a target for his slander."

Graham had a hard time within THE POST family. Herblock was adamantly pro-Stevenson and anti-Nixon; some staffers wanted to run an ad in the paper saying they were for Stevenson but Graham talked them out of it; finally, the publisher's wife quietly told him after the Marshall incident that she could not go along with his position but would say nothing publicly.

The month before the Marshall incident came the Nixon "secret fund" affair. The New York *Post* first reported the $18,235 fund provided by wealthy Nixon partisans to help with his office and travel expenses. Nixon retorted that "communists and crooks" were trying to "smear" him. As the furor mounted, and it appeared that Nixon might be forced off the ticket, an editorial called for Nixon's withdrawal. But Nixon fought back, making his emotional "Checkers" speech on television and radio, and Eisenhower declared him "completely vindicated." In another editorial Graham wrote that Nixon had "eloquently and movingly answered" charges that he had used the fund for "personal enjoyment" and hence this was not a case "involving moral turpitude" but rather "an error of judgment, however unwitting."

To many of Graham's friends, this was a great letdown. His tolerance of Nixon, whom his paper had attacked both in cartoons and editorials for his conduct in Congress and in earlier election campaigns, demonstrated the publisher's stubborn streak once he mapped out a line of reasoning. To some, however, it seemed that he was trimming and doing so, at least in part, to rid the paper and himself of the radical tag that their enemies had pinned on them. Elliston, recuperating from a heart attack, wanted to switch endorsement to Stevenson. After Graham determined to stick with the Republican ticket, he refused to print Herblock's drawing of Ike saying "naughty, naughty" to Nixon and McCarthy, drawn as two youthful smear artists with buckets and dripping brushes in their hands. However, Herblock's cartoons were syndicated and the "naughty, naughty" one appeared in other newspapers. Until the election, THE POST used only reprints of his earlier cartoons.

Five days before the election Graham acted as master of ceremonies at a Citizens for Eisenhower-Nixon rally. A reporter described the publisher as saying that he supported Eisenhower because postwar Washington had taught him the truth of Lord Acton's statement that "power tends to corrupt"; because he considered a change necessary to perpetuate the two-party system; and, finally, because he wanted none of his friends or family "to be candidates for experiments in radioactivity."

Eisenhower, inaugurated on January 20, 1953, as the first GOP President in 20 years, "unleashed" Chiang Kai-shek to harass the Chinese on the mainland, a step THE POST termed "the honest thing to do." But an editorial warned that Chiang "wants a war" between the United States and the Soviet Union whereas "the only end that ought to be envisaged is a disengagement from Asia with honor." The war between the French and the Viet Minh in Indochina, now in its seventh year, was a "stalemate," POST readers were told in a dispatch by Homer Bigart. Eisenhower soon was assuring the French that the United States "intends to help them wind up" the war, Kuhn reported. In the last Truman years, as Communist strength increased in Indochina, THE POST had declared it "utterly unrealistic" to commit a land army to the jungles of Indochina. But the country "could accept a share of the burden under a U.N. command if the nations with forces and bases near at hand would assume the major responsibility."

On March 6 Stalin died and Herblock won a second Pulitzer with a drawing of the figure of death saying to the dictator, "You were always a great friend of mine, Joseph." The new premier, Georgi Malenkov, spoke softly to the West. THE POST was wary: "There may have been a change of Soviet tactics, initiated by Stalin and dramatized by Malenkov, but until there is some practical demonstration to the contrary it is fair to assume that the basic strategy remains the same." Nevertheless, the paper praised Eisenhower's initial olive branch proffer to the new Kremlin leaders. But when Churchill, once again Britain's Prime Minister, called for exploring the Malenkov overtures at a "summit" meeting, both Eisenhower and THE POST reacted negatively.

In the spring of 1953 Kuhn quit THE POST to free-lance and his diplomatic beat was turned over to Roberts. In 1954 he followed Secretary of State John Foster Dulles to the Big Four foreign ministers' conference in Berlin. The conference got nowhere on the German and Austrian issues, but did produce an Indochina meeting with Communist China in attendance. By now, the Korean War had been ended, a Japanese peace treaty signed, and Greece and Turkey admitted to NATO. But the Shah of Iran had to flee his capital in the face of an internal Communist threat, returning to his throne only after CIA intervention, although no one outside a handful in the government would know of that for a long time. The Egyptian military, having deposed King Farouk, began to pressure the British to evacuate the Suez Canal zone and a new figure came to power in Cairo, Gamal Abdel Nasser.

In Moscow, Malenkov said that continuation of the Cold War would mean a "new world slaughter" that would result in the destruction of "world civilization." But Malenkov soon was ousted; a new man was rising in the Kremlin hierarchy, 59-year-old Nikita S. Khrushchev. He became first secretary of the Communist Party on the same day in 1953 that 36-year-old Senator John F. Kennedy married 24-year-old Jacqueline Bouvier, described in THE POST as "a former Washington newspaperwoman" because she had been the *Times-Herald*'s "inquiring photographer." In THE POST the wedding story got the bigger display.

THE POST marked its 75th birthday in the December between Eisenhower's election and his inauguration. With 840 employees, it had come a long way; it now was a happy, even a happy-go-lucky shop. The staff, both news and business, was infused with a spirit of drive and determination to make it the best, if not the biggest, paper in the capital. The man responsible was Graham, called "Phil" by practically everybody, who had "the gift of empathy," as Bill Brinkley put it. He would come down from his seventh-floor office to the news and editorial fifth floor, meander about to chat, drop a news tip, suggest an idea for a story or editorial. Or he would wander through the sixth-floor advertising offices, asking why his paper did not have a particular advertiser or how the classified columns might be fattened.

It was still hard going even though *Time* called THE POST the capital's "most independent and vigorous paper." Circulation in 1952 had not yet broken the 200,000 mark, trailing both the *Times-Herald* and the *Star;* advertising had passed the *Times Herald* but was far behind the *Star* and still amounted to only about a quarter of the total for the city's four newspapers.

Looking back on THE POST of this era, Ferdinand Kuhn remarked that

> it looked best in its freedom from tradition, conformity or habit in its handling of news and editorials. The reader could never be sure what he would find in his *Post* each morning, whether it was some brilliant piece of reporting and editing or some mess of horrid news judgment . . . The worst side of *The Post* in those years was its all-pervasive sloppiness. Stor-

> ies were edited in sloppy fashion, incompletely checked for accuracy, often chopped without regard to their meaning.

It was all true, and Graham knew it, too. Nonetheless, many performed mightily to improve the paper, among them Jack Burness and Molly Parker. Burness, chief librarian from 1936 to 1963, and whose wife Anne long was Wiggins' secretary, built the clipping file from virtually nothing to over two million items; he had an incredible ability to find any one of them. Molly Parker, who had come to THE POST in 1918 as its sole switchboard operator and who served as chief operator from 1929 to 1970, was renowned for her ability to locate reporters and their news sources in obscure and unlikely places.

When Frank Dennis left in the fall of 1952 his job was divided by making Friendly the new assistant managing editor–day and James Cutlip assistant managing editor–night. It was an odd but effective combination: Friendly, the erudite editor and probing newsman, and Cutlip, the old-style master of getting whatever it was into print in a hurry in the evening hours. Wiggins now had the additional help he desperately needed. At the same time, Harold Kneeland, a skilled practitioner, became Sunday and feature editor. A year earlier Graham had plucked reporter Elsie Carper out of the city room to make her personnel director, a post she held for six years before returning to writing. Graham, she recalled, "knew everyone in the building, made sure he met all new employees, helped them through all sorts of family and health problems, gave advice, found them the best medical attention."

Soon after Eisenhower's inauguration Elliston resigned from his editorial page post to become contributing editor, writing a Sunday column until near his death in 1957. Elliston had won a Pulitzer Prize for editorial writing in 1949 but in 1952 he suffered a heart attack and then a stroke. Rather ruthlessly, Graham cut his salary when he became only a contributor on the grounds that his wife had money and the paper was poor. Graham offered the editorship to his friend James (Scotty) Reston, then the New York *Times'* stellar diplomatic reporter. Reston was tempted but Arthur Krock relinquished his post as the paper's Washington bureau chief to Reston to keep him at the *Times.* Graham had to find someone else. To the surprise of many he chose the youngest member of THE POST's editorial staff, Robert H. Estabrook, then 34.

Estabrook, an Iowan just out of the army, had come to the paper in 1946 to handle letters to the editor for Elliston, and then had joined the editorial writers. Graham now gave him the title of editor of the editorial page. The choice was both good and bad. Estabrook was an indefatigable worker, a human vacuum cleaner in conducting interviews at home and abroad, but, unlike Elliston, he was not a stylist, had difficulty getting on with some of the other editorial writers, tended to do too much of the writing himself, and, above all, always felt insecure with Graham. Though both Graham and Meyer opened all sorts of doors for Estabrook, he tended to be stiff and uncomfortable in the world of society and wealth and out of place among many of Graham's friends. But like everybody else, he looked on Graham as a brilliant leader whose tips and suggestions he faithfully followed.

Just before his promotion, Estabrook wrote an editorial that caused Pan American World Airways to cancel advertising. Graham told him not to worry. The publisher wrote Pan Am's Juan Trippe: "I really think it is most unwise for a . . . leading American corporation to indulge in the legal right" of not running advertisements. "Necessarily, it amounts to saying that all of the protestations by Mr. Truman et al. are correct — namely, that newspapers are responsive to the wishes of large advertisers." Eventually Pan Am ads returned.

By June 1953, the 20th anniversary of Meyer's purchase of THE POST, both daily and Sunday circulation at last had passed 200,000. That year Graham finally ended a practice that had long annoyed the capital's influential Jewish population, especially important in the local business world. He replied to one complaining reader that the paper had "at the request of various Jewish organizations" stopped using words like "restricted" in advertising copy; but he added, "Even here I have received many letters of complaint from Jewish people saying that they would rather know about such conditions to avoid the embarrassment of looking at advertised houses."

As the paper grew in influence, it was obvious that its lack of foreign correspondents was a glaring weakness. For many years André Visson had written a Washington editorial page column of sophisticated comment on foreign affairs but Graham canceled it in 1953. That fall the publisher made a six-week tour of Western Europe; from Rome he wrote back to Meyer: "What I wouldn't give to have $100,000 a year to spend on three or four good correspondents overseas. We won't be doing a proper job in the capital until we manage that." In Paris, Graham again was captivated by David Bruce, the American ambassador. A year later, after the purchase of the *Times-Herald,* Graham with Meyer's approval proposed that Bruce join in both ownership and management of THE POST but the flattered diplomat declined with much appreciation.

As soon as Eisenhower came to the White House, Graham and his paper both supported and pushed and prodded the President and his administration. THE POST began running the column of Roscoe Drummond, the New York *Herald Tribune*'s liberal Republican writer. Graham called in his due bills for having supported Ike, using Sherman Adams, the President's chief of staff, to seek an Eisenhower endorsement for home rule, to expedite the city's redevelopment projects, and to try to make the administration stand up to McCarthy and the Republican right wing.

On February 17, just after Ike's inauguration, Agnes Meyer in an Atlantic City, New Jersey, speech blasted McCarthy and Illinois Republican Representative Harold Velde, the new chairman of the House Un-American Activities Committee. McCarthy, she said, had been "using the techniques of insinuation against innocent people," had "debauched the Senate's power of investigation" and "stirred up hatred." McCarthy replied: "I would waste no time reading speeches by the management of the Washington Daily Worker, much less answer them." Velde responded with a statement declaring that *Pravda,* Moscow's Communist Party paper, had quoted Mrs. Meyer as writing a warmly pro-Russian letter to a propaganda magazine, *Soviet Russia Today.* Mrs. Meyer called this an "outright falsehood." THE POST checked the files of both *Pravda* and the magazine and discovered that such a letter had been written by a Mrs. G. S. Mayer of British Columbia, Canada. Velde acknowledged the mistake, blaming it on a staff member. THE POST retorted that he had retracted "tardily and whiningly."

Graham's opposition to McCarthy, as Friendly later observed, was "instant, unremitting and total." McCarthy's opposition to THE POST also was unremitting and total and frequently instant. After he grilled James A. Wechsler, editor of the New York *Post* and a strong anti-McCarthyite, the American Society of Newspaper Editors named an 11-man committee to investigate. When they reported in August 1953, there was a split of opinion as to whether McCarthy was infringing on freedom of the press. A four-man minority, led by THE POST's Wiggins who was the full committee's chairman, pulled no punches; their statement included: "A press that is under the necessity of accounting to government for its opinions is not a free press."

The day the report appeared, THE POST editorialized that McCarthy's "attempt at intimidation" of the press in the Wechsler case should "be recognized for what it is." Three days later McCarthy declared it was incumbent on the ASNE members who had not signed the Wiggins statement to "investigate the extent" to which Wiggins "has prostituted and endangered freedom of the press by false, vicious, intemperate attacks upon anyone who dares to expose any of the undercover Communists." Wiggins retorted that "nothing would please me more" than to have such a probe of THE POST's "full, accurate and fair news coverage and editorial comment on the public career of Senator McCarthy."

In the fall Murrey Marder determined that McCarthy's guilt-by-association charges against Army Signal Corps employees at Fort Monmouth, New Jersey, were baseless. When Marder told Wiggins that the story he was about to write could raise a new storm against THE POST, Wiggins responded: "Murrey, you write what you have; we'll worry about what happens to the paper." The army was forced to concede there was no proven evidence of Communists at Monmouth. In turn, McCarthy expanded his attack on the military at what became known as the Army-McCarthy hearings, a television magnet for millions.

The Eisenhower administration had become so subservient to McCarthy's increasingly arrogant demands that THE POST reported in September that "Federal employe morale is the worst in fifty years." Ten days later, when McCarthy married former aide Jean Kerr, administration officials turned out in force, including Nixon, Adams, Deputy Attorney General William P. Rogers, and Allen Dulles, head of the CIA. The Eisenhowers, however, declined an invitation.

By mid-January 1954, McCarthy held the nation in thrall. Gallup reported that 50 percent viewed him favorably, 29 percent unfavorably, with 21 percent having no opinion; but only 38 percent said they approved "of the methods" he used, while 47 percent disapproved and the rest had no opinion. The atmosphere in Washington was bitter, corrosive, and divisive, even within families.

Privately as well as publicly, Graham fought the senator. He made campaign contributions to liberal Republican senatorial and gubernatorial candidates. He wrote Adams at the White House that Army Secretary Robert Stevens, who had tried to compromise with McCarthy, should be allowed to resign, and suggested that the President issue a statement to include: "I feel impelled to make clear that the tactics of Senator McCarthy are in direct opposition to my fundamental beliefs, and that they represent a flat contradiction of the decent goals of this Administration." Graham added to Adams: "Excuse what must seem to be rank effrontery. But do believe me that if you do not now break specifically with this monster you will become his pawns."

This same line of reasoning thundered forth in an editorial titled "Walking With the Devil." Estabrook wrote it after Graham suggested the theme.

> There is only one man in the country with the stature and voice to speak out in clarion tones for the things decent

> Americans believe in. That is President Eisenhower himself . . . Either the President must disavow, in the most unequivocal terms, McCarthyism and everything it stands for, or he and his Administration will be regarded by the public as having joined hands with it . . . For if he should elect to walk with the Devil, he will lose the support of millions of independent, fair-minded Americans of both parties who elected him as a spokesman of moderation; and he will walk alone.

Ike, however, was determined, as he said privately, not to "get down in the gutter" with the senator. When his press conference response was mild, an editorial said that "instead of grappling with the monster that is defying the Administration at home and destroying its prestige abroad, Mr. Eisenhower spoke only in generalities about 'justice and fair play.'" Herblock produced a powerful cartoon: McCarthy, dark-faced and with a bloody meat ax in hand, standing before Eisenhower, who had drawn from his scabbard a white feather. The caption: "Have a Care, Sir."

Graham's focus was on destroying McCarthyism; one fight was enough. So in late 1953 he refused to permit use of a Barth editorial attacking the FBI's technique of gathering all kinds of irrelevant data in its investigations. J. Edgar Hoover, in fact, had written Graham in 1952 praising an editorial opposing publication of raw Civil Service Commission files. Barth's editorial was not used but he wrote a similar piece for *Harper's* magazine of March 1954 and he rejected Graham's plea to withdraw it. The article created considerable discussion; Graham's relations with Barth henceforth were cool.

As the McCarthy issue was coming to a climax, Graham had to switch his attention, for the Washington *Times-Herald* proved to be for sale.

On Monday, January 25, 1954, Eugene Meyer, now 78, received a letter marked "personal" from Palm Beach, Florida.

> Dear Eugene:
> I am wondering whether you expect to be in Palm Beach anytime soon for I would like very much to talk to you about a business matter of importance to you. Please let me know.
> With kindest regards to you and Mrs. Meyer,
> Sincerely yours,
> Kent Cooper

Cooper, the former general manager of the Associated Press, was living in retirement in Palm Beach. Meyer had a hunch about Cooper's letter. Unable to show it to Graham, then in Jacksonville, Meyer took it to POST Business Manager Sweeterman who commented: "I'm probably thinking the same thing you are. Mr. Cooper is a good friend of Colonel McCormick, lives near him or on his property in Palm Beach, and he could be talking about the *Times-Herald.*"

Meyer called Cooper. "Kent," he said, "this 'business matter' to which you refer, is it in the field of journalism?" Cooper said that it was. "Is it in Washington?" Again Cooper said yes. "I have been thinking of going to Florida this week, in the next couple of days," Meyer said and Cooper asked him to call on his arrival.

Thus began THE POST's purchase of the *Times-Herald,* a move that gave THE POST a morning monopoly in the national capital, doubled its circulation, skyrocketed its advertising, and thereby produced a healthy financial basis on which it could, and would, become one of the world's major newspapers. The purchase capped Eugene Meyer's two-decade gamble with THE POST and it left no doubt that Philip Graham, now 39, would be a major figure in American journalism.

When Meyer, Graham, and Sweeterman met Cooper in Palm Beach, Cooper explained that McCormick was fed up with the *Times-Herald* and wanted to know if Meyer was interested in buying it.

"Yes, I am," said Meyer. "How much does the Colonel want for it?"

Cooper explained that McCormick wanted what he had put into it — the $4,500,000 purchase price plus what he had spent on additions to the *Times-Herald* building on H Street and for new presses, a total of $8,500,000. There was no haggle over price. "That's all right with me," said Meyer. Cooper saw McCormick, then also in Palm Beach, that evening and reported back next morning that it was a deal. Meyer suggested an immediate agreement be drawn up, but the colonel said one of his men would get in touch with THE POST in March.

There followed six weeks of utter — and agonizing — silence before contact was made by a Chicago *Tribune* vice president. Next ensued a series of meetings with lawyers for both papers. One of the lawyers was Frederick S. (Fritz) Beebe of the New York firm of Cravath, Swaine and Moore, whom Graham earlier had hired as THE POST's New York counsel and who became a major company executive. As the deal neared completion, Graham called in his six top executives: Sweeterman, Wiggins, Advertising Director Bernard, Circulation Director Gladstein, Production Manager Harry Eybers, and Radio-Television Chief John S. Hayes. "If it works," Graham said of the deal, "in three days we'll be publishing in the afternoon." The *Times-Herald* then was printing around the clock with a 4 P.M. edition and many plans had to be readied.

The deal called for a down payment of $1,500,000 and the other $7 million by the end of the year, plus $1.8 million for severance pay for *Times-Herald* employees not hired by THE POST, and for some other miscellaneous charges. On March 15 Colonel McCormick presided at a meeting of *Times-Herald* directors when the news was first disclosed to the others. One thunderstruck director was Mrs. Ruth McCormick Miller (Bazy) Tankersley, the colonel's niece and former *Times-Herald* editor. The sale was approved; but in response to Bazy's anguished plea she was given 45 hours to raise money to buy the paper herself, provided she would not disclose why she was trying to raise it. She frantically phoned conservative millionaires such as Sears, Roebuck chairman Robert Wood, ex-ambassador Joseph P. Kennedy, and Texas oilmen H. L. Hunt, Sid Richardson, Hugh Roy Cullen, and Clint Murchison. She obtained pledges of about $4 million but McCormick said "no" and the Tribune Company directors approved the sale. Hayes delivered the initial payment in Chicago and phoned Graham on a specially installed line: "I've got it. We're all set. Let me tell you about . . ." Graham broke in: "Good-bye, we're on our way" and slammed down the phone. His wife, standing at his side, let out a whoop of joy. The time was 12:44 P.M., St. Patrick's Day, Wednesday, March 17, 1954.

The extraordinary fact, of course, was that Robert R. McCormick, the right-wing isolationist conservative, had sold out to Eugene Meyer, the internationalist whose paper had a liberal, even ultraliberal, reputation. The papers had feuded for years and had presented Washington readers with such diverse accounts of the news and editorial opinions that they hardly seemed to be reflecting the same events. A year and a half before the sale a POST editorial had attacked McCormick for deserting candidate Eisenhower, characterizing the publisher as one of a number of "right-wing oddities."

The simple fact was that McCormick, then 73 and in failing health, was losing money on the *Times-Herald* with the prospect of even greater deficits ahead. He had said in 1949 that he had bought the paper for the purpose of "bringing the United States to Washington." What he brought was the Chicago *Tribune*'s typography, strident and slanted stories reflecting the Republican right wing, and simplified spelling — "sherif," "fotograf," "burocrat," and so on. The new *Times-Herald* did not catch on and Bazy's involvement, or at least the disclosure of it, in a 1951 McCarthy smear campaign that helped defeat Maryland Senator Tydings had soured the colonel. On the other hand, Meyer and McCormick were "contemporaries," Frank C. Waldrop, the *Times-Herald*'s last editor, wrote in a later biography of McCormick.

> They could regard each other as Yalemen who had earned their "Y" in life after graduation. And in journalism, Meyer had shown himself worthy of McCormick's respect. He had been a tough competitor, he had learned while doing, and shown himself under stress to be a gentleman.

So, why not sell to Meyer?

Walter Lippmann wired: "Hooray for the canary that swallowed the cat." And on the day the transaction was completed Meyer dropped in at the snack bar for a cup of coffee. He searched vainly through his pockets and then turned to a printer: "Could you lend me a nickel? I just bought a newspaper."

# 7

# World Capital Triumph and Tragedy 1954–1963

Three hours and one minute after the merger was consummated, the first edition of the combined WASHINGTON POST AND TIMES-HERALD hit the streets. It was 3:45 on the afternoon of March 17, 1954. Fifteen minutes later an official announcement of the sale was given to the press associations. A magazine columnist expressed the general astonishment:

> The unique feature of the deal is that it came about without a breath of rumor or warning. That is unprecedented in this town, which usually appears to be made up exclusively of people who live by their ability to foretell coming events. Even the advance guard of gossipers were taken unawares of this one.

Eugene Meyer, wearing a pressman's cap of folded newsprint, was allowed to start the first run after the pressmen's union made him an honorary member. It was a slimmed-down 16-page edition bare of advertisements, the only way to make a quick demonstration that the deed was done and to head off possible invocation of the Clayton Antitrust Act by the Department of Justice. During the interval between consummation and publication, one of THE POST's lawyers, Gerhard Gesell of Covington & Burling, formalized a transaction to avoid that threat: THE POST bought the stock of the *Times-Herald*, a move that made it subject to the antitrust law, but simultaneously liquidated that company thus taking over its assets, a move then not subject to the law. An angry assistant attorney general demanded that THE POST maintain separate publication of the two papers "until we investigate." He was told it was impossible; the *Times-Herald,* as a company, had been dissolved and the combined paper already was on the street. Attorney General Herbert Brownell later reviewed the case, concluded that it was too late to take any action, and privately let Graham know there would be no government prosecution.

On Thursday, March 18, subscribers to both papers received a fat 64-page newspaper on their doorsteps. Indeed, for several days many received two copies until subscription lists could be merged. The production strain was enormous and both THE POST's L Street presses and those of the *Times-Herald* six blocks away on H Street had to be used for more than seven years. The *Times-Herald*'s initial daily "green streak" edition had come out around 4 P.M. and the combined paper kept to this schedule for the first few days. But the product was sloppily thrown together and the early paper was abandoned for a somewhat less chaotic 7 P.M. edition. This lasted nine months before publication time was moved back to 9:30 P.M.

The point of all this strain was simple: to keep as much of the *Times-Herald*'s circulation as possible, for the amount of advertising would be affected by the new circulation figures and financial success would depend on that ad revenue. Given the diametrically opposite approaches in the news and editorial columns of the two papers, it was widely assumed, in and out of THE POST, that many former *Times-Herald* readers simply would not stomach a combined paper molded in THE POST's image. The assumption was wrong.

Of the *Times-Herald*'s daily circulation of 253,000, the combined paper picked up 180,000; of its Sunday 250,000, the combined paper added 200,000 — the *Star* a mere 8000. The remainder represented duplicate circulation, some who quit reading any newspaper, and a few *Times-Herald* afternoon readers who switched to the six-day *Daily News.* Because such a high proportion of the aggregate circulation was retained, the merger was the most amazingly successful in modern American journalism. Within four months, the combined paper was boasting that with 85 percent of the premerger separate circulations its new totals were 381,417 daily and 393,580 on Sundays. It had vaulted to ninth in morning and twenty-sixth in Sunday circulation among all the nation's newspapers. In this critical advance, circulation boss Harry Gladstein, an administrative genius, received able assistance from *Times-Herald* Circulation Manager Harry A. (Happy) Robinson.

The *Star*'s reaction — total complacency — surprised POST management. More than two decades later former *Star* Editor Newbold Noyes, Jr., explained that *Star* President Samuel H. Kauffmann had "refused to respond in any competitive way . . . He wanted to play it cool, sit back and watch the balance sheet . . . He didn't believe the *Post* would hold any of [the *Times-Herald's*] circulation . . . In our group the highest guess was that they would hold 80,000 and I think Sam thought they would hold 5,000."

The first day's merged paper carried on page 1 the story of the purchase; a message signed by Meyer and Graham recognizing that "only as we conduct our affairs with integrity, courage and high purpose can we earn the respect of the people, the community and the Nation we live to serve"; and a telegram from Colonel McCormick pleading illness for his sale and adding: "Mr. Meyer needs no endorsement from me, but I bespeak for everybody the fullest possible cooperation." Next day an editorial said that the owners were "fully cognizant" of their "enlarged obligations." For those who wondered about the policy of the combined paper it declared:

> Editorially we shall continue our devotion to the cause of constitutional government, to the protection of civil liberties of each citizen as the safeguard of the civil liberties of every citizen, to home rule in Washington as the just due of Americans, and to international cooperation as the only safe national policy in the atomic age . . . As an independent newspaper we shall continue to treat the issues as we see them, to deal with measures rather than men, and to espouse causes irrespective of political considerations or labels such as "conservative" or "liberal."

In short, the editorial and news policies of the combined paper would be those of THE POST alone.

Habit is a major characteristic of newspaper readers and Graham shrewdly played on that. He knew a lot of *Times-Herald* readers would buy the combined paper simply because they wanted a morning paper and there now was no other. More important, he knew that many newspaper readers turn first not to page 1 or the editorial page but to the sports and comic pages. Thus, his first move was to assure that the combined paper would carry all the *Times-Herald* comics, two pages of them along with the two pages from THE POST, and the chief sportswriters and features from the *Times-Herald.* The 16 new comic strips included the popular Dick Tracy, Moon Mullins, Brenda Starr, Li'l Abner, Barney Google, Gasoline Alley, Orphan Annie, Blondie, the Phantom, and Bringing Up Father. Features included the *Times-Herald's* Inquiring Camera Girl, George Dixon's humor column, George Sokolsky's conservative political column, Victor Riesel's conservative labor column, a daily picture page, Bob Addie's daily sports column, and Joseph Brocator (known as Paddock) who offered racing picks — plus such syndicated columnists as Bob Considine, Dorothy Kilgallen, and Louella Parsons. On Sundays the combined paper included the *American Weekly* tabloid along with *Parade* and two sections of color comics. The only *Times-Herald* columnist instantly rejected was Westbrook Pegler.

If these back-of-the-paper additions were sufficient to help bring over vast numbers of former *Times-Herald* readers, some serious-minded subscribers worried about the effects of a morning monopoly in the nation's capital. Three weeks after the merger a letter to the editor appeared from Patrick Murphy Malin, executive director of the American Civil Liberties Union. He noted that "increased responsibility is placed on the existing newspaper to maintain for the public diversity, both in the selection of news and the presentation of opinion through special columns, even though a particular opinion may not agree with the editorial policy of the newspaper." To his letter was added an editor's note quoting a Graham message to an unidentified person:

> We must be doubly careful, in news and even through independent commentators, to present a full picture of all points of view. We must be quick to correct our errors when they occur, as they inevitably will. Yet with all this, we cannot abdicate another responsibility — namely, of saying what we think, and saying it fully, so long as we restrict this opinion to our editorial columns.

That was the goal. The reality, however, was that THE WASHINGTON POST AND TIMES-HERALD, in its editorial posture, remained liberal and internationalist, and in its news presentation essentially the same. A slight contrast was provided by Sokolsky and Riesel and, from time to time, by other writers espousing anti-liberal and anti-internationalist viewpoints.

Although the *Times-Herald* purchase instantly propelled the combined paper ahead of both the evening and Sunday *Star* in circulation, it took five years for advertising to follow. The 1955 total was up by 12,467,000 lines over the premerger year of 1953 while the *Star*'s total rose only 3,258,000 lines; still, the *Star* lead in 1955 was 8,731,000 lines. But the ad trend would be inexorable: up for THE POST AND TIMES-HERALD and down for the *Star*. In 1955 his colleagues presented to Advertising Director Bernard a tin cup as a reminder of the long years he had had to beg for ads. Now those days were gone forever. The gap steadily closed, and in 1959 the inevitable occurred: THE POST AND TIMES-HERALD passed the *Star* and from then on the combined paper rushed ahead in advertising and increased its lead in circulation.

In all this John W. Sweeterman played a critical role as head of THE POST's business operations. Graham had great confidence in him, remarking that he "could run General Motors." At the merger Sweeterman quickly ordered all of both THE POST's and the *Times-Herald*'s previously scheduled advertising into the combined paper, charging only the old single-paper rates for the rest of the initial month. Because so much more newsprint was being used this cost money but it earned good will. Sweeterman insisted on retaining *Times-Herald* features to hold conservative readers and he asked, and received, from Graham a commitment to keep the *Times-Herald* logotype on page 1 for ten years. (It was reduced the first time 17 days after the merger and finally to minuscule size but it was not eliminated until January 1, 1974.) Sweeterman at first questioned but later accepted a key move in 1957 suggested by Real Estate Advertising Director George DeLozier to move that important section from Sunday to Saturday in order to get the jump on the *Star*'s rival Saturday afternoon pages. Once the higher circulation seemed assured, Sweeterman boosted advertising rates accordingly. That produced some howls from businessmen but the huge new audience gave them no alternative but to patronize THE POST.

One of Sweeterman's major contributions was his persistent effort to build a Sunday paper "package" in both premerger and later years. Surveys had shown that THE POST had the capital's quality readership but that, premerger, it lacked the bulk of the middle class that advertisers wanted to reach. Reasoning correctly that on Sundays readers wanted not just news but variety and entertainment, and in bulk, Sweeterman was instrumental in turning the Show section into a tabloid, adding a television section, creating a separate classified ad section, producing two sets of comic pages, and, later, in starting *Potomac*, the local Sunday supplement.

Long-term financial success was assured by the merger but the cost of buying the *Times-Herald* and making the transformation had been considerable. The newsprint bill alone soared in two years from $2,900,000 to $7,500,000. The paper lost $238,000 in 1954 but it made something over $2,000,000 a year in 1955, 1956, and 1957.

The combined paper, especially on Sundays, was a monster by old POST standards and a monumental task for production boss Harry Eybers and his able assistant, E. J. (Neal) Greenwald, who concluded a 47-year career at THE POST in 1972. The first Sunday after consolidation the 228-page edition, counting supplements, weighed two pounds five ounces. By 1957 a Sunday paper in December comprised 334 pages and weighed three and a quarter pounds.

Providentially, the merger increased the "news hole," the space available for news and features, from a daily average of about 108 columns to about 150. Helping to fill this additional space were many reporters and desk men who came over from the *Times-Herald,* 45 percent of whose total work force made the move. In addition to sportswriter Addie, the new additions included William Brady, who became night city editor; Harry Gabbett, a talented and whimsical reporter and rewrite man; Richard Darcy, who became director of photography; photographers Jim McNamara and Joe Heiberger; Albon Hailey, a POST reporter before the war; sportswriters Maury Fitzgerald and Hugh Brannen, and many desk men.

Among those added on the business side was the amiable W. Frank Gatewood, local advertising manager at the *Times-Herald,* who became assistant advertising director and, in time, advertising director and a company vice president. The year after the merger James J. Daly came from New York to be classified advertising manager and, later, the paper's business manager and a vice president. Buoyed by the massive new circulation, Daly was immensely successful in increasing the highly lucrative classified advertising on which the *Star* so long had had a hammerlock.

Presiding over the transition, Graham was at his sparkling, intuitive best. Although he had Meyer and Sweeterman advising on financial and business problems and Wiggins and Friendly on news and features, Graham set the tone. There was no bragging about killing the often despised rival paper; instead there was much declaration of purpose to meet the responsibility of morning monopoly journalism, in part to discourage anyone from trying to start a rival paper.

Wiggins, who in 1955 became executive editor, and Friendly, who then succeeded him as managing editor, began to cull out the weaker *Times-Herald* features but, on Graham's insistence, at a pace that was hardly noticeable. The technique with the comic strips was to move an intended victim from one of the four comic pages (later spread over five to accommodate more high-priced ads) to a classified page. After readers tired of trying to find this or that strip, few noticed it had been dropped. An exception was a Friendly decision to drop the inherited daily horoscope; a furor of protest recalled it for a while longer. The daily page 3, known within THE POST shop as the "blood, guts and semen page" because it was a collection of lurid tales that THE POST had used to counter, although never to equal, the *Times-Herald* offerings, slowly was cleaned up and eventually eliminated.

The transitional task was vast for every department, often with chaotic results. To get the immense number of papers off the presses in two buildings, the various sections frequently appeared in confusing sequences. To meet the required early deadlines, writing and editing were hasty, often sloppy and incomplete. Despite strain and struggle, the spirit was upbeat; at long last success had arrived and there would be more rewards for all, both financially and in journalistic pride. The news and editorial staff increased from 160 to more than 200 and Graham made a point of meeting the new people; he remained "Phil" to everyone, old and new. The 1954 annual POST Christmas party across L Street at the Statler Hotel was by far the cheeriest yet. In his annual report to employees early in 1955 Graham pronounced 1954 "the year of all years." He also disclosed that he owned a majority of the voting stock with his wife holding the minority.

The exhilaration sweeping through the paper reached a peak when Graham appeared on *Time* magazine's cover for April 16, 1956. Who could do else than beam at *Time*'s laudatory words:

> Across the presidential breakfast tray and over the coverlets and coffee cups of the most influential people in the world's most influential city looms the capital's most influential paper: the *Washington Post and Times-Herald* . . . From Foggy Bottom to the fog on the Hill, Washington reaches for the *Post* as Broadway reaches for *Variety* or bankers for the *Wall Street Journal.*

The "quick-witted" publisher was described as having a "Lincolnesque look" and "staffers" were said to "like his flair for an old soldier's easy profanity, his first-name familiarity and quickness to bestow praise."

Graham was planning a $5.5 million addition to the L Street building. In March 1956 an unprecedented five-year agreement with the Washington Newspaper Guild helped buy labor peace; a 1962 contract would bring the highest top minimum wages in the industry — $175 a week for editors and reporters. (Labor relations for the paper were handled by Adrian S. Fisher and Lawrence W. Kennelly, with help from Gerald W. Siegel, and later by James Daly.) On June 19, 1955, to mark the 22nd anniversary of his purchase of THE POST, Meyer and his wife gave to all 711 company employees with five years' service (at both the paper and the television-radio stations and including those who had come from the *Times-Herald*) nearly $500,000 worth of nonvoting POST stock in blocks ranging from 4 to 20 shares. Meyer commented that "some people in similar situations remember their old associates in their wills. But Mrs.

Meyer and I both thought that a rather melancholy approach to things. Besides, neither of us has any plan to relieve you of our companionship for some time." These gifts added to the general feeling of gain from the paper's new success, save for those trade unionists leery of this blurring of labor-management relationships. One share initially worth $52.96 skyrocketed to a value of $1154.80 by the time The Washington Post Company went public in 1971. For some senior employees not eligible for executive stock options Graham established a confidential payroll through a New York bank to hide the large raises he gave them.

The article in *Time* magazine, however, had also pointed out some POST problems: "Its local staff is still undermanned and stretched thin; its seven-man national bureau (one-third the size of the New York *Times* bureau) does a spotty job; it has never had its own foreign correspondents." Publisher Graham, *Time* concluded, "has great power and responsibility. He realizes this, and aims beyond it. He dreams of greatness for his paper. 'I want independence and institutionalism,' he says. 'Before I die, I should like to see the *Post* like *La Prensa* of Buenos Aires, the *Times* of London or the New York *Times,* with a sense of vocation on the part of the people who write and edit it, and with a continuity of fundamental principles."

For Graham no problem was insurmountable. For those who worked for him, and many would say "I love that guy," he was the inspiring boss. It was a time of triumph to be savored, if only one had time to catch a breath. In the first three and a half years after the merger the paper gained a momentum that would carry it forward despite the tragedy that struck its leader.

While THE WASHINGTON POST was facing and resolving the problems of the merger, the city, metropolitan area, nation, and world were alive with news for editors, reporters, and editorial writers to cope with. The career of Senator Joseph R. McCarthy was reaching its climax, the United States was edging toward intervention in Indochina, a presidential election was in the offing, and the Supreme Court's decision on school desegregation created both hope and violence.

The eight-column black banner in the first issue of the combined paper read: IKE BACKS STEVENS IN ROW. The President had told a press conference he stood behind Army Secretary Robert T. Stevens after McCarthy had charged him with "blackmail" in the course of the televised Army-McCarthy hearings. Murrey Marder was writing the daily news stories with Warren Unna providing a running summary of each day's testimony, together filling many POST columns during the 36 days of hearings. But McCarthy's power effectively was ended on December 2, 1954, when the Senate voted, 67 to 22, to censure him.

THE POST called the vote "a vindication of the Senate's honor," adding: "Mr. McCarthy has opened the eyes of the country — and, we trust, of the Senate — to the evils of unbridled and unsupervised investigation. It remains for the Senate (and for the House of Representatives as well, of course) to bring its investigating procedures into conformity with the American constitutional system and established American standards of justice." This had been the theme of countless Barth editorials throughout the McCarthy hysteria. When McCarthy died on May 2, 1957, by then in virtual obscurity, Estabrook wrote that "his monument is a noun that has come to be a synonym for reckless slander. His memory cannot be divorced from a trail of shattered careers and groveling agencies, of cultivated suspicions that set Americans blindly against Americans, of a humiliating debasement of America's standing in the free world."

THE POST's relentless and determined pursuit of McCarthy led the paper into what proved to be a highly embarrassing incident. In 1954 a man named Paul H. Hughes who claimed to be on McCarthy's staff approached Wiggins and Friendly through civil rights attorney Joseph L. Rauh, Jr. Hughes contended that he had evidence the senator was paying for information from the State Department and the Pentagon. At Friendly's request Rauh and others advanced Hughes expense money. But a check by Marder then found Hughes' documents to be either unsupportable, untrue, or forgeries. THE POST's role became public when Hughes was indicted and tried on unrelated charges. In a statement the paper said that while the accusations had been "most plausibly tendered," THE POST "did not print one single word of, or use in any way, these unsubstantiated charges." Privately, Graham and Friendly presented Wiggins with a gold clock inscribed "Pro Prudentia" because his skepticism had prevented a POST disaster. Ironically, months earlier columnist Kluttz had been approached by Hughes but had failed to report this to his superiors.

As the McCarthy case moved to its climax, two foreign policy issues threatened to involve the United States in war: the French disaster in Indochina and the Chinese Communist assault on the off-shore islands, most notably Quemoy.

On page 7 of the first day's combined POST AND TIMES-HERALD a headline read: VIET MINH SHOCK TROOPS CLOSE IN AGAINST BESIEGED DIEN BIEN PHU FORT. On the second page of the local news section Vice President Nixon was reported to have told students of Washington's

Dunbar High School that the way the current struggle for Asia turned out "will in the long run determine whether we remain free or go under totalitarian rule." Eisenhower at a press conference first mentioned the "falling domino" principle. "You have a row of dominoes set up, he said," wrote Folliard, "and you knock over the first one, making it a certainty that the last one will go over very quickly, too. His point was that the loss of Indochina would start a disintegration in Southeast Asia that would have the most profound influence on the free world." THE POST was skeptical.

> The hard truth of the matter is, first, that without the wholehearted support of the peoples of the Associated States [Vietnam, Laos, and Cambodia], without a reliable and crusading native army with a dependable officer corps, a military victory, even with American support, in that area is difficult if not impossible of achievement.

There had been minor mentions of the French colony during and after World War II. Now Indochina came to page 1, culminating in the French defeat at Dien Bien Phu in May 1954. From the concurrent Geneva Conference, Roberts described the first week as "a major defeat for American diplomacy . . . There is every evidence that Indochina now is heading into Communist hands, certainly far more of it than they have won on the battlefield, perhaps, in the end, all of it." Putting together what he learned in Geneva, Paris, London, and Washington, Roberts on July 7 disclosed that the Eisenhower administration had "set a tentative date [April 28] for an air strike to aid the then besieged fortress of Dienbienphu." In a long chronology he pieced together the secret American diplomatic and military moves. The Indochina story created a sensation; it was partially confirmed at the time and fully confirmed 17 years later with the publication of the Pentagon Papers.

The Indochina truce and partition into North and South Vietnam came in July. THE POST commented: "The truce probably represents a realistic accommodation with the Communists on the basis of power in the region. But there is no blinking the fact that it brings another 11 million persons and 60,000 square miles behind the Iron Curtain." Not only were the editors convinced that the Indochina Communists were agents of Moscow but they urged a stand be made at the partition line.

Within the next six weeks Premier Chou En-lai declared that China would "liberate" Taiwan and Communist guns on the mainland began to shell Quemoy, an off-shore island under Chiang Kai-shek's control. On November 8 Roberts disclosed that Eisenhower had rejected a proposal approved, 3 to 1, by the Joint Chiefs of Staff to let Chiang's forces bomb the mainland, and if an all-out Communist attack on Quemoy developed, to permit American planes to do the same. A year later two FBI agents turned up at THE POST to ask the reporter where he had gotten his information about such secret National Security Council deliberations. On page 1 in the New York *Times* James Reston described this as a threat to freedom of the press. Graham wrote Reston that THE POST had put the story inside because this, like similar previous inquiries, had been turned aside "when we were able to assure them that we had not handled any secret documents or seen any secret codes."

While these events were occurring in Asia, the French rejected the European army scheme (EDC). Among the most bitter of American officials was Walter Bedell Smith, then about to leave the government after having headed the CIA and served as Undersecretary of State. At a farewell dinner tendered by 14 newsmen Smith blurted out: "We spent 70 million French francs [about $200,000] trying to buy members of the French Assembly to vote for EDC." The dinner was given on an off-the-record basis. Roberts circulated a memo to Graham, Wiggins, and Friendly but none of them for a moment considered disclosing this fragment of secret Eisenhower administration machinations. All four accepted restraint as necessary while East and West were locked in Cold War conflict. EDC's defeat, THE POST declared, "undoubtedly . . . constitutes the greatest Soviet triumph in postwar Europe."

Nonetheless, the paper favored dealing with the Russians and in succeeding months strongly prodded the administration toward the 1955 Geneva Summit Conference where Eisenhower first encountered Nikita Khrushchev. In November 1954 Estabrook asked editorially, "Are we resilient enough to seize the chance for abatement of the cold war if such chance exists?" Graham pounced on Estabrook, warning him against embracing the Soviet term "coexistence" which, "I submit, is every ounce a bastard idea, sired by Wish and mothered by Cold War–weariness. The Soviet state has inherently evil and dangerous characteristics which have not been even slightly altered." Nevertheless, two days later Estabrook wrote that the "best guarantees of coexistence are patience, vigilance, and a full armory . . . If the Soviet Union is sincere in wanting to reduce tensions, the way to do it is by specific steps in the form of self-enforcing agreements. One such step . . . would be a peace treaty with Austria and the withdrawal of Russian troops." The Kremlin's agreement to that treaty produced the Geneva summit.

Estabrook and Roberts went to the July summit, aided by Edmund Taylor, the paper's stringer in Paris. Many Americans were opposed even to Eisenhower's meeting Khrushchev; Dulles was wary lest the rapprochement dilute the fear that helped bind the Western allies. Herblock drew Dulles wrapped in overcoat and blankets while a cheery Ike in sports clothes told the Soviet leader on the phone: "Yes, We'll Be There, Rain and Shine." At Geneva, Ike unveiled his "open skies" plan for mutual aerial reconnaissance and an exchange of military blueprints, designed to end American fear of a "nuclear Pearl Harbor." Khrushchev took it as an espionage plan. Estabrook wrote: "In effect, Mr. Eisenhower is asking in one swoop to lift the Iron Curtain."

A year after the summit Khrushchev began "destalinization" in his famous secret speech to the 20th Party Congress; this led to a relaxation in Eastern Europe that produced a Polish crisis and then the bloody rebellion in Hungary. Simultaneously, Israel, in connivance with France and Britain and without any of them telling the United States, plunged into war with Egypt over Nasser's takeover of the Suez Canal. THE POST sympathized with the Hungarian rebels and excoriated the European allies for their folly in Egypt, backing Eisenhower's pressure to force them and Israel to withdraw.

On July 11, 1956, THE POST reported a Moscow protest that American military planes coming in from the west via East Germany and Poland had flown for up to two and a half hours over several Russian cities. Dulles said he knew nothing of this. An evasive but technically correct formal reply said that "no United States military planes" could have overflown the Soviet Union. What Moscow, in fact, was protesting were the first flights of the CIA's high-level reconnaissance plane, the U-2. Sometime later, before Francis Gary Powers' ill-fated 1959 flight, both Wiggins and Roberts independently learned of the U-2's existence and activities. Together with Friendly they decided, in what they considered the national interest, to publish nothing.

Eisenhower was an immensely popular President. It was big news when his Gallup poll approval rating, a constant POST feature, dropped to 61 percent during the 1954 Army-McCarthy hearings. (Truman's once had sunk to a mere 23 percent.) In 1957, after Ike publicly accepted such gifts for his farm as a tractor, hogs, cattle, and a chest of silver, Senator Wayne Morse attacked the President as "politically immoral." There was no editorial protest, however, although later when Mamie Eisenhower accepted pelts for a beaver coat an editorial mildly remonstrated that "the line should be drawn somewhere short of accepting tractors and furs for coats." Morse was a frequent needler, too, of THE POST. One letter, which contended that the paper could "dish it out but not take it," brought this Graham response: "What elevates my temperature was your suggestion that we intentionally doctored our news story to fit our editorial view. We are often dumb but we don't cheat."

The midterm 1954 election produced a Democratic Congress, returning Sam Rayburn to the House speakership and elevating Lyndon Johnson to Senate majority leader. During the campaign Nixon declared that Acheson's policy had been responsible for the "loss" of China and if China had not been lost there would have been no Korean War and no subsequent crisis in Indochina. Such campaign tactics led Herblock to draw his most biting Nixon cartoon: a group of political welcomers stood by saying "Here He Comes Now" while a shadow-faced Nixon, suitcase in hand, crawled out of a sewer.

The President's heart attack in September 1955 caught the paper in an unhappy moment: the news came in time for the Sunday paper but the Outlook section containing Herblock's cartoon already had been printed. Herblock had depicted Nixon climbing on Ike's back, saying "You're Going to Run Again, Aren't We?" A hasty editorial, placed on page 1, titled "Get Well, Mr. President," included a note that the cartoon already printed was "characteristic of the almost uniform presumption of his continued good health."

When Ike recuperated and announced he would run, THE POST spoke the truth: "If it were merely a question of personal popularity, Mr. Eisenhower might now be elected by acclamation." THE POST reverted to its traditional policy of nonendorsement. The presidential choice, an editorial said, was between "two high-minded men" but "let us state frankly our distaste for Mr. Nixon."

The bitterness engendered by the campaign, especially by Nixon, led former President Truman to write a stinging letter about the Vice President to Folliard. As a member of the prestigious Gridiron Club of Washington newsmen (the first woman was not admitted until 1975), Folliard had the task of inviting Truman to a club dinner. Truman replied that he could not be present, saying:

> The reason is that I will not sit at the same table with Nixon. He has never refuted his statement that I was a traitor; but even if he did, my feelings about him would remain the same . . . I regret it very much for there is nothing I would like better than being there, but I just cannot sit with that fellow, or with his boss either.

Nixon never had directly called Truman a traitor but he had implied it by saying that Truman, Acheson, and Stevenson were "traitors to the high principles in which many of the nation's Democrats believe." As for "his boss," Truman had soured on Eisenhower, especially for his failure to stand up for General Marshall in 1952 against the McCarthyite slanders.

On page 1 of the first day's combined WASHINGTON POST AND TIMES-HERALD Shirley Povich wrote from Orlando, Florida:

> Seven Cuban Negro players in the Washington farm system camp at nearby Winter Garden today were ordered to "get out of town by sundown" . . . This year marked the first attempt of the Washington club to train its Negro players at Winter Garden with other farm talent . . . City Clerk E. M. (Doc) Tanner . . . said: "We're just trying to avoid trouble." . . . Police Chief Mann who issued the "By Sundown" ultimatum [said]: "You know what this section is like around here."

Two months later the issue of the Negro's place in American society entered a new phase with the Supreme Court's unanimous decision in *Brown* v. *Board of Education,* outlawing segregation in the nation's public schools. For THE POST this would call for detailed reporting in both the city of Washington and in Maryland and Virginia. Wiggins and Friendly put City Editor Ben Gilbert in charge of coverage although the story had national ramifications. As it turned out, the District and nearby Maryland schools integrated with minimal difficulty but Virginia took much longer. Editorially, from the day of the decision, THE POST was totally on the side of the Court's ruling. Graham never interfered with what Estabrook and Barth wrote, although Estabrook had the feeling the publisher would have preferred going slower editorially. The initial editorial included:

> The Supreme Court's resolution yesterday of the school segregation cases affords all Americans an occasion for pride and gratitude. The decision will prove, we are sure — whatever transient difficulties it may create and whatever irritations it may arouse — a profoundly healthy and healing one. It will serve — and speedily — to close an ancient wound too long allowed to fester. It will bring to an end a painful disparity between American principles and American practices. It will help to refurbish American prestige in a world which looks to this land for moral inspiration and restore the faith of Americans themselves in their own great values and traditions.

In Washington blacks already were a majority in the public schools at the time of the court ruling — 57 percent in the school year 1953–1954 — since the white flight to the suburbs had been well under way before the ruling. Now the pace increased; the 1960 census showed 53.9 percent of the total population was black, a huge rise from the 35 percent of a decade earlier.

Eisenhower, although he refused to say that he considered the Court decision to be the right one, did declare that he wanted the federal city to have a "model" desegregation plan. This eased the way for the Board of Education to vote abolition of its separate schools. At the end of the 1955–1956 school year an editorial declared that desegregation "has been accomplished here with surprising ease, understanding and good sense, and it has been accomplished without disrupting the school system."

The major problem, in THE POST's circulation area, was across the Potomac in Virginia where Senator Harry F. Byrd, Sr., in February 1956, called for "massive resistance." To cover the story in Virginia and elsewhere in the South, Gilbert made a fortuitous choice. He picked Robert E. Baker, a towering Philadelphian who had come to THE POST from the Fredericksburg, Virginia, *Free Lance–Star* to which he returned in 1976. His soft voice, easy gait and southern charm, together with a deep sensitivity about, and understanding of, the race issue, made him one of the paper's outstanding reporters, in the right spot at a critical moment. Gilbert's instructions to Baker: "You've got to forget that you're white and are dealing with Negroes. Adopt a different skin color — have a green skin. Write so that both Negroes and whites still will understand what you are talking about."

Baker, who had covered some of Washington's racial problems, first reported from Richmond as the legislature sought to avoid integration. Then Gilbert sent him to Montgomery, Alabama, where blacks were boycotting the city bus line because Rosa Parks, a 42-year-old black woman, had been arrested when she refused to move to the back of a bus. In a roundup on February 26, 1956, Baker first introduced POST readers to a "27-year-old Negro pastor of the Dexter Avenue Baptist Church and an active NAACP member," the president of the newly formed Montgomery Improvement Association; he was the Reverend Martin Luther King, Jr.

At the conclusion of a nine-week tour of the South in 1956, Baker described an "unhappy area of tension, unrest and fear." Most important, he depicted the two extremes demanding, on the one side, "immediate and outright compliance" with the Court mandate and, on the other, those "who vow they will never comply." Between them was "a middle ground. On it are many Southerners, dedicated to law and human decency, who live in uneasy silence today because it is unpopular and unrewarding, in the present climate, to suffer the squeeze of the two extremes. It would seem they hold the answer." They did, but it would be a long time coming.

In Richmond, Governor Thomas G. Stanley declared that same July that "there shall be no mixing of the races in the public schools, anywhere in Virginia." Stanley found an ally in Representative James C. Davis, a Georgia Democrat, who began an investigation of Washington's public schools. The array of witnesses telling horror stories of integration was covered in detail by POST reporters Eve Edstrom and Grace Bassett. Gilbert had other reporters checking each accusation so rebuttals could appear daily along with the charges. The Davis hearings, for all their bias, did bring out black problems. "Many of the Negro children," a story reported the chief attendance officer as saying, "found they were unable to compete. Much of their bad conduct, she said, results from the frustration of finding out they weren't doing as well as they thought."

In September Eisenhower signed the Civil Rights Act of 1957, chiefly designed to give some federal protection to would-be black voters in the South and to establish a Civil Rights Commission, the first such act in 82 years. A POST editorial called the measure "a personal triumph" for Majority Leader Johnson, lauding his "consummate skill" in sensing "the legislative weather" and in finding "a common ground for agreement between South and North that extended across party lines." The same week a major crisis erupted over integration of Central High School in Little Rock, Arkansas. It soon made Governor Orval Faubus and President Eisenhower antagonists, with the President ordering federal troops to the city to protect Negro pupils. Baker rushed to Little Rock, later aided by Richard Lyons, to cover the story which reached its peak on September 25. Next day's POST banners and Baker's lead:

> 9 LITTLE ROCK NEGRO PUPILS INTEGRATED
> WITH AID OF 350 TOUGH PARATROOPERS;
> TROOPS COOLLY OUST DEFIANT ONLOOKERS
>
> This city learned today how the United States can enforce a school desegregation order the hard way. It was a spectacular, unbelievable, and sad sight.

Time was pressing and Baker had to dictate this and other stories off the top of his head, recalling, he said years later, the advice of wise old John J. Riseling who had told him: "The most valuable tool in the English language for a reporter is a period. Don't embellish, just tell what happened and let people there tell what happened." Back in Washington, Managing Editor Friendly, unbeknownst to Baker, put the reporter's full name — Robert E. Lee Baker — on these stories in hopes it might help protect him from the mob which was hassling newsmen. At one point Baker helped rescue a New York *Times* reporter from a mob who threatened to "get" the outsider.

Editorially, THE POST said the issue at Little Rock was "basically the same as that supposedly settled at Appomattox 92 years ago. No consequence of firmness can be half so grievous as the consequence of allowing the sabotage of the Union." Other editorials were equally firm but reasoned, temperate, and explanatory. The editors knew they had a lot of readers who viewed the changes in American racial patterns, at the least, with misgivings and, at the most, with bitterness and fear.

Unknown to Baker in Little Rock, his publisher had thrown himself into the struggle to make integration work without violence. Graham explained in an October 6 letter to Joseph Alsop that he became involved because of "frantic calls . . . from Joe Rauh and others." Graham explained the reasoning behind his attitude in a letter to a Tennessee friend who had asked why anyone should back the Supreme Court ruling:

> I would say there are two sincere reasons, and then there are undoubtedly some bad ones. The first sincere one is the Christian Doctrine that men are made in God's image; this is reflected in our American traditions. I think it really causes us terrible inner turmoil when we not only do not practice what we preach, but refuse to even consider starting to practice what we preach. The second reason is a more "practical one"; some people consider it very major, though I consider the first one more important. The second reason is that most of the people in the world happen not to be white people; that the Communist conspiracy is trying very hard to get most of the people in the world on its side so that it can break down our system of freedom; and that unless we look better in the world we are going to commit suicide.

The "inner turmoil" the publisher saw in others was very much in himself. Rauh became aware of it when Graham called him at 3 A.M. to get the unlisted phone number of Thurgood Marshall, then the chief lawyer for the NAACP. The publisher in his letter to Alsop said that he "spent about sixteen hours a day on phone as sort of self-appointed, quite unwarranted, needler of White House and Justice Department." Graham had talked to Faubus and many others and had used Folliard, then with the President at Newport, Rhode Island, to relay a message to Eisenhower that a number of the President's friends thought he ought to give up his golfing, return to his White House desk, and take charge of the crisis. Eisenhower did fly back if only long enough to appear before television cameras in his office to explain why he had sent in the troops and to declare that "mob rule cannot be allowed to override the decisions of the courts."

When the crisis was over, the publisher sent a note to Gilbert praising "your genius as a city editor. We have had fine, perceptive and balanced reporting and editing of stories which relate to an inherently vicious and grotesquely confusing situation. I can hardly imagine a more difficult job better done."

The trauma of dealing with Little Rock caused Graham to lose the stability he had always maintained despite such nervous habits as 40 cigarettes a day and the compulsion to have at his fingertips the problems of the nation, even the world, as well as those of running a now very large enterprise. His brother, William A. Graham, years later was quoted in the Miami *Herald* as believing that "his disillusionment after Little Rock was the first step toward the manic-depressive." That such a tendency may long have been latent might be read from a letter he had written home on May 5, 1945, while in the Philippines during World War II: "Yesterday I was saturated with gloom and had been for some days and could see nothing bright at all presently or for some time to come in the world. Today for no good reason I feel quite jubilant, life seems better and easier; and all in all I feel that it is my oyster."

One medical expert on depression has written that "there is an array of true depressive mental disorders, traceable to biochemical disturbances and usually occurring in cycles. These may be bipolar — periods of depression alternate with bursts of frenzied activity." Graham's Little Rock activity was visibly manic; failure to prevent violence was a terrible blow to him. He told key assistants and three personal aides, Joseph Paull, Charles Paradise, and De Vee Fisher, that he had had a nervous breakdown and was going to the family farm, Glen Welby, near Marshall, Virginia, to recuperate. Graham was away from the office from October 29 through the end of 1957. In 1958 he was in and out most of the year and the next year it was much the same; he was back during most of 1960. His moods were alternately depressed and euphoric.

When he first went to Glen Welby, Graham ordered the running of

THE POST to be shared by Business Manager Sweeterman and Editor Wiggins. Only they and a few others at the paper knew that their boss was seriously ill. When he did appear at the office, Graham seemingly was his usual charming and dynamic self, able to make major decisions some of which were among his most brilliant. The paper's momentum, plus such spurts of activity, carried The Washington Post Company forward successfully despite increasing evidence of Graham's often puzzling and bizarre conduct. Not until the Kennedy era was well under way did Graham finally succumb to the last fatal stage of manic depression. From Little Rock on, those at THE POST who knew of Graham's troubles referred among themselves to "problem A."

After the segregationists' failure at Little Rock their counterparts in Virginia likewise had to face the inevitable. In the 1957 election the Byrd machine candidate, J. Lindsay Almond, made defiant speeches against integration and swore to uphold "massive resistance," although he privately told Bob Baker that he knew such resistance must crumble and that as governor he would not preside over dissolution of the public school system. Baker passed all this on to editorial writers Estabrook and Barth and the paper proceeded to compliment Almond on a moderate statement he made in northern Virginia. During an October speech at Danville in southside Virginia, however, Almond lashed out at THE POST for "deliberate distortion" of his moderate statement. In midsentence he spotted Baker arriving and switched to declare: "But there is one reporter who is not an outsider on *The Washington Post* and here he is, Robert E. Lee Baker. He is a man of integrity and I trust he'll take my words back across the Mason-Dixon line and tell them we don't need their advice."

Once governor, Almond closed some schools that federal judges ordered integrated. But in November 1958 Baker reported that Almond was beginning to turn away from "massive resistance." Then, on February 3, 1959, THE POST's eight-column headline read: VIRGINIA'S DESEGREGATION IS PEACEFUL AS 21 NEGROES ENTER 7 WHITE SCHOOLS. Baker began: "Virginia entered a new era yesterday with traditional respect for law and order . . . There were no pickets, no mobs, no violence and only minor incidents within the schools."

Almond had sounded off against "the living stench of sadism, sex, immorality and juvenile pregnancy infesting the mixed schools" of the District; THE POST called this a "despicable and unforgiveable distortion of the truth." But the fact was that the city's public schools were deteriorating. An editorial conceded:

> It would be idle to pretend that desegregation did not cause many problems, scholastic and social. But desegregation did not, contrary to uninformed impressions, lower school standards and attainments. What it really did was expose how low the standards had been in the previously separated Negro schools.

During the 381-day Montgomery bus boycott, THE POST's first editorial recognition of Martin Luther King, Jr., had referred to him as "a voice of moderation and sanity . . . his restrained leadership . . . is a luminous example of how an oppressed group can successfully assert its rights without employing the poison of violence." In the South, King encouraged the sit-in movement in early 1960. In June sit-ins came to northern Virginia covered by Elsie Carper and Susanna McBee. They described Negroes and whites, together, waiting patiently but fruitlessly to be served at the food counters in Arlington stores of the area's two major drug chains, Peoples and Drug Fair. By now these chains had dropped all bars to blacks in Washington and nearby Maryland but they said Virginia law forbade them to do so. Within two weeks, however, McBee was reporting that all major Arlington retail organizations, led by Woolworth's, had desegregated their lunch counters. Alexandria stores were next to follow. The last such battle came at the Glen Echo Amusement Park in Montgomery County, Maryland. Five Negroes protesting segregation were hustled off the merry-go-round and arrested for trespassing. Mass picketing ensued. A guard challenged Laurence Henry, a black Howard University divinity student, with: "What race do you belong to?" He replied, "I belong to the human race." In March 1961 the amusement park reopened on an integrated basis but was closed five years later after a racial incident. Eventually, it became a public park.

The second Eisenhower administration was marred by a series of disasters. In the fall of 1957, barely a month after Little Rock, came the launching of the first man-made satellite which introduced to the world the Russian word "sputnik." This was followed by Eisenhower's stroke, publicized failures in launching American satellites and missiles, charges that the administration had allowed a "missile gap" to develop, an economic recession, and the disgrace and resignation of Sherman Adams, Ike's White House chief of staff, for accepting gifts from Bernard Goldfine in exchange for favors. Vice President Nixon was stoned by leftists in Latin America, Secretary Dulles was forced to resign because of a fatal cancer, and Francis Gary Powers' U-2 was shot down, wrecking the planned 1960 Big Four Summit Conference. The only favorable international development, from the American point of view, was the beginning of the Sino-Soviet dispute — a fact the Eisenhower administration refused to accept.

Graham contributed another headache to the administration when, during one of his brief stays at the office during 1958, he received in great secrecy a tip from Lyndon Johnson. It was a copy of a letter the Republican National Committeeman from Texas had sent to oil and gas millionaires in the Lone Star State, inviting them to a $100-a-plate dinner at Houston to honor Representative Joseph W. Martin, Jr., the GOP House leader from Massachusetts. The letter described how much Martin had done for the oil and gas industries of Texas and stated that the congressman was now ready to rally his troops to help pass a bill to ease federal control over producers of natural gas, a billion-dollar bonanza. Folliard was sent to Houston. His story of the blatant affair and of the $100,000 lobbying fund raised at the dinner, appearing on page 1, was a bombshell. Speaker Rayburn correctly pronounced a one-sentence verdict: "The gas bill is as dead as slavery." THE POST had rendered a notable public service.

THE POST long had badly needed its own foreign correspondents and Graham finally authorized the first foreign bureau, in London, to which Murrey Marder was assigned at the beginning of 1957 for a two-year stint. Graham provided Marder with a rundown on 33 British, French, and other European leaders he knew with letters to all of them. Still financially cautious, the publisher charged half the bureau's cost to WTOP and Marder had to break his work for THE POST to do telephoned radio spots for more than a year, this at a time when overseas calls sometimes took hours to complete. When the money-minded Sweeterman visited Britain he said to Marder, "Walter Lippmann works in Washington. Why do we have to have you in London?"

On October 5, 1957, THE POST headlined:

SPACE SATELLITE LAUNCHED BY RUSSIANS,
CIRCLING EARTH AT 18,000 MILES AN HOUR;
IS TRACKED NEAR WASHINGTON BY NAVY

The first editorial called sputnik "one of the great breakthroughs of modern science . . . The clear meaning of recent events is that the United States is trailing seriously behind in the missile race." On December 20 THE POST added a new alarm when Roberts wrote that the still top-secret Gaither Report "pictures the nation moving in frightening course to the status of a second-class power. It shows an America exposed to an almost immediate threat from the missile-bristling Soviet Union." This long and frightening story was the result of interviews by Roberts, with able assists from Friendly, of a number of Gaither panel members who were willing, in the wake of sputnik, to disclose the sense of the document because they feared for their country. The Gaither committee, however, had relied on what turned out to be incomplete government intelligence from which they had extrapolated the threat beyond actuality and on which they built a case for a massive arms and civil defense program. Disclosure of the report's central points, however, spurred Congress, with wide public backing, to accelerate the missile program. On the last day of January 1958 the United States successfully launched a satellite of its own, called "Explorer," and public faith began to be restored. And only in this year did THE POST hire its first qualified science reporter, Edward Gamarekian, who could explain with sophistication the laws of space and such new discoveries as the earth's radiation belt.

In December 1958 Senator Humphrey met Nikita Khrushchev in the Kremlin. Upon his return, Humphrey was the guest at a newsman's dinner where he proved unusually taciturn because he was husbanding his stories for a *Life* magazine article. One story he did tell was so astonishing that Roberts later dogged him until he agreed it could be printed. In an editorial page column THE POST printed for the first time startling news of the Sino-Soviet breach — an assault by the Soviet leader on China's 26,000 rural communes as "reactionary." After Humphrey recounted the same story in his *Life* article, Khrushchev told a Party Congress the senator had made up "inventions" and was a "compiler of fabrications, Baron Munchausen." But indeed the Sino-Soviet split was under way. THE POST had no resident Kremlinologist or Sinologist but in early 1959 it began to run analytical articles by Victor Zorza of the Manchester *Guardian* who in subsequent years became a major provider of valuable insights on both the Soviet Union and China.

In the wake of sputnik and a new Khrushchev ultimatum on Berlin, Eisenhower invited the Soviet leader to visit the United States in September 1959. To help cover this exciting story THE POST took on Thomas P. Whitney, a Russian-speaking former government official and Associated Press reporter in Moscow. The day Khrushchev arrived in Washington the paper turned out most of the staff to produce 17 stories. Whitney and Roberts joined the caravan around the country, pouring out column after column as the paper gave more space to this seeming man-from-Mars than to any single event that had preceded it in THE POST's entire history.

But then THE POST of May 6, 1960, headlined:

RED AIRMEN GUN DOWN U. S. PLANE;
CHILL HITS EAST-WEST SUMMIT SCENE

The administration trapped itself in a series of lies about Powers and his U-2. After Eisenhower took responsibility, justifying the secret flights by declaring that "no one wants another Pearl Harbor," an editorial said, "The simple truth is that the United States, having been caught in the act, must now take its medicine."

To cover the aborted Paris summit, where Khrushchev met only once with Eisenhower, de Gaulle, and Macmillan, THE POST fielded the largest team ever for an international gathering: Roberts and Marder from Washington, Baker from London, and two full-time stringers, Waverley Root in Paris and Flora Lewis from Bonn. For the first time the paper was effectively competing head to head with the New York *Times* on a critical foreign policy story, operating a close-knit, highly cooperative bureau.

Hubert H. Humphrey formally announced his presidential candidacy on December 30, 1959, and John F. Kennedy followed three days later. THE POST called Humphrey "an experienced executive and legislator, an able proponent of ideas as well as ideals, an energetic delver into national and international affairs, and a living demonstration of the freedom of speech." Kennedy was credited with a "tenacity of purpose and maturity of judgment . . . an acute awareness of the great issues of the day . . . His statement on the religious issue seems to us admirable. He wholeheartedly supports the First Amendment with its guarantee of religious freedom and its separation of church and state."

On the Republican side New York Governor Nelson A. Rockefeller dropped out after an unpromising early campaign, leaving the field to Vice President Nixon. An editorial said that "there is a curious ambivalence in the impression Mr. Nixon has created, particularly among the independents to whom he necessarily must appeal. The image of him as a dynamic statesman is inconsistent with the image of him as a not-too-scrupulous climber with a lead-pipe campaign technique and what is called an instinct for the jugular."

Cartoonist Herblock had suffered a heart attack in mid-September 1959 but he returned to work the following January, primed for new assaults on Nixon that grew progressively rougher. An early admirer of Kennedy, Herblock depicted him in heroic mold. Molly Thayer, a long-time friend of Mrs. Kennedy's, favorably described the Kennedy family life, accompanied by the flattering photographs of staffer Charles Del Vecchio. In West Virginia, in the midst of the U-2 crisis, Kennedy won what Carroll Kilpatrick termed "a smashing victory" over Humphrey and was on his way to the nomination.

Nothing was more natural than publisher Graham's attraction to Kennedy. In his *A Thousand Days* Arthur M. Schlesinger, Jr., recounted that Graham saw Kennedy "as another man of power; and he was captivated by Kennedy's candor, detachment and intellectual force." They had been on an easy "Jack" and "Phil" relationship for at least three years.

On June 21, 1960, Kennedy came to an off-the-record luncheon in THE POST's executive dining room with Graham and various editors and reporters. The shrewd Folliard, who had been covering elections and presidents since the Coolidge era, knew how to probe for a story. "Jack," he said, "if you win the Democratic nomination and Nixon wins the Republican nomination, would you be willing to debate Nixon on television?" "Yes, I would," responded the senator. Reminded that the Vice President had quite a reputation as a debater, Kennedy said he knew that, adding: "I think I can take Nixon." Folliard thus had a gem of a story which would be carefully hoarded until the right moment after the nomination, a story that launched the politically important Nixon-Kennedy debates. Roberts somewhat bent the rules of the luncheon to write a column in which he said that "Kennedy insists he would not himself take second place . . . and he grants to Johnson the same determination. Hence, while he does not oppose the idea of Johnson as his running mate, he thinks it rather inconceivable."

But Graham didn't think it inconceivable. His friendship with LBJ had preceded that with JFK; in 1956 Graham had sketched out for Johnson what LBJ as President privately described as "the basis of the Great Society programs." Graham had drafted a memo advising LBJ on a "strategy of getting off the defensive" by offering a civil rights program "which goes a bit beyond [Senator Richard] Russell and yet far short of Humphrey" and by making "a poetical yet realistic" speech "about our national promise. The big things to be done. The inherent strength and character of our people. Land and water and forests to be conserved. Cities and towns and villages to be rehabilitated and slums to be decimated. Education to be strengthened and supported." A year later LBJ wrote Graham about the civil rights bill debate: "You stepped into the breach at the critical hour. That is something I will never forget and I wish there were some way of telling the country that your contribution to an effective enforceable bill was decisive." Graham sent LBJ Henry A. Kissinger's *Nuclear Weapons and Foreign Policy,* calling it "a thick, ponderous book which you *must* read . . . It is absolutely essential for you to dog through it." LBJ did so, replying that "I find that it has a profound effect on my own thinking." Graham sent both LBJ and JFK Germaine Tillion's *Algeria,* a provocative account of French activities there, telling Kennedy that "you can read it in one hour, while Jackie should need only fifty minutes."

Graham was as pragmatic about Johnson's chances for the 1960 nomination as he had been about civil rights legislation; he saw Kennedy as the choice and he was ready to urge Johnson to accept second place. To the Los Angeles convention the publisher led a large POST contingent: Friendly, Estabrook, Roberts, Folliard, Albright, Kilpatrick, Carper, Lyons, Gilbert, some city-side reporters, photographer Del Vecchio, and, for the women's pages, Maxine Cheshire and Molly Thayer. It was by far the largest POST group yet to cover such a gathering.

On July 12, two days before the formal nomination, Folliard wrote the lead-all beginning: "It's Kennedy on the first ballot." Further down on page 1, under Lyons' by-line, another story began: "The word here tonight is that Sen. John F. Kennedy will offer the vice presidential nomination to Senate Majority Leader Lyndon B. Johnson." It was a startling story and there was general skepticism when word of it reached Los Angeles. LBJ, who had said that "the vice presidency is a good place for a young man who needs experience. It is a good place for a young man who needs training," was still attacking Kennedy and most Johnson partisans were indignant at the very thought he might take the second spot.

Graham wrote a detailed memoir of his activities at the convention, published after his death as an appendix to Theodore H. White's *The Making of the President, 1964,* and then in THE POST. Graham had given it to White after disagreeing with White's account in his 1960 book. The critical paragraphs described how Graham and columnist Joseph Alsop were involved on July 11:

> At Joe's urging, I accompanied him to Kennedy's suite on the ninth floor of the Biltmore where, after considerable delay . . . Kennedy appeared and we went with him into a living room for the five minutes we had asked for.
>
> At Joe's request, I did the greatest portion of our talking and urged Kennedy to offer the Vice Presidency to Johnson. He immediately agreed, so immediately as to leave me doubting the easy triumph, and I therefore restated the matter, urging him not to count on Johnson's turning it down but to offer the VPship so persuasively as to win Johnson over. Kennedy was decisive in saying that was his intention, point-

> ing out that Johnson would help the ticket not only in the South but in important segments of the Party all over the country . . .
>
> On the basis of this I agreed with Al Friendly and Chal Roberts that the *Post* could write for Tuesday that "the word in Los Angeles is that Kennedy will offer the VPship to Lyndon Johnson" but forbade them writing more strongly in order not to embarrass the Kennedy confidence.

Only four hours before the presidential nomination balloting was to begin, Kennedy worried out loud to Graham that he was some 20 votes shy and "asked if I thought he could get any Johnson votes out of the Vice-Presidency offer . . . At this point," Graham recounted, "I said he'd never miss by any twenty votes, that his nomination was assured by *res ipsa loquitur* [the thing speaks for itself]. Whereupon, in the midst of traffic jam and Convention hubbub, his face became a student's face and he asked, 'What does that mean?' "

As the lengthy Graham memorandum demonstrated, there was much more to the publisher's often frenzied activities at the convention, none of which appeared in either THE POST or Alsop's columns. Graham was, it would later be clear, in a manic phase of his illness, doubtless accounting for the even more than usual boldness in involving himself in high politics.

The last story to go out of THE POST's bureau at the convention was Folliard's, appearing July 18, saying the presidential nominee might challenge Nixon to a television debate after the GOP nomination was assured. The Grahams left Los Angeles but the staffers, whose admiration for their boss now was at a peak, enjoyed a final feast together in the euphoria of a first-rate job despite the problems of a three-hour time difference from Washington where Wiggins had held the presses for last-minute stories.

From Los Angeles most of the staffers went to Chicago for the Republican convention, joined by Wiggins while Friendly remained in Washington to run the shop. The Grahams also went to Chicago but the publisher's investment was with the Democrats. In February he had written Wiggins:

> As for Ike, if he's sore at us, who can be surprised. All presidents are sore as they near end of office and unfortunately we've had to be critical and he's almost as thin-skinned as Lyndon . . . I am so infuriated by his incompetence that I am frequently awful about him verbally in front of our staff, so

> I am particularly sensitive to need for our paper not to reflect this kind of intemperance. (I don't think we've done so to date in paper.)

Later, after Kennedy's election, the publisher would characterize the Eisenhower era as "eight years of the dreariest and phoniest mediocrity I ever hope to live through."

After the nomination of Nixon and Henry Cabot Lodge, the American representative at the United Nations, an editorial included:

> It will be no surprise to readers of this newspaper that there are qualities about Mr. Nixon which we have not liked. He has seemed on many occasions to be an extraordinarily divisive man with little scruple or sensitivity, and we have doubted his ability to call forth national unity and respect . . . At the same time we have no doubt whatever of Mr. Nixon's awesome capabilities and penchant for hard work.

In early August, when Nixon sought but failed to win a steelworkers' union endorsement, Herblock drew him as a sour-faced fox among the grapes he could not reach. To a reader who protested, Graham replied:

> My feeling is that Herblock is the most gifted political cartoonist of our times. By definition, he, therefore, cannot be an "organization man." Being an old reactionary and individualist, I am all for people who simply have to be individualistic . . . And I think — though it will amaze you — that Herblock probably considers himself frustrated and suffocated by our policy.

After the first televised Nixon-Kennedy debate on September 26, an editorial said, "Of the two performances Mr. Nixon's probably was the smoother" while "Mr. Kennedy was crisp and to the point, but his comments suffered somewhat from machine-gun delivery." Still later, Folliard wrote that "there was much talk, even among his [Nixon's] friends, that he looked worn and haggard" and blame was being laid on his television makeup.

THE POST announced it would once again not formally endorse a candidate. "Hindsight also has convinced us," the editorial added, "that it might have been wiser for an independent newspaper in the Nation's Capital to have avoided formal endorsement" of Eisenhower in 1952. The election-eve editorial called the "really basic distinction" between the candidates to be about "the role of Government." Nixon was "tied broadly to the belief holding that Government best which governs least.

Mr. Kennedy believes that the problems facing the country in the space age pose new challenges and require new responsibilities of government. That philosophical difference is enormously important, and it represents the fundamental choice before the voters on Tuesday."

Wiggins sought balanced campaign coverage, putting out as he had done in earlier campaigns a memorandum that included: "The news columns of *The Washington Post* must bring to readers fair and impartial accounts of public events and unbiased and objective interpretations of them. The news columns are without political affiliation. Coverage should not be influenced by our editorial page or by our personal inclinations and wishes." But given Herblock's biting anti-Nixon and pro-Kennedy cartoons as well as laudatory editorials and articles, POST readers had no doubt as to the paper's choice.

A few days before the balloting Drew Pearson's column revealed defense contractor Howard Hughes' $205,000 loan to Donald Nixon, the Vice President's brother. Friendly was for publishing the column but Graham and Wiggins vetoed it on the grounds that if the story were incorrect it would backlash to help elect Nixon. The story was correct. The final Gallup poll gave Kennedy 49 percent, Nixon 48 with 3 percent undecided — too close to call. Election night the final edition headlined KENNEDY NEAR VICTORY over Folliard's cautious story that he was "moving toward election." Graham, remembering 1948, would not let Folliard call the outcome "for a few thousand lousy papers." Even when Nixon conceded the next day, THE POST still did not itself say that Kennedy had been elected.

On December 11, THE POST was first to report that Dean Rusk would be the new Secretary of State. Roberts had narrowed down the choice and was prepared to predict his likely appointment when Graham, in Roberts' presence, called the President-elect at Palm Beach. Kennedy gave confirmation. When the story appeared Kennedy called for Press Secretary Pierre Salinger: "Stop everything you're doing. I want the name of the person responsible for this and I want it today. This has got to stop." Salinger canvassed the few who knew of the choice and in two hours phoned back: "I have caught the leaker," he said. "All right, who is it?" "You." "What do you mean, me?" Salinger asked if Kennedy hadn't discussed the appointment the evening before on the phone with Graham. "I did talk to Graham about it last night." "Did you tell him he couldn't use the story?" There was a long silence, Salinger later recounted in his own book, before Kennedy chuckled and replied: "No, I guess I didn't."

THE WASHINGTON POST in the years from the *Times-Herald* acquisition to the Kennedy inaugural was by no means totally concerned with threats of war, the finale of McCarthyism, racial strife, and electoral politics. When rhymster Ogden Nash came to the capital, Harry Gabbett recorded his visit:

*Ogden Nash, the free-wheeling poet*
*Showed up in Our Town last night, ostensibly*
*to tell all, but actually to admit he*
*doesn't knoet.*

. . .

*Candy is dandy*
*But liquor is quicker*
*He thinks are his lines that are oftenest*
*quoted*
*But, alas, nearly everyone follows them up*
*by identifying Dorothy Parker as the*
*woman by whom they were wroted.*

After the State Department moved into its new building in 1960, the Defense Department, with the Pentagon already full, snatched up temporary structures vacated by the diplomats. This led reporter James Carberry to pronounce a Parkinson's law for tempos: "Government expands to fill the space available to it."

There even was congressional humor of sorts in the long struggle to throw another bridge across the Potomac. The Senate in 1957 voted for a tunnel, whereupon the House turned it into a drawbridge and finally into the absurdity of a fixed span with a draw — before sending the measure back to committee in confusion.

The airline shuttle from Washington to New York resulted from a reporter's trip to Latin America in 1959. Reporter Roberts described a nonreservation hourly service between Rio and São Paulo, almost exactly the New York–Washington distance. Civil Aeronautics Board officials read the story, called for details from Brazil, and ordered similar service between the nation's political and business centers. The shuttle began in 1961. The next year the city's new airport, Dulles International, opened and THE POST correctly called it "a thing of beauty and a joy to use."

In 1954 the American Legion convened in the capital and 750,000 watched "the greatest parade since 1865" when the victorious Union Army had marched along Pennsylvania Avenue; this time 125,000 participated and the parade lasted until 1:24 A.M. Later the same year 150,000 Catholics gathered at the Washington Monument to pay homage to the Blessed Mother of the Immaculate Conception, with the chief speaker Fulton J. Sheen, long a Washington fixture and now auxiliary bishop of New York and a "TV and radio orator." Queen Elizabeth and Prince Philip dazzled the city in 1957. They journeyed to College Park, Maryland, to visit a Giant supermarket and to see Maryland beat the University of North Carolina in football.

In May 1959 the Bolshoi Ballet appeared in Washington and POST critic Jean Battey reported "a tumult of approval" for Galina Ulanova in *The Dying Swan.* Two days later Mr. and Mrs. William A. Walker ran into protests that they were "beatniks," a new word in the paper, when they tried to open their Coffee and Confusion shop at 945 K Street Northwest. Phil Casey, in describing them, pictured something new on the capital scene: "They see themselves only as down-the-line protestors against materialism, conformity, standardization, emphasis on security and fear of individuality." Their language, Casey went on, was "filled with 'man' and 'like' and 'cool' . . . The Washington beat group, according to them, numbers about 200 or so. It includes the bearded and the barefooted, the conventionally nonconformists and devoted nonconformists."

THE POST helped kill a memorial to Franklin D. Roosevelt. A 1960 plan called for eight huge, free-standing tablets with selections from his speeches, to be erected on a 27-acre site in West Potomac Park. Frederick Gutheim, who was the first to contribute architectural criticism, wrote that the slabs looked like "a set of book ends — just out of the deep freeze." The coup de grâce was administered by Estabrook who described the monument as "instant Stonehenge."

A 1955 transit strike threat led THE POST to blame "the stubbornness and greed of the Wolfson management of the Capital Transit Co." which had refused to offer even a penny in wage increases. Once the strike began the paper attacked the company for its "harkback to the robber baron days" and what it termed Wolfson's "public be damned attitude." For 53 days the public struggled through the strike, exacerbated by a heat wave, before Congress ended it by withdrawing Wolfson's franchise. The commissioners then let Wolfson sell his company for $13,540,000 to O. Roy Chalk. Employees got their pay raise; cash fares remained at 20 cents but tokens went from 16 to 19 cents and the weekly pass from 75 to 90 cents.

Wolfson brought a $30 million libel action against THE POST over three editorials, written by Graham, Wiggins, and Estabrook. The case was settled in 1958 with an editorial saying the paper "had never intended" to charge Wolfson or his company with lacking "integrity" or doing "anything illegal" but that "both sides remain in sincere disagreement as to whether the editorials were fairly or libelously expressed."

THE POST contributed $25,000 to a Wolfson charity, a hospital in Jacksonville, Florida, where Graham's company owned a television station.

THE POST campaigned tirelessly for District home rule, but the Southern Democratic–Republican coalition in the House remained adamantly opposed. After Hawaii and Alaska won statehood, THE POST tried once more on April 27, 1959, with an editorial that consumed the entire available space. It rebutted all the old objections and then touched on the critical issue:

> The only other argument against the bill that seems to influence some members of Congress is the large percentage of Negroes in the District's population. Actual experience has shown that there is little disposition on the part of Negroes to vote as a block, unless that is necessary for protection of their rights. But in any event a general denial of suffrage in order to prevent Negroes from voting is the very negation of democracy — the counsel of despair.

THE POST was full of stories demonstrating the city's needs. Eve Edstrom, a perceptive reporter with a knack for personalizing human tragedies, in 1955 described the "national disgrace" of the city's receiving home for children. Two years later her stories on the lack of hot lunches for District elementary school children forced the city to take part in the federal program. In 1959 Edstrom opened a long account of the "face of poverty behind Washington's facade" in these human terms:

> A teacher complains about the constant tardiness of a child. But no one mentions that the child's home has no clock.
>
> A social worker counsels a mother on how to market wisely. But no one mentions that the mother's home has no icebox.
>
> A child care worker deplores the toilet habits of a youngster. But no one mentions that the child's home has no workable lavatory.

On June 22, 1954, on page 1 THE POST ran an AP story from San Francisco: "Smoking a pack or more of cigarettes daily cuts the life span and doubles the death rate from cancer and heart attacks in men 50 to 70, the American Cancer Society reported today." On July 12, 1957, the Public Health Service issued a public warning that excessive cigarette smoking could cause lung cancer, medical reporter Nate Haseltine recounted next day. Not until late 1959, however, did THE POST begin to do investigative reporting on public health. That year Morton Mintz described in a five-part series the health hazards of automobile exhaust fumes, going on the next year to campaign for antismog devices on cars.

In 1959 THE POST also explored at length the coming of the Pill and its potential effect on the population explosion. But such stories were the exception; for the most part the paper was oblivious to changing social mores of its readers. Perhaps it was the surface lull of the Eisenhower era: in 1955 editorial page columnist Malvina Lindsay quoted a foreign visitor as asking, "Why are your [college] students so tame. Don't they ever march, riot, get arrested?" Two years later Jean Rogers reported a study that found "a dominant characteristic of the current student generation" to be that they were "gloriously contented both in regard to their present day-to-day activity, and their outlook for the future."

The social whirl in Washington and much of its cultural life were chronicled in the For and About Women section under the able editorship of Marie Sauer. No editor was more possessive of her turf. In 1952 she had lost a battle to name the section For and About People because the paper's advertisers preferred the stress on women's activities and Wiggins wanted to build up the news in that section. Sauer was insistent that whatever her staff reported should be printed only in her section, no matter the scope of the news; the joke around town was that if the President resigned in a speech to a woman's club the readers would find the news in her section only. But Sauer could never win an argument with Graham to let her report his own newsworthy parties, although he did provide her with tips.

Molly Thayer wrote from Washington and abroad, as both a staffer and a free lance. She knew the Arab world, she fearlessly covered rebellions in Iraq and Lebanon, and she introduced readers to sheiks and their courts. Once she invented a newly arrived family of wealth, the Wintouns, who were making a splash with cocktail parties and treasure hunts. Mrs. Thayer began receiving calls from the socially ambitious who wanted to know how to get on the Wintouns' list, even a call from the National Symphony wondering if they would like to buy an orchestra box. Wiggins was not amused by the spoof. Always a party town for society and officialdom, Washington in 1954, so a story reported, had an estimated 200 cocktail parties a day or about 73,000 a year at embassies, hotels, restaurants, and private homes. In 1957 columnist George Dixon quipped that the word "brunch" in Washington really was "a telescoping of 'brew' and 'punch.' "

Culturally, the capital still was looked down upon by New Yorkers and others. There were a few local celebrities: in 1955 Douglas Wallop saw his book, *The Year the Yankees Lost the Pennant,* open at the National as the successful musical *Damn Yankees.* Later the same year Margaret Landon, author of *Anna and the King of Siam,* saw it open as *The King and I.* In 1958 Archibald MacLeish's *J.B.*, a modern retelling of the story of Job, had its premier at the National. Drama Critic Coe wrote that its basic flaw was that "Job is the same man at the end as he was in the beginning." MacLeish wrote Graham that Coe had "hit or stumbled on a weakness in the play we had not observed. At this stage there can be no greater service to a playwright and a director, and though it cost me three days and nights of work I am profoundly grateful to him."

In 1962, 674,000 people flocked to the National Gallery of Art to see a stellar attraction, Leonardo da Vinci's Mona Lisa. The loan of the Louvre's most famous painting was the result of Eddie Folliard's suggestion to French Cultural Minister André Malraux with an assist from Jacqueline Kennedy. Folliard flew to Paris to escort the painting, writing during the crossing on the liner *France* a series of fanciful interviews with the masterpiece:

> What do you think about all this fuss in Paris? . . . One commentator in Paris had this to say — "You don't ask a beautiful woman to come to you — you go to see her."
>
> Well, not everybody would agree that I am beautiful. Vallentin said that my face was a very commonplace one. But Vassari said that, at least as Leonardo painted me, I was very beautiful. What do you think?
>
> Well, as we say in the States, I think you are a lot of woman.

In 1957 plans were unveiled for a new, long-needed cultural center. Coe was a constant advocate, successfully backing the proposed Foggy Bottom site on the Potomac against efforts, including POST editorials, to locate it on the Mall or along Pennsylvania Avenue. In 1959 architect Edward Durell Stone's initial concept was made public but not until the Kennedy administration did the center get its crucial boost. Roger Stevens was named board chairman by JFK and the President helped raise $500,000 by speaking on closed-circuit television to a series of dinners around the nation. Some of the words that THE POST reported he spoke that evening were carved on a marble outer wall of what became the John F. Kennedy Center for the Performing Arts:

> I am certain that after the dust of centuries has passed over our cities, we, too, will be remembered not for victories or

> defeats in battle or in politics, but for our contribution to the human spirit.

When Coe called for further presidential aid for the center, Kennedy sent him a handwritten note: "We will get it done." The morning after the President was assassinated Coe suggested the center be named for him.

Presidents continued to open the Senators' baseball season but the team, like the football Redskins, was second rate or worse. College football was more successful: the Maryland Terrapins of suburban College Park journeyed to the 1955 Orange Bowl but they lost to Oklahoma, 20 to 6. Coach James M. Tatum then quit after what THE POST called the best ten-year record in the nation, 73 wins, 13 losses, and 4 ties, including five bowl games and one national championship. The Senators did stir interest with a quartet of home-run hitters but they never found the pitching to support the batters. In 1957 Roy Sievers hit 42 homers but the team finished last in the American League. In 1959 Sievers, Harmon Killebrew, Bob Allison, and Jim Lemon were dubbed "the fearsome foursome" with a total of 126 homers. But again the team finished in the cellar.

Clark Griffith, "the old fox," died in 1955 at 85. Soon new franchises were being considered by the big leagues. Although young Calvin Griffith swore the club "has never considered and does not contemplate" moving to another city, rumors of a shift continued. In 1959 Griffith announced a move to Minneapolis, then reneged after a public outcry joined in by THE POST. Finally, in 1960, he did move to Minneapolis, a new baseball city, with Washington getting an expansion team franchise. Sportswriter Bob Addie expressed the local fans' feeling:

> *Once we had a franchise*
> *And the bloom was on the rose.*
> *But Griffith transferred all our men*
> *To where the River Money flows.*

Publisher Graham helped the new club management keep a team in the capital by getting his wife and mother-in-law to buy $300,000 worth of stock. Business Manager Sweeterman joined the club's board to protect their interests. Meanwhile, Congress voted approval of a new stadium for both baseball and football, located at the end of East Capitol Street along the Anacostia River. The Redskins inaugurated it on October 1, 1961, by losing, 24–21, to the New York Giants before 36,767 fans. The initial baseball game, with President Kennedy tossing the first ball, was a Senators' victory over the Detroit Tigers, 4–1, on April 9, 1962, before 44,383, "the largest crowd ever to see a professional sports event in the National Capital." The state of sports, however, was epitomized that September 2 with a headline: MILLENNIUM! REDSKINS, NATS WIN. The stadium proved to be a money loser and a financial drain on city taxpayers.

For John F. Kennedy and his good friend Philip L. Graham inauguration day 1961 was a moment of triumph. Not since the days of Warren Harding and Ned McLean, 40 years earlier, had THE WASHINGTON POST been so "in" at the White House. Once again triumph turned into tragedy for President and publisher.

THE POST banner that morning: SNOW CRIPPLES INAUGURAL CITY. Eight inches had left 175 cars abandoned on Pennsylvania Avenue alone. On inaugural eve, before the army moved in to help clear streets, Kennedy could not get through to Graham's house for a merry party with most of the new officials and the press. But POST reporters made it about town. Jean White wrote that at the tea at Walter Lippmann's on Woodley Road the guest list "read like an intellectual who's who of writers, artists, composers, philosophers, scientists and musicians. It was a thinking man's party. You could not turn around without bumping into a Nobel or Pulitzer prize winner."

Graham had been a political kingmaker. He also had successfully sent Kennedy "a few suggestions" for appointments, the Treasury for C. Douglas Dillon, the coveted London ambassadorial post for David Bruce, and other jobs for other friends. To Jacqueline Kennedy he later presented the camera she had used as the *Times-Herald*'s inquiring photographer, an item that had come to THE POST with the purchase of that paper. Graham had advised LBJ, as Vice President–elect, how to handle his visits to Adenauer and de Gaulle, describing both as "great" as "they are . . . difficult and complicated." Jean Monnet, he joshed LBJ, was "too intellectually brilliant for a cowboy like you to understand." Later he found the Johnsons their new home, The Elms, and made sure that the sales agreement negated restrictive covenants. On October 3, 1961, the President, flanked by Graham and Wiggins, spoke at THE POST's book and author luncheon on publication of *The Adams Papers.* (Enid Reque year after year ran these lunches.)

THE POST now was stunningly successful financially. In 1959 it ranked seventh in advertising among all the nation's newspapers and it advanced to sixth in 1962. By 1960 Sunday circulation was over 460,000 and the daily finally had topped 400,000, far ahead of the *Star* and the six-day *News.* The newsstand price on Sundays had been raised from 15 to 20 cents in the fall of 1955 and on January 6, 1958, the daily price went from 5 cents, the rate since 1944, to 10 cents.

On this secure financial base Graham increased his staff in all parts of the paper. In February 1961 he promoted Wiggins from executive editor to editor and Sweeterman from general manager to publisher, with Graham now using the title of president. Wiggins' news staff budget, only $670,000 for 1947, had soared by 1962 to $2,889,281. The addition to the L Street building was nearing completion. *Potomac,* the local Sunday magazine supplement, was inaugurated on February 5, 1961, with Paul Herron as editor.

In March 1961 Graham bought *Newsweek* magazine from the Astor Foundation and other stockholders at the suggestion and urging of, among others, Benjamin C. Bradlee, the former POST city reporter now in the magazine's Washington bureau. It cost $15 million, the deal including a 45 percent interest in a San Diego, California, television and radio station subsequently sold for around $2.5 million. The month after the *Newsweek* purchase Frederick S. (Fritz) Beebe, the New York lawyer who had helped in the *Times-Herald* acquisition and had urged consideration of the magazine purchase, became The Washington Post Company's board chairman. When Beebe came over full time, Graham wrote: "Now I am completely free of duties! Eureka!" In this euphoric mood there was one cloud; Katharine Graham that same April was ordered to bed for several months with a small spot of tuberculosis on one lung.

As THE POST had hurtled forward, Eugene Meyer had withdrawn almost totally. In 1958 a big party marked the 25th anniversary of his acquisition of the paper. A plaque already had been placed in THE POST lobby on behalf of his employees calling him "A Newspaperman of Conscience." But his health was deteriorating and he died on July 17, 1959, at 83. Meyer had served every President from Wilson to Eisenhower but his enduring monument was THE WASHINGTON POST. Herblock drew a banner flying over the capital inscribed with Meyer's words: "A newspaper should serve the conscience of its community."

The Kennedy administration began in such a whirlwind that THE POST "temporarily" shifted Carroll Kilpatrick to help Eddie Folliard at the White House; he would be assigned there for 14 years. On April 17 came the Bay of Pigs invasion, a debacle that tarnished the new administration. THE POST had performed miserably, failing to send reporters to Florida and Guatemala as the New York *Times* had done to find out what was up. On April 11 Roberts wrote only that "Cubans are about to fight Cubans for the control of their island nation, and the anti-Castro forces have the blessing of the Kennedy Administration," although six days earlier Kennedy had made clear to him that the Central Intelligence Agency was deeply involved. The fact was that Graham, Wiggins, Friendly, and Roberts found no fault with such a CIA operation and hoped it would succeed in what they perceived as the national interest. Editorially, the paper on April 22 declared that the events in Cuba were "only one chapter in the long history of freedom, which has encompassed many greater disasters and darker days before men have combined their wit and determination to write a brighter sequel." Only on May 1 did an editorial speak of "the Cuban misadventure" and next day of "the appalling mistake of judgment." Graham pulled one critical Estabrook editorial out of the paper without telling his editorial page editor.

Khrushchev was emboldened by the Bay of Pigs and at his Vienna meeting with Kennedy in June he created yet another Berlin crisis. But Kennedy, much to THE POST's chagrin, chose to leak his alarm first to Reston in the New York *Times.* Back in Washington, the President shared his fears with Graham and the publisher ordered a series, "Beleaguered Bastion," to explain the crisis.

When the Russians exploded a massive nuclear bomb in a threatening test, Wiggins wrote an editorial, titled "In Memoriam" and placed between black bars, discussing the expected long-term genetic damage from fallout. The editorial concluded: "It is too late to do more than mourn the loss; but it is not too late to find in this misfortune new resolve that such a blasphemy against creation must not be repeated." By now Howard Simons had come to the paper as its science writer and he delved into the meaning of such massive nuclear tests. In his Christmas poem that year Friendly included these lines:

*Don't sing out, Khrush, or Chou En-lai,*
*"Here's strontium-ninety in your eye."*
*Don't bid us signal your Workers' Heaven*
*With cesium-one-thirty-seven.*
*(We know how sweet you've mulled the wine*
*with radioactive iodine.)*

The exact relationship in Kennedy's mind between the disgrace of the Bay of Pigs, Khrushchev's pressure on Berlin and his accompanying nuclear threats, and the President's approval of the venture in Vietnam will never be known. On February 9, 1962, THE POST reported the announcement that the United States had set up a new command known as MACV (Military Assistance Command, Vietnam), and that 4000 Americans now were in that country in a military support effort.

A February 25 editorial expressed the paper's justification for the Vietnam venture as well as a sense of wariness.

> We must ask ourselves if the United States is ready for the great-power burden which Great Britain carried for so long . . . We must make sufficient inquiry to learn if we are ready to send good men and brave men to dusty deaths in troubled places all over the globe . . . We must take up our great-power burdens and fight our proxy wars with an awareness that the pursuit of these military purposes endangers not only our forces in the field but our institutions and our beliefs at home. Out of that awareness there ought to come new precautions against the corrosive belief that representative institutions, in such crises, are more encumbering and embarrassing baggage with which practical diplomats and soldiers can safely dispense.

Basically, THE POST editorially supported the gradual involvement in Vietnam. Yet not until mid-1963 did a staff reporter go to Saigon and even then Warren Unna did not stay long enough to dig into what was occurring. In 1964 THE POST belatedly opened a one-man bureau in Saigon.

The Cuban missile crisis of October 1962 caught THE POST, like the Kennedy administration, by surprise. Rumors of Soviet missiles being sent to Cuba, coming from refugees and magnified by Republicans as the midterm election neared, were dismissed by both as essentially political statements. In fact, Berlin was more on reportorial minds than was Cuba.

On Saturday evening, October 20, Friendly was having a black tie dinner at his Georgetown home when Walter Lippmann phoned to say something serious was afoot but he knew not what. Friendly called Marder at home and then left for the office where he got Arthur Schlesinger, now working in the White House, on the phone. Schlesinger said only that the situation was "tense and tight." Meanwhile, Marder had rushed to the State Department, found the executive floor ablaze, and encountered Assistant Secretary Harlan Cleveland who, in a verbal sparring match, implied the crisis was over Cuba, not Berlin, and commented that the situation was "pretty rough." With other bits and pieces the astute Marder wrote an unsigned story that led the Sunday paper:

> Large-scale movements of United States Marines were reported yesterday in the Florida Keys and at Marine bases in

> the South. The movements were believed to be in connection with the Cuban situation.
>
> These movements coincide with numerous indications in Washington last night that a major international development was in the making.

As it happened, the White House had waved off the New York *Times* but failed to call THE POST; only THE POST had even this part of the story on Sunday. That day Kennedy called Graham to get the paper at least to avoid further pinpointing Cuba. The publisher then challenged Marder's conviction that Cuba was at issue and they argued at some length. The outcome was that, on Graham's orders, Cuba was left out of Marder's Monday lead although he adroitly managed to slide past Graham's instructions in the second paragraph. Under an eight-column banner, MAJOR U.S. DECISION IS AWAITED, Marder, again without a by-line, began:

> Official Washington yesterday wrapped itself in one of the tightest cloaks of secrecy ever seen in peace-time while key policymakers worked out a major international decision they were forbidden to discuss.
>
> At the White House and the State and Defense departments, officials refused to confirm or deny reports published in *The Washington Post* yesterday that Cuba is the focus of the extraordinary operation.

Further down, after including speculation about Berlin to meet Graham's orders, Marder reported that the government was "preparing to issue an order tightening the American quarantine on shipping to Communist Cuba" and that officials had refused to confirm or deny — a device for writing what the reporter believes to be true — whether "some new and intensive pressure on Cuba, perhaps in the form of a threat, warning or ultimatum is being readied."

Once Kennedy disclosed the nature of the Cuban crisis in his October 22 speech, highly credible stories and analysis pieces boosted the paper's internal morale and its standing with readers. A year earlier Graham had established a joint national news service with fellow publisher Otis Chandler of the Los Angeles *Times.* Thus POST missile crisis stories were widely used across the country and abroad, further heightening the competition with the New York *Times* which long had had its own similar news service.

Murrey Marder, a wartime marine combat correspondent, had come to THE POST in 1946, first as a local and then a national reporter. As meticulous a journalist as any who ever worked for the paper, although sometimes an agonizingly slow writer, Marder gradually moved into diplomacy. After his stint in London, he had come home for full-time foreign affairs reporting. After Roberts' 1971 retirement Marder worked in tandem first with Marilyn Berger and then with Don Oberdorfer.

The Kennedy era ended on both a high note, the American University "world peace" speech and the signing of the limited nuclear test-ban treaty, and on the uncertainty of the deepening involvement in Vietnam. THE POST strongly backed both the speech and the treaty as breaks in the Cold War. On Vietnam the paper wavered. A September 11, 1963, editorial noted Kennedy's decision "that we should not now withdraw" and went on: "It is a decision that may be right, now, but it is one that we must keep in a state of day-to-day review."

But when Defense Secretary Robert S. McNamara and General Maxwell Taylor returned from Saigon in October to say it should be possible to withdraw American forces by the end of 1965, THE POST called this a "most unfortunate" statement, adding: "This kind of groundless prophecy may have the political merit of pleasing those who wish to get our troops home at the same time it gratifies those who wish to keep them there. It has no other merit."

Following the overthrow and murder of Ngo Dinh Diem, Federal Diary columnist Kluttz, on a tour of the American bureaucracy in Asia, cabled from Saigon that "a mood of hopefulness and cautious optimism has replaced tension and frustration in the American community here since the coup." The Kluttz column appeared in the November 22 paper, the day of Kennedy's assassination. That paper also carried Folliard's report from Houston that the President had begun a "nonpolitical" tour of Texas "accompanied by wrangling Democrats who couldn't think about anything but politics." The veteran reporter was riding in the press bus that afternoon and out of the confusion he put together a dramatic account of the tragedy. THE POST published an eight-page extra, its first since Pearl Harbor, on the street three and a half hours after Wiggins gave the order.

Ten days after he entered the White House, Kennedy named Frank Reeves, the District Democratic national committeeman, to be a presidential assistant with the publicized intention of appointing him the city's first black commissioner on July 1. In June, when the formal appointment was made, THE POST called Reeves "well qualified," adding that "the fact that he is a Negro reflects a long overdue recognition that Negroes constitute a majority of this city's population." But the appointment turned to embarrassment and the nomination had to be withdrawn when it became known that Reeves had failed to pay all his federal income taxes. In his place, Kennedy named another black, John B. Duncan, the recorder of deeds.

Duncan, like Reeves, was an old-style, conservative black, prepared to work for whites within the system. But there were new and more aggressive leaders moving up in Washington, as elsewhere in the nation. In mid-1961 Stephen S. Rosenfeld, a new man at THE POST, quoted Sterling Tucker of the Urban League: "The employment noose is tight on the Negro's neck. There's been little change over the years. The Negro population is more sophisticated and desires higher opportunities. Patience is running out." The same day Julius Hobson of the Congress of Racial Equality set as a goal a "climate" in which Negroes would feel as eligible for hiring, training, and promotion as their ambitions and abilities permitted. Both Tucker and Hobson would become major figures in the capital's elected political structure.

The upper-crust Metropolitan Club in mid-1961 lifted its ban on black guests, but not on black members. The next January the Cosmos Club, called by THE POST "an exclusive organization of the intellectual elite," refused to accept the black writer Carl Rowan, and such members as John Kenneth Galbraith, Edward R. Murrow, Howard K. Smith, Bruce Catton, and Jerome Wiesner handed in resignations. The club admitted the first black later in 1962. More important, the growing black majority in Washington resented the fact that the police department in late 1961 had only 370 Negroes among its 2800-man force. An editorial remarked that "there is an understandable feeling among Negroes that the force is not yet altogether free of racial prejudice and discrimination." The White House police accepted its first black in 1961.

On the evening of April 27, 1962, Graham and Attorney General Robert F. Kennedy happened to be seated together at a press dinner. Kennedy startled Graham by saying that Washington was on the verge of a racial explosion and that the city's two civilian commissioners were doing nothing to head it off. The publisher set up a small civic group, including Tucker and Joseph Rauh, and had City Editor Gilbert produce a memo, drafted by Eve Edstrom, which led to a recommendation that the President name a White House adviser for national capital affairs.

Graham's civic group recommended Charles Horsky, a public-minded lawyer at Covington & Burling, for the White House post and the President gave Graham his approval. The post, held by Horsky for five years and by his successors until its abolition in 1975, served as an important means of pressing Congress in the President's name and in stirring the bureaucracy to make available to the city a host of federal grants and other aid.

Horsky was sworn in with public fanfare in September; the first explosion came on Thanksgiving day, November 22, 1962. At the new stadium that day 50,033 watched St. John's College High, a mostly white Catholic parochial school, defeat Eastern High, a largely Negro city school, in the annual city championship game jointly sponsored by the Touchdown Club, a group of football enthusiasts, and THE POST. Next morning the paper reported on page 1 that "at least 32 persons were injured yesterday in widespread fighting which erupted" after the game's end. Far down in the account was a statement that "the racial element was involved." Wiggins, Friendly, and Gilbert had agreed to play down the racial angle, a violation of Wiggins' own precepts on covering the news. Only when THE POST, three days later, ran a letter to the editor from Simeon Booker, its former Negro reporter now the correspondent of *Ebony, Tan,* and *Jet,* did readers get their first clear picture of what actually had occurred. Booker described "groups of toughs" beating whites in "the explosion of hate" which "stemmed mostly from my own people" aroused by losing the game although the outburst was "not entirely racial." The majority of blacks, he wrote, "opposed the misconduct, many were hurt trying to defend whites."

A January 1963 citizens' report cited an "atmosphere of lawlessness" in the public schools. "Fear rages through many school buildings which have become tramping grounds for outside influences, including thugs, hoodlums and persons of the lowest character . . . Students receive little discipline, little guidance and little incentive to develop strong citizenship qualities." An editorial the day the report came out called it a "shocker" but insisted that "the trouble is not a consequence of school desegregation; it is a hangover from segregation in the past, from continuing segregation in residence and work opportunities and from a failure to bring Negroes into full participation in the life of the schools and of the community generally."

The stadium riot — that word only gradually crept into THE POST — put an end to the paper's somewhat Pollyannish attitude toward the city's racial problems. Stories began to appear that delved deeply into school problems as well as black joblessness, housing, and crime. By mid-1963 the race problem clearly was national in scope. President Kennedy, James E. Clayton reported, was being urged "to take drastic steps immediately in an effort to head off a national crisis in race relations as serious in its dimensions as any domestic crisis since the Great Depression." That summer Alabama Governor George C. Wallace stood in the door of the state university, Bob Baker reported from

Tuscaloosa, "and forced the Federal Government to bring troops on the campus before two Negro students were enrolled." The President told the nation that "the fires of frustration and discord are burning in every city"; civil rights leader Medgar Evers was slain in Mississippi; electric cattle prods were used against black protesters in Gadsen, Alabama; Archbishop Patrick A. O'Boyle of Washington urged the 350,000 Catholics in his diocese to pray for God's help in meeting the national racial crisis; the National Guard was called out after racial shootings on Maryland's Eastern Shore; and the March on Washington was organized.

The march was conceived by A. Philip Randolph, then 74, who 22 years earlier had used the threat of such a gathering to pressure Franklin Roosevelt. Baker wrote that "there is some feeling of apprehension as Wednesday approaches." All liquor stores were ordered shut for the day. An army of POST reporters was deployed by Friendly and Gilbert; Marya Mannes, the critic-essayist, was hired to write a mood piece. The August 29, 1963, headline:

MAMMOTH RALLY OF 200,000 JAMS MALL
IN SOLEMN, ORDERLY PLEA FOR EQUALITY

Susanna McBee reported that the "loudest and most consistent applause came for Dr. King" and his moving "I have a dream" speech. Mannes wrote of the rally, in which several thousand whites took part:

> It was a wonderful and immensely important thing that happened here. And the only pity of it was that the people who fled it, the people who deplored it, the people who resented it, missed one of the great democratic expressions of this century; a people claiming, with immense control and dignity, the American rights long denied them.

A march, however impressive, cannot resolve specific issues or problems. The year before in the capital, when the last streetcar was retired, armed robberies of bus drivers had begun. Over many decades THE POST had advocated gun control and after Kennedy's assassination this became a running, although fruitless, battle with the National Rifle Association. Alan Barth alone wrote more than 1000 such editorials, 77 of them on consecutive days. A typical 1962 version said the NRA "takes a dour view of any proposition tending to restrict the inalienable right of Americans to shoot it out with each other."

Barth also strongly defended what became known as the Mallory Rule, a court ruling that a suspect held by police was entitled to prompt arraignment and that a confession extorted from him through prolonged questioning before arraignment was invalid. The city's police strongly objected, contending, as one official told Congress, that "thousands of guilty persons will go free." But THE POST argued that restraints on the police "mark the essential distinction between a police state and a free society." Andrew R. Mallory, whose name the rule bore, in 1958 surrendered on another charge only after his demand was granted that police reporter Al Lewis be on hand to make sure he was not beaten. Lewis had so many stories on page 1, including the surrender account, that Graham proclaimed an "Alfred E. Lewis Day" at THE POST.

The final Graham years sparkled with new POST talent, many exclusive stories, and a feeling of high camaraderie — despite an occasional sign to the staff that something was wrong with their boss.

One addition was Thomas K. Wolfe, Jr., who as Tom Wolfe would become a younger-generation favorite. He was 28 when Friendly hired him in 1959 but Gilbert never really knew what to do with Wolfe's offbeat talent. Gifted with drawing pen as well as words, Wolfe perceptively reported from Cuba in mid-1960 that the island was run by Communists. But for the most part Wolfe was a lonely rebel at THE POST; if he had come a decade later, he might have stayed longer, so different would be the nation and the paper. He was a magazine writer, or developing into one, and there was no place on THE POST for him in the serious world of editors like Wiggins and Gilbert. Another young reporter briefly at THE POST was Peter Benchley who went on to earn a fortune by writing *Jaws*.

More to the editors' liking was Laurence Stern, who came in 1952, worked his way through local and suburban news, and got his first big break covering the Maryland legislature in 1961. Maryland, he soon discovered, was the only state with no supervision over building and loan associations and had become "a mecca for high-promotional, save-by-mail associations which operate outside the scope of Federal regulation." Stern helped force a cleanup of the political tie-ins between Democratic politicians and the savings and loans. It was Graham who had first spotted an obscure Stern item and had ordered vigorous pursuit.

With Helen Dewar as Stern's counterpart on Virginia news and a growing number of suburban reporters, THE POST often tied together related stories on zoning, schools, transportation, and other area-wide interests. THE POST's distribution in the suburbs gave it either the first or second largest circulation of any daily in those states, as well as first in Washington. Wiggins' steadfast rule was that THE POST must first of all cover its readers' local interests. This was a fundamentally sound premise but one that constantly irked those writing on national and international affairs who felt their competition was not with the Washington *Star* but with the New York *Times.*

Another reporter who broke through in this period was Morton Mintz who had come to the paper in 1958. On July 12, 1962, he disclosed the thalidomide horror and made a national heroine of Frances Kelsey, a 47-year-old, $13,550-a-year civil servant. Mintz wrote his full measure of indignation:

> This is the story of how the skepticism and stubbornness of a Government physician prevented what could have been an appalling American tragedy, the birth of hundreds or indeed thousands of armless and legless children . . . What she did was refuse to be hurried into approving an application for marketing a new drug. She regarded its safety as unproved, despite considerable data arguing that it was ultra safe.

A Senate committee opened a drug probe and President Kennedy gave Dr. Kelsey a medal. Wiggins had picked up the first rumblings of the thalidomide scandal from British newspapers and put Mintz to probing; about the same time Bernard Nossiter heard about Kelsey's work from a senatorial aide and passed a memo to Mintz. The reporter was on his way to becoming perhaps the nation's most respected in the long-neglected consumer area of public health.

Bernard D. (Bud) Nossiter, with a Harvard master's in economics and an ability to explain with sophistication business-labor-government relationships, came to THE POST in 1955, hired by Friendly who himself had pioneered economic reporting in the New Deal years. At the end of the 1950s Nossiter was the first reporter on a major newspaper to alert readers to the importance of administered prices — the ability of a few firms in a concentrated industry to raise prices even in a recession. In that he had Wiggins' strong backing, but Graham, then cementing the paper's relationship with big advertisers after the *Times-Herald* purchase, was leery of Nossiter's incisive probing into hitherto journalistically taboo areas. At an economic conference in Latin America Nossiter was introduced to the Cuban revolutionary Che Guevara as THE POST correspondent. Guevara: "Ah, the *Pravda* of the United States."

Many talented writers like Marder, Wolfe, Stern, Mintz, and Nossiter were individualists and some of them prickly personalities as well. A great strength of the paper was that enterprising, "self-starting" reporters were given wide range to examine what they, not just the editors, felt was important. A great weakness was the inevitable lapse back into routine after a burst of energetic reporting; there was not enough sustained reporting and editing nor, despite the now much larger staff, enough reportorial defense in depth. Among those who came during this period were two talented blacks, Luther Jackson and Dorothy Butler Gilliam. Glendy Culligan succeeded Walter Karig as book editor, Marie Smith joined the women's pages and Frank Porter the business pages; Elinor Lee handled the food sections and Paul Herron, followed by John B. Willmann, the real estate sections. Of all the special sections, the editors allowed only food, travel, and real estate to remain largely a reflection of the advertisers.

Only after the *Times-Herald* purchase did THE POST make its first effort overseas, initially with Marder in London. The second full-time bureau, in New Delhi, was established in 1962 by Selig Harrison. American Ambassador John Kenneth Galbraith circumvented the State Department by leaking to Harrison for use in THE POST stories he wanted Kennedy to know about. From 1960 Warren Unna covered the Asian scene from Washington, a Friendly idea, where he found the embassies and international organizations fertile sources. In charge of these as well as other overseas cable reports was Philip Foisie who had come to THE POST in 1955 as a desk man and then became cable editor, foreign editor, and finally assistant managing editor for foreign news. A serious and most conscientious journalist, Foisie would preside well over THE POST's coming explosion of bureaus abroad.

Dan Kurzman, first a Middle East stringer and then an able foreign affairs reporter, was an abrasive personality. He was done out of a beat in 1963 by a Kennedy call to Wiggins. Kurzman had learned of an impending British legal ruling that would deprive leftist Prime Minister Cheddi Jagan of his parliamentary majority in British Guiana, later Guyana. The President heard that Kurzman had the story and phoned Wiggins to say it was correct but "if you print it we will have the first Communist regime in South America." Feeling he could not turn down the implied presidential request, Wiggins, with Kurzman's consent, killed the story.

By mid-1961 Graham was totally at odds with Estabrook and wanted to fire him. To prevent that, Wiggins sent Estabrook to London and himself took over running the editorial page. This largely left to Friendly the news and feature operations. A man of erudition and sophistication with a facile and witty pen, Friendly was an imaginative editor constantly on the prowl for talent to improve the paper's professionalism. He gave both the news pages and the Sunday Outlook section a liberal tone and an intellectual cast with a new emphasis on analytical pieces and stories ranging from archaeology and architecture to mathematics and nuclear science. He had a warm and engaging personality but he was less of an administrator than an inspirator, a worrier over the conflict between free press and fair trial. Although an editor with a strong competitive instinct, he had a greater interest in national and foreign than in local and sports news. He and the publisher first met when Graham came to Washington as a law clerk; the Grahams and Friendlys became social friends and the two men found their interests and personalities easily meshed. Graham boosted Friendly up the ladder; he would be managing editor for a decade and become one of the largest nonfamily stockholders in the Post Company. Friendly looked to Wiggins as a journalistic father and together, with Graham's encouragement and leadership, they propelled THE POST into a national newspaper of renown. Wiggins planned and expected that when he retired Friendly would succeed him as editor. Al Friendly, without doubt, presided over a transition from an essentially provincial and local paper with a fine editorial page to a POST poised on the brink of greatness.

Graham was a man bursting with ideas. In 1955, two years before his crackup, he made a speech at the University of Chicago on the "high cost of politics." Alarmed at reports of "the financial interests that racketeers had in political campaigns," he argued that expenditure laws produced "manipulations and evasions" because they were "patently laughable" in an age of increasingly costly campaigning. He proposed a public drive to get millions of families to make small contributions of "untainted money" to "revolutionize American politics." The speech stirred much interest but, despite a good deal of support in Congress and elsewhere, it was an idea whose time had not yet come.

The publisher also frequently spoke of the press. At the University of Minnesota School of Journalism in 1960 he pronounced American newspapers

> stale and disoriented. Not in techniques for we are encased in and fascinated by techniques. Our staleness and our disorientation is caused rather by our basic assumptions. They are shallow, out of date and almost entirely unexamined because we all of us spend all our time with techniques . . . We have probably not spent one hour asking: What *are* we doing? Where *are* we going? Our most passionate energies are expended tinkering with the superstructure, with none left over for contemplating the foundation.

In answer to a question about pressures on newspapers, Graham responded, "This sissy talk about pressure is parochial. I love pressures because I learn from them." But his inner pressures kept him from making that examination of basic assumptions, although he did give a clue to his thinking that same year in a letter to Clare Luce. "It's all us journalists who cause people to be surprised at the unsurprisable. We do everything in one dimension. You make a few of those hyperbolic speeches of yours and we turn you into your speeches."

As a publisher, Graham personally was much too close to the Kennedy administration and too protective of it. That, coupled with a sympathetic attitude toward the President by some on the paper who wrote about his administration, resulted in far less critical reporting and editorializing than should have been the role of the capital's leading newspaper.

After the onset of his illness the publisher went through cycles: sometimes he was turbulent and erratic; at other times, brilliant. Increasingly in 1962–1963 he was either withdrawn in depression or impulsive in mania. In upswing periods he bought *Newsweek* in 1961 and in 1963, for $8.4 million, a 49 percent interest in the Bowater Mersey Paper Company, a Nova Scotia firm that supplied the bulk of his paper's newsprint. Another purchase, *Art News* magazine, was sold at a loss after his death; an effort to buy a Sioux Falls, South Dakota, newspaper failed to come off as did his efforts to hire Stewart Alsop from the *Saturday Evening Post,* Philip L. Geyelin from the *Wall Street Journal,* and Mary McGrory from the Washington *Star.* He did take over national distribution of Walter Lippmann's column and talked the aging columnist into writing for *Newsweek* as well. He switched THE POST's legal business from Covington & Burling to William P. Rogers' firm. He became a fanatical backer of a congressman's plan to build a national aquarium in Washington to "celebrate Nature," Graham said in a speech, "along with our Zoo and Opera." Herblock ridiculed the idea in a cartoon and when an editorial did the same, Graham ordered Gilbert to buy a $100 fish tank for the chief editorial writer's office.

Graham bought or leased a series of airplanes, traveling restlessly about the country making speeches or investigating new properties to buy. In the spring of 1961 a British journalist described him as "the fastest talker I have yet heard in this fast-talking country. He has the same powers of pitter-patter as a master solo comic. His speech is designed to amuse, to tease, and sometimes to outrage. He cannot keep still. He cannot keep silent. With this wild and restless brilliance he must play Pied Piper to every man and woman that comes into his ken."

In early 1963 Graham moved out of the family home, took up with a *Newsweek* secretary in Paris, Robin Webb, and traveled with her until he broke off the relationship and she returned to her home in Australia. At times he told friends and POST people that he intended to divorce his wife and marry the girl. There were embarrassing public scenes and his behavior became a topic of conversation and concern among his friends, from President Kennedy down.

In the winter of 1962–1963 Graham intervened in the long New York newspaper strike on the side of the printers' union. He drafted an editorial for THE POST that Wiggins considered so one-sided he refused to run it and told the publisher that he would quit if the piece appeared. Graham backed down — he had always disliked scenes and fights — but Wiggins became even more the number one target of his enmity. The publisher wanted to fire Wiggins and he told Friendly to take over the editor's post but Friendly would have none of it. Friendly agonized over how to help Graham. The pressure and burden on Wiggins was immense but he was determined to hold the paper together and he did. Because Graham was either away so much or unavailable for long periods, management fell to the combination of Wiggins and Sweeterman with Beebe, in the last years, helping on financial matters and sometimes arbitrating differences. Without Graham to settle Wiggins-Sweeterman money disputes, Sweeterman usually had the last word in his own determination to keep the paper highly profitable.

At the time of the New York strike President Kennedy, to whom Graham had made a flood of phone calls, discussed the publisher with Benjamin Bradlee, then *Newsweek*'s Washington bureau chief. In his 1975 book, *Conversations with Kennedy,* Bradlee recalled:

> Holding his thumb and forefinger close together, the president said "The line is so damn narrow between rationality and irrationality in Phil."

Bradlee wrote that "when he was well," Graham "was one of the most naturally attractive, witty, and brilliant men I've ever known — and a natural friend for Kennedy, as JFK was a natural friend for Graham. They shared humor, understanding of the uses and abuses of power, charm, common goals for America, and much more. The strain that Graham's illness was putting on their friendship, and Kennedy's loyalty to him and to his wife, were sad and moving." Kennedy fruitlessly called other friends of Graham to ask what they might do to help him. After the publisher wrote a laudatory POST article about Kennedy and his Cuban missile crisis policy, the President on March 28, 1963, sent him a thank-you note and added, "I hope you come by some day soon."

But when Graham took to berating Kennedy over the phone, asking "Do you know who you're talking to?" the President replied, "I know I'm not talking to the Phil Graham I have so much admiration for."

At a dinner in Phoenix, Arizona, Graham attacked fellow publishers so wildly that his associates had to forcibly fly him back to Washington. He drank excessively. He knew he was a manic depressive and in rational periods would tearfully ask what had made him turn on his best friends and on his wife and whether they thought he could ever return to running the paper. Graham went to see "Scotty" Reston "to see if my faith could help him," as Reston recalled, "but my faith was not strong enough." Rumors that THE POST was for sale brought inquiries from the *Star* and at least one prospective purchaser flew to Washington. Graham was three times committed, twice voluntarily, to Chestnut Lodge, a Rockville, Maryland, private institution for psychiatric care, the last time on June 20, 1963.

On August 3, a Saturday, with his doctor's permission and his wife believing him "quite noticeably much better," he left Chestnut Lodge with Katharine to drive to their Glen Welby, Virginia, farm for a weekend outing. As THE POST reported the next day: "Shortly after 1 P.M., while Mrs. Graham was in her room upstairs, Mr. Graham killed himself with a .28-gauge sportsman's shotgun. He was alone in a first-floor room. The only other persons in the house were the servants." Philip Leslie Graham was only 48.

During his last months the agony for Katharine Graham had been excruciating. She had talked with her husband for hours on end, visited him at Chestnut Lodge, and encouraged selected friends to see him from time to time. She had endured his manic slurs, the gossip, the talk of divorce. At one point her mother, Agnes Meyer, by then a widow, had given a massive party to which all of political Washington was invited and came in a show of support for Katharine.

A Karl Meyer editorial, in consultation with Wiggins who was away, was printed between black bars. Speaking of this "gallant figure" and the paper's total "sense of loss," it included this discerning paragraph:

> To his associates on this newspaper, Mr. Graham was as much a friend as an employer. There was no detail of journalism he regarded as too trifling to engage his concern. His rangy figure and quicksilver wit were as familiar a part of our enterprise as the fonts of type in our composing room. In all that he dealt with at *The Washington Post* and its related ventures, he was broadly liberal, eminently practical and endowed with an intuitive grasp of coming needs.

Arthur Schlesinger, who knew the publisher well, wrote in *A Thousand Days* that Graham

> was one of the brilliant and tragic figures of my generation . . . Phil Graham was a man of quite extraordinary vitality, audacity and charm, who charged everything he said or did with an electric excitement. He joined an exceptional gift for intimacy with a restless desire to provoke and challenge his intimates. He knew everybody and was intimidated by nobody. He was fascinated by power and by other men who were fascinated by power. Yet power for its own sake gave him only fleeting satisfaction. He wanted to *do* things. His sense of the general welfare was strong and usually sound; and he was a forceful manager of people and situations in what he conceived as the public interest.

To services at the National Cathedral on August 6 came President Kennedy, members of the Cabinet, Supreme Court, and Congress, friends from the city government and the press. Next day one of the publisher's college roommates, Senator George Smathers, was quoted in THE POST as saying: "If Phil Graham had any fault or weakness, I think it would be that of being too greatly concerned about the problems of other people, and of all humanity, and he resented and brooded over the fact that he could do nothing about many of them."

The man so many remembered once wrote fellow publisher Joseph Pulitzer, Jr.: "Remember that it is possible to be a good publisher and a happy publisher at the same time." And he wrote labor leader Walter Reuther: "The way of the progressive — who eschews the easy answers of extremists — is hard. But it is the only hopeful path for civilized man." Phil Graham had been such a good and happy publisher and such a civilized man.

# 8

# Maturity
# Katharine Graham's Turn
# 1963-1972

When THE WASHINGTON POST was sold at bankruptcy on June 1, 1933, it was exam time at Miss Madeira's school for young ladies across the Potomac in Virginia. Katharine Meyer — Kate, as her father called her — was 15 days short of her 16th birthday when she joined in the student guessing about who might have bought the paper. By June 13, when THE POST announced that Eugene Meyer was the new owner, Kate was at the family home in Mt. Kisco, New York. She overheard mother asking father what he intended to do with the paper. "Oh, darling," said Agnes Meyer in response to a puzzled look, "didn't anyone tell you? We bought the *Post.*"

Thirty years later, on the death of her husband, Katharine Meyer Graham, just turned 46, became controlling owner of the paper and its related communications enterprises. As she later recounted, she felt "unprepared," "nervous and uncertain," "paralyzed," and "in a state of absolute terror."

Born in New York City on June 16, 1917, Katharine Meyer was fourth of five children, one son and four daughters. Her father, already a millionaire, established munificent trust funds for each child. Kate had a French governess and she was sent to the proper private schools for the wealthy, Potomac in Washington and then Miss Madeira's where, as she later put it with approval, there was a "curious hair shirt discipline." When she went off to Vassar in 1934 she was "an unquestioning Republican" who, like her parents, had supported Hoover over Roosevelt. But like so many other collegians of the time she turned ardent New Dealer by the end of her freshman year.

Meyer family life, she recalled, was "characterized by what might be called 'discussions.' In proportion to our lack of experience we of the younger generation contributed heat and dogmatic assertions to these discussions, whatever the topic. The noise at our table was often such that nervous indigestion and sometimes a manifest tremor were the unhappy fate of the timid guest who took things too seriously." Some summers there were pack trips, with a retinue of servants, organized by "Ma," or trips to Europe ordained by "Pa." One summer, when her siblings fled the capital, she came back to Washington to be an unpaid copy girl in THE POST's women's department.

Ma was "sort of a Viking," her daughter recalled. Kate was dressed in "ribbed stockings when no one else wore them, and other agonizing things." Ma cared more about people and issues and responsibilities. She told her children: "You can't sit around the house and be rich. You must do something." To daughter "she came on so strong you wilted. Ma did hold up almost impossible standards and I thought everyone else was living up to them. I thought I was this peasant walking around among brilliant people." Only on much later reflection would mother appear to have been "a marvelous example."

If Ma was demanding, Pa was more subtle. It never occurred to Kate that father could think she might someday take over the newspaper; he was too much the male chauvinist, she came to believe, perhaps because he distrusted his own wife's judgment. Yet Alice Roosevelt Longworth remembered Eugene Meyer saying one day in the Coolidge era: "You watch my little Kate; she'll surprise you."

Kate found Vassar too confining, and besides it was an all-girls school. Pa decided she had been playing, not working, and he encouraged her to transfer to the University of Chicago for her last two years. Both father and daughter were attracted by the creative educational leadership of Robert M. Hutchins. Meyer wrote Hutchins that "she has in mind to become a professional journalist." He advised Kate to avoid joining clubs with labels. She wrote that fellow students were all talking about a new comic strip, Terry and the Pirates. He checked, found none of the Washington papers yet had it, and promptly added it to THE POST.

In the spring of her senior year, Meyer suggested she come to work at THE POST. "You ought to be in on the job of putting it to the top. It is much better sport fighting to get there than trying to stay there after you have gotten there." But Kate was not yet ready for the family fold. Economics professor Paul H. Douglas, later a senator, encouraged her to get a newspaper job and she did, on her own, at the Chicago *Times.* But before she could begin she joined Pa on a train trip to San Francisco. "I fell in love with that city. I chucked my pride and asked my father to help me get a job there. The San Francisco *News,*" a Scripps-Howard afternoon paper, "said they would take me for two months." She remained for seven and a half months, at $21 a week.

San Francisco was in the midst of a major strike when she arrived. A *News* executive recalled assigning her "to a routine employer-labor meeting, and she phoned in such an excellent account that she promptly was sent on more and more important stories . . . Miss Meyer showed a remarkable grasp of the issues and events. Soon she was our chief outside reporter on the strike. Seldom have we seen anyone take hold of a tough assignment as she did."

The 21-year-old reporter took her job very seriously. After the lead of one of her first stories had been changed, she wrote Pa that "I was a little discouraged at that but the assistant city editor wanted it the way I wrote it at first. The city editor had it changed. Felt better when the news editor came up especially and introduced himself and said it was a darned good piece of restrained writing and not to be discouraged because they had changed the lead."

At the University of Chicago a fellow student recalled Kay Meyer as "a tall diffident, shy young woman who walked with long, confident strides dressed 'down' in sweaters and skirts," hanging out "Saturday nights at Hanley's Bar, the campus boite for professors and students, stretching a glass of beer (dutch treat)." At Chicago she was a member of the liberal, anti-Communist wing of the American Student Union. In San Francisco by day she was fascinated by Harry Bridges, the left-wing labor leader, but by night she was in evening gown for the gala opening of the opera or for dinner in Del Monte's Bali Room. These appearances made the society pages, with photographs, prompting Pa to write: "I want to advise not going out every night; for the work you have to do in the day, late hours every night on social jaunts will wreck your otherwise good health."

Pa went further. He came out to San Francisco "and suggested that I work on *The Post.*" *Time* magazine got wind of the move and on April 24, 1939, along with her photo in gold lamé evening gown, reported: "To Washington, D.C. went comely, 21-year-old Katherine Meyer, daughter of Publisher Eugene Meyer, to handle for $25 a week the 'Letters to the Editor' department of her father's *Post.* Said Father Meyer: 'If it doesn't work, we'll get rid of her.'" *Time* misspelled her first name, as did a POST house ad eight months later in which she was pictured with the editorial staff.

Miss Meyer, as she was known to the staff, edited the incoming letters, helped to make up the editorial page, and began writing editorials. That year, 1939, she wrote 103, ranging from the perils of the Rocky Mountain tick to a defense of Archibald MacLeish when he was charged with being a "fellow traveler." She tried humor: an editorial on changing female waistlines remarked that "in this case not even haste makes waist." She quoted Sophocles: "the truth is the strongest argument." Editor Felix Morley noted in his diary that she was "a well-poised and intelligent girl who evidently was to be groomed as the eventual owner-publisher."

While writing editorials she met Philip Graham who had come to Washington in the fall of 1939 to clerk for Justice Reed. Married on June 5, 1940, they set up housekeeping in Burleith, just outside of Georgetown. When his wife hinted that she would like to quit her job so she could learn to cook, he responded: "My God. I don't think I could stand having you wait around with a pie for me to come home from the Court. You continue to work and we'll pay a maid with what you make." So she moved into THE POST's Sunday department to write about Pan American Day and the Cherry Blossom Festival. There also were more substantial pieces in the brains section on the battle over radio fees for songwriters and on the pre–Pearl Harbor struggles between the America First Committee and the Committee to Defend America by Aiding the Allies. On the eve of FDR's third inaugural she wrote of Mrs. Roosevelt's "disarming honesty, dignity and intelligent interest." On June 10, 1941, THE POST pictured her at the microphone in a spelling bee between the Women's National Press Club and the male National Press Club but neglected to tell what was the word at issue or whether she knew how to spell it.

When she reviewed *The Other Germany* by Erika and Klaus Mann someone misspelled her by-line; obviously she wasn't putting it on her stories herself. After Pearl Harbor, as the men left for the war, she helped in the circulation department, going from school to school recruiting carrier boys. She took telephone complaints from subscribers. One caller told her, "If you can't get me the paper promptly delivered, I'll have to complain to my good friend, Eugene Meyer." Her reply: "I'm glad to hear you're his friend, but I've never heard him mention you and I'm his daughter." About this time her father remarked to a friend that of his five children "Kate's the only one like me. She's got a hard mind. She'd make a great businessman."

In 1943 she went with her husband, now in the Army Air Corps, to a post at Sioux Falls, South Dakota, and then to the Air Corps intelligence school at Harrisburg, Pennsylvania, before he left in mid-1944 for the Southwest Pacific. There were children, too. She lost their first baby, but Elizabeth (Lally) and Donald were born during the war and William and Stephen afterward. When her husband returned from the war to begin taking over THE POST, "I really felt I was put on earth to take care of Phil Graham. He was so glamorous that I was perfectly happy just to clean up after him. I did all the scutwork: paid the bills, ran the house, drove the children. I was always the butt of family jokes. You know, good old Mom, plodding along. And I accepted it. That's the way I viewed myself." Besides tennis and bridge and parties there were "good works" for dependent children, the Health and Welfare Council, the Children's Convalescent Home, the Washington Gallery of Modern Art, the Junior Village study committee. President Truman named her to the city's Sesquicentennial Commission.

Once her husband moved to THE POST she stopped working there herself. In late 1947, however, Graham conceived the idea of a Sunday digest of current magazine articles and he inveigled his wife to write The Magazine Rack column. She did so for nearly three years. Once she got in a family dig. Of an article about Washington in *Junior Bazaar* she wrote that "Philip Graham of this paper rather hogs the camera while his wife, who writes a magazine column, lurks in the background."

Katharine Graham did lurk in the background, submerging her own personality. A friend recalled her as "the awkward, ill-at-ease woman standing at Phil's side at those painful company parties." Another remembered her as "dowdy, dumpy almost, in a shapeless dress and a nervous manner, smothered by her husband," less man and wife than "prince and attendant." Although she now held a minority of THE POST voting stock, it was he who held the majority. Although she was in on the purchase of the *Times-Herald,* her father and husband had managed it. Although she was with her husband when he bought *Newsweek* and expanded into other ventures, she gave consent rather than advice. Her mother continued to put her down. One day at the Mt. Kisco house, Mrs. Meyer was talking to her son-in-law when her daughter came up, several children in tow. "Pardon us, dear," said Ma, "we're having an *intellectual* conversation."

After her husband's 1957 crackup, his health became her major concern. A 1961 bout with tuberculosis kept her in bed for three months. And there were four children to raise. When her husband died they were 20, 18, 15, and 11, the older two at college. Her father was dead, her mother 76. She had inherited THE WASHINGTON POST.

"When my husband died I had three choices," she recounted. "I could sell it. I could find somebody else to run it. Or I could go to work. And that was no choice at all. I went to work." Although "the vultures were flying around" with offers to buy, "it was simply inconceivable to me to dismantle all that my father and my husband had built with such labor and such love."

Katharine Graham was not totally unprepared but "my credentials were pathetically thin" and "I had to use the Montessori method — learn by doing" because "I was the new girl in school. And I didn't even know how to give directions to a secretary." There were two major areas to conquer: the news and editorial operation and the business and financial side of the paper. Fortunately she could count on Fritz Beebe to oversee the magazine and broadcasting properties, leaving her free first of all to get a handle on THE POST. The centerpiece of the corporation, the newspaper, was producing nearly two-thirds of the corporate profits.

"It took me some while," she remembered, "to cease thinking constantly of a certain scene from the old musical comedy, *The Vagabond King*. You may recall the moment when the suddenly enthroned vagabond — for the first time dressed in royal robes — descends the great stairs, slowly and anxiously, tensely eyeing on either side the rows of archers with their drawn bows and inscrutable faces." Ten years after she took over she was asked on a television show what had been "the toughest part." She replied, "I wasn't trained." And when she was asked whether she was terrified, she said, "Congealed."

Immediately after her husband's death, Mrs. Graham met with her board of directors, all company officials, to say that "I want you all to know that I know what you've been through this past year." Leaving management in the hands of Sweeterman and Wiggins, she spent a month sailing the Aegean with her mother and daughter, the Earl Warrens, and the Drew Pearsons. Later she commended Sweeterman and Wiggins for having "held the rudder steady through some difficult moments — through Phil's illness and death and my newness. Let's face it — this must have been the worst cross of all." On September 20, 1963, she formally assumed the company presidency, saying she would be guided by her father's dictum:

> The newspaper's duty is to its readers and to the public at large, and not to the private interests of its owner. In the pursuit of truth, the newspaper shall be prepared to make sacrifices of its material fortunes, if such course be necessary for the public good. The newspaper shall not be the ally of any special interest, but shall be fair and free and wholesome in its outlook on public affairs and public men.

Men. "I had deferred to men for ages. They *knew* better," she said. She carried on the tradition of editorial luncheons with the men but "the first time I opened my mouth, I nearly died . . . My worst moments were the public appearances. Speeches and interviews were the hardest thing for me to learn; I wasn't very articulate."

She consulted men outside the company whom she trusted, especially Walter Lippmann and James Reston. Reston asked, "Don't you want to leave your children a greater newspaper than you inherited?" and that "made me realize I could do things I hadn't envisioned." During an upheaval at the New York *Times* Reston was tempted by her offer to join THE POST in a managerial role while continuing his column, but in the end he couldn't bear to leave his paper. She followed Lippmann's advice to devote an hour each morning before going to the office to reading THE POST and glancing at the rival *Times.* "Then, instead of trying to study all the strange subjects that are reported," suggested the columnist, "make a note of the stories in the *Post* or *Times* that interest you particularly and that you want to know more about. Make a point of calling in the reporter who covers it and have him explain it to you. In this way . . . you'll be informed on the news . . . and you will get to know better than you probably would any other way the people who actually write the paper." Finally, "I wouldn't try to worry out everything myself. Not everybody, by any means, understands everything, and nobody expects you to do that."

The next year — 1964 — Mrs. Graham began to catch the swing of things, at least on the news side of her paper. She also was spending two days a week in New York with *Newsweek,* and less time with the television and radio stations. In February she wrote a friend that "of course, it isn't like having Phil running" the paper and the magazine "but I feel like the President of the United States [Lyndon Johnson] who said to Congress, 'I am the only President you've got.' " In May she wrote another friend: "I think at first I had a tendency to compare myself unfavorably with Phil at his best. Since I really know that almost nobody could live up to this kind of standard, I have become somewhat reconciled to doing this job in the only way I can do it — as myself." By then she was signing her mail "Katharine Graham," no longer "Mrs. Philip L. Graham." As she once wrote in a letter of condolence: "There is no recovery really from grief — even the void left by having to take care of someone who isn't well; but after some time passes, you become someone else."

A few days after her husband died Mrs. Graham had asked both Editor Wiggins and Managing Editor Friendly what she should do. They both replied, "Run the paper." To them she said, "You're my team." Wiggins continued for just over five years; Friendly for only two years until Benjamin C. Bradlee was brought in as his deputy and then, three months later, his successor.

The final Friendly years, especially 1964, were full of excitement. THE POST sent a full crew to San Francisco for Barry Goldwater's nomination and to Atlantic City for Johnson's. The chief political reporting was done by Julius Duscha. Johnson became the most accessible of presidents and POST reporters, especially National Bureau Chief Roberts, were frequently at the White House. On April 15, 1964, the President had a group of POST executives, editors, reporters, and editorial writers, headed by Mrs. Graham and Beebe, to lunch in the family dining room. LBJ often was on the phone to the publisher and it was difficult to escape his embrace especially when he spent so much time expounding and explaining his policies.

Mrs. Graham went to both conventions and at the end of the Democratic conclave, as she was waiting at the airport, she was swept up by Johnson and flown off in Air Force One to his Texas ranch. In THE POST her name appeared in a Kilpatrick story only in a list of those going to the ranch, but among press and politicians the presidential act made a big splash. She admitted to being "goggle-eyed" to find herself flying from Austin to the ranch in a helicopter with only the President, the vice-presidential nominee, and their wives.

Mrs. Graham's notes on the visit recounted that at the ranch Lady Bird Johnson

> turned to me and said, "Kay, I don't know how to tell you to ring for breakfast in the morning. We used to have a real simple system in the house but it has all been replaced and I don't understand it." One of the Secret Service men was walking alongside of us and she asked him how I could ring the kitchen. He replied, "Just ask the operator, ma'am, and he can get you anyplace in the world." I laughed, "And can he get me something as simple as the kitchen?" And he said, "Yes, he could."

When it was over she wrote a friend that she had gone "with huge interest and joy." To Johnson she wrote: "I feel exactly as though I were the heroine of one's childhood fairy tales, put on a magic carpet and carried in three swift jet hours into Never Never Land."

That summer she traveled awhile with POST political reporters covering the two candidates. A British interviewer that year found her "tremendous fun to talk to. In her deep, slow drawl she is as witty as she is informed." That fall in Wiggins' presence, she told the President that

THE POST would not endorse him. When tears welled in LBJ's eyes, she added, "Oh, we're for you 100 percent." Wiggins was appalled at her remark; he knew his new boss still had a lot to learn. Editorially the paper endorsed no one.

THE POST covered the 1964 race riots in northern cities only with press association stories. It did better in the South, sending Richard Corrigan to Mississippi after northern young people instituted a "freedom summer" program. Editorially, THE POST was torn. It maintained its strong pro–civil rights stance but it also warned that some northerners seemed to be needlessly courting disaster. "Let them ask themselves with some humility what action, however fastidiously legal, they are entitled to take that could inflame passions and explode sparks in the political tinder box of this menacing summer." Two weeks later Mrs. Graham expressed, in a letter, her fear that "the students will be used by extremists who want very much to see the state occupied by federal troops. Phil was too much of a Southerner, having grown up there, for me not to have a heavy sense of the counter bitterness and resentment of the South if this becomes necessary. I worry that the students from the North, courageous and enterprising as they may be, haven't any understanding of the size and scope of racial problems in the South and of the resentment of Southerners. I don't mean the thugs but the decent ones." Fortunately, no federal troops became involved.

There was violence in 1965 when blacks marched in Selma, Alabama. William Chapman and Thomas R. Kendrick wrote from Alabama and Rasa Gustaitis covered the sympathy marches in Washington. The paper was much slower, however, in recognizing the unrest at the Berkeley campus in California and it was very late in understanding the relationship to the war in Vietnam. A 1964 editorial was concerned chiefly with those "few students who made a travesty of the free-speech case by displaying obscene words on the campus."

THE POST deserved criticism for its delay in covering the Vietnam War. Not until mid-1964, long after the New York *Times,* did THE POST open a Saigon bureau, and then it sent a Canadian, John Maffre, whose nationality complicated his reporting problems. Editorially the paper stood with LBJ. The editorial position was set by Wiggins although there was constant discussion with other editorial writers. In these years, especially after LBJ's 1964 landslide, the President's Great Society programs were highly exciting to POST editors, reporters, and editorial writers. The war, to most, was an annoying intrusion. It seemed possible, as Johnson would insist, to have both guns and butter. Katharine Graham went to Vietnam on a round-the-world *Newsweek* trip in early 1965 and she returned home as fully a believer in the war's rightness as was Wiggins who never went to see for himself. He felt she was emphatically in accord with him in these years, and she was.

James Russell Wiggins was not a mindless hawk; he was repelled by the all-out war proponents. Essentially, like many of his generation within the administration, Wiggins was influenced by memory of the democracies' failure to check the aggression that had led to World War II. This was a central theme of POST editorials on Vietnam and no amount of argument that Vietnam bore no resemblance to Europe could shake Wiggins from his principle. Walter Lippmann, still a powerful journalistic force on THE POST's op-ed page, wrote in March 1964 that "we must not and we can not withdraw." But by February 1965 he concluded that American power in the Pacific had been "diminished because we have become entrapped in a land war." From then on POST editorials and Lippmann columns grew more divergent.

Wiggins did not call for total victory; rather, he wanted a negotiated peace. But the fatal flaw in his editorial argument was the same as that of the American government: by a negotiated peace was meant a non-Communist, preferably an anti-Communist, South Vietnam whereas to the Communists that outcome represented capitulation to yet another foreign invader. After the Communist attack on the American base at Pleiku in February 1965, an editorial thundered that such violent acts "disclose with dreadful clarity that South Vietnam is not an isolated battlefield but a part of a long war which the Communist world seems determined to continue until every vestige of Western power and influence have been driven from Asia . . . [It is] now clear that withdrawal from South Vietnam would not gain peace, but only lead to another war."

When Marguerite Higgins, the hawkish New York *Herald Tribune* correspondent, congratulated Mrs. Graham on that editorial, the publisher responded that "I agree more than ever after having been through that part of the world." When Johnson sent the marines to Vietnam in April 1965 another editorial put the Wiggins case: "The whole prospect is unpleasant, unpalatable, unlovely, unhappy — and unavoidable as long as North Viet-Nam will consent to nothing but the complete conquest of South Viet-Nam."

That June Wiggins made his only visit to the Soviet Union. He was shocked by the stiff-arm responses he received from a North Vietnamese diplomat in Moscow and he was repelled by what he described in print as the "bellicosity and truculence and querulousness of [Soviet] officialdom and of the press" on the whole range of Soviet-American issues, including Vietnam. In short, his trip reinforced his belief that LBJ was right when he said that "we did not choose to be the guardian at the gate but there is no one else."

THE POST, however, was not quite monolithic. In June 1965 Murrey Marder in a massive takeout on the crisis in the Dominican Republic spread over five pages in the Outlook section wrote that "perhaps, above all, these events have underlined the limitations on the ability of the mightiest nation in the world to work its will in one of the smallest." Next day Laurence Stern described the current stereotype of Johnson as that of "a fast-drawing cowboy who is impatient with the complexities of a world sundered by the forces of nationalism, revolution and big power policies."

Wiggins' support of LBJ on the war was a thing apart. When the President's chief aide, Walter Jenkins, was caught in a homosexual act two of Johnson's close friends, attorneys Abe Fortas and Clark Clifford, came to see Wiggins and Friendly (and their counterparts at the *Star*) to ask that the story be withheld. Just as Wiggins was saying that that was impossible, a copy boy brought him the first wire service story on the case. Later, when Senator Edward Kennedy came to see Wiggins after an editorial criticized the senator's recommendation of the unqualified Francis X. Morrissey to be a federal judge, Kennedy explained: "My brother [the late President] promised my father he would make Morrissey a judge." Wiggins: "I didn't promise your father anything."

In addition to the Saigon bureau the most notable new overseas post during the last years of the Friendly regime was that in Moscow. It was first filled by Stephen S. Rosenfeld, the young Russian-speaking city-side reporter and editorial writer whom Friendly had hired five years earlier with just such a post in mind.

Salaries now were going up for many as a 1964 Newspaper Guild contract raised to $200, the highest in the industry, the minimum weekly pay for the most experienced reporters and photographers. Ben Gilbert was still city editor and his side of the paper was much concerned with plans for a Washington subway; a 25-mile system finally was authorized by Congress in August 1965. The previous year Friendly hired the paper's first full-time architectural critic, Wolf Von Eckardt, who helped stir and then build interest in urban design as a way to improve the quality of life. A Von Eckardt editorial called the new Rayburn office building on Capitol Hill "unquestionably the most expensive office space in the long and lamentable history of architectural debauchery."

William Raspberry, a Mississippi-born black reporter who eventually became a nationally syndicated columnist, got his start when Friendly and Gilbert took him on as a teletype operator in 1962. Soon he was writing local civil rights stories and he was one of several to alternate in writing an area Potomac Watch column beginning in early 1965; others were George Lardner, Jr., Alan Desoff, Dan Morgan, and Jesse

W. Lewis, another young black reporter. Early in 1966 Raspberry took over the column as his own at Gilbert's suggestion. Wiggins' concept of the column was to have "a Walter Lippmann for the District" and Mrs. Graham years later told Raspberry he had "really fulfilled that job description." In 1974 *Time* called Raspberry "the most respected black voice on any white U.S. newspaper."

There were changes of morals and mores for THE POST to begin to describe. In 1965 Robert L. Asher wrote of

> the fantastic collection of night spots along M street [in Georgetown] that now lures hundreds of boisterous, gyrating youths . . . some dressed to the teeth, some in T shirts and slacks and others in who-can-tell-what-sex getup. The bearded pseudobeat and his stringy-blonde chick . . . The honky-tonk thunder of overamplified guitars mounts with each heavy-handed blast of drums as the young throngs cluster on the sidewalk to check out admission prices and ready their "I.D." cards . . . The music, the beer and the atmosphere cater to their legitimate desires for "action," and the name Georgetown keeps it respectable if parents ever ask where they're headed.

The day this appeared Theater Critic Coe's cabled story from the Berlin film festival included: "I am up to my eyeballs in sex and violence. I've watched sex on beds, under beds and in beds, in parks, jungles and cars." The new frankness ended old newspaper taboos. Jean White's account of rape appeared on page 1 of July 24, 1965: "A woman raped repeatedly in a Georgetown park area last week has assailed medical procedures that she feels coldly ignored the victims." Hospitals, she added, said they must have "a semen smear from the victim to detect the presence of sperm."

When Mrs. Graham came back from her 1965 round-the-world trip she heard that her magazine's Washington bureau chief for the last four years had turned down a promotion because it entailed moving to New York. She had learned intuitively from her husband to talk to promising people, so she now invited Benjamin Crowninshield Bradlee to lunch at the F Street Club. This April conversation was to lead to her first major change at THE POST, one that had repercussions for years to come.

She asked Bradlee what he had in mind for his long-term future. He replied that if THE POST's managing editorship ever became available,

"I'd give my left one for it." She answered that such a change might someday be possible, she'd have to think about it. She consulted Beebe, Reston, and Lippmann and found all three critical of Friendly who had held the job for a decade. This confirmed her own sense that something was wrong at the paper — that Friendly no longer had the necessary zest and zip. She noted that he was growing deaf and she joined in Beebe's complaint that he was taking two months off a year — the normal vacation month plus an extra her husband had awarded him for travel and contemplation and which he spent at a home in Turkey. Lippmann told her he felt Bradlee could do great things for the paper. By late June she had decided to bring Bradlee in as deputy managing editor with the intention of his succeeding Friendly in perhaps a year or two. When she broke the news to Wiggins and Friendly, both were unhappy. Bradlee felt that six months would be long enough as deputy but he came to THE POST without any firm timetable. He was given the title of deputy managing editor for national and foreign news. Gilbert was made deputy for local news, a way of telling Gilbert, who had hoped to succeed Friendly, that he never would become managing editor. Bradlee came to work on August 1, 1965, 25 days before his 44th birthday. Friendly was 53.

There followed an uncomfortable three months as the staff watched the obvious drama. Bradlee plunged in energetically, coming back to the office every evening and staying to 1 A.M. to monitor or change the paper's stories and layout. When Friendly was away for two months, including a visit to Turkey in October, Bradlee made it evident that he was in charge. There were no Friendly-Bradlee run-ins; it simply became a question of when Bradlee would take over. Friendly told him not to be in a hurry but he was in a hurry. It was not long before Mrs. Graham decided that sooner was better than later and she used Lippmann to break the news over lunch at the Metropolitan Club. He asked Friendly, "Have you thought about returning to writing?" Friendly got the message and after lunch went to Mrs. Graham's office. He recounted Lippmann's remark, then asked: "Is that what you want?" "Yes." He was hurt: "I'd rather have heard it from you."

On November 4, in one of those disingenuous stories newspapers have so often written about their own affairs, THE POST quoted Mrs. Graham as saying that Friendly "asked to be relieved of executive duties and to resume an earlier career of reporting and writing on national and international affairs." Bradlee became managing editor and Friendly associate editor, continuing as vice president and a member of the Post Company's board of directors. Nobody at THE POST was fooled when Friendly was listed on the revamped masthead ahead of

Bradlee. Many who knew of the long Friendly relationship with Philip Graham believed that this act of dropping the pilot he had named represented an unconscious declaration of independence by his widow. True or not, the move was based on a shrewd judgment that the paper needed a major infusion of new managerial vigor. As Beebe put it, "She wants to rule, not merely reign, but she wants to do it with the help of a lot of other people."

Friendly spent several not-so-happy months writing stories that Bradlee saw were given good display. He moved to London in January 1967 to become roving correspondent. He soon discovered that he did, in fact, enjoy a return to reporting and he capped his career by winning a Pulitzer Prize for coverage of the Six-Day War in 1967. He retired at 60 at the end of 1971.

Ben Bradlee came on as a self-confident, no-nonsense guy, all macho and "don't cross me." A strapping six foot plus, he exuded toughness, vigor, charisma. He has been described in print as easily mistaken for a bookie, as witty and charming and as looking "like the Hollywood version of an international jewel thief." With a deep voice and a certain swagger he quickly dominated THE POST newsroom. Often brusque, his language was, and remains, crude at times. In his 1975 book, *Conversations with Kennedy,* he wrote that such language as his and the late President's had been "formed in the crucible of life" during World War II. Yet he also had an air of erudition and sophistication partly because of his flawless French. Ben Bagdikian, who worked awhile for him, described Bradlee as "irritated and bored with serious ideas but quick and contemporaneous in his tastes." He would admit to being no intellectual but he never suffered easily stories making that point. Doubtless, he remains more at home at a Redskins game than at the ballet.

A proper Massachusetts WASP by birth, a product of St. Mark's and Harvard, he served under fire on a navy destroyer in the South Pacific in World War II. With three associates he next helped run, for two years, a New Hampshire weekly — "One of our stories put the state comptroller behind bars for mishandling funds" — before he first came to THE POST in 1949 for a two-and-a-half-year stint as a city desk reporter. He showed both interest and talent in producing crime stories but then he went off to France to serve two years as press attaché in the American Embassy in Paris and next to join *Newsweek* for 12 years. He worked out of Paris the first four years, then became a Washington bureau reporter, and finally bureau chief, the post he held when he helped persuade Philip Graham to buy the magazine.

To THE POST Bradlee brought much of the magazine flair and style.

To old-timers, used to the Friendly emphasis on the often heavy substance in news coverage, newsmagazines seemed "all sizzle and no steak." In short, it soon was evident that Bradlee's prime aim was impact. "I want to have some impact on this town and this country," he said early on. "I want to know they are reading us. Impact." The fist was likely to smack the other palm with that statement. Bradlee had always been bored with institutional stories and he never strove to make sure that the paper contained the nitty-gritty of each day's news.

Not a conceptual thinker, he came, he later said, with no worked-out battle plan. As one of his close friends put it: "[He operates] intuitively, not systematically, there is never any architecture to it." He did, and does, encourage imaginative writing and a relentless examination of both public and private institutions. Mrs. Graham found "a driving quality" in Bradlee, something that was "very much what we were looking for." She told one interviewer she had hired him "for his ability as a talent finder, because I essentially think that is what any business is all about."

Talent he did find. He continues to be a hot-property man, collecting what he calls journalistic "horseflesh" much in the fashion of a Hollywood movie mogul collecting stars. Because he could turn a phrase handsomely himself, Bradlee wanted good writing as well as good reporting. Ben Bradlee clearly proved to be the right man at the right time and he was such a success that he became the best-known editor in THE POST's first 100 years.

More and better reporters and editors cost money and Mrs. Graham provided it. The news budget began to soar. Instead of rising by increments of $100,000 or $200,000 a year it now rose by half a million dollars or more. When he first came as deputy managing editor Bradlee brought with him from *Newsweek* Ward Just, a gifted writer, and Hobart Rowen, a seasoned business and economics writer and editor, and he quickly hired Stanley Karnow to man a new Hong Kong bureau. After he succeeded Friendly, Bradlee rather quickly added Richard Harwood, Nicholas von Hoffman, and David Broder — all high-powered reporters with established reputations. He took on such fancy writers as Jimmy Breslin and Henry Fairlie for special occasions. He began revamping the news desks which badly needed new talent. David Laventhol, Kenneth Johnson, and Jack Lemmon were among key additions as assistant and night managing editors, while old-timers like Kenneth Harter and B. F. Henry prepared to retire. In the years 1966–1969 about 50 new positions on the news side were created as Bradlee's budget rose by $2.25 million to $7,295,087 for 1969. Laurence Stern, whom Bradlee had known from his earlier POST years, became national news editor succeeding Edwin Gritz. That is the key position for handling all Washington-originated stories other than metropolitan area local news. One of Stern's problems as editor was his reluctance to give up writing.

The infusion of new people led to two immediate changes. One was creative tension, a magazine technique that tended to replace team cooperation among reporters and editors with competition between them for individual enterprise. The other was a sense of "them" versus "us," the new Bradlee men versus the holdover Friendly team. "They'd be happier if we all left," commented one who gritted his teeth, stuck it out, and in time won major promotion. It took perhaps three or four years for this sense of division to dissipate.

Of all the new people Dick Harwood, a blustery, profane, tough-talking ex-marine and Nieman fellow, was the most critical of the paper before he had joined it. He added considerably to rancor and unhappiness by making clear his denigration, culminating in his remark that the pre-Bradlee POST had been "a schlock newspaper." "Schlock," a Yiddish word, means "cheap; trashy" and "something of cheap or inferior quality; junk." Bradlee was always careful to avoid such gratuitous remarks, saying that THE POST had been a far better paper than most people thought, especially given the tight budgets. Yet Harwood, for all his bluster, was just the kind of first-rate reporter the paper needed. Until 1968, when he succeeded Stern as national editor, he was the paper's chief generalist, writing perceptively on a wide range of subjects from wrongdoing in Congress to the first full POST takeout on J. Edgar Hoover and doing a stint of war coverage in Vietnam.

Many years later after his retirement, Editor Wiggins commented on those who denigrated THE POST of the past: "Perspectives in history are like perspectives in architecture: the foreground inevitably occupies a much larger area than the remote background."

What Mrs. Graham did in installing Bradlee and giving him her backing was to create a new journalistic environment at the newspaper. As she once said, "The owner of a publishing enterprise can create an ambiance, but others must fill this environment." In that respect she was right in replacing Friendly with Bradlee, as Friendly in the fullness of time agreed. A 1966 *Time* story declared that "by financing an uninhibited hiring spree," she had "pumped new life into the paper." *Time* also quoted her as saying, "I don't play girl editor. I don't tell people what to do all the time. I'm interested in finding people, developing them, giving them leeway and backing them up."

Bradlee's magazine approach aided by Dave Laventhol's imaginative skill at newspaper layout gave THE POST a face lifting, especially on page 1. In 1966 the paper was awarded the Ayer Cup for makeup and printing excellence. David Levine's cartoons of Washington's powerful illustrated personality pieces. The end of the Philip Graham limit on story jumps from page 1 facilitated a richer mix for readers. Bradlee sent his own photographer, Wally McNamee, to Vietnam soon after dispatching Ward Just as the new reporter. On columnist George Dixon's death in December 1965, Bradlee's old friend from Paris days, humorist Art Buchwald, succeeded to Dixon's space on the op-ed page, soon becoming one of the paper's best-read features.

Bradlee's quest for impact sometimes had unexpected results. In 1965 he bought serial rights to the *Penkovsky Papers,* revelations about an executed Soviet spy who had worked for the United States. After 12 of 14 installments had been printed the Soviet Union called their publication "an intentional act in the spirit of the worst traditions of the cold war" and demanded a halt to the series. Wiggins' reaction was cold fury. "We refuse to accept the inadmissible suggestion," read THE POST response, "that this newspaper must not print material which the Soviet government may find inacceptable. Newspapers in the United States, the Soviet government should know by this time, are not to be told by governments, either foreign or domestic, what they 'must' print or 'must not' print." Twelve days later, after the series was completed, the paper's Moscow correspondent, Stephen Rosenfeld, was expelled. Wiggins would not permit anyone to replace him for a year and a half, and he was Bradlee's boss when he wanted to exercise that authority. A decade later the *Penkovsky Papers* were shown to have been a CIA product, based on what the spy had disclosed. Rosenfeld in a column wondered whether the CIA had produced the book to "deflect the American public" from the closer relations John Kennedy had begun to achieve with Moscow; it was not inconceivable.

Sustained impact came from the typewriter of Nicholas von Hoffman, among those Bradlee hired in the spring of 1966. Over the next decade his vivid prose, often intentionally provocative, produced more angry letters to the editor than the work of any other single reporter in the paper's history. In the late 1960s and early 1970s he became a favorite of the New Left and of some of the youth cults. At THE POST some adored him; others considered him a menace to journalism. His contribution, until he began to fade after the end of the Nixon era, was substantial: by the very power of his words, the details of his reporting, and the outrage of his expressed beliefs he forced uncounted POST readers to examine a life style that repelled them, especially when it became that of their own middle-class offspring.

Von Hoffman began for THE POST with vivid accounts of the plight of poor southern blacks. He had an ear for dialogue so sharp that some felt he must be inventing the words. In 1966 he did the paper's first reporting on the emerging drug scene in San Francisco. In 1967 during three months with the so-called flower children and dope peddlers of that city's Haight-Ashbury district von Hoffman so intrigued Bradlee with his reports that the managing editor flew there to spend three nights with his reporter. Von Hoffman's series of 16 stories were words aflame on page 1:

> There never were any flower children. It was the biggest fraud ever perpetrated on the American public, and it's your fault, you, the mass media . . . This community is based on dope, not love . . . The colloquial language of the Haight is the speech of the ghetto interspersed with a few expressions from two fugitive minorities: the homosexuals and the underworld.

Back home at THE POST Bradlee fired a copy boy for selling marijuana in the news room and a reporter for dealing in cocaine outside the building.

In mid-1966 von Hoffman described Martin Luther King, Jr., as "leader, symbol, bridge, bearer of the true charisma, prophet of justice, witness of love" with "that famous face, bronze, flattened, almond-eyed, like a Benin mask." His most striking descriptive story was that on King's funeral:

> The Rev. Dr. Martin Luther King Jr. led his last march today. He was in a cherrywood coffin, carried in an old farm wagon hitched to a pair of downhome mules.
>
> The march began at Ebenezer Baptist Church where he and his father had pastored for so many years and ended at Southview Cemetery, a burial ground founded by Negroes because they couldn't get in the front gates of the white cemetery.

In citing these paragraphs, Katharine Graham commented that "this style of reporting is immensely productive when handled skillfully." Indeed, it was the only style that could compete with the television eye in describing such emotion-packed events. But there was resistance at THE POST to the von Hoffman story from Ben Gilbert who didn't want National Editor Stern to lead the paper with it. Stern said the story would do just that or he would quit; Bradlee ruled for Stern.

Bradlee hired or rescued from obscurity a host of editors and writers.

He made Geoffrey Wolff book editor but Wolff, like Just, eventually gave up newspapers for novel writing. Bradlee never mourned those who departed, with perhaps the exception of Just. Morton Mintz, at Stern's urging, was given a new freedom to pursue his investigative reporting especially in the field of drugs. A prime Mintz target, on safety grounds, was the Pill; his critics said he was responsible for a lot of unwanted children. George C. Wilson replaced the retiring John G. Norris at the Pentagon. Retirements of Eddie Folliard, Chief Photographer Hugh Miller, and Night City Editor John J. Riseling at the end of 1966 — together they had given over 130 years to THE POST — helped open the way for younger people. Among the youngsters who made it to page 1 in this period were Robert Kaiser, Peter Osnos, Peter Jay, Louis Diuguid, John Goshko, Jim Hoagland, and Thomas W. Lippman, all of whom later became foreign correspondents. Walter Pincus took over editorship of *Potomac.* William Gildea and Kenneth Denlinger began careers in sports. John MacKenzie started a decade of covering the Supreme Court. Amid this explosion of talent some never made it in the competitive, tension-filled whirl of Bradlee's fifth floor. They felt "used up like Kleenex," as one put it.

In 1966 The Washington Post Company bought from Whitney Communications for an undisclosed sum a 45 percent interest in the New York *Herald Tribune*'s Paris edition, just before the parent paper folded in Manhattan. Within another year the New York *Times* killed its own European edition, joining Whitney and THE POST as co-owners of what was renamed the *International Herald Tribune.* The paper, still called the *"Trib,"* is a Paris-edited compendium of the major stories from America's two leading dailies plus the Los Angeles *Times* and the wire services. It circulates principally in Western Europe but as far east as Southeast Asia. Buying into the *Trib* represented a major new source of prestige for THE POST as a paper and for its reporters abroad. For the first time many important governmental, business, and press people discovered that there was another must-read American paper besides the *Times.* In this period THE POST also opened new bureaus in Tokyo, with Richard Halloran, and at the United Nations, with Bob Estabrook, who had come back from London to write editorials for Wiggins. Estabrook covered Canada as well, until his 1971 retirement.

Wiggins devoted most of his time to the editorial page. When the little red book, *The Sayings of Chairman Mao,* became something of a rage in the United States, Bradlee took to calling his editor "Chairman Wiggins." Various Wiggins aphorisms — "The customer is entitled to one clear shot at the naked facts" — were set in type and proofs thumbtacked on the walls of Bradlee's office. It was fun and jollity but there was no humor in the growing breach at THE POST over the war in Vietnam. An increasing number of younger staffers became vocally disenchanted with both the war and THE POST's editorial support of it as Wiggins dug in his heels, much like President Johnson.

In a memorable analysis piece on December 5, 1965, Murrey Marder hung the term "credibility gap" on Lyndon Johnson.

> Creeping signs of doubt and cynicism about Administration pronouncements, especially in its foreign policy, are privately troubling some of the Government's usually stalwart supporters. The problem could be called a credibility gap. It represents a perceptibly growing disquiet, misgiving or skepticism about the candor or validity of official declarations.

Marder did not simply write that the administration was lying about the war; typically, he spelled it out item by item. The same month Walter Lippmann was even more direct: "We are in deepening trouble because we are too proud to face up to the reality, too proud to recognize a mistake." The other op-ed page regulars, except for Marquis Childs, were hawks on the war: Joseph Alsop, Rowland Evans and Robert Novak, and William S. White whose column was carefully read because he often floated the thoughts of his close friend LBJ.

In his role as editorial page editor, Wiggins held daily sessions in his office with his writers, usually half a dozen, following the practice of his predecessors back to Felix Morley. Each editor had his own style of running these meetings; in Wiggins' nine years the editorial conference was a debate, sometimes of great intensity and heat. Wiggins was a strong personality yet everyone had his say. He also used outside experts for some editorials: for economics, Yale professor and later Federal Reserve Board member Henry Wallich, and then Harvey H. Segal who later joined the staff; and Donald Zagoria, a Columbia University Russian expert. Once, after listening to Zagoria argue a particular point, Wiggins, with a growing pussycat smile, reached up to his bookshelf to pull down Zagoria's major work and cite him against himself. Wiggins generally had outread his staff, at least in history and politics.

The editor could write as fast as he read and his prose, as one colleague put it, "had a powerful Victorian roll, reminiscent of Macaulay." Examples: "Such candor is not the prelude to American despair and defeat. It is the essential preliminary to the perfection of policies better suited to meet the challenge." "If we abandon principle to get peace we will wind up with neither peace nor principle." Both quotations had to do with Vietnam, increasingly the subject of his typewriter until he left in the fall of 1968. THE POST editorial board, from Morley's time on, had divided subject matter by the interests of various writers plus their accretions of interest at the editor's suggestion or someone's absence or departure. Wiggins himself commanded foreign affairs as the battle outside THE POST over the war began to seep under the paper's own doors. None of the others could mount a challenge to his stand sufficient to move him despite increasing efforts to do so. Although Wiggins frequently criticized administration secrecy and constantly warned against excessive use of force, his central themes were those of the administration. A 1966 example: "We are in South Vietnam to preserve the right of a small people to govern themselves and make their own choices." This reasoning he followed to the bitter end, although the perceptive Just wrote from Vietnam a month after that editorial that "we are here defending freedom as we understand it for people who don't." Just was correct.

Of the dozen full-time and almost that many short-term POST reporters to go to Vietnam in the 11 years the paper maintained a bureau there, Ward Just made the most waves. Mrs. Graham praised him because, for one thing, "not a single person on the *Post* could tell where he stood from his news stories." The best in his 19 months there were vignettes about the men in the field, some of them deliberately bloody and raw. His intention, he said after it was all over, had been "to send notes over the wall to the average reader that war is a bloody business." When Just was wounded in mid-1966 Bradlee cabled him to come home. He frantically replied that to leave the war would be "like coitus interruptus"; but he did come home to recuperate, then returned. On one home leave he and Wiggins met for an hour, each trying to tell the other the war that he saw. They were ships passing in the night. When Just ended his tour he summarized on June 4, 1967: "This war is not being won, and by any reasonable estimate, it is not going to be won in the foreseeable future. It may be unwinnable." The story, the lead in the Sunday Outlook section, would have created more of a stir if it had not appeared the day the Six-Day War began in the Middle East.

Just's prose had a powerful appeal and some felt, in retrospect, that it created the first real tension within THE POST. Among the editorial writers, Alan Barth signaled his dismay by taping to his office wall a photograph of a South Vietnamese half-track dragging the body of a dead Vietcong along a road. There was, however, no signal of disapproval from the publisher. Mrs. Graham, like her editor, was constantly exposed to the arguments of the war believers from LBJ on down. Although in August 1967 she wrote a friend that "I am beginning to be greatly concerned" about the increasingly heavy American bombing and "where it is leading us," she made no objections to Wiggins at the editorial conferences she frequently attended. A year and a half later, in an oral history tape for the LBJ library, she commented that on Vietnam "we supported him [the President] longer than almost any paper in the country."

So did Herblock — by not attacking. His war cartoons in 1965–1967 were critical of the effect of the war on domestic programs, opposed escalation of the conflict, and, as peace efforts began, showed impatience at the American posture. He was critical of the Saigon junta for its lack of respect for civil rights, as he constantly was critical of Franco's Spain and the Greek colonels, but he did not attack Johnson's management of the war or his war aims. In short, while other cartoonists were turning against the war, Herblock never unleashed his pen.

Wiggins expected to retire on his 65th birthday in December 1968. Mrs. Graham urged him to take on Philip L. Geyelin, the respected diplomatic reporter of the *Wall Street Journal,* as a writer with the intent of making him editorial page editor when Wiggins left. Geyelin came in early 1967. He had been to Vietnam and he had concluded that the war was unwinnable. But he favored gradually turning the conflict back to the Vietnamese rather than a precipitous American withdrawal. Coming from a background he described as "unrelievedly Republican, Protestant, Social Register," he was a man of personal polish and social entrée in Washington as well as a perceptive reporter and writer. Geyelin told Mrs. Graham during a long interview that he would prefer an editorial page with what he later described as "a little perspective — a measured application of reason and logic and documented argument." She wanted only one promise: "Don't surprise me." A major editorial pronouncement or change of policy would be talked over in advance. Wiggins' style was pungent polemics, Geyelin's suave skepticism. In late 1967 Geyelin became editorial page editor under Wiggins.

Fortunately THE POST by 1968 had so expanded its staff in quantity and quality that it could cope with what turned out to be perhaps the most turbulent and tragic year since World War II. It was the year of the North Korean capture of the American spy ship *Pueblo;* the Communist Tet offensive in South Vietnam; LBJ's announcement that he would not run again, following Eugene McCarthy's amazingly successful primary challenge; the assassination of Martin Luther King, Jr., and the resulting racial rioting across the nation, including death and destruction in the capital that came within 10 blocks of the White House; the assassination of Robert F. Kennedy at the moment of his triumph in the California presidential primary; the Democratic convention from which Hubert H. Humphrey emerged as the party's candidate after incredible political turmoil and physical violence; the almost concurrent Soviet invasion of Czechoslovakia to end Alexander Dubček's efforts to create "Communism with a human face"; the first manned flights to and around the moon; the nomination of Abe Fortas to be Chief Justice of the United States, blocked in the Senate; the election of Richard M. Nixon and Spiro T. Agnew and the choice of Henry A. Kissinger as White House assistant for national security.

There were less spectacular events of substance. In Rome Pope Paul VI upheld the Catholic Church's ban on contraception and in Washington Francis Cardinal O'Boyle relieved 41 priests who protested the decree. An editorial by Ward Just, back from the war, commented that the church and the cardinal were "out of joint with this century . . . The Catholic intellectual, torn between St. Paul and Teilhard de Chardin, will choose the latter; sometimes he will leave the church altogether." A few years later Colman McCarthy, an editorial writer hired by Geyelin and who had been both a pro golfer and a layman in a Trappist monastery, began a series, "Thinkers and Their Thoughts." Sample from one on W. E. B. Du Bois: "In setting out to establish truth, Du Bois joined all incurable idealists in history — he believed that once the truth surfaced men would believe it. That, of course, is why idealists generally burn out so early. Society's veins can take only the smallest injection of truth, and definitely not in the huge doses administered by the likes of Du Bois."

For those who wanted entertainment, THE POST provided plenty of alternatives. Page 2 of *Parade* became a best-read part of the paper because its Personality Parade column contained such tidbits as: "Q. Is it true that Elizabeth Taylor and Richard Burton are loaded most of the time? A. From time to time the Burtons are filled with good spirits."

When Mrs. Graham, on a trip to South America, phoned in a tip that Jacqueline Kennedy might marry Aristotle Onassis, Bradlee pitched in with calls to his old Kennedy family friends. A dozen denied it, only Truman Capote said it was true. Bradlee wouldn't risk the story — and missed the scoop. Maxine Cheshire flew off to detail the wedding. Her Jackie-O and other Kennedy family stories were so recurrent well into the Nixon era that they added to criticism that the paper longed for a return to Camelot. Cheshire's column was called Very Interesting People. Some felt it simply bitchy, others amusing; but the town read it and the gossip competition between Cheshire and the *Star*'s Betty Beale was intense.

In the capital city itself things seemed to go from bad to worse. A long

John Anderson editorial on January 3, 1967, called for "a profound reform of the city government" with a single executive:

> In our schools, there are illiterate seventh-graders. In our municipal hospitals, there are patients who are dying for want of modern equipment. The housing shortage is worse than it was a decade ago, and the remedy is a volume of new houses utterly beyond the city's present capacity. The tuberculosis rate is rising. The reasons are much deeper than a simple lack of money. This city persists in holding in bleak welfare institutions a greater proportion of its children than any other city or county in the United States; it knows that institutions are bad for children, and it also knows that institutions cost more per child than other healthier alternatives. The city spends as much on its police as other American cities, and more than most; but the prevalence of crime makes citizens fearful to walk the streets.

Five months later President Johnson, by executive order, instituted an appointive mayor-council government. An elected school board and an elected, nonvoting delegate to the House of Representatives were both approved by Congress. Then southern opposition in the House finally collapsed and Congress voted a considerable degree of home rule for Washington, "the last colony," as home rule proponents had labeled it. These developments, strongly backed by THE POST, were, of course, related to the sea change in American race relations. New black leaders took over as Walter Fauntroy became the first delegate to Congress in a century and Walter E. Washington the first appointed, and then elected, mayor.

Washington was a close friend and the personal choice of Ben Gilbert, now deputy managing editor. When Johnson agreed to appoint him Gilbert wanted nothing printed until the actual appointment; Bradlee would have none of that. Without telling her that Washington was to get the job, he had Elsie Carper check around. She soon discovered the facts and wrote the story which Bradlee printed despite protests by Gilbert and Joseph A. Califano, Jr., the White House liaison man for the city. Califano phoned Mrs. Graham, pleading, she said, "not to print it because if we printed it, it wouldn't happen." But she backed Bradlee. "We just had to think about what our job was," she recalled, "and our job wasn't to make Walter Washington mayor." Here was a major divergence on her part from the civic and political role her husband had played — a divergence strongly urged on her by Bradlee. After the incident Gilbert complained of "a lack of confidence" in him. He was made an editorial writer, with the title of associate editor, and given a pay boost. He left THE POST in April 1970, later becoming a key assistant to the mayor.

Gilbert's last major task at THE POST was to compile, with the help chiefly of Leonard Downie, Jr., and Jesse W. Lewis, Jr., a book on the 1968 riots and the paper's coverage. First word of the King shooting reached Washington by radio at 7:16 P.M. on April 4, four days after LBJ said he wouldn't run again. From the moment of the assassination until June 24, THE POST deployed just about every available body to cover this expression of rage and militancy. In all, about 100 reporters, photographers, and editors were involved, including 14 blacks. City Editor Stephen Isaacs mobilized and ran the staff, with able help at night from Assistant City Editor Bill Brady.

Gilbert's preparations for trouble proved very helpful. He provided staffers with detailed instructions on how to cover civil disorders, and a good many reporters needed this help.

> A hand moving quickly into a pocket to pull out a [press] pass may be misunderstood. Thus we have designed our own pass, which can be hung around the neck for ready identification . . . Our fleet model photographic cars without any ornamentation look like official cars and can be targets. They are now being repainted two-tone and "unstandardized" in other ways . . . It has been the consensus of those in the field [covering riots elsewhere the year before] that hard hats may make the wearer a target . . . We are seeking the broadest possible perspective in our reporting of racial unrest and find that inter-racial teams are especially valuable in riot situations.

The news that King had been shot came as THE POST's first edition was being closed and many reporters were leaving the newsroom for the night. But Hollie I. West, a black reporter, arrived at the critical corner of 14th and U streets, in the center of Washington's Harlem, just after word came at 8:19 P.M. that King was dead. Two other black reporters to whom Gilbert gave special credit were Robert C. Maynard, later an editorial writer, and Bill Raspberry, the columnist. Raspberry along with Bob Kaiser and Carl Bernstein had fled a dinner party to rush to the office on their own at first word of the shooting. A black photographer, Matthew Lewis, with Ken Feil, Stephen Northrup, and Frank Hoy, took the first day's pictures, and many more. Joe Heiberger,

Jim McNamara, Douglas Chevalier, and Ellsworth Davis all took part in the risky photographing of later days. (Lewis won the 1974 Pulitzer Prize for his *Potomac* magazine color-feature work. In 1977 he became assistant managing editor for photography.)

The lead story on the first day's troubles, an unsigned composite of many hands, began: "Tense, milling crowds of Negroes — angered by the slaying of the Rev. Dr. Martin Luther King — swarmed along 14th street's inner-city strip last night and early today, wrecking and looting stores and heckling policemen." A Barth editorial declared that "those who are responsible for this vile deed have killed an unoffending, God-fearing and innocent man of great goodwill; they have also killed something in the spirit and heart of the American people where lived the bright hope for reconciliation between the races."

On the second day Just wrote: "When the news of the riots spread, the first instinct of the white citizens was to leave downtown. Government buildings closed down and shops shuttered. By three P.M., the routes leading out of Washington were clogged with cars." Mayor Washington ordered a downtown curfew; it lasted six days. THE POST estimated that about 20,000 people, 90 percent of them black, rioted, looted, and did an estimated $24 million in property damage. In all about 1000 fires were set, 13,600 soldiers and national guardsmen were called in to restore and maintain order, 7600 were arrested. Remarkably, only 12 persons died, 7 of them in fires. Of the 12, 6 were policemen, firemen, or soldiers. There was almost no shooting; overwhelming force, mass arrests, and tear gas carried the day.

The closest the looters came to the White House was the Lewis & Thos. Saltz clothing store, less than two blocks away. Phil Casey reported black power spokesman Stokely Carmichael telling a press conference that "when white America killed Dr. King last night she declared war on us . . . We have to retaliate for the death of our leaders." A Bill Raspberry column was a confession: "Many of my militant friends tell me that I am a dreamer, that the American system will never work for any but a chosen few Negroes. I hope for the sake of us all that America will prove them wrong."

On Sunday, June 4, 1967, THE POST carried on page 1 what proved to be Friendly's Pulitzer Prize–winning story strongly hinting that the Israelis were about to strike. "Diplomatic procedures to solve the Middle East crisis are seen by the Israeli government as being close to failure and in any event proceeding on an unacceptably prolonged time table," he began circuitously to get past the Israeli censor. "The decision, it was learned here tonight from a uniquely informed source, now rests with Israel alone." His source was an Israeli Foreign Office official named Moshe Bitan.

Back home the President began sending troops into Detroit to halt what a July editorial called "this fourth summer of slum riots." The editorial posed "the real question" as "whether a nation of free men can achieve order and social justice as well." Next day in Cambridge, on Maryland's Eastern Shore, Richard Homan quoted H. Rap Brown as urging Negroes "to burn and shoot."

The following week Senate Foreign Relations Committee Chairman J. William Fulbright introduced a resolution declaring that a "national commitment" could result only from "affirmative action" by the Congress as well as by the President. When LBJ increased American troop strength in Vietnam to 525,000 an editorial termed that "a sensible response" to the request of field commanders. Fulbright called THE POST "a newspaper which has obsequiously supported the administration's policy on Vietnam." THE POST's London correspondent, Karl Meyer, caught the American scene in an Outlook piece: "It is like wandering uninvited into someone else's nightmare to return to the United States on home leave after spending 27 months on alien soil. The first melancholy impression is that the Ugly American has been replaced by the Ugly America — ugly in mood, ugly in appearance, and ugly in the face she turns to a non-comprehending world."

Walter Lippmann, now 77, left Washington in the spring of 1967 after three decades in the capital. He was bitter about President Johnson. "I feel he misled me," he told Andrew J. Glass. It was impossible, he said, "for an objective newspaperman to be a friend of a President. Cronyism is a sure sign that something is wrong and that the public is not getting the whole journalistic truth." When Glass asked him to comment on rumors that LBJ had driven him from Washington, Lippmann retorted, "I wouldn't give him that satisfaction." LBJ was slipping to a new low in the polls. House Republican Leader Gerald Ford demanded that Johnson reveal why American airmen were "handcuffed by secret restraint" on their bombing of North Vietnam. Nguyen Van Thieu was elected president of South Vietnam and Wiggins editorialized that "the outcome . . . must be welcomed as a strong plus in the struggle to save South Vietnam as a political entity entitled to determine its own future."

There were divided reactions when Muhammad Ali refused to be inducted into the army and when Dr. Benjamin Spock was indicted for conspiring to encourage draft violations. Some 55,000 rallied in Washington against the war and there was violence at the Pentagon. Joseph Alsop warned that the "sure and certain consequence" of accepting the "nonsense" of the antiwar movement would be "a third world war." Wiggins accepted a November 14, 1967, Geyelin editorial chiding LBJ for his tough talk about dissenters: "[The President would not get cooperation] by denigrating or disdaining those whose questions are relevant and whose anguish is real. By that approach he can only hope to generate more — and more inflammable — dissent."

Johnson by now had become so angry with Mrs. Graham, apparently because of what both her paper and *Newsweek* were writing about him and the war, that there was what she recalled as a long period "of almost non-speak, and bolts of lightning coming out of the White House." In mid-1966 she wrote him to deny that she had told her editors that he was "trying to buy me with dinners" and that they "shouldn't pay any attention to this." LBJ sent back a frosty reply. On December 8, 1967, after the President had fired Defense Secretary Robert S. McNamara for turning from hawk to dove, she wrote Johnson:

> These times are so difficult that my heart bleeds for you. I think so often of the story you tell of Phil's letter to Jack Kennedy after the Bay of Pigs. [Her husband had written Kennedy what Graham called a "cheer up" note.] Of course there has been no such parallel event — quite the contrary. And yet it seems that the burdens you bear, the issues you confront, the delicate line you must tread, are almost too much for one human being. The only thanks you ever seem to receive is a deafening chorus of carping criticism.
>
> Unlike Phil, I find it hard to express emotion. I can't write in the eloquent words he used. But I want you to know I am among the many people in this country who believe in you and are behind you with trust and devotion.

If the President felt the publisher's sympathetic words would guarantee softer treatment from her newspaper, however, he was mistaken; hers were personal, not institutional, thoughts. Hardly a month later Marie Smith recorded that singer Eartha Kitt had confronted Lady Bird Johnson at a White House luncheon with: "You sent the best of this country off to be shot and maimed." Mrs. Johnson called Kitt "the shrill voice of anger and dissent" but a POST editorial commented that "many will think" Kitt's remarks "quite relevant and pertinent."

It was against this background of rising dissent in the United States, and at THE POST, that the Communists launched their Tet offensive of January 30, 1968.

Two weeks earlier, THE POST's Saigon bureau had been doubled

— from one man to two. Lee Lescaze, a soft-spoken, unspectacular, but highly competent reporter, had succeeded Just. He was joined by Peter Braestrup, recently a New York *Times* man in Bangkok, whom Bradlee and Foisie made bureau chief. Braestrup preferred to write military developments rather than "mood" or analysis pieces often asked for by the paper's foreign desk under Foisie. He was recommended to Bradlee and Mrs. Graham by columnist Alsop on the grounds that the paper had been sending only young reporters who had no experience in warfare and thus were unable to see that the United States and South Vietnam were winning, not losing.

The shocking surprise of a nationwide offensive resolved the doubts of many Americans who were beginning to believe the war a hopeless enterprise, whatever its rights or wrongs. At THE POST, Wiggins was an editor besieged. Most important, Herblock drew his first critical cartoon. He ridiculed the administration claim of victory by picturing the chaos of attack amid which a mimeograph machine in "Headquarters Saigon" was grinding out such statements as "We now have the initiative," "The enemy offensive has been foiled," and "Besides, we knew about it in advance."

On Saturday evening March 9 a number of POST men were attending the annual Gridiron dinner at the Statler Hilton across L Street from their office. Between acts Bradlee was told by phone that the New York *Times* was appearing with a Sunday story that General William Westmoreland had requested 206,000 more American troops. Marder was in the office seeking both explanation and confirmation. Bradlee told Roberts and at the next entr'acte they cornered in the halls and men's room enough officials to confirm the *Times* account. This plus Marder's own sources enabled him to write a cautious story about an "intense debate" within the administration on "sending up to 200,000 more troops." It was a catch-up story and every journalist would know it. Bradlee was very unhappy. About the war itself he seemed to others to have no opinion; it was simply an event to cover, and to cover better than the *Times.*

The way THE POST knew what the *Times* was printing that evening was that each night it received from New York via UPI wirephoto a picture of page 1 of the *Times*' first edition, on the street early enough for THE POST to catch up in its main edition. The *Times* received a similar facsimile from Washington.

The POST versus *Times* competition had begun in the mid-1950s, following THE POST purchase of the *Times-Herald.* After the New York *Herald Tribune*'s demise in 1966, *Times* editors and reporters found THE POST their only serious news competition, especially in Washington-generated stories both domestic and foreign. In this competitive situation "Ben came in with his dukes up," James Reston remembered. One thing Bradlee did was to end the taboo against one paper writing about another's internal problems. A week after Tet began Dick Harwood described the effort of the *Times'* main office in New York to recapture control of its Washington bureau by replacing Tom Wicker with James Greenfield, a move that didn't quite come off. THE POST headline jabbed the *Times'* most sacred motto: A NEW YORK TIMES COUP THAT WAS ALMOST FIT TO PRINT.

The *Times,* however, had what Geyelin termed "cruising speed" whereas THE POST did its best work in spurts, then often seemed to fall back in exhaustion or torpor. The *Times* had many more correspondents abroad, too; the 1977 figures were 12 for THE POST and about three times that many for the *Times.* But numbers sometimes were a disadvantage; when a major story broke with many angles from different capitals the *Times* would confront the reader with myriad stories and vast detail, but no single story that pulled it all together. THE POST, partly out of necessity, began in the early Bradlee years to turn to a lead-all written in Washington that described the essence of the story with necessary sidebars or takeouts from reporters abroad. This technique was successful in the Six-Day War and the invasion of Czechoslovakia but unfortunately it was seldom used in presenting the confusing news from Vietnam.

The New York *Times* was the nation's only newspaper of record, something THE POST has never been nor sought to be. The *Times* has an unparalleled advantage because of the universally used *Times Index.* Not until 1972 was there a POST *Index* for similar use; published not by THE POST, however, but by Bell & Howell which prepared microfilm of each day's paper. The *Times* had, and continues to have, another advantage: it is distributed, even at a financial loss, to many newsstands around the United States and, importantly, to many colleges and universities where THE POST is unobtainable. Although the number of papers involved is relatively small, they go to influential and potentially influential people. Only through its excellent joint news service with the Los Angeles *Times* does THE POST match the New York *Times.* This daily wire means that major POST stories reach newspapers all over the country and in many nations abroad. The news service plus THE POST's share of the *International Herald Tribune* did much to put THE POST in head-to-head competition with the *Times.* And that pleased nobody more than Bradlee who from his first day was constantly on the outlook for ways to outpoint — or out-impact — the *Times.*

As the two papers grew more and more competitive, they also diverged editorially about the war. The *Times* became a leader of the dove forces, THE POST, or at least Wiggins, stuck with LBJ. After Tet, POST editorial conferences sometimes became shouting matches. As one who was there put it: "The national divisiveness of the Vietnam debate was repeated at our 11 o'clock meetings." Phil Geyelin's tactic was to take two steps forward in an editorial, then concede to Wiggins one step back. This way THE POST did begin to change policy as Geyelin editorials argued for making the United States "progressively superlative" in Vietnam.

Then, suddenly, on September 24, 1968, while he was vacationing in Maine, Wiggins received a call from LBJ. The President told him he had been criticizing public officials and second-guessing the government during his 21 years at THE POST and he thought it only fair that Wiggins now give others a chance to second-guess him. LBJ wanted him to be the new ambassador to the United Nations. When he accepted the offer, a Geyelin editorial warned Wiggins' new UN colleagues that "a debate with him is, shall we say, an experience." Those who were the most bitter over his support of the war called the UN job nothing but a payoff. To POST people abroad the publisher wrote of Wiggins: "He has been a pillar of sense, a source of wisdom and a good friend, as well as a brilliant journalist." But six years later she began a letter about Vietnam this way: "As one who was wrong too long and backed an editor who was wrong even longer . . ."

Wiggins' sudden departure forced some quick decisions. Bradlee was named executive editor. The editorial page became the responsibility of Geyelin who reported directly to Mrs. Graham. A new managing editor had to be found and, by chance, Eugene Patterson, the Pulitzer Prize–winning editor of the Atlanta *Constitution,* had just left that paper. Mrs. Graham and Bradlee quickly agreed on him and he came that same September. But Patterson, a Georgian two years Bradlee's junior, never found the rough-and-tumble competitiveness of Bradlee's shop to his taste. As executive editor Bradlee continued to be, in effect, managing editor; he could find no really different role. Once Patterson asked him, "Ben, get off my back." From below, Patterson felt hostility from Howard Simons, the science writer who had become assistant managing editor and who had hoped for the job when it went to Patterson. He got it when Patterson left after three years. About the time Patterson came to THE POST Harwood succeeded Stern as national news editor and Steve Isaacs became the first metropolitan editor, a post created to combine direction of both city and suburban editors and reporters. Harry Rosenfeld became foreign editor and Philip Foisie moved up to assistant managing editor for foreign news operations. Ken

Johnson became executive news editor and Jack Lemmon succeeded him as news editor. Bradlee's management team was proliferating and new titles had to be created. The increasing number, however, tended to depreciate their meaning and value.

In early 1969 there were similar shifts on the paper's business side. Frank Gatewood retired and Harry Gladstein moved from circulation boss to business manager with Jack Patterson the new circulation director. The biggest change was at the top.

If Katharine Graham, when she took over THE POST, had enough feel for the news operation to see the need for, and to find, Bradlee, her sense of the business operation was close to nonexistent. As her father long ago had said of himself, she made every mistake in the book.

John W. Sweeterman had the title of publisher and executive vice president when Philip Graham died. He ran the paper well on the financial level and many who knew him felt that he expected to run the entire paper for Graham's widow. Instead, as one put it, "the arrival of the little lady" appalled him. He was a rather authoritarian, dominating male. "If I as much as asked a question, he took my head off," she recalled. "He reduced me to tears." There were exceptions: Once Wiggins insisted that a story about a murder contain the name of the store, Montgomery Ward, where the gun had been purchased. Sweeterman objected. The issue went to Mrs. Graham who ruled for Wiggins.

The paper was doing so well she could afford to leave business management in Sweeterman's hands. In 1963 THE POST had about 49 percent of the total advertising linage of the city's three dailies. By 1969, when Sweeterman gave up his publisher's post, the figure was over 55 percent. Circulation likewise boomed: the daily figure grew to more than half again as much as the *Star*'s; the Sunday total to almost double the *Star* figure. In financial terms, pretax corporate profits nearly doubled in the 1963–1969 period. In 1969 the paper's profits accounted for more than 58 percent of the corporate total although POST revenue was less than 45 percent of the total. In other words, THE POST was the most profitable part of the enterprise. In 1966 when THE POST advanced to third nationally in total advertising linage, behind only the Los Angeles *Times* and the New York *Times,* 85 percent of its $60 million revenue came from advertising and 15 percent from circulation.

In 1968 Sweeterman, now 61, told Mrs. Graham and Beebe he wanted to take early retirement in a year. Beebe and William P. Rogers, the former Attorney General and later Secretary of State who then was the paper's counsel and a board member, suggested Sweeterman stay on to complete plans for the much needed new building. So on March 1, 1969, he became vice chairman of the Board (Beebe remained as chairman) of The Washington Post Company. Sweeterman told Mrs. Graham that "you're going to run" the paper and "you should be the publisher." She took that title, used by both her father and husband. Announcement of Sweeterman's new post and of his successor was dressed up as a Sweeterman promotion. But when his office was moved out of THE POST building to rented space in an annex everyone knew that once again the newspaper was not being honest with its readers about itself.

To succeed Sweeterman, Mrs. Graham chose Paul R. Ignatius, outgoing navy secretary, on the recommendation of his former boss and her close friend, Robert McNamara. It was a bad choice. Ignatius knew nothing about the newspaper business. On weekends, when she thought he ought to be doing such things as riding the circulation trucks to learn, he was at his farm. On increasingly important labor negotiations, Ignatius relied heavily on James Daly who, some in management felt, gave away far too much to the unions. There were many new production problems and Ignatius could not seem to get them under control. He lasted until November 1971, less than two years. The announcement said he was "resigning" but in truth his contract was bought out for $150,000.

For the 1968 presidential campaign there was a new team: Broder, Harwood, and Just, with Broder now the full-time man on politics. Mrs. Graham remarked that he "eats, sleeps and lives American politics. It's his cottage industry." Friendly had wanted to hire him from the Washington *Star* but Wiggins then had a no-raiding rule which he strictly enforced as to both the *Star* and the New York *Times.* By the time Bradlee hired him at 36 Broder had switched to the *Times.* A meticulous man who injected humor, but seldom acerbity, into his knowledgeable reporting, Broder now began to travel regularly more than 100,000 miles a year in search of the headwaters of American politics at the state and local level. Each year he laid out the paper's campaign and election coverage plans.

At midnight on June 5, Senator Robert Kennedy was assassinated in San Francisco just as he was savoring his California primary victory. Harwood was nearby, ran to see how seriously Kennedy was wounded, then dashed for a phone to call his office where at 3 A.M. THE POST was about to close up. Bradlee was still at the office and he stopped the presses to take a Harwood-dictated new lead on the Kennedy story for the street sale final edition.

When Kennedy had announced he was running, an editorial had described him as "the bold, perhaps even brash, combatant happily released from the tormenting confines of indecision and inactivity."

Harwood came to greatly admire him and others on the staff felt likewise. But Kennedy and Wiggins did not hit it off. Once Kennedy came to see Wiggins because he felt the editor did not understand his statement on the war. As they talked, Kennedy finally blurted out, "Why do you hate me so, Mr. Wiggins?" Wiggins, who denied any such feeling, disagreed with Kennedy's switch from hawk to dove and he was distrustful of the emotions the senator aroused among younger Americans. Following the murder THE POST once again cried out in a Barth editorial the hope that "the ownership of deadly firearms may at last be brought within the rule of reason and law." Once again, the cry was in vain.

When the Democrats chose Humphrey, Broder's lead story correctly noted that the nomination's value had been "diminished by the bitterness of feeling on the convention floor and by the bloody fighting in downtown Chicago between troops and police and thousands of anti-war, anti-Humphrey demonstrators." Nick von Hoffman, naturally, was in the midst of the uproar. Mayor Richard Daley, he wrote, "was bellowing about hippies, newsmen, assassins and Communists. The cops were wiping the blood off their night sticks and looking around for anybody else who wanted a crack on the noggin . . . The children of the rich and the suburban well-to-do make up most of the amorphous cultural entity that is called the New Left." Von Hoffman reported, as THE POST printed it on September 1, that several thousand had gathered in front of the Hilton Hotel to chant "f— — you LBJ, f— — you LBJ."

When Richard Nixon won the GOP nomination an editorial declared that THE POST's old adversary had shown "an admirable understanding and restraint in his public approach to Vietnam; a commendable comprehension of some aspects of the Nation's social ills." But in private "he has revealed a disquieting disregard for principle, not to say good sense, in his discussion of the war, of the courts, of open housing and gun control and other things. As well as we ought to know him by now, he remains remarkably unknown."

He was not unknown to Herblock. While Nixon campaigned for the nomination, the cartoonist returned to the battle. After the nomination, Nixon's vice-presidential choice, Maryland Governor Spiro T. Agnew, called Humphrey "squishy soft" on the war. Next day Herblock had a smiling Nixon watching as Agnew smear-painted on a wall: "Humphrey is soft on communism and soft on law and order." The caption: "An Apt Pupil."

Agnew, to THE POST, was a local boy. In 1966 editorials all but formally endorsed him for governor. The reason was simple: the Democratic nomination had been captured by George P. Mahoney on a platform of "your home is your castle — protect it." THE POST said Agnew had "a credible record in government" as the Baltimore County executive and had "avoided the expedient appeal to bigotry" of his opponent. It was Broder who on May 17 provided a shocker when he wrote that Agnew was "the latest and most interesting addition" to Nixon's list of possible running mates. Nixon had floated Agnew's name in a chat with Broder in Oregon. But when he actually was picked at the convention, Broder said later, "my jaw dropped just like everybody else's." Nonetheless, the Agnew story gave Broder a big boost to a national reputation as the top political reporter in the United States. He won the Pulitzer Prize for his 1972 commentary. Editorially, THE POST began to sour on Agnew as governor and when he was nominated for Vice President the paper commented that he would have "an uphill task . . . in convincing the electorate that he does have the mature political judgement and the ability to cope with complex world problems."

By fall Ward Just had become an editorial writer and his most memorable shaft was aimed at Agnew. On September 25 THE POST said that "you can view Agnew with alarm, or you can point to him with pride, but for now we prefer to look on with horrified fascination." The stinger: "Nixon's decision . . . to name Agnew . . . may come to be regarded as perhaps the most eccentric political appointment since the Roman emperor Caligula named his horse a consul." Agnew never got over it. Four years later, amid the gathering Watergate storm, he wrote Mrs. Graham: "It is difficult to admire a newspaper that characterizes one as Caligula's horse, but I think you are charming."

Nixon came to THE POST for lunch in July 1968 with Mrs. Graham, editors, and reporters but the old differences remained. Gallup's final poll gave Nixon 42 percent, Humphrey 40, George C. Wallace 14, with 4 percent undecided. On election day Broder's story said the campaign had ended "in an atmosphere of total uncertainty." On election night, as the results showed it was even closer than Gallup had figured, Broder speculated in print that the choice might end up in the House. When it was clear Nixon had won, a Geyelin editorial said that because Nixon "has fully earned the opportunity to test himself, he has also earned encouragement, cooperation, good wishes and an open mind among those whose security and welfare have been placed in such large measure in his hands."

Before Nixon's nomination Editor Wiggins had sent cartoonist Herblock a razor and a poem suggesting he shave Nixon's five o'clock shadow, but the face seemed to grow darker as the campaign progressed. After Nixon's election, however, Herblock yielded to the extent of drawing his own office with a barber's pole and a sign on the wall:

"This shop gives to every new President of the United States a free shave. H. Block proprietor." Herblock simply had seen the man for what he was way back in his first congressional years and he never swerved from his merciless judgment. In all of Nixon's career he probably never had a more implacable or more effective foe. Politician and cartoonist met only casually, and unintentionally, a couple of times. On several occasions Nixon canceled his POST subscription; he explained that "I don't want the girls to be upset" by Herblock's blasts. Once, on giving that explanation to Roberts, Nixon added that he read THE POST as soon as he got to the office — he then was Vice President — and he asked that his regards be passed on to the cartoonist. Then, reflecting on Herblock's drawings of him, Nixon commented, "You know, a lot of people think I'm a prick, but I'm really not."

On Monday, January 6, 1969, two weeks before Nixon's first inauguration, THE POST introduced Bradlee's major structural change in the newspaper: the Style section. It was another example of his desire for impact and that it had. Newspapers all over the country examined what THE POST was doing and there were many imitations. From POST readers there were howls of complaint as well as shouts of praise.

Newspapers like THE POST were traditionally divided into hard news and soft. Soft included the women's pages, movie, television, theater, book, art and other cultural news and reviews, advice columns, puzzles, weekly travel and food sections. At THE POST the For and About Women section had been run for the past 23 years by Marie Sauer who was retiring. Looked down on by most of the paper's male reporters, Sauer's female — and occasional male — reporters were largely limited to coverage of social events and interviewing wives and secretaries of important men. "But," as Judith Martin, one of her youngsters who became a Style regular, put it, "she taught us how to make these into opportunities for gathering hard news . . . I quickly learned that it was easier to talk my way into some place I didn't belong, grab the President of the United States, and ask him some awful question no one else would dare to, than it was to go back and have to admit to Miss Sauer (we never called her anything else) that I hadn't done it." In the 1960s Sauer's reporters could cover Coretta King but not Martin Luther King, Jr., the Women's Strike for Peace but not student protests.

Two things made Style possible. "We had become convinced," Bradlee said, "that traditional women's news bored the ass off all of us. One more picture of Mrs. Dean Rusk attending the national day of some embassy (101 of them) and we'd all cut our throats. Same for dieting, parties that had no sociological purpose . . . or reporting teas, state societies, etc." He acknowledged that the women's movement helped induce change because "most of us had been listening to intelligent women, intelligent wives." Mrs. Graham, too, was highly conscious of the women's rights movement. She put up $20,000 to help found *Ms.* magazine, but she made it clear she preferred to be addressed as "Mrs." This also was the time of the counterculture movement and many younger POST people were swept up in it.

Bradlee had an idea, a concept, about Style as "modern, vital, swinging" or, as Larry Stern described it, "something to be fun and pizzaz." Bradlee was applying the "back of the book" newsmagazine technique from his years at *Newsweek*, packaging in one section of THE POST what had been called cultural news or reviews scattered through the paper. Details, however, bored Bradlee, a man of markedly short attention span. Fortunately he put in charge Assistant Managing Editor David Laventhol who already had dressed up THE POST's page 1 typographically. In effect, Style now gave the arts and the critics a daily front page and section of their own and multiple Sunday sections. The first day's page 1 had as its lead story B. J. Phillips' account of a 26-year-old woman kidnapper; over it Laventhol ran a huge "Wanted by the FBI" poster, a startling attention-getter. Indeed, many complained that Style's graphics, including the satirical work of such caricaturists as Vint Lawrence and John Twohey, often seemed more important than its written substance.

In its first year Style was, as Howard Simons put it, "a mixed-up, identity-crisis-ridden, constantly traumatized and perhaps mismanaged section." The staff, as a later Style editor, Thomas R. Kendrick, described it, was "uniquely diverse, non-interchangeable (a motley assemblage of individuals with roaring talent for certain tasks, howling weaknesses for others)." There were plots and counterplots within the staff and a seemingly endless change of editors and subeditors. The purpose of Style, said Bradlee, was "to relate to what people do and can do in their spare time, to what people could do, to what others are doing. We are very interested in parties, but not as social events as much as expressions of this culture at this time in history." It was not easy to translate these themes into stories and layouts. Everyone from Mrs. Graham on down seemed to be kibitzing: there was too much culture and not enough society, or when that was changed, the whole thing was too elitist. Mrs. Graham, who said she wanted Style to be a "unisex section," once let Bradlee know her displeasure: "Clothes, fashions, interiors and the frothy side . . . are all taking a hosing . . . I am quite fed up with the really heedless eggheadedness of Style."

There was a long shakedown cruise before Style calmed down. Elsie

Carper, Larry Stern, William Cooper all gave it an unsuccessful editing try. Not until Tom Kendrick, a strong editor, took over in mid-1972 for a four-year term did Style reach maturity. He was succeeded by Shelby Coffey whose editorship of *Potomac* magazine then went to Marion Clark.

Style was launched at the turbulent end of the 1960s and its staffers argued over everything from unisex bathrooms to advocacy journalism. There was much talk around the country of "the new journalism" popularized by one-time POST reporter Tom Wolfe. As Kendrick put it, some "often confused style with advocacy." The theme of Style, however, was as old as journalism: people, what they do, what it means, important or trivial but interestingly told and presented. Many stories ran much too long. There were charges of racism and arguments as to whether there were enough, or too many, stories about black Washington. There were stories about abortion, homosexuality, unmarried parents, and other hitherto taboo subjects. THE POST, with Bradlee's approval, now was willing — even avid — to print such stories, however much they shocked many readers and brought protests and cancellations. There was no doubt Style had impact, if too often the section was superficially trendy or reflective of some current radical chic. Style was at its best when it offered the unexpected, ranging from sorrow to satire.

Nick von Hoffman, whose advocacy grew so obvious in his news stories that Bradlee turned him into a columnist, now appeared in Style. He briefly was a disaster as the section's culture editor. His columns, usually with big display on page 1 of Style, caused constant uproar. A July 1969 description of the "now-people" as "with it, where it's at, groovy, sexy, beautiful, swinging, mellow, hip and hep" concluded that "then-people" were "old, ugly, square, plastic, out of it, programmed, sold out and copped out."

To complainants Bradlee replied that "he does not write to please or soothe. Like Mencken, he writes to prod, and sometimes to outrage." Mrs. Graham, in a memo to Bradlee, said she was "willing and eager to stand still for Nick whom I consider first rate and worth the gaff and of interest to the young and the black whom we need to attract. But I am not willing to use the rest of the section to appeal to 1% of our readers." She developed a standard reply to the outraged that went like this: "We think von Hoffman, almost alone among American journalists, is telling us what it is in the minds of the vast youthful segment of our nation which we little understand but often greatly resent when its misunderstanding of us threatens the fabric of the society. It is our feeling that we must know what those alienated Americans are thinking before we can intelligently respond with our own thoughts and actions." She had tried once at Harvard to talk with a trio of leftist Students for a Democratic Society (SDS) "and found them so rigid and difficult." One of her own boys, too, at the time was going through a difficult college phase.

Style also included the Thursday food section. From 1953 to 1970 under Elinor Lee's editorship food news began to move away from industry-oriented stories and recipes. When the section was swept into Style it totally broke from the past. In 1972 William E. Rice, a former POST reporter, returned as food coordinator after two years in France attending the Cordon Bleu school. In 1974 Marian Burros, a *News* and then a *Star* veteran, came as food editor. An effective critic of the industry regulatory commissions and of junk food processors, Burros wrote on consumer issues in the food field, a long-neglected area, while Rice concentrated on food makers, recipes, and wines. The section at last was free from its advertisers' domination. *Potomac* magazine's influential weekly restaurant review for seven years was written by Donald Dresden until he was succeeded at the beginning of 1977 by Phyllis C. Richman who wrote, and well, for a wider audience.

Television coverage, both industry news and advance program reviews, was considerably extended in 1975–1977 when Sander Vanocur, a well-known TV newsman, was the chief reviewer. Before the amazingly successful serialization of Alex Haley's *Roots,* in early 1977, Vanocur predicted that "television will never be the same" after that "quite revolutionary" production. THE POST earlier had serialized the book. Vanocur was succeeded by Tom Shales and John Carmody wrote an expanded TV column on each day's news and programs.

Of all the arts that exploded in the 1970s none did so more than dance, partly because of television presentations of ballet artists. The POST's Alan M. Kriegsman won the Pulitzer Prize for criticism in 1975. He was cited for such reviews as those of Rudolf Nureyev and Margot Fonteyn. It was the first Pulitzer ever for a Washington critic and the first for a Style writer.

From the beginning of Style, profiles of the great and the obscure in the worlds of politics, entertainment, sports, society, and just about anything else were a staple. As Michael Kernan put it, "[Style] always has clung like a ferret to the one attribute all our heterogeneous readers have in common: they're people. And people will always read about people." Style had many fine portraitists able to "go far beyond the recorded statements of an interview to probe personality and lifestyle." Among them have been Kernan, Jeanette Smyth, Myra MacPherson, Henry Mitchell, Henry Allen, Judy Bachrach, and Tom Zito. And then there was, and is, Sally Quinn.

An army brat, Quinn was hired in 1969 with no journalistic experience but with plenty of nerve, talent, and a first-class sense of what a story is and how to write it engagingly. She quickly established herself, so much so that she was hired away in a blaze of publicity by the "CBS Morning News." It was a mismatch and Quinn returned to THE POST to become the star of Style, writing about everyone from a rapist to Rosalynn and Jimmy Carter. Despite some caterwauling that she got special treatment and the best assignments because she had become Bradlee's roommate, as they both put it, Quinn's interviews generally were perceptive portraits. Muhammad Ali: "He interviews like he fights. Slow, wary, defensive at first." Alice Roosevelt Longworth at 90: "[She] can still laugh at herself and laughing at herself gives her license to laugh at others." Rudolf Nureyev: "He has a fabulous behind. Women follow him around and stare at his fanny as blatantly as some men would stare at a woman's bosom." The major justifiable criticism of Quinn was that her stories seemed seldom to be edited; rather, they ran on and on, a disservice to any reporter and especially to one so good as Quinn.

Daily and Sunday book reviews also became part of Style, as did the Sunday travel section edited by Morris D. Rosenberg. In 1967 THE POST joined the New York *Herald Tribune* to produce a Sunday tabloid, *Book Week,* as a rival to the New York *Times'* fat Sunday book section. After the *Herald Tribune*'s demise this evolved into *Book World,* at first published with the Chicago *Tribune;* in 1972 *Book World* moved to Washington as strictly a POST magazine. But in none of these formats was it financially successful, so dominant was the *Times,* and in late 1973 the separate tabloid was killed. *Book World* then was folded into a Style section. William McPherson began editing the book pages, daily and Sunday, in 1972, winning a Pulitzer prize in 1977 for distinguished criticism. A growing number of Washington area writers — an increasing number of them POST staffers — and development of some local publishers added to the pressures on McPherson's precious space into which he managed to squeeze around 1000 reviews a year.

Some Style stories Mrs. Graham found "tasteless," "snide," or "grisly" and some gossip items simply "bitchy." Maxine Cheshire's VIP column became a Style feature and it was chock-full of Kennedy family stories and talk of Henry Kissinger's movie starlet dinner dates. Of the Kissinger items Mrs. Graham told a British television audience: "Every now and then he'd call me up in a fury and say: couldn't she stop, and it wasn't fair, and it wasn't true." When a rumor got into print that Mrs. Graham "had something going" with British Prime Minister Edward Heath she phoned Kissinger, so she said, to say: "Henry, guess what's happened to me. Move over please."

Style, however, had a lot more to offer, if one read it carefully. Three days before Nixon's inauguration, Marie Smith reported that not only did he like "ketchup on his cottage cheese" but, "He is never without a tape recorder within reach on which to record thoughts and ideas on whatever subject pops into his mind or comes up in a conversation." Smith quoted his secretary, Rose Mary Woods: "The ideas he dictates into the machine and the memos are fantastic."

The section also contained, after a transfer from the op-ed page, Art Buchwald's satirical Capitol Punishment column. Sample: During the 1977 coffee price rise, "People began to toast each other with their cups, and waiters showed the can the coffee came from, before they poured it from a pot wrapped in a white napkin . . . Connoisseurs . . . would say such things as 'It's an unassuming little Maxwell House, but I think you'll be amused by its presumption.' "

Others among the early Style writers and editors were Leroy Aarons, Lon Tuck, Mary Wiegers Russell, Jean White, and Thomas Grubisich. Coe continued with the theater and Hume with music. In 1969 Gary Arnold was signed on as the chief movie critic and he quickly proved to be highly controversial. In a column on the ten best films of 1969 he wrote that "at the moment I think the abrasive pictures, the ones that are concerned or worked up — often to the point of confusion — about contemporary life, are more important to see and encourage." His power as the critic of the city's leading paper to make or break new films has been enormous. Sample reviews: *Butch Cassidy and the Sundance Kid* — "Shallow . . . overdressed . . . alienating." *Z* — "Revive[s] that abandoned but still commercially and dramatically potent genre of political melodrama." Worth seeing "even though you know that it's not likely to put a dent in Greek tourism, let alone the Greek [colonels'] regime." *Patton* — "Oddly evasive . . . Is it left, right, confused or non-existent?" *M*A*S*H* — "Irreverent and farcical and surreally funny, but it's also loose and informal and surprisingly humane." *Love Story* — "Apparently many people — perhaps a clear majority of the human race — are not just willing to be sapped by this sappy material . . . It's a smug tear-jerker, worth resisting on principle, because it's been so deliberately designed as a mass-cultured bromide, a reactionary bridge over all the troubled political and artistic waters of the last few years."

Wolf Von Eckardt, whose Cityscape column ran in Style, campaigned against the proposed "national square" at the White House end of Pennsylvania Avenue and he criticized the new Kennedy Center as "this Brobdingnagian shoebox with its golden matchstick ornament." The National Cathedral's west rose window, on the other hand, was "surely one of the masterpieces of Christendom."

As much as strong opinions in POST columns raised hackles, stories about explicit sex and the use of hitherto banned obscenities infuriated many readers. These things were not confined to Style any more than to THE POST. They reflected what was occurring "out there" and the paper's stories were reflecting life, however unpleasant this slice of it seemed to so many, particularly older, readers.

There were local court battles over an underground newspaper called the *Free Press* which, THE POST recounted, ran cartoons depicting "a naked judge masturbating" and showing "genitals and various sexual practices." An article by William Greider, one of the paper's most talented new writers, described Jerry Rubin as "a leading actor-director-producer in the freak rebellion" and reported that he "uses words like f— — and s— — in his speeches to kids, delighted with the fact that adult newspapers and TV always bleep them out." From Amsterdam Karl Meyer reported on the making of pornographic movies. There were City Life stories on the flood of "adult" book and film stores taking over the city's 14th Street strip and the resulting "sexploitation." When Myra MacPherson described homosexuality at the Pentagon in 1971 it was the top story in Style. In 1968 Ann Landers' advice column was lured from the rival afternoon *News* and for a while it alternated with Mary Haworth's considerably less frank column until Haworth retired. By 1971 Landers was discussing male homosexuals and lesbians.

Bradlee's own tongue was more than salty yet he sought a rule of reason. To a 1973 inquiry on "conditions under which vulgarities are printed," he replied, "Tastes constantly change, and what is permissible and mandatory today would have been impossible even a few years ago. The trial of [the pornographic movie] *Deep Throat* is not comprehensible without words like 'fellatio.' When the Prime Minister of Canada, in the well of Parliament, tells an opposition deputy to 'fuck off,' it is printable news by any standard, I would think. Certainly, by mine. In general, we avoid titillation at all costs; we avoid the leering vulgarity; we insist that any vulgarity be essentially relevant to understanding." As vulgar language became old hat in America its appearance in THE POST began to decrease; it no longer had the shock value younger writers had found in using it.

What Bradlee called "spin" or "tilt" on POST stories that gave the paper a liberal image in its news columns was something else again. When one of his most able foreign correspondents complained that his story had been cut up, Bradlee responded that

> we are not trying to make this paper flatter. We are trying to make it fairer. What you interpret as an effort to remove flavor, individuality and allusion is in fact an effort to remove the tipped hand, the veiled stand, the editorial phrases that make your position clear while they cloud the news . . . If we flattened [your] vivid writing to colorless mush, the *Washington Post* would be a loser. We want flair, audacity and a flashing quality to wax in this paper. You've got those qualities. They're valued. But we're talking here about something entirely different: tilt. Tilt flaws the effort we're making to become a newspaper distinguished by flavor, individuality and allusion — while being, above all, fair.

Finding good reporters who could write sparkling copy was less difficult than finding good editors who could direct and control such reporters. Once Bradlee wrote a description of the kind of city editor he'd like to find.

> Someone strong in conceiving stories, strong in motivating a talented staff, strong in personal relationships, especially with young staffers. Someone with modern ideas and imagination, but with old-fashioned devotion to accuracy, fairness, and good writing. Someone with outstanding commitment to excellence and hard work, to this newspaper and its people. A little flair, a lot of toughness and a lot of hunger would be OK with me, too.

One outside critic who got under THE POST's skin was Ben Bagdikian and as a result he became a national editor. In a 1967 *Columbia Journalism Review* article he wrote that "nobody edits the paper" and "*The Post* is irritating because it comes within a lunge of greatness as a newspaper but it is not great. It is tantalizing because it has all the rare ingredients needed and lacks the easy things." Mrs. Graham responded to Bagdikian that "the main charge that the paper is unedited is one Russ and Ben and I are already worried about and agree with . . . The charge that we sometimes let opinion creep into the news columns I find painful because I think it's a cardinal sin. It's also one we are working on." (The iconoclastic I. F. Stone once cracked that "*The Post* is the most exciting paper in town — you never can tell where you'll find a front-page story.") Bagdikian came to the paper in 1971 but he was better as a scholar and critic than in helping to produce a daily, with the notable exception of the Pentagon Papers later that year.

At the outset relations between the Nixon administration and THE POST were, if not cordial, at least workable. The President's initial stance on ending the Vietnam War won editorial support and Nixon sent a pleasant thank-you note to Steve Rosenfeld in February for an editorial page column stating that the President's performance thus far had been so flawless that it was "deeply troubling to inveterate Nixon knockers." In June when Mrs. Graham was honored by the American Newspaper Women's Club Nixon wrote her that that was "a just tribute to your outstanding career and example. We are glad to count ourselves among your admirers." Nixon administration figures — Cabinet secretaries Rogers, Richardson, Mitchell, and Finch, White House assistants Kissinger, Ehrlichman, and Moynihan — were among those who tasted her hospitality. When Attorney General John Mitchell was misquoted in a 1970 story by Ken W. Clawson (the only POST employee who went to work for the Nixon White House) and the paper ran a page 1 correction, Mitchell wrote Mrs. Graham: "Now you can see why I say *The Post* is the best paper in the country."

But it couldn't last. There were editorial expressions of unhappiness at Nixon's slow pace of troop withdrawal and some very firm words opposing his antimissile plans. There was a skirmish in the fall of 1969 over Nixon's nomination of Clement F. Haynesworth, Jr., to the Supreme Court, and a major battle the following January when he put forward G. Harrold Carswell. In the fall of 1969, too, Vice President Agnew began sounding off against "impudent snobs," and the next summer he took on THE POST directly.

POST coverage of the Supreme Court by a succession of reporters was not a full-time job until James Clayton was given that beat in 1960. Philip Graham, who had been hearing complaints about the Court coverage from Justice Frankfurter, sent Clayton to Harvard Law School for six months of auditing courses. By the time Nixon made his Court nominations Clayton was an editorial writer and comment fell to him. THE POST had run a bitter Barth editorial when the Senate failed to confirm Abe Fortas as Chief Justice, blaming it in part on "a desire to discipline the Court of libertarian decisions which protected basic constitutional rights to freedom of expression and to due process in criminal proceedings." When Fortas was forced to resign in disgrace an editorial spoke of "grave improprieties" on his part. Haynesworth was named to the Fortas vacancy. As conflicts of interest were disclosed THE POST first called on him to withdraw, but when he refused an editorial concluded that "reluctantly, we think the Senate should confirm." The day that appeared the Senate rejected the nomination, 55 to 45.

The paper's reaction to Carswell was much stronger. His record on civil rights was called "considerably worse" than Haynesworth's and his "intellectual credentials . . . measurably inferior." Clayton then examined in great detail hundreds of Carswell's lower-court decisions to show a poor record of disposition on appeal: he was upheld in 84 percent of criminal cases but in only 34 percent of civil cases and 33 percent of habeas and other similar cases. THE POST kept up a drumbeat of criticism, concluding on April 6, 1970, that "the evidence in this case is so strong, the record so clear that there should not be the slightest qualms in the Senate about rejecting this nomination outright . . . to confirm him would be to send yet one more signal of indifference at best, and contempt at worst, not just for minorities already short on hope, but for values and institutions which are in urgent need of more, not less, respect." Clayton's editorials and a flood of pro and con letters to the editor on Carswell made the paper a focal point in the 11-week battle. On April 9 the Senate rejected the nomination, 51 to 45.

The Paris negotiations on Vietnam were laboriously monitored chiefly by Marder who, in all, spent some ten months following each minute twist and turn. Roberts also was involved and he was being fed by Henry Kissinger in Washington. On one occasion Nixon asked some of his staff to find out Roberts' source for a Vietnam story; they wouldn't tell him because they knew it was Kissinger. But both Marder and Roberts completely missed the importance of a New York *Times* story on May 9, 1969, that revealed the initial secret American bombing of Cambodia and provoked that same evening the first Nixon wiretaps.

For a second time THE POST's Moscow correspondent was expelled. Anthony Shub increasingly annoyed the Russians with his critical reporting on dissidents and on differences within the Kremlin leadership. He was expelled May 21, 1969, after two years, only two months before he was due for reassignment. An editorial called this an "abrupt, not to say rude, ouster," adding that "it is more discouraging than irritating, to us, that the Russians still cannot abide a dedicated journalist doing an honest job." When Rosenfeld had been expelled over the *Penkovsky Papers,* Wiggins had refused to reopen the bureau for a year and a half. But now Bradlee, on Foisie's urging, sent Anthony Astrachan to Moscow at once. Despite POST problems with Moscow, the paper editorially backed the Ostpolitik of Willy Brandt and strongly backed the beginning of the Strategic Arms Limitation Talks (SALT) with the Soviet Union.

In this last area, as in several others, the editorial expert was Meg Greenfield. A Seattle native whose wit and whimsy tended to conceal firm views and iron will, Greenfield was hired by Geyelin on July 1, 1968, on the collapse of *Reporter* magazine where she had worked for a decade. She was promoted to deputy editor of the editorial page and was so listed on the masthead on June 1, 1969; she quickly gained a reputation as perhaps the best pencil editor of another writer's copy that the page had ever had. Mrs. Graham called her thinking "independent and uninfluenced by trends or molds. Her judgment is very dispassionate." Greenfield and the publisher found they had the same interested but wary attitude toward some aspects of women's liberation and that they were simpatico on many other accounts. Geyelin and Greenfield, as he once put it, worked "like two people at the piano playing 'Chopsticks.' " In mid-1974 Greenfield became a regular columnist for *Newsweek*, giving her a national audience and recognition beyond her continuing work at THE POST. Geyelin won the Pulitzer Prize for 1969 editorial writing, the third such prize to a POST editorial page editor.

Mrs. Graham's own relationship to the editorial page she described this way in 1977:

> The publisher's influence now tends to be exercised at one remove, through the selection of an editorial page editor and the professional relationship which they evolve. There must ge a general harmony of minds about approaches to the issues, about the management of the editorial page, and about its tone — the proportions of indignation and dispassionate analysis, the amount of humor, the degree of informality. There must also be general agreement on how to respond to criticism, listen to the community and correct mistakes.

While Mrs. Graham occasionally attended editorial conferences, she made it explicitly clear that in asking questions she was not setting an editorial line; on that Geyelin had the last word, although his staff had a high degree of authority in fields of expertise. In 1977 the other writers were John Anderson, Robert Asher, James Clayton, Carrie Johnson, Colman McCarthy, Robert Maynard, Stephen Rosenfeld, and Wolf Von Eckardt. When Maynard and Von Eckardt left they were succeeded by two blacks, Patricia Mathews and Lee Daniels. Occasionally Geyelin made use of outsiders; in 1971–1972, Alice Rivlin, later director of the congressional budget office, was a visiting editorial writer.

The tone of the editorial page changed with the shift from Wiggins to Geyelin. Wiggins believed in expressing opinion and doing so in strong terms; Geyelin believed more in explanation and reason than in trying to sway, say, a vote in Congress. "What newspaper readers need now more than ever," he said in a 1972 speech, "is a little perspective

— a measured application of reason and logic and documented argument." Or, as he put it in 1976, "while people may not mind being told what a *newspaper* thinks, they don't feel the need to be told what *they* should think."

On November 13, 1969, Nixon made a tough speech on Vietnam in which he asked for support of "the great silent majority." Soon Vice President Agnew was assailing "instant analysis" of the Nixon speech by television commentators. "Perhaps it is time," he said in a Des Moines, Iowa, speech, "that the networks were made more responsive to the views of the nation and more responsive to the people they serve." A POST editorial spoke of Agnew's "tirade" while conceding that "there is a decent and respectable case to be made" that what Agnew had called "a tiny and closed fraternity of privileged men" did represent "a concentration in power over American public opinion unknown in American history." Next came a reaction to Nixon and Agnew in the form of the "new Mobe" rally, headlined as LARGEST IN WASHINGTON HISTORY, against the war. When Nixon brushed off the demonstration by saying it had been "a fine afternoon for watching football," an editorial commented that "we have not heard the likes of that since Marie Antoinette."

Then on November 20 in Montgomery, Alabama, Agnew let go at The Washington Post Company "as an example of a trend toward monopolization," as THE POST recounted it. Letters to the editor were more pro- than anti-Agnew. Sample: "Like all bullies you can dish it out but you can't take it." Mrs. Graham's response was that THE POST, *Newsweek*, and WTOP, all cited by Agnew, "decidedly do not," as he had charged, "grind out the same editorial line." Rather, she said, "they compete vigorously with one another. They disagree on many issues."

It was against this backdrop that on November 10, 1969, Assistant Managing Editor Foisie proposed that THE POST create the job of ombudsman, an idea and word from Sweden. Foisie suggested hiring an outsider. Geyelin was against an internal ombudsman, arguing that the problem was to "come to terms, not with Agnew, but with what we all perceive to be an authentic crisis of public confidence in the news media." The answer was "to make the paper less remote, less lofty, less arrogant, less insensitive, in the public eye." One way to do so Geyelin initiated in January 1969: an effective, occasional editorial titled "F.Y.I." (for your information) about errors, criticisms, and other internal POST matters.

Typical of the buffeting the paper now was receiving was a letter to the editor appearing after Maxine Cheshire had printed the texts of letters stolen from Jacqueline Onassis that were to have been sold at public auction: "I don't know of any newspaper that is more self-righteous than *The Washington Post,* or any newspaper that shouts any louder about individual rights, but when it comes to someone else's rights that you think might interfere with your vaunted freedom of the press, then it's a different story."

Agnew gloried in that kind of reaction against the newspapers, especially THE POST and the New York *Times.* After the American invasion of Cambodia and the Kent State killings produced editorials and cartoons not to his liking, the Vice President sounded off in Houston, Texas, on "the hysterical view from the *Post*'s Ivory Tower where that master of sick invective, Herblock, also lives." A Greenfield editorial in reply: "Mr. Agnew is a threat to the administration and to its chances of governing wisely and well — he is not a threat to the press." The day Agnew spoke Mrs. Graham also made a speech: "Despite all the snarling official din, the free press is alive, well — and kicking like mad. For one thing, there exists incontrovertible proof — from the time of the first loud criticisms of the Vietnam war to the clamor of this moment — that America's dissenters can dissent more effectively than their suppressors can suppress . . . Our political leaders may regard us as pernicious enemies but the radical left no less passionately regards us as sycophants and tools of our political leaders."

After Agnew's resignation Mrs. Graham said of him: "He made the media self-conscious and compelled us to reflect on how we operate and why we had come to be so mistrusted and misunderstood." In mid-June 1970, when the battle was raging, Harwood produced a long internal POST memo of his own and other highly astringent opinions. Examples:

*Harwood:* "Our standards are subjective and whimsical. They reflect *our* tastes, values, prejudices, opinions and conveniences . . . We are a 'white' newspaper in a Southern or crypto-Southern area of circulation . . . There are millions of Poles and Italians and Chicanos and farmers and coal miners out there but very few in our newsroom . . . Our coverage of the New Culture has been so extensive — in the news columns, in Style, on the editorial pages, in the literary, art, theater, and movie columns — that we may sometimes appear to be a New Culture organ."

*William Greider:* "Agnew had spoken of Eastern bias but it is really cultural. It turns up in the columns of *The Post, Times* and other members of the media axis. The core of it is the unspoken assumption that the rest of the country is filled with boobs, simple folk who look eastward for their model of the nobler goals, but can be expected to do the wrong thing."

*Peter Osnos:* "We are, for the most part, a collection of Easterners, middle and upper-middle class, well-educated, relatively sophisticated, generally liberal. This shows in our reporting."

*Carl Bernstein:* "Our view of the world as reflected in *The Post* is very parochial and filtered. It is not based on first hand observation of the country."

*Anonymous reader:* "You give too much publicity to radical oddballs . . . You get the idea from reading *The Post* that there isn't a decent idea or person living on earth."

*Richard Scammon,* the election analyst: "You sometimes get the feeling reading the *WP* that it is edited for Maoist college students and black militants."

*William Raspberry:* "If you were a Martian and read nothing but the *WP* you would think this city is inhabited by five kinds of people — Georgetown and northwest whites, black militants at 14th and U, black criminals, black welfare mothers. What is there in the paper for the big black middle class out there between 16th street and Catholic University? What is there in the paper for the white plumber? Practically nothing. These people don't make happenings so they are ignored and we get a false image of our community."

In his wildest dreams Spiro Agnew could not have imagined what depths of introspection he had stirred. In mid-1970 Harwood well described these times in a piece that began:

> The age of Aquarius is not a happy time for the American military establishment. Flower children are in the streets. Wars are unfashionable. In circles of the New Left, men in uniform have come to symbolize the "corruption" of American life, the distortion of national priorities, the "darker impulses" of the American soul. In colleges and high schools new heroes have emerged whose battle cry is, "Resist!" Politicians decry "militarism," priests and doctors and lawyers encourage draft evasion, military recruiters are driven from college campuses, ROTC buildings are stoned and burned.

THE POST was printing plenty of stories corroborating all these scenes.

In September 1970 Bradlee created the job of ombudsman with Harwood giving up the national editorship to take the post. Harwood flooded Bradlee and others with memos questioning everything from Jack Anderson columns and late race results in sports to the use of the term "Establishment" and the word "beatnik." He found that the paper's chief problem was "incompleteness," meaning superficiality or one-dimensional reporting, and inconsistency, meaning the application of different standards to different events. He complained about the paper's declining to run a horoscope — Bradlee reinstated it in 1976 as "the purest entertainment, and nothing else" — while devoting the front page of Style "to 'scurrilous' predictions by a 'self-styled witch.' " This was a reference to a Sally Quinn piece. But Harwood and his successor ombudsmen, Bagdikian, Maynard, and Charles B. Seib, found criticism sometimes resented, memos often disregarded. It was easier to point to flaws than to get much done about them. However, Harwood's editorial page articles, titled "The News Business," for the first time began to explain to readers why "newspapers make mistakes every day" and that such errors are born of human failing rather than some sort of plot to alter or suppress the news.

One constant criticism from the outside was that THE POST was far easier on the Kennedy family than on Nixon and Agnew; this was especially so after Senator Edward M. Kennedy's car accident at Chappaquiddick cost the life of a young woman companion. The news reached Washington as the world was about to watch the televised first landing of men on the moon. Nonetheless, Harwood pounced on the story instantly, soon joined by Stern, and they wrote as completely and thoroughly as anyone. An editorial said the senator must tell all "because it is crucial to dispel the impression given by his silence that there is something he is trying to hide." However, hundreds of letters flowed in, "most of them," Bradlee said, "accusing *The Post* of inadequate reporting about Chappaquiddick, most of them from persons who have no apparent way of reading *The Post,* and most of them obviously not interested in answers."

In the 1970 congressional elections Agnew was Nixon's "cutting edge" but the Republicans failed to win control of the Senate. Dave Broder commented that "President Nixon faces an extremely tough battle for re-election in 1972 against a Democratic Party whose hopes for victory were enhanced Tuesday by a massive infusion of strength in the state capitals and a revival of support from both Dixie and the union halls." Little did Broder know of Nixon's reelection plans.

Events were moving rapidly. In South Vietnam there were signs of some form of coalition regime emerging and a POST editorial saw as necessary "some sharing of power, some achievement by both sides of some part of their original objectives." When Nixon promised to bring home 100,000 more men, a Geyelin editorial on April 9, 1971, declared that most Americans "want to be told *how* we are going to get out of this mess, not *who* is getting us out, and still less *who* got us in. They want to see some terminal point. And instead they are being toyed with, tantalized with a momentary vision of total withdrawal, and then told in the next breath that it is impossible, not only to fix a certain date, but even to promise it will happen at all."

Suddenly table tennis became world news. It was the beginning of the Sino-American overtures, heartily endorsed by THE POST. Among the three American newsmen allowed to enter China (it was no longer compulsory at THE POST to call it "Communist China" or "Red China") to cover the Ping-Pong matches was John Saar of *Life* magazine in Hong Kong; in 1975 he became THE POST's man in Tokyo.

The 1971 May Day weekend antiwar demonstration produced mass arrests. Jim Mann and Tom Huth described a camp out in West Potomac Park, swept by police, where "at dawn's light . . . about 45,000 people were dancing, nodding their heads to music, making love, drinking wine and smoking pot." Paul Valentine's lead story on May 4 was more serious:

> More than 7,000 persons were arrested in widespread hit-and-run skirmishes with police and federal troops in Washington yesterday as anti-war protestors made an unprecedented attempt to bring the government to a physical halt.
>
> By most accounts, including those of protest organizers, the disruption plan generally failed.
>
> The arrests, made while police fired tear gas through much of downtown Washington and military helicopters whirred across city skies, were greater in number than those in any single event in the nation's history, research indicated.

THE POST now was so rich in manpower it could blanket the city for such an event plus having researchers in the office rummaging through files. There were nine by-lined articles on related stories that day.

Police arrested some 12,000 people — 7000 on that single day — and many were held without charges for as long as 36 hours. The effort to disrupt the government, said an editorial, could not be

> an excuse for the prosecutors to set themselves up as judge and jury and to punish people by holding them in confinement, illegally, beyond any period sanctioned by any law or any court. That may appeal to some people as rough and ready justice; and no better than the demonstrators deserved. But to us it is a gross abuse of the principles of equal

> justice under law which, in turn, are fundamental to the very system that the demonstrations were designed to paralyze.

THE POST of Sunday, June 13, 1971, accented the Saturday White House rose garden wedding of Tricia Nixon and Edward Cox. Two events of more importance, however, were about to provide Katharine Graham with her first major test as publisher of the capital's leading newspaper. That morning the New York *Times* began publication of what quickly became known as the Pentagon Papers; and in two days The Washington Post Company would issue its prospectus for going public, that is, offering the public 1,354,000 shares of its class B stock and disclosing for the first time its financial details. The two events intertwined when THE POST, five days after the *Times,* began to run its own excerpts from the documents despite the clear threat of government legal action that could seriously damage the company financially.

The Pentagon Papers, a massive study ordered by Defense Secretary McNamara, was formally titled *History of U.S. Decision-Making Process on Vietnam Policy, 1945–1967.* Daniel Ellsberg, a hawk-turned-dove, had given the *Times* 7000 pages of the papers, but not the four volumes dealing with diplomatic negotiations, three months before they began to appear in that paper. The *Times* began printing each day more than six pages about the papers including texts of hitherto top-secret documents.

It took the Nixon administration three days to go to court and obtain an order halting publication pending a fuller hearing. It took THE POST four days to get hold of some of the papers for itself and to prepare to run its own stories. As Sanford J. Ungar, its reporter for the judicial proceedings, put it in his book *The Papers and The Papers,* detailing much of the affair, THE POST was "feeling egg on its well-respected, well-connected face after the *Times*'s weekend scoop." The material was confirmatory of many reports and rumors about what the United States had done in Vietnam and revelatory of the cynicism and deceit of the Kennedy and Johnson administrations. It could not, therefore, be ignored. So for three days Roberts and Marder rewrote the *Times* accounts with due, but painful, credit to its rival.

While this was going on, National Editor Bagdikian, who knew Ellsberg, was after the papers for THE POST. Before he flew to a Boston rendezvous with Ellsberg on June 16 he checked with Bradlee on the promise he had given Ellsberg over the phone that THE POST would publish the papers if it got them. Bradlee had replied: "If we don't publish, there's going to be a new executive editor of *The Washington Post.*"

What Bagdikian got and brought to Bradlee's Georgetown house was a disorganized mass of some 4400 pages, mostly copies of copies. The top-secret security labels had been obliterated, many of the pages lacked numbers. Bradlee had summoned Roberts, Marder, Don Oberdorfer, two secretaries, Geyelin, Greenfield, and Deputy Managing Editor Howard Simons. As soon as Bagdikian arrived the reporters began collating the papers, dividing them up and deciding who would write what.

Nearly three years later in a speech, Bradlee said he had

> wondered at what exact moment did I myself confront freedom of the press as a passionate, personal immediate reality instead of a glorious concept, lovingly taught but cherished from afar, from a seat in the audience instead of a role on this vital stage. The moment was 10:30 A.M. Thursday morning, June 17, 1971, when silver-haired Ben Bagdikian, his shoulders bending under the burden of two heavy cartons, staggered up the stairs of my house . . . and dropped the Pentagon Papers on my living room floor. For the next 14 hours, freedom of the press, and all the legal baggage which surrounds it and tends to make it impersonal and remote, became as vivid and personal to me and my colleagues at *The Washington Post* as life itself.

Time obviously was of the essence; instead of the three months the *Times* had had to absorb the papers, organize, and write its stories, THE POST now had part of a single day. One quick decision was to write the stories from the documents now available but not to print textually any documents that the government already had claimed, in moving against the *Times*, were vital national security secrets. All the POST people assumed the government would move at any moment against their paper as well.

Three reporters fell to work in Bradlee's dimly lit library, papers in stacks on chairs, tables, and floor. At the same time, two POST lawyers, Roger Clark and Anthony Essaye of Royal, Koegel, and Wells, the paper's New York law firm of which Secretary of State Rogers had been the senior partner, were in the Bradlee living room listing reasons for not publishing anything. They argued for awaiting the outcome of the *Times* case. Arguing for publication were Bradlee, Bagdikian, Geyelin, Greenfield, and Simons. In one degree or another, all the editors felt at this moment that their newspaper had reached a critical moment: it would either go on to be the great national newspaper they wanted it to be or it would timidly decline to publish and become the laughing-stock of the trade. The fiercely competitive Bradlee desperately wanted what he called "a piece of the action," and if that meant a roaring battle over freedom of the press, well, so much the better; at least the *Times* would not have all the glory for itself. Bradlee toyed with the idea of propelling Mrs. Graham to publish by threatening to resign but it never came to that.

The arguments for and against publication were made, in the first instance, to Frederick Beebe, board chairman of the parent Washington Post Company, who had flown down from New York to attend a party at Mrs. Graham's house but had quickly detoured to Bradlee's. Around 8 P.M., after Roberts had given Bradlee the first part of his story to send down to the office for the main late-city edition, Simons came running into the library to say, "Hey fellows, I think we're losing the battle." All three rushed into the living room to hear a startling proposal, born of the lawyers' feeling that to publish would be to violate a specific statute. This was coupled with Beebe's worry about the effect of the litigation on the impending sale of POST stock. Bagdikian later wrote that Beebe said to him:

> You may feel responsible for freedom of the press, and I'm committed to that, too. But I have a responsibility that you don't. I have to worry about stock in a 193 million dollar corporation. Our contract with the underwriters can be canceled if the corporation has a catastrophic event, and it's been determined by the courts that a criminal indictment is a catastrophic event. And if we get convicted we lose all our broadcast properties because a felon may not hold a broadcast license.

Instead of publishing immediately, it was suggested THE POST notify Attorney General Mitchell that it had the papers and intended to publish in a day or two. At this the three reporters exploded in the tension-filled room. Roberts, who was due to retire at the end of the month, equated the proposal with "crawling on your belly" to the Attorney General; he threatened to quit immediately and publicly disassociate himself if publication were barred. Oberdorfer called the proposal "the shittiest idea I've ever heard." Marder argued that THE POST had no alternative but to publish; since everyone would know it had the papers, it would end up more damned professionally for not publishing than it could be jeopardized legally by publishing. Finally, Beebe and Bradlee knew they had to put the question to Mrs. Graham. They phoned her from the kitchen and when the call reached her she was on the lawn of her home amid several hundred guests. It was getting late. Roberts' story was being set in type and Managing Editor Patterson was standing by at the office for word whether it would go into Friday's paper. Bradlee argued that nonpublication would make the paper out a coward. Geyelin told his boss that to hold back would demoralize the staff and diminish the paper. Greenfield, too, urged publication.

Beebe, more a shrewd corporate lawyer than a businessman, had decided that The Post Company had to go public and had sold that idea to Mrs. Graham. The company was obligated to pay off in cash many millions of dollars in stock options and, besides, there was the threat of devastating inheritance taxes. As Beebe had presented it to her, there was no choice and she had agreed. At the moment of the phone call a $33 million public stock offering had been made but the underwriting agreement had not yet been consummated.

At the end of the Beebe-Bradlee-Geyelin-Graham conversation Beebe said to Mrs. Graham, "I think I wouldn't [publish] but it's up to you to decide." She paused, then said to Bradlee who was on an extension, "Okay, go ahead, go ahead!"

Five years later, in reflecting on those hectic moments, Mrs. Graham commented that if Beebe had given her a flat "no" she never would have agreed to publish. It had been a very close thing but in the crunch the publisher came down on the right side, and THE POST was on its way to a national reputation it had never had before.

Friday's POST devoted the upper left half of page 1 to Roberts' lengthy story headlined DOCUMENTS REVEAL U.S. EFFORT IN '54 TO DELAY VIET ELECTION. Above the by-line were the tip-off words: "First of a Series." The *Times* series had not yet touched on this part of the Indochina story so THE POST had managed an exclusive while the *Times* was enjoined from printing anything. On Saturday, the *Times* ran a front-page account of Roberts' story and later in court it cited this fact to argue that it was being put at a disadvantage by the injunction. The AP story also noted that the POST's news service had carried an advisory message with the story saying the study on which the story was based was the subject of the government's injunction against the *Times.* The advisory then added: "In the judgement of *The Washington Post* editors, nothing in this article could be used to the injury of the United States." The AP added, truthfully, that "the parts of the study disclosed by *The Post* today contained little not already known and published over the years since the Eisenhower Administration."

But the story had come from the Pentagon Papers, they were top secret, and the Nixon administration did not know what might come next. So at 3 P.M. that Friday afternoon Bradlee received a phone call from William H. Rehnquist, then an assistant attorney general and later a Supreme Court justice, relaying the Attorney General's message:

> I have been advised by the Secretary of Defense that the material published in *The Washington Post* on June 18 . . . contains information relating to the national defense of the United States and bears a top-secret classification. As such, publication of this information is directly prohibited by the provisions of the Espionage Law, Title 18, United States Code, Section 793. Moreover, further publication of information of this character will cause irreparable injury to the defense interests of the United States. Accordingly, I respectfully request that you publish no further information of this character and advise me that you have made arrangements for the return of these documents to the Department of Defense.

While Mrs. Graham and others listened in his office, Bradlee responded: "I'm sure you will understand that I must respectfully decline." The issue of free press and national security was now joined at THE POST as well as at the *Times.* Morale in the fifth-floor newsroom had reached a new high. And the battle with the government now seemed to overshadow the subject matter of the papers.

The second POST article, by Marder, detailing some of the Johnson administration's deceptions during bombing pauses, barely made it into print. Judge Gerhard Gesell ruled for the paper that criminal prosecution, not a restraining injunction, should have been the government's remedy, if indeed it had a case. By nightfall a three-judge Court of Appeals panel had the case and, while the presses were rolling with Marder's story at the top of page 1, the majority ruled for the government. The presses were halted but Beebe, still at the courthouse, asked for and got a clarification — a ruling that the injunction applied only to further stories. That day's paper also carried a story from New York by MacKenzie on the government's claim in court that the *Times* articles had produced diplomatic and security "disaster."

That same Friday POST reporters were deployed everywhere there might be a Pentagon Papers angle. Since it was possible that the Court of Appeals ruling would be appealed at once to Chief Justice Warren Burger in his capacity as circuit judge for the District of Columbia, THE POST assigned Spencer Rich, normally the Senate reporter, and Martin Weil, a Metro reporter, to check at Burger's home. He lived in a wooded area of suburban Arlington, Virginia. Around 11:30 P.M. Rich and Weil knocked on the door, to be greeted by the Chief Justice in a bathrobe, carrying a long-barreled revolver, the muzzle pointed down. He agreed that the reporters should wait, if they must, on the street, which they did to no avail. Bradlee decided that the story of this encounter was one that should not be published.

The legal maneuvering involving THE POST in Washington and the *Times* in New York led to the Supreme Court where the two cases were argued jointly on June 26. By then the government's ability to win judicial restraint orders, almost unprecedented in American history, had kept the *Times* from publishing further stories for 12 days and THE POST for 7. At THE POST stories were being written and stockpiled. Meanwhile other newspapers had obtained some of the documents, and two papers, the Boston *Globe* and the St. Louis *Post-Dispatch*, likewise had been restrained. By the time the case was argued before the nine justices the issue of press versus government was being treated in both newspapers and television as much more important — and it was — than the contents of the Pentagon Papers. However, some newspapers editorially criticized use of the papers and some would not run stories furnished them by the *Times* and THE POST.

In all the proceedings the burden of the government's case was that publication "could be used to the injury of the United States and to the advantage of a foreign power," as the suit against THE POST charged. The counterargument was that the papers really were no more than history and no such possible injury was involved. At a closed hearing in Gesell's court POST military affairs reporter George C. Wilson provided a series of rebuttals from published stories and books to demonstrate that much of what was in the documents already had become known. POST and *Times* reporters provided affidavits to show the courts that government officials constantly leaked classified information to newspapers.

The issue before the Supreme Court, in essence, as Justice Potter Stewart put it, was whether disclosures from the Pentagon Papers would pose "such grave and immediate danger" as to permit an exception to the historic rule against prior restraint. Solicitor General Erwin Griswold told the Court that publication "will affect lives . . . the process of the termination of the war . . . the process of recovering prisoners of war." The newspapers' attorneys countered that the record — some of which was presented in sealed form — failed to make any such case. (Nor did any subsequent event justify that claim.)

On Thursday, July 1, THE POST's eight-column banner read: COURT RULES FOR NEWSPAPERS, 6–3. MacKenzie's account said that "the justices summed up their action by stating that the government had failed to meet its 'heavy burden' of justifying prior restraints against the press in light of cherished First Amendment freedoms." The stays were lifted at once and THE POST ran, on page 1, three held-up stories from the documents.

The editorial that day, written by Geyelin, was titled "The Pentagon Papers: Free — At Last." Geyelin noted Justice Byron White's opinion that the government had mistakenly chosen the injunction route rather than relying on criminal penalties after publication, a clear and continuing threat to the American press. Most important, said the editorial,

> the very uniqueness of this affair, in other words, has grossly distorted the realities, which are that the government has a very broad grant of authority to conduct its activities in secret, and enormous powers to preserve its essential secrets, and an impressive record of doing so. That it failed to do so in this case was never an argument, in our view, for suspending the First Amendment rights of the press to exercise its own judgement in the handling of these documents. Still less was it an argument for denying the public its right to be informed.

The editorial quoted with approval Judge Gesell's declaration that "it is the purpose and the effect of the First Amendment to expose to the public the maximum amount of information on which sound judgement can be made by the electorate."

At THE POST there were cheers and applause when Managing Editor Patterson jumped on a desk to call out: "We win, and so does the New York *Times.*" Mrs. Graham declared: "We are extremely gratified not only from the point of view of newspapers, which was not the least of our concerns, but gratified from the point of view of government, good government, and the public's right to know, which is what we were concerned with."

Bradlee posted a jubilant memorandum to the staff: "There is just no way of saying how proud I am of this wonderful newspaper and everyone on it. The guts and energy and responsibility of everyone involved in this fight, and the sense that you all were involved, has impressed me more than anything in my life. You were beautiful." He did not mention his supreme satisfaction: although THE POST had not matched the *Times'* great scoop, for which it would win a Pulitzer Prize, it had pulled up even in the court battle; in short, it had had impact.

It is, of course, impossible to be certain, but it is probable that Philip Graham would not have taken the risk that Katharine Graham took. Quite probably James Russell Wiggins would not have printed the papers even if they had been handed to THE POST first. In other words, the Pentagon Papers case proved to be a benchmark for the new regime at THE POST, a venerable newspaper in its ninety-fourth year.

There was a lot of fallout. For one, THE POST switched to a Washington law firm headed by Edward Bennett Williams, Paul Connolly, and Joseph A. Califano, Jr. The legal fees for the paper amounted to some $85,000. At THE POST Mrs. Graham radiated a new sense of self-confidence and Ben Bradlee was even more firmly in the catbird seat.

It was evident that the Nixon administration was bitter and that it was determined to jail Ellsberg who, two days after the court ruling, publicly stated that he had been the source for all the newspapers. But no one imagined that the Nixon White House would create a band of so-called plumbers who, that September, would burglarize the office of Ellsberg's psychiatrist and, the next June, the office of the Democratic National Committee in the Watergate office building.

There was a clue, however, to this mood and it came directly to THE POST. Ken W. Clawson, who covered the Justice Department, attended the gala opening of the new Wolf Trap cultural center the evening after THE POST reported the Court decision. After the concert Clawson went to the home of Deputy Attorney General Richard G. Kleindienst, with whom he was on good terms, and Kleindienst "asked me to privately convey" a "message to Mrs. Graham." He did so next morning by memorandum.

Kleindienst's remarks pointedly centered on possible Justice Department criminal prosecution, as Justice White had suggested, of the newspapers and specifically THE POST. He invited the publisher to discuss informally the still unpublished parts of the Pentagon Papers relating (1) what Communist governments had done as go-betweens in Vietnam peace negotiations and (2) indicating that the United States could intercept and read communications between foreign governments. On July 2 Clawson reported on page 1 that Attorney General Mitchell had said the government would prosecute "all those who have violated federal criminal" laws. In a later speech Bradlee said of Kleindienst's message that it "sounded then — and now — a little like blackmail."

In retrospect, however, the most fascinating part of the Kleindienst warning to Mrs. Graham had to do with President Nixon. In his memo Clawson quoted Kleindienst:

> The President is going to pick up a stick and start fighting back. I know he would go to the people on this. If he does, the big issue of the 1972 campaign may not be Vietnam or the economic situation, but whether an arrogant press is free to undermine the security of this country without check.

Mrs. Graham took all of this as a threat to her company and there were some efforts, through Secretary of State Rogers, to mollify the government though nothing came of it. Mitchell later denied to her that Kleindienst had meant any threat, suggesting that his deputy and the reporter might have had too much to drink that evening.

By 1971 THE POST was loaded with talent and "needed time for digestion," Bradlee said, although he always seemed to find the money when someone he wanted was available. Pulitzer Prize–winners Nick Kotz of the Des Moines *Register* and Haynes Johnson of the Washington *Star* both came although Kotz stayed only briefly. Richard Wald was hired in 1967 as an assistant managing editor but soon decided THE POST was not for him. He later became president of NBC News. Many staffers were shuffled around, some until they decided to quit, others to good purpose. In the latter group was Dan Morgan who went from city reporter to foreign correspondent in Europe and then back home to be the expert on agriculture. Kenneth Turan began in sports, went to *Potomac* and then to Style. Leonard Downie, Jr., began as a Metro reporter in 1965 and rose to Metro editor, in charge of all local coverage in both the city and the suburbs. Jim Hoagland, after three years as a city reporter, became the Africa correspondent, winning a Pulitzer for his 1971 reporting. Downie and Hoagland had collaborated on a 1969 series on Washington slum real estate speculators. Downie wrote exposés of the city's inadequate court system and of corruption among local savings and loan officials. This latter series brought an advertising boycott that cost the paper several hundred thousand dollars in ad revenue.

THE POST's Metro staff, said a 1975 article in the *Washington Monthly,* "is crammed with people who would be stars on most other papers and who are desperate to show their talent." This outside view found "more creative thinking and innovative thinking" on the Metro page, as the City Life page was renamed, "than in the big leagues of the national section."

One local reporter's by-line gave Mrs. Graham a start: Eugene Meyer. When she encountered him in an elevator she introduced herself and asked: "Don't you have a middle initial?" His by-line became: Eugene L. Meyer. He was no relation.

Retirements made room for some of the newcomers. After writing 8700 Federal Diary columns Jerry Kluttz turned that job over to Mike Causey. On the business side G. S. (Steve) Phillips, who had been at THE POST almost 50 years, capping his career as the company's secretary-treasurer, was succeeded by Robert P. Thome and, in time, by Martin Cohen.

In 1973 the company created The Washington Post Writers Group, run by William B. Dickinson, Jr., and Laura Longley Babb, to originate and market columns, features, and books mostly by staff members. In part the idea was to provide, through syndication, additional income for THE POST's stars.

In 1972, when Shirley Povich and William Gildea were in Munich for the Olympic games, they found themselves covering the massacre of Israeli athletes. At home there had been two major sports changes in Washington: Vince Lombardi came to manage the Redskins, Ted Williams the Senators. But Lombardi died after a single season and the baseball club was moved to Texas. When the move was announced on September 22, 1971, George Minot, Jr., told it all in his lead: "The Washington Senators died at age 71 tonight." Lombardi, the master coach, turned the Skins around and his successor, George Allen, did even better. Professional football had the Washington area in its emotional grip and POST coverage reached massive proportions. Televised games even seemed to help circulation; on Mondays after a Sunday televised game the paper consistently sold four or five thousand more copies than when the game was blacked out locally. Bradlee figured viewers wanted either to second-guess POST writers or to see how they explained something unclear on the tube.

In 1974 Shirley Povich retired and his This Morning sports column eventually was shared by Ken Denlinger and Dave Kindred. Povich continued to write, however, especially about baseball and boxing.

Metropolitan Washington's population reached 3 million as THE POST neared its centennial. The racial mix for the entire area remained roughly 70 percent white and 30 percent black but in the city itself blacks comprised more than 71 percent of the total. The capital's problems — crime, eroding tax base, lack of housing, public school deterioration, racial tension — paralleled those in many other cities.

Not long after the newly elected municipal government was sworn in on January 2, 1975, THE POST began to treat its actions, and inactions, without regard to the fact that the leaders were mostly black. Mayor

Washington and some of his top aides came under searching inquiry by black reporters as well as white. When city officials resorted to racial innuendo to defend themselves against criticism there was strong editorial rebuttal. Columnist Richard Cohen in 1976 described "what has become standard operating procedure at the District Building: When under attack yell racism, or at the very least imply it." THE POST handled local news with a high degree of sympathy for the historical and sociological background of the black community but the paper held up a standard for government by blacks comparable to that by whites.

In his 1968 campaign Nixon stung the city by calling it "the crime capital of the world." During his first term the paper for some months brought together city crime reports in a column called Crime and Justice. It was a shocking collection of daily robbings, stabbings, assaults, thefts, arrests, and indictments. City officials and businessmen complained that the column was adding to fears of suburbanites about coming into the city. THE POST tried in vain to obtain comparable data from suburban jurisdictions before it abandoned the column and once again scattered crime stories throughout the paper.

To an inquiring fellow publisher Mrs. Graham replied that "many residents of Washington feel that crime shouldn't be reported because it hurts business and the tourist trade, as indeed I fear it does. Therefore it hurts us, too, which I deplore. The only thing that would hurt us more as a newspaper and a community is not reporting what we know is happening."

Editorially, THE POST began to examine more sympathetically such anticrime measures as preventive detention, stringent bail requirements, and financial aid to crime victims, yet without departing from the paper's long-held civil libertarian standards.

In both reporting and editorials, THE POST sought to create a metropolitan approach to problems, especially transportation as the city's multibillion-dollar subway first began operations in 1976. But editorial support for commuter taxes, much desired by the city, was limited to a regional tax to finance the continuing bus and subway deficits.

On February 7, 1972, nine black reporters handed Bradlee a list of 20 questions to which they wanted answers in four days. Samples: "Why are there no black originating editors on the foreign, national, sports, financial and Style desks, and only one . . . on the metropolitan desk? Why was a white reporter assigned to cover the [Representative Shirley] Chisholm campaign after two black reporters suggested coverage and volunteered for the assignment?" At a meeting a week later Bradlee replied: "We are not meeting here because someone has been assigned to cover Mrs. Chisholm instead of someone else. We are not meeting here because there are no black journalists on the news desk. You are here because you feel seriously aggrieved, and discriminated against — because you feel that *The Washington Post,* as an institution, and some of its managers are consciously or unconsciously racist . . . As professional communicators we have failed. We have lost our way in a forest of suspicion and misunderstanding."

Thus the civil rights movement hit home at THE POST and women's liberation soon followed. Bradlee's initial response was that THE POST "now employs more black editors, reporters and photographers than any newspaper in America," 21 of them, and that of all the 396 newsroom employees, 37, or 9.3 percent, were black. The protesters, who became known as the Metro Seven after two dropped out, wanted many, many more. They filed charges of discrimination with the federal Equal Employment Opportunity Commission. As Bill Raspberry wrote in a column:

> *The Post,* it must be said, has done more than any other white newspaper in the country, both in terms of its editorial policy and in terms of its newsroom hiring practices. And when you do more, more is expected of you. The expectation is, in fact, a compliment.
>
> The Metro [Seven] and the rest of *The Post*'s black staff are paying their employer the ultimate compliment when they ask — and confidently expect — *The Washington Post* to do what no other white newspaper has done: to stop being just a white newspaper.

Back in 1968 before the riots in Washington, the National Advisory Commission on Civil Disorders had blamed the news media for contributing to "the black-white schism in this country." After the local riots later that year, in which THE POST relied heavily on its black staff members, the paper had taken on additional blacks, including its first black editorial writer, Roger Wilkins. But as Bradlee later acknowledged, THE POST still had "a red-neck streak" especially on some news desks and sensitive blacks often had a hard time from some editors. A letter of support for the Metro Seven signed by other black staffers showed that more was involved than jobs. "The lack of black participation in the shaping of the news about the society in which they play so vital a role has led to unfortunate distortions of the basic posture of the community on such vital questions as crime in the streets and the busing of school children." As Leon Dash, one of the blacks, told Bradlee, they aimed "to shake your tree."

After some acrimony and legal arguments, the EEOC's local office issued a finding of discrimination in THE POST's employment practices on the basis of race. POST attorneys swept this aside as "mistakes of fact and unsupportable conclusions." In the end the commission voted, 3 to 2, not to prosecute the paper.

Newsroom blacks were the most articulate at THE POST but the racial problem affected the entire paper. At the time of their protest there were 609 full- and part-time minority employees, or 21 percent of the paper's total employment of 2858. But they were unevenly distributed because of discriminatory practices by some unions. At the management level it was privately recognized that "our performance in black hiring has not lived up to our intentions. We have talked a lot and thought a lot, but we haven't worked a lot or spent a lot on black hiring and promotion." This memorandum to THE POST's then president, John Prescott, came from Donald Graham, the publisher's son who was beginning to work his way through the newspaper.

The response to the Metro Seven was a firmer commitment to recruiting, hiring, promoting, and creating new job slots for blacks. A two-year intern program was established to give an opportunity to reporters with no previous experience to demonstrate they were capable of becoming regular staffers. But on one point Bradlee was very firm: "There will be no mandatory quotas, except on quality, and no mandatory timetables, as long as I am the executive editor of *The Washington Post.*" By January 1977 full- and part-time minority employees totaled 807, or 27 percent of the 2962 work force.

World War II had brought women into the newsroom but when the men returned few were able to hang on. The creation of Style gave women an important and expanding area for reporting and editing. In mid-1970 when, as Bradlee put it, "the meaningful equality and dignity of women is properly under scrutiny . . . by all thoughtful people," he ended the use of what had come to be called sexist terminology. "Words like 'divorcée,' 'grandmother,' 'blonde' (or 'brunette'), or 'housewife,' should be avoided in all stories where, if a man were involved, the words 'divorcé,' 'grandfather,' 'blond,' or 'householder' would be inapplicable. In other words, they should be avoided. Words like 'vivacious,' 'pert,' 'dimpled,' or 'cute' have long since become clichés, and are droppable on that count alone." In early 1972 there was a Style ruckus over use of a backside view of a group of Playboy bunnies and the photo was yanked between editions. And when an unmarried woman reporter inquired of her editor whether there would be a fuss because she was going to have a baby, she was told that was her business, not THE

POST's. Newspaper mores and morals probably always have been more liberal than those of the nation generally; this certainly was true at THE POST in the late 1960s and early 1970s.

Bradlee responded to the women protesters as he had to the blacks. In 1970, as reported in THE POST, he pledged to increase substantially "as fast as possible, consistent with quality and opportunity," the role of women newsroom employees, particularly in top- and middle-management positions. A Newsroom Equal Employment Opportunity Committee composed of respected white and black employees was appointed to report publicly from time to time. The burden of the committee's first report in late 1972 was to urge management to break out of "its normal pattern of recruitment . . . now badly lopsided in favor of white males." THE POST in 1974 was charged in an EEOC finding with discrimination against women, particularly in promotion opportunities. Soon the Style section reached a rough male-female parity and there were many more women elsewhere in the news operation. By January 1976 almost 20 percent of all news employees were women.

Old job barriers against both blacks and women were ended in the sports department. By early 1977 the paper had two black men and two white women in sports. Both women, Joan Ryan and Nancy Scannell, won acceptance with the exception of entry to locker rooms. The first time Scannell went to Kennedy Stadium it took a combined escort of Shirley Povich and Sports Editor James Clayton to break the all-male tradition.

Mrs. Graham was acutely aware of a responsibility to advance women at her paper. By early 1976 she could say that 46 percent of those hired by THE POST the previous year had been members of minority groups. "We have made it plain to all managers at *The Post* that future promotions here will depend, among other things, on their affirmative action records." THE POST, she also said, "employs more black newsroom professionals than any other newspaper in the United States." As Leon Dash had predicted, the blacks had shaken THE POST's tree.

Bradlee insisted that "quality is the key word" in hiring blacks and he defined a person of quality as "someone who can carry the coal in a tough, competitive journalistic situation." One black POST reporter noted, correctly, that while the paper had done "a good job of hiring black reporters that are just starting out," few experienced blacks were hired. Another black, Joel Dreyfus, remarked that "you're expected to see things and report them in exactly the same way a white reporter does." Some blacks at THE POST viewed others there as "essentially aracial" and felt that "one can not afford the luxury of being aracial." Dreyfus applied for the job of Los Angeles bureau chief but Bradlee rejected him in a note that included:

Ever since you joined the paper, you have been critical of its managers, their attitudes on racial matters, their personnel policies, their assignments. You have made it clear that you prefer not to become a team player, but to stay outside and try to change the paper in your own image. Editors have invariably respected your talents, if not always your performance. But they have always resented your attitudes. When jobs have opened up that interested you, you invariably applied and were critical of us when your application was denied. When jobs opened up where we wanted you, you invariably turned us down and were critical of us for offering you jobs you considered beneath you.

This is how you gained the reputation you have among the editors here, the reputation of being a gifted journalist who is also a pain in the ass. All of us would love to have — and will have — as our Los Angeles bureau chief a gifted journalist. None of us wants a pain in the ass out there.

# 9

# Fame
# Watergate and Beyond
# 1972–1977

What came to be known as Watergate began for THE WASHINGTON POST with an 8:15 A.M. phone call on Saturday, June 17, 1972, from Joseph A. Califano, Jr., then general counsel of the Democratic National Committee, to Howard Simons, the paper's managing editor, alerting him to a break-in at the party headquarters in the Watergate office building. THE POST's handling of the story from that day on was to have a more profound effect on the paper than any other event in its first century. As the involvement of THE POST's publisher in the Teapot Dome scandal half a century earlier had proved a turning point toward the paper's worst disaster, so THE POST's leading role in uncovering the scandals of the Nixon administration proved to be its greatest triumph.

Simons' reaction to Califano's call was that most basic to journalism: here's a good story, let's dig it out. Simons put the paper to work. His first call was to Metro Editor Harry Rosenfeld. In turn Rosenfeld called his city editor, Barry Sussman. Before Sussman was out of bed he called Alfred E. Lewis, the veteran police reporter, and told him to go at once to the Watergate office building where five men had been arrested during the night. Then Sussman called Bob Woodward to ask him to come into the office at once. Sussman and Rosenfeld had agreed to put these two on the story.

Lewis had begun covering police in Washington six years before Woodward was born. He arrived at the Watergate with the acting chief of police, went upstairs with him to the Democratic committee suite, and stayed during the whole day's investigation while all other reporters had to wait outside. Lewis' name appeared on the next day's account but there were eight other contributors to the lengthy story: Bob Woodward, Carl Bernstein, Bart Barnes, Kirk Scharfenberg, Martin Weil,

Claudia Levy, Abbott Combes, and Tim O'Brien. The main story — there were two sidebars inside — ran at the top left side of page 1 of the 306-page Sunday POST under the headline:

5 HELD IN PLOT TO BUG
DEMOCRATS' OFFICE HERE

The New York *Times* ran an unsigned account of the break-in, tucked between ads on page 30 of its even fatter Sunday paper. If THE POST's judgment was superior, and it was, THE POST had the advantage in that Watergate began as a police story in its own city where it was well staffed and well connected, whereas the *Times* staffers in Washington were national rather than local reporters. The first story was worth page 1 not just because a political party's headquarters had been broken into five months before a presidential election but because Lewis, Woodward, and the others filled it with exciting and tantalizing news including the CIA connection of burglar James McCord. The next day THE POST's night police reporter, Eugene Bachinski, used his contacts around 3 A.M. to get an exclusive look at notebooks taken by the police from the burglars, thus providing the first tie between Howard Hunt and the White House. It was Woodward, then 29 and on THE POST only nine months, who was in court when McCord admitted his CIA connection. It also was Woodward who tied down the Hunt–White House relationship by some simple telephoning.

Two things made possible the Watergate reporting: many civil servants demonstrated that they had a higher loyalty than to the current occupant of the White House; and the persistence of POST reporters, most notably Bob Woodward and his partner Carl Bernstein, who together soon became known around the newspaper as "Woodstein." The element of luck is often present in successful reporting but as Bradlee pointed out after THE POST won its Pulitzer, "The best reporters make their own luck. My favorite reporters and editors are driven right out of their chairs by the electric excitement of a good story. They literally stalk the story, looking for a piece of it. Woodward and Bernstein join that select company." The story of how they stalked Watergate they themselves reported in their book, *All the President's Men,* told from the reporters' standpoint. Barry Sussman recounted the story as a deeply involved editor in *The Great Coverup;* and Leonard Downie, Jr., in *The New Muckrakers* described the interplay between reporters and editors.

When he got the first tip Simons called Metro Editor Rosenfeld rather than National Editor Harwood simply because the story began as a local crime. Although Metro had more reporters it rated as second fiddle to national. At the time of the break-in the Democratic convention was only weeks away and the national staff was concentrating on that quadrennial POST favorite, the presidential election. Some 40 men and women were headed to the convention and plans were being drawn for fall campaign coverage. In a sense, Watergate fell by default to Metro, or at least stayed there because of national's election concentration. Later on, Harwood expressed a belief that the Woodstein reporting was jeopardizing the paper's future or at least would end up making THE POST look ridiculous. When the story ballooned Bradlee seriously considered turning coverage over to national, but Simons insisted it stay with Metro and it did. The end result was a massive morale rise among the Metro staff even though only a few of its reporters were involved.

The first Woodstein joint by-line appeared on July 3. Thereafter the by-line generally alternated with Bernstein's name first one day and Woodward's first the next. Rosenfeld and Sussman had agreed to put Woodward on the break-in story the first day but Bernstein simply horned his way in. They were indeed "the odd couple," as some at THE POST first dubbed them. Woodward had unsuccessfully pestered Rosenfeld for a job when he got out of the navy, then had gone to work at the suburban Montgomery *Sentinel.* Six months later Rosenfeld hired him. Bernstein had come to THE POST in 1966 and one of his by-lined stories that year described a suburban plague of toilet paper strung on houses, trees, and cars. He graduated to antiwar protests, the Eisenhower funeral, and communes in the capital. With longish hair and general slouch, he would have looked at home in a commune, whereas Woodward was a nattily dressed square. Watergate historian J. Anthony Lukas described the pair as "a kind of journalistic centaur with an aristocratic Republican head and runty Jewish hind quarters." What they had in common was an intense, persistent work ethic. Since both then were single they did what older, more attached reporters did not like to do — work long days, weekends, and nights, sometimes all night.

Bernstein was an easy and imaginative writer; Sussman later described him as a reporter who "sometimes found universal truths in ordinary fires or auto accidents." Woodward was a rather awkward, stilted writer, but somehow the more cautious Woodward and the more conceptual Bernstein came to a superb working arrangement. They rewrote each other's draft stories which then were labored over by the imaginative Sussman and by Rosenfeld, a strong pencil editor with a knack at finding holes in stories and forcing reporters to fill them.

Simons saw the story's potential from the first moment and kept both editors and reporters on the track. Bradlee provided the essential backing and protection for reporters and editors, even when they faltered. His public bravado in the face of both skepticism and denial gave THE POST an image of a paper determined to root out the truth whatever the cost. In the beginning Simons was far more involved than Bradlee, insisting on a full-time investigative team which Sussman selected: Woodward and Bernstein. Mrs. Graham later described the "rules which *The Post*'s editors laid down" for Watergate: "First, every bit of information attributed to an unnamed source had to be supported by at least one other independent source. Second, nothing reported by another media would be repeated in *The Post* unless it could be independently verified. Third, every word of every story had to be read by at least one of three senior editors before it went into print."

Of all the Woodstein sources one of Woodward's was the prize and his identity their most closely guarded secret. On May 15, five weeks before Watergate and the day George Wallace was shot in nearby Laurel, Maryland, during his presidential campaign, THE POST was having trouble learning the identity of the man who had fired at the Alabama governor. Woodward told Sussman he had "a friend" who might be able to help. In fact he was no help but this was the first appearance of the man who became famous as Deep Throat. He next appeared June 19 when the second-day Watergate story was being written, to tell Woodward that Howard Hunt definitely was involved. In their book, Bernstein and Woodward described him as "a source in the Executive Branch who had access to information at CRP [Committee for the Re-election of the President] as well as at the White House." He would talk only to Woodward and only on "deep background" so Simons dubbed him "Deep Throat," the name of the celebrated pornographic movie, which Simons had not seen. Many skeptics have doubted whether such a person really existed or whether he was invented to cover several persons who provided information. Woodward insisted that "there is a Deep Throat, and he is not a composite" and that "Carl knows" his identity. It is hardly conceivable that a tough editor like Bradlee would risk his paper's reputation on a cub reporter's unidentified source but the most he would say was that "I have never said whether or not I knew his identity." Mrs. Graham repeatedly said she did not know who Deep Throat was. At one point when her paper was feeling the heat she did ask Woodward to tell her. He replied that he would if she wanted but she said "she was only kidding, she didn't really want to carry that burden around with her." (In 1975 when an anonymous source supplied THE POST and other papers with confidential files of the American Medical Association reporters dubbed him "Sore Throat." But it didn't catch on.)

It is unquestionably true, as Bradlee wrote, that reporters and editors working on Watergate "could be no better than the publisher will let them be." Probably no publisher has received such a vote of approval for conduct under intense fire as did Katharine Graham from within her own paper. As expressive as any was a note from Roger Wilkins, author of many Watergate editorials: "You hired Benny and the rest, who made the tough decisions and, more than anybody else around here, you had to take the heat for what the 5th floor was doing. None of us has much of an inkling of what it took for you to hang tough, but whatever the cost, you did it."

At a private luncheon in July 1973, three days after Nixon's White House taping system was disclosed, Mrs. Graham remarked: "Being so far out in front on the story meant that for months *The Post*'s position was very lonely and exposed. No matter how careful we were, there was always the nagging possibility that we were wrong, being set up, being misled." Yet "one of the indications that we were really onto something was the intensity of the pressure on us to cease and desist." On one occasion she was told by a friend with administration connections that phones of several POST reporters and editors were tapped at the office but a check, costing $5000, failed to turn up any taps.

When it was all over Mrs. Graham publicly admitted to "many moments of anxiety." In private she wrote to a friend abroad of "an unbelieveable two years of pressured existence — the first in particular, when one never dreamt it would all come out . . . It was painfully obvious they were out to destroy us . . . I must say, there was a blood-chilling moment when Henry Kissinger said to me, looking at me with incredulity, 'Don't you believe we are going to get re-elected?' "

Pressure on THE POST peaked, as Nixon's re-election campaign peaked, in late October. For two weeks beginning on October 10 THE POST presented a run of sensational stories. First was a long and detailed Woodstein disclosure that the FBI had established that the initial Watergate break-in "stemmed from a massive campaign of political spying and sabotage . . . directed by officials of the White House and the Committee for Re-election of the President." Up to this point POST stories had been reporting bits and pieces; now the whole puzzle was becoming recognizable. Bradlee became more directly engaged in Watergate coverage and at luncheon the day that story appeared he told Woodward that "our cocks are on the chopping block now and I just want to know a little more about this." In rapid succession Woodstein stories focused on the activities of Dwight Chapin, Herbert Kalmbach, and H. R. Haldeman. The Haldeman story contained a serious error in fact on which THE POST's opponents pounced, for a time obscuring the link the account provided between Nixon's chief of staff and a secret campaign cash fund. The two reporters also came dangerously close to serious trouble with Judge John Sirica when, with Bradlee's approval, they talked to several Watergate grand jurors.

Prior to the October 10 story the White House had tried to brush off POST stories as based on "hearsay." On October 16 came a violent administration counterattack. Bradlee later said that the week of October 15 to 25 "probably ranks as the longest of the last 30 months for all of us here at *The Post*." Under the headline GOP HITS POST FOR 'HEARSAY' Bernstein and Woodward described on page 1 the "separate attacks" by Nixon Campaign Manager Clark MacGregor, Republican National Chairman Robert Dole, and White House press secretary Ronald Ziegler. MacGregor used the toughest language: "*The Washington Post*'s credibility has today sunk lower than that of George McGovern . . . Using innuendo, third-person hearsay, unsubstantiated charges, anonymous sources and huge scare headlines, *The Post* has maliciously sought to give the appearance of a direct connection between the White House and the Watergate . . . a charge which *The Post* knows, and half a dozen investigations have found . . . to be false. The hallmark of *The Post*'s campaign is hypocrisy, and its celebrated double standard is today visible for all to see."

That same day Dole slammed away at "a barrage of unfounded and unsubstantiated allegations [by McGovern] and his partner-in-mudslinging, *The Washington Post.*" Dole also charged that Mrs. Graham had said at a dinner that her paper opposed Nixon "because I hate him." She categorically denied any such conversation. Four days before Nixon's great triumph at the polls she replied to a letter from John D. Ehrlichman which repeated the "hate" remark:

> What appears in *The Post* is not a reflection of my personal feeling. And by the same token, I would add that my continuing and genuine pride in the paper's performance over the past few months — the period that seems to be at issue — does not proceed from some sense that it has gratified my personal whim. It proceeds from my belief that the editors and reporters have fulfilled the highest standards of professional duty and responsibility.

On October 25, the day of the Haldeman story, Ziegler attacked THE POST for "shabby journalism" and Bradlee as anti-Nixon. On October 29 Vice President Agnew charged that THE POST "has engaged in a veritable paroxysm of individual vendettas against the President."

The charge that THE POST was carrying McGovern's political water was conclusive to those who disliked the paper for its liberalism. Although the Woodstein stories were available to the 220 domestic news service subscribers many editors simply would not print them; something more than half did use the October 10 story but many editors buried it on inside pages. As Haynes Johnson wrote the following spring, "The people still wanted to believe the White House, still could not accept what had happened." By the time of THE POST's October burst of stories other publications, notably the Los Angeles *Times* and *Time* magazine, had come up with exclusive Watergate stories. The television networks for the most part repeated what the print media disclosed. In the summer and fall of 1972 television's most familiar Watergate lead-in phrase came to be: "*The Washington Post* reported this morning . . ." Ben Bagdikian, who had left THE POST to become a media critic, pointed out that "no more than 14 reporters" of the 2200 regularly working in Washington did any substantial work on the story.

The next spring, after new revelations forced Ziegler to call all previous White House statements "inoperative," he publicly apologized to Woodward and Bernstein. MacGregor admitted he had not known the facts when he attacked THE POST and had only been parroting the White House. Dole never apologized. As Bradlee put it, "The plain truth chases the big lie forlornly."

For six weeks after the election THE POST had no further story. Many readers and some, too, who worked at the paper were saying this only proved that the disclosures had been part of the McGovern campaign. In this period until the dam broke on Nixon in the spring of 1973 THE POST was the target of White House retribution. Nixon gave an exclusive interview to a Washington *Star-News* reporter. THE POST's veteran society reporter, Dorothy McCardle, was banned for 28 days from covering White House social functions, a move so petty it rebounded. Mrs. Graham described her as "cooling her heels in her evening dress all alone in the White House press room while parties went on without her." The *Star-News* ran an editorial saying it would not allow itself to be a White House tool for revenge against its competitor and would not cover functions until Mrs. McCardle was allowed to return; the ban soon was lifted. More serious, a *Star-News* reporter had told Bernstein before election day that White House hatchet man Charles Colson had told him, "As soon as the election is behind us, we're going to really shove it to *The Post.*"

As the Nixon tapes would show, the attack on THE POST had been planned at least as early as September 15, 1972. On that day, in a conversation with Haldeman and John Dean, the President had said of THE

POST: "It's going to have its problems . . . The main thing is the *Post* is going to have damnable, damnable problems out of this one. They have a television station . . . and they're going to have to get it renewed." When Haldeman added, "They've got a radio station, too," Nixon went on, "Does that come up, too? The point is, when does it come up?" Dean replied, "I don't know. But the practice of non-licensees filing on top of licensees has certainly gotten more . . . active in the, this area." And Nixon: "And it's going to be God damn active here . . . Well, the game has to be played awfully rough."

In January 1973 challenges were filed before the Federal Communications Commission to renewal of The Washington Post Company's licenses to operate its two Florida television stations up for renewal that year, WJXT in Jacksonville and WPLG in Miami. In an affidavit filed with the FCC in June 1974 Mrs. Graham said that "all the people challenging" the renewals were Nixon administration supporters or sympathizers. Two principals in the Miami challenge, for example, were law partners of former Senator George Smathers who had introduced Nixon to the man who became his close friend, C. G. (Bebe) Rebozo. Ironically, Smathers had been a college roommate of Mrs. Graham's husband. In her affidavit the publisher said she believed the challenges had been filed as "a part of a White House–inspired effort to injure the . . . company in retaliation for its Watergate coverage." The challengers denied any such connection or intention but the stock market read it Mrs. Graham's way: POST stock fell from a high of $38 a share to $21.

Thirteen days after Nixon's private promise of "damnable, damnable problems" for THE POST his former Attorney General, John Mitchell, received a call from Bernstein at 11:30 P.M. When the reporter read him the Woodstein story saying that while in office he had "personally controlled a secret Republican fund that was used to gather information about the Democrats," Mitchell erupted: "All that crap you're putting it in the paper? It's all been denied. Jesus. Katie Graham is gonna get her tit caught in a big fat wringer if that's published. Good Christ. That's the most sickening thing I've ever heard." On Bradlee's order only the words "her tit" were omitted from the September 29 story.

In the midst of the October run of major Watergate exclusives and two days before MacGregor, Dole, and Ziegler raked the newspaper, THE WASHINGTON POST dedicated its new $25 million building. Fronting on 15th Street Northwest and four blocks from the White House, the structure was joined to the old L Street building to more than double the space for both the 2600 employees and additional mechanical equipment. The principal speaker was William P. Rogers, former POST lawyer and board member, long-time close Nixon friend, now Secretary of State. He declared that "this is the home of a newspaper with a great tradition — a dedication to the public good." That tradition, he said, had been begun by Eugene Meyer, carried on by Philip Graham, "and now strikingly enhanced under the leadership of Kay Graham." The secretary and the publisher did not miss the incongruity of the day. In introducing Rogers, Mrs. Graham compared asking him to asking the President of Egypt to keynote a Jewish convention. Rogers responded by noting the paper's articles "attacking the Administration of which I am proud to be a part." He added: *"The Post* doesn't reflect Government policy, in fact doesn't even acknowledge that we have a policy." (A few weeks later architectural critic Von Eckardt wrote in THE POST that the building was "somewhat brutal in its massiveness" and while excellent to work in an architectural "disappointment.")

THE POST was on the defensive until December 8 when a Woodstein story tied Howard Hunt's White House office to one of the Watergate burglars. In the following weeks the whole story began to flood out — at the burglars' trial, in a New York *Times* story first disclosing hush money was being paid some of the burglars, in James McCord's letter to Judge Sirica. Simons phoned Mrs. Graham in Hong Kong to tell her of McCord's important corroboration of the Woodstein reasoning. Next came L. Patrick Gray's FBI confirmation hearing and, finally, John Dean and Jeb Stuart Magruder telling all to the Senate Watergate Committee while an enthralled nation watched on television. Now Watergate was everybody's story. Whereas the generally lonely Woodstein stories had appeared on page 1 under one- or two- or occasionally three-column headlines, the massive disclosures now rated double eight-column banner lines.

In early 1973 the CRP tried to obtain by subpoena what Mrs. Graham called "the contents of our newsroom, [the] chance to rummage through our files, flip through our reporters' notes, and pore over every scrap of material we had gathered in our months-long investigation" and to disclose "the names of sources we had promised to protect." When this effort was defeated in court the publisher used it as a reference point to explain that

> confidentiality is not a personal privilege for reporters, but a vital component of the public's right to know. It serves not the private interests of journalists, but the immense public interest in learning the news. The Watergate scandals illustrate this in what I think is a most compelling way, for an enormous portion of the information which *Post* reporters

> and others have brought to light . . . was gleaned, necessarily, from sources whose identity could not be divulged.

As the possibility of Nixon's impeachment emerged, his Vice President was disclosed to have been a small-time felon. Lou Cannon wrote that whereas many felt Nixon was "too smart" to be involved in Watergate crimes, surely Agnew was "too honest" to cheat. First word of the truth came in April 1973 from Woodward's friend Deep Throat: Agnew had taken a bribe while Vice President, the amount was $2500 and he had put an envelope containing the cash in a desk drawer in his Executive Office Building office. This report came to THE POST nearly a month before the time when federal prosecutors later conceded they had received the first hint of such kickbacks and nearly two months before they learned any specifics. At THE POST the Agnew story was largely a job for two contemporaries of Woodward and Bernstein, Richard M. Cohen and Edward Walsh, assigned to cover Maryland news for the Metro desk. Six days after Agnew was formally, but secretly, notified on August 1 that he was under investigation, the story surfaced in both the *Wall Street Journal* and THE POST. Cohen and Bernstein were the writers.

Agnew, who had been castigating the press, now became its victim as leak after leak disclosed his money-grubbing past. An August 22 POST editorial by Meg Greenfield declared that the Vice President was "well within his rights to be powerfully annoyed if those charged with the responsibility for the investigation are acting in a way careless of the protections that are due him." The editorial said that the paper would continue to report the investigation but that it expected the government to protect its own "legitimate secrets." In other words, the government should not leak such a damning case but if it does we will print it. POST columnist Broder chastised his own paper for such a posture. The leaks went on until Broder himself on September 18 wrote the lead story on page 1: Agnew had been discussing resignation from the second highest office in the land. Broder's by-line by now had such authority that few could doubt that Agnew was finished. On September 22 Cohen and Cannon disclosed that, despite all his statements that he would never quit, Agnew was plea bargaining. Agnew's lawyers tried to learn the source of the damaging leaks by subpoenas for Cohen and other reporters. Bradlee told a meeting in Simons' office the day the subpoenas were served that "it goes without saying that *The Washington Post* will not reveal its sources. We will go to jail first." In her affidavit to the court Mrs. Graham boldly asserted that she had "ultimate responsibility for the custody" of Cohen's notes. Privately, she was prepared to go to jail, if it came to that. But the issue became moot when Agnew resigned on October 10. Next day Herblock drew Agnew folding a tent labeled "Agnew Scandals" beside a much bigger tent marked "Nixon Scandals." The cartoonist's title: "The Side-Show Closes." Within the next ten days Nixon fired Special Prosecutor Archibald Cox; Attorney General Elliot Richardson and his deputy, William Ruckelshaus, resigned; and Nixon was headed toward the final stages of his decline and fall. Two days after Agnew's resignation Nixon chose Representative Gerald R. Ford of Michigan as Vice President, under terms of the new 25th Amendment.

THE POST learned on April 12, 1973, that it would receive the Pulitzer Prize for public service. The Woodstein stories had been submitted in two categories, but the jurors had switched them into the public service category. Woodward and Bernstein received all the other major reporting awards for 1972. When word came of the Pulitzer, Bradlee called a news staff meeting to announce it, to the accompaniment of loud cheering.

Professionally, the greatest satisfaction was THE POST's triumph over the New York *Times.* At the very beginning the *Times* had followed the White House's deliberately false clue of a Cuban connection. Not for many months did the *Times* begin to challenge POST reporting. In the interval the *Times'* editors in New York nightly waited with far more anxiety for the wirephoto transmission of THE POST's front page than the other way around. The *Times,* as one magazine account put it, was not always a graceful loser: learning of the major October 10, 1972, story, the *Times* rewrote it after its accuracy was confirmed "in such a way that *The Washington Post's* name did not appear until the article had jumped [to a page] inside the paper." The day Haldeman and Ehrlichman resigned Bradlee strode through the newsroom shouting to Woodward: "Not bad, Bob! Not half bad!" Simons was more cautious: "Don't gloat. We can't afford to gloat." At another moment of POST exuberance Bradlee shouted out: "Eat your heart out, Abe!" in a reference to his rival on the *Times,* Managing Editor Abe Rosenthal, who had beaten him to the Pentagon Papers.

Hard-working, intellectual Howard Simons was hardly a shrinking violet but he was overshadowed by Bradlee, especially on Watergate. POST staffers, however, gave him high marks for imagination, craftsmanship, and for widening the horizons of the paper's subeditors. One put the truth this way: "You can't afford a Ben Bradlee unless you have a Howard Simons to do the daily work."

Woodward and Bernstein's reporting provided the cutting edge, editorials pushed and prodded, and Herblock rained hammer blows at

Nixon and his crew, drawing some of the most powerful cartoons of his career. His routine was to make several preliminary pencil sketches on newsprint copy paper, then walk from his office into the newsroom to show them to perhaps three or four reporters, those he trusted the most or those who were working on the story he was commenting on. In part he wanted to be sure he had made no factual error, in part he wanted to gauge reactions. The final pen-and-ink product usually came off his drawing board just at deadline time.

As the early Watergate stories began to be confirmed, especially by the presidential tapes, the newspaper itself became a news item. Reporters and television crews swarmed into the newsroom and POST people, especially Bradlee, became national, even international, celebrities. The publication of *All the President's Men* and then the motion picture of the same name, which had its world première at the Kennedy Center on April 4, 1976, further enhanced THE POST's reputation.

A year before the film's première, Style carried a long piece, ordered by Bradlee, by-lined Tom Shales, Tom Zito, and Jeanette Smith and worked over by numerous editors. It detailed the movie-newspaper interplay, especially the impact of the movie-making on THE POST. Although no shooting was permitted inside the POST building, Robert Redford (who played Woodward), Dustin Hoffman (Bernstein), and Jason Robards (Bradlee) spent considerable time in the newsroom soaking up the atmosphere and learning something of the news business, as POST employees from all floors came to gawk. The film glamorized Bradlee more than anyone; Mrs. Graham did not appear and she was mentioned only when the movie John Mitchell warned Bernstein that "Katie Graham" was headed for trouble with "a big fat wringer." The film was generally acclaimed by journalists for presenting the most honest picture in cinema history of how they really behave. At a cost of $450,000 the movie newsroom was an exact duplicate of THE POST's, down to the desks covered with real POST litter that had been shipped to the Burbank, California, lot. Of all the reviews, mostly raves, probably none was more critical than the paper's own Gary Arnold's. He found the film "engrossing and enjoyable" but picked it apart for a too "restrictive framework" that omitted many scenes from the book.

Although she fully supported Woodward and Bernstein, Mrs. Graham was publicly critical after Watergate of what she called "a new and rather indiscriminate emphasis on disclosure as the index of fitness for public office." She commented that Watergate had "made the press too much a party to events, too much an actor in the drama . . . to see conspiracy and cover-up in everything is as myopic as to believe that no conspiracies and cover-ups exist . . . it's not the business of the press to uphold institutions, to reform them, or to make policy. Our job is to relate what's happening, as fairly and completely as we can — whether or not that is what people want to hear and what officials want the people to hear." And: "In the past two years, I fear, we may have acquired some tendencies toward over-involvement that we had better overcome. But we had better not yield to the temptation to go on re-fighting the last war and see conspiracy and cover-up where they do not exist."

The publisher, as she indicated in a post-Watergate letter, felt that "a lot of the administration mud and deliberate attacks on the press has stuck — people do think we are unfair and too powerful and that someone should control or at least judge us." She was not beguiled by the flood of friendly letters congratulating her on "the magnitude of your accomplishment, your fortitude, and just plain guts," as one writer put it, or saying "you should run for president."

To Woodward and Bernstein she sent a handwritten letter just after Nixon's resignation:

> . . . all things considered, it's miraculous. I concede all the things we *must* concede — incredible amounts of luck, sources willing and even finally a few eager to talk and help — I concede the role of the courts, grand juries, and congressional committees — *we* didn't bring *him* down — those institutions and holders of office did, as we all keep repeating — But I believe if the story pre-election and post hadn't continued McCord might well not have written his letter. I concede by that time too you had been joined and sustained by other reporting — But it was still an extraordinary, gutsy, hard, brilliant piece of journalism — and I want to say this to you both despite all the accompanying crap that has fallen all over us and especially you. Lastly, you've both made it fun and we've all kept the demon pomposity in moderate if far from complete control. The sound of our own voices, while listened to by us with some awe and even some admiration, is receding — And if it isn't, there are all sorts of stark realities before us to restore balance and defy hubris.

The Woodstein team produced a second book, *The Final Days,* demonstrating again their reportorial talents. (To television interviewer David Frost on May 25, 1977, Nixon bitterly described the book as "contemptible journalism" and both the book and its authors as "trash.") In it they acknowledged the help of Scott Armstrong and Al

Kamen. Woodward had helped Armstrong, an old friend, to get an investigator's job on the Senate Watergate Committee. In July 1974 Armstrong was one of the two junior Watergate committee staffers to question Alexander Butterfield, who told them that Nixon had taped all his White House conversations. Woodward learned this the next day, two days before Butterfield disclosed it to an amazed nation. But the reporter was hesitant and when he sought Bradlee's advice Bradlee let a big one slip through his hands. Woodward asked Bradlee how he would rate such a story, and his boss replied "B-plus," adding that he didn't think it worth too much effort to verify. When the story broke Bradlee told Woodward, "Okay. It's worth more than a B-plus." In 1976 Woodward got Bradlee to hire Armstrong as an investigative reporter.

After their triumph the decompression problem was difficult for Woodward and Bernstein. Finally, Carl Bernstein resigned from THE POST at the end of 1976 to write books but Bob Woodward soldiered on to turn up more exclusive stories, especially about the CIA. One story neither Woodstein nor anyone else has yet written, however, is a verified explanation of exactly what had motivated the Watergate burglary in the first place.

When the end came THE POST on August 9, 1974, bannered NIXON RESIGNS in 168-point type, unmatched since March 5, 1953, when the line had read STALIN IS DEAD.

Within the newspaper some egos had been expanded, others bruised; some reporters and editors felt unappreciated, others gloried in the limelight even though they had nothing to do with the Watergate story. Bumper stickers had appeared in the capital proclaiming "Thank God for *The Washington Post.*" Another said: "Gerald Ford — I got my job through *The Washington Post.*" Privately as well as publicly the relationship between Mrs. Graham and her executive editor had become even closer than ever. Bradlee thanked her for "just being around, for laughing, for worrying, for teasing and being teased, for encouraging, for being warm and human." She told him:

> The reason you and I get along so well, notwithstanding the fact that we are both innately endowed with a primordial urge — not at all competitive, mind you — to be No. 1, is because of this — our routes run parallel and synchronize . . . I know I'm No. 1 because you are No. 1. You know that I know that I am No. 1 because you are No. 1.

As 1974, the final Watergate year, began, THE POST had 2750 employees, more than half the company's total of 4835. The paper's march to financial success and dominance in the capital in the four decades since Eugene Meyer had bought it was strikingly shown in these figures:

| POST advertising linage as a percentage of all Washington papers: | Daily circulation as a percentage of all Washington papers | Sunday circulation as a percentage of all Washington papers: |
|---|---|---|
| 1933 | | |
| 13.9 of 5 papers | 12.3 of 5 | 18.2 of 3 |
| 1943 | | |
| 22.3 of 4 papers | 24.0 of 4 | 26.0 of 3 |
| 1953 | | |
| 24.9 of 4 papers | 24.3 of 4 | 26.6 of 3 |
| 1963 | | |
| 48.9 of 3 papers | 46.7 of 3 | 60.1 of 2 |
| 1973 | | |
| 65.8 of 2 papers | 56.6 of 2 | 67.1 of 2 |

But these figures did not tell the whole story. The Washington Post Company's net income for 1973 was over $13 million, highest ever, and the dividend had been doubled. But the newspaper division profits had leveled off whereas magazine and radio-television profits continued to grow. The reason, as management saw it, was the ever-rising cost of production, especially wages in the mechanical departments increased by restrictive union practices which management called featherbedding.

THE POST set as its long-range goal a return to a 15 percent operating, pretax margin, which equated to about 7 1/2 percent after taxes. The paper had achieved such profitability in the 1960s but margins had declined to about 9 percent. Public references to the 15 percent figure created a belief among some employees that the company had come to be dominated by a "bottom line" — profitability — philosophy, a charge Mrs. Graham repeatedly and vehemently denied. In her first appearance before security analysts in January 1972, six months after the company had gone public, Mrs. Graham had declared that "the first order of business at *The Washington*

*Post* is to maximize profits from our existing operations." She went on to say that "some costs resist more stubbornly than others. The most frustrating kind are those imposed by archaic union practices that deprive the company of the savings we ought to achieve from modern technology. This is a problem we are determined to solve; we hope it can be solved in an amicable, constructive, spirit. In any event, we fully intend to deal with it."

First, however, the publisher had to learn far more about her business than what went on in the newsroom. In mid-1968, when she first began to grapple with the mechanical side, she confessed that "somehow the technology of publishing is the hardest one to grasp." To a fellow publisher she wrote: "I have just started to become interested in newspaper production . . . I should have started ages ago but there were so many things to learn at the beginning. I think it's the most important area for top management to keep up with and it's hard to do it when one's education in technological language is so deficient. But I hope to close the ignorance gap before too long." Although in 1968 she went to an IBM computer school for seven days, in mid-1973 she was still calling herself "a devout non-technocrat."

THE POST was late moving into new technologies. In early 1974 the company told stockholders that "by the late seventies" it planned "to have installed a computerized composition system that will be both faster and significantly less costly than present methods." The company noted that "the prospect of this technological change is essential to an understanding of *The Post*'s most difficult labor problem." This was a reference to a form of make-work or featherbedding known as "reproduce" or "bogus," long embedded in POST contracts with the Columbia Typographical Union 101. When advertising matter was brought in from outside already set in type THE POST's printers nonetheless reset it, proofread it, made corrections, and then threw their work away.

After purchase of the *Times-Herald* sent POST profits soaring, management opted to pay out more rather than take strikes. What strikes there had been, in 1949, 1958, 1966, 1968 when the paper lost three days, and 1969, had been called by pressmen or stereotypers. Printers began in 1967 to employ the slowdown tactic to get their way at contract time. They found that it worked because management would not risk being shut down.

Production of the paper deteriorated from the late 1960s onward. The paper came off the presses later and later, frequently so late newsboys could not deliver it before school time. It was full of egregious typographical errors about which both readers and advertisers complained.

Labor relations were getting worse as management felt frustrated and the unions dug in to hold or improve their benefits. Mrs. Graham's decisiveness on matters involving the news side were in sharp contrast to her well-perceived indecisiveness in business matters. Bradlee had been a great find but she couldn't seem to match him on the business side.

During a slowdown in late 1971 some of the printers altered classified ads to include explicit sexual epithets aimed at the publisher. Management began to feel it must regain the control it had lost over its own production plant. At the end of 1971 Mrs. Graham replaced Ignatius with John S. Prescott, Jr., a Knight newspaper chain executive, as the new POST president. His first major task was to develop "equality at the bargaining table." This meant creating a capacity to put out a newspaper without union labor, that is, to be able for the first time to take a strike and go on publishing. Prescott put Kenneth Johnson, one of Bradlee's former news editors, in charge of Project X, a plan to train nonunion white collar business employees to run the presses. This was done at Southern Production Program in Oklahoma City, a publisher-supported organization well known for its antiunion bias. THE POST also established its own training school — the printers called it a "scab school" — to teach others the use of newly purchased cold type machinery. Cold type computerized photocomposition, a replacement of the hot type produced by linotype, already was in use at many other newspapers, including the Washington *Star.* Finally, Prescott hired a well-known, tough labor negotiator, Lawrence A. Wallace.

A test of company-union strength came in late 1973 over dismissal of a printer for taking part in a slowdown. The other printers refused either to work or leave; and THE POST called in federal marshals to evict them. Nonunion employees then prepared a 40-page paper in cold type and other nonunion employees were ready to man the presses. James A. Dugan, the tough-talking head of Local 6 of the Newspaper and Graphic Communications Union, the pressmen, told Prescott his men would print the paper. Instead the pressmen outfoxed management by staging a sit-down strike in the pressroom until the printer was reinstated; then they ran off a mere 90,000 papers. The three days' lost or curtailed production represented a loss to THE POST of around $700,000. From then on there was enduring management suspicion of Dugan and his men, many of them younger militants who also worked at the *Star,* came from other cities, and felt no loyalty to THE POST.

Management believed the pressmen were taking advantage of a generous contract to put in excessive and expensive overtime — in 1974 the average pressman earned over $22,000 — and to require employment of far more men than really needed to run the presses safely and efficiently. Delay of the press starting time meant overtime; sabotage, the deliberate breaking of the paper rolls feeding THE POST's nine presses, also meant overtime. There were legitimate union complaints about working conditions, involving dirt, noise, and badly designed work space, about which management did little or nothing. To the union leaders and many of the men, the company simply was out to bust their union as other newspapers had busted the same union in half a dozen cities in the past decade or so.

In April 1974 more than 800 news and commercial employees, members of the Newspaper Guild, walked out for 16 days. They did not set up a picket line, however, hoping to win this first-ever Guild strike against THE POST by "withholding excellence," a phrase reflective of pride in the paper's Watergate performance. Among Guild demands was a top minimum for experienced reporters, editors, and ad salesmen of $500 a week; the company offered $470.47. The strike was a disastrous failure. Privately, Mrs. Graham commented that "the Guild is talking about 'excellence,' but we have in fact built in a bureaucracy of high minimums," making it impossible to get rid of those "who can't earn" such salaries anywhere else. "And it is difficult because of the high minimums to reward enough real ability and length of service." During the strike she went to work taking ads over the phone and non-Guild employees wrote stories and headlines, filling the remaining columns with wire service copy. The paper was much slimmer but the strike actually made about $250,000 for THE POST because payroll savings exceeded lost revenue. In the end the majority voted to go back to work for substantially what the company had offered originally.

Bradlee asked a distinguished student of journalism, George E. Reedy, to probe the strike and tell him why it had occurred. The confidential report he received explained the "withholding excellence" rationale this way:

> Generally speaking, you are cast in the role of the champion of "excellence" and Prescott in the role of champion of "the bottom line" . . . they think they see you losing, and, to them, this means that "excellence" is losing.

Reedy gave this broader picture:

> To most of the employees, she [Mrs. Graham] has something of the aura of a hereditary monarch. They regard the internal life of *The Washington Post* as a political struggle for her favor. To most of them, she is a benevolent ruler who would

> resolve all controversies in their favor providing she was aware of the facts . . . There is a small minority . . . who regard her as a "tough babe" that has inherited a great institution from her father and is determined to concentrate solely on making money from it, without regard to the "traditions" of the man who built it.

The report was equally frank about staff attitudes toward Bradlee:

> The allegation is that you "play favorites" and glory in pitting people against each other to a point where the office resembles a snake pit. In many instances, this may well be nothing but the alibi of the second-rate. But nevertheless, it is a widespread perception.

The month before the Guild strike Mrs. Graham had told security analysts that it had been "mainly costs and manpower assigned to production — not editorial extravagance — that has held down *The Post*'s profitability in recent years." Then she added: "Figuratively speaking, I want to win a Pulitzer prize for management." When the Guild strike collapsed, Mrs. Graham remarked that its "real significance" was that the paper "overcame a reputation for willingness to avoid a strike at almost any price" by demonstrating that it was "willing to take a strike if necessary to demonstrate our determination to keep our costs under reasonable control." Business publications began to analyze her management. *Forbes* magazine in mid-1974 commented that "a few years ago the best that could have been said of the Washington Post Company's performance was that it rated a gentleman's C in profitability. Today *The Post* would rate a solid B within its industry."

In late 1974 after lengthy negotiations Prescott came to terms in a six-year contract with the printers. The agreement allowed THE POST a free hand to introduce cold type technology in exchange for cash bonuses for early retirements, lifetime job guarantees, retraining programs for those who chose to remain, and a union shop for the indefinite future. THE POST made cash payments totaling $2.6 million for the accumulated reproduce, or bogus, and that practice finally was ended. As a result of this contract the number of printers at THE POST dropped from 773 in 1974 to 534 in 1977.

The printers had accepted the new reality at THE WASHINGTON POST; the pressmen would not. The result was a bitter 139-day strike that ended in a company victory over the union but which severely shook THE POST and left a chillness between management and many of its union employees.

Negotiations for a new pressmen's contract to replace the one expiring at midnight on September 30, 1975, deadlocked on THE POST's demand for substantive changes in work-rule restrictions and union refusal to yield on any basic issue. Although management had its specially trained employees standing by to put out a paper in case of a strike, the general expectation was that work would go on as negotiations continued after midnight. Instead, at about 4:35 A.M. on October 1, at the end of the night pressrun, several pressmen jumped Night Foreman James Hover, beat him, and threatened to kill him. A number of others, in about a 20-minute period, sabotaged all 72 units of THE POST's nine presses and started a fire on one of them after disabling some of the automatic fire extinguishers, although others put out the blaze before it could spread. THE POST had been put out of business.

When it was all over the story of the strike was told, at Bradlee's order, in a massive report by Robert G. Kaiser that filled all six pages of Outlook on February 29, 1976. Nine POST unions, all except the Guild, walked out when the pressmen left, refusing to cross the pressmen's picket line. Many union members expected the company once again to give in to pressure but this time it was different. The Guild voted three times during the course of the strike and each time, though by ever-narrowing margins, the majority declined to join the walkout. The membership was deeply divided over union loyalty and solidarity, the trashing of the presses, and the leadership of its Washington-Baltimore local. The continuing presence of the Guild majority was a major factor in the production of a respectable paper but Guild members realized that even without them management could have gotten out a paper. The sabotage of the first night, widely reported in the *Star* and on television and radio, proved to be crucial in creating a negative public attitude toward the pressmen. Dugan would concede only that some of his men "just went crazy and panicked."

POST employees who continued to work were spat upon, punched, hit by pieces of wood, and verbally harassed as they crossed the picket line, despite the presence of large numbers of police. Some employees had their car tires slashed, others received threatening phone calls at home. The son of foreman Hover was badly beaten by two masked men on a rural highway. Windows were broken in THE POST's lobby. The company beefed up its force of private police and new passes were issued to enter the 15th Street building. All of this produced a siege mentality both inside and out. Some stores that continued to advertise despite threats were harassed by union members who disrupted the stock on shelves.

Before the strike Mrs. Graham had replaced John Prescott with Mark

Meagher, a youthful-looking accountant who had joined the company as financial vice president under Fritz Beebe. Mrs. Graham gave him the title of general manager of the newspaper, rather than president, on the grounds that the former better described the job. During the strike Meagher was THE POST's spokesman, appearing on television and in interviews as a bland and moderate counter to Dugan's acerbic and belligerent tones.

THE POST lost one day's publication before it found six small newspapers from Charlottesville, Virginia, to Chambersburg, Pennsylvania, all within 200 miles of Washington, willing and able to print part of each night's run. For two weeks helicopters picked up POST-prepared photographs or negatives of the pages from the 15th Street building's roof, whisked them to the nearby papers, and trucked the resulting 24-page product back to the capital where the nonunion circulation distributors delivered them to newsboys and newsgirls. Where it had taken 1220 craft union workers to produce the paper before the strike, the job was done by a makeshift force ranging from 210 to 375. By October 6 one POST press had been repaired to run off 100,000 papers; after that, capacity steadily increased while pickets marched outside. The Oklahoma-trained amateur crews, including some women, began to run THE POST's presses. As Kaiser reported, "[What] proved crucial to *The Post*'s prosperity [was] the esprit de corps of its non-union employees."

Production of the paper was the job of Assistant General Manager Donald Graham, the publisher's son, then 30. By November 14, a 56-page paper was being printed at THE POST. As many as 200 employees slept on cots in the building, doing normal jobs by day, eating in a catered dining room and then in coveralls doing production jobs at night. On Thanksgiving the paper ran 184 pages, 104 of them printed in advance by the Miami *Herald* and trucked up from Florida. Other sections were printed in West Virginia and Ohio after being assembled by POST editors working at the Richmond, Virginia, *Times-Dispatch*. THE POST did not use the facilities of the Trenton, New Jersey, *Times*, a daily it had bought in October 1974. It was said Trenton was too far away.

Mrs. Graham worked most Saturday nights taking classified ads or in the mailroom gluing papers for mail subscribers. News executives — Bradlee, Simons, Geyelin, Greenfield, and the assistant managing editors — all exempt from Guild membership — did double duty of some kind or other along with their regular jobs. During a December union rally outside THE POST building a stereotypers' union executive carried a sign saying, "Phil Shot the Wrong Graham." When Mrs. Graham saw it she exclaimed, "Oh God, not that."

Efforts to mediate were fruitless and on December 4, 1975, the pressmen rejected, 249 to 5, what the company called its "final offer," a slight modification of its initial proposal. Thereupon THE POST began advertising for "temporary replacements" and more than 700 applicants appeared outside the building in a line that bisected the pickets. Ultimately, 20 pressmen and 29 stereotypers resigned from their unions to return to work. One pressman was so depressed he killed himself. The strike collapsed on February 16, 1976, after the mailers' union voted to accept a new contract. The printers, technically only respecting the mailers' picket line, thereupon crossed the pressmen's line. When it was apparent that management had won, Meagher told the New York *Times* that "we were muscled and we muscled back and in that brute strength kind of perspective — looking at the casualties — I think you have to see that you have one union dead on the battlefield, and others that have been chastened by the combat."

The Guild emerged from the strike not only chastened but seriously weakened. More than 200 of its members resigned, many forming an independent union that made a strong showing against the Guild in a representation election. After the Guild contract expired in April 1976, the company posted a cost-of-living raise that again made THE POST's top minimum, $504.25 a week, the highest in the industry. Fifteen pressmen were indicted on charges of rioting and destruction of property in the pressroom. Fourteen pleaded guilty to misdemeanor charges in exchange for abandonment of the felony charges; the fifteenth pleaded guilty to simple assault in a strike-related incident. Six received jail or detention sentences of up to one year and eight were fined up to $750. In mid-1976 Dugan was defeated for reelection as head of the pressmen's local; the new press crew next year voted to decertify the union, 146 to 1. The union indeed was busted at THE POST, largely because of its own stupidity.

The strike, said Mrs. Graham at the May 1976 stockholders meeting, had been "a sad time in the history of the newspaper." But it had been necessary to "make a stand to keep costs under control" by eliminating "featherbedding." Stockholders "owe continued economic viability" to a "tiny cadre" of some 200 management workers who had worked double jobs to keep the paper going. The strike cost the company "about $800,000" in the last quarter of 1975, Post Company president Larry H. Israel reported. A substantial part of the strike loss, including damage to the presses, was covered by insurance.

Mrs. Graham emerged from the strike even more of a national figure. Kaiser wrote in THE POST a year after the strike had begun that she had become "something of a hero among her fellow publishers, even those who despise the moderately liberal policies proclaimed by her newspaper's editorial page. 'It's funny, isn't it,' Mrs. Graham said in an interview, commenting on this irony. 'I sort of wear two hats.' "

Donald Graham had the task of working out personnel policies in the nonunion pressroom. Of the new workers many were young, many were black, and a few were women. The fact that the pressmen's union had no black journeymen at THE POST was one reason it failed to gain widespread backing, among either liberal Guild members or leaders of the city's largely black government.

A most interested observer of the strike was the Washington *Star* which in 1970 had lost money for the first time. A 1971 loss of nearly $4.5 million, known only to the family owners, impelled the *Star* to buy out its six-day afternoon competition, Scripps-Howard's tabloid *Daily News,* on July 12, 1972. Instead of helping, the merger propelled the renamed *Star-News* further into the red as too few new ads followed the circulation gains. In 1970–1973 the paper lost nearly $15.5 million. The result was the 1974 sale of a controlling interest to Joe L. Albritton, a Texas banking millionaire. He won economy concessions from the unions, a four-day work week from the Guild instead of layoffs, and took on THE POST for its liberal slant by advertising "Get It Straight From *The Star.*" Albritton brought in new editors and the paper began to shine in makeup and reporting, often giving THE POST much needed and healthy competition on both local and national stories. Still, the paper lost a whopping $7.7 million in 1974 and the red ink continued into 1975. Thus when THE POST strike began on October 1, 1975, the *Star* (as Albritton named it once again) was in a precarious position. In a hasty call to Albritton, later regretted, Mrs. Graham asked him to print her paper on his presses. Not only would there have been a pressrun conflict on Saturdays and Sundays but the pressmen clearly would have shut down the *Star.* The view was widespread in Washington that if that occurred the *Star* probably would never again publish. Albritton refused the request. But his paper got an economic shot in the arm in October as circulation and advertising both rose at THE POST's expense and for a month the *Star* was in the black.

In his account of the strike Kaiser wrote that "some businessmen in Washington said — not for quotation — that they didn't mind seeing *The Post* squirming under the pressure of the strike . . . Some thought the paper was too smug, too quick to raise advertising rates and too sloppy in the production of ads. Others disliked *The Post* for its politics." Nonetheless, within a year after the strike's end virtually all the advertising lost to the *Star* had been regained. In 1976 THE POST carried 66.2 percent of the total ad linage as against 70 percent just before the strike;

more important, THE POST was collecting more than 80 percent of the advertising-dollar revenue going to the two papers. Circulation, which fell during the strike while the *Star*'s grew, soon bounced back: for the six-month period ending March 31, 1977, THE POST's daily circulation averaged 555,030 and the Sunday total was 766,241, both the highest ever. Comparable *Star* figures were 375,583 and 374,251, both down from a year earlier but up from levels before THE POST strike.

After the strike POST readers complained that they were receiving a badly inked paper or one that smeared more than normal for high-speed printing. Probably most complaints concerned the atrocious word breaks or hyphenizations that resulted from increased use of computerized typesetting. Letters to the editor referred to this "carnage of crippled language" and "verbal mayhem." Words were being arbitrarily chopped in two at the ends of lines of type: je-ans, co-me, se-ating, don-'t, se-en, bed-raggled, Mar-yland. District Line columnist Bill Gold explained that it all depended on the computer's instructions for dividing words and he told readers to be patient: "I am content to endure improper word divisions for a while if that will ultimately help us produce better newspapers . . . We are now in a transition period. The technological advances that will emerge from it will, I think, make our temporary unhappiness worthwhile." But that was small solace to a reader who wrote: "The periodic educational crusades by your fine newspaper lamenting 'Johnny's' inability to read and write are tarnished . . . by the fact you daily expose Johnny to an underworld of one-syllable fractures, root word dismemberments, and one-letter mutations."

Richard Harwood, who in 1976 became deputy managing editor to rank third behind Bradlee and Simons, wrote in a post-Watergate memo to Bradlee that "we are in a position now to put more of a muckraking stamp on *The Post.*" Bradlee preferred to speak of "a provocative paper" rather than of "muckraking" but the effect was the same. All sections of THE POST now sought to probe beneath the flow of news and to expose wrongdoing. Some resulting stories were major accomplishments, others all too clearly showed the strain to find error or chicanery.

Haynes Johnson had once written that newspapers have "two functions, both vital: to report what is the news of the day, fully and fairly, and also to go beyond these events, and draw a larger portrait." After Watergate the emphasis was on that "larger portrait." Bradlee said THE POST must ask: "What does our reader already know from TV and what do we tell him after that?" He responded to charges that the paper considered politicians guilty until they proved their innocence by saying: "I do not assume that a politician is normally engaged in trying to do things adverse to the people's interests, and that our job is to discover and expose those malfeasances. I do believe that the politician is normally engaged in trying to do things favorable to his own interest, and that our job is to explore the difference between that interest and the public interest."

Before Watergate Mrs. Graham had worried that "a paper edited by people largely preoccupied with political and social issues will get more and more egg-headed and less and less broad based." After Watergate the publisher's preoccupation was the new hostility toward the press because of its increasing suspicion of any form of secrecy: "Many people, especially in government and business, assume the press is hostile, uninformed and likely to distort or sensationalize everything. Many reporters and editors, on the other hand, assume that everything secret is scandalous, and every claim of confidentiality is a cover-up." The post-Watergate reporting by her newspaper brought home these differences.

Among POST staffers there were differing reactions. One commented that "it may be that we are so hell-bent for exposure we forget our explaining role." Others felt there had been "too much gung-ho spirit." Some argued that THE POST was indulging in "much more criticism by innuendo . . . much more concern about what we can get away with and less about whether we should try to get away with it." Older staffers spoke of what one termed "a lack of heritage," an attitude on the part of newer editors and reporters that "there was no *Washington Post* before Watergate or, possibly, before Bradlee."

Investigative reporting was not new at THE POST, even if some there thought it was. The result of Watergate was to give it both a new impetus and a new approach. This new approach was described by one of its practioners, Metro Editor Len Downie, in his book on muckrakers: "Editors must deal with an investigative reporter's stories in an adversary way, since an investigative reporter does not record an event in objective fashion. He subsequently presents what amounts to his theory of the evidence against someone he believes has done something wrong. He can be no more impartial about his inquiry than a good police detective or prosecutor, no matter how hard he tries. It is up to the editor to maintain the distance that the reporter has lost and bring to the story the skepticism that the reporter can no longer muster."

This approach put a tremendous burden on editors to excise what Bradlee had described as the "tilt" in stories. Critics argued, and with a good deal of merit, that muckraking was producing more, not less, tilt.

It was an argument, in fact, as old as journalism because it went to the continuing problem of how to draw that elusive line between fairness and unfairness.

That Watergate was followed by some major POST reporting in the muckraking style was undeniable. In 1976 alone the paper exposed the fact that Representative Wayne Hays had kept Elizabeth Ray on his staff at $14,000 a year to serve as his mistress; that New York's Chase Manhattan and First National City banks had been placed on a secret list of problem banks by the Comptroller of the Currency; and that the South Korean government had set up a secret system to bribe, or attempt to bribe, members of Congress. THE POST also had a share in such important stories as a federal grand jury's probe of Maryland Governor Marvin Mandel, leading to his indictment and trial, and disclosure of many irregularities in the District government involving Mayor Washington's close friends and associates.

The Hays story began with a chance train encounter between Marion Clark, a reporter and later editor of *Potomac*, and Elizabeth Ray more than a year and a half before she and Rudy Maxa wrote their first joint story. It involved a lot of dogged reporting and the result was not just to end Hays' career but also to add pressure on Congress to monitor the ethics of its members. The banking stories were very different in origin; they were the product of months of obtaining and fine-combing documents by Ronald Kessler who had been hired for just such investigative reporting. Kessler already had made a name for himself and THE POST with stories on sweetheart relationships between local hospitals and their directors, on the Postal Service's deficiencies, and on exorbitant real estate settlement costs. Later he disclosed how some local bank officials and directors gave themselves preferential treatment. The Korean money story — sometimes called "Koreagate" — was first of all the work of Style columnist Maxine Cheshire. Aided by Scott Armstrong and others, the Cheshire stories went far beyond mystery moneyman Tongsun Park to raise major foreign policy questions about United States–South Korea relationships.

The Hays and Korean stories proved to be less sensitive than the banking stories for a newspaper which is itself a profit-making business dealing with many banks. Citibank Chairman Walter Wriston lambasted "journalistic voyeurism" but Mrs. Graham defended Kessler's stories as "very salutary" in "challenging habits of secrecy" in "an area the public should know more about."

Of all the paper's post-Watergate critics none was more penetrating than THE POST's own ombudsman. In 1975 Bob Maynard had moved to editorial writing; he was succeeded by Charles B. Seib, the *Star*'s managing editor and the first ombudsman to be given the extra measure of freedom insured by a long-term contract. He continued the internal memoranda as well as explaining to readers some of the paper's foibles, sometimes using his op-ed column to criticize failure to correct error. A regular page 2 space for corrections finally was established in 1976. As the paper's internal gadfly Seib also wrote about muckraking stories he felt had "achieved impact at the expense of accuracy." In a January 1976 column Seib described the "intense" POST versus New York *Times* rivalry and how THE POST was influenced by that rivalry to play down a major *Times* story, Seymour Hersh's disclosure of the CIA's domestic spying activities. He likewise showed how the *Times* had tried to knock down THE POST's exposé of the weakness of the two New York banks. "Such are the games newspapers — even great newspapers — play," Seib concluded. In early 1977, after THE POST announced, without adequate explanation, that company president Larry Israel had resigned, Seib criticized "the feared watchdog" for becoming "a pussycat in its own yard." (Company statements later showed that Israel would receive $450,000 in "termination" payments, a $200,000 "severance payment" and about $20,000 a year in retirement benefits when he reaches 65.) Seib also pointed out the paper's failure to probe the key story of the "Winter of '77": "Was there a true shortage of natural gas or was it a phony?" This public exposure of inner POST workings, its faults and failures, represented a major and praiseworthy break with the traditional American press posture of hear-no-evil, see-no-evil, and certainly speak-no-evil-about-my-own-newspaper.

One point of frequent criticism was the paper's use of photographs, especially those that readers felt represented excessive violence, nudity, or invasion of privacy. As Seib explained it, in many cases use of such a photo was likely to be argued at length until Bradlee or Simons decided that it had, or did not have, a relevance that could not be ignored.

Arthur Ellis began at THE POST in 1930, three years before Meyer's purchase, and remained to become chief photographer, his sensitive portraits a continuing feature. Charles Del Vecchio, famous for his action shots, came in 1935. But THE POST's photographic staff really began to grow only after the *Times-Herald* purchase. By 1977 the staff consisted of a director of photography, two picture editors, two female and 18 male photographers, and a lab technician. Newspaper pictures at THE POST, as elsewhere, too long were simply an adjunct to stories or only a device to break up a solid page of type. Al Friendly had begun the use of the picture story and intelligent use of photos increased in the Bradlee era, especially with the advent of Style.

THE POST editorial page had become less passionate, less automatically liberal, certainly less willing to accept, as it so long had, the theme that a federal approach to national problems was the route to solution or that the United States required a vast establishment to support a major role abroad. While editorial policy shifted as national attitudes changed, the page remained faithful to both civil liberties and international cooperation.

Phil Geyelin's prescription for reasoned editorials sometimes left readers uncertain. The prime examples were editorials before presidential elections. In 1952 THE POST clearly endorsed Eisenhower. In 1960, 1964, and 1968, as Geyelin explained it, "We did not exactly endorse, and we did not exactly *not* endorse. We added things up on both sides of the ledger and then declined to offer a bottom line." In 1972 "we thought we had said rather plainly that we didn't think Richard Nixon should be elected but the message was delivered in six long editorials, and somewhere along the line it was lost." At the time Woodward and Bernstein were closing in on Nixon and many readers deduced THE POST was trying to elect George McGovern.

In 1976 Jimmy Carter came out of nowhere to win nomination and election. Carter's name had first appeared in THE POST in a June 23, 1966, list of "other" candidates running for governor of Georgia, the year he lost. David Broder confessed in 1976 that other political writers and other papers — meaning first of all the rival New York *Times* — had been ahead of THE POST in spotting the Carter phenomenon. In March 1976 the candidate came to Mrs. Graham's home for lunch with editors and reporters. She was "interested, but puzzled." Carter promptly wrote the requisite thank-you letter: "Your personal friendship, and the hospitality of your own home meant a lot to me." But he misspelled her first name. In her paper columnist Joseph Kraft called Carter "a pig in a poke" and columnist Nick von Hoffman derided "Jimmy Peanut" as "the gleamy-toothed, bushy-tailed anointed chipmunk of the Lord."

Herblock was not so much pro-Carter as anti various Carter primary opponents except his favorite, Representative Morris Udall. In the fall he was anti–President Ford. In 1977 Herblock explained that he considered his cartoon to be "a signed expression of personal opinion . . . like a column or other signed articles — as distinguished from the editorials, which express the policy" of THE POST. To the two 1976 conventions the paper sent the largest contingents ever, some 35 editors, reporters, photographers, and others. Broder's preelection summary forecast the narrow Carter victory.

In October, Broder had described "the dilemma some voters see in choosing Carter. His presidency, they perceive, is full of promise, yes, but also full of risk." As to Ford, "they know . . . they will be both safe — and sorry." THE POST's October 31 editorial, the joint work of Geyelin and Greenfield, once again added up the plusses and minuses but failed to draw a bottom line beyond a reference to "this modest and tentative case for Mr. Carter's credentials." The editorial ended: "If this doesn't strike you as much of an endorsement, well, that's fine: It isn't meant to be. Not being in the business of manufacturing or marketing candidates, we offer no warranties. We offer only an indication of what we think should go into the difficult and consequential choice for President that voters will be making on Tuesday."

There was no confusion that same day, however, about Herblock's cartoon: a terrified voter was having a nightmare — Ford's running mate, Senator Robert Dole, was taking the presidential oath of office as a smiling Ford and John Connally stood by, and the recognizable arms of Richard Nixon were thrust out from behind a pillar.

Geyelin's view that the primary purpose of an editorial page was "to inform, to illuminate, even to educate" was applied as well to the op-ed page and its writers. Many new writers were introduced to readers, including a major new columnist, George Will. During the 1972 campaign Geyelin had asked William Safire, a Nixon speechwriter, and Frank Mankiewicz, McGovern's campaign director, to write rival pieces. An unexpected result was that the New York *Times,* then worrying like THE POST that its columnists were generally too liberal in the face of Agnewesque attacks, hired Safire. Geyelin had dickered with Safire but then found an articulate, witty, and knowledgeable conservative voice in Will who in 1977 won the Pulitzer Prize for Commentary.

Bradlee showed no interest in the editorial page and he had gladly surrendered control of the op-ed page. He repeatedly declared that he had "no partisan political philosophy" and even that "I don't care who the President is," a statement he made on national television five days after Nixon's resignation. When pressed on that, Bradlee replied that "I think it was perfectly clear from the context that I meant I do not care what party produces the President. I do not prefer one man to another." He was pleased, however, in late 1974 to escort Mrs. Graham to a Ford White House dinner, widely reported as marking the end of presidential displeasure with the powerful POST. Bradlee rejected a bid to join the prestigious Gridiron Club and he later offered this general view: "The older I get, the more finely tuned my sense of conflict of interest seems to become. I don't think executive editors in charge of news should have anything to do with editorials; I don't think editors should be officers of the company. I don't think editors should join any civic groups, clubs, institutions. I truly believe that people on the business side of newspapers shouldn't, either." To business-side officials, however, joining was both a way of life and a business necessity. Mrs. Graham, boss of both sides, went most of the way with the Bradlee dictum. She turned down many offers of board memberships at local universities except for George Washington where her husband had served and in the nation's most prestigious companies except for Allied Chemical, a business created by her father. Her rationale was that she wanted to join one business board to learn how other firms worked and that Allied could be joined "fairly safely" since she was not a major stockholder. In 1976, when Allied was involved in the kepone scandal in Virginia, THE POST repeatedly reported that its publisher was a company director. She turned down membership in most local organizations. In 1968–1972 she was a director of the Anacostia Assistance Corporation, a group which provided seed money for black businesses in a poor area of the capital. With attorneys Edward Bennett Williams and Joseph A. Califano, Jr., she worked on local crime problems, helping in part to get more police for the city. But she found such semisecret civil roles "awkward" for a publisher and largely discontinued them.

Mrs. Graham, a registered Democrat, thought her son Don wiser to refuse any party designation. Within a few years of taking over THE POST she discontinued her husband's practice of making political contributions to liberal Republicans and middle-of-the-road Democrats.

Watergate fame flooded THE POST with job applicants, as many as 1600 for 15 summer internships alone. As Bradlee put it to one hopeful, "People aren't leaving THE POST these days, and our problem is that you can fit only so much caviar in one box."

Still, new people were hired and older hands shifted about. Lewis Simons was expelled from India for his honest reporting. From Hong Kong, Jay Mathews skillfully interpreted China's post-Mao turmoil. Jonathan Randal survived the perils of covering Lebanon's civil war. Richard M. Cohen in 1976 began a three-times-a-week Metro column that shone with wry wit and family nostalgia. Edward Walsh covered the Ford White House and Austin Scott joined him for the Carter era. Style was enriched by Nina Hyde on fashions, Henry Mitchell's Earthman column, and Sarah Booth Conroy on design. George Solomon became sports editor and that section added Sports II, an idea of Howard Simons for weekly coverage of participatory activities for just about anyone. For four months in 1977 THE POST ran The Gossip Column in Style, an imitation of the Star's Ear column. Many readers, and many Post staffers, felt that such an arch collection of small talk tended to cheapen the newspaper. It also had the unhappy effect of encouraging gossipy imitation in such otherwise new and useful additions as the PostScript column and The TV Column.

Comic strips continued to be a prime attraction. When the paper dropped Winnie Winkle and Orphan Annie in 1975 there were protesting letters. One Annie fan: "Without wishing to sound paranoid . . . it does seem to me that the lineup on your comic page is coming more and more to reflect the policies of your editorial page." When Dick Tracy and Li'l Abner were dropped the next year, high school pickets appeared at THE POST. Both strips were snapped up by the *Star.*

Comics were not being switched to bring them in line with editorials but rather with reader interest, as shown by surveys, and with social change. Charles Schulz's Snoopy remained a dog for all seasons but Gary Trudeau's Doonesbury proved to be too far out on the social fringes for some readers, a bonanza for others. THE POST did not censor Trudeau, as some papers did, when his characters ventured into homosexuality and unmarried sex nor, with one exception, when his Watergate-era strips provided brilliant insight into the Nixon White House siege mentality. The exception: a 1973 strip in which a character pronounced a "guilty! guilty! guilty!" verdict on John Mitchell before a real-life jury had reached the decision that would make him the second Cabinet member to go to prison. Said Managing Editor Simons: "If anyone is going to find any defendant guilty, it's going to be the due process of justice, not a comic strip artist. We cannot have one standard for the news pages and another for the comics." Simon's action produced over 500 protesting phone calls but ombudsman Maynard wrote in THE POST that Trudeau had "stepped across the line." Fewer and fewer strips remained "comic"; more and more became means of social or even political comment, a fact recognized in 1975 when Trudeau was awarded a Pulitzer Prize.

In the 1970s, inflation in general and rising newsprint costs in particular made it imperative to find ways to cut expenses and prevent advertising rates from rising so high that many firms could not afford to use the paper. By 1976 THE POST was consuming nearly 3000 tons of newsprint a week, or about 750 rolls a day, or 30 truckloads. The price of newsprint in 1974–1977 rose more than 33 percent. The size of the page, 16 7/8 by 27 1/2 inches in 1939, was down to 14 3/4 by 23 3/8 inches by 1977. In 1975 classified ad columns were increased from nine to ten per page without reducing the number of characters or the cost per line. That same year the paper began zoned editions of its Thursday feature section, called the Weekly. Advertisers could buy space in only that part of the paper going to District, Maryland, or Virginia readers.

Most apparent to readers was the switch on August 2, 1976, from the conventional eight-column page to a new format of six news columns or nine advertising columns per page, known as "six on nine." This change, being made by many newspapers, reduced the daily number of pages enough to save about 5 percent in newsprint or $2.4 million annually. It also meant 12.5 percent more ad lines per page. The wider columns were easier to read and the total news wordage per page was about the same as before. THE POST retained the option it frequently exercised to go to eight columns on page 1, either to begin more stories there or for better photographic display. Even with all these changes, however, THE POST remained a huge paper: in an ad-fat pre-Christmas week in 1976 it printed 814 standard-sized pages plus the feature tabloids and numerous ad supplements often printed in other places and trucked to Washington.

Shortly before the 1975 pressmen's strike a study of the paper's circulation trends since 1961 showed that daily sales had leveled off although the Sunday figure continued to grow. The gross figures, and especially the big lead over the *Star,* were gratifying but the trend had some disturbing aspects. The number of area households receiving the daily paper had dropped from 57 percent in 1960 to 49 percent in 1970; comparable Sunday figures were 60 and 57 percent. "With every price increase we whiten the readership another shade," the survey concluded. Between 1968 and 1975 the cost of the seven-day, home-delivered paper rose from $2.60 per month to $5 and in early 1977 it went to $5.60 for four weeks. Bradlee once had quipped that THE POST was read by "100,000 policy makers and 100,000 policy players." Donald Graham now added: "No longer — perhaps . . . never . . . but our present policy player total is going down, not up." Of total circulation in late 1975 only 23.5 percent was inside the District. Inner-city blacks and less affluent whites were not readers. Mrs. Graham stressed that "our base is local and our primary purpose is to be a local newspaper" and she told Bradlee that "we must . . . try to make the paper indispensable" for those with low incomes as well as for the affluent. However, with the coming of major technological changes in newspaper production, THE POST began to prepare for publication in the suburbs. Ten acre sites were purchased near Alexandria, Virginia, and beyond Silver Spring, Maryland, for potential use as satellite printing plants at some indefinite time in the future.

The Washington Post Company in 1976 ranked 452nd on *Fortune* magazine's list of the 500 largest American companies, ranked by sales. Its 1976 revenue from all sources surpassed a third of a billion dollars of which 40 percent represented POST income. In December 1976 the company stock was split 2 for 1, the dividend raised, and on the American Stock Exchange the share price soon reached a new high.

Mrs. Graham referred to the paper as "the cornerstone" of the company. On Fritz Beebe's death in 1973, corporate headquarters was moved from New York to Washington and there Mrs. Graham spent most of her time. She continued to drop handwritten notes of praise or concern to editors and reporters: "Our quality and professionalism are tops and as usual you were so important to it." "It is truly only the people with passion in the world who ever create anything or get anything decent done." It was no surprise when she strode through the building to drop in on editors or business executives, just as had her father and her husband. But there were so many new faces, so many more names to remember; THE POST had grown big and in many ways impersonal. Almost everyone had called her husband "Phil," not many called her "Kay." To one and all she repeatedly equated excellence with profitability. The 100-year history of THE POST demonstrated that without profitability there could be little excellence; but it also demonstrated that profitability did not guarantee excellence. As one veteran staff member put it: "A quality newspaper in a commercially noncompetitive situation like *The Post* depends on an eleemosynary instinct. That does not go with the bottom line."

As she surveyed her great success in terms of both excellence and profitability, Katharine Graham was not as lacking in that instinct, not as bottom line–minded as some thought. In a 1976 letter she conceded that "size really has many disadvantages — and so in fact oddly does success. Although we all pursue it, it's a problem I'd rather deal with than not." To a close friend that same year she explained some of her feelings about her company: "It is family oriented — and that makes me nervous as I look around me at other family businesses and what becomes of them. I also see what replaces them when they go downhill. I am trying hard to get strong, able managers around me in an effort to combine the advantages of both."

All the Post Company's class A common stock remains in Graham family hands with Mrs. Graham having voting rights to 50.1 percent. Since class A stockholders elect a majority of the directors, she alone controls the company. Owners of the publicly traded class B stock elect a minority of directors. This combination of family and public ownership but with firm family control appears likely to continue indefinitely.

Katharine Graham reached 60 in THE POST's centennial year, a powerful and glamorous figure in the national capital and in the world of communications. Early in 1977, after an abortive effort to buy *New York* magazine and other publications, she was described on page 1 of her own newspaper by two of her reporters as "a pillar of [the] Washington political and social establishment." By the rules of the times for women in the news THE POST referred to her simply as "Graham" without the "Mrs." (Post style for decades had been to use "Miss" or "Mrs." at all times but "Mr." only for the deceased, the clergy, and the President. During the 1976 campaign Bradlee finally abolished the use of "Mr." for the President.)

Mrs. Graham was the first woman director of the American Newspaper Publishers Association and in 1974 she was elected the first woman director of the Associated Press. To a congratulator she replied: "I really am rather pleased about the A.P. I don't know quite why except we inheritors like to do something on our own." She became the recipient of a string of honorary degrees. She finally mastered speechmaking although she disliked television appearances, contending that she was "an awful lead balloon." She became as adept as her father and husband in dealing with those in the business world who thought her newspaper too liberal. To one businessman who complained about a story she returned this salvo:

> What I do is back the editors. Since all of us are humanly fallible, when I get a complaint or alarm, I check it out or ask them to. If the story is accurate, I conceive our job to entail printing it, whether it harms friendships or anything else. If an editor starts censoring stories because they might hurt this person or that cause, it's very damaging to the newspaper and the informational job that is our obligation. I just want to emphasize this — because in my business I can't have any friends except those who understand this.

The fact that the publisher was a woman meant both acclaim and strain. She was featured in the women's magazines. But within the Post Company she recognized "an additional sexist problem . . . If I do something unexpected, male executives tend to react more than normally by asking 'who has gotten to her.' I'm sure I'm too defensive about this — but I try to say very clearly where an idea comes from, even if it has been adopted by me and has become mine."

Mrs. Graham continues to move in an international world of statesmen and politicians, artists and actors, bankers and industrialists, publishers and editors. She entertains in her spacious Georgetown house, her Virginia farm, and her newly acquired Martha's Vineyard estate. Dinners, lunches, weekends, all are expertly woven into her schedule by an extraordinary personal secretary, Elizabeth (Liz) Hylton. Women's magazines have called her "the most powerful woman in

America" to which she responded that "it makes me think of a female weight lifter." She has appeared as number 14 on a list of the "most influential" people in America; New York *Times* publisher Arthur Sulzberger was number 13. Her old friend McGeorge Bundy, now president of the Ford Foundation, was credited in a London paper with saying that she might just be the most powerful woman in the world since Queen Victoria.

In 1965 Truman Capote gave a flamboyant masked ball for Mrs. Graham, proclaimed at least by the jet set as the party of the century. She found it "cozy and glamorous" and she said that it had made her "feel younger and gayer than I am most days." Her appearance, her clothes all became news of a sort. She paid attention to both but couldn't avoid the publicity. "It doesn't help my job," she commented in 1975, "when I get into print for where I am at dinner or what I have on my back."

The Pentagon Papers battle and then Watergate turned a well-known publisher into an international celebrity, no matter how she felt about it. Her male escorts — Clayton Fritchey, Clay Felker, Warren Buffett among them — were carefully scrutinized but she has not remarried. Fritchey married her close friend Polly Wisner.

Katharine Graham, associated with THE WASHINGTON POST for nearly four decades, has never forgotten the role of the press. On occasion she has quoted from *Henry IV, Part 2:* "Yet, the first bringing of unwelcome news hath but a losing office, and his tongue ever after as a sullen bell." She has constantly sought to make the public understand that newspapers are the messengers, not the originators, of bad news, that freedom of the press means not special privilege for journalists but knowledge for the public.

She can be sharp and unsmiling, charming and radiant. She has said that "learning and laughing" are the things she enjoys most. Those who haven't measured up to expectations did not last long; those who have were handsomely rewarded. Perhaps her special characteristic has been her drive, exhibited, unexpectedly, in a letter to a friend about hairdressers.

> . . . my hairdresser had just gone out of business leaving me stranded on the beach and desperate. I mean desperate. I tried at least six. My own requirements are simple. Whoever has the dubious benefits of my trade must only be first rate, silent, nice, take me at any time of the day or night I arrive, get me in and out under an hour, have good manicurists who don't cut your fingers to ribbons and always let me have one hand free to hold the reading. Surprisingly difficult the latter

> requirement, as most of them will die rather than let you keep the hand she is not working on out of the finger bowl.

When THE WASHINGTON POST bought the *Times-Herald* in 1954, Donald Edward Graham was five weeks short of nine years old. His grandfather, Eugene Meyer, remarked that "the real significance of this event is that it makes the paper safe for Donnie."

Twenty-two and a half years later Donald Graham became general manager of the newspaper his grandfather had rescued from bankruptcy. If the remark made grandpa appear prescient, it meant nothing to grandson, who learned of it only in 1974 when he read Merlo Pusey's biography of Meyer. While Graham grew up in a household flooded with both fascinating people and newspaper talk, it was without any inner feeling that someday he would take over the paper; nor did his parents thrust the idea upon him. Nonetheless, in THE POST's 100th year he is the heir apparent.

Don Graham, as he prefers to be called, was born in Washington on April 22, 1945, second child and eldest son of Philip and Katharine Graham. His siblings are engaged in other pursuits. He attended proper and demanding St. Alban's private school. The headmaster wrote his father that he was "a very unusual human being . . . Be very proud and very grateful." He spent the summer after graduation in Tanganyika, now Tanzania, helping to build a church for an Episcopal mission.

Graham's father died a year later, the summer after his freshman year at Harvard. Three years later, in 1966, he graduated from Harvard magna cum laude, having majored in English history and literature. In his senior year he was president (editor) of the *Crimson,* the university daily.

Two months after graduation Graham was drafted, serving two years in the army. In January 1967, at 21 and already in uniform, he married Mary Wissler, a Radcliffe graduate who had worked with him on the *Crimson.* When her husband was sent to Vietnam she went to law school; after graduation she worked awhile for the government until the birth of their first child. In his year in Vietnam Graham became a spec 5 in public information in the 1st Cavalry Division, working on the division paper and magazine, part of the time in Tokyo. Graham saw little combat but from his photographic work he saw what combat was doing to Vietnam.

When Graham graduated from Harvard the United States was bombing North Vietnam, the Johnson administration was being accused of an "arrogance of power," and POST editorials were declaring that American withdrawal was "no longer a meaningful political alternative." Graham also was against unilateral withdrawal and thus went to Vietnam in the belief that he had an obligation to serve. Seeing the conflict, however, rather quickly changed his mind; he concluded that the war was having ruinous effects in the United States and in Vietnam. But when he returned home his change of heart did not lead him into antiwar protests.

Graham came back to the United States in time to join THE POST contingent at the 1968 Miami Beach convention that nominated Richard Nixon. By now he realized that he should, and would, join the family enterprise as its eventual boss. But he decided "to do something first to learn about the city" he had been away from for six years and to do so "from another angle than that of a newspaperman." So he joined Washington's metropolitan police force. His first 4 months were spent at the police academy, the last 14 as a patrolman walking a beat in the old ninth precinct, partly on Capitol Hill and partly in adjacent slum areas. Friends reported he was so conscientious that on his days off he carried a police revolver, as per regulations. He did not promise not to write about his experiences; he simply resolved not to do so and he didn't. A book review he did for THE POST some years later indicated he had come to sympathize with the policeman's problems.

In January 1971 Graham finally came to The Washington Post Company. He began as a Metro reporter on the paper where, among other things, he helped cover the May Day demonstrations. In a year and a half he also took turns as a makeup editor, in the accounting department, as an assistant circulation home-delivery manager, in the promotion department, in classified and retail advertising, and as an assistant production manager. He then spent ten months at *Newsweek* as a reporter in the Los Angeles bureau and as a writer and in the business office in New York. He returned to THE POST in mid-1974 to be assistant managing editor for sports.

Sports was Graham's first real managerial challenge and his colleagues gave him good marks. In his year in that job he spruced up the page design, revamped the staff, and tore down a glass partition that symbolized the long-time separation of sportswriters from the rest of those in the newsroom. He accelerated a process already under way of moving reporters in and out of sports. He ran a highly successful contest to find a new horse racing handicapper. Probably most important was the knowledge he gained of middle-level management problems.

While still in sports Graham was added to the company board of directors. In 1975 he became assistant general manager of the newspaper, under Mark Meagher. He held that job during the pressmen's strike, working tirelessly to continue publishing the newspaper. Quite evidently he earned the respect of his peers and of his mother. On December 1, 1976, he was named general manager of THE POST, although he still reported to Meagher who became president of the parent company's newspaper division. Under Meagher and Graham now were the seven POST operating vice presidents: John M. Dower for communications, Christopher M. Little as counsel, Robert M. McCormick for advertising, Jack F. Patterson for circulation, Virgil P. Schroeder for operations, William A. Spartin for administration, and Lawrence A. Wallace for labor relations.

As Graham moved up THE POST escalator, speculation rode with him as to when there would be a transition. His mother gave a public answer in a 1976 interview: "Donnie will take over when he's ready. And when *I'm* ready." Mother and son are in agreement on that. The expectation as THE POST neared its centennial was that Katharine Graham, sometime in the next few years, would yield the role of POST publisher to her son and then confine herself to corporate management. But not right away.

Tall and slim like his father and with his mother's sense of toughness and determination, Donald Graham at 32 retains a boyish look and engaging smile. POST people consider him "terribly approachable" and find it easy to call him "Don." His gentlemanly, even nice-guy, appearance and conscientious air only partially hide a forceful determination and a healthy ambition.

THE WASHINGTON POST has survived and grown to greatness in a city long known as "the graveyard of journalism." Today a POST editor, reporter, or editorial writer can move a President or the Congress, influence the courts, cleanse a regulatory agency, affect elections, protect the public interest in myriad ways — or, as Katharine Graham has cautioned, the paper can "distort events, destroy reputations and influence public opinion recklessly." This vast power and the newspaper's use of it over the century has engendered every response from adulation to hatred. So it is today.

The history of THE WASHINGTON POST surely has demonstrated that it is the owner-publisher who sets the tone. Katharine Graham has done that courageously and well. Next it will be Donald Graham's turn.

# Bibliography
# Index

# Bibliography


BOOKS

Abels, Jules. *Out of the Jaws of Victory.* New York: Henry Holt, 1959.

Adams, Samuel Hopkins. *Incredible Era.* Boston: Houghton Mifflin, 1939.

Allen, Frederick Lewis. *Only Yesterday.* New York: Harper, 1957.

Babb, Laura Longley, ed. *Writing in Style.* Boston: Houghton Mifflin, 1975.

______. *Of the Press, by the Press, for the Press, and Others Too.* Boston: Houghton Mifflin, 1976.

______. *The Editorial Page.* Boston: Houghton Mifflin, 1977.

Baker, Ray Stannard. *Life and Letters of Woodrow Wilson.* Vols. 7 and 8. New York: Reprint House International, 1927–1939.

Barth, Alan. *The Loyalty of Free Men.* New York: Viking, 1951.

Bennett, Ira E. *Editorials from* The Washington Post, *1917–20.* Washington, D.C.: The Washington Post, 1921.

Bernstein, Carl, and Bob Woodward. *All the President's Men.* New York: Simon and Schuster, 1974.

Block, Herbert L. (Herblock). *The Herblock Book.* Boston: Beacon Press, 1952.

______. *Herblock's Here and Now.* New York: Simon and Schuster, 1955.

______. *Herblock's Special for Today.* New York: Simon and Schuster, 1958.

______. *Straight Herblock.* New York: Simon and Schuster, 1964.

______. *The Herblock Gallery.* New York: Simon and Schuster, 1968.

______. *Herblock's State of the Union.* New York: Simon and Schuster, 1972.

______. *Herblock Special Report.* New York: Norton, 1974.

Bradlee, Benjamin C. *Conversations with Kennedy.* New York: Norton, 1975.

Brown, George Rothwell. *Washington: A Not Too Serious History.* Baltimore: Norman, 1930.

Butt, Archie. *Taft and Roosevelt: The Intimate Letters of Archie Butt.* 2 vols. Garden City, N.Y.: Doubleday, 1930.

Butterfield, Roger. *The American Past.* New York: Simon and Schuster, 1947.

Cable, Mary. *The Avenue of the Presidents.* Boston: Houghton Mifflin, 1969.

Carpenter, Frank G. *Carp's Washington.* New York: McGraw-Hill, 1960.

Cohen, Richard M., and Jules Witcover. *A Heartbeat Away.* New York: Viking, 1974.

Daugherty, Harry M. *The Inside Story of the Harding Tragedy.* New York: Churchill, 1932.

Downes, Randolph C. *The Rise of Warren Gamaliel Harding, 1865–1920.* Columbus, Ohio: Ohio State University Press, 1970.

Downie, Leonard, Jr. *The New Muckrakers.* Washington, D.C.: New Republic, 1976.

Federal Writers' Project. *Washington: City and Capital.* Washington, D.C.: Government Printing Office, 1937.

Friendly, Alfred, and Ronald L. Goldfarb. *Crime and Publicity.* New York: Twentieth Century Fund, 1967.

Gallagher, Edward J. *Stilson Hutchins: 1838–1912.* Laconia, N.H.: Citizen Publishing, 1965.

Gilbert, Ben W. *Ten Blocks from the White House.* New York: Praeger, 1968.

Green, Constance McLaughlin. *Washington, Village and Capital, 1800–1878.* Princeton, N.J.: Princeton University Press, 1962.

———. *Washington, Capital City, 1879–1950.* Princeton, N.J.: Princeton University Press, 1963.

Hart, Scott. *Washington at War: 1941–45.* Englewood Cliffs, N.J.: Prentice-Hall, 1970.

Healy, Paul F. *Cissy.* Garden City, N.Y.: Doubleday, 1966.

Hess, Stephen, and Milton Kaplan. *The Ungentlemanly Art.* New York: Macmillan, 1975.

Hoge, Alice Albright. *Cissy Patterson.* New York: Random House, 1966.

Hoover, Irving Hood. *Forty-Two Years in the White House.* Boston: Houghton Mifflin, 1934.

Hutchins, Stilson, and Joseph West Moore. *The National Capital, Past and Present.* Washington, D.C.: Post Publishing, 1885.

Ickes, Harold L. *The Secret Diary of Harold L. Ickes.* Vols. 1 and 2. New York: Simon and Schuster, 1953–1954.

Johnson, Willis F. *George Harvey: A Passionate Patriot.* Boston: Houghton Mifflin, 1929.

Keogh, James. *President Nixon and the Press.* New York: Funk & Wagnalls, 1972.

King, Homer W. *Pulitzer's Prize Editor: John A. Cockerill.* Durham, N.C.: Duke University Press, 1965.

Koenig, Louis G. *The Invisible Presidency.* New York: Rinehart, 1960.

Lewis, Lloyd, and Henry Justin Smith. *Oscar Wilde Discovers America.* New York: Harcourt, Brace, 1936.

Longworth, Alice Roosevelt. *Crowded Hours.* New York: Scribner's, 1933.

Lorant, Stefan. *The Glorious Burden.* New York: Harper & Row, 1968.

McLean, Evalyn Walsh (with Boyden Sparkes). *Father Struck It Rich.* Boston: Little, Brown, 1936.

Manchester, William. *The Glory and the Dream.* Boston: Little, Brown, 1973.

Mazo, Earl, and Stephen Hess. *Nixon: A Political Portrait.* New York: Popular Library, 1968.

Meyer, Agnes E. *Out of These Roots.* Boston: Little, Brown, 1953.

Millis, Walter, ed. *The Forrestal Diaries.* New York: Viking, 1951.

Morison, Elting M., et al., eds. *The Letters of Theodore Roosevelt.* Cambridge, Mass.: Harvard University Press, 1951–1954.

Morison, Samuel Eliot, Henry Steele Commager, and William E. Leuchtenburg. *The Growth of the American Republic.* Vol. 2. New York: Oxford University Press, 1969.

Mott, Frank L. *American Journalism: A History: 1690–1960.* New York: Macmillan, 1962.

Nixon, Richard M. *Six Crises.* Garden City, N.Y.: Doubleday, 1962.

Patch, Susan Steinem. *Blue Mystery: The Story of the Hope Diamond.* Washington, D.C.: Smithsonian Institution, 1976.

Pearson, Drew. *Diaries 1949–1959.* Ed. Tyler Abell. New York: Holt, Rinehart and Winston, 1974.

[Pearson, Drew, and Robert S. Allen.] *Washington Merry-Go-Round.* New York: Horace Liveright, 1931.

Peterson, H. C. *Propaganda for War.* Norman, Okla.: University of Oklahoma, 1939.

Pilat, Oliver. *Drew Pearson.* New York: Harper's Magazine Press, 1973.

Pollard, James E. *The Presidents and the Press.* New York: Macmillan, 1947.

______. *The Presidents and the Press: Truman and Johnson.* Washington, D.C.: Public Affairs Press, 1964.

Povich, Shirley. *The Washington Senators.* New York: G. P. Putnam's Sons, 1954.

______. *All These Mornings.* Englewood Cliffs, N.J.: Prentice-Hall, 1969.

Pringle, Henry F. *The Life and Times of William Howard Taft.* 2 vols. New York: Farrar & Rinehart, 1939.

Pusey, Merlo J. *Eugene Meyer.* New York: Knopf, 1974.

Roberts, Chalmers M. *Washington Past and Present.* Washington, D.C.: Public Affairs Press, 1950.

______. *First Rough Draft: A Journalist's Journal of Our Times.* New York: Praeger, 1973.

Rosten, Leo C. *The Washington Correspondents.* New York: Harcourt, Brace, 1937.

Russell, Francis. *The Shadow of Blooming Grove.* New York: McGraw-Hill, 1968.

Salinger, Pierre. *With Kennedy.* Garden City, N.Y.: Doubleday, 1966.

Schlesinger, Arthur, Jr. *A Thousand Days.* Boston: Houghton Mifflin, 1965.

Simons, Howard, and Joseph A. Califano, Jr., eds. *The Media and the Law.* New York: Praeger, 1976.

Slauson, Allan B., ed. *A History of the City of Washington.* Washington, D.C.: Washington Post, 1903.

Smith, Gene. *When the Cheering Stopped.* New York: William Morrow, 1964.

Stern, Philip M. *The Oppenheimer Case.* New York: Harper & Row, 1969.

Sullivan, Mark. *Our Times.* 6 vols. New York: Charles Scribner's Sons, 1926–1935.

Sussman, Barry. *The Great Coverup.* New York: Crowell, 1974.

Ungar, Sanford J. *The Papers and The Papers.* New York: Dutton, 1972.

United States Commission on Civil Rights. *Report.* Washington, D.C.: Government Printing Office, 1959.

United States Senate. *Investigation of Hon. Harry M. Daugherty, Formerly Attorney General of the United States.* Hearings before the Select Committee on Investigation of the Attorney General.

Washington, D.C.: Government Printing Office, 1924.

———. *Leases Upon Naval Oil Reserves.* Hearings before the Committee on Public Lands and Surveys, 68th Congress, Part 10. Washington, D.C.: Government Printing Office, 1924.

Villard, Oswald Garrison. *Some Newspapers and Newspapermen.* Plainview, New York: Books for Libraries (reprint), 1926.

———. *The Disappearing Daily.* New York: Knopf, 1944.

Waldrop, Frank C. *McCormick of Chicago.* Englewood Cliffs, N.J.: Prentice-Hall, 1966.

Washow, Arthur I. *From Race Riot to Sit-In.* Garden City, N.Y.: Doubleday, 1966.

White, Theodore H. *The Making of the President, 1964.* New York: Atheneum, 1965.

Zacharias, Ellis M. *Secret Mission.* New York: G. P. Putman's Sons, 1946.

## MAGAZINE ARTICLES

Fallows, James. "Big Ben." *Esquire,* April 1976.

Howard, Jane. "Katharine Graham: The Power That Didn't Corrupt." *Ms.,* October 1974.

McBee, Susanna. "Katharine Graham and How She Grew." *McCall's,* September 1971.

Morley, Felix. "Europe on the Eve," *Modern Age,* Spring 1974.

Peck, Evans. "The Many-Sided McLean," *Cosmopolitan,* February 1911.

"The Rise of the Washington Post," *Fortune,* December 1944.

Sherman, Norman, " 'Who the Hell Was That?' 'He's the Editor of the Post.' 'Jesus, I Thought He Was Your Bookie.' " *Washingtonian,* July 1974.

Viorst, Judith. "Katharine Graham." *Washingtonian,* September 1967.

# Index